HISTORICAL WRITINGS ON THE SIKHS
(1784-2011)

Historical Writings on the Sikhs (1784-2011)

Western Enterprise and Indian Response

J. S. GREWAL

MANOHAR
2012

First published 2012

ISBN 978-81-7304-953-8

Published by
Ajay Kumar Jain *for*
Manohar Publishers & Distributors
4753/23 Ansari Road, Daryaganj,
New Delhi 110 002

Printed at
Salasar Imaging Systems
Delhi 110 035

Contents

Preface

This volume consists of five parts. The first two relate to works of the British, European and American writers who laid the foundations of modern Sikh studies in the broad framework of colonial, 'orientalist', and evangelical concerns. Next three parts deal with works of the Indian historians who appropriated the Western legacy and tried to improve upon it in the broad framework of socio-religious resurgence and 'nationalism' during the colonial period. The last part focuses on the widening scope of historical studies on the Sikhs and the issues being debated by the Western and Indian scholars during the past six decades.

There is a good deal of diversity in the interpretations of the Sikh past by the historians, whether Western or Indian. Their historical thinking was embedded in their socio-political situations, their world-views and assumptions, and their attitudes and purposes. These differences lend a large measure of fascination to their works and make us aware of the nature and character of our heritage as researchers in the area of Sikh studies.

My interest in historical writing on the Sikhs goes back to the early 1960s. Over the decades I have become indebted to a large number of scholars and institutions for interaction and help. I am thankful to all of them. I am thankful to two young scholars who have helped me in preparing this volume for publication: Dr Sheena Pall and Dr Karamjit Kaur Malhotra. I am thankful also to Ms Parneet Minhas for preparing the press copy with diligence and care.

Professor Indu Banga has given valuable suggestions for the contents of this volume and its organization. I am grateful to her.

4 October 2011 J.S. GREWAL

Prologue

My interest in historiography began with my doctoral thesis on British historical writing on medieval India.[1] An article on 'J.D. Cunningham and His Predecessors on the Sikhs' was my first publication on a work of Sikh history.[2] In the late 1960s I began to take interest in historical writing on the Sikhs.[3] A rather comprehensive statement on the state of Sikh studies was made in 1973 in a lecture delivered at the Christian Institute of Sikh Studies, Baring Union Christian College, Batala.[4] An account of the historians of Maharaja Ranjit Singh was published in 1980.[5] A monograph on *Guru Nanak in Western Scholarship* was published by the Indian Institute of Advanced Study in 1992, covering the works of writers from James Browne in the late eighteenth to W.H. McLeod in the late twentieth century.[6] A more elaborate analysis of the works of Western and Sikh writers was published in 1998 as the first part of the *Contesting Interpretations of the Sikh Tradition*.[7]

Meanwhile, other publications on the historians of the Sikhs have come out. A volume edited by Fauja Singh and published in 1978 contains fourteen articles by seven contributors: five by S.K. Bajaj, three by Fauja Singh himself, two by S.S. Bal and one each by A.C. Arora, N.G. Barrier, A.C. Banerjee, and myself. These articles cover twenty-two works, eighteen by European writers and four by Indian historians. Among the former are Browne, Polier, Forster, Malcolm, Prinsep, Murray, Smyth, Steinbach, Gardner, Honingberger, M'Gregor, Cunningham, Griffin, Trumpp, Macauliffe, Gordon, Bingley and Payne. Not all of them are historians. Among the Indian historians are Syad Muhammad Latif, Sita Ram Kohli, Indubhusan Banerjee, and Gokul Chand Narang. The book is useful for both students and historians.[8]

Gianeshwar Khurana has examined the development of British historiography of the Sikhs up to 1849. He looks upon A.L.H. Polier, George Forster and James Browne as 'the pioneers', and John Malcolm as laying 'the foundation'. H.T. Prinsep added 'a new dimension' by covering the political life of Maharaja Ranjit Singh. W.G. Osborne is seen as depicting 'men and manners' at the court of Ranjit Singh. Henry Steinbach makes 'a plea for annexation'. H.T. Thornton's work 'echoes the official version' of the First Anglo-Sikh War. M'Gregor concentrated on 'contemporary history', writing largely on the events of the first Sikh War. G. Carmichael Smyth questioned the legitimacy of the successors of Ranjit Singh. With Joseph Davey Cunningham's *History of the Sikhs* comes 'the culmination' of early British historical writing of the Sikhs. Khurana's book presents a continuous account of 'British historiography of the Sikh power' in the time of the East India Company.[9]

Darshan Singh's *Western Perspectives on the Sikh Religion* covers the period from the late eighteenth to the late twentieth century. He has surveyed Western writings with some information on most of the authors from A.L.H. Polier to W.H. McLeod. He talks of the origin and nature of 'orientalism', the problems of Christian writers in studying non-Christian religions, their evangelical and political purposes, their views on Guru Nanak, the Sikh faith, and the evolution of the Sikh religious tradition. Darshan Singh goes into their relatively favourable view of the Sikh faith, their predispositions, their ignorance of the primary sources, their concern mainly with Sikh theology, and their limitations in understanding Sikh religious practices. This comprehensive treatment, though confined to religion, is nonetheless useful to the historian.[10]

The present volume covers the period from the late eighteenth to the beginning of the present century. The first five chapters relate to the time of the East India Company up to the annexation of the Punjab to the British empire in 1849. The beginning of British interest in the Sikhs synchronized with the rise of the East India Company into a political power in Bengal and the emergence of the Sikhs as a political power in the Punjab. All the Europeans who took interest in the contemporary Sikhs and their past were connected with the East

India Company, especially with Warren Hastings who looked upon the Sikhs as a potential threat to British political interests in India. Thus, the beginning of British interest in the Sikhs was a compliment to their political power. However, this does not provide the whole explanation. British interest in the Sikhs was also a reflection of the importance which the British intelligentsia had come to attach to history as knowledge of the past for understanding the present. For a proper appraisal of the Sikh power it was considered necessary to know the Sikh past. Intellectual curiosity was, thus, closely aligned with political purposes.

During the first half of the nineteenth century, the Sikh power became increasingly important for the British. Lord Minto subscribed to the policy of non-intervention but he was keen to make an exception in the case of the Sikhs because Ranjit Singh was increasing his influence towards Delhi. The Sikh rulers on the Delhi side of the Sutlej were taken under protection and Ranjit Singh was confined to the other side. John Malcolm's *Sketch of the Sikhs* was a product of this phase. Within a decade then Ranjit Singh unified the former Mughal province of Lahore, and conquered Kashmir and a large part of the province of Multan. In the 1820s he carried his arms beyond the Indus, and after 1830, turned his eyes towards Sind. William Bentinck was anxious to contain Ranjit Singh. H.T. Prinsep provided an assessment of Ranjit Singh at this juncture. The decade after Ranjit Singh's death was marked by two Sikh wars and the subversion of the sovereign Sikh state. It was also the decade in which the works of W.G. Osborne, W.L. M'Gregor, G.C. Smyth and H.H. Wilson were published, largely in justification of British policies and measures. The only historian who struck a different note was J.D. Cunningham.

After the annexation, the British administrators and military officers were interested in the Sikhs as subject people: the Sikh rulers and aristocrats, and Sikhs as soldiers and collaborators. Lepel Griffin and a number of army officers wrote on the Sikhs. The Sikh religion appeared nonetheless to be relevant for policies to be evolved in relation to the Sikhs. Two Western writers showed much more interest in the Sikh religious tradition than in the past Sikh politics, or in the contemporary Sikhs: Ernest Trumpp and M.A. Macauliffe. Their work was supplemented by the American missionaries, J.C. Archer and C.H. Loehlin.

The third part of the book relates to early Indian responses to Western enterprise. The writers of the last decade of the nineteenth and the first two decades of the twentieth century were not yet influenced by 'nationalism'. Syad Muhammad Latif wrote as a Punjabi loyalist, identifying himself with Muslims. Three Sikh writers responded to the work of all their predecessors in order to put forth interpretations of their own.

The fourth part deals with two historians from Bengal: Indubhusan Banerjee and Narendra Krishna Sinha. Between them, they covered the period from Guru Nanak to Maharaja Ranjit Singh, the former concentrating on the early Sikh tradition and the latter on the political history of the Sikhs during the eighteenth century and in the time of Ranjit Singh. They were deeply influenced by the rise of nationalism. Whereas Banerjee wrote from the angle of 'Hindu' nationalism, Sinha looked at the political history of the Sikhs from the standpoint of 'Indian' nationalism.

The native historians of the Punjab are taken up in the fifth part. Gukul Chand Narang wrote clearly from the Hindu viewpoint, maintaining his stand throughout his work. An alternative title for his *Transformation of Sikhism* was 'How the Sikhs became a political power'. Hari Ram Gupta concentrated on the eighteenth century, much more than did Sinha. In his works it is possible to perceive an identification of 'national' with 'Hindu' viewpoint. G.L. Chopra and Sita Ram Kohli focused on Ranjit Singh, going into much greater detail than Sinha. In their works it is possible to perceive a strong Punjabi sentiment. Sita Ram Kohli alone wrote on the last decade of Sikh rule, with great empathy for the Khalsa.

What is common to the Indian historians is their conviction that their understanding and their interpretation of the Sikh past was more meaningful than that of the Western writers. Adopting Western methodology, they created 'modern' historical writing. This heritage from the colonial period has been reinforced, expanded, and enriched after India's Independence.

The sixth part deals with contemporary historical writing on the Sikhs. *A Short History of the Sikhs* by Teja Singh and Ganda Singh is analysed as a sort of transition from the colonial to the contemporary period. In the past five or six decades the scope of Sikh studies has expanded enormously. A brief analysis of fifteen selected monographs and comment on half a dozen general histories are expected to illustrate the widening scope and character of contemporary historical writing. This is supplemented by a brief discussion of recent controversies over a number of basic issues in Sikh studies.

NOTES

1. The subject of my doctoral thesis submitted to the University of London in 1962, was 'British Historical Writing on Medieval India from Alexander Dow to Mountstuart Elphinstone'. A revised and enlarged version of this thesis was published by the Oxford University Press in 1970 as *Muslim Rule in India: The Assessments of British Historians.*
2. For a revised version of the article on J.D. Cunningham published in 1964 in the *Bengal Past and Present,* see J.S. Grewal, *The Sikhs: Ideology, Institutions and Identity,* New Delhi: Oxford University Press, 2009. For Cunningham's treatment of the Khalsa, see J.S. Grewal, 'Emergence of a Nation: The Khalsa for Cunningham', *The Khalsa: Sikh and Non-Sikh Perspectives,* ed. J.S. Grewal, New Delhi: Manohar, 2004.
3. I wrote some short articles on 'Toynbee's Interpretation of Sikh History', (*Punjab History Conference Proceedings,* Patiala: Punjabi University, 1969) and 'Indubhusan Banerjee's Evolution of the Khalsa' (*Historians and Historiography of the Sikhs,* ed. Fauja Singh, New Delhi: Oriental Publishers, 1978), besides a few other articles for the *Encyclopaedia of Sikhism,* ed. Harbans Singh, Patiala: Punjabi University (Smyth's 'A History of the Reigning Family of Lahore' in vol. II), pp. 279-81; M'Gregor's 'The History of the Sikhs' in vol. II (pp. 211-12); Gough's 'Sikhs and the Sikh Wars' in vol. IV (pp. 183-5); and Malcolm's 'Sketch of the Sikhs' in vol. IV (pp. 218-20).
4. For a revised version of the 'State of Sikh Studies', see J.S. Grewal, 'A Brief History of Sikh Studies in English', *Studying the Sikhs: Issues for North America,* ed. John Stratton Hawley and Gurinder Singh Mann, Albany: State University of New York Press, 1993.
5. J.S. Grewal, 'The Historians of Maharaja Ranjit Singh', *Journal of Regional History,* Amritsar: Guru Nanak Dev University, 1980.
6. J.S. Grewal, *Guru Nanak in Western Scholarship,* Shimla: Indian Institute of Advanced Study, 1992.
7. J.S. Grewal, *Contesting Interpretations of the Sikh Tradition,* New Delhi: Manohar, 1998.
8. Fauja Singh (ed.), *Historians and Historiography of the Sikhs,* New Delhi: Oriental Publishers, 1978.

9. Gianeshwar Khurana, *British Historiography on the Sikh Power in Punjab*, New Delhi: Allied Publishers, 1985.
10. Darshan Singh, *Western Perspectives on the Sikh Religion*, Amritsar: Singh Brothers, 2004 (2nd edn.).

PART ONE

Under the East India Company

CHAPTER ONE

The Beginnings
Wilkins, Polier, Forster and Browne

The *Early European Accounts of the Sikhs,* edited by Ganda Singh, was published as 'an important source-book for Sikh-history'.[1] Apart from Father Jerome Xavier's brief statement on Guru Arjan's martyrdom in Lahore in 1606 and a short statement of John Surman and Edward Stephenson on the massacre of Banda and his companions in Delhi in 1716, this volume contains half a dozen publications of the last quarter of the eighteenth century, which provide information not only on the contemporary events related to the Sikhs but also on their past.

Amandeep Singh Madra and Paramjit Singh refer to Ganda Singh's work as a source of inspiration for their own work which contains 'every surviving written text' on the Sikhs between 1606 and 1809. They classify nearly 40 texts as coming from missionaries, company men, travellers, military men, orientalists and others. The bulk of the texts relate to contemporary situation, with only a cursory reference to the Sikh past. All the 'eye witness accounts of the Sikhs' edited by Madra and Singh are fascinating and certainly useful for the present-day historians of the Sikhs.[2] Our present concern, however, is only with those writers who presented the late eighteenth-century Sikhs in a historical perspective. We propose to take up only four such 'texts'. In terms of the classification by Madra and Singh, two of the writers were Company men, Antoine Louis-Henri Polier and James Browne; one of them was a traveller, George Forster; and the fourth was an orientalist, Charles Wilkins. They all wrote in the 1780s and their texts were published before the end of the eighteenth century.[3]

I. CHARLES WILKINS: 'THE SEEKS AND THEIR COLLEGE AT PATNA'

Charles Wilkins joined the service of the East India Company as 'a writer' in 1770. As one of the 'bright young men' of Warren Hastings he learnt Sanskrit under his patronage and wrote a grammar in 1779. Wilkins' translation of the *Bhagavadgita* established his reputation as an orientalist. While discoursing with a gentleman in Calcutta on 'that sect of people who are distinguished from the worshippers of Brahma and the followers of Mahommed by the appellation of Seek', he was informed that a considerable number of them had settled in Patna where they had a College for teaching the tenets of their philosophy. On his way to Benares, Wilkins stopped at Patna and visited the College of the Sikhs for a couple of hours. His observations, recorded at Benares on 1 March 1781, were published in the first volume of the *Asiatick Researches* in 1788.[4]

Reaching the College, Wilkins discovered that Sikh worship was open to all; and he had to remove his shoes before entering the place of worship. The noon service was performed by *kirtan* with *shabads* from the *Adi Granth*, followed by formal *ardas*. At the end, *karha parsad* prepared with flour, brown sugar and clarified butter was distributed in the assembly without any distinction. Some of the principal men among them were probably visitors from the Punjab. Wilkins' description of the service and the hall which served as the place of worship is full of interesting details, including a reference to what actually could be the portraits of the Gurus which looked like pictures of Musalman princes.[5]

What Wilkins gathered from his conversation with the Sikhs in the College is no less significant. He records the common belief that there was a dispute between Hindus and Musalmans about the disposal of Guru Nanak's body after his death, but they did not find his body when they removed the sheet that covered it. Wilkins assumed that the Sikh scripture was composed by Guru Nanak; its language is mentioned as that of the Punjab, and its script as Gurmukhi. There were several copies of it in the hall for worship. About its teachings, Wilkins was told that 'there is but one God, omnipotent and omnipresent; filling all space, and pervading all matter; and that he is to be worshipped and invoked'. The ethical dimension of the message was conveyed by the idea that good and bad deeds were taken into account after death for reward or punishment. The Sikh scripture commends universal toleration; it forbids dispute with those of another persuasion and crimes against society; it inculcates universal philanthropy and a general hospitality to strangers and travellers. Wilkins was told that there was another book which was 'now held in almost as much esteem as the former'. An extract in praise of the Deity from this second book struck Wilkins as close to Hindvi, with many Sanskrit words. The main features of the mode of initiation into the Sikh faith were the following: five or more Sikhs assembled together in any place; water sweetened with sugar, sprinkled over the body and into the eyes of the person initiated; and instruction in the chief canons of the faith was imparted to him. Wilkins' appreciative observations left the impression that the Sikhs had their own scripture or scriptures, a simple form of worship, a new ceremony of initiation and a distinct identity of their own.[6]

II. ANTOINE-LOUIS HENRI POLIER: 'THE SIQUES'

Like Wilkins, Polier combined his own observation with oral evidence collected from various sources for a paper that was read before the Asiatic Society of Bengal in December 1787 as 'History of the Seeks'. It had been written at about the same time as Wilkins' observations on the Sikhs. Polier had come to India in 1757 and started his early career as a cadet under Robert Clive who was fighting against the French. He was posted to Bengal in 1761, and allowed to go to Awadh on a secondment in 1766. He resigned from the Company's service in 1775 and took service with Shah Alam II in Delhi in 1776. It was there that he began to collect information on the Sikhs who presented a threat to all non-Sikh territories in their neighbourhood.[7] As pointed out by Ganda Singh, Polier's paper, 'The Siques', was the first 'connected account of the Sikh people written by a European'.[8]

Polier placed the origin of the Sikhs in the time of Akbar when Guru Nanak came to have many followers called Sikhs (disciples); they acknowledged him as the head of 'a new sect'. They never tried to rise against the Mughal authority until the reign of Bahadur Shah when Guru Gobind Singh laid the foundation of 'a kind of Republic'. Originally, and in general, the Sikhs were cultivators of land. They belonged to the tribe called Jatts who were hard working but turbulent in disposition. One of the lowest 'tribes' amongst the Hindus, the Jatts were numerous in the north-west of India. The troubles and rebellions during the reign of Bahadur Shah gave the Sikhs an opportunity of rising under the leadership of 'Guru Govind'. Eventually, the emperor Farrukh Siyar took notice of his activities and sent an army in or about 1715 under the command of Abdus Samad Khan, the governor of Lahore, to exterminate the Sikhs. He took 'Guru Govind' prisoner, and sent him to Delhi where he was put to death. His followers were persecuted with such a vigour that the very name Sikh seemed to have become extinct.[9]

The Sikhs were heard of again some time after the invasion of Nadir Shah. Mir Mannu took rigorous measures against them and might have destroyed them altogether but his deputy Kaura Mal remained helpful to them. Dina Beg Khan did not suppress them for his own reasons. After Mir Mannu's death, struggle for the governorship of Lahore and the intrigues of Mir Mannu's widow resulted in anarchy and confusion. The Sikhs began to grow formidable and to assume independence. They formed themselves into a kind of Republic and in the course of a few years established their government in the provinces of Lahore and Multan. Polier's account has many factual errors, and appears to have been based on oral evidence.[10]

Polier gives a lot more space to Ahmad Shah Abdali. He took notice of the progress of the Sikhs and the manner in which they treated Muslims and Islam, profaning their places of worship and converting them to the Sikh faith. He thought of chastizing them. With the support of the Muslim nobles of Hindustan he defeated the Marathas, and turned his attention to the Sikhs. They were defeated wherever they presented themselves. They were obliged to seek shelter in jungles, but they kept hovering round the Afghans and cutting off their stragglers. Ahmad Shah Abdali razed their famous place of worship to the ground. The holy tank was filled up. For three to four years he caused much destruction but failed to subdue them effectively. He was distracted by revolts in other parts of his empire. His governors in the Punjab were overwhelmed by the Sikhs who destroyed mosques and compelled the Durranis to dig and restore the famous tank in Amritsar. The Sikhs fully established their religion and national councils. Ahmad Shah Abdali did not have the time needed to subdue the Sikhs completely and he abandoned the project. His son, Taimur Shah, lost Multan to the Sikhs, but he recovered it later. Whatever his reasons, Taimur Shah did not try to recover the territories occupied by the Sikhs.[11]

Polier explains the rise and progress of the Sikhs in negative terms. It could be attributed not so much to their bravery, conduct or military knowledge, as to the anarchy and confusion that had desolated the Mughal empire for six or seven decades since the death of Aurangzeb, more particularly due to the weak government of Muhammad Shah, Ahmad Shah and Alamgir Sani. The last emperor was the weakest and the most wretched of them all.[12]

Polier was interested primarily in the contemporary Sikhs who are given as much space as all their past history. Polier comments on the army of the Sikhs, their civil government, their hard life, food and dress, and their beliefs and practices. This part of his essay is extremely interesting and useful for a historical study of the late eighteenth-century Sikhs. However, we may notice it only briefly to understand the nature of Polier's interest. The Sikhs were not so formidable militarily as they were generally represented. They never engaged Ahmad Shah Abdali in a pitched battle even though they were far more numerous than the Afghans. The government of the Sikhs was an aristocracy in which all the chiefs, great and small, looked upon themselves as perfectly equal in all the public concerns. Polier refers to their Deit or Council as Gurmatta held annually at Amritsar, Lahore or some other place. He refers to *rakhi* as tribute. The possessions of the Sikh chiefs were well cultivated and the revenue in general was collected in kind.[13]

The Sikhs abhorred smoking of tobacco but drank *bhang* and spirits freely; they wore blue turbans and iron bracelets on their wrists. The Sikh faith had a 'taint' of the Hindu religion: they venerated the cow and abstained scrupulously from beef; they paid some respect to idols, but their great object of worship was their own saints, called Gurus. Their only symbol was Vaheguru. About the mode of initiation, Polier says that the converts were made to drink out of a pan in which the feet of those present had been washed. The Sikhs kept their hair and beard uncut. They had started pilgrimages to Ganges in addition to the famous tank at Amritsar.[14]

In Polier's assessment, the Sikhs were the terror and plague of the northern parts of India. They encouraged the *zamindars* and cultivators under others to revolt, which made them troublesome. If they were not attacked soon in their own territories, their tenets and manners would be adopted by the *zamindars* of the provinces of Delhi and Agra. The combined forces of Najaf Khan and Taimur Shah could reduce the Sikhs effectively. Polier closes his essay with the prophecy made by one of their Gurus that white men from the West would destroy the power of the Sikhs who now believed that the Europeans would fulfil that prophecy.[15]

On the whole, Polier's information on the Sikhs appears to have been collected from non-Sikhs who were neither sympathetic nor accurate. He himself had no appreciation for their religion and no respect for their power. Nor had he any scruples against the destruction of their states. The prophecy of their Guru, whether or not actually current among the Sikhs, was in tune with Polier's own hope for the future.

III. GEORGE FORSTER: *A JOURNEY FROM BENGAL TO ENGLAND*

Not much later than Polier's account, George Forster wrote about the Sikhs early in 1783. A civil servant on the Madras establishment of the East India Company, Forster was on a short visit to Benares in August 1782 for conducting investigation into the Hindu religion. He had read Nathaniel Halhed's *Code of Gentoo Laws,* but his own interest was wider. Before the end of 1782 he was on the move in the guise of a Georgian, and not an English man, for safety to reach Europe through Asian countries by land, and into Russia by the Caspian Sea. On 6 March 1783 he crossed the Jamuna to arrive at Nahan two days later. He crossed the Sutlej on 23 March to reach Bilaspur. Before reaching Jammu in April, Forster wrote a long letter on the history of the Sikhs, 'this new and extraordinary people who, within a period of twenty years, have conquered a tract of country, extending in certain directions from the Ganges to the Indus'.[16] Evidently, the rise of the Sikhs to political power was the primary reason for Forster's interest in the Sikh past.

In his comments on the contemporary Sikhs, Forster quotes a passage from a 'memoir' written by Polier at Delhi in 1777 on the Sikhs and their 'military capacity'.[17] Elsewhere he refers to the 'records of the Sikhs', without mentioning any specific source. In any case, his account of the Sikhs is more detailed than Polier's, and a broad outline of Sikh history appears to emerge from it. The year of Guru Nanak's birth at Talwandi is given correctly as 1469, and that of his death as 1539. He appeared to have possessed qualities which enabled him to institute 'a new system of religion'. His tenets forbid the worship of idols. The place of public prayer ordained by him was a simple construction, with the *Granth* as the only object. The prayer was addressed directly to God, the sole ruler of the universe. There were many essential differences between the religious code of the Hindus and that of the Sikhs, but there were also strong features of similarity in the groundwork. Admission of proselytes from all castes and creeds to the Sikh faith was an essential 'deviation' from the Hindu system. In the patterns of connubium and commensality there was no change. Among the contemporary Sikhs, only the sacred *parsad* was eaten together without any distinction of tribe or caste.[18]

Guru Nanak travelled for fifteen years through most of the kingdoms of India to preach his doctrine and, according to the Sikh tradition, he went into Persia and Arabia. He was accompanied by the Muslim musician Mardana who became his disciple. It was said that he was apprehended by the soldiers of Babur in one of his expeditions but he was treated with respect and indulgence in view of the sanctity of his character. The followers of Guru Nanak in his lifetime were neither numerous nor powerful, and that was the reason why the contemporary writers do not refer to them. At the place where Guru Nanak had died on the bank of the Ravi, a vast concourse of people assembled annually to perform certain ceremonies in commemoration of his death.[19]

Guru Nanak did not leave the charge of his mission with either of his two sons but with his disciple Angad who was also entrusted with the propagation of his message. Guru Angad died at Khadur in 1542[20] to be succeeded by Guru Amar Das who propagated the teachings of Guru Nanak at Goindwal till the end of his life in 1574. His son-in-law, Guru Ram Das received some marks of favour from Akbar and founded the town of Ramdaspur on land granted by him. He repaired and embellished the tank known as *amritsar*. He compiled the history and precepts of his predecessors, adding his own commentaries. He died at Ramdaspur in 1581 to be succeeded by his son, Guru Arjan, who died at Lahore in 1606 due to the rigours of confinement by a Hindu favourite of emperor Jahangir on his orders.[21]

Guru Hargobind, the only son and successor of Guru Arjan, was actuated by revenge. With the aid of his enthusiastic supporters he dragged the emperor's Hindu favourite from his house and put him to death in Lahore itself. For fear of the emperor's reaction, Guru Hargobind moved to Kartarpur and collected an armed body for defence. According to the Sikh records, he defeated a force of Jahangir that had been sent to punish him for his rebellion. But Forster is sceptical about his military achievements. He goes on to say that probably the Mughal officer Mahabat Khan effected the submission of the Sikhs to the emperor; Guru Hargobind was imprisoned in the fort of Gwalior but set at liberty after a short confinement. Henceforth, he did not disturb the peace of the Mughal government and died at Kiratpur in 1644.[22]

The Sikhs accepted Har Rai, a grandson of Guru Hargobind, as their Guru. He died at Kiratpur in 1661. There was a contest for succession among his two sons: Ram Rai and Har Krishan. They appealed to the court of law at Delhi and presented their claims. The court allowed the Sikhs to nominate their Guru and they elected Har Krishan. A short time after his investiture Guru Har Krishan died at Delhi in 1664. He was succeeded by Guru Tegh Bahadur who was 'persecuted' by Ram Rai with Aurangzeb's support. After two years of imprisonment in Delhi, Guru Tegh Bahadur was released through the intercession of Raja Jai Singh. The Guru and his Sikhs accompanied Raja Jai Singh to Bengal. According to the Sikh records, Ram Rai kept up his hostility towards Guru Tegh Bahadur who was arrested, brought to Delhi, and executed in 1675. Forster is sceptical about the Sikh version that the Guru was punished without any criminal charge against him. Partial to their Guru the Sikhs appeared to misrepresent Aurangzeb. Forster admits, however, that he could not find any evidence of crime on the part of Guru Tegh Bahadur.[23]

Guru Gobind Singh, the only son and successor of Guru Tegh Bahadur, left Patna, went into the territories of Srinagar (Garhwal), fought a battle against the Raja, and left for the Punjab where a marauding Hindu chief welcomed him. Guru Gobind Singh helped this chief against the bordering landholders, often in opposition to the forces of the Mughal government. Due to his 'predatory conduct' the Mughal governor of Sirhind, Wazir Khan, drove him out of his place of residence. Vigorously pressed by the imperial troops, he was compelled to save himself by speedy flight. His two younger sons were put to death in cold blood by Wazir Khan. The Guru found a safe retreat in the Lakhi Jungle, and returned to his former residence after some time. According to the Sikhs, he received marks of favour from Bahadur Shah who gave him a command in the army which he was leading against his brother, Kam Bakhsh, in the south. At Nander, Guru Gobind Singh was assaulted by a Pathan soldier and died of wounds in 1708. No successor was appointed because he had left no male heirs. In any case, the Sikhs believed that no one was to be nominated after the tenth Guru.[24]

A disciple named Banda, who had accompanied Guru Gobind Singh, returned to the Punjab and raised a small force on the basis of his connection with the Guru. His successes drew the whole body of the Sikh nation to his standard. They attacked Wazir Khan who was killed in the battle. The victorious Sikhs satiated their revenge by destroying the inhabitants of Sirhind, overthrowing their mosques, and digging out their graves. A body of the Sikhs invaded the Doab and occupied the town and territory of Saharanpur. Banda crossed the Sutlej but he was repulsed by Shams Khan, the imperial officer. The Sikhs who had conquered Saharanpur were defeated by the imperial forces near Delhi. A division of the imperial army defeated the Sikhs in a battle near Sirhind and obliged Banda to give up his conquests. However, the Sikhs could not be conquered during the reign of Bahadur Shah. His successor, Jahandar Shah, could only make a feeble effort against the Sikhs. In the time of Farrukh Siyar, Abdus Samad Khan, the governor of Lahore, captured Banda and his followers and sent them to Delhi where they met a deserved fate for their savage and often unprovoked cruelties. 'Yet they met it with an undaunted firmness, and died amidst the wondering praise of the populace'.[25]

After relating the origin of the Sikhs, with a chronological account of the ten Gurus and Banda's attempt 'to establish an independent dominion', Forster talks of certain 'ordinances' established by the Gurus. He refers to the ceremony of initiation, concluding with instructions laying down the religious, moral and political duties of a Sikh. The first part of the initiation denoted the equality of the followers of Guru Nanak; it was designed to destroy the essentially inegalitarian principle of the Hindu religion. However, this objective was only partially achieved. The military order among the Sikhs allowed their hair and beard to grow long; they wore iron bracelets on their wrists, and prohibited the use of tobacco. These regulations had become primary and almost formed the essence of their creed. Widows were expressly forbidden to destroy themselves at the death of their husbands, and they were permitted to remarry. But many women were seen ascending the funeral pyre because Hindu converts to the Sikh faith still adhered to this practice. A lamentation for the death of any person was regarded as criminal. The Sikhs subscribed to the belief in transmigration.[26]

The Sikh nation was composed of two distinct orders: the *Khulasa* and the *Khalsa*. The former adhered to the institutions of Guru Nanak and were generally occupied in civil and domestic duties. They cut-off the hair of their heads and beards and resembled the ordinary class of Hindus. The *Khalsa* belonged to the 'modern order' founded by Guru Gobind Singh who imparted a military spirit to his followers. Mostly Jatts and Gujjars, they affixed the word Singh to their names, kept uncut hair, wore an iron bracelet, and abhorred tobacco. They were visibly distinct from the *Khulasa*. Forster was informed that matrimonial connections were occasionally formed between the *Khulasa* Sikhs and Hindus.[27]

After the defeat and death of Banda, the power of the Sikhs was destroyed and their sect, ostensibly, extirpated. Farrukh Siyar issued a general order now to put all those Sikhs to the sword who refused to accept Islam. The Sikhs who still adhered to their faith left the Punjab plains and took refuge in the hills. Sikh forces appeared in arms at the time of Nadir Shah's return from Delhi when his rear was attacked by parties of Sikh cavalry to acquire a large plunder. Even at their lowest ebb, the Sikhs had continued to resort secretly to *amritsar*. The spark that lay concealed now burst forth and produced a flame which was never to be extinguished. Their favourite place of worship rose into the capital of a small territory. Alarmed at the increase in their power, Mir Mannu made a vigorous attack on them but Kaura Mal, who was a *Khulasa* Sikh, diverted him from his objective of destroying Sikh power.

Adina Beg Khan was successful in his campaign against the Sikhs in 1749 but Kaura Mal effected accommodation between the Sikhs and the governor of Lahore. The death of Mir Mannu was followed by competition for the governorship of Lahore, and the Sikhs were able to increase their power. However, during the governorship of Adina Beg Khan the Sikhs were rarely seen interrupting the peace of his government.[28]

Ahmad Shah Durrani came in 1756 to recover the Punjab. Adina Beg Khan fled into the mountains. On his suggestion, a huge army of the Marathas moved into the Punjab in 1757 or 1758. After the occupation, the Marathas appointed Adina Beg Khan as their governor but he died soon afterwards. Ahmad Shah defeated the Marathas in the battle of Panipat in 1761. Early in 1762 he killed 25,000 Sikhs in a single battle, razed Amritsar to the ground, and choked up the sacred tank with its ruins. On Ahmad Shah's departure from the Punjab, the Sikhs defeated his administrators and even occupied Lahore. Its mosques were destroyed and the Afghans in chains were forced to cleanse the tank at Amritsar. Forster is sceptical about the Sikh claim that the Sikhs had obliged Ahmad Shah to retreat after a battle near Amritsar in 1762. Ahmad Shah came again in 1763 to drive the Sikhs from the plains of Lahore. In 1764, however, the Sikhs occupied territories from the Indus to the neighbourhood of Delhi. In the three years following Ahmad Shah failed against the Sikhs. After 1767, he relinquished the design of subduing them. In 1782, the Sikhs were ruling over territories between the northern mountains and Multan and between the Indus and the Ganges.[29]

Having outlined the first territorial establishment of the Sikhs and the extension of their spacious dominions, Forster observes that during their struggle against the superior resources of the Mughals or the Afghans the Sikhs retained their high spirits, resourcefulness, and perseverance to rise superior to the most powerful ruler of the time. The other factors which accounted for their success included a general decline in Mughal power, internecine intrigues, and defection of the distant governors, which resulted in a common relaxation of allegiance in pursuit of individual interests. The role of Kaura Mal in a critical situation and the distracted state of Ahmad Shah's dominions were also helpful to the Sikhs.[30]

Forster talks about the form of the civil and military government of the Sikhs, their tactics in battle, the state of agriculture and commerce in their dominions, their general character, their attitude towards Muslims, and their discordant interests. According to Forster, no distinct term could be applied to the form of the Sikh government. It appeared to be aristocratic but a large vein of popular power could be discerned in many of its parts. An equality of rank was maintained in their civil society, which no class of men, however wealthy or powerful, was suffered to infringe. In their council, every member was free to express his opinion. However, the grand assembly was now rarely convened. Numerous heads or chiefs of states pursued their independent interests, without any regard to general policy. There was no cooperation at the 'national level'. Nevertheless, a cause for maintaining their power and faith could combine them in their efforts under a capable leader who could raise the standard of monarchy on the ruins of their commonwealth. If that were to happen, Forster had no doubt that the Sikhs would be advanced to 'the first rank' among the native rulers of India. They could, thus, become 'a terror to the surrounding states'.[31]

Forster's account of the Sikhs is not free from errors or inadequacies. However, it makes a substantial advance over Polier's account, particularly in its historical part. This may be due partly to the Sikh sources he used. Indeed, he refers to Sikh records at several places in his account and to historical tracts of the Sikhs in the preface. But he does not appear to have personally read any written source. His attitude towards received information was critical. He claims that his 'history' was 'either founded on received tradition or on those legends which have the least exceptionable claims to credit'.[32] Forster aimed at rational explanation on the basis of evidence that he regarded as credible. In his narrative he presents strictly what he regarded as historical facts.

IV. JAMES BROWNE: *HISTORY OF THE ORIGIN AND PROGRESS OF THE SICKS*

James Browne was the first writer to make use of a literary work directly for his *History of the Origin and Progress of the Sicks*. In fact, he gave his own translation of this work in Persian commissioned by him. He refers to 'two Hindu natives of Lahore' as its authors. Ganda Singh has identified them as Budh Singh of Lahore and Ajaib Singh Suraj of Malerkotla, and their work as *Risala-i Nanak Shah Darvesh*. Budh Singh was actually in the service of James Browne. The original *Risala* is now in the British Library.[33]

Browne had joined the army of the East India Company in 1765 when he was about 21 years old. He became Lieutenant in 1767 and Captain in 1771. He was appointed Collector of the 'Jungle Terry districts' in 1774. He was promoted to the rank of Major in 1781. From the Company's point of view the political situation in Delhi appeared to be deteriorating and Warren Hastings appointed Browne in August 1782 as his Agent to the imperial court. On 1 March 1785, he was recalled by Sir John McPherson who had succeeded Warren Hastings in January. Browne left for England in 1786, and in September 1787 he submitted to John Motteux, the Chairman of the Court of Directors of the Company, a copy of the *History of the Origin and Progress of the Sicks*, together with His *Description of the Jungle Terry Districts*. Browne's *History* was published by the Company in 1788 as *India Tracts*. Browne was promoted to the rank of Lieutenant-Colonel in 1788 itself.[34]

Browne tells us that during the time of his residence in Delhi as the English Minister at the Court of His Majesty, Shah Alam, he took every opportunity to acquire knowledge of the strength, resources, disposition, and the constitution of the states bordering on the provinces of Agra and Dehli, by seeking out the best informed men among the subjects of those states. The first and the most important among them was 'the great irregular Aristocracy of Sicks' who had established themselves as rulers 'in complete possession' of all the countries between the Attock and Sutlej and extended their excursions to the frontiers of the Vizier's dominions. The primary reason for Browne's interest in the Sikhs, thus, was political, a candid acknowledgement of their political power.

Browne concludes his statement about the Persian manuscript by pointing out its limitation: it did not contain any information on the manners and customs of the Sikhs. For these 'heads', he had collected information from other sources orally. The 'Introduction' to his *History of the Origin and Progress of the Sicks* is based on the information he had collected.[35]

Browne refers to the Sikhs as being originally the common inhabitants of the provinces of Lahore and Multan, belonging mostly to the 'Jaut' tribe. About the Sikh doctrine, he observes that it was introduced by Guru Nanak. It appeared 'to bear that kind of relation to the Hindoo religion, which the Protestant does to the Romish'; all the essential principles were retained, but most of its ceremonies were dropped and the subordinate objects of veneration were removed.[36] Browne had virtually no evidence on the essential principles of the Sikh faith but then he had no way of knowing it.

Browne makes a general statement about the development of the Sikhs from a pacifist sect into a militant organization against the government.

> At first, the sect was merely speculative, quiet, inoffensive, and unarmed: they were first persecuted by the barbarous bigotry of Aurungzebe; and persecution, as will ever be the case, gave strength to that which it meant to destroy; the Sicks from necessity confederated together, and finding that their peaceable deportment did not secure them from oppression, they took up arms to defend themselves against a tyrannical government and as will always happen where the common rights of humanity are violated, a hero arose, whose courage and ability directed the efforts of his injured followers, to a just, though severe revenge.

He further observes that as the Mughal government declined, the Sikhs continued to gain strength despite the repeated attempts to suppress them. They combined the political with the religious principle and opened admission to all. The immediate advantages of protection and independence attracted new entrants. They levied contribution from their neighbours who did not come into their fraternity.[37]

The government of the Sikhs, according to Browne; was 'aristocratical, but very irregular and imperfect'. The body of the people was divided under a number of chiefs, who possessed portions of the country and enjoyed distinct authority in their respective districts, uncontrolled by any superior power. They assembled together on particular occasions for organizing campaigns against others or for defence. Their meetings were tumultuous and the leader to command their joint forces during the expedition was chosen by majority, generally from among the chiefs whose territories were the most considerable. His authority was rather ill-obeyed by so many other chiefs who possessed smaller territories but thought of themselves as perfectly equal. During his temporary elevation, the leader was barely given the dignity of a first among equals.[38]

Browne talks of a coin struck by Jassa Singh, which had to be replaced. According to him, when the Sikhs expelled Ahmad Shah Durrani from the province and occupied Lahore, Jassa Singh (Ahluwalia) struck a rupee at the mint of Lahore in his own name. This coin wore an inscription in Persian to the effect that 'Jassa Kalal' had conquered the country of Ahmad and struck coin through God's grace. This inscription carried the implication that Jassa Singh (Ahluwalia) was the sovereign ruler of the Sikhs. This coin remained current for about fifteen years before it was recalled, and in its place a new coin was struck after a collective decision of the Sikh chiefs. The new coin carried an inscription in Persian to the effect that Guru Gobind Singh received three things from Guru Nanak: the *degh*, the sword, and rapid victory.[39] The coin of 'Jassa Kalal' became controversial in the twentieth century and its authenticity stands rejected.

Browne was familiar with the words *Gurmata*, *Khalsaji* and *Dal Khalsa*. He equates the first with his 'Diet', the second with his 'Confederacy' or the State and the third with 'the Army of the state'.[40] These terms were becoming current in the late eighteenth century and their echoes can be heard even in the twentieth century. The polity of the Sikhs during the late eighteenth century was not easy to conceptualize.

Browne makes the general observation that the territories under Sikh rule were in a state of high cultivation. The rate of land revenue was moderate and it was mostly collected in kind. During an internal dispute, the husbandman was never molested. Trade was in a low state. The principal manufactures were fine cloth and excellent arms, both produced in Lahore. The Sikh cavalry was remarkably good. The Sikhs generally had 'a manly boldness in their manner and conversation, very unlike the other inhabitants of Hindostan, owing no doubt to the freedom of their government'. They did not smoke tobacco but drank spirits and *bhang* to excess. They let the hair and beard grow to full length and wore a steel ring round one of the wrists. They confirmed all their engagements in the name of the Guru. The initiation ceremony was meant to abolish every distinction. Their past indicated that their power was bound to expand, making them in the end to be exceedingly formidable to all their neighbours.[41]

The map given by Browne was 'designed principally as a political chart, to show the extent of the dominions of the Sicks, and the places where the chiefs reside'. Thirty chiefs and their places of residence figure in the list prepared by Browne. Better known among these chiefs are Raja Gajpat Singh of Karnal, Bhanga Singh of Thanesar, Karam Singh of Shahabad, Gurdit Singh of Ambala, Jassa Singh of Sirhind, Hamir Singh of Nabha, Raja Sahib Singh of Patiala and Rai Singh of Buria between the Jamuna and the Sutlej; in the Jalandhar Doab, Jassa Singh of Kapurthala, and Tara Singh Gheba of Nakodar; in the Bari Doab, Gujjar Singh, Sobha Singh and Lehna Singh of Lahore; in the Rachna Doab, Mahan Singh; in the remaining two Doabs, Mahan Singh and Gujjar Singh. The total force of all the Sikh chiefs was close to 100,000, with cavalry constituting about 75 per cent of the force. In terms of the number of horse and foot under each chief, Raja Sahib Singh was at the top in the Sutlej-Jamuna Divide, with 4,500 horse and 1,500 foot; in the Jalandhar Doab, Jassa Singh of Kapurthala commanded 3,000 horse and 1,000 foot; in the remaining Doabs, Mahan Singh commanded 15,000 horse and 5,000 foot. Most of the chiefs listed commanded 1,000 to 3,000 horse and foot. The chief to command the lowest number was Khushal Singh of Garh Shankar, with 150 horse and 50 foot. It is not the accuracy of the chart that is so important as the care and concern with which it was prepared. It reflects the depth of Browne's primary interest.[42]

Towards the end of his narrative, Browne provides information on the events that took place after the last event mentioned in the *Risala-i Nanak Shah Darvesh*: the loss of Multan by Taimur Shah in the beginning of his reign and its recovery in 1779; the tribute collected by the Sikh chiefs from the Raja of Jammu in 1785; and the treaty signed by Mahadji Sindhia with the Sikh chiefs of the Sutlej-Jamuna Divide. Browne managed to obtain a copy of this treaty and sent it to the Acting Governor-General MacPherson on 9 April 1785. He did not know what use was made of this information but 'surely a confederacy of two such formidable powers as the Sicks and the Mahrattas, close to the Vizier's frontier, must afford matter for very serious apprehension to every person who is anxious for the safety of the Company's possessions in

India, which are intimately connected with those of the Vizier, that prosperity or calamity must be in common to them both'. Thus, the interests of the Company were of paramount importance for Browne in his search for knowledge about the Sikhs, present and past.[43]

In Ganda Singh's *Early European Accounts of the Sikhs,* Browne's *History of the Origin and Progress of the Sicks* covers 31 pages. The translation of the *Risala,* covering 20 pages, contains ample annotation by Ganda Singh. Even so, the translated narrative forms a substantial portion of Browne's *History*. Incidentally, the annotation reveals the factual errors and misconceptions of the *Risala*. Guru Nanak's death, for example, is placed in the reign of Babur in 1529. Nevertheless, what is sought to be underlined by the authors of the *Risala* is the fact that Guru Nanak at the time of his death was recognized by a considerable number of people called 'Sikhs' as their preceptor (Guru). In the list of his successors we find the name of Ram Rai instead of Guru Hargobind, and Guru Tegh Bahadur is stated to have been born in 1662 as the son of Guru Har Krishan. The Sikhs began to call Guru Tegh Bahadur 'the true king' and he was summoned to the imperial court where Aurangzeb ordered his execution. Born after the death of Guru Tegh Bahadur, Guru Gobind Singh, conceived at the age of 20 an ardent desire for revenge. He performed a number of superstitious rites on the advice of Brahmans, eventually to hear a voice from heaven that his followers, and he in his lifetime, would take revenge and also arrive at 'the highest point of strength and dominion'. For some time, Guru Gobind Singh's mind was 'disordered', but recovering his reason he put on a dress of blue colour, let his hair and beard grow, and instructed his followers to do likewise. He also directed them to arm themselves in expectation of the fulfilment of the prophecy of their success. Guru Gobind Singh introduced a new ceremony of initiation called *pahul,* marked by the use of a dagger and a certain incantation. This *pahul* was drunk by all from a common bowl. The number of Sikhs began to increase rapidly. Aurangzeb sent an order to Wazir Khan of Sirhind to suppress the threatening insurrection. However, before he received the order, Guru Gobind Singh died at Patna. Wazir Khan pursued the Sikhs escorting the young sons and their grandmother to a safe place, captured the two children, and put them in confinement. Eventually, they were butchered before the eyes of their grandmother who died of grief.[44]

Banda Bairagi appears in the narrative as a friend of Guru Gobind Singh. This was the reason for the former's determination to seek revenge. He inspired the most powerful and zealous Sikhs of the Guru with the same spirit. He himself became a Sikh. Aurangzeb's death, followed by the war of succession, gave Banda the opportunity to collect an irregular but large army of Sikhs to attack Wazir Khan. In a battle fought away from Sirhind, Wazir Khan was killed and his army was defeated. Diwan Sucha Nanda, on whose advice the sons of Guru Gobind Singh had been butchered, was torn into pieces. Mosques and tombs were destroyed. In a short time then the country from Panipat to the neighbourhood of Lahore came under the control of the Sikhs. Bahadur Shah was in the south but hearing of this revolt he moved with his whole force towards Sirhind, sending an advance army under Sultan Kuli Khan. He was ordered to put to the sword every man who had unshorn hair and a flowing beard, 'the characteristic external of the Sicks'. Sultan Kuli Khan defeated a unit of the Sikh army before coming to battle with Banda. Finding the Sikhs disarrayed due to a determined attack by the imperial troops, Banda took refuge in the fort of Lohgarh. The imperial army laid siege to the fort, and Bahadur Shah arrived with the whole army. Many Sikhs died fighting in defence and a number of them were made prisoners and sent to Delhi. There they were publicly executed in 1718 after having been offered the option of Islam which they rejected out of contempt. Banda was among them.[45]

Abdus Samad Khan was the governor of Lahore at this time and the Sikhs virtually disappeared from the province during his tenure. In the time of Zakariya Khan they carried on a kind of predatory war in the foothills as if to try the temper of the government. In 1838, Nadir Shah invaded India. The Sikhs began to commit depredations on all sides plundering the property of those who had fled to avoid the Persian army. The Sikhs fortified themselves near the village Dallewal on the bank of the Ravi. After Nadir Shah's return to Persia, Zakariya Khan appointed Adina Beg Khan as the *faujdar* of the Bari Doab. Though he could have done so, Adina Beg Khan did not wholly suppress the Sikhs who had seized several places in different parts of the province. They began to visit the holy tank at Amritsar.[46]

Zakariya Khan died at this time and his elder son was appointed as the *subedar* of Lahore. His younger brother entered into dispute with him. In this situation the Sikhs increased their strength. Ahmad Shah Durrani, who had proclaimed himself to be the successor of Nadir Shah after his assassination, claimed the territories which the Mughal emperor had ceded to Nadir Shah. He came to Lahore. Shah Nawaz Khan, the younger son of Zakariya Khan, submitted to him. Ahmad Shah proclaimed himself to be the master of the province, and returned to Kandahar. During these troubles the Sikh chiefs Jassa Singh Kalal, Charhat Singh and 'Kirwar' Singh got together about 5,000 horse, and to this army, with which they had made themselves masters of the Bari Doab, they gave the name of *Dal Khalsaji*, or the Army of the State.[47]

Muin ul-Mulk or Mir Mannu was appointed to the governorship of Lahore and Multan by the Mughal emperor Ahmad Shah who had succeeded Muhammad Shah. Mir Mannu appointed Adina Beg Khan as the *faujdar* of Jalandhar Doab and he became active against the Sikhs. However, more and more people in distress began to join the *Dal Khalsa*. In 1750, Ahmad Shah Durrani invaded India again and defeated Mir Mannu, seized Lahore and levied heavy contribution. But he reappointed Mir Mannu as his own governor. He tried to suppress the Sikhs but he died in 1752. At Delhi too, the emperor Ahmad Shah was deposed and Alamgir Sani was placed on the throne. The reins of government became entirely relaxed, and the Sikhs gathered new strength.[48]

Ahmad Shah Durrani invaded India in 1755. The Sikhs had become very numerous by this time. They did not oppose the Afghan army but they plundered the stragglers. Ahmad Shah Durrani marched on to Delhi and plundered the city. Then he plundered Mathura and returned to Kandahar. He appointed a chief named Ahmad Khan to command in Sirhind and his own son Taimur Shah, as the *subedar* of Lahore and Multan, with the support of an army under the command of Jahan Khan. In his religious zeal, Jahan Khan destroyed the Sikh sacred structures at Amritsar and filled up the holy tank. The Sikh chiefs gathered together and blockaded the city of Lahore. Jahan Khan came out several time to give battle but felt obliged to retreat. On this occasion, Jassa Singh Kalal, the commander-in-chief of the *Dal Khalsa*, struck rupees in his own name at the royal mint at Lahore, with the inscription that Jassa Kalal had conquered the country of Ahmad and struck this coin with the grace of God.[49]

The court of Delhi appointed Adina Beg Khan as the *subedar* of Lahore, but the force with which he was provided was so weak that he was not prepared to encounter the Sikhs. He stayed near Sirhind and applied to Raghnath Rao to assist him. The Maratha chief marched to Sirhind. The Sikh chiefs who had been persuaded to join him plundered the town of Sirhind, and the Marathas thought of taking action against them. Adina Beg Khan informed the Sikh chiefs in time and they marched away. The Sikh leaders at Lahore did not think their army could match the Marathas and they left the city. The Marathas occupied the provinces of Lahore and Multan but retreated before Ahmad Shah Durrani in 1758. Durrani reached Delhi and defeated the Marathas in a battle. The battle of Panipat was fought then in 1760 in which the Marathas received such a blow that they had not recovered from it when Browne was writing his account. The Sikhs were more powerful and active in the Punjab now. As soon as Ahmad Shah Durrani crossed the Sutlej, the Sikhs began to plunder the stragglers. In this manner he continued to march up to Attock. The Sikhs who were pursuing him returned to Lahore to blockade the city. Buland Khan evacuated Lahore. The Sikhs took the city and all the country from the Indus to Sirhind.[50]

In 1761 Ahmad Shah Durrani came to the Punjab primarily to deal with the Sikhs. At a place called Barnala he put great numbers of the Sikhs to the sword. But they assembled again in 1762 and ousted the governors appointed by him: Raja Kabuli Mal from Lahore and Sa'adat Yar Khan from the Jalandhar Doab. They attacked Malerkotla and killed Hinghun (Bhikhan) Khan. They attacked Zain Khan, the Durrani *faujdar* at Sirhind. The city was sacked with particular enthusiasm for being the place where Guru Gurbind Singh's children had been butchered. Ahmad Shah Durrani marched from Kabul towards Delhi, avoiding interruption from the Sikhs. He had not yet reached Delhi when he was informed by Najib-ud-Daulah that he had concluded a peace with Jawahar Singh and the Shah's presence in the neighbourhood of Delhi might renew the calamities for the city. The Shah marched back to his own country. But the Sikhs were determined to oppose him and a pitched battle was fought near Amritsar, with great losses on both sides. In the morning, Ahmad Shah Durrani retreated quietly. The Sikhs expelled his administrators from the Punjab, held a general 'diet' at Amritsar, and resolved to recall the 'Jassa Kalal' coin and to strike in future the coin with the names of Guru Nanak and Guru Gobind Singh. 'Thus, was the divine pleasure notified to Guru Gobind Singh fulfilled; and thus had Providence raised up the Sikhs in consideration of the piety and charity of Guru Nanak.' The Sikh sovereignty was a reward of Sikh piety.[51]

On the whole, Browne's *History of the Origin and Progress of the Sicks* gets neatly divided into two almost equal parts: his own information, and his translation of the *Risala-i Nanak Shah Darvesh*. His own observations are largely on contemporary Sikhs. They relate to the form of polity, government and administration, the army and material resources, manners and morals, and the religious beliefs and practices of the Sikhs. All these aspects of life appeared to be relevant for an assessment of the Sikhs as a political power and the future course of their political élan. The *Risala* starts with Guru Nanak and ends with the declaration of Sikh sovereignty by striking the coin in the name of the Gurus. In spite of the large gaps, factual errors, misconceptions and inadequacies which mark the *Risala*, it projects a development in chronological order, with patches of information that appear to have come from written sources. Furthermore, these written sources were not 'Sikh' but Persian. In a sense, thus, Browne's work complements the work of Forster who used 'Sikh' and not Persian records.

Ganda Singh noticed that John Malcolm, W.L. M'Gregor and Joseph Davey Cunningham relied considerably on Browne's *History*, and the result was not very happy. 'Many a mistake of the Persian manuscript translated by Browne have come to be repeated.'[52] It may be added that Ganda Singh's own 'source-book' was based on the assumption that these early European sources were still useful to the historian if they were used carefully and critically. The basic importance of these sources now is not their historiographical part but their evidence on the contemporary Sikhs, that is, for the history of the Sikhs during the late eighteenth century.

NOTES

1. Ganda Singh (ed.), *Early European Accounts of the Sikhs*, Calcutta: Firma K.L. Mukhopadhayaya, 1962, Preface.

2. Amandeep Singh Madra and Paramjit Singh (eds.), *"Sicques, Tigers or Thieves": Eyewitness Accounts of the Sikhs (1606-1809)*, New York: Palgrave Macmillan, 2004. The quoted part of the title comes from the words used by George Forster in his *Journey*.
3. We have not taken up these works in the order of their publication but in the order of the time of their composition, starting with Charles Wilkins who stands distinguished as the only author writing on the basis of his short visit to a Sikh institution outside the Punjab.
4. Madra and Singh, *"Sicques, Tigers, or Thieves"*, pp. 291-4.
5. Ibid., pp. 294-5.
6. Ibid., pp. 295-6.
7. Ibid., pp. 67-72.
8. Ganda Singh, *Early European Accounts*, pp. 53.
9. Madra and Singh, *"Sicques, Tigers, or Thieves"*, pp. 77-8.
10. Ibid., p. 78.
11. Ibid., pp. 78-9.
12. Ibid., pp. 79-80.
13. Ibid., pp. 80-1.
14. Ibid., pp. 81-2.
15. Ibid., p. 82.
16. George Forster, *A Journey from Bengal to England, through the Northern Part of India, Kashmire, Afghanistan, and Persia, and into Russia by the Caspian Sea*, 2 vols., Patiala: Punjab Languages Department, 1970 (rpt.), vol. I, pp. 73, 78, 88, 98, 102, 108, 241.
17. Ibid., pp. 333-5. In the Preface to his work, Forster mentions his obligation to Colonel Polier for 'large historical tracts of the Sicques'.
18. Ibid., pp. 292-5.
19. Ibid., pp. 295-6.
20. The correct date is 1552. In view of the accuracy of several other dates given by Forster, the year '1542' may be a misprint.
21. Forster, *A Journey from Bengal to England*, pp. 296-8.
22. Ibid., pp. 298-9.
23. Ibid., pp. 299-300.
24. Ibid., pp. 300-3.
25. Ibid., pp. 303-6.
26. Ibid., pp. 306-9.
27. Ibid., pp. 309-12.
28. Ibid., pp. 312-17.
29. Ibid., pp. 317-26.
30. Ibid., pp. 326-8.
31. Ibid., pp. 329-40.
32. Ibid., pp. 291-2.

33. Ganda Singh, *Early European Accounts of the Sikhs*, pp. 5, 13.
34. Ibid., pp. 1-5. Madra and Singh, *"Sicques, Tigers, and Thieves"*, pp. 89-93.
35. Ganda Singh, *Early European Accounts of the Sikhs*, p. 13.
36. Ibid., pp. 13-14.
37. Ibid., p. 14.
38. Ibid., pp. 14-15.
39. Ibid., pp. 15-16.
40. Ibid., pp. 16-17.
41. Ibid., pp. 17-19.
42. Ibid., p. 43.
43. Ibid., pp. 41-2.
44. Ibid., pp. 13-28.
45. Ibid., pp. 28-31.
46. Ibid., pp. 31-2.
47. Ibid., pp. 32-3.
48. Ibid., pp. 34-5.
49. Ibid., pp. 35-6.
50. Ibid., pp. 36-8.
51. Ibid., pp. 38-41.
52. Ibid., p. 6. For Polier, Forster and Browne, see also Fauja Singh, 'Early European Writers: Browne, Polier, Forster and Malcolm', *Historians and Historiography of the Sikhs*, ed. Fauja Singh, New Delhi: Oriental Publishers, 1978, pp. 1-15. Gianeshwar Khurana, 'The Pioneers', *British Historiography on the Sikh Power in Punjab*, New Delhi: Allied Publishers, 1985, pp. 1-16.

CHAPTER TWO

John Malcolm
A Sketch of the Sikhs

I. INTRODUCTORY

First published in the eleventh volume of the *Asiatick Researches,* John Malcolm's *Sketch of the Sikhs* was published as a book in 1812.[1] He had started collecting materials on the Sikhs in 1805 when he was with the British army in the Punjab. Besides the information collected within the Sikh territories and his own personal observations, Malcolm obtained a copy of the *Adi Granth* from a Sikh chief and some 'historical tracts'. The material was enriched later by Dr. Leyden with a translation of several tracts by Sikh authors in Punjabi and 'Duggar' dialects on their history and religion. Malcolm's initial intention was to collect more materials for a history of the Sikhs but eventually he decided to publish 'a short and hasty sketch' which, though defective, could be 'useful at a moment when every information regarding the Sikhs' was important. It could serve as a step towards a fuller history of the Sikhs by some other writer.[2] The historical context made the Sikhs an important subject for the British.

Malcolm was critical of both Sikh and Muslim writers, the former for their 'enthusiastic admiration' of the Gurus and the latter for misrepresenting them. Nevertheless, he gave preference to the Sikh writers on a pragmatic consideration: 'In every research into the general history of mankind, it is of the most essential importance to hear what a nation has to say of itself'. Apart from its historical utility the self-image of a people had a value for friendly intercourse between nations. He was aware that the British had to deal with the Sikhs for diplomatic and political purposes.[3]

Malcolm had several European predecessors but, in his view, 'none of them had possessed opportunities of obtaining more than very general information'.[4] Two of the 'several historical accounts of the Sikhs' are mentioned by Malcolm in the body of his *Sketch*: the account given by Major Browne and Forster's *Travels*.[5] Malcolm refers to 'Muhammadan historians', 'Muhammadan authors' and 'Muhammadan writers' in general and makes a specific reference to only the *Seir Mutakhkerin* (*Siyar al-Mutakhirin*), a work dealing with the 'later Mughala'.[6] There is a general reference to the 'historians of Ahmed Shah' and a specific reference to Bernier.[7] In all probability, Malcolm was familiar with some of the literature on medieval India published in England during the late eighteenth century.

Much more often, Malcolm refers to 'Sikh authors', 'several Sikh authors', 'all Sikh writers', 'different Sikh authors', and the 'biographers' of Guru Nanak.[8] He refers to the *Adi Granth* but he does not appear to be familiar with its contents. At one place he refers to *Pran Sancli (Pran Sangali)* as a part of the *Adi Granth*.[9] He was aware that the *Adi Granth* had not been translated into English.[10] The only composition from the *Adi Granth*, given in English translation, is *So Dar*.[11] Malcolm refers to *Dasama Padshah ka Granth*,[12] and to an English translation of the *Vichitra Natac* (*Bachittar Natak*).[13] The passage on the 'protection of all-steel' (*sarb-loh ki rachhchha*) is also quoted with translation in English.[14] The authors referred to are Bhai Gurdas Bhalla and Nand (probably Bhai Nand Lal). The quotations given by Malcolm leave no doubt that he used the *Vars* of Bhai Gurdas. There is also a quotation from the *Var* of the second Bhai Gurdas.[15] One of the Sikh works referred to is Bhacta Malli (*Bhagat Mal*); another is *Gyana Ratnawali* (*Gian Ratnavali*).[16] The latter is attributed to Bhai Gurdas, and it contains a quotation from his *Vars*.[17] At one place 'Bhai Guru Das Bhalla' is mentioned as a Sikh author of respectability but he is writing on Guru Gobind Singh.[18] At another place he is writing on Guru Gobind Singh and his sons.[19] But Bhai Gurdas had died several decades before the birth of Guru Gobind Singh. The life of Guru Gobind Singh, according to Malcolm, is based on his own works and the works of the Sikh writers like 'Nand' and Bhai Gurdas.[20] Malcolm was not clear about Bhai Gurdas. He refers also to Sikh priests as his informants,[21] and to a work written in 'Duggar' or the hill dialect.[22] Evidently, a remarkable feature of Malcolm's *Sketch* is his use of Sikh sources, though at second hand.

The full title of Malcolm's work is *A Sketch of the History and Present State of the Sikhs; with Observations on Their Religious Institutions, Usages, Manners, and Character*. It is divided into three sections. The first section of about hundred pages deals with the history of the Sikhs from the time of Guru Nanak to 1805. The second section of less than fifty pages relates to what may be called the polity and social order of the Sikhs. The third section of over fifty pages deals with the religion of the Sikhs. The scope of Malcolm's work, thus, is quite wide. Consequently, his treatment of Sikh history, polity, society and religion remains rather sketchy.

II. EARLY SIKH HISTORY

More than two-thirds of the space in the first section of Malcolm's *Sketch* is given to the Gurus: a quarter of this space is given to Guru Nanak, another quarter to his successors up to Guru Tegh Bahadur, and one-half to Guru Gobind Singh. As for Guru Nanak, Malcolm refers to his birth, his early life, his marriage, his sons, his service in the granary of Daulat Khan Lodhi, his travels, his stay at Kartarpur, and the nomination of Lehna as his successor. Based professedly on Sikh sources, this account is quite impressive. It seems, however, that Malcolm had not actually read his sources. He makes mistakes which are not likely to be there in the Sikh sources referred to as *Bhagat Mal, Gian Ratnavali* and Guru Nanak's 'biographers'. For example, Guru Nanak's two sons are named Sri Chand and Lakshmi Das but the former is made the father of Dharam Chand who is presented as the founder of the sect of the Udasis and whose descendants were known as Nanak-putras. Lakshmi Das, on the other hand, 'left neither heirs nor reputation'.[23] The *Pran Sangali,* which was neither a composition of Guru Nanak nor included in the *Granth Sahib,* is stated to have been incorporated in the *Adi Granth* as Guru Nanak's composition.[24] The place where he finally came to stay is mentioned as 'Kirtipur'.[25]

Malcolm was not prepared to judge 'the character' of Guru Nanak on the authority of the accounts in his possession because the compositions of Guru Nanak had not yet been translated. In other words, it was necessary to study the compositions of Guru Nanak for a correct judgement. Nevertheless, Malcolm comes to conclude that Guru Nanak was 'a man of more than common genius'. His aim was to blend the 'jarring elements' of his times (Hindus and Muslims) in peaceful union through mild persuasion. He tried to overcome all obstacles by the force of reason and humanity. His success did not rouse the bigotry of the 'intolerant and tyrannical Muhammadan government under which he lived'.[26]

Guru Angad taught the same doctrine as Guru Nanak and his compositions too are included in the *Adi Granth*. He was succeeded by a disciple, Amar Das, and not by his sons. Amar Das was distinguished for his activity in propagating the teachings of Guru Nanak. The number of his followers increased and with their help he established 'some temporal power' and separated the Sikhs from the Udasis who were regarded as heretical at that time. Guru Amar Das was succeeded by his son-in-law Ram Das who, according to Malcolm, did not found Ramdaspur (Amritsar) but only made some improvements at Amritsar. Contrary to his Sikh authorities Malcolm believed that Ramdaspur was an ancient town, known as Chak. Guru Ram Das 'added much to its population, and built a famous tank, or reservoir of water, which he called Amritsar, a name signifying the water of immortality'. It had become so sacred that it gave its name and imparted its sanctity to the town of Ramdaspur, the sacred city of the Sikh nation now 'known by the name of Amritsar'.[27]

After his death at Amritsar in 1581, Guru Ram Das was succeeded by his son, Guru Arjan, who made himself famous by compiling the *Adi Granth*. This name was given to the compilation to distinguish it from the *Dasama Padshah ka Granth* composed by Guru Gobind Singh. Malcolm believed that originally the *Adi Granth* contained the compositions of the first five Gurus, and some small portions were 'subsequently added by thirteen different persons, whose numbers, however, are reduced, by the Sikh authors, to twelve and a half: the last contributor to this sacred volume being a woman'.[28] Apparently, the informants of Malcolm looked upon the hymn of Mira Bai as a part of the *Adi Granth*.

Guru Arjan was the first Guru to give a 'consistent form and order to the religion of the Sikhs'. It united them more closely and increased their number. However, this proved to be fatal for himself. It excited the jealousy of the Muhammadan government and 'he was made its sacrifice'. His 'martyrdom' was caused by the hatred of a rival Hindu zealot whose writings he had refused to include in the *Adi Granth*. Nonetheless, it was considered by the Sikhs as an atrocious murder committed by the Muhammadan government. An inoffensive and peaceable sect till then, the Sikhs took up arms under Guru Hargobind, the son of Guru Arjan, and wreaked their vengeance upon all those persons who they thought were concerned with the death of their Guru.[29]

Malcolm points out that the name of Guru Hargobind does not figure in Major Browne's translation of his Persian source. The evidence of Bhai Gurdas cited by Malcolm makes it very clear that Guru Hargobind was a great warrior and a destroyer of armies. Malcolm argues that Guru Hargobind's contest against the Muslim chiefs of the Punjab could not have been of great magnitude, or importance, because the contemporary Muslim writers did not take much notice of it. Nevertheless, it was the first fruit of that spirit of hostility which was to mark the wars between the followers of Guru Nanak and the followers of Muhammad. It was Guru Hargobind's 'anxious wish to inspire his followers with the most irreconcilable hatred of their oppressors'. Thus, a great change in 'the Sikh commonwealth' occurred in the time of Guru Hargobind. He wore two swords, it was said, to avenge the death of his father and to destroy the 'miracles of Muhammed'.[30] This refers to the popular notion of *miri* (temporal authority) and *piri* (spiritual authority) but, as presented by Malcolm, it underscores *miri*.

The Sikh records of their history from the death of Guru Hargobind to that of Guru Tegh Bahadur, according to Malcolm, were contradictory and unsatisfactory, and appeared to merit little attention. The sect was almost crushed in their first effort to attain power. The Mughal empire was at its zenith under Aurangzeb and the Sikhs were rendered still weaker by their own internal dissensions. The time of Guru Har Rai passed without any remarkable event but a violent contest arose after his death between Guru Har Krishan and Ram Rai first and then between Guru Tegh Bahadur and Ram Rai. The author of the *Seir Mutakhherin* attributed the execution of Guru Tegh Bahadur to his crimes against the state but the Sikh authors attributed it to the implacable rancour, jealousy and ambition of Ram Rai. Guru Tegh

Bahadur was summoned from Patna and publicly put to death without even the allegation of a crime other than that of an undaunted assertion of the truth of his faith.[31]

III. GURU GOBIND SINGH

After the death of Guru Tegh Bahadur, the history of the Sikhs assumed a new aspect. They laid aside their peaceable habits and swore eternal war against their oppressive rulers. Guru Gobind Singh devoted his life to this purpose. However, there was no point in following his life in all its detail. It was sufficient, for the purpose of the *Sketch* 'to state the essential changes which he effected in his tribe, and the consequences of his innovations'.[32]

Guru Hargobind had taken up arms in self-defence. For Guru Gobind Singh, this was not enough. His objective was to arm 'the whole population of the country, and to make worldly wealth and rank an object to which Hindus, of every class, might aspire'. Subverting the hoary institutions of Brahma, he opened the dazzling prospect of earthly glory to men of the lowest tribe, like the Ranghretas. Guru Gobind Singh's object was 'to make all Sikhs equal'. By giving them the title of Singh (lion) he equated them with the Rajputs, the first military class of Hindus. Every Sikh felt himself 'at once elevated to rank with the highest, by this proud appellation'. They were required to devote themselves to arms, to have steel about them all the time, to wear a blue dress, to allow their hair to grow, and to exclaim *Vaheguruji ka Khalsa, Vaheguruji ki fateh* (the Khalsa belong to God, and God's is the victory). This exclamation reminded them of the obligation they owed to the community as a whole, and of the faith to which they were committed. Malcolm refers to the views expressed by Sikhs and Muslims on the uncut hair and the blue dress and suggests that the real purpose of Guru Gobind Singh was 'to separate his followers from all other classes of India, as much by their appearance as by their religion'.[33]

Guru Gobind Singh inculcated his tenets by his works in the *Dasama Padshah ka Granth*. Its scope was not limited to religious subjects. It was written to stir up a spirit of valour and emulation among his followers. It was 'at least as much revered, among the Sikhs, as the *Adi Granth*'. Guru Gobind Singh was said to have instituted the *Gurmata* or state council among the Sikhs. Its foundation gave the form of a federative republic to the commonwealth of the Sikhs and roused them from their indolent habits 'by giving them a personal share in the government, and placing within the reach of every individual the attainment of rank and influence in the state'. Malcolm refers to the ceremony for invoking the aid of the Goddess but remarks that it would be 'tedious to dwell on such fables'.[34]

Malcolm makes no distinction between the pre-Khalsa and the post-Khalsa battles of Guru Gobind Singh. The battle against the chief of Garhwal is mentioned both before and after the institution of the Khalsa. Guru Gobind Singh, though victorious, was unable to maintain himself against the chief and went to the Punjab where he was warmly welcomed by a Hindu chief in rebellion against the government. He gave Makhowal and several other villages to the Guru who settled there with his followers and repaid the chief by aiding him in his depredations.[35] The evidence of the *Bachittar Natak* (Wondrous Drama) is presented after the institution of the Khalsa. In this work, Guru Gobind Singh describes with great animation his own feats and that of his friends (in the battle of Bhangani), the first of his actions in which the arrows of his Sikhs were victorious over the sabres of the Muhammadans. This battle is mistakenly assumed to have been fought against 'the emperor'. Hayat Khan and Najabat Khan, who are killed in the battle, are mentioned as 'two of the principal chiefs of the emperor's army'.[36] Malcolm is grossly mistaken in treating one and the same event as two different episodes.

The success of Guru Gobind Singh increased the number of his followers whom he established at Anandpur, Kahlur, and the towns in their vicinity. Malcolm did not know that Makhowal adjoined Anandpur and that Kahlur was not a town but a state. He goes on to add that the followers of the Guru remained there till called to the aid of Raja Bhim Chand who was supposed to be the chief of Nadaun. Malcolm did not know that Bhim Chand was the chief of Kahlur (Bilaspur). In fact, he refers to Sansar Chand, the chief of Kangra, as a successor of Bhim Chand. Possibly, the translation of the *Bachittar Natak* used by Malcolm was defective. Malcolm refers to the victory of the allies (Bhim Chand and Guru Gobind Singh) in the battle of Nadaun and goes on to mention the unsuccessful expeditions of the son of Dilawar Khan and Husain Khan against Guru Gobind Singh.

They were followed by Dilawar Khan and Rustam Khan and, still later, by Bahadur Shah (Prince Mu'azzam). Guru Gobind Singh hammers the point that they who deserted him in this crisis suffered pain and misery and they who were faithful to him remained safe. Malcolm notes 'a remarkable passage' in the *Bachittar Natak* in which Guru Gobind Singh appears to acknowledge the supremacy of the Mughal emperor.[37] On this last point, however, Malcolm was misled by the translation.

Malcolm gives an account of Guru Gobind Singh's war with the Raja of Kahlur on the basis of a work written in 'Duggar', a hill dialect. The Rajas of Kahlur, Jaswal and others were defeated and disgraced in several actions by Guru Gobind Singh and they made a representation against him to Aurangzeb. The combined forces of the hill chiefs and the Mughal commandants obliged Guru Gobind Singh and his followers to leave their fortresses which were occupied by their enemies. The 'Raja' of Chamkaur received Guru Gobind Singh in a kind and friendly manner. But the governor of Sirhind inhumanly massacred the younger sons of the Guru. Incidentally, Malcolm refers to the *faujdar* of Sirhind as 'Faujdar Khan' instead of Wazir Khan and refers to 'Wazir Khan' as another person. The Mughal army and the hill Rajas besieged Chamkaur. Guru Gobind Singh called upon Bhavani Durga for aid. The elder son of Guru Gobind Singh, called both Ajit Singh and Ranjit Singh by Malcolm, attacked the besiegers commanded by Khwajah Muhammad and Nahar Khan, and died fighting. Guru Gobind Singh himself performed prodigious feats of valour but eventually had to leave Chamkaur, taking advantage of a dark night. Malcolm refers to 'the Punjabi narrative' of Bhai Gurdas Bhalla and other Sikh authors as his authorities and adds that the sons of Guru Gobind Singh 'adorned their sacred strings, by converting them into sword-belts'.[38] Apart from some obvious factual errors, Malcolm is mistaken about Bhai Gurdas Bhalla who had died long before the birth of Guru Gobind Singh.

The accounts of the last few years of Guru Gobind Singh's life were 'contradictory and imperfect'. It was clear, however, that he performed no actions worthy of record after his flight from Chamkaur. The inactivity of his declining years could best be explained on the assumption of his 'mental distraction, in consequence of deep distress and disappointment'. Even in a distracted state of mind he could continue 'that wandering and adventurous life to which he had been so early accustomed'.[39] Malcolm tried to make the best sense of the evidence at his disposal, little realizing that it was extremely defective, as we can see with the advantage of hindsight.

IV. AFTER GURU GOBIND SINGH

Guru Gobind Singh was 'the last acknowledged religious ruler' of the Sikhs. His devoted follower and friend, Banda, resolved to avenge his wrongs. After plundering the country and defeating most of the petty Muhammadan chiefs, he fought against 'Faujdar Khan, the governor of the province of Sirhind'. A severe contest resulted in the victory of the Sikh leader. 'Faujdar Khan' was killed in battle and Sirhind was destroyed in brutal rage. The Sikhs subdued all the country between the Sutlej and the Jamuna and made inroads into the province of Saharanpur. Had Bahadur Shah not quitted the Deccan in 1710, the whole of Hindustan would have been subdued by 'these merciless invaders'. Sultan Kuli Khan defeated the Sikhs at Panipat but the death of Bahadur Shah created a confusion that was favourable to the Sikhs. Banda defeated Islam Khan, the viceroy of Lahore, and one of Banda's followers killed Bayazid Khan, the governor of Sirhind. Abdus Samad Khan was appointed by the emperor Farrukh Siyar against the Sikhs. He besieged Lohgarh where Banda and his supporters had taken refuge. Eventually they surrendered and were sent to Delhi where they were executed. The author of the *Seir Mutakherin* praises the intrepidity with which they faced death. However, Malcolm looks upon Banda as a cruel and ferocious man who imparted to his followers a feeling of merciless resentment which he cherished against 'the whole Muhammadan race'. His memory was not revered by the Sikhs for a different reason: intoxicated with victory, he tried to change the religious institutions and laws of Guru Gobind Singh, like the blue dress, meat diet and the Khalsa exclamation. The Akalis (as staunch followers of Guru Gobind Singh) opposed Banda on those issues and triumphed after his death. Malcolm mentions the year 1710 but no other date in connection with Banda. That may be the reason why he did not realize that his account of Banda left a wide gap between his success in 1710 and his execution in 1716.

Malcolm was aware of the huge gap in his sources between the death of Banda and the invasion of India by Nadir Shah, a span of twenty-three years. The Mughal government tried 'to extirpate the race, of the Sikhs'. Those who refused to abandon their identity and submit to the Mughal authorities took refuge in the hills. At the time of Nadir Shah's invasion they plundered those people who were trying to escape into the hills in order to avoid being plundered by the Persian invader. The Sikhs now left the hills and built a fort on the Ravi. From there, they harassed and plundered the rear of Nadir Shah's army on its return from Delhi. The number of Sikhs began to increase and they began to visit Amritsar. It was foreign to the objective of Malcolm's *Sketch* to enter into any detail of the efforts by which the Sikhs rose into power. It was enough for his purpose to 'glance at the principal events'.[41]

Malcolm equates *gurmata* with 'national council' but does not attach any great importance to it. There were a number of *sardars* or chiefs among the Sikhs, each followed by a small or large number of followers and acting independently of one another. The function of the *gurmata* was to select a military leader for a common campaign. Such a mode of government was little calculated to give the required strength. Their usages, their ardent faith, the power of their enemies and the oppression they endured supplied the place of ordinances. 'To unite and to act in one body, and on one principle, was, with the first Sikhs, a law of necessity: it was, amid the dangers with which they were surrounded, their only hope of success, and their sole means of preservation'. These causes, combined with weakness and internal quarrels of their enemies, explain the success of the Sikhs rather than their boasted constitution. They occupied territories in the Bari and Jalandhar Doabs during the first Afghan invasion in 1746 (actually 1748). They received severe checks from Mir Mannu as the governor of Lahore. But for the counsel of Kaura Mal, who was a Khulasa Sikh, Mir Mannu would have destroyed them. Adina Beg Khan defeated the Sikhs near Makhowal but entered into a secret understanding with them, not only before but also after the death of Mir Mannu which gave the Sikhs the opportunity to occupy territories on a larger scale and a firmer footing.[42]

Ahmad Shah Abdali appointed his son Taimur Khan as the governor of Lahore to deal with the Sikhs. He destroyed Amritsar and filled up the sacred tank, and polluted all their places of worship. In retaliation, the Sikhs obliged Taimur Khan to leave Lahore where a coin was struck in the name of Jassa Singh Kalal. Adina Beg Khan invited the Marathas who advanced to Lahore and expelled both the Sikhs and Afghans from the principal towns of the provinces of Sirhind and Lahore. They appointed Adina Beg Khan as governor but he died soon afterwards. The Sikhs made themselves masters of the province again. Ahmad Shah Abdali defeated the Marathas in the battle of Panipat and massacred over 20,000 Sikhs in February 1762. Amritsar was razed to the ground and the sacred tank was again choked with its ruins. The Sikhs defeated the Afghan General who was left behind by Ahmad Shah, and occupied Lahore. Ahmad Shah retook Lahore in 1763. The Sikhs again expelled the Afghan garrison from the Punjab and began to rule over it.[43]

After Ahmad Shah Abdali's death, the Afghans presented no threat to the Sikhs. The hostilities of the Sikhs were first directed against the Muslim chiefs of the Punjab who were either conquered or made subordinate. Before long, every village became the object of dispute among the Sikh chiefs themselves. In such a state it was obvious that the Sikhs could be formidable only to the most weak and distracted governments. They continued to plunder the upper provinces of Hindustan but only till the establishment of the power of Daulat Rao Sindhia. His French Generals would have conquered the Punjab if the British had not intervened. When Malcolm came to the Punjab in 1805 with Lord Lake in pursuit of Holkar he actually observed the state of the Sikh nation and found it 'weak and distracted, in degree that could hardly have been imagined'. A *gurmata* was called but it was attended by a few chiefs. The majority of the absentees were bold enough in their offers 'to resist any resolution to which this council might come'. The first section of Malcolm's *Sketch* ends with the remark: 'every shadow of that concord, which formed the strength of the Sikh nation, seemed to be extinguished'.[44]

V. POLITY AND SOCIAL ORDER

In the second section of his *Sketch of the Sikhs*, Malcolm gives 'a cursory view' of the government, manners and habits of the Sikhs. He refers to the possessions of the Sikh chiefs in Malwa, Jalandhar Doab, Bari Doab, Rachna Doab, Sindh Sagar Doab and the province of Multan. Mentioned among the notable Sikh chiefs are Sahib Singh of Patiala, Bhanga Singh of Thanesar, Bhag Singh of Jind, Bhai Lal Singh of

Kaithal, Ranjit Singh of Lahore, Fateh Singh Ahluwalia, and Jodh Singh Ramgarhia.[45] The notable omissions are Jaswant Singh of Nabha and Sada Kaur of Batala. It is interesting to note that, like his predecessors, Malcolm makes no reference to any *misl*.

The government of the Sikhs could in theory be termed a theocracy. They obey a temporal chief but he preserves his power and authority by professing himself to be 'the servant of the Khalsa' or government through the national council of which every chief is a member and which functions in the interests of the commonwealth. The Akalis played the most important role in the functioning of the national council as a supreme authority over the federative republic of the Sikh chiefs. They had the sole direction of all religious affairs at Amritsar. They could accuse the chiefs of 'crimes' (defaults) and impose fines (*tankhah*) upon them. In the case of their refusal, the Akalis prevented them from performing their ablutions, or going through any of their religious ceremonies at Amritsar. The Akalis had great interest in maintaining both the religion and government of the Sikhs as established by Guru Gobind Singh. 'Should Amritsar cease to be a place of resort, or be no longer considered as the religious capital of the state, in which all questions that involve the general interests of the commonwealth are to be decided, this formidable order would at once fall from that power and consideration which they now possess, to a level with other mendicants'.[46]

Contrary to the general impression, Malcolm did not actually see any *gurmata* on the ground. An account of this custom was given to him by a Sikh priest. The assembly was convened by the Akalis. When the chiefs and principal leaders were seated, the *Adi Granth* and the *Dasama Padshah Ka Granth* were placed before them. An *ardas* was made and the sacred food was distributed. The proposition was put before the chiefs by the Akalis and Generals were chosen to lead the Dal Khalsa against the common enemy. This, obviously, is a description of the *gurmata* as a past mode. Malcolm had only heard that the first *gurmata* had been assembled by Guru Gobind Singh and the latest was called in 1805 when the British army pursued Holkar into the Punjab.[47] It was actually a meeting of the chiefs.

Malcolm maintained that all Sikh chiefs had Hindu ancestry and, because of the historical background of animosity towards Muslim rulers, they did not treat their Muslim subjects in the same way as the other subjects. The Muslim subjects of the Sikh territories were all poor, and they appeared to be an oppressed and despised lot. They tilled the land, they were employed to carry burdens, and to do all kinds of labour. They were not allowed to eat beef or to say their prayers aloud. The mosques which had escaped destruction were not frequented. By contrast as it were, the lower order of Sikhs were more happy. They were protected from the tyranny and violence of the chiefs by the precepts of their common religion. They could leave a leader they disliked. The lowest Sikh horseman usually assumed a very independent style. The highest chief treated his military followers with attention and conciliation. The civil, financial and diplomatic affairs of the Sikh chiefs were looked after by the *khulasa* (non-Khalsa) Sikhs who were the followers of Guru Nanak and not devoted to arms.[48]

Malcolm noticed that Ranjit Singh was the most eminent Sikh chief in 1805. However, even he could muster no more than 8,000 troopers, including those of his subordinate chiefs and *jagirdars*. Malcolm goes on to add that Ranjit Singh's army was now more numerous but it was composed of materials which had 'no natural cohesion': 'the first serious check which it meets, will probably cause its dissolution.' Malcolm makes brief comments on the cultivation, commerce, administration of justice, disputes about property, the character of the Sikhs, the Sikh soldier, the Sikh merchant, the Akali, Shahids and Nirmalas, the Nanak-putras, intermarriage, food and drinks, intoxicants, the conduct of Sikh men towards their women, the Sikh horsemen, education of the Sikhs, the strength of their armies and the attitude of the Sikh chiefs towards the common people. Malcolm's comments are relevant for a present-day historian of the late eighteenth- or the early nineteenth-century Sikhs.[49]

VI. RELIGION OF THE SIKHS

The third section of Malcolm's *Sketch of the Sikhs* is devoted to the religion of the Sikhs, a subject that was curious and important, and rather difficult to grasp. It was a pure 'deism', grounded on the most sublime general truths but it was blended with the absurdities of Hindu mythology and fables of Islam. Guru Nanak wanted to reform and not to destroy the religion of his ancestors. At the same time he was actuated by 'reconciling the jarring faiths' of Brahma and Muhammad. He called upon Muslims to abandon slaughter of cows and persecution of Hindus. He appreciated the Sufis, especially Kabir who upheld the doctrine of equality. Guru Nanak stood for toleration and was against war. He was known for austerities and treated polytheism with respect, and even veneration. He spoke of Muhammad with moderation.[50]

Malcolm states emphatically that Guru Nanak was a Hindu reformer. He made no material invasion of either the civil or religious usages of the Hindus, and his only desire was to restore a degenerated nation to their original pure worship of one God. Guru Nanak 'may be considered more in the light of a reformer than of a subverter of the Hindu religion'. Malcolm makes these categorical statements without having read Guru Nanak's compositions which, according to Malcolm himself, were the only source for correct judgement. He goes on to add that those Sikhs who did not accept the tenets of Guru Gobind Singh were 'hardly to be distinguished from the great mass of Hindu population'.[51]

'It was reserved for Guru Gobind to give a new character to the religion of his followers.' However, he did this not by making any material change in the tenets of Guru Nanak but by establishing institutions and usages which separated the Sikhs from Hindus and destroyed at one blow a system of civil polity that had withstood the shock of ages. He called upon Hindus to discard caste distinctions and to take up arms against the oppressive Muhammadan government. Every Khalsa Singh was equal, and 'had a like title to the good things of this world, and to the blessings of a future life'.[52] The Khalsa were different from the earlier Sikhs not due to their religious beliefs but due to their social attitudes and political aspirations.

It was impossible to reconcile the religion and usages of Guru Gobind Singh with the beliefs of the Hindus but he mixed their mythology with his own tenets even more than Guru Nanak. In order to conciliate the Hindus in a situation of opposition to Muslims he worshipped at Hindu sacred shrines; he adopted blue dress due to veneration for Durga Bhavani. Malcolm is emphatic nonetheless that 'wherever the religion of Guru Gobind prevails, the institutions of Brahma must fall'. The ordinances of Guru Gobind Singh with regard to admission of proselytes, abolition of caste distinctions, meat diet, devotion to arms and the form of worship could not be reconciled with Hindu mythology. Sikhism of Guru Gobind Singh had no appeal for Brahmans and upper castes but it was popular with the lower orders.[53]

After portrarying its general character, Malcolm turns to a more detailed view of the origin, progress, tenets and forms of the Sikh religion. He concentrates on Guru Nanak and Guru Gobind Singh for detail. Bhai Gurdas is quoted on the four *yugas,* underscoring the errors into which the Hindus had fallen. There is a passage on Islam too. The Hindus and Muslims were 'alike excited by pride, enmity, and avarice'. The world was in a distracted state and God sent Guru Nanak 'to enlighten and improve a degenerate and corrupt age'. He made the Supreme God known to all. He blended the four castes into one and established one mode of salutation. Malcolm interprets the statements of Bhai Gurdas in terms of 'reform'. After performing penance, Guru Nanak began his travels for 'spreading his doctrine over the world'. In his debate with the *siddhas* on Sumeru, a divine voice exclaimed that Guru Nanak would form his own sect in the Kali Age. He instructed the Muslims at Mecca that both Hindus and Muslims were unacceptable to God without true piety. His biographers admired the courageous independence with which he announced his religion. The quotations given by Malcolm are suggestive of transcendence of contemporary forms of religious belief and practice by the message of Guru Nanak. Malcolm concludes that Guru Nanak 'professed veneration and respect, but refused adoration to the founders of both the religions'.[54] Malcolm seems to contradict his own view that Guru Nanak was a Hindu reformer.

Guru Nanak's interview with the Supreme God is described by 'the Sikh author'. God told him that he was sent to the world to bear witness to God's name. When Nanak expressed his incompetence for such a task, God assured him that he would be Nanak's Guru and Nanak 'shalt be a Guru to all mankind'. His sect would be distinct from that of the *bairagis,* the *yogis,* the *sanyasis,* and the Muhammadans, with its own form of salutation and place of worship. Commissioned by God, Guru Nanak 'came to give light and freedom to the universe'. Malcolm suggests that this 'divine origin' indicated that Sikh faith was 'the religion of peace' (and not an original dispensation). Malcolm goes on to say that Guru Nanak accepted the validity of the Qur'an and the Vedas but rejected the validity of the beliefs and practices of contemporary Hindus and Muslims. He 'borrowed indifferently from the Koran and the Hindu Sastras; and his example was followed by his successor'.[55] Malcolm's evidence, however, does not lead to the inferences he draws.

The only composition of Guru Nanak quoted by Malcolm is the *So Dar* (the divine court) in which Ishar, Brahma and Devi sing God's praises (as his creation). This composition showed that Guru Nanak's religion was grounded on 'a principle of pure deism' (uncompromizing monotheism). However, the followers of Guru Nanak deviated from his position by making 'an adoration to his name'. They considered him 'as the selected instrument of God to make known the true faith to fallen men'; they gave him divine honours; they performed pilgrimage to his tomb and addressed him in their prayers as their saviour and mediator. Yet Malcolm goes on to state that the religious tenets and usages of the Sikhs continued as they had been established by Guru Nanak till the time of Guru Gobind Singh.[56]

Guru Gobind Singh did not alter the fundamental principals of the established faith but he made a complete change in the sacred usages and civil habits of his followers and gave them an entirely new character. The Sikhs retained all their veneration for Guru Nanak and they deemed Guru Gobind Singh to be equally exalted by the immediate favour and protection of the Divinity. The *Dasama Padshah Ka Granth* written by Guru Gobind Singh was considered in every respect as holy as the *Adi Granth*. Guru Gobind Singh's 'pretensions' to the rank of a prophet are found in his *Bachittar Natak*. Malcolm quotes a passage that conveys the impression of 'his divine mission'.[57] Malcolm did not believe in the possibility of revelation. Therefore, he treated such claims as 'pretension', missing the point that the claim implied originally, and independence.

Guru Gobind Singh introduced a new rite of *pahul* for initiation into the Khalsa, with the obligation to bear the epithet Singh, to bear arms for the defence of the Khalsa commonwealth, to destroy its enemies, to keep uncut hair, and to wear a blue dress. The great sanctity of uncut hair is underlined through an incident in which Malcolm was a participant. The mode of initiation is described by Malcolm on the authority of a Sikh writer. Some of its important features are the following: sugar stirred in water by a dagger while compositions from the *Adi Granth* and *Dasama Padshah Ka Granth* are recited; instruction to keep uncut hair and to wear a blue dress; presentation of five weapons, exclamation of *Vaheguruji ka Khalsa, Vaheguruji ki fateh*; no intercourse with the Minas, the Dhir Mallias, the Masandias, the Ram Raiyas, the destroyers of their own daughters (*kurimar*), and those who shaved their head and beards as a rite of *bhaddan*; reverence to all gurdwaras, especially the Harmandar Sahib at Amritsar; and the injunction to pay devotions to the Khalsa, or state, and prefer its interests to one's own. These and some other instructions mentioned by Malcolm indicate that his source was a *Rahitnama*. His reference to 'Nand' may be a reference to a *Rahitnama* attributed to Bhai Nand Lal. After initiating five Sikhs, Guru Gobind Singh asked them to initiate him in the same manner. The sanctity of the five was hammered by the Sikh author who stated that Guru Gobind Singh had exclaimed at the time of his death that 'wherever five Sikhs are assembled, there I also shall be present'.[58]

The leading tenet of Guru Gobind Singh's religious institutions, according to Malcolm, was devotion to arms. Bhavani Durga had told Guru Gobind Singh in a dream that he would conquer the country of the Muhammadans with the sword given to him by the goddess. Guru Gobind Singh exclaimed: 'This steel shall be the guard to me and my followers, because, in its lustre, the splendour of the countenance, O goddess! is always reflected'. The source used by Malcolm also stated that Guru Gobind Singh told his followers that it was right to slay a Muhammadan in battle and to destroy the countries ruled by Muhammadans.[59] Bhai Gurdas (the second) gives expression to a 'spirit of hostility' against Muslims when he praises the Khalsa for abolishing *namaz* and slaying Sultans, reducing mirs and pirs to silence, and confounding the mullas and qazis. Bhai Gurdas also says that in this way 'the third sect' was established and increased greatly in might.[60] Malcolm misses the significance of the claim of the Khalsa to be the 'third sect' (the two other being Hindus and Muslims).

Malcolm takes notice of the paradox of Guru Gobind rejecting the worship of idols and constantly alluding to Hindu mythology, so much so that it was 'often difficult to separate his purer belief from their gross idolatry'. It was clear nonetheless that Guru Gobind Singh 'separated his followers for ever from the Hindus'. The Sikh opinion of Guru Gobind Singh was reflected in the *Var* of Bhai Gurdas (the second).

> He meditated on the Creator himself, invisible, eternal, and incomprehensible. He established the Khalsa, his own sect, and, by exhibiting singular energy, leaving the hair on his head, and seizing the scimitar, he smote every wicked person.[61]
>
> No Sirdar could stand in battle against him, but all of them fled; and, whether Hindu Rajas, or Muhammadan lords, became like dust in his presence. The mountains, hearing of him, were struck with terror; the whole world was affrighted, and the people fled from their habitations.[62]

The religious institutions of Guru Gobind Singh proved to be the appropriate means of attaining the end he had in view. Banda Bahadur failed to alter those institutions. The spirit of equality, which was the vital principle of the Khalsa, would tend to preserve those institutions. Malcolm refers to the Sikh tradition that Guru Gobind Singh declared from his death bed that he had 'delivered over the Khalsa (commonwealth) to God who never dies'. They should read the *Granth* and attend to its tenets: 'whoever remains true to the state, him will I aid'. The Sikhs believed in the dying words of Guru Gobind Singh that they were placed under the special care of God. Their attachment to this mysterious principle led them to consider the Khalsa as a theocracy. Malcolm was inclined to conclude that the Sikhs were most likely to offer 'a very serious obstacle, if not an insuperable barrier, to the designs of any of their chiefs, who may hereafter endeavour to establish an absolute power over the whole nation'.[63] Ironically, by the time of the publication of *A Sketch of the Sikhs,* the British had recognized Ranjit Singh as the sole sovereign on his side of the river Sutlej. All the surviving Sikh chiefs had become subordinate to him.

Malcolm's *Sketch of the Sikhs* is distinguished from the work of his predecessors by a considerable use of Sikh sources on the religion of the Sikhs. The scope of his work is also much larger. His account of Sikh history is clearer, though still marked by many a factual error and misconstruction. His account of Sikh polity makes no advance upon the descriptions of his predecessors. In the Sikh social order he emphasizes the difference between the Khalsa Singhs and the rest of the Sikhs.

He notices a few categories among the former but tends to ignore the sectarian differences among the latter. His account of the Sikh religion is more detailed than that of his predecessors but his conceptualization of Sikh beliefs and practices is not clear. The evidence he cites in support of his view of Sikhism as a Hindu reform does not lead to this inference.

NOTES

1. Lt. Col. (John) Malcolm, *A Sketch of the Sikhs*, New Delhi: Asian Educational Services, 1986 (rpt.), 'Advertisement'. (First published by John Murray, London, 1812.)
2. Ibid., pp. 1-3.
3. Ibid., pp. 4-6.
4. Ibid., p. 1.
5. Ibid., pp. 34-5n, 70n, 90n.
6. Ibid., pp. 22n, 38n, 39n, 65n, 69, 81n.
7. Ibid., pp. 101, 108n.
8. Ibid., pp. 8n, 9, 14n, 17n, 100, 159, 165n.
9. Ibid., p. 19n.
10. Ibid., p. 22.
11. Ibid., pp. 169-71n.
12. Ibid., pp. 31 & n, 51-2, 173.
13. Ibid., pp. 55n, 173.
14. Ibid., p. 117.
15. Ibid., pp. 20, 21, 36n, 152 & n, 190n.
16. Ibid., pp. 14n, 16n, 30n.
17. Ibid., pp. 20, 21, 34-5n.
18. Ibid., p. 43n.
19. Ibid., pp. 67-8n.
20. Ibid., p. 69.
21. Ibid., pp. 122n, 128n.
22. Ibid., p. 63.
23. Ibid., p. 8.
24. Ibid., p. 18 & n.
25. Ibid., p. 21 & n.
26. Ibid., pp. 22-4.
27. Ibid., pp. 24-30.
28. Ibid., pp. 30-1 & n.
29. Ibid., pp. 32-3.
30. Ibid., pp. 33-5 & n.
31. Ibid., pp. 36-41 & nn.

32. Ibid., pp. 41-4.
33. Ibid., pp. 44-51.
34. Ibid., pp. 51-3 & n.
35. Ibid., pp. 42-3.
36. Ibid., 54-7 & nn.
37. Ibid., pp. 57-63 & nn.
38. Ibid., pp. 63-9 & nn.
39. Ibid., pp. 69-75 & nn.
40. Ibid., pp. 76-84 & nn.
41. Ibid., pp. 85-8.
42. Ibid., pp. 89-93 & nn.
43. Ibid., pp. 93-101.
44. Ibid., pp. 101-7 & nn.
45. Ibid., pp. 108-14.
46. Ibid., pp. 114-20.
47. Ibid., pp. 120-3.
48. Ibid., pp. 123-5 & nn.
49. Ibid., pp. 125-43 & nn.
50. Ibid., pp. 144-7.
51. Ibid., pp. 147-8.
52. Ibid., pp. 148-50.
53. Ibid., pp. 150-1.
54. Ibid., pp. 152-62.
55. Ibid., pp. 162-7.
56. Ibid., pp. 168-72.
57. Ibid., pp. 173-9.
58. Ibid., pp. 179-86.
59. Ibid., pp. 186-8 & nn.
60. Ibid., pp. 192-4.
61. Ibid., pp. 190-1.
62. Ibid., p. 191.
63. Ibid., pp. 192-7. For Malcolm, see also Fauja Singh, 'Early European Writers: Browne, Polier, Forster and Malcolm', *Historians and Historiography of the Sikhs*, ed. Fauja Singh, New Delhi: Oriental Publishers, 1978, pp. 15-20. Gianeshwar Khurana, 'The Foundation', *British Historiography on the Sikh Power in Punjab*, New Delhi: Allied Publishers, 1985, pp. 17-34.

CHAPTER THREE

Henry T. Prinsep on the Political Life of Ranjit Singh

After the meeting at Ropar between Lord William Bentinck and Maharaja Ranjit Singh in 1831, H.T. Prinsep composed his *Origin of the Sikh Power in the Punjab and Political Life of Maharaja Ranjit Singh* which was published in 1834. It was almost an official publication. Much of the material had been collected by Captain Murray, the British political agent at Ludhiana and his successor Captain Wade. In the first two chapters, he talks of the decline of the Mughal sovereignty and the rise of the Sikh *misls* in the Punjab. In the third chapter which covers the phase from 1773 to 1791, he begins to concentrate on the ancestors of Ranjit Singh. Then seven chapters are devoted to the rise of Ranjit Singh from 1794 to 1831. The character of Ranjit Singh and his policy are discussed in the eleventh chapter, and an Appendix reproduces Murray's account of the manners, rules, and customs of the Sikhs. At the end, there are a score of notes and an index of persons.

I. THE SIKHS BECOME MASTERS OF THE PUNJAB

According to Prinsep, the Marathas undermined the Mughal power in the reign of Muhammad Shah and the invasion of Nadir Shah gave a violent shock to its stability. The inroads of Ahmad Shah Abdali, though meant to check the Hindu vigour, nevertheless accelerated the fall of the dynasty of Babur. In this context, the Jat *zamindars* of the Punjab, driven to desperation by extortion, took to the faith and tenets of Guru Gobind Singh in increasing numbers; they took *pahul*, kept long hair and flowing beards, renounced tobacco, adopted the exclamation of *Vaheguruji ki fateh*, and took up the sword, forming small bodies of highwaymen (*dharwi*). They had formed their own *deras* before any official notice was taken of their activity. Yahiya Khan and his *diwan,* Lakhpat Rai, tried to suppress them after the latter's brother Jaspat Rai was killed by the Sikhs. Lakhpat Rai took action against the Sikhs and the heads of Sikh prisoners were struck off at *Nakhas* in Lahore, now called *Sahidganj,* with a *samadh* in honour of Bhai Tara Singh.[1]

Yahiya Khan's younger brother, Shah Nawaz Khan, rose in revolt and established himself at Lahore with Kaura Mal as his *diwan*. For fear of the possible consequences, Shah Nawaz opened correspondence with Ahmad Shah Durrani who had succeeded Nadir Shah and occupied Kabul. When the Delhi Wazir Qamruddin Khan wrote to Shah Nawaz to return to allegiance to the hereditary sovereign of his family, the young man's pride was touched and he decided to oppose Ahmad Shah Durrani. But after some resistance he fled to Delhi. Ahmad Shah moved on towards Delhi, and faced the Mughal army at Manupur near Sirhind. The *wazir,* Qamruddin, was killed but his son, Mir Mannu, repulsed the Durrani attack. Ahmad Shah retraced his steps and Mir Mannu became the governor of Lahore and Multan as Muin ul-Mulk. The invasion was favourable for the further rise of the Sikhs. Mir Mannu had to attack Ram Raumi at Amritsar to capture it.[2]

Ahmad Shah Durrani again crossed the Indus after the rains in 1748 and Mir Mannu promised to pay the revenues of the four *parganas* of Parsarur, Gujrat, Sialkot and Aurangabad (which had been ceded to Nadir Shah). Against Mir Mannu's wishes, the governorship of Multan was given to Shah Nawaz Khan by the Mughal emperor. Mir Mannu sent his *diwan,* Kaura Mal, against him. Shah Nawaz was defeated and slain. Ahmad Shah Durrani came once again in 1751-2. Kaura Mal was killed during a retreat from the battle. Mir Mannu submitted to Ahmad Shah who reinstated him as his own governor for Lahore and Multan. He died before long and his widow tried to govern in the name of their infant son and then on her own. But she was unable to check the Sikhs who had become increasingly audacious with the increase in their numbers. They created anarchy and confusion in the province.[3]

In 1755-6, Ahmad Shah Durrani marched on to Delhi, plundered Mathura as well, formed a matrimonial connection with the imperial family, and seized Sirhind and the Punjab. He appointed his son, Taimur

Shah, as the governor at Lahore, with Jahan Khan to support him. Adina Beg Khan invited Malhar Rao Holkar. The Marathas overran the whole country up to the Indus and returned to Delhi with the main body, leaving a detachment in occupation of Lahore and appointing Adina Beg Khan as the governor in 1758. Adina Beg Khan died soon after. The Marathas were now the ruling power of Hindustan, and no one ventured to take the field against them. Ahmad Shah defeated Dattaji Sindhia and Malhar Rao Holkar near Delhi and defeated the whole of the Maratha army at Panipat on 7 January 1761. The Maratha commander Sadasheo Rao Bhao was killed in the battle and tens of thousands perished in action or flight. The Maratha ambition and power were destroyed. Ahmad Shah returned to Kabul, appointing Zain Khan at Sirhind and Khwaja Ubaid at Lahore.[4]

Prinsep goes into the early career of Charhat Singh before he attracted the attention of Khwaja Ubaid. The other Sikh chiefs went to his support and Khwaja Ubaid barely escaped with his life. The Sikh chiefs and their followers met at Amritsar and resolved to invest Jandiala, the place of the Niranjani 'guru' who was helping Ahmad Shah Abdali against the Sikhs. Ahmad Shah came in November 1762 and, after a long and rapid march, attacked the Sikhs near Malerkotla. Their losses were estimated at 25,000 to 30,000 men. A conservative estimate by a Musalman of Malerkotla, who was in the action, did not exceed 12,000. The event was known as the bloody carnage (*ghallughara*). On his return, Ahmad Shah blew up the Harmandar with gunpowder, filled the sacred tank, and polluted it with the blood and entrails of cows and bullocks.[5]

After Ahmad Shah Abdali's departure, the Sikhs reappeared in the field. Through a *gurmata* at Amritsar, they resolved to march against Kasur which they sacked. In December 1763, they attacked Zain Khan of Sirhind; he was defeated and killed, and Sirhind was razed to the ground. 'Not a house was left standing, and even to this day it was deemed a meritorious act by a Sikh, to pull down three bricks from any standing wall of Sirhind, and convey them to the Sutlej or Jamuna to be cast there into the river.' Ahmad Shah re-appeared in January 1764. The Sikhs dispersed and Raja Ala Singh obtained the ruins of Sirhind from Bhai Buddh Singh in exchange for a few productive villages. Ahmad

Shah returned to Kabul without suppressing the Sikhs. His governor, Kabuli Mal, was compelled to fly and Lahore was divided by Lahna Singh, Gujjar Singh, and Sobha Singh among themselves. Ahmad Shah came again and gave the title of 'Maharaja Rajgan, Mahendra Bahadur' to Ala Singh's successor, Amar Singh. But the Sikhs remained undisputed masters of the Punjab. After Ahmad Shah's death in 1773, Taimur Shah made no attempt to recover Lahore.[6] Prinsep's narrative is better than that of any of his predecessors though it is not free from factual errors.

II. THE *MISLDARI* SYSTEM

For the first time in British historical writing on the Sikhs, Prinsep talks of the *misldari* system. Since he does not give any reference to his sources it is not easy to identify them. According to him, the Sikh chiefs (*sardars*) were followed into the field by relations, friends and volunteers, and ordinarily not by hired retainers. Most of them looked upon themselves as partners and associates in each enterprise, and regarded the lands acquired as a common property in which each was to have his share in accordance with the degree of his contribution towards its acquisition. These associations were called *misls,* carrying the implication that they were 'confederacies of equals' under the chief of their own selection. The chief was to lead in the war and act as an arbiter in peace; he was respected and treated with deference by the inferior *sardars* but they owned no obligation to obey beyond what they considered to be for their mutual benefit or for the well-being of the *misl*. Each confederacy had its distinguishing title.[7]

Prinsep was also the first historian to talk of twelve *misls*. In terms of the number of horses, the Nishanwala and Karora-Singhia *misls* were at the top, with 12,000 horse each. The first was headed by Sangat Singh and Mohr Singh as the standard bearer of the Dal; the second was led by Karora Singh and later by Bhagel Singh. Their territories were in the Sutlej-Jamuna Divide. They were followed by the Bhangi *misl,* with 10,000 horse, led by Hari Singh, Jhanda Singh and Ganda Singh. Next to the Bhangi was Kanhiya *misl,* with 8,000 horse, led by Jai Singh. They were followed by the Dallewalia *misl,* with 7,500 horse, led by Tara Singh Gheba. The Phulkian and Bhaikian *misl* was headed by Ala Singh, and later by Amar Singh, and it commanded 5,000 horse. The Ramgarhia and Ahluwalia *misls* came next, with 3,000 horse each. The former was led by Jassa Singh Thoka and the latter by Jassa Singh Kalal. The Faizullapuria and Sukarchakia *misls* stood bracketed, with 2,500 horse each. The former was headed by Kapur Singh and Khushal Singh and the latter by Charhat Singh. At the bottom of the scale were the Nakkais, and the Shahids and Nihangs, with 2,000 horse each. Altogether, the 12 *misls* commanded 69,500 horse. Prinsep comments that the *misl* of Charhat Singh held the last place, and it was formed probably after the successful defence of Gujarauli (Gujranwala).[8]

Every *misl* acted independently, or in concert, as necessity or inclination suggested. There was generally an assembly of the chiefs called the Sarbat Khalsa; it was held twice a year at Amritsar on the Baisakhi and the Diwali. A special council, called *gurmata,* was held to take decisions on important expeditions or on a matter of more than ordinary importance. When joint forces of the *misls* took the field for a predatory enterprise, or to collect *rakha* (blackmail), the army assumed the designation of Dal of the Khalsa. When the *misls* acquired territorial possessions, it became the first duty of the chiefs to partition out the lands, towns, and villages amongst those who considered themselves as having made the conquest in common (*shamil*). Every leader (*sarkarda*) of the smallest party of horse demanded his share in proportion to his contribution to the acquisition. This was the only way of recompense because these leaders received no pay from the chief. The chief's portion (*sardari*) was divided off first and the remainder was separated into parcels (*pattis*) for each *sarkarda*; these were again parcelled out to inferior leaders in accordance with the number of horse they had brought into the field. 'Each took his portion as a co-sharer, and held it in absolute independence.'[9]

Prinsep goes on to add that this state of things could not last long. When the link of a common enemy and common danger was removed, and the chiefs were converted from needy adventurers into lords of domains, discords and mutual plunderings began due to temper, ambition or avarice. In matters of internal strife within the *misl,* every one was free to choose his own side, and either party would deem it fair to fortify itself with any aid it could command from without. In other words, internal conflicts within a *misl* could lead to conflict with another *misl*.[10]

Prinsep was also the first historian to talk of tenures during the *misldari* system. The *pattidari* has already been mentioned: every associate of a rank lower than that of the *sardar* in a *misl* got his share in the territory down even to a single horseman who equipped and mounted himself. The *pattidar* and the *sardar* stood in relationship of reciprocal aid for mutual protection and defence as the only condition of the tenure. However, a *pattidar* could not sell his tenure to a stranger. He could leave his tenure to any of his male relations. There were three other tenures: *misldari*, *tabadari*, and *jagirdari*. The land assigned as a reward for cooperation was called *misldari*. It was not held in dependence; if the *misldar* was dissatisfied he could transfer his possessions to another chief. In other words, the *misldar* was a leader who had joined the *sardar* voluntarily and got his share; he could leave the *misl* to join another if and when he liked. A *tabadar* on the other hand was a retainer, completely subservient to the chief; his lands were liable to forfeiture for an act of rebellion or even disobedience. His position entirely depended on the pleasure of the chief. *Jagirs* were given to needy relations, dependents, and soldiers who deserved well; the holders of *jagir* were called upon for their personal services at all times with the contingents maintained by them as a condition of the tenure. They were under the power of the *sardar* even more than the *tabadars*. The lands in both the cases were parts of the *sardari* lands. The fifth category was formed by the religious and charitable grants, given to Sodhis and Bedis, temples, and *pirzadas*. They were no different from what was found all over India.[11]

It is important to note that the head or the chief is the *sardar* and the *misldar* of Prinsep is a *sarkarda,* or inferior leader, and not the head of the *misl*. The smallest unit of the *misl* is a single horseman. That is why Prinsep talks of 70,000 sovereigns in the provinces of Lahore and Sirhind. In his view, no class could find happiness under them. It is interesting to note that Prinsep compares the *misldari* system with what has come to be known as 'feudalism', in England and France. He had no good opinion of European 'feudalism' either.[12] We may add that Prinsep's conceptualization of Sikh polity in the late eighteenth century has remained popular with modern historians of the Sikhs but seldom actually understood.

III. RANJIT SINGH'S INHERITANCE AND EARLY CONQUESTS

Prinsep was not interested in the squabbles and feuds of the chiefs except those in which the ancestors of Ranjit Singh were involved. One of these was the support given by Charhat Singh to Brij Raj Dev of Jammu against his younger brother Mian Dalel Singh who was their father's favourite. The Bhangi Chief Jhanda Singh was supporting the latter. Charhat Singh was killed by the malfunction of his own gun. His elder son, Mahan Singh, succeeded to the *sardari.* A sweeper was bribed to kill Jhanda Singh who was mortally wounded. These events are placed by Prinsep in 1774. A subordinate *sardar,* Dharam Singh, tried to become independent but he suffered forfeiture of his lands for this contumacy. Mahan Singh was married in 1776 at Badrukhan to the daughter of Raja Gajpat Singh of Jind. In association with Jai Singh in 1778, Mahan Singh captured Rasul Nagar, called Ram Nagar by the Sikhs. It was a possession of Pir Muhammad Chattha, also called Mancharia. Ranjit Singh was born on 2 November 1780. An attack of smallpox left him one eyed, with marks on his face. While the Bhangi chief was away to defend Multan, Mahan Singh sacked Jammu and brought back a large spoil in gold and valuables of all kinds. Jai Singh Kanhiya who wanted a share in the spoils, treated Mahan Singh with contempt. Mahan Singh called Jassa Singh Ramgarhia from the wilds of Hansi and Hissar. He had been ousted earlier by Jai Singh from his territories in the Bari and the Jalandhar Doab. Their combined forces attacked Batala. In the battle that followed, Jai Singh's son Gurbakhsh Singh was killed. Jai Singh had to relinquish control over the Ramgarhia territory, and over the fort of Kangra which was restored to Sansar Chand who had joined Mahan Singh against Jai Singh. On the initiative of Sada Kaur, the widow of Gurbakhsh Singh, her daughter Mahtab Kaur was betrothed to Ranjit Singh.[13]

Mahan Singh's last action was the siege of Sodhara in 1791. It belonged to Sahib Singh, son of Gujjar Singh Bhangi, to whom Mahan Singh's sister was married. The ties of affinity had little influence in restraining his ambition. Early in 1792, Mahan Singh fell seriously ill and returned to Gujranwala where he died at the young age of 27. Ranjit Singh succeeded him at the age of 12. His mother became regent, assisted by Lakha or Lakhpat Singh as the *diwan*. Ranjit Singh contracted a second marriage with the daughter of the Nakkai Chief, Khazan Singh. At the age of 17, Ranjit Singh assumed the command of affairs, dismissed the *diwan* under the guidance of Dal Singh, the maternal uncle of his father. Diwan Lakha was slain by *zamindars,* not without suspicion of connivance.[14]

During the invasions of Shah Zaman in 1795, 1796 and 1797-8, Ranjit Singh was one of the chiefs on his route, who retreated before him. But, unlike them, he led an expedition across the Sutlej to reduce towns and villages to his authority. Upon Shah Zaman's retirement from Lahore, Ranjit Singh entertained the design of occupying Lahore which was in joint possession of Chet Singh, Mohar Singh and Sahib Singh. Prinsep chooses to follow Wade rather than Murray in stating that Ranjit Singh received a grant from Shah Zaman for the occupation of Lahore in return for extricating eight of his twelve guns from the bed of river Jhelum. Some of the eminent men of Lahore, like Mir Muhkam, Muhammad Ashiq and Mir Shadi, were persuaded to approach Ranjit Singh for taking over Lahore with their help. The city was occupied by him without opposition. He established his own authority, giving *jagirs* to the three co-partners. Prinsep did not know that Sahib Singh was the same person as the Sahib Singh of Gujrat, nor was he aware that they were not co-partners. He goes on to add that Sahib Singh of Gujrat, Gulab Singh Bhangi of Amritsar, and Nizamuddin of Kasur joined their forces to recover Lahore; their march towards Lahore was stopped by Ranjit Singh at Bhasin where the two sides remained encamped until the allies dispersed after the death of Gulab Singh. They failed to take Lahore.[15]

Ranjit Singh's career of conquest and consolidation of his power started in 1801-2 when he compelled Nizamuddin of Kasur to become his feudatory. Then he exchanged turbans with Fateh Singh Ahluwalia as a permanent ally. After the birth of Prince Kharak Singh in 1802, Ranjit Singh obliged Jassa Singh, son of Karam Singh Dulu, the chief of Chiniot, to hand over his territory; he was given a trifling allowance for maintenance. Towards the end of the year, Ranjit Singh occupied Lohgarh and other possessions of Mai Sukhan, the widow of Gulab Singh, in and around Amritsar. She fled with her minor son Gurdit Singh, and sank to indigence and obscurity. Called for help by Sada

Kaur against Sansar Chand of Kangra who had occupied some of her villages, Ranjit Singh expelled the mountaineers and occupied three districts of Budh Singh Bhagat (Bagga), the Sikh chief of Sujanpur. The widow of Char (Chuhar) Mal of Phagwara was deprived of her territory which was given to Fateh Singh Ahluwalia in an exchange. Tribute was taken from Tara Singh Gheba, Dharam Singh of Amritsar, and Buddh Singh Faizullapuria. Dal Singh died and Akalgarh was taken over by Ranjit Singh, along with his territory. In 1804, Ahmad Khan, the chief of Jhang, made his submission; tribute was taken also from the Baloch Chiefs of Sahiwal and Kot Maharaja.[16]

Early in 1805, Ranjit Singh performed ablutions in the Ganges at Hardwar. After the Dussehra, he demanded Rs. 1,20,000 as tribute from the chief of Jhang. Before the negotiations were concluded, Ranjit Singh heard of Jaswant Rao Holkar's flight to Amritsar, with Lord Lake in pursuit. Ranjit Singh reached Amritsar, treated Holkar in a friendly manner, but did not encourage him. He made his terms in a treaty signed with Lord Lake on 24 December. Friendly engagements were exchanged by Lord Lake with Ranjit Singh and Fateh Singh Ahluwalia; the Maratha and British armies returned to Hindustan in Januray 1806. Prinsep does not, however, refer explicitly to the treaty signed by Lake with Ranjit Singh and Fateh Singh together on the first of January.[17]

Raja Bhag Singh of Jind, the maternal uncle of Ranjit Singh, invited him to settle a dispute between Nabha and Patiala with regard to the village Doladdi. On his way to Nabha, Ranjit Singh occupied Ludhiana which belonged to Rani Nur un-Nisa, the mother of Rai Ilias (of Raikot), and seized Sahnewal which belonged to 'another defenceless widow'. Patiala troops were driven out of Doladdi. Both Raja Sahib Singh of Patiala and Raja Jaswant Singh of Nabha satisfied Ranjit Singh's greed and he removed 'the scourge of his ill-organized all-ravaging army' back into the Punjab.[18]

In 1807, the possessions of Nar Singh (Chamiari) were seized after his death and his son was given a *jagir* for subsistence. Qutbuddin of Kasur surrendered at discretion; Kasur and his other territories were taken over, except a small territory on the south of the Sutlej. Ranjit Singh took tribute from Nawab Muzaffar Khan of Multan, sent a force against Dinanagar and took exactions from some of the chiefs of the area who were under Sada Kaur's protection. She took offence, which became the basis of her growing differences with Ranjit Singh. The Rani of Patiala invited him to espouse her cause against her husband. Ranjit Singh crossed the Sutlej and seized the remaining territory of Ilias Rai and distributed it among his dependents and allies. Before he reached Patiala, the Rani had been reconciled but Ranjit Singh insisted on taking the promised gun and necklace. Naraingarh was conquered and given to Fateh Singh. On the death of Tara Singh Gheba, his possessions were taken over by Ranjit Singh, making a small provision for his family.[19]

IV. CHECK IN THE EAST AND EXPANSION IN THE WEST

In 1808, Ranjit Singh seized three important forts: Pathankot, Sialkot and Sheikhupura. His extensive usurpations alarmed the Sikh chiefs of Malwa. Raja Bhag Singh of Jind, Bhai Lal Singh of Kaithal, and the Vakil of Patiala met the British Resident, Seton, in Delhi to solicit British protection. The answer they received was not decisive but they were encouraged to hope that Ranjit Singh would not be allowed to extend his usurpations eastward. Ranjit Singh came to know of the mission and tried to re-assure the Malwa chiefs. In view of the alarm of an invasion of India by 'Napolean Bounaparte', Lord Minto determined to send Charles Metcalfe to Lahore. Metcalfe met Ranjit Singh at Kasur in September 1808 but before any serious discussion of the matter could take place, Ranjit Singh broke up his camp, crossed the Sutlej, occupied Faridkot, and proceeded against the Musalman Chief of Malerkotla. Metcalfe accompanied him to Faridkot but refused to go any further. Ranjit Singh seized Ambala and its dependencies, which were made over to the chiefs of Nabha and Kaithal. He extracted tribute from Shahabad and Thanesar. The government at Calcutta decided in October to declare that the country between the Jamuna and the Sutlej was under British protection. Ranjit Singh could retain his possessions acquired before Metcalfe's mission but not what he had seized in 1808. A body of troops under Colonel David Ochterlony reached Ludhiana in February 1809. Ranjit Singh had maintained all along that the Jamuna and not Sutlej was the proper boundary of the British possessions. The arrival of Ochterlony with troops opened his eyes to a new danger. A little later the Akalis under Phula Singh were routed at Amritsar by a small body of trained troops accompanying Metcalfe. This incident made a strong impression on Ranjit Singh who could see that his own troops were unfit to cope with those under European discipline, and he accepted peace and friendship at the sacrifices demanded. Prinsep's comment on the situation is significant. Had the danger been more imminent, it would probably have been deemed politic 'to extend our direct influence further into the Punjab, in reduction of the power of a chief who showed himself so unfriendly'. The perceived threat from Napoleon was there no more. A treaty was concluded with Ranjit Singh on 25 April 1809. The first article of the treaty was its best part from Ranjit Singh's viewpoint. It talked of 'perpetual friendship' between the British government and the state of Lahore which was to be considered by the British 'to be on the footing of the most favoured powers'; the British government was to have 'no concern with the territories and subjects of the Raja (Ranjit Singh) to the northward of the river Sutlej'. By implication, the British recognized Ranjit Singh not only as a sovereign but as the sole sovereign on his side of the Sutlej.[20]

Prinsep makes another significant comment at the close of the chapter: 'there is now established between the two powers as complete and perfect a good-fellowship as can exist with states constituted like those of India'. It was based on no better foundation than 'the personal character of Ranjit Singh' and his personal conviction that the British government desired to see him prosperous and powerful, and 'would regard the extinction of his rule, and the confusion and convulsions which must follow, as a serious evil of mischievous influence to itself'. Having prepared the reader to hear more on this important subject, Prinsep promises to say 'more hereafter'.[21]

Before returning to Ranjit Singh, Prinsep talks about the affairs of the states under British protection, justifying British intervention. Within four months of the Treaty of Amritsar, Ranjit Singh occupied the fort of Kangra for saving Sansar Chand from the Gurkhas. Before the end of the year, Ranjit Singh seized the *jagir* of Baghel Singh's eldest widow in the Jalandhar Doab, and the districts of Buddh Singh Faizullapuria. On the death of Jodh Singh of Wazirabad, his son was confirmed in his position on the payment of a heavy tribute. Before long, however,

Wazirabad was taken over. On a dispute between Sahib Singh and his son, Gujrat and other territories of the chief were confiscated. Tribute was collected from the Baloch and other Muslim chiefs in the Chaj Doab. Fateh Khan of Sahiwal was sent in chains to Lahore and the whole of his estate was sequestered. The Gilani and Bukhari Sayyads of Uch paid tribute to Ranjit Singh. The country of Multan was ravaged, and Muzaffar Khan paid Rs. 80,000 as tribute. Nidhan Singh Hattu and Bagh Singh Hallowalia lost their territories. The former was given a *jagir* later when a *jagir* was given to Sahib Singh too. Before the end of 1811, only four *misls* were left in the Punjab: the Sukarchakia, the Kanhiya, the Ramgarhia and the Ahluwalia. The last three had ranged under Ranjit Singh's standards.[22]

In 1812, Kanwar Kharak Singh was married to the daughter of Jaimal Singh of Fatehgarh from whom Ranjit Singh had taken Pathankot. Colonel Ochterlony attended the marriage, along with the Rajas of Nabha, Jind and Kaithal. After all the ceremonies connected with marriage were over, an expedition was sent against Bhimbar and Rajauri under the nominal command of Kharak Singh. Sujanpur was taken over from Buddh Singh (Bagga). On Jaimal Singh's death, his territories were taken over. In November, the chiefs of Bhimbar and Rajauri submitted to Ranjit Singh. In March 1813, Ranjit Singh's troops occupied the fort of Attock. In resentment, Wazir Fateh Khan refused to give the share he had promised out of the booty obtained from Kashmir. Later on, he blockaded the fort. Diwan Mohkam Chand and Ghausi Khan defeated the Afghans. In the rains of 1813, an expedition was sent to Kashmir but it turned out to be unsuccessful. The hill territory of Haripur was confiscated and Raja Bhup Chand was given a small *jagir*.[23]

In April 1814, Ram Dial was chosen for the conquest of Kashmir. He penetrated into the valley but his supplies were cut-off. Azim Khan, Wazir Fateh Khan's brother, allowed Ram Dial to retire safety in consideration of his professed friendship for Ram Dial's grandfather, Diwan Mohkam Chand. In April 1815, Ram Dial and Dal Singh ravaged the territories of Multan and Bahawalpur to exact tribute. After the Dussehera, the two commandants ravaged Bhimbar and Rajauri as a punishment for their role during the Kashmir expedition. Early in 1816, Raja Bir Singh of Nurpur was deprived of his territory and given a *jagir*. Ranjit Singh then moved with the army into the territories of Multan and Bahawalpur. Hafiz Ahmad Khan, the chief of Bhakkar and Leia, refused to pay tribute. His forts, Khangarh and Mahmudkot, were occupied. The territory of Ahmad Khan of Jhang were taken over and farmed out to Lala Sukh Dial for Rs. 1,60,000.[24]

After the Dussehra of 1816, the territories and *jagirs* of Bir Singh and Diwan Singh, the brothers of Jodh Singh Ramgarhia, worth Rs. 5,00,000 a year were confiscated. In 1817, Ram Lal, the brother of Khushal Singh, was compelled to take *pahul* as Ram Singh. After the Dussehra, Misar Diwan Chand was sent for the reduction of Multan under the nominal command of Kharak Singh. He occupied the city of Multan and closely invested the citadel. In June 1818, Akali Sadhu Singh advanced without orders with a few companions and attacked the Afghans, and overpowered them. The citadel was sacked and immense booty fell into the hands of the troops engaged in the assault. Ranjit Singh appointed Sukh Dial to the civil government of Multan. Most of the spoil was later recovered from the troops. Sarfaraz Khan and his wounded brother Zulfiqar Khan were conducted to Lahore and Ranjit Singh gave them a small stipend for subsistence. Raja Govind Chand of Datarpur died and his territory was annexed; his son eventually accepted a *jagir*. The occupation of Peshawar before the end of 1818 proved to be temporary.[25]

In 1819, Ranjit Singh made preparations for the second expedition to Kashmir. Misar Diwan Chand was selected for the command. A second army was placed under the command of Kharak Singh. Early in June, Diwan Chand occupied Rajauri and Punchh. In July, he advanced to the Kashmir valley and attacked the Afghans. The Misar's victory was complete. On the news of this success, the cities of Lahore and Amritsar were illuminated for three nights. Moti Ram was sent as governor. Before the end of 1819, Dera Ghazi Khan was wrested and farmed to the chief of Bahawalpur. Ranjit Singh extorted from Ahmad Khan of Mankera, the horse named *safed pari*. Moti Ram was replaced by Hari Singh Nalwa. Rawalpindi was annexed, dispossessing its chief Nand Singh.[26]

Mankera was conquered in 1821. For ten years then, most of the events related to the trans-Indus: the ongoing tussle for the control of Peshawar, the pacification of the Gandgarh and Darband area by Hari

Singh Nalwa, and the holy war of Sayyad Ahmad from 1827 to 1831. In a whole chapter then, Prinsep describes Lieutenant Burnes' mission through Sind up the Indus and the Ravi to Lahore, Ranjit Singh's mission to Lord William Bentinck at Simla, the meeting between the Governor-General and Ranjit Singh at Ropar in October 1831, and the commercial treaty concluded by the British in 1832 with Mir Murad Ali Khan of Hyderabad in Sind and Mir Rustam Ali Khan of Khairpur.[27] Ranjit Singh's ambition with regard to Sind was frustrated.

V. SCANDALS AND THE ARMY

Two aspects of Prinsep's work we have not mentioned so far: the scandals attached to Ranjit Singh, and his interest in the army. Ranjit Singh's mother was accused of having led a life of profligate indulgence and Ranjit Singh connived at her being put to death. He was following his father's example. Here, Prinsep accepts Wade's version in preference to Murray's.[28] It must be added that Prinsep seldom misses the opportunity of mentioning such scandals which have been repeated by later historians without any credible evidence.

Ranjit Singh reached Lahore in December 1807 to be presented by Mahtab Kaur with the twins, Sher Singh and Tara Singh. Mahtab Kaur's fidelity had been suspected for some time by her husband and he never fully acknowledged the twins as his offsprings. Prinsep refers to the rumour that the boys were procured by Sada Kaur from a carpenter and a weaver, and produced as born to her daughter. She had circulated the report that Mahtab Kaur was pregnant and people were prepared to hear of the birth of the children. Sher Singh was recognized as a prince for the expedition against Sayyad Ahmad but Tara Singh was treated by Ranjit Singh with uniform neglect.[29]

In 1816, Ranjit Singh had to attend to some domestic matters. His second wife, the mother of Prince Kharak Singh, was accused of scandalous improprieties, particularly of a notorious and close intimacy with Bhayya Ram Singh, the *diwan* of Prince Kharak Singh for his large *jagirs*. On the charge of mismanagement and extortion, the *diwan* was thrown into imprisonment, and ordered to give accounts of the *jagirs*; Prince Kharak Singh's mother was directed to fix her residence in the fort of Sheikhupura.[30]

Finally, Ranjit Singh led a most dissolute life. His debaucheries, particularly during the Holi and Dussehra, were shameless. Talked about all over Hindustan, they were worse than what was reported in the history of ancient Rome. He paraded in streets in a state of inebriety, with courtesans on his elephant. One of them, called Moran, acquired notoriety by her shamelessness. A coin was struck in her name. After Moran, Ranjit Singh turned his affection to Jamadar Khushal Singh and his brothers who were employed in state service. Prinsep refers to the notorious addiction of the Sikhs to pederasty and other unnatural lusts. He justifies his interest in scandals in the name of truth. History 'forbids the veil being thrown altogether over such facts and traits of character, howsoever revolting it may be to allude to them.' Though justly tainted with the foul blemish, the reputation of Ranjit Singh does not suffer in the eyes of his nation.[31] Prinsep judged Ranjit Singh and the other Sikh chiefs from what he assumed to be the British norms.

According to Prinsep, Ranjit Singh began to modernize his army on the British model after the encounter of Metcalfe's troops with the Akalis at Amritsar. For this purpose he entertained Purbias or the natives of the Gangetic provinces. He procured deserters from the British ranks. His artillery was also formed into a separate corps under a *darogha*. The cavalry was divided into two classes: the Ghurcharha Sawar and the Ghurcharha-i-Khas. The first was paid in money and the second in *jagirs,* and both were mounted on state horses. A few years later, Ranjit Singh devoted his attention to regular battalions and formed a corps of Sikhs, called *Orderly Khas,* to whom he gave superior pay. A horse artillery was also formed. In 1815, Ranjit Singh recruited the Gurkhas whose valour was impressive, and who were well adapted to hill warfare. In 1822, Ranjit Singh began to employ Europeans for military service. The Italian Ventura and the French Allard were the first to be employed on handsome salaries. The first was an infantry colonel in the French army and the second held a similar rank in the cavalry. They were set to train troops in European methods of exercise and manoeuvre. In 1833, Ventura was commanding 10,000 men in a separate command. His quarrel with Prince Kharak Singh proved to be injurious when the Prince succeeded his father. General Court joined Ranjit Singh's service, following the example of Ventura and Allard.[32]

VI. PRINSEP'S INFERENCES AND REFLECTIONS

In the last chapter of his book, Prinsep talks of the character and policy of Ranjit Singh, his revenues, and the strength of his army, and he makes some general observations. The empirical evidence presented in the earlier chapters was assumed to support his observations and explanation. Ranjit Singh had no education in any branch of learning or science but he had learnt enough to transact business rapidly. His memory was excellent and he was always watchful. He had great power of dissimulation so that he could veil subtle designs and even treachery. He was personally brave but his plans were neither bold nor adventurous. He was 'selfish, sensual and licentious in the extreme; disregardful of all ties of blood or friendship in the pursuit of his ambition or pleasure; and profligately greedy.' He plundered and reduced to misery, without the slightest feeling or remorse, widows, orphans and families possessing claims to consideration and respect.[32] Even Sada Kaur was treated in a shameless manner.[33]

Prinsep underlines that avarice and the desire of hoarding had become the ruling passions of Ranjit Singh by the time he was writing. He was known to break out into fits of passion and to use personal violence, but he had never awarded capital punishment to anyone. His love of horses was extreme. He seemed to take pleasure in seeing his courtiers and establishments decorated in jewels and handsome dresses. The splendour of his Darbar was very striking. He was not a fanatic but he listened to the *Granth* being read before him daily for a certain number of hours. He was superstitious enough to consult astrologers on all occasions.[34]

Ranjit Singh did not evolve any constitution or fixed form of government. There was no law, written or oral, and no courts of justice. The *gurmata* or the old council of the Sikhs had been entirely discontinued. The last council was held in 1805 when Holkar had fled to the Punjab. Ranjit Singh's government had become 'a pure despotism', with the army forming the whole machinery of administration. The whole power and authority was centred in a single individual. Prinsep goes on to add that 'upon his being removed from the scene, unless there be another to fill his place, with equal energy, and command over the attachment and affections of his dependents, which it is feared is not the character of Kharak Singh, everything must necessarily fall into confusion'. To put it simply, Prinsep anticipated political instability after the death of Ranjit Singh as something inevitable.[35]

The territorial possessions of Ranjit Singh covered the entire fork of the Punjab between the Indus and the Sutlej; he held Kashmir and Ladakh. The Rajas of the hills were tributary to him. He possessed 45 *ta'aluqas* on the east of the Sutlej; on the west of the Indus, he held Khairabad, Akora, Peshawar, Dera Ghazi Khan (farmed to the Nawab of Bahawalpur), Dera Ismail Khan (assigned to Hafiz Ahmad Khan of Mankera); and he levied tribute from the Baloch chiefs of Tonk and Sangar. The total revenues of Ranjit Singh amounted to Rs. 2,58,09,500 a year, coming from land revenue and tribute, customs and *mohrana*. Out of this total, revenues worth Rs. 1,09,28,000 were alienated in *jagirs*. Prinsep remarks that the province was not as productive as it had been under the Mughals. Ranjit Singh had hoarded wealth worth Rs. 10 crore.[35]

The military force of the Lahore state amounted to 82,014 horse and foot. Of this total force, the cavalry of the *jagirdars* accounted for 27,312 horse. The number of infantry variously armed and equipped was 26,950. The remaining 27,752 horse and foot constituted the regular army, with 12,811 cavalrymen under Allard and 14,752 of disciplined infantry. The regular army was the real strength of Ranjit Singh. In the artillery under a *darogha*, there were 376 guns and 370 swivels. Only the heavy train called *Jinsi* was distinct from the rest of the army. Prinsep reiterates that Ranjit Singh's government was not based on any solid form and institutions and, after his removal from the scene, it was not easy to carry on the machinery of his government and the army. With the British on one side and the Afghans on the other, the dominions of Ranjit Singh were most unlikely to expand any further.[37]

On the whole, Prinsep's work gives a lot of factual information. But all this information is not necessarily correct. Furthermore, he gives running comments on persons and their actions and expresses his attitudes through the language he uses. It is safe to suggest that he had no sympathy or empathy with Ranjit Singh. The professed goodwill of the British for Ranjit Singh is not reflected in Prinsep's work. If anything, he maligns Ranjit Singh by treating what could be merely rumours and gossip as established facts. He dwells on scandals which come to have a bearing on the issue of legitimacy. For Prinsep, only Kharak Singh and his son were the legitimate progeny of Ranjit Singh. Prinsep's interest in the army and revenue resources is obviously related to an assessment of Ranjit Singh's striking power and sustained resistance. This assessment itself gets related to his political imagination: the British were sure to have a problem after the death of Ranjit Singh. By implication, the formulation of a new policy with regard to the Punjab was necessary.

NOTES

1. Henry T. Prinsep, *Origin of the Sikh Power in the Punjab and Political Life of Maharaja Ranjit Singh with an Account of the Religion, Laws and Customs of the Sikhs,* Patiala: Punjab Languages Department, 1970 (rpt.), pp. 1-4.
2. Ibid., pp. 4-7.
3. Ibid., pp. 7-12.
4. Ibid., pp. 12-16.
5. Ibid., pp. 17-20.
6. Ibid., pp. 20-3.
7. Ibid., p. 23.
8. Ibid., pp. 23-6.
9. Ibid., p. 26.
10. Ibid., pp. 26-7.
11. Ibid., pp. 27-9.
12. Ibid., p. 29.
13. Ibid., pp. 30-7.
14. Ibid., pp. 37-9.
15. Ibid., pp. 40-2.
16. Ibid., pp. 42-5.
17. Ibid., pp. 45-6.
18. Ibid., pp. 46-7.
19. Ibid., pp. 48-50.
20. Ibid., pp. 50-5.
21. Ibid., p. 56.
22. Ibid., pp. 57-70.
23. Ibid., pp. 71-80.
24. Ibid., pp. 83-9.
25. Ibid., pp. 89-95.
26. Ibid., pp. 96-100.
27. Ibid., pp. 102-4.

28. Ibid., pp. 38-9.
29. Ibid., p. 50.
30. Ibid., pp. 88-9.
31. Ibid., pp. 67-8.
32. Ibid., pp. 62, 104-6.
33. Ibid., pp. 101-2, 106-7, 141-2.
34. Ibid., pp. 142-4.
35. Ibid., pp. 144-5.
36. Ibid., pp. 145-7.
37. Ibid., pp. 147-9. For Henry T. Prinsep, see also, S.K. Bajaj, 'Prinsep, Murray and Smyth', *Historians and Historiography of the Sikhs*, ed. Fauja Singh, New Delhi: Oriental Publishers, 1978, pp. 24-31. Gianeshwar Khurana, 'A New Dimension', *British Historiography of the Sikh Power in Punjab*, New Delhi: Allied Publishers, 1985, pp. 32-51.

CHAPTER FOUR

Intensive Interest in Sikh Affairs

Osborne, M'Gregor, Smyth, and Wilson

The decade after the death of Ranjit Singh was marked by the production of a large volume of literature on the Punjab in various forms, including historical works. Already before 1839, British interest in Afghanistan was increasing. The geographical position of the Punjab, the political developments within the state, the first Sikh War, and the issue of annexation of the kingdom of Ranjit Singh kept the Sikhs at the centre of British Indian politics until the truncated dominions of Ranjit Singh were annexed to the British empire after the second Sikh War in 1849.[1]

The writers of this decade were aware of the importance of their work for British Indian politics even when they did not set out deliberately to influence the course of British policies. The East India Directors sponsored the publication of Edward Thornton's *Gazetteer of the Countries Adjacent to India on the North-West* because the subject had acquired 'a new and extraordinary interest'.[2] An English translation of Baron Charles Hugel's *Travels in Kashmir and Punjab* was expected to throw light on 'the proper line of policy to be pursued by the Government of India, in relation to the Punjab'.[3] Extracts from the works of Malcolm and Steinbach were brought out by a publisher of Calcutta in 1846 as *The History of the Sikhs* with an imposing subtitle.[4] A publisher in London employed T.H. Thornton on a complete and revised edition of Prinsep's work called forth by the 'recent events in the Punjab'.[5] The second volume of Thornton's *History of the Punjab, and the Rise, Progress and Present Condition of the Sect and Nation of the Sikhs* was devoted to the events leading to the Sikh War and the campaign of the Sutlej.

The writers of the time tended as a rule to support and justify the official lines of policy. Steinbach favoured an outright annexation of the Sikh kingdom to the British empire.[6] The *Calcutta Review* described the Anglo-Sikh war as a Sikh invasion of British India and characterized it as 'the violent agonies of a young and profligate state which has died by its own hand in the mad moment of a national debauch.'[7] Major-General Caulfield argued that the 'natural' frontiers of British India and the stability of British rule in India demanded a complete annexation of the Punjab.[8] Montague Gore grounded himself on the unprovoked aggression and flagrant perfidy of the Sikhs and argued that no trust could be placed in 'this treacherous and unprincipled race'; all their cis-Indus territories, he suggested, should be annexed.[9] *The Edinburgh Review* thought of the annexation of the Punjab as the 'consummation' of conquest and its extraordinary necessity.[10]

The historians of the time glorified the success of British arms in the Punjab and justified British policy towards the Sikhs. We propose to discuss the works of W.G. Osborne, W.L. M'Gregor and G.C. Smyth and the views of H.H. Wilson on Sikh institutions as the immediate background for *A History of the Sikhs* by J.D. Cunningham who presented a contrast to their works.

I. W.G. OSBORNE

'It is a melancholy thing to contemplate the future probable state of this beautiful country. On the death of Ranjit Singh, which in the common course of nature must take place in a few years, his throne will become an object of contention between two rival candidates of equal power and pretentions.' This was what W.G. Osborne recorded in May 1838. The rival candidates were Sher Singh and Kharak Singh; the former, a natural son of Ranjit Singh, was seen as a good and proven warrior supported by all the influence, wealth and talents of Raja Dhian Singh; and the latter, the rightful son and heir of Ranjit Singh, who possessed little talent or courage but who was supported by all the Sikh chiefs bound by gratitude to Ranjit Singh for past favours, and their hatred of Raja Dhian Singh. After Ranjit Singh's death, a protracted and bloody war was inevitable; it could be terminated only by a third and stronger power which was without any doubt the British government. Both the claimants to the throne shared a common hatred for the British: none of them was expected to be friendly as a ruler. Therefore, the only option was that the Punjab should be 'our own'. Osborne goes on the add that the East India Company had 'swallowed too many camels to strain at this gnat.'[11]

Captain W.G. Osborne 'Military Secretary to the Earl of Auckland' was a member of the mission sent by the Governor-General to Ranjit Singh in May 1838. He refers to his work, *The Court and Camp of Runjeet Sing*, published in 1840, as 'a hasty journal, written to beguile the tedium of a camp life, and without the remotest intention of publication'. However, 'the present excited state of the country beyond our north-western frontier' made it an object of more than ordinary interest because it embodied a familiar intercourse with a ruler of an extraordinary character and, more than that, the peculiar position of his kingdom.[12]

The historical background outlined by Osborne reveals his reliance on Prinsep. Except in the first couple of pages, all his information is there in Prinsep's *Origins of Sikh Power in the Punjab and Political Life of Maharaja Ranjit Singh*. Though he was writing after 1838, Osborne's outline ends with the meeting between Lord William Bentinck and Ranjit Singh in October 1831. His assessment of Ranjit Singh's character and personality remains close to that of Prinsep, though couched in mild language.[13]

The mission of which Osborne was a member was sent by Auckland to the Court of Ranjit Singh in view of the suspected designs of Russia and the ambiguous conduct of Dost Muhammad. The objective was to replace Dost Muhammad by Shah Shuja at Kabul, and Ranjit Singh's consent and support was considered to be necessary. In other words, the British wanted Ranjit Singh to enter into the agreement which came to be known as the Tripartite Treaty. He seems to have signed this treaty rather reluctantly.

Osborne describes persons and places graphically in his journal. Among the most important men at the court were Kharak Singh, Sher Singh, Dhian Singh, Suchet Singh, Hira Singh, and Faqir Azizuddin. We can hear loud echoes of Prinsep even in the journal of Osborne. In the case of Prince Sher Singh, the Maharaja 'strongly denies the paternity'. In the footnote, Osborne explains that the conjugal fidelity of Mahtab

Kaur had been suspected already before she presented Sher Singh and Tara Singh to the Maharaja as his sons; he did not own up to them. But Osborne himself refers to 'Raja Sher Singh' seated on the right hand of the Maharaja while Raja Hira Singh was seated on the left, and no other individual was allowed a seat. Raja Hira Singh's extraordinary influence over Ranjit Singh was acquired in 'a manner which in any other country would render him infamous for ever, here he is universally looked up to and respected'. Ranjit Singh was extremely fond of Kashmiri girls. He fell violently in love with 'the Lotus'. She received seven good villages from the Maharaja. He asked Osborne to pick any of the girls to take with him. The prettiest of Kashmiri girls attended upon him and his guests. About two years earlier, he had fallen violently in love with one of these fair cup-bearers and actually married her.[14]

Like Prinsep, Osborne was deeply interested in the army of Ranjit Singh. Being on the scene, he could observe things in depth and detail. He talks of Ranjit Singh's Ghurcharhas 'handsomely dressed in chain armour and quilted jackets, made of rich silk of either a bright yellow, green, or scarlet colour'. Sardar Lehna Singh (Majithia), a clever mechanic, was successful in casting shrapnel shells. Unlike Ranjit Singh, the Sikhs were supposed to be generally deficient in personal courage. The regiments in Peshawar were in a state of open mutiny for want of pay for 18 to 22 months. Osborne attributed this to Ranjit Singh's avarice: he had six million sterling in his treasury at Amritsar.[15]

On the first of June, Osborne saw about 2,000 men under arms, 'a fine looking body of men, dressed in white jackets and trousers, with black belts and pouches'; they were wearing the yellow Sikh turban which they were not prepared to discard for a cap. They were beautifully steady on parade, and fired with greater precision and regularity than any other troops Osborne had ever seen. 'They are finer men, I think, than the Company's Sipahis, have fewer prejudices than most Indians.' Osborne remarks that, despite the impression to the contrary, Ranjit Singh's troop at times had fought well. The Sikh army possessed great advantage over that of the East India Company: 'thirty thousand of their troops could be moved with more facility, and less expense and loss of time, than Company's three regiments on this side of the Sutlej'.[16]

Ranjit Singh claimed to have a regiment of Gurkhas. Osborne claims to have discovered that only one man in twenty was a real Gurkha; the rest had come mostly from Kashmir. On the third of June, Osborne saw the artillery practice, and found twelve horse artillery guns of different calibres but well horsed and equipped. These were not the best guns Ranjit Singh possessed. He was trying out his own shells. At 500 yards the practice was indifferent but at 800 and 1,200 yards it was excellent. 'Many of the shells exploded exactly over the curtain'. Ranjit Singh told Osborne that in 1826, during the siege of Bharatpur, its ruler had offered him Rs. 100,000 for everyday of march and Rs. 50,000 for every day he remained with the Jat Chief, with 20,000 men. However, Ranjit Singh was not tempted. In retrospect, he thought that he had done well in not accepting the advice of the people around him.[17]

On 22 June, Osborne saw Ranjit Singh's trained infantry of 12,000 men, spread over a vast area up to the gates of the city. 'I never saw so straight or beautiful a line with any troops.' They were dressed in white with black cross belts, and either a red or a yellow silk turban 'armed with muskets and bayonets of excellent manufacture from Ranjit Singh's foundry at Lahore'. Their movements were steady but much too slow. Osborne comments that 'a European light infantry would find little difficulty in working round them'. Osborne gives an example to show 'how little dependence can be placed on their discipline, in a case of emergency'. However, he thought that it required only good officers and regular pay to make the Sikh army very powerful and serviceable. Osborne was not inclined to agree with those who accused the Sikhs of want of courage; they had fought the Afghans hand to hand and beaten them on more than one occasion. Significantly, Osborne adds: 'what they would do against our own Sipahis must remain a matter of uncertainty; though I confess I think, if equally well officered and led, they would prove efficient troops in every way'. Ranjit Singh knew that his regular infantry, upwards of 20,000, armed and disciplined like Europeans, had done more towards keeping his refractory *sardars* in order, than the fear of ten times their number of irregular forces would have done.[18]

Osborne saw the artillery drawn up on the opposite bank of the river. It consisted of a battery of fifty-three horse artillery, nine-pounders, cast in brass in Ranjit Singh's own foundry at Lahore, from the patterns of those presented to him by Lord William Bentinck. No Indian power had possessed so large and well disciplined a corps. It had already become by far the best and most powerful arm of the Sikh nation. The regular infantry, raised and drilled by General Ventura, had soldier-like appearance and good discipline. However, the same success had not attended the efforts of General Allard for the regular cavalry due to the parsimony of the Maharaja. On the first of July, Osborne saw the parade of a brigade of infantry, cavalry, and horse artillery under the command of Sardar Gulab Singh. Ranjit Singh insisted on having Osborne's view of the parade. He mentioned to the Maharaja that the only mistake he noticed was the system of making his skirmishers fire together in volleys by words of command; each man should fire individually, as soon as he had taken his aim and felt certain of the mark, without waiting for his comrades. Another mistake pointed out by Osborne related to the cavalry protecting the guns: they should stand on the flanks and not in the rear. Ranjit Singh saw the propriety of both these observations and gave orders for the change at the spot.[19]

The Governor-General's letter to the Maharaja was read to him by W.H. McNaughten on 31 May. It related to the part he was expected to take in concert with the British government for the restoration of Shah Shuja ul-Mulk to the throne of Kabul. Dhian Singh showed his dissatisfaction with the idea of any alliance, but only by shakes of the head. But Ranjit Singh agreed to the arrangement with apparent cordiality and eagerness. Osborne thought, however, that he would think of some gain for himself for allowing the British troops to pass through his country. Indeed, on 19 June, Osborne observed that the 'old lion has turned sulky, and refuses to sign the treaty, wishing to stipulate for all sorts of concessions'. The mission had no authority to make any changes and it was necessary to refer the matter to the headquarters. The principal *sardars* were opposed to the alliance. Nevertheless, Osborne remarked on 19 June that he would eventually agree: 'Ranjit has too much sense not to feel that all his power—nay, his very kingdom itself—depends upon his being on good terms with us.' Osborne left Lahore on 13 July.[20]

A meeting was arranged between the Governor-General and the Maharaja at Ferozepore on 30 November 1838. Lord Auckland appeared with the imposing magnificence of an Indian potentate. The bodyguards of Ranjit Singh had long beards down to their waists. A letter written by Osborne on 3 January 1839, after the Governor-

General's visit to the Maharaja in December 1838, was meant to show the Maharaja's friendly disposition towards the English. Osborne received the military order of the 'Ranjit Star of the Punjab.' He feared that he would soon have to inform of the old man's death. The Maharaja's illness increased on 20 July 1839 and he breathed his last on 27 July. Kharak Singh succeeded to the throne quietly and without the slightest opposition, in accordance with the wishes of Ranjit Singh. His four wives and five Kashmiri slave girls burnt themselves with his body. Dhian Singh threw himself on the pile but he was dragged away by force. Ranjit Singh's death caused a great sensation. For Osborne, it increased the risk for the treasure and the supplies to the army of the Indus passing through the Punjab, with many powerful and almost independent chiefs in the country. Kharak Singh was no substitute for Ranjit Singh.[21]

II. W.L. M'GREGOR

The History of the Sikhs by W.L. M'Gregor was published in two volumes in 1846. His professed purpose was to record 'every fact' connected with the history of the Sikhs and to present a 'complete history' of Ranjit Singh. The first volume is devoted entirely to these two themes. Besides a longish introduction, this volume contains eighteen chapters. The first chapter is given to Guru Nanak and the second, to his eight successors. To Guru Gobind Singh, however, are given four chapters. One chapter is given to Banda Bahadur and one to the history of the Sikhs after Banda's death till the establishment of 'confederacies.' In three chapters then are described six *misls:* the Bhangi, the Faizullapuria, the Ramgarhia, the Kanhiya, the Ahluwalia and the Sukarchakia. Seven chapters are then devoted to Ranjit Singh. In the second volume, a little more than four chapters of about forty pages contain an account of the successors of Ranjit Singh. The rest of the volume relates to Sikh War in the reign of Maharaja Dulip Singh.

M'Gregor had little appreciation for the Sikhs as a people. The religious doctrines inculcated by Guru Nanak were marked by simplicity and purity, and it had been his zealous desire to remove 'all the abuses and idolatries of the Hindoos, and the intolerance of the Mussulmans.' But he presented only 'an imperfect code of religion' which was 'finite in its application'. Furthermore, the simplicity of the Sikhs as a people was lost when they became warlike under Guru Gobind Singh. The followers of Guru Gobind Singh in the days of M'Gregor were 'like other pagan and barbarous nations, victims of their evil propensities'; 'their morality is even below that of the blood-thirsty Moslems, for they are guilty of crime in the sight of God and man'.[22]

Nevertheless, following his predecessors, M'Gregor did not deny the title of greatness to Guru Gobind Singh. At the outset of his pontificate Guru Gobind Singh propitiated the Goddess and instituted the Khalsa to avenge the death of his father. He waged a successful war against the hill chiefs and occupied a large chunk of territory. He was dislodged from Anandpur only by the Mughal forces but even against them he was successful in his last battle. Eventually, the Mughal emperor was prepared to come to terms with him through a personal meeting which did not take place because of the emperor's death. This account was derived from 'Musalman historians'. The impression formed by M'Gregor on the basis of their evidence is expressed by him in the following terms:

> If we consider the work which Govind accomplished, both in reforming his religion and instituting a new code of law for his followers; his personal bravery under all circumstances; his persevering endurance amidst difficulties, which would have disheartened others, and overwhelmed when in inextricable distress; and, lastly, his final victory over his powerful enemies by the very men who had previously forsaken him, we need not be surprised that the Sikhs venerate his memory. He was, undoubtedly, a great man.[23]

In M'Gregor's account, Banda Bairagi is commissioned by Guru Gobind Singh to avenge himself upon the oppressors of Guru Gobind Singh. A man of undoubted valour and cool courage, Banda fulfilled the order of Guru Gobind Singh by destroying Sirhind and murdering its inhabitants to avenge the death of his sons; he took full revenge also on the Muslim inhabitants of the Punjab. 'Seldom in the annals of the most barbarous nations do we find traces of such savage slaughter and devastation, as marked the progress of this Byragee'. Like the Persian chroniclers, M'Gregor could not see any good qualities in Banda; and like them again, he failed to see that Banda had established an independent state in a large part of the Punjab.[24]

The history of the Sikhs after Banda is given very briefly by M'Gregor. The true followers of Guru Gobind Singh resisted Banda's attempt to introduce changes in the practices of the Khalsa and they separated themselves from Banda. They were nearly annihilated by Abdus Samad Khan but somehow they survived all persecutory measures adopted by the Mughal governors of Lahore. Their numbers and strength increased particularly after Nadir Shah's invasion and, eventually, they ousted the governors of Ahmad Shah Abdali from the Punjab, occupying the country from Saharanpur in the east to Attock in the west and from Jammu and Kangra in the north to Multan and Sindh in the south. 'Each independent Sirdar kept possession of his own territory, nor encroached on that of his neighbour. In some instances, pergunnahs, or districts, were divided between two, and each received half the revenue of the whole.' Afterwards however the *sardars* began to quarrel among themselves for extension of territory. After repeated contests the country became 'the property of a few of the most powerful'. And these were the *sardars* of *misls.* M'Gregor then describes each of the six *misls* of the Punjab between the rivers Sutlej and Indus; the other *misls,* having 'long ago merged into the protected Sikh states', did not properly belong to the history of the Sikhs in M'Gregor's opinion. His account of the Sikh *misls* proper is based almost entirely on Ahmad Shah's *Tarikh-i Hind.*[25]

M'Gregor brings the narrative of the military career of Ranjit Singh up to his meeting with Bentinck in 1831 and remarks that the sketch of the life of the Maharaja he has presented differs in respect to dates from that given by Prinsep, 'but the authority we have followed appears, in many parts, the same as that from which Murray and Wade derived their information'.[26] This is followed by a description of the relations of Ranjit Singh with the British government based on M'Gregor's 'paper' on the court of Ranjit Singh drawn up by him in 1838 for Lord Auckland. It was meant 'to elucidate the character of the Maharaja, and the friendly feelings which at all times existed between him and the British'.[27] M'Gregor underlined that Ranjit Singh's state would provide the most effective buffer between Russia and the British empire in India. He is appreciative of the character of the Maharaja, and describes his courtiers. Towards the end of the first volume M'Gregor states that he has not copied Prinsep or the reports of Murray and Wade. 'Our first source of information was a history of the Maharaja kept by a Musalman family in the Punjab, natives of Wittala, and carefully translated by ourselves from the work rendered into Oordoo by our worthly friend Abdoolashah'. M'Gregor had thought of leaving out the military career of Ranjit Singh but he decided to write 'a continuous history'. He apologizes to the readers 'if they do not find anything new' in this part of his work. However, on the basis of his own observation and experience he has given the character of the Maharaja 'in its true light', besides his views regarding his British allies. None among the princes of the East ever preserved his alliance with greater zeal than Ranjit Singh and 'the British Government in India was not unmindful of this when securing to his son the throne of Lahore'.[28]

The second volume of M'Gregor's *History* starts with the death of Ranjit Singh and the reign of Kharak Singh. *The* real line of Ranjit Singh, according to M'Gregor, was extinct after Nau Nihal Singh's death. But the British were prepared to acknowledge any ruler installed by the Sikhs at Lahore, 'provided he could establish and maintain a government which would prevent any infringement of the treaty or aggression across the Sutlej'. A brief outline of the events at Lahore after the death of Nau Nihal Singh is meant to show that there was no control over the army in the reign of Dulip Singh; its *panchas* were the real rulers of the country. The history of the Sikhs during the reign of Dulip Singh was of 'vast importance' to the civilized nations of Europe precisely because it was during his reign that 'the Sikh power had become so arrogant' that 'it aimed at the conquest of Hindostan and imagined itself capable of overthrowing the British supremacy'. In this volume there is hardly any 'history of the Sikhs'. The Sikh war is described and discussed simply and purely from the contemporary British viewpoint.[29]

A clue to an understanding of M'Gregor's *History of the Sikhs* is provided by its dedication to Lord Gough and the officers of the Army of the Sutlej as a token of admiration for the invincible courage they displayed in the fields of Mudki, Ferozeshah, Aliwal and Sabraon, 'to render justice to all those enlightened men and gallant spirits, whose skill and intrepidity combined to repel the insolent invasion of a rebellious army and to consolidate the British power in the north-west of India'.[30] Obviously, M'Gregor's primary purpose was to write about the Sikh War of 1845-6 to vindicate the measures and policies of the British rulers of India as well as to commemorate the actions of the British officers and soldiers.

In November 1845 reports of the intended Sikh invasion of British territories were spread daily and the news-writers at Lahore gave minute accounts of the hostile preparations, but the British government did not believe that such an event could occur. Therefore, when the Sikhs crossed the Sutlej, there was no time for 'extensive preparations'. Fortunately, Lord Ellenborough had established a large force at Ambala which could be available at a moment's notice. The Governor-General Hardinge issued his manifesto of war, and confiscated Dulip Singh's possessions on the British side of the Sutlej. An 'unprovoked aggression' called for punishment. The first encounter at Mudki was indecisive; it resulted in the deaths of Sir Robert Sale, Sir John McCaskill, and many other officers. Had the Khalsa troops encountered a less desperate resistance, they would have rallied on the day following but Tej Singh thought that retreat to his entrenched camp would be safer. Therefore, the Khalsa troops joined the camp at Pherushahr. M'Gregor gives the account of the battle of Mudki written by the British Commander-in-Chief on 18 December 1845, treating the official version as more authentic than any other.[31]

The Sikhs were confident of their strength and resources and they looked upon the British as hardly their equals. M'Gregor finds it difficult to explain why the Sikh troops did not attack Ferozepore when Sir John Littler could hardly have held it against a siege. Lal Singh appeared to be responsible for this inaction on the part of the Sikhs but M'Gregor was not sure of the real cause. 'We are almost tempted to believe that the Sikh leaders wished to keep their troops together, in order that the British might have a full and fair opportunity of destroying them'. M'Gregor states that the Punjabi Muslims did not like Sikh rule and the Muslim officers of the Sikh army were mere mercenaries. The Sikhs, on the hand, were 'fighting upon religious principles'. Even when defeated they were bound by the obligation 'to lay down their sword but with their lives'. The British were informed of the disposition of the Sikh army at Pherushahr but 'the information given on native authority' turned out to be wrong. The Sikh guns could not be silenced by the British and the infantry had to advance to capture them. 'Never in the annals of warfare in India had matters attained such a threatening crisis'. The British officers had the greatest difficulty in getting their men to advance. The hard-contested battle of Pherushahr would have been won by the Sikhs but for 'the indomitable bravery of the British infantry'. All the British regiments suffered heavy losses.[32]

After the defeat at Pherushahr, the Sikhs appealed to Gulab Singh for assistance but the Raja had a 'deep game to play'. He obeyed the summons but he was determined not to mix himself up with 'the ill-judged opposition offered to the British'. Compared with the entrenchments at Pherushahr, the works at Sabraon were '*fortifications*'. Even when at particular points their entrenchments were mastered with the bayonet, the Sikhs strove to regain them by 'the fiercest conflict sword in hand'. Eventually, they were defeated. 'In their efforts to reach the right bank through the deepened water, they suffered a terrible carnage from our horse artillery'. The carnage at Sabraon had no parallel in the annals of warfare. No fewer than 13 British officers were killed and 101 wounded. The last battle of the War terminated in the final defeat of the Sikhs 'who had crossed the river in the vain hope of conquering Hindostan'.[33]

M'Gregor reproduces the proclamation made by Lord Hardinge at Kasur on 14 February 1846. This proclamation refers to the 'unprovoked aggression' of the Sikhs and 'the forebearance and moderation of the British Government' in their treatment of the state founded by 'the late Maharaja Runjeet Singh, the faithful ally of the British power'. The wily Gulab Singh became the mediator between 'the fallen state of Lahore, and the victorious Governor-General of India'. He brought Maharaja Dulip Singh from Lahore to make a personal submission to the Governor-General. M'Gregor states that annexation of the entire state was 'impracticable': it was truncated. And the army was reduced in strength. M'Gregor gives the text of various notifications, orders and treaties. The treaty signed with 'Maharaja Gulab Singh' gave him Jammu and Kashmir 'in independent possession' under British supremacy, with a token tribute of one horse, twelve shawl goats, and three pairs of Kashmir shawls.[34]

In his 'general remarks', M'Gregor goes on to justify the arrangements made. The country was entirely in the hands of the paramount power. British troops were posted in the Punjab to preserve the semblance of a government, 'but in reality to keep possession of the advantages already gained, until the season of the year shall enable the Governor-General to annex the whole country to the British possessions, if such a step be deemed necessary'. In any case, this experiment was most unlikely to be successful. Sooner or later the British standards would again be unfurled, and the Indus, and not the Beas, become the frontier barrier of British possessions in the east. M'Gregor talks of the measures to be adopted 'in case it becomes necessary for the British to subjugate the whole of the Punjab'. No means were to be overlooked for curbing 'the disorderly and treacherous spirit of the Sikhs': force alone could accomplish this. The principles of economy should be overlooked for a time: 'The acquisition of the Punjab, with Indus forming our boundary on the west, will no doubt tend to consolidate our vast empire, and ensure a permanency of peace and its countless blessings.'[35]

In the last hundred pages of his *History*, M'Gregor reports on some of the happenings during the early months of British presence in the Punjab. Significantly, he does so on the assumption that the British had come to stay. In a chapter on 'the British garrison at Lahore' he talks of the Sikhs having been conquered and discomfited still cherished the hope of retaliating and their spirit urged them 'to seek for the lives of the British'. Their powerful prejudice regarding the cow led the authorities at Lahore to forbid the slaughter of cows or bullocks for the supply of beef to the British roops. 'For an army to be thus dictated by its prostrate foe, appears to be somewhat absurd'. It impressed the Sikhs with a belief that 'our present position at Lahore is one of sufferance.' The British garrison should inflict condign punishment on all offenders. The Akalis and disaffected Sikhs were most likely to congregate and discuss their affairs at the sacred tank of their Gurus. The garrison at Lahore must be prepared to crush every disturbance in the very bud, no matter from what source it may arise'. Incidentally, M'Gregor suggested that the money of Raja Suchet Singh lodged at Ferozepore should be conveyed to the Company's treasury rather than be given to Gulab Singh.[36]

At the end of his book M'Gregor says that if its second edition was published he would be able to correct errors and add many more facts regarding the Sikh campaign of 1845 and 1846. He had done this already in the last six chapters of the book. The communications of the Governor-General to the Secret Committee laid before the Parliament provided 'many particulars regarding the origin of the Sikh campaign'. The additional information highlights the commendable role of the Governor-General, the Commander-in-Chief, Brigadier Wheeler, Major Broadfoot, and Captain Nicholson. It was not the Lahore government but 'a mutinous Sikh army' that made war upon the British. Therefore, the Governor-General did full justice to the 'pacific intentions' of Rani Jindan and her son. M'Gregor gives information on the defiance of the *qiladar* of the fort of Kangra and its final fall. He talks again of the Sutlej campaign to highlight the role of Major-General Joseph Thackwell. He goes on to add 'some particulars not generally known' about the artillery at Pherushahr. M'Gregor provides some information on the Jalandhar Doab and emphasizes that it gets cut-off from the rest of the Punjab during the rainy season. The unruly Sikhs made no secret of their intentions to rise against the British at an opportune time. Therefore, the British troops at Lahore and in the Jalandhar Doab should be adequate to meet such an eventuality. M'Gregor picks up the threads of the siege of Kangra to highlight the role of Major Lawrence. For the battle of Pherushahr, again, he turns to Sir Harry Smith for 'accurate information'. It was not artillery opposed to artillery, nor cavalry to infantry, but 'a body of European infantry fighting against all the three arms' that won the War.[37] Thus, on every issue related to the Sikh War, M'Gregor was keen to present the British official view and to uphold it to the end of his work.

III. MAJOR CARMICHAEL SMYTH

A *History of the Reigning Family of Lahore with Some Accounts of the Jummoo Rajas, the Seik Soldiers and Their Sirdars,* edited by Major Carmichael Smyth of the Third Bengal Light Infantry, 'with Notes on Malcolm, Prinsep, Lawrence, Steinbach, M'Gregor, and the *Calcutta Review*', was compiled 'partly from native manuscripts, and partly from information collected from Seik Sirdars, and European officers in the Seik service; but chiefly from the notes of a Captain Gardner of the Seik Artillery who has for several years past supplied important information to the British Government without betraying his own'. Undertaken at the suggestion of Major Broadfoot, it was dedicated 'to the memory of Major Broadfoot', Agent to the Governor-General of India on the North-Western Frontier; his moral courage in counsel was equal to his undaunted conduct in the field. Smyth adds later on that Dr Archibald Gordon of the Political Department had suggested the idea before Major Broadfoot's 'recommendation'.[38] We may be sure that Captain Gardner provided 'important information' to Major Broadfoot who passed it on to Major Smyth.

The contents of Smyth's work make it clear that his primary purpose was to use the information provided by Gardner. The core of the book consists of the 'Secret History of the Lahore Durbar' in 12 chapters which have headings and numbers in the 'contents' and the text. This core is preceded by two un-numbered chapters entitled 'History of Runjeet Singh's Family' and 'Early History of Runjeet Singh'. These are followed by an un-numbered chapter on 'the war with the British'. All these chapters relate to Sikh history. The rest of his work was to give interesting or useful information without any regard to its strict relevance to Sikh history. His 'Miscellaneous Notices' related to Akali Phula Singh, the mutiny in Kashmir, Zorawar Singh, and revolt of the Sudhan Afghans, and Fateh Khan Tiwana. The part on 'the Lords of the Hills' is followed by an Appendix that contains extracts from Malcolm's *Sketch of the Sikhs,* Prinsep's *Life of Runjeet Singh,* Henry Lawrence's *Punjab Adventurer* and Steinbach's *Punjab,* the *Medical and Literary Journal* for January 1845 and the *Calcutta Review* for August 1844, with comments called 'notes'. These notes are meant to give comprehensive information.

However, the Appendix does not end here. It gives information on 15 other themes: productions of the Punjab and the hill states, mineralogical productions, Hindu, Muslim and Sikh castes in the Punjab, estimates of the population of cities, estimated population of different districts, the *sardars* and chiefs killed after the death of Ranjit Singh, those who died naturally, those who were killed in the battles with the British, and those living at Lahore, an abstract showing the distribution of the Sikh army on 1 July 1844, the boundary of the Punjab in 1845, the principal *sardars* and chiefs of the Dogra faction and their opponents, the numerical strength of the standing army of the Punjab in 1845, foreign officers in Sikh service, the state revenues collected in 1844, products and manufactures, and articles procurable in the Punjab with their prices. The bulk of the 297 subscribers for Smyth's work belonged to the British Indian army.

The importance given by Smyth to 'the lords of the hills' did not mean that he had any admiration for them. The Jammu family was the source of all intrigues. There was every reason to believe that Captain Gardner could give further information to prove that the Dogra chiefs were at the bottom of the Kabul insurrection. The history of the Dogra family was also an account of their 'iniquities'. After knowing Gulab Singh's 'atrocities', the public would be greatly surprised that the British government had entered into a treaty with 'such a monster'. During his 26 years in India Smyth had never heard of 'so infamous a miscreant' as the Raja of Jammu.[39]

The character of Gulab Singh, as revealed in the early days of his power, was 'the most repulsive it is possible to imagine'. He was ambitious, avaricious, and cruel by nature; he exercised the most ruthless barbarities and committed the most horrible atrocities. Yet he was courteous and polite in demeanour, and suave in manners. He was a good soldier and a prudent commander. Dhian Singh was active, enterprising, brave, energetic and intrepid; he was ever employed in bold and manly pursuits. His ambition knew no bounds, but he was moderate and regular in his habits. He could shamelessly sacrifice everything, even his life and honour, to his ambition and the thirst for aggrandizement. Suchet Singh knew better how to fight than to command; he was a most licentious debauchee and shameless defiler of women. Hira Singh, a pet of Ranjit Singh, was his most loving victim; he was a mixture of strange and contradictory ingredients. He was inseparable from Misar Jalla, his sole adviser, sworn friend and protector, tutor and master, father and brother.[40]

Smyth projected the reigning family of Lahore in no better light. He presents Ranjit Singh's great grandfather as a highway robber. Charhat Singh's wife was unfaithful to him. Mahan Singh put his mother to death 'with his own hands' because she had been long suspected of 'a criminal intercourse' with yet another man. Mahan Singh was said to have expressed strong doubts about the paternity of Ranjit Singh himself because of his mother's liaison with his father's *diwan*. The mother-in-law of Ranjit Singh as well as his mother were chiefly aided and influenced 'by their paramours'. Ranjit Singh 'followed the example of his father by putting his mother to death'. The first important event of his life was the occupation of Lahore and the story of his subsequent career was well known. Smyth refers briefly to a few events related to Holker's visit to the Punjab, the treaty of Ranjit Singh with the English, and his major conquests.[41]

In the first two chapters of the history of the reigning family of Lahore, also called 'Secret History of the Lahore Durbar', which was based on the reports of Captain Gardner, Smyth narrates the events from the death of Maharaja Ranjit Singh to the accession of Prince Sher Singh as the Maharaja. Some years before Ranjit Singh's death, Raja Dhian Singh had come to hold 'the reins of government entirely in his own hands'. He was enjoined by Ranjit Singh to place Prince Kharak Singh on the throne. Soon afterwards, however, there was a breach between the minister and Maharaja Kharak Singh who doted on one Chet Singh. Raja Dhian Singh conspired with his brothers, the Sandhanwalia *sardars*, and Prince Nau Nihal Singh to murder Chet Singh. After his assassination, Nau Nihal Singh was 'proclaimed king'. Kharak Singh was confined to the palace and slowly poisoned. After his funeral, Nau Nihal Singh was struck by the beams, stones and tiles of a gateway that collapsed suddenly. A *palaki* was ready to convey him into the fort where no one was allowed to see him, not even his wives. Nau Nihal Singh died in the sole custody of Raja Dhian Singh who was inwardly hoping to place Prince Sher Singh on the throne. The Sandhanwalias, openly, and Raja Gulab Singh, outwardly, supported Chand Kaur, Nau Nihal Singh's mother. The Dogras were apparently divided among themselves but they were actually in league. Raja Gulab Singh succeeded for some time and then Sher Singh was called by Raja Dhian Singh and, after a show of force, a compromise was worked out. Raja Gulab Singh was a great gainer. Eventually, he secured for himself a *jagir* worth Rs. 9,00,000 a year under the pretence of holding it for Chand Kaur, and all her money and valuables under the pretence of keeping them safely at Jammu. Smyth's comment at the end of the second chapter sums up the position:[42]

> The deep policy of the Jummoo brothers was now beginning to develop itself. They had got rid of the unfortunate Kurruck Singh, and of his active ambitious son, Nau Nihal Singh; the Rani Chand Kaur had been set aside, and Sher Singh was placed on the throne simply that he might be the more completely in the power of these his worst enemies. It now only remained to dispose of the new

Maharaja, to replace whom Dhian Singh had in his hand a young child, the reputed though not the real son, of Ranjit Singh, and then, with the Khalsa troops entirely at his command, Raja Dhian Singh, aided by his brothers, would be supreme.

At the outset of Maharaja Sher Singh's reign, his *mukhtar*, Jawala Singh, appeared to aspire to power at the court. The Dogra brothers were bent on his destruction. Their first step was to rob him of the confidence of the Maharaja. Then he was fettered and thrown into a dungeon where he died of torture. On Maharaja Sher Singh's secret orders, the slave girls of Chand Kaur killed her. On the intercession of Bhai Ram Singh, Attar Singh Sandhanwalia and his nephew Ajit Singh were recalled from exile and Lehna Singh was released from imprisonment. Raja Dhian Singh conspired with the Sandhanwalias to place a newly discovered, reputed son of Maharaja Ranjit Singh on the throne in place of Sher Singh. The Sandhanwalias exposed Raja Dhian Singh's disloyalty to Maharaja Sher Singh who agreed to the elimination of Dhian Singh. The Sandhanwalias murdered Maharaja Sher Singh and his son Partap Singh, and they murdered Dhian Singh too. Hira Singh induced the whole Khalsa force to side with him. He came into power and proclaimed the boy Dulip Singh to be the Maharaja.[43]

Raja Suchet Singh was not reconciled to the *wazarat* of his nephew, Raja Hira Singh. Like his brother Dhian Singh, Suchet Singh had risen to favour in the court of Ranjit Singh by 'the most infamous means'. They had secured his patronage by the most criminal compliance with his desires.

Suchet Singh had been the favourite of several court ladies, including some of the widows of Ranjit Singh. Rani Jindan, the mother of the young Maharaja, was one of them. She promised to bestow *wazarat* on Suchet Singh. Misar Jalla was afraid that he would be displaced from power as he had been supplanted in love. Hira Singh issued orders that Suchet Singh should not be allowed to enter the *zanana* without permission from the *wazir*. Suchet Singh's indignation knew no bounds. However, Gulab Singh persuaded him to accompany him to Jammu. There, he adopted Gulab Singh's son Mian Ranbir Singh as his son.[44]

Raja Gulab Singh used forged letters to implicate Princes Kashmira Singh and Pashaura Singh in a conspiracy against the Maharaja and his *wazir*. Gulab Singh was ordered to attack them at Gujranwala and Sialkot. His troops occupied Gujranwala but they were defeated at Sialkot. The Khalsa were persuaded to move against the reputed sons of Maharaja Ranjit Singh. Sialkot was taken. The Khalsa swore vengeance against Raja Hira Singh, and all the Dogras, if any harm came to the two princes. Hira Singh accepted some other conditions too imposed by the Khalsa. In this situation, Suchet Singh thought of replacing his nephew. However, the army did not support him and in the end he was slain by the troops sent against him by Raja Hira Singh. Princes Kashmira Singh and Pashaura Singh joined the camp of Bhai Bir Singh where some other refractory *sardars* were present. Sardar Attar Singh Sandhanwalia was among them. Raja Hira Singh sent Khalsa battalions against them. Bhai Bir Singh, Attar Singh Sandhanwalia and Prince Kashmira Singh were killed in the conflict. Pashaura Singh had surrendered a day before the battle and his *jagir* was restored to him.[45]

Raja Hira Singh and Misar Jalla used to send for Rani Jindan at night and compel her to allow 'criminal intercourse' with her. It was also discovered that Jalla was trying to poison her under the pretence of medication. Jawahar Singh, the Rani's brother, and *sardars* and soldiers were all against Hira Singh and Jalla. They tried to escape but on their way to Jammu they were overtaken and slain. The head of Hira Singh was exposed on the Lahauri Gate. The head of Jalla was carried about in the city for some days.[46]

Jawahar Singh and his supporters thought of reducing all those places which were held by Hira Singh and Gulab Singh. Troops against Jasrota, Samba, Ramnagar, and other places were sent under Lal Singh, Sham Singh Attariwala, Fateh Singh Mann, and Sultan Mahmud Khan. They marched towards Jammu. Fateh Singh Mann was treacherously killed and the Sikh troops invaded Jammu. Gulab Singh submitted, pleaded innocent, and appealed to the greed of the troops. The Khalsa army got divided into two bodies, and marched towards Lahore. Meanwhile, at the instigation of Avitabile, Pashaura Singh had marched towards the capital. He was persuaded by the Khalsa camp to return to Sialkot. The *panchas* of the army assembled to escort Gulab Singh to the palace. However, Jawahar Singh was able to undermine his position and secured the *wazarat* formally for himself. Gulab Singh was asked to pay Rs. 35,00,000 to the state and give up the territories of Suchet Singh and the property of Hira Singh. After a few months he left the capital for Jammu.[47]

The Khalsa declared that they would proclaim Prince Pashaura Singh as the rightful heir to the throne, and Jawahar Singh responded by promising a golden necklace worth Rs. 25 to every army man. The Khalsa persuaded Pashaura Singh to return with some valuable presents from the court. Jawahar Singh later on used the services of Sardar Chatter Singh and Fateh Khan Tiwana to get rid of Pashaura Singh. They tricked him into leaving the fort of Attock. He was detached from his troops and taken back to the fort, strangled and thrown into the Indus. Jawahar Singh was elated on receiving the news but the Khalsa were furious. On 21 September 1845, Jawahar Singh was escorted to the camp to be killed there before the eyes of Rani Jindan and Maharaja Dulip Singh.[48]

After the murder of Jawahar Singh, Lal Singh, son of Jassa Misar, was so favoured by Rani Jindan that he became virtually the head of the government. He was formally appointed *wazir* when the invasion of the British territories was planned. In November 1845, the Council confirmed Lal Singh as *wazir* and Sardar Tej Singh as the commander-in-chief in deference to the wishes of the Rani. All the *sardars, panchas* and officers were requested to swear by the *Granth Sahib* at the *samadh* of Maharaja Ranjit Singh to remain faithful to Maharaja Dulip Singh and obedient to Raja Lal Singh and Sardar Tej Singh. Then orders were issued to march the army towards the Sutlej. Smyth describes the battles rather briefly. The Khalsa soldiers entertained strong suspicions that their late defeats had been brought on by the treachery of 'their chiefs, prompted by the Ranee, who sought their destruction in revenge for the death of her brother'. The conduct of Tej Singh in the war appeared to be treasonous. His order to retreat at Pherushahr was inexplicable on any other supposition than that of treachery. He was also the first to quit the bloody field of Sabraon. There were other such stories. Smyth concludes his account of the Sikh War on a note scepticism: 'It is possible, however, that many of these stories, attributing treachery and cowardice to Teja Singh, may have their origin in the distrust and ill-will with which he was regarded by the army, and therefore they are not to be implicitly relied upon.'[49]

There is no doubt that Smyth's narrative of the years from the death of Maharaja Ranjit Singh to the first Sikh War is more detailed than any earlier narrative. Would that alone, however, have prompted the publication of his book? In his 'Introduction' to the work, Smyth asserts that it was absurd to expect that the Raj of Ranjit Singh would last. The appellation of 'the old Robber' was more appropriate for him rather than the 'old Lion'. In the *Punjaub Adventurer*, Dhian Singh foretells the destruction of the Raj and all the bloodshed that ensued. 'What a country the Punjab was then to have between us and Cabull! What a nation to form our alliance with!' They were on the brink of a revolution, and their government depended 'on the life of a decrepit debauchee'. How could the British look to such people for support?[50] Smyth's narrative of the events of the 1840s was meant to provide the evidence in support of his view, and the view of many others among his contemporaries, that the state of Lahore could not serve any purpose as a buffer state. It had lost its *raison d'être*.

Smyth argues that the treaty of the British with Maharaja Ranjit Singh had ended with the death of Nau Nihal Singh. It was well known that Sher Singh was not the son of the Maharaja. Even Dulip Singh was not his son, though he was the son of Rani Jindan. Smyth himself states that he was induced to undertake this *History* 'to bring forth all these facts'. With regard to the War, he was neither of the opinion that the Sikhs had made an unprovoked attack nor that the British government had acted towards them with great forbearance. In his view, the British as 'the paramount authority' should have adopted coercive measures with the Sikhs. No half measures should have been pursued, and no middle course should have been taken. The implication is clear enough: outright annexation of the Punjab. The British would not have been in India now if Lord Wellesley had troubled his head about 'what they would say at home'. Smyth is critical of the Government of India not for waging the war but for leaving the task half-finished.[51]

IV. HORACE HAYMAN WILSON

In 1848, Horace Hayman Wilson, the Bodin Professor of Sanskrit at Oxford, contributed an article on 'Civil and Religious Institutions of the Sikhs' to the *Journal of the Royal Asiatic Society* in compliance with a wish expressed by some of the members of the Asiatic Society. Lord Auckland was its President at that time. The article was based on the works of Charles Wilkins, John Malcolm, H.T. Prinsep, Garcin de Tassy, the *Travels* of Moorcroft, Burnes, Jacquement and Baron von Hugel, the fictional *Adventures of an Officer in the Punjab* by Major Henry Lawrence, and the *Dabistan-i Mazahib*, a work on religions of the world, in English translation. Wilson was conscious of the fact that all his sources were 'already in print'. His purpose was to focus on 'the institutions of the Sikhs which distinguish them from the Hindus in general'.[52]

Wilson starts with a general statement on the popular religious movements, initiated by thoughtful and benevolent individuals belonging to the unlearned classes of the people of India, who were dissatisfied with the prevalent religious practices and the distinctions of caste. They attempted to reform these defects, and to reduce 'the existing systems of belief to a few simple elements of faith and worship in which Brahman and the Shudra, the Muhammadan and Hindu might cordially combine'. These reformers were not deeply versed in the Vedas and the Qur'an but they were well grounded in the speculative tenets of the two systems 'which they sought to amalgamate'. They retained the doctrine of transmigration, and grafted upon it the Vedantic principle of emanation and the Sufi idea of love. They wrote hymns in the vernacular dialects, addressed to the imagination and feelings of the common people. Their compositions were preserved as the literature of the creed of a large portion of the agricultural population of north India. The teacher whose instructions exercised the most durable influence on a considerable body of people was Guru Nanak.[53]

However, Guru Nanak was 'the nominal founder of the religion and nation of the Sikhs'. The development of the nation was aided by 'political events'. To make this point clear, Wilson takes up the ten Gurus and their contribution towards the general development of the movement, which is not free from factual errors and misperceptions. Though Guru Angad kept his followers together 'as a distinct body', Guru Amar Das came to have some temporal power and built a fort. His secular aggrandizement alienated the 'orthodox' Sikhs and they became Udasis or Nirmalas. It was chiefly from these categories of Sikhs that teachers of Guru Nanak's theism were to be found in almost every considerable city of Hindustan, either singly or assembled in convents (*sangats*).[54]

The successors of Guru Amar Das, who propagated the doctrines of Guru Nanak unmolested under the early Mughal rulers, seemed to have risen rapidly in temporal as well as spiritual consideration. Guru Ram Das enjoyed the favour of Akbar, and enlarged and improved an ancient city which came to be called Ramdaspur after his name. He constructed a large tank, called *amritsar,* which gave its name and sanctity later to the city of Amritsar. Guru Arjan compiled the *Adi Granth* which, apart from the compositions of his predecessors, contained contributions from 13 other authors, like Kabir, Shaikh Farid, Ramanand and Mira Bai, and other well-known sectarian or Vaishnava teachers. For Wilson, the exposition of the Sikh faith in the *Adi Granth* was so vague that it did not deserve 'the appellation of a faith'. There was no systematic exposition of the doctrines, no condensed creed, and no rules for ritual observances. The name *Adi Granth* was meant to distinguish it from the later compilation known as the *Daswen Padshah ka Granth,* the Book of the Tenth King.[55]

The wealth and consideration attained by the Sikh Gurus drew upon them the jealousy and persecution of the Muhammadans and Guru Arjan was thrown into prison where he died, or he was put to death. This was resented by the Sikhs of the province. They took up arms under Guru Hargobind, and exacted vengeance from all who were regarded as hostile to them. However, it was regarded as a mere local disturbance, involving no political crisis. The persecuting spirit continued. For some, it was a retribution because the Sikhs had become plunderers and robbers and they suffered due to this. Guru Tegh Bahadur was publicly put to death in 1675. The cause, according to Sikh authorities, was the instigation of a competitor for Guruship. According to Muslim writers, it was due to offences against the law, a life of predatory violence. At the time of his death, the Sikhs had almost disappeared, 'except a few inoffensive sectarians or scattered bands of banditti'.[56]

The succession of Guru Gobind Singh constituted the most important era 'in the political progress of the Sikhs'. He changed the whole character of the community, turning it into an armed confederacy, a military republic. The worship of the 'steel' was combined with that of the book. Instead of uniting Muslims and Hindus into one fraternity, he made his disciples vow an implacable hatred of Muslims. He abrogated the distinctions of caste finally, opened his ranks to every person, including the very lowest of Hindus, and assigned to them the name Singh, or lion, which was peculiar to the Rajput Hindus. His followers were enjoined to have steel around them, to wear a blue dress, to let their hair grow, and to use the salutation of *Vaheguruji ka Khalsa, Vaheguruji ki Fateh*. Even the Udasis and Nirmalas, who were the more genuine descendants of Guru Nanak, began to use this salutation.[57]

Guru Gobind Singh composed the *Daswen Padshah ka Granth* with the works of various writers. Its contents were more of a martial nature than of a moral or speculative complexion. It was chiefly in the same language as the *Adi Granth*. Guru Gobind Singh also made the first attempt at political organization of the Sikhs by the institution of *gurmata*, or federal council of chiefs, which assembled periodically at Amritsar. Indiscriminate ravages as well as the religious tenets of Guru Gobind Singh provoked the enmity of the generals of Aurangzeb and the hill Rajas, and he was reduced to great distress. After the loss of his friends and children he became a solitary fugitive. He seems to have been compelled by the Mughal administrators to lead the life of a mendicant wanderer. He was killed in the Deccan in 1708.[58]

Banda, a *bairagi*, inflicted a ferocious vengeance for the discomfiture and death of 'his friend and teacher' on his enemies. He took and demolished Sirhind, and spread desolation in Saharanpur. Appointed by Farrukh Siyar for the task, Abdus Samad Khan completely routed Banda. Besieged in Lohgarh, Banda surrendered; he was sent to Delhi and put to death. So rigorous was the persecution of the Sikhs after Banda's death that they were almost exterminated in the plains. They re-appeared only after the invasion of Nadir Shah when they began to plunder and build forts. The repeated incursions of Ahmad Shah Abdali resulted in an increase in their numbers and eventually their independence.[59]

The Sikh constitution grew naturally out of their political situation. When they were successful as a fighting unit, they remained located in the country which they had ravaged, and divided it among themselves.

A larger portion of the conquered territory was set apart for the leader, and portions were distributed to everyone who had taken a prominent share in the expedition. Another peculiarity of the Sikh constitution was the partition of the lands among the relatives. In this manner sprang up voluntary associations called *misls* which were twelve in number in the palmy days of the Sikh confederacy. The notion of a unity of interests, or national identity, was designated as the Khalsa, the Church Militant. It was a sort of abstract theocracy. This imaginary unity was maintained by Ranjit Singh when the term Khalsa was applied to his temporal government.[60]

Wilson gives a sketch of Ranjit Singh's rise into power as the best way of illustrating the characteristics of the Sikh confederacy. Charhat Singh's father was a Jat farmer but Charhat Singh became a petty chief by joining the Sikh movement. He was supported by fellow chiefs when the Afghan governor of Lahore tried to dislodge him from his fort near Gajrauli (Gujranwala). This enabled Charhat Singh to extend his acquisitions. His *misl* was one of the least considerable, with 2,500 horse, when several other *misls* furnished 10,000 to 12,000 horse. His son, Mahan Singh, extended the power of the confederacy even though he died in 1792 at the age of 27. Ranjit Singh improved his resources by marrying the daughter of Sada Kaur. He got the grant of Lahore from Shah Zaman which induced the Muslims of Lahore to support him in his design of occupying Lahore. His advance towards the east was checked by the British but he made extensive conquests on his side of the Sutlej, including Multan and Kashmir, Little Tibet and territories across the Indus. A kingdom composed of heterogeneous materials could be held together only by military force. The rottenness of the system was revealed by the instability after his death due to military violence and individual ambition. In this process, the successors of Ranjit Singh perished. However, the soldiery had been pretty well destroyed and the Khalsa were left in a state of utter imbecility. Were it not kept alive by the undeserved protection of the British, their power would become spontaneously extinct at no distant period.[61]

Having outlined the history of the Sikhs from the early sixteenth century to the 1840s, in a way summing up his predecessors, Wilson addresses himself to the primary issue: were the Sikh institutions distinguishable from those of the Hindus in general? The political organization of the Sikhs (which appeared to have some connection with the changes introduced by Guru Gobind Singh) received a death blow from Ranjit Singh who established a monarchy of a despotic character. The *misls* were destroyed and the *gurmata* was forgotten. The Sikh religion had not preserved much of its original character. Its elements then were a mystical deism, contemplative worship, peace and good-will, and amalgamation of Hindus and Muslims. There was not much of dogma or precept, and the doctrines of Sikhism were inculcated through the medium of mystical and moral verses in a popular style. Guru Nanak did not seem to have abolished the caste system formally but he received proselytes from every order. He treated the Qu'ran with reverence and acknowledged the whole scheme of the Hindu mythology. His followers do that to 'the present day'. They did not worship images but they worshipped the book. They did not question the existence of Brahma, Vishnu and Shiva. The myths relating to them, especially Vishnu, as popularized from the Puranas in vernacular compositions, constituted much of their favourite literature. There was little difference between a Nirmala Sikh and an orthodox Hindu of the Vaishnava sect, except in the mode of performing public worship and in the profession of benevolent sentiments for all mankind. It may be pointed out that Wilson is not talking of the Khalsa but of the denominations like the Nirmala (and the Udasi) who were supposed to 'profess the pure Sikh faith'.[62]

The followers of Guru Gobind Singh too were not 'unbelievers in the Hindu mythology'. They received all Puranic legends as true, especially those of the Goddess Bhavani who was prominent for her fierce and martial character. Guru Gobind Singh was an assiduous worshipper of the Goddess. In the account of his own mission in the *Bachittar Natak*, he talks of a previous life in which he meditated on Kalika as well as Mahakal. The 'wicked', who were to be destroyed, were equated with Muslims. Wilson quotes an injunction, supposed to be one of the Guru's injunctions, to the effect that it was right to slay a Musalman. He adds, however, that Musalmans could be admitted to the faith despite the deadly enmity of the Sikhs towards them. Anyway, the benevolent spirit of the teachings of Guru Nanak had been sacrificed, as also the sanctity of the caste distinctions. However, the Sikhs observed within limits the domestic usages of the Hindu tribes. The Sikhs from Jat and Gujjar background still ate with Hindu Jats and Gujjars and intermarried with them. The Sikhs had a stronger prejudice against beef. Smoking was also prohibited but there was no restriction on the use of *bhang*, opium and liquor, or even to drunkenness. Nor was this the only vice to which the Sikhs were addicted. No reverence was paid to Guru Nanak's pure code of ethics. Consequently, 'no race in India is more flagrantly demoralized than the Lions of the Punjab'.[63]

Baron Hugel had described the tank and the Harmandar in which a copy of the *Adi Granth* was preserved. In its precincts were several small structures in which the Sikh Udasis and Nirmalas were seated. Fronting the tank was the chief gathering place of the Akalis whose insolence made it dangerous to approach the holy precincts. Outside the Punjab, however, there was no objection to the presence of European visitors. Wilson refers to Wilkin's visit to Patna and his observations. Wilson himself had a similar experience in Benares where he observed the service in the house of a Nirmala priest. The Sikhs in the gathering were settled in the city but some of them were visitors from the Punjab. The local Sikhs had adopted the Sikh ritual, or grafted it upon Vaishnava tenets. Hari and Ram were familiar names in their invocations. The Sikhs visited the holy cities like Benares, Mathura and Hardwar as pilgrims, just as they visited their own holy shrines. They also observed the Holi and the Dussehra. The Diwali at Amritsar was popular among the Sikhs. Murray (in Prinsep's book) gives a description of *pahul* which is different from that given by Malcolm.[64]

At the end, Wilson comes to the conclusion that the Sikh religion scarcely deserved the name of a religious faith. A vague notion of God pervades the poetry of Guru Nanak, defined by negatives. The worship of God was found only in the hymns chanted at the daily service. Ram and Hari, the popular names of Vishnu, appear frequently and the existence of the Hindu divinites was not disputed; the characters given to them by the Hindus and the legends told of them were devoutly credited; and there were probably some esoteric rites in which worship of the Tantras was privately practised. The great distinction between 'the Sikhs and the other Hindus' was the abolition of the distinctions of caste and, consequently, extinction of many of the restraints of the orthodox Hindu system which supplied at least imperfectly a code of faith and practice. The worship of the Book and of the Sword, and the moral declamations of the *Adi Granth* have led to laxity of conduct and disregard of both religious and moral obligations which Wilson thought were as great, if not greater than the superstitions and multiplied ceremonial of the Brahman.[65]

Wilson, thus, looked upon the beliefs and practices of the Sikhs as having close affinity with the beliefs and practices of the Hindus in general, and as deplorable as the beliefs and practices of the orthodox Hindus. He tried to make the best sense of the religious beliefs and practices of the Sikhs found in Malcolm's *Sketch of the Sikhs,* just as he relied heavily upon Prinsep's depiction of Sikh polity and the political career of Ranjit Singh. Wilson had studied the Puranas, especially the *Vishnu Purana,* but had read neither the *Adi Granth* nor the *Daswen Padshah ka Granth.* He saw closer affinity between the Sikh and the Puranic tradition than what was warranted by his own sources even though not free from errors of fact and perception. His work on the whole carried the implication that there were no 'Sikh' institutions to sustain the 'Sikh' state unsupported by the British.

V. A GENERAL OBSERVATION

All the four writers discussed here subscribed to the idea of annexation of the kingdom of Lahore to the British empire. Osborne refers to the expansionist policies of the East India Company which had 'swallowed many camels' and should not hesitate to swallow 'this gnat'. M'Gregor justified the British action against the Lahore Darbar and appreciated the arrangements made after the Sikh War, but argued that the Indus, rather than the Beas, was a more desirable boundary for the British empire in India. Smyth asserted that no treaty existed between the British and the illegitimate successors of Ranjit Singh and, therefore, the British had every right to conquer the Punjab. Wilson put forward the view that there was nothing distinctive in the civil and religious institutions of the Sikhs and that the Lahore state was kept alive by the undeserved protection of the British. He looked upon Sikhism as more or less a sect of the Hindus.

NOTES

1. See, for example, *The Calcutta Review*, vol. I, no. 2, pp. 449- 507; no. 3, pp. 153-208; vol. II, no. 4, pp. 469-535; vol. III, no. 6, 'Notices', pp. i-vi, xiv-xxii; vol. V, no. 10, pp. 48-72; 'Notices', pp. viii-xxii; vol. VI, no. 11, pp. 241-304; vol. IX, no. 18, pp. 511-24; vol. X, no. 19, pp. 1-21. *The Quarterly Review*, vol. LXXVIII, no. 155, pp. 175-225. *The Edinburgh Review*, vol. LXXXIX, pp. 184-221; Charles Masson, *Narratives of Various Journeys*, London, 1842; H.M.L. Lawrence, *Adventures of an Officer in the Punjab*, 2 vols., Calcutta: 1846; General Caulfield, *The Punjab and the Indian Army*, London, 1846; C.M. Wade, *History of the Campaign on the Sutlej*, London, 1846; C.M. Wade, *Notes on the State of Our Relations with the Punjab and the Best Mode of Their Settlement*, Isle of Wight: Ryde, 1848. R.B. Smith, *Agricultural Resources of the Punjab*, London, 1849; Lt. Col. John Briggs, *What Are We to do with the Punjab*? London: James Madden, 1849.
2. Edward Thornton, *A Gazetteer of the Countries Adjacent to India on the North West*, London: Annen & Co., 1844, Preface.
3. T.B. Jarvis (ed.), *Travels in Kashmir and Punjab*, London, 1845, Preface, p. iii.
4. 'A concise account of the Punjab and Kashmir, its topography, climate and productions, customs, manners and character of the people, commerce, manufactures, history and religious institutions, government, administration of the laws, revenue, extent of population, etc. etc. etc.'
5. Thomas Henry Thornton, *History of the Punjab and The Rise and Progress and Present Condition of the Sect and Nation of the Sikhs*, 2 vols., London: Annen & Co., Preface, 1846, pp. x-xi.
6. Steinbach, *The Punjaub*, London: Smith, Elder and Co., 1846, Preface, p. iv, passim.
7. *The Calcutta Review*, vol. VI, no. 11, 241.
8. Caulfield, *The Punjab and the Indian Army*, pp. 3-6, 7-8.
9. Montague Gore, *Remarks on the Present State of the Punjab*, London: James Ridgeway, 1849, Preface, pp. iii-xi, 18, 20, 25.
10. *The Edinburgh Review*, vol. LXXXIX, p. 220.
11. W.G. Osborne, *The Camp and Court of Ranjeet Sing*, reprinted as *Ranjit Singh: The Lion of the Punjab*, Calcutta: Susil Gupta (India) Ltd., 1952 (rpt.), pp. 22-3. This book was first published by Henry Colburn, London, 1840.
12. Ibid., Preface.
13. Ibid., Introduction.
14. Ibid., pp. 26 & ii, 27, 30, 35, 37, 70.
15. Ibid., pp. 28, 31, 32.
16. Ibid., pp. 39, 40.
17. Ibid., pp. 40, 45.
18. Ibid., pp. 58-9.

19. Ibid., pp. 60-8.
20. Ibid., pp. 38, 55, 56, 74.
21. Ibid., pp. 75-81. For W.G. Osborne, see also, Gianeshwar Khurana, 'Men and Manners', *British Historiography on the Sikh Power in Punjab*, New Delhi: Allied Publishers, 1985, pp. 52-63.
22. W.L. M'Gregor, *The History of the Sikhs: The Lives of the Gooroos, The History of Independent Sirdars, Or Missuls and the Life of the Great Founder of the Sikh Monarchy, Maharaja Ranjit Singh*, New Delhi: Rupa & Co., 2007 (rpt.), pp. 46-7. This book was first published in two volumes by James Madden, London, 1846.
23. Ibid., p. 101.
24. Ibid., pp. 105-12.
25. Ibid., pp. 113-201.
26. Ibid., p. 201.
27. Ibid., p. 202.
28. Ibid., p. 291.
29. Ibid., vol. II, pp. 10-42.
30. The dedication stands omitted in the two volumes reprinted together by Rupa & Co.
31. Ibid., vol. II, pp. 42-76.
32. Ibid., pp. 76-128.
33. Ibid., pp. 149-95.
34. Ibid., pp. 196-250.
35. Ibid., pp. 250-74.
36. Ibid., pp. 275-92.
37. Ibid., pp. 293-376. For W.L. M'Gregor, see S.S. Bal, 'W.L. M'Gregor', *Historians and Historiography of the Sikhs*, ed. Fauja Singh, New Delhi: Oriental Publishers, 1978, pp. 59-84. Gianeshwar Khurana, 'Contemporary History', *British Historiography on the Sikh Power in Punjab*, New Delhi: Allied Publishers, 1985, pp. 91-106.
38. G. Carmichael Smyth, *A History of the Reigning Family of Lahore*, Patiala: Punjab Languages Department, 1970 (rpt.), full title, Dedication, Preface and Introduction, pp. xvii, xxx. This book was first published by W. Thacker and Co., Calcutta, 1847.
39. Ibid., Introduction, p. xx.
40. Ibid., pp. 257-63.
41. Ibid., pp. 1-23.
42. lbid., pp. 24-61.
43. Ibid., pp. 65-97.
44. Ibid., pp. 98-102.
45. Ibid., pp. 102-20.
46. Ibid., pp. 120-32.

47. Ibid., pp. 133-4.
48. Ibid., pp. 141-54.
49. Ibid., pp. 160, 167-84.
50. Ibid., pp. xxvii-xxviii.
51. Ibid., pp. xvii-xxi. For Smyth, see also, S.K. Bajaj, 'Prinsep, Murray and Smyth', *Historians and Historiography of the Sikhs*, ed. Fauja Singh, New Delhi: Oriental Publishers, 1978, pp. 31-4.
52. *The Sikh Religion: A Symposium*, Calcutta: Susil Gupta (India) Private Ltd., 1958 (rpt.), pp. vii, 56, 57, 66, 69. First printed as 'A Summary Account of the Religious Institutions of the Sikhs', *Journal of the Royal Asiatick Society*, London, 1848 (vol. IX, art. III, pp. 43-59).
53. Ibid., p. 54.
54. Ibid., pp. 54-5.
55. Ibid., pp. 55-6, 58.
56. Ibid., p. 57.
57. Ibid., p. 58.
58. Ibid., pp. 58-9.
59. Ibid., pp. 59-60.
60. Ibid., pp. 60-1.
61 Ibid., pp. 62-4.
62. Ibid., p. 64.
63. Ibid., pp. 64-6.
64. Ibid., pp. 66-8.
65. Ibid., pp. 68-9.

CHAPTER FIVE

J.D. Cunningham's Classic
A History of the Sikhs

I. INTRODUCTORY

Writing in December 1848 at Bhopal, J.D. Cunningham tells the reader that he thought of writing a history of the Sikhs in 1844 when he was required to draw up reports on the British connection with the states on the Sutlej and especially on the military resources of the Punjab. He had been appointed assistant to Colonel Claude Wade, the political agent of the Governor-General, Lord Auckland, at Ludhiana, who was in-charge of British relations with the Punjab and the chiefs of Afghanistan. Cunningham was also required as an engineer to make Ferozepur a defensible post due to its military importance. In 1838, he was present at the interview between Maharaja Ranjit Singh and Lord Auckland. In 1839 he accompanied Colonel Wade to escort Prince Taimur to Peshawar. In 1840 he was made administrator of the Ludhiana district and accompanied Colonel Wheeler who escorted Dost Muhammad Khan back to Ludhiana. Towards the end of 1841 he was sent to Tibet to see that the Rajas of Jammu surrendered certain territories which they had seized so that the British trade with Ladakh was restored to its old footing. He was present at the interviews between Lord Ellenborough and Dost Muhammad Khan at Ludhiana. In December 1842 he was present at the interview between Lord Ellenborough and the Sikh chiefs. He was in-charge of Ambala before he was made personal assistant to Colonel Richmond as the political agent in place of Clark who had replaced Colonel Wade in 1840. On the appointment of Major Broadfoot as the political agent in 1844, and during the greater part of 1845, Cunningham was employed in the Bahawalpur territory in connection with boundary disputes between the Daudputras and the Rajputs of Bikaner and Jaisalmer.

Cunningham goes on to add that, when the war with the Sikhs broke out towards the end of 1845, he was required by Sir Charles Napier to join his army which was to cooperate with the main army. After the battle of Pherushahr, he was summoned to Lord Gough's headquarters. He was accompanying Sir Harry Smith when the skirmish at Baddowal took place and he was present at the battle of Aliwal. He was present also at the battle of Sabraon when he was acting as an aid-de-camp to the Governor-General, Lord Hardinge. He remained attached to the headquarters of the Commander-in-Chief until the army broke up at Lahore. He was 'unexpectedly' appointed to the political agency of Bhopal by Lord Hardinge. Thus, he had lived, as he says, among the Sikh people for eight years during a very important period of their history. 'He had intercourse, under variety of circumstances, with all classes of men, and he had at the same time free access to all the public records bearing on the affairs of the frontier.' His residence in Malwa was 'of advantage' to him in the composition of his work.[2]

The second edition of Cunningham's *History of the Sikhs* came out in 1853, after his death. However, his preface to this edition was written in October 1849, a little over seven months after the publication of his book in March 1849 on the eve of the annexation of the Punjab to the British Indian empire. In this preface Cunningham says that his principal object in writing this history had 'not always been understood'. Therefore, he thought it right to state that 'his main endeavour was to give Sikhism its place in the general history of humanity'. A secondary object was to give some account of the British relations with the Sikhs and, in part, with the Afghans. Cunningham also noted that his public critics had remarked that he 'leans unduly towards the Sikhs'; his criticism of the East India Company as its delegate was 'at the least strange'. He responds to these views by stating that he had 'constantly endeavoured to keep his readers alive to that undercurrent of feeling or principle which moves the Sikh people collectively, and which will usually rise superior to the crimes and follies of individuals.'[3]

Cunningham gives a clear expression to his own outlook on, and his attitude towards, the policies and measures of the East India Company in India.

The glory to England is indeed great of her Eastern Dominion, and she may justly feel proud of the increasing excellence of her sway over subject nations; but this general expression of the sense and desire of the English people does not show that every proceeding of her delegates is necessarily fitting and farseeing. The extension of supremacy, and not the extinction of dynasties, should be the aim and scope of English sway in the East. England should reign over kings rather than rule over subjects.[4]

Already in July 1849, Cunningham had been removed from political service for having made 'unauthorized use of official documents entrusted to his charge as a public officer' in his *History*. Under pressure from Lord Hardinge, Hobhouse had written to Dalhousie to call Cunningham's explanation for unauthorized use of official documents and, in the event of his failure to furnish a satisfactory reply, to dismiss him. The ostensible reason for Cunningham's removal from political service was his *History* but there was a deeper cause. In February 1843, the political agent at Ludhiana, A.F. Richmond had been asked by Lord Ellenborough, the Governor-General, to supply specific information about the army and forts of the Punjab and the political condition of the country, including the hill states. Richmond entrusted this duty to his assistant, J.D. Cunningham. A report was completed by Cunningham in September as 'Some Account of the Political Conditions and Military Resources of the Punjab'. Meanwhile, in July 1844, Lord Hardinge had replaced Ellenborough. He did not appreciate Cunningham's sympathetic attitude towards the Sikhs. He wrote to Ellenborough in March 1845 that Richmond was in Cunningham's hands and he had been taking latitude and power which, if proved, would induce him to remove Cunningham immediately: 'He is a perfect Sikh'. Despite Richmond's strong recommendation, Hardinge did not appoint Cunningham in his place. He appointed Major Broadfoot who was overbearing and aggressive in his attitude towards the Sikh chiefs. He did not need Cunningham's assistance. Hardinge remained distrustful of Cunningham. That was why he was made Political Agent at Bhopal in March 1846 through an order issued from 'Camp Lahore'.[5] Hardinge's remark on Cunningham's *History of the Sikhs* is quite telling: 'The book justifies the step I took in pitch forking our friend to Bhopal. It proves his Sikh partialities'. He goes on to add, 'he has not forgotten that I had sent him to another agency'.[6]

The contemporary criticism of Cunningham's *History of the Sikhs*, whether genuine or orchestrated, dwelt on three aspects of his work: his Sikh sympathies, his criticism of the East India Company, and his academic merit as a historian. One of his critics was Henry Lawrence. In an unfinished article he wrote: 'The author has written in an anti-English spirit more as a Sikh than a Christian, more as a Punjabee than an Englishman'. He believed that Cunningham's treatment of Sikhism was reprehensible; he felt like 'a martyr' (because of his removal to Bhopal), and he had sharp disagreements with his senior, Major Broadfoot.[7] Cunningham's critic in the *Calcutta Review* remarked that he had written his *History* 'for the most part as a Sikh historian would write it'. His abilities had been wasted for a contemptible purpose: he had preferred 'the Sikh cause and the Sikh religion to his own'. He was almost a follower of Gobind; 'almost is the *Granth* his gospel'. His 'plain-speaking' in discussing British policy was misdirected but he had consulted many unpublished sources of Sikh history besides a careful study of every published work.[8] A reviewer of Cunningham's book in *The Times* lamented that his heart was with the Sikhs throughout his work, and that his view was opposed to the generally accepted notion of the Sikhs and the Sikh War. However, the reviewer appreciated the 'fullness of details' in his work.[9] The *Athenaeum* appreciated the 'scrupulous care of a man of science' and his sound judgement in selecting his facts with a strict regard to historical truth.[10] In our analysis of Cunningham's *History of the Sikhs* we propose to keep these three perspectives in view.

II. GURU NANAK AND HIS LEGACY

Cunningham traces the history of the Sikhs 'from the origin of the nation to the battles of the Sutlej' in nine chapters. The first chapter describes the country and its people, including the Sikhs. The second chapter places Guru Nanak in the context of the religious history of India. The third chapter relates to the successors of Guru Nanak and 'the modification of Sikhism' under Guru Gobind Singh; it ends with Banda's execution in 1716. The fourth chapter narrates the political struggle leading to the establishment of 'Sikh independence', covering half a century from 1716 to 1764. The fifth chapter covers the phase from 1765 to 1809, narrating the political activity of the Sikhs, the ascendancy of Ranjit Singh, and his alliance with the English. Two chapters then relate to Maharaja Ranjit Singh. The eighth chapter covers the years from 1839 to 1845, that is, from the death of Ranjit Singh to the eve of the first Sikh War. The last chapter, on 'the War with the English', covers a few months of 1845-6. In terms of space, the last two chapters cover less than a third of the whole narrative. Ranjit Singh gets about a fourth. A little less than half of the narrative covers the first three centuries of Sikh history. Then there are more than 40 appendices covering more than a fifth of the whole book which has an unusually large number of footnotes.

Cunningham observes at the outset that the followers of Guru Nanak and Guru Gobind Singh 'have now become a nation'. The reference surely is to their distinct identity and the fact that they had acquired political power. On the composition of the Khalsa and their distribution in space, Cunningham states that the Jatts of Majha and Malwa were mostly Sikh; between the Jamuna and the Jhelum, they appeared to form about a third of the Jatt population, the rest being equally divided between Islam and Brahmanism. Around Bhatinda and Sunam 'the priest, the soldier, the mechanic, the shopkeeper, and the ploughman are equally Sikh'. The 'poor and contemned races', who were treated as outcaste, regarded themselves as 'inferior members of the Sikh community'. Cunningham emphasizes the importance of the characteristics of 'race and religion' far more than the role of individuals. Different from their contemporary Indians, the Sikhs were converts of 'a new religion' which was 'the seal' of the double dispensation of Islam and the Indian religious tradition: 'their enthusiasm was still fresh, and their faith was still an active and a living principle'. Cunningham points out that 'the feeling of the Sikh people' deserved the attention of the English as 'a civilized nation' and as 'a paramount government'. The Sikhs were not numerous. However, their strength was not to be estimated by tens of thousands but by 'the unity and energy of religious fervor and warlike temperament'. Ascribing special importance to the Jatt component, Cunningham states that 'religious reformation and political ascendancy' had given 'spirit to their industry and activity and purpose to their courage'. Like the other members of the race, the Khatri and Arora Sikhs too were enterprising as merchants, governors, and leaders of armies. It was important for Cunningham to note that the Sikhs continued to make converts in the territories under their political control.[11]

For the background and the context of Guru Nanak's mission, Cunningham starts with the glorious achievement of the Hindus in literature, philosophy and sciences. In his view, Buddhism was a modified form of 'the ancient faith of India'. The Brahmans succeeded in expelling the Buddhist faith from India. The victory of Hinduism, however, proved to be costly: monasticism and worship of idols became an integral part of the Hindu religious tradition; the doctrine of *maya*, or illusion, brought to the fore by Shankaracharya, was eagerly adopted by subsequent reformers and given 'a moral or religious application'. This was the state of the Hindu faith and polity a thousand years after Christ. The Brahmans had 'isolated themselves from the soldiers and the peasants, and they had destroyed their own unity by admitting a virtual plurality of gods, and giving assemblies of ascetics a preeminence over communities of pious householders'.[12]

The Turkish invasions started early in the eleventh century, and Hindustan became a separate portion of the Islamic world in the thirteenth. During the next 150 years the whole of India was subdued and the influx of Mughals and Afghans continued during this period. The influence of 'a new people' began gradually to prevail on the minds of the masses and even the learned were obliged to rethink. The new people were as good warriors as the Kshatriyas, if not better, and they despised the sanctity of the Brahmans; they proclaimed the unity of God and denounced the worship of idols. 'Thus custom jarred with custom, and opinion with opinion.' A few fell back with confidence upon the revealed books, the Qur'an and the Vedas, but 'the public' became agitated and found no consolation in the prescriptions of the Brahman or the Mulla.[13]

The first result of the tension was the appearance of a considerable sect of Ramanand who was a follower of Ramanuja. The heroic Rama was made the object of devotion and the idea of equality before God was propagated in the middle Gangetic plain. Ramanand admitted all classes of people as his disciples and declared that the true votary was raised above the social forms and became free and liberated. Gorakh Nath popularized 'Yog' in the Punjab, teaching that intense mental abstraction etheralized the body even of the most lowly so that his spirit gradually united with Shiva, the all-pervading soul of the world. In the next generation, or around 1450, Kabir assailed the worship of idols, the authority of the Islamic and Brahmanical scriptures, and the exclusive use of a learned language. He addressed both Hindus and Muslims, urging them to call upon the invisible God and to strive after inward purity. The world as *maya* was the source of deceit and illusion. Kabir admitted outward conformity and was inclined to look upon Rama or Vishnu as the most perfect type of God. He further limited the scope of reform by subscribing to the ideal of renunciation. The use of spoken language by Kabir made his writings extensively popular among 'the lower orders of India.' Chaitanya in Bengal admitted all classes of people as members of his sect and insisted that *bhakti* chastened the most impure; he allowed marriage and secular occupations to his followers. Vallabhacharya gave a further impulse to the reformation in progress he taught that married teachers were admissible and the householder was to be preferred.[14]

Cunningham emphasizes that the Hindu mind was no longer stagnant or retrogressive in the early sixteenth century. Leavened with Islam, it changed and quickened for a new development. 'Ramanand and Gorakh had preached religious equality, and Chaitan had repeated that faith levelled caste. Kubeer had denounced images, and appealed to the people in their own tongue, and Vullabh had taught that effectual devotion was compatible with the ordinary duties of the world.' However, all these reformers aimed chiefly at emancipation from priestcraft or from idolatry and polytheism. They formed assemblies of quietists and did not call upon their followers to discard every social form and religious trammel in order to rouse 'a new people freed from the debasing corruption of ages.' They appear to have been impressed with the nothingness of earthly life and, therefore, they did not entertain the idea of improving the social condition. 'They perfected forms of dissent rather than planted the germs of nations.' Their sects remained where they left them, without further progress of any significance.[15]

Guru Nanak was among these religious reformers but with a difference. In the frequently quoted words of Cunningham,

> It was reserved for *Nanuk* to perceive the true principles of reform, and to lay those broad foundations which enabled his successor *Govind* to fire the minds

of his countrymen with a new nationality, and to give practical effect to the doctrine that the lowest is equal with the highest, in race as in creed, in political rights as in religious hopes.[16]

Narrating briefly the life of Guru Nanak, Cunningham points out that he appropriated the good points of the preceding reformers and avoided their grave errors. His conception of God was different from that of Ramanand or Kabir. His God is One, the sole timeless being; 'the creator, the self-existent, the incomprehensible, and the everlasting'. He is the ultimate idea or cause of all we know and behold. The prophets like Muhammad and the deities like Shiva and Vishnu were his creation. Guru Nanak emphasized the importance of good works and righteous conduct for liberation but liberation could not be attained without God's grace. The state of liberation was a state of bliss arising from the dwelling of the soul with God; the cycle of transmigration ended with the attainment of liberation.[17]

Guru Nanak did not claim to be a prophet of the semitic tradition or an incarnation of the Indian tradition. He declared himself to be the slave, the humble messenger of the Almighty. Making use of universal truth as his sole instrument, he made his mission 'applicable to all times and places'. He emphasized that renunciation was not necessary and that in the eyes of God the devout householder was equal to the pious hermit. 'Thus Nanuk extricated his followers from the accumulated errors of ages, and enjoined upon them devotion of thought and excellence of conduct as the first of duties.' In its immediate effect, his reform was religious and moral. Whether or not he possessed clear views of social amelioration or political advancement was not very important. 'He left the progress of his people to the operation of time'. His concern was to present his followers contracting into a sect and his comprehensive principles narrowing into monastic distinctions. Guru Nanak's choice of Angad as his successor, in preference to his son Sri Chand, who founded the Hindu sect of Udasis, was quite deliberate.[18]

III. FROM GURU ANGAD TO BANDA BAHADUR

Cunningham states that little was known of the ministry of Guru Angad (1539-52). He committed to writing what he heard about Guru

Nanak from Bala Sandhu, and his own compositions which were later incorporated in the *Granth*; he chose Amar Das as his successor. Guru Amar Das separated the active and domestic Sikhs from the passive and recluse Udasis, and he discountenanced the practice of *sati*. Before his death in 1574, he chose his son-in-law Ram Das to be his successor. Guru Ram Das dug a reservoir called *amritsar* and founded the town called Ramdaspur. When he died in 1581, the number of Sikhs was still very small.[19]

Guru Arjan, the son and successor of Guru Ram Das, was 'perhaps the first who clearly understood the wide import of the teachings of Nanuk, or who perceived how applicable they were to every state of life and to every condition of society'. He made Ramdaspur the proper seat of his followers; it became a populous city, and a great place of pilgrimage for the Sikh people. He compiled the *Granth* which gave to his followers fixed rules of religious and moral conduct. He reduced the customary offerings of his followers, who were now found in every province and every city, to a systematic tax collected through the authorized representatives of the Guru. The Sikhs became accustomed to 'a regular government'. Guru Arjan sent his followers into foreign countries for trade, especially in horses. The rebel Prince Khusrau's visit to Guru Arjan was presented to Jahangir by the finance minister Chandu Shah, who was an enemy of the Guru, as his political ambition, and Guru Arjan was fined and imprisoned, which led to his death in 1606. Cunningham says that the principles of Guru Nanak took a firm hold on the minds of the Sikhs during the ministry of Guru Arjan. He refers to the writings of Bhai Gurdas who refers to the objective of Guru Nanak of a fusion of Muslims and Hindus 'into common observers of a new and better creed' as 'the active principle of a multitude'. For Bhai Gurdas, Guru Nanak becomes 'the proclaimed instrument of God for the redemption of the world'.[20]

On the death of Guru Arjan, his elder brother Prithi Chand made an attempt to be recognized as the Guru. Though he did not succeed, he continued to retain a few followers and 'thus sowed the first fertile seeds of dissent'. Guru Arjan's son and successor, Guru Hargobind, probably got Chandu Shah killed either on his own or on the emperor's authority. It is certain, however, that in a short time he became a military leader and grasped a sword to march with his devoted followers among the troops of the empire, or boldly led them to oppose and overcome provincial governors or personal enemies. He became a hunter and an eater of flesh; his followers imitated him in these robust practices. Cunningham comments that Guru Nanak had sanctioned or enjoined secular occupations upon his follower and Guru Arjan carried the injunction into practice; 'the impulse thus given speedily extended and became general'. Guru Hargobind had 800 horses, 300 mounted followers, and a guard of 60 matchlock-men. The impulse given to the Sikhs went a long way to separate them from all Hindu sects; there was little danger of their relapsing into 'the limited merit or utility of monks and mendicants'. Cunningham refers to Guru Hargobind's imprisonment, his employment under the Mughal government, and his battles. During his ministry, the Sikhs increased greatly in numbers. The fiscal policy of Guru Arjan and the armed system of Guru Hargobind 'formed them into a kind of separate state within the empire'.[21]

Cunningham's brief account of Guru Har Rai, Guru Har Krishan and Guru Tegh Bahadur suggests increasing intervention in their affairs by Aurangzeb, ending in the execution of Guru Tegh Bahadur in 1675. His violent end and his last injunction to his son and successor, Guru Gobind Singh, made a deep impression on the mind of the youthful Guru and after a good deal of introspection he conceived the noble idea of moulding the vanquished Hindus into a new and aspiring people. Study and reflection enlarged his mind and he resolved upon giving 'precision and aim to the broad and general institutions of Nanuk'. In the heart of a powerful empire he set himself the task of subverting it. He was bold, systematic and optimistic. His *Bachittar Natak* reveals his mission: 'to declare perfect faith, to extend virtue, and to destroy evil'. Cunningham's comment on the episode of the Goddess is significant. Guru Gobind Singh's mode of presenting his mission in the *Bachittar Natak* was extended by his followers to give 'an earthly close to his celestial vision'.[22]

A new faith was declared, that of the Khalsa. All social distinctions were abolished. A new form of initiation was introduced. The basic tenet of the Khalsa included worship of one God, belief in Guru Nanak and his successors, the watchword of *Vaheguru*, reverence for the *Granth*, unshorn hair, naming themselves 'Singhs', devotion to steel, bearing arms and waging war, and no intercourse with dissenters, the

Masandis, the killers of infant daughters and those who cut-off their hair. Guru Gobind Singh made himself 'master of the imagination of his followers'. He established a 'theocracy' but he had yet to vanquish the armies of a great emperor. His design was not really wild or senseless. Shivaji had roused the slumbering spirit of the Marathas. Guru Gobind Singh added religious fervour to warlike temper and his design of founding a kingdom of Jatts upon the waning glories of Aurangzeb's dominions 'does not appear to have been idly conceived or rashly undertaken'. Cunningham places all the battles of Guru Gobind Singh after the institution of the Khalsa. He talks of 'the book of the Tenth King' having been composed at Damdama. There are some other factual errors too. Before his death at Nander in 1708, Guru Gobind Singh abolished personal Guruship. He proclaimed: 'He who wishes to behold the Gooroo, let him search the Grunt'h of Nanuk. The Gooroo will dwell with the Khalsa; be firm and be faithful; wherever five Sikhs are gathered together there will I also be present.'[23]

Cunningham remarks that success is not 'always the measure of greatness'. Guru Gobind Singh did not live to see his own ends accomplished,

> but he effectually roused the dormant energies of a vanquished people, and filled them with a lofty although fitful longing for social freedom and national ascendancy, the proper adjuncts of that purity of worship which had been preached by Nanuk. Govind saw what was yet vital, and relumed it with Promethean fire.

This insight was based on what Cunningham observed in his own times. A living spirit possessed the whole Sikh people. Their elevated minds and the amplitude of their physical features were the result of what Guru Gobind Singh had done. In language and everyday customs, the Sikhs were essentially Hindu, 'yet, in religious faith and worldly aspirations, they are wholly different from other Indians, and they are bound together by a community of inward sentiment and of outward object unknown elsewhere'. [24]

Banda, a chosen disciple of Guru Gobind Singh, carried Guru Gobind Singh's intentions forward. He put to flight the Mughal authorities in the neighbourhood of Sirhind and then defeated and killed its governor. He occupied the entire country between the Sutlej and the Jamuna, and laid waste the district of Saharanpur. The emperor marched against him and besieged his new stronghold. However, Banda escaped with his followers, and established himself near Jammu. After the death of Bahadur Shah, Banda occupied the old places but Abdus Samad Khan defeated him. Banda retreated again but finally he was besieged, captured, taken to Delhi and executed. Cunningham observes that the memory of Banda was not held in much esteem by the Sikhs. 'He did not perhaps comprehend the general nature of Nanuk's and Govind's reforms; the spirit of sectarianism possessed him.' He introduced changes in accordance with his own ascetical and Hindu notions. His innovations were resisted by the more zealous Sikhs, which caused 'the memory of an able and enterprising leader to be generally neglected'.[25]

Cunningham comments at the end of the first two centuries of Sikh history that the Sikh faith had become established as a prevailing sentiment and guiding principle to work its way in the world. Guru Nanak disengaged his followers from Hindu and Muslim superstitions and made them free on a broad basis of religious and moral purity. Guru Amar Das preserved the infant community from declining into a sect of quietists or ascetics. Guru Arjan gave his increasing followers a written rule of conduct and civil organization. Guru Hargobind added the use of arms and a military system. Guru Gobind Singh bestowed upon them a distinct political existence, and inspired them with the desire of being socially free and nationally independent. No further legislation was required.[26] Guruship was vested in the *Granth* and the Khalsa.

IV. THE SIKH STRUGGLE FOR INDEPENDENCE

As for the Sikh struggle for independence, Cunningham starts with the decline of the Mughal empire, which was helpful to the Sikhs. The tenets of Guru Nanak and Guru Gobind Singh had taken root in the hearts of the people: 'The peasant and the mechanic nursed their faith in secret, and the more ardent clung to the hope of ample revenge and speedy victory.' During the invasion of Nadir Shah the Sikhs collected in small bands and plundered the stragglers of the Persian army. Some Sikhs then established a small fort at Dallewal on the Ravi. They levied contributions around Eminabad and they were attacked. A larger force pursued and defeated them. Many of the Sikh prisoners were brought to Lahore and executed at a place that came to be known as Shahidganj. Political change brought Ahmad Shah Abdali to Lahore and his defeat by the Mughal army brought Mir Mannu to Lahore as the Mughal governor. During this time, the Sikhs built the fort called Ram Rauni in Amritsar and declared the birth of a new power in the state. This was the Dal Khalsa or army of the theocracy of Singhs.[27]

The successive invasions of Ahmad Shah Abdali and capture of territories by the Afghans weakened the administration of the province. Mir Mannu's death in 1752 was followed by further distractions and Ahmad Shah Abdali appointed his son Taimur to disperse the Sikhs. The prince failed to suppress them and they occupied Lahore temporarily. Jassa Singh Kalal struck a coin in his name. Adina Beg Khan invited the Marathas. The Sikhs evacuated Lahore, and the Afghan garrisons retired leaving the Punjab in the hands of the Marathas. Adina Beg was made the governor but he died a few months later. The loss of the Punjab brought Ahmad Shah to the banks of the Jamuna and he destroyed the Maratha dreams of supremacy in north India. His great victory at Panipat in the beginning of 1761 struck a blow on the power of the Marathas in Hindustan, and the power of the Peshwa among the Marathas.[28]

During Ahmad Shah Abdali's campaign the Sikhs hovered round his army. The absence of all regular government gave them additional strength and they became masters of their own villages and began to erect forts for keeping the outsiders in check. Among others, Charhat Singh established a stronghold at Gujranwala. When the Afghan governor, Khwaja Ubaid, went to reduce it in 1762, the Sikhs assembled for its relief. The Afghans were repulsed, and they fled to Lahore. The 'army of the Khalsa' assembled at Amritsar and held a 'diet' (*gurmata*), ravaged Malerkotla, and invested Jandiala. Ahmad Shah reached Lahore towards the end of 1762 and killed 12,000 to 25,000 men in a single action against the Sikhs. The event was known as *ghallughara* or great disaster. Ahmad Shah gratified his resentment further by destroying and desecrating the temple at Amritsar.[29]

However, the Sikhs were not cast down. Their number increased and they had a vague feeling that they were 'a people'; all were bent on revenge and their leaders were ambitious of dominion and fame. They plundered Kasur and killed the chief of Malerkotla. They defeated Zain Khan, the Afghan governor of Sirhind, and occupied the plains from the Sutlej and the Jamuna. Sirhind itself was totally destroyed. Ahmad Shah Abdali failed to suppress the Sikhs. They ousted the Afghan administrators and occupied the whole country from the Sutlej to the Jhelum. The Sikh chiefs then assembled at Amritsar and proclaimed their own sway by striking a coin with an inscription to the effect that Guru Gobind Singh received from Guru Nanak *'deg, tegh* and *fateh'* (grace, power and rapid victory).[30]

Cunningham refers to the system of government evolved by the Sikhs as 'theocratic confederate feudalism'. Every year on the occasion of Diwali, the whole Sikh people (*Sarbat Khalsa*) met at Amritsar. The assembly of chiefs was called *gurmata*. They owned no subjection to one another, and they were imperfectly obeyed by the followers. However, there was a chain of dependence that was acknowledged by all as the law. The federate chiefs partitioned their joint conquests equally among themselves, and divided their respective shares among their own leaders of bands; these leaders subdivided their portions among their own dependents. This federative feudalism was theocratic in the sense that God was believed to be the only helper and the only judge. However, this constitution was not fixed. 'It would be idle to call an everchanging state of alliance and dependence by the name of a constitution.' It was soon clear that the strong were ever ready to make themselves obeyed and to appropriate all within their power. Yet every member continued to defer to the mystic Khalsa. Cunningham refers to the twelve *misls* into which the Sikh territories were said to have been divided. 'The confederacies did not all exist in their full strength at the same time'. The names of the *misls* were derived from 'the name, the village, the district, or progenitor of the first or most eminent chief, or some peculiarity of custom or of leadership'. The Nishananias and Shahids scarcely formed *misls* 'in the conventional meaning of the term, but complimentary bodies set apart and honoured by all for particular reasons'. Not all the *misls* were equal in terms of their possessions or power. The Akalis did not belong to any *misl,* and they did not acknowledge an earthly governor. They took upon themselves the authority of censors, and they inspired awe and respect.[31] Clearly, Cunningham tried to form his own idea of Sikh polity during the eighteenth century which was not easy to conceptualize.

V. SIKH RULE AND THE RISE OF RANJIT SINGH

The political activity of the Sikh chiefs and the interaction of the English with the Sikhs form the subject of Cunningham's account of the phase from 1765 to 1809. Ahmad Shah Abdali could neither overcome nor conciliate the Sikh chiefs. The Sukarchakias under Charhat Singh, aided by the Bhangis, occupied Rohtas and Rawalpindi, and the Bhangis occupied Multan. Jhanda Singh Bhangi made Jammu a tributary. Jai Singh occupied the fort of Kangra, and established his authority over the neighbouring Rajas and Thakurs. In 1778-9, however, the Bhangis lost Multan to Taimur who had succeeded Ahmad Shah Abdali in 1773. Amar Singh of Patiala extended his territories in Haryana, some of which were lost by his successor after his death in 1781. The Sikhs remained active in the Ganga-Jamuna Doab. They were predominant from the frontiers of Awadh to the Indus. Mahan Singh Sukarchakia became 'the most influential chief of the Punjab' before his death in 1792.[32]

Shah Zaman succeeded to the throne of Kabul in 1793 and revived the aspiration to establish an Indian empire. In 1795 he moved to Hasan Abdal and his advance party recovered the fort of Rohtas. In 1797, he reached Lahore, 'but the Sikhs were perhaps less dismayed than the beaten Mahrattas and the ill-informed English'. Shah Zaman came again in 1798 but left Lahore early in 1799 without achieving anything. Ranjit Singh played a leading role in this situation. Like some other historians, Cunningham states that he extricated heavy artillery of Shah Zaman from the flooded Jhelum and procured a royal investiture of the capital of Lahore. 'Thenceforward the history of the Sikhs gradually centres in their great Maharaja'.[33]

Before taking up the narrative of Ranjit Singh's achievements, Cunningham takes up the revival of the Maratha power in upper India and the appearance of the English on the scene. Mahadji Sindhia raised regular brigades and restored the Maratha power in northern India. He entered into an engagement with the Sikhs for a joint conquest on both sides of the Jamuna. Under Daulat Rao Sindhia, General Perron, who had succeeded De Boigne, obliged George Thomas to surrender early in 1802. General Perron's successor Bourquin formed an engagement with Ranjit Singh for a joint expedition to the Indus. In 1803, the English defeated the Marathas. Sir David Ochterloney defended Delhi against Jaswant Rao Holkar and defeated him in the battle of Deeg. In 1805, however, Jaswant Rao Holkar and Amir Khan again moved northward. Lord Lake defeated them. They came towards the Punjab, but Ranjit Singh did not support Holkar. Towards the end of 1805, an arrangement was arrived at, which allowed Holkar to return quietly to central India. On 1 January 1806, Lieutenant-Colonel John Malcolm, under the authority of Lord Lake, and Sardar Fateh Singh Ahluwalia for himself and as plenipotentiary of Sardar Ranjit Singh concluded an agreement to the effect that Holkar should be compelled to retire from Amritsar, and that so long as the two chiefs conducted themselves as friends the English would never form plans to seize their territories.[34]

By this time Ranjit Singh's authority had become predominant among the Sikh people. He had obliged Nizamuddin Khan of Kasur to become his feudatory in 1801-2. He entered into a friendly alliance with Fateh Singh Ahluwalia in 1802, and they took Amritsar. In 1803 and 1804, Ranjit Singh repulsed Sansar Chand of Kangra. He received homage from the chiefs of Jhang, Sahiwal and Multan in 1804-5. Cunningham's comment on 'the Sikhs' at this time is significant:

> The genuine spirit of Sikhism had again sought the dwelling of the peasant to reproduce itself in another form; the rude system of mixed independence and confederacy, was unsuited to an extended dominion; it had served its ends of immediate agglomeration, and the '*Misls*' were in effect dissolved.

Ranjit Singh alone was desirous of excluding both the Marathas and English from the Punjab. They could be an obstacle to his ambition of founding a military monarchy.[35]

> In truth, Runjeet Singh laboured, with more or less of intelligent design, to give unity and coherence to diverse atoms and scattered elements; to mould the increasing Sikh nation into a well ordered state or commonwealth as Govind had developed a sect into a people, and had given application and purpose to the general institutions of Nanuk.[36]

After the treaty of Ranjit Singh and Fateh Singh with the English in 1806 and before the treaty of Amritsar in 1809, Ranjit Singh had emerged as the most powerful Sikh chief. Towards the end of 1806, he settled the dispute between Nabha and Patiala as an arbitrator acceptable to both the sides. In 1807, Kutbuddin of Kasur surrendered at Ranjit Singh's discretion and he was given a small tract of land across the Sutlej for his maintenance. Proceeding towards Multan, Ranjit Singh captured the city but not yet the fort when the Nawab of Multan paid tribute. Ranjit Singh then crossed the Sutlej to settle a domestic dispute at Patiala, conquered Naraingarh, and took over the territories of the old chief Tara Singh who had died. In 1808, Ranjit Singh took over the territories of some Sikh chiefs of the Punjab proper. His activities frightened the chiefs of Patiala, Jind and Kaithal and their deputation approached the British Resident at Delhi for protection. They received no positive assurances but they were led to hope that they would not be deserted in the hour of need. They made their own terms with Ranjit Singh.[37]

Lord Cornwallis was averse to any treaties with rulers beyond the Jamuna. In 1808, however, the perceived threat of the subjugation of India by the French led Lord Minto to seek alliances even beyond the Indus. While Mountstuart Elphinstone was sent to Shah Shuja at Kabul, Charles Metcalfe was sent on a mission to Ranjit Singh. When Metcalfe met him at Kasur in September 1808, Ranjit Singh affected to consider himself as the head of the whole Sikh people, with the claim of supremacy over Sirhind. He crossed the Sutlej for the third time, seized Faridkot and Ambala, levied exactions in Malerkotla and Thanesar, and formed a symbolic alliance with the Raja of Patiala. Metcalfe did not follow him beyond the Sutlej. The Governor-General ordered a detachment of troops to the Sutlej to support Metcalfe in his negotiations and to confine him to his side of the river. Meanwhile, the threat from Napolean appeared to have vanished and the Governor-General made it known that the object of the English had become limited to the security of the country south of the Sutlej. In February 1809, David Ochterloney issued a proclamation that the cis-Sutlej states were under British protection. Ranjit Singh signed the Treaty of Amritsar on 25 April 1809 as 'the now single Chief of Lahore'. He retained his conquests made in the cis-Sutlej area before 1808 and confined his ambition for the future to the north and north-west of the river without any interference from the English.[38]

VI. CONQUEST AND CONSOLIDATION

Cunningham narrates the political history of Ranjit Singh for 15 years, from 1809 to 1824. His carefully constructed narrative is full of details in a chorological order, punctuated by some general observations at places. By the end of 1816, the northern plains and lower hills of the Punjab had been fairly reduced to obedience and order, and Ranjit Singh's territories were bounded on the south and the west by the confederacies of Kabul. Multan was conquered in 1818, and Peshawar was temporarily occupied. Kashmir was conquered in 1819. Dera Ghazi Khan was seized soon after. Dera Ismail Khan was conquered in 1821 and the chief of Mankera was made a feudatory with some territory across the Indus. By the end of 1823, Ranjit Singh had brought under his sway the three Muslim provinces of Kashmir, Multan and Peshawar; he was supreme in the hills and plains of the Punjab proper, and the mass of his dominions had been acquired.[39]

About the government of Ranjit Singh, Cunningham observes that he did not introduce any legislation. Such a task neither suited the Maharaja's genius nor that of the Sikh nation.

> Ranjeet Singh grasped the more obvious characteristics of the impulse given by Nanuk and Govind; he dexterously turned them to the purposes of his own material ambition, and he appeared to be an absolute monarch in the midst of willing and obedient subjects. But he knew that he merely directed into a particular channel a power which he could neither destroy nor control, and that, to prevent the Sikhs turning upon himself, or contending with one another, he must regularly engage them in conquest and remote warfare.

The first political system of the Sikhs had crumbled to pieces, partly through its own defects, partly owing to its contact with a well-ordered and civilized government, and partly due to the ascendancy of one superior mind.[40]

Ranjit Singh took from the land as much as it could readily yield, and he took from merchants as much as they could profitably give. He put down open marauding. The Sikh peasantry enjoyed a light assessment; no local officer dared to oppress a member of the Khalsa. Ranjit Singh did not ordinarily punish men who took redress into their own hands. The whole wealth and energies of the people were devoted to war, and to the preparation of military means and equipment. It suited the mass of the Sikh population. Ranjit Singh never arrogated to himself the title or powers of a despot. He attributed every achievement to the favour of God, and he styled himself and the people collectively the 'Khalsa' or commonwealth of Gobind. He carefully concealed his own name and his own motives, and every thing was done for the sake of the Guru, for the advantage of the Khalsa, and in the name of God whether in showing reverence to a descendant of the Gurus, rewarding a soldier for his long beard, restraining the Akalis, or acquiring a province.[41]

Cunningham does not attribute the superiority of the Sikh army under Ranjit Singh to the labours of Ventura, Allard, Court and Avitabile. The Sikh owed his excellence as a soldier 'to his own hardihood of character, to that spirit of adaptation which distinguishes every new people, and to that feeling of a common interest and destiny planted in him by his great teachers'. The religious faith of the Sikh sustained him under any adversity, and assured him of an ultimate triumph. Even in the eighteenth century the Sikhs seemed intuitively to have adopted the matchlock in place of the bow and the spear. Ranjit Singh was said to have gone to see the order of Lord Lake's army in 1805; in 1809, he praised the disciplined soldiers of Metcalfe's small escort which had repulsed the Akalis. He began to give attention to the formation of regular infantry. In 1812, two regiments of Sikhs were drilled by men who had resigned or deserted the British service. By degrees the infantry service came to be preferred. Before Ranjit Singh's death it came to be regarded as 'the proper warlike array of his people'. They were perhaps more readily brought to serve guns than to stand in even ranks as footmen. General Allard and General Ventura gave a moderate degree of precision and completeness to a system already introduced.[42]

Detailing the domestic relations of Ranjit Singh and the opprobrium heaped upon him and his countrymen as 'the practitioners of every immorality', Cunningham observes that such excesses were exceptional to the general usage, 'and those who vilify the Sikhs at one time, and describe their long and rapid marches at another, should remember the contradiction, and reflect that what common sense and better feelings of our nature have always condemned, can never be the ordinary practice of a nation'.

It was illogical to apply the character of a few dissolute chiefs and licentious soldiers to 'the thousands of hardy peasants and industrious mechanics'. Cunningham, however, concedes, that Ranjit Singh 'yielded more than was becoming to the promptings of his appetites' and that he laid himself open also to the charge of 'extravagant partiality and favoritism'. The Khalsa being unwilling to be subservient to him, he sought strangers 'whose applause would be more ready if less sincere, and in whom he could repose some confidence as the creatures of his favour.' The first among them was Jamadar Khushal Singh, followed by the Jamwal brothers Gulab Singh, Dhian Singh and Suchet Singh, who were raised to the rank of Rajas. They were the most conspicuous persons in the Lahore court but the mind of Ranjit Singh was 'never prostrate before that of others'. There were others who enjoyed his esteem and confidence, like Sawan Mal, Hari Singh Nalwa, and Desa Singh Majithia.[43]

VII. THE LAST PHASE OF RANJIT SINGH'S REIGN

Cunningham's account of the last 15 years of Ranjit Singh's reign is prefaced by the remark that he had become master of the Punjab almost unheeded by the English, but the position and views of the English had changed since they had asked his aid against the armies of Napolean. With the laudable design of diffusing wealth and of linking remote provinces together in the strong and useful bonds of commerce,

> they were about to enter upon schemes of navigation and of trade, which caused them to deprecate the ambition of the king of the Sikhs, and led them, by sure yet unforeseen steps, to absorb his dominion in their own, and to grasp, perhaps inscrutably to chasten, with the cold unfeeling hand of worldly rule, the youthful spirit of social change and religious reformation evoked by the genius of Nanuk and Govind.[44]

In other words, Anglo-Sikh relations were on the eve of entering a new phase, not because of any change in the policy of Ranjit Singh but that of the British.

Cunningham refers briefly to the affairs of Ranjit Singh in relation to Peshawar, Nepal, and Sindh. He then refers to a few matters of dispute between the Lahore Darbar and the English. Ranjit Singh claimed his supremacy over Chamkaur, Anandpur, Wadni, and Ferozepur. His claims to Chamkaur, Anandpur and Wadni were admitted but not to Ferozepur 'which the English continued to admire as a commanding position'. Ranjit Singh's connection with the English was becoming more and more close.[45]

Before coming to the meeting of the Maharaja with the Governor-General at Ropar, Cunningham refers to 'a formidable insurrection' organized by Syed Ahmad in the neighbourhood of Peshawar. In his war against infidels he acted as if he meant by unbelievers 'the Sikhs alone'; he was careful not to offend the English. In 1826 he left Delhi with 500 attendants, and passing through Sindh and Kandhar he reached Panjtar where the *ghazis* were hailed by the Yusufzais as deliverers. Their attacks were repulsed by Buddh Singh Sandhanwalia first and then by Prince Sher Singh and General Ventura, and by Hari Singh Nalwa and General Allard. However, the *ghazis* defeated the Barakzai governor of Peshawar, Sultan Muhammad Khan, and occupied Peshawar. Syed Ahmad proclaimed himself to be the Caliph and struck coins in the name of 'Ahmad the Just'. He was soon obliged to relinquish Peshawar. In May 1831 he was slain at Balakot. The Yusufzais expelled his *ghazis* and they returned to Hindustan in disguise. The fame of Ranjit was now at its height and 'his friendship was sought by distant sovereigns'. Among them were the rulers of Balochistan and Herat. The English themselves were about to flatter him for 'the fulfilment of their expanding views of just influence and profitable commerce'.[46]

The meeting between Lord William Bentinck and Maharaja Ranjit Singh took place in October 1831. The Governor-General's object was to give the world an impression of complete unanimity between the two states, and the Maharaja wished to strengthen his own authority and his dynasty by being acknowledged by the predominant English rulers as the proper head of the 'Khalsa'. Ranjit Singh gave a hint of his schemes with regard to Sind but the Governor-General did not divulge that his own agent was already on the way to the chiefs of Sind. Cunningham comments that Ranjit Singh 'may or may not have felt that he was distrusted, but as he was to be a party to the opening of the navigation of the Indus, and as the project had been matured, it would have better suited the character and position of the British Government had no concealment been attempted'.[47]

The Governor-General had directed Colonel Pottinger to negotiate with the Amirs of Sind the opening of the river Indus to all boats. Two months later, towards the end of 1831, he wrote to the Maharaja that he wished to draw closer the commercial relations of the two states. Captain Wade, the political agent at Ludhiana, was directed to induce Ranjit Singh to accept the proposition. The Maharaja was mistrustful and had his eye on Shikarpur. But he perceived that the Governor-General had resolved upon his course and gave his assent to the common use of the Sutlej and the Indus, and to residence of a British officer at Mithankot to superintend the navigation. He did not conceal his opinion from Wade that the commercial measures of the English had really restricted his political power. He was actually out of humour with the English about Sind.[48]

In 1832, Shah Shuja agreed to relinquish his nominal supremacy over the Amirs of Sind and to waive his right to Peshawar, and other areas across the Indus which had been conquered by Ranjit Singh, in return for assistance in men and money to enable him to regain the throne of Kabul. Ranjit Singh wanted the English to be a party to an engagement with the Shah. The British became neutral. Eventually, an alliance was entered into. The areas beyond the Indus in the possession of Ranjit Singh were formally ceded to him, but Shah Shuja's expedition to Kabul ended in his defeat and he returned to his old asylum at Ludhiana in March 1835. Meanwhile, Ranjit Singh had established his direct control over Peshawar in May 1834 with the intention of retaining it as a part of his dominions.[49]

Ranjit Singh's fondest hopes were in the direction of Sind. But the English had formed a treaty of navigation with the Amirs of Sind and the designs of Ranjit Singh were not pleasing to them. In August 1836, the Multan governor took possession of Rojhan, defeated the Mazaris, and occupied a fort called Ken to the south of Rojhan. Ranjit Singh was thus gradually feeling his way by force. The views of the English with regard to Sind were inevitably becoming political as much as commercial. The political agent was directed to use every means short of aggression to induce the Maharaja to abandon his designs against Shikarpur. The Maharaja yielded at last, though he was urged by his chiefs not to agree. However, he was not inclined to relinquish Rojhan and it came to be formally regarded as a Sikh possession in 1838.[50]

Cunningham takes up the relations of the English government with the Barakzai rulers of Afghanistan till the war of Dost Muhammad Khan against Maharaja Ranjit Singh after the occupation of Peshawar by the Sikhs. Dost Muhammad suffered much in general estimation by withdrawing from his encounter with the Sikhs. In April 1837, the Afghans attacked Jamrud and they were repulsed, but Hari Singh Nalwa was mortally wounded. His death caused some anxiety in Lahore. The Maharaja promptly roused his people to exertion. He advanced personally to Rohtas. He had scarcely vindicated his supremacy on the frontier by filling the valley of Peshawar with troops 'when the English interfered to embitter the short remainder of his life, and to set bounds to his ambition on the west, as they had already done on the east and south'.[51]

In the beginning of 1838 the Governor-General did not contemplate the restoration of Shah Shuja but in four months the scheme was adopted. In May, Sir William Macnaughten was sent to Maharaja Ranjit Singh to unfold the views of the British government. The Maharaja disliked the scheme which obliged him to resign all hope of Shikarpur, and he did not like to be 'enclosed within the iron arms of the English rule'. He suddenly broke up the camp at Adinanagar, leaving the British envoys to follow at their leisure or to return to Simla. When he was told that an expedition would be undertaken whether or not he chose to share in it, the triple alliance was formed for the subversion of the power of the Barakzais. 'Ostensibly Runjeet Singh had reached the summit of his ambition; he was acknowledged as the arbiter in the fate of that empire which had tyrannized over his peasant forefather, and he was treated with the greatest distinction by the foreign paramounts of India'. But his health had become seriously impaired and he felt that he was 'in truth fairly in collusion with the English'. He heard of the fall of Kandhar in April 1839. His health continued to decline, and he died on

27 June at the age of 59, before the final success of 'a campaign in which he was an unwilling partner'.[52]

At the end, Cunningham gives his assessment of Maharaja Ranjit Singh's achievement and his legacy. Ranjit Singh found the Punjab a waning confederacy, a prey to the factions of its chiefs, pressed by the Afghans and the Marathas, and ready to submit to English supremacy. He consolidated the numerous petty states into a kingdom, wrested from Kabul the fairest of its provinces, and gave to the English no cause for interference. He found the military array of his country a mass of horsemen, brave but ignorant of the art of war, and he left it with 50,000 disciplined soldiers, 50,000 well-armed militia, and more than 300 pieces of cannon for the field. His rule was founded on the feelings of the people, and it involved the joint action of the principles of military order and territorial extension. When 'a limit had been set to Sikh dominions, and his own commanding genius was no more, the vital spirit of his race began to consume itself in domestic contentions'.[53]

VIII. THE LAHORE DARBAR AFTER RANJIT SINGH

Cunningham devotes a little over 50 pages to the years from Ranjit Singh's death in June 1839 to the death of Jawahar Singh in 1845. During these years the affairs of the Lahore Darbar became increasingly linked with the British and Cunningham's narrative takes into account this intricate web. Therefore, the events in the kingdom of Lahore and the attitude and activities of the British may be taken up together.

Kharak Singh was recognized as the Maharaja of the Punjab, with Raja Dhian Singh as his *wazir*. Prince Nau Nihal Singh was not opposed to this arrangement but the ascendancy of Chet Singh over the Maharaja, and Kharak Singh's own desire to rest upon the influence of the British agent, brought Nau Nihal Singh and Raja Dhian Singh together, first for the destruction of Chet Singh and then for the removal of Colonel Wade from Ludhiana. Nau Nihal Singh's great aim was to destroy or reduce the power of the Jammu Rajas who were all powerful in the hills, but his attention was distracted by disputes with the English authorities over matters related to both Dost Muhammad Khan and Shah Shuja. When he became free from the danger from the side of the English, Maharaja Kharak Singh died on 5 November 1840 at the age of thirty-eight. The day that dazzled Nau Nihal Singh with the crown proved to be the last day of his life: after the cremation of his father, he was crushed by the fall of a gateway. He was in his twentieth year and promised to be an able and vigorous ruler. Had his life been spared and had not the English partly forestalled him, 'he would have found an ample scope for his ambition in Sind, in Afghanistan, and beyond the Hindoo Koosh; and he might perhaps, at last have boasted that the inroads of Mehmood and of Tymoor had been fully avenged by the aroused peasants of India'.[54]

Raja Dhian Singh and the British agent thought of Prince Sher Singh as a suitable successor, but his paternity was more than doubtful; he possessed no commanding and popular qualities, and the Rajas of Jammu were odious to the majority of the Sikh chiefs. Chand Kaur, the widow of Maharaja Kharak Singh and the mother of Prince Nau Nihal Singh, assumed the functions of regent, supported by several men of reputation, especially the Sandhanwalia *sardars*. She spurned all proposals of marriage and 'loudly asserted her own right to supreme power'. The widow of Nau Nihal Singh was declared to be pregnant. Raja Dhian Singh began to rethink about the claims of Sher Singh. The English authorities were informed that there was another son of Maharaja Ranjit Singh. Rani Jindan, a favourite wife or concubine of Maharaja Ranjit Singh, had given birth to a son named Dulip in 1838. The Governor-General did not acknowledge Mai Chand Kaur as the sovereign of the country but he treated her government as *de facto*. He made no declaration with regard to the Lahore succession. Sher Singh sounded the British agent about his eventual recognition and he was satisfied with the reply that 'the friends of thirty-two years wished to see a strong government in the Punjab'. Sher Singh had gained over some divisions of the army, and he appeared at Lahore on 14 January 1841. Raja Dhian Singh, who had left for Jammu, returned to Lahore on 18 January and a compromise was worked out. Sher Singh was proclaimed as the Maharaja, with Dhian Singh as the *wazir*.[55]

Maharaja Sher Singh was unable to command the soldiers. Some officers were killed and civilians were plundered by them. The English watched the confusion with anxiety. Their agent in Kabul proposed to give the trans-Indus Sikh territories to Shah Shuja. The British political agent proposed to march to Lahore with 12,000 men to beat and disperse a rebel army in order to strengthen the sovereignty of Sher Singh, and to take 'the cis-Sutlej districts and forty lakhs of rupees in coin as the price of his aid'. Neither Maharaja Sher Singh nor the Governor-General desired such intervention. But the opinion got abroad that overtures had been made to the English. Sardar Lehna Singh Sandhanwalia in the Mandi hills was imprisoned by his own men 'on the charge of conspiracy with his refugee brother to introduce the supremacy of strangers'.[56]

The army was no longer willing to be an instrument of the government; it looked upon itself, and was regarded by others, as the representative body of the Sikh people. The efficiency of the army as a disciplined force was not much impaired; a higher feeling possessed the men, and increased alacrity and resolution supplied the place of exact training. As a general rule the troops were obedient to their officers, but the position of a regiment, a brigade, a division, or the whole army relatively to the executive government of the country, was determined by a committee, or an assemblage of committees, termed the *panchayat*. Thus, the Sikh people were 'enabled to interfere with effect, and with some degree of consistency, in the nomination and in the removal of their rulers'. However, their resolutions were often unstable or unwise, and the representatives of different divisions could take opposite sides from conviction or prejudice; they could also be bribed and cajoled by able and unscrupulous men like Raja Gulab Singh.[57]

The British authorities, generally, had a low opinion of the Sikh soldiers. Before the end of 1841, insurrection broke out in Kabul and the British troops were beaten by the Afghans. But no confidence was placed in the efficiency and the friendship of the Sikhs; the mode in which their aid was sought and used served only 'to sink the Lahore army lower than before in British estimation'. The disinclination of the Sikhs to fight the battles of strangers communicated itself to the mercenary soldiers of the English. Maharaja Sher Singh was willing to help even beyond the limited degree of the relevant article of the tripartite treaty. But the Sikhs were held inferior in warlike spirit to the soldiers of Jammu. When the Khyber Pass was forced in April 1842, the Sikhs acquitted themselves to the satisfaction of the English General. The Governor-General wanted to thank Maharaja Sher Singh in person but the Maharaja was not inclined to meet him. The boy prince, Partap Singh, reached Ferozepore and he was visited by Lord Ellenborough.[58]

The English government urged the restoration of the Sandhanwalia chiefs to favour and Maharaja Sher Singh was not averse to reconciliation. Sardar Ajit Singh and his uncles again took their old place at the court of Lahore. Ajit Singh became a boon companion of the Maharaja. The Sandhanwalias and Raja Dhian Singh tried to use each other against Maharaja Sher Singh. On 15 September 1843, Ajit Singh shot his sovereign dead and Lehna Singh took the life of Prince Partap Singh. They joined Dhian Singh and proceeded with him to the citadel to proclaim a new king. Dhian Singh became the dupe of his accomplices and he was shot dead. His son, Raja Hira Singh, promised rewards to the army to avenge the death of its friend, and the soldiers responded to his call. The citadel was assaulted, Lehna Singh and Ajit Singh were killed, Dulip Singh was proclaimed Maharaja, and Hira Singh was raised to the high office of *wazir*.[59]

Hira Singh added two rupees and a half to the pay of the common soldiers. 'The army felt that it had become the master of the state.' He was beset by difficulties from Fateh Khan Tiwana, Princes Kashmira Singh and Pashaura Singh, Jawahar Singh, and Raja Suchet Singh. Sardar Attar Singh Sandhanwalia had escaped into British territory. Bhai Bir Singh, who was influential among the Sikhs, was opposed to Hira Singh. When the princes and Sardar Attar Singh joined Bhai Bir Singh at his *dera*, Hira Singh sent a large force against them. In the action that followed, Attar Singh and Kashmira Singh were killed along with Bhai Bir Singh. Hira Singh had appealed to the anti-British feeling of the army. The English government confirmed its suspicions by resuming the village Mauran (which had been given by Raja Jaswant Singh of Nabha to Maharaja Ranjit Singh in exchange), and by retaining the treasure of Raja Suchet Singh, estimated at Rs. 1,500,000, in Ferozepur.[60]

Hira Singh's successes surpassed the general expectation but the person who directed his measures was Pandit Jalla who proceeded too hastily in some matters and attempted to do too much at one time. He forgot that the chiefs whom he was trying to crush were Sikhs and that the word 'Khalsa' could be used to unite the high and the low. He showed no respect even for the *sardars* of ability and means. He used some expressions of disrespect towards the mother of the Maharaja. Jawahar Singh, Rani Jindan's brother, was treated by Jalla with neglect and contempt. The Rani and her brother appealed to the army, the children of the Khalsa, against Jalla and his master. Hira Singh perceived that his rule was at an end. They fled from the capital on 21 December 1844 but they were captured and slain.[61]

Rani Jindan, her brother Jawahar Singh and her favourite Lal Singh were now the most influential members of administration. The services of the troops were rewarded by adding half a rupee to the monthly pay of the common soldier. Raja Gulab Singh was obliged to agree to pay in all a fine of Rs. 6,800,000. In his presence, Jawahar Singh was installed as *wazir* on 14 May 1845. Maharaja Dulip Singh was betrothed to the daughter of Sardar Chattar Singh Attariwala on 10 July. Prince Pashaura Singh tried to rally a party around him at Sialkot. Sardar Chattar Singh was sent against him. He submitted on 30 August but he was put to death on Jawahar Singh's instigation. This last triumph was fatal to Jawahar Singh; anger was added to the contempt in which he was always held. The *panchayats* met in council and resolved that Jawahar Singh should die 'as a traitor to the commonwealth'. He was put to death on 21 September.[62]

After Jawahar Singh's death, no one seemed willing to become the *wazir*. Raja Gulab Singh was urged to repair to the capital but he was overawed. Rani Jindan held a regular court, and the army reposed confidence in three courtiers: Diwan Dina Nath, the paymaster Bhagat Ram, and Faqir Nuruddin. However, the advantage of a responsible head was apparent. By degrees the soldiers were worked upon to wage war with the English. Raja Lal Singh was nominated *wazir*, and Sardar Tej Singh was reconfirmed in his office of commander-in-chief. These arrangements were made in November 1845, and the stage was set for war with the English.[63]

IX. THE FIRST SIKH WAR

Cunningham's last chapter relates to 'war with the English'. The Indian public, in view of the progressive expansion of the British empire in India, was prepared to hear the annexation of another kingdom; the selfish Sikh chiefs had always desired a degree of interference that should guarantee to them the easy enjoyment of their possessions; the English government had long expected to be forced into a war with the overbearing soldiery of the Punjab. Until within two or three months of the first battles, the Sikh soldiery had not thought of fighting with the paramount power of Hindustan, and even then the rude yeomen considered that they were about to enter a war 'purely defensive', though it was in every way congenial to 'their feelings of youthful pride and national jealousy'.[64]

Cunningham goes on to add 'that India is far behind Europe in civilization, and that political morality or moderation is as little appreciated in the East in these days as it was in Christendom in the middle ages'. The Sikhs feared the ambition of their great and growing neighbour. They did not understand why they should be dreaded when internal commotions had reduced their comparative inferiority still lower, or why inefficiency of rule should be construed as dangerous. Defensive measures of the British took the form of aggressive preparations in the eyes of the Sikhs, and they came to the conclusion that their country was to be invaded. To this general persuasion was added the particular bearing of the British government towards the Punjab itself. Till 1838, the garrison at Ludhiana had formed the only body of armed men near the Sikh frontier. Addition to the troops at Ferozepore as well Ludhiana was seen by the Sikhs as a threat. They were not informed of the preparations being made but they were known, and appeared 'to denote a campaign, not of defence, but of aggression'.[65]

There were other factors which appeared to the Sikhs to indicate that the fixed policy of English was territorial aggrandizement and that the immediate object of their ambition was the conquest of Lahore. In November 1844 Major Broadfoot, who had made a stormy passage through the Punjab in 1842, was appointed political agent at Ludhiana. One of his first acts was to declare the cis-Sutlej possessions of Lahore to be under British protection. He acted on this assumption when he interfered authoritatively in the affairs of the Sodhis of Anandpur. He ordered a troop of horse, who had crossed the Sutlej near Ferozepore to proceed to Kot Kapura, to recross the river; assuming that they were delaying, even a shot was fired at them. Every act of Broadfoot was considered 'to denote a foregone resolution, and to be conceived in a spirit of enmity rather than of good will'.[66]

Cunningham goes on to state that the Sikh army and the Sikh people were convinced that war was inevitable, but the members of the Sikh government knew that no interference was likely 'without an overt act of hostility on their part'. In fact, Maharaja Sher Singh, the Sandhanwalia *sardars,* and others, had been ready to become tributary, and to lean for support upon foreigners. The predominance of the army now presented a new danger to the territorial chiefs. Lal Singh, Tej Singh, and many others, were conscious of their inability to control the troops. 'These men considered that their only chance of retaining power was to have the army removed by inducing it to engage in a contest, which they believed would end in its dispersion'. Had the British made no military preparations, mercenary men like Lal Singh and Tej Singh would not have succeeded in inciting the army against the British. The sequestration of two villages near Ludhiana and the rapid approach of the Governor-General to the frontier left no doubt in the minds of the army *panchayats*. Before the end of November 1845, troops began to move in detachments from Lahore and to cross the Sutlej on 11 December. A portion of the army took up position within a few miles of Ferozepore on 14 December 1845.[67]

A certain degree of criticism of the British measures is implicit in Cunningham's narrative of the causes of the war. His criticism becomes explicit in the statement that follows. The initiative was taken by the Sikhs but 'the policy pursued by the English themselves for several years was not in reality well calculated to insure a continuation of pacific relations'. Logically, therefore, they could not 'be held wholly blameless'. They also knew that the war would result in 'their own aggrandizement'.

The proceedings of the English, indeed, did not exhibit that punctilious adherence to the spirit of first relations which allows no change of circumstances to cause a departure from arrangements which had, in the progress of time, come to be regarded by a weaker power as essentially bound up with its independence. Nor did the acts of the English seem marked by that high wisdom and sure foresight, which should distinguish the career of intelligent rulers acquainted with actual life, and the examples of history. Significantly, Cunningham traces a change in the British attitude to the treaties of commerce and navigation which had been urged upon the Sikhs despite their 'dislike to such bonds of unequal union'. They were withheld not only from Sind but also from Afghanistan and Tibet, which were left open to the ambition of the English.[68]

The English in their confidence continued to hold a low opinion of the martial qualities of the Sikhs. They also mistook the form which the long-expected aggression of the Sikhs would assume. The treasonable views of the chiefs and the unity and depth of feeling of the troops were not fully appreciated. What the English anticipated was a desultory warfare, and they made no adequate arrangements for food and ammunition, and carriage and hospital stores.[69]

In his description of the battles, Cunningham highlights the treachery of the Sikh leaders and the valour of the Sikh soldiers. With reference to the situation at Ferozepore, he observes that the object of Lal Singh and Tej Singh was 'not to compromise themselves with the English by destroying an isolated division, but to get their own troops dispersed by the converging forces of their opponents'. They assured the local British authorities of 'their secret and efficient good-will'. There was an enthusiastic unity of purpose in the Sikh army, but it was 'headed by men not only ignorant of warfare, but studiously treacherous towards their followers'. The youthful Khalsa was active and strong but the soldiers had never before met so great a foe as the English, and their tactics were modified by involuntary awe of the British army. At Mudki on 18 December, 'Lal Singh headed the attack, but, in accordance with his original design, he involved his followers in an engagement, and then left them to fight as their undirected valour might attempt'. The Sikhs were repulsed but the success of the English was not complete.[70]

At Pherushahr on 21 December, the resistance met by the English was wholly unexpected. Battalion after battalion was hurled back with shattered ranks. Darkness threw the English into confusion; men of all regiments and arms were mixed together; Generals were doubtful of the fact or of the extent of their own success, and Colonels did not know what had become of the regiments they commanded. The position of the English was one of real danger and great perplexity. 'On that memorable night the English were hardly masters of the ground on which they stood.' On the day following, the second army of the Sikhs approached in battle-array. It was commanded by Tej Singh. His object was 'to have the dreaded army of the Khalsa overcome and dispersed';

he delayed until Lal Singh's force was everywhere put to flight, and the opponents had again ranged themselves round their colours.' He made feints rather than a resolute attack, and after some time he 'precipitately fled, leaving his subordinates without orders and without an object'. If the Sikhs had boldly pressed forward, the English would have been forced to retreat.[71]

After the skirmish with the detachment under Sir Harry Smith near Baddowal, the Sikhs did not pursue him because they were without a leader 'or without one who wished to see the English beaten'. This skirmish added to the belief that the dreaded army of the English had 'at last been foiled by the skill and valor of the disciples of Govind'. The Sikhs were elated, and the presence of European prisoners added to their triumph. 'Lal Singh and Tej Singh shrank within themselves with fear'. At Aliwal, the English were victorious; their cavalry charge was timely and bold, 'but the ground was more thickly strewn with the bodies of victorious horsemen than of beaten infantry'.[72]

On behalf of the Lahore Darbar, Gulab Singh entered into negotiations with the English leaders. The Govenor-General was not displeased that the Lahore authorities were ready to yield. He truly felt for various reasons that it was difficult and risky to subjugate the Punjab in one season. The English intimated to Gulab Singh their readiness to acknowledge a Sikh sovereignty in Lahore after the army had been disbanded. Gulab Singh declared his inability to deal with the troops. The views of the two sides were in some sort met by an understanding that 'the Sikh army should be attacked by the English, and that when beaten it should be openly abandoned by its own government'. It was further understood that the British would be allowed to cross the Sutlej unopposed and the road to the capital laid open to the victors. 'Under such circumstances of discreet policy and shameless treason was the battle of Subraon fought'.[73]

At Sabraon, as in the other battles 'the soldiers did everything and the leaders nothing'. There was no mind to guide and inspire them. The grey-headed chief Sham Singh of Atari made known his resolution to die in the first conflict with 'the enemies of his race' as a sacrifice of propitiation to the spirit of Guru Gobind Singh and to the genius of his mystic commonwealth. Sham Singh repeatedly rallied his shattered ranks, and at last fell as a martyr on a heap of his slain countrymen.

The traitor Tej Singh, instead of leading fresh men to sustain the failing strength of the troops on his right, fled on the first assault and, either accidentally or by design, sank a boat in the middle of the bridge of communication to make it useless. 'No Sikh offered to submit, and no disciple of Govind asked for quarter'. The victors looked in wonder upon the formidable courage of the vanquished. On 10 February 1846 the victory of the English was complete.[74]

On 15 February Raja Gulab Singh and other chiefs were received by the Governor-General at Kasur. They were told that Dulip Singh would continue 'to be regarded as a friendly sovereign' but the country between the Sutlej and the Beas would be retained by the conquerors; an indemnity of 1,500,000 sterling should be paid by the Lahore government. The terms were reluctantly agreed upon. The Maharaja tendered his submission in person, and the British army arrived at Lahore on 20 February. The citadel was garrisoned by English regiments. Gulab Singh congratulated himself on 'the approaching success of all his treasons'; his object simply was his own aggrandizement 'at the expense of Sikh independence'. Kashmir and the hill states from the Beas to the Indus were transferred to him for a million pounds. 'This transaction was scarcely 'worthy of the British name and greatness'. Lal Singh became minister once more, but he did not feel safe. As a further departure from the original scheme, a British force was to be kept in Lahore till the end of 1846. Before the year ended, it was decided that the British force should remain at Lahore till the Maharaja came of age.[75] Portions of the Sikh army were paid up and disbanded when the Governor-General and the Commander-in-Chief were in Lahore. 'The soldiers showed neither the despondency of mutinous rebels nor the effrontery and indifference of mercenaries, and their manly deportment added lustre to that valour which the victors had dearly felt and generously extolled.'

They still thought of the future destiny of the Khalsa. Thus, 'the spirit of progress which collectively animated them yielded with a murmur to the superior genius of England and civilization, to be chastened by the rough hand of power, and perhaps to be moulded to noblest purposes by the informing touch of knowledge and philosophy'.

Cunningham closed his *History of the Sikhs* with the hope of a better future for the Sikhs.[76]

X. ELABORATE ANNOTATION

That Cunningham was earnestly interested in history is evident from his 41 appendices. Nine of these relate to Indian history and seventeen to texts of treaties and proclamations. There are genealogical tables of the Lahore and Jammu families. The remaining thirteen appendices relate to Sikh history, including a genealogical table of the Gurus. The themes of a dozen appendices are Guru Nanak's philosophical allusions, the terms *raj, jog, deg* and *tegh*, caste among the Sikhs, rites of initiation into Sikhism, the exclamation *Vah Guru* and the expression *deg, tegh, fateh*, Sikh devotion to steel and the term *Sachcha Padshah*, distinctive usages of the Sikhs, the *Adi Granth*, the *Daswen Padshah ka Granth*, some principles of belief and practice, the letters attributed to Guru Nanak and Guru Gobind Singh, and Sikh sects, orders or denominations. Thus, Cunningham's interest in the Sikh tradition is wide in scope, with a certain degree of depth.

Cunningham refers to H.H. Wilson thinking 'slightly of the doctrines of Nanuk' which, in Wilson's view, were mere metaphysical notions founded on the abstractions of Sufism and the Vedanta philosophy. Cunningham points out that it was difficult for any one to write about 'omnipotence of God and the hopes of man' without laying himself open to the charge of belonging to one speculative school or another. Like Jeremiah and Paul, Guru Nanak simply desired to underline the greatness and goodness of God. Cunningham goes on to add that Wilson's view was contrary to that of the author of the *Dabistan* who emphasizes the difference between Sikhism and Brahmanism. It was important in this connection to remember that the Sikhs regarded the mission of Guru Nanak and Guru Gobind Singh as 'the consummation of all other dispensations', including Islam. Guru Nanak refers to Hindu notions but he was not an idolater. 'In truth, all religious systems not possessed of a body of literature themselves seek elsewhere for support in such matters'. The position of Sikhism in this respect was no different from that of early Christianity.[77]

Cunningham refers to Malcolm's view that Guru Hargobind armed the Sikhs due to his personal feelings of revenge for the death of his father. However, the martial array of the Guru did not strike the author of the *Dabistan* as strange or unusual. The Sikhs themselves connect the modification of Guru Nanak's system with the double nature of the mythology of Janak. In the anecdote of Bhai Buddha, he blesses Guru Arjan's wife with 'a son who would be master of both of the Deg and Tegh; that is, simply of a vessel for food and a sword, but typically of grace and power, the terms corresponding in significance with the "Raj" and "Jog" of Junnuk, the "Peeree" and "Meeree" of Indian Mahomedans'. Thus, Guru Hargobind is said to have worn two swords, one to denote his spiritual power and the other his temporal power. The personal feelings of Guru Hargobind could have some share for leading the Sikhs to take up arms, but this could not be the whole explanation. The belief that Guru Nanak was an incarnation of the legendary Raja Janak carried the implication that the founder of Sikhism was the master of both temporal and spiritual authority (*raj* and *jog* or *miri* and *piri*).[78]

On caste among the Sikhs, Cunningham quotes Guru Nanak 'Think not of caste: abase thyself, and attain to salvation'; also, 'God will not ask man of what race he is; he will ask him what has he done?' Another quotation from Guru Nanak refers to his preference for goodness over caste. Guru Amar Das is quoted to the effect that people talk of four castes but all human beings are the seed of God. Guru Ram Das asserts that liberation is open to all alike whether a Brahman or a Shudra. Guru Gobind Singh (in a *Rahitnama*) says that all 'the four races' shall be one. The Sikhs ate the *prasad* in common. In all this evidence, more importance is assigned to 'religious unity and truth' than to 'political equality'. It may be justly observed, says Cunningham, that Guru Gobind Singh abolished caste 'rather by implication than by a direct enactment'. The Guru nowhere says that Brahmans and Shudras were to intermarry, or that they should interdine. However, the statements on caste appeared to lay 'a good foundation for the practical obliteration of all differences'.[79]

About the rites of initiation into Sikhism, Cunningham makes only one new statement that, sometimes women were initiated through the baptism of the sword, though a one-edged dagger was used for mingling sugar and water.[80] For the exclamation *Vah Guru, Vah Guru Ki Fateh* or *Vah Guru Ka Khalsa,* Cunningham states that if Guru Gobind Singh 'did not ordain it as the proper salutation of believers', it arose naturally out of the notions diffused by him. Cunningham goes on to add that the origin of 'Wah Guru' given by the author of the *Gur-Ratnavali* was 'fanciful and trivial'.[81]

For Sikh devotion to steel, Cunningham observes that the implements of various callings in India were in a manner worshipped, like the plough, the loom, and the pen. Guru Gobind Singh withdrew his followers from such practices and urged them 'to regard the sword as *their* principal stay in the world'. The term *Sachcha Padshah* could be explained in the same way. A spiritual king, or Guru, 'rules the eternal soul, or guides it to salvation, while the temporal monarch controls our finite faculties only'.[82]

The distinctive usages of the Sikhs are seen by Cunningham chiefly in contrast with those of the Hindus. He observes that unshorn hair and blue dress did not appear as direct injunctions of Guru Gobind Singh 'in any extant writing'. They seemed chiefly to have derived their distinction from custom or usage. The propriety of wearing a blue dress was regarded as less obligatory in the time of Cunningham than formerly. Both appeared to have originated in opposition to Hinduism. Similarly, no Sikh would wear clothes of a *suhi* colour, dyed with safflower. The Sikhs wore a kind of breeches (*kachh*) instead of girding up their loins after the manner of the Hindus. The Sikh women were distinguished from Hindu women by some variety of dress, but chiefly by higher top-knot of hair.[83]

Cunningham notes that the *Adi Granth* contains many allusions 'illustrative of the condition of society, and of the religious feelings of the times'. Its teachings emphasize that God was to be worshipped in spirit and in truth, with little reference to particular forms, and that salvation was not attainable without grace, faith and good works. The works of the Bhagats, Bhatts and Doms, apart from those of the Gurus, were, included in the *Adi Granth*. There was some doubt about the authenticity of some works appended to the volume. Originally compiled by Guru Arjan, the *Granth* received a few additions at the hands of his successors. The script used throughout was Gurmukhi but the language generally used was 'the Hindee of Upper India' rather than the particular dialect of the Punjab. Some portions were in Sanskrit. The language of Guru Arjan, and largely of Guru Nanak too, was held to be the pure language of the region. Cunningham notes the contents of the *Adi Granth* in some detail, which shows that he was familiar with the broad contents of the scripture.[84]

Like the *Adi Granth*, the *Daswen Padshah ka Granth* (Book of the Tenth King) was metrical throughout; it was written in Braj but in Gurmukhi script. The concluding portion was in Persian. The *Bachittar Natak* was written by Guru Gobind Singh himself. Some other compositions were also attributed to him but the remainder, which was by far the larger part, was said to have been composed by four scribes in his service, partly, perhaps, on the basis of his dictation. Cunningham notes the contents of this *Granth* in detail which indicates that the contents were broadly the same as in the present *Dasam Granth*. It was more mythological and worldly in its contents than the *Adi Granth*.[85]

Cunningham uses extracts from both the *Granths* to illustrate some principles of Sikh belief and practice. These extracts relate to a large number of themes, like Godhead, incarnation, saints and prophets, the Hindu *avtars*, Muhammad, *siddhs* and *pirs*, images and the worship of saints, miracles, transmigration, faith, grace, predestination, the Vedas, the Puranas, and the Qur'an, asceticism, caste, food, Brahmans, infanticide, and *sati*. The Sikh Gurus were not to be worshipped. Cunningham's understanding of Sikhism and Sikh ideology appears to have been informed by his understanding of this scriptural evidence. Added to these are Bhai Gurdas' understanding of the mission of Guru Nanak, and the representation of Guru Gobind Singh's mission in the *Bachittar Natak*.[86] None of Cunningham's predecessors had appreciated or used all this evidence.

Finally, Cunningham takes notice of two letters attributed to Guru Nanak, and of two *Rahitnamas*. The former were actually written in the early or mid-eighteenth century and attributed to Guru Nanak. The first of these refers to a great king's preoccupation with wealth and riches, collected by plundering the earth and spent in pleasure at the cost of justice and good governance. The second refers to the rise of the Khalsa in the future to establish their rule in the Punjab first and then in Hindustan and the countries in its West up to Mecca and Madina (the Islamic world). The *Rahitnamas*, were not composed by Guru Gobind Singh but they could be held 'to represent his views and the principles of Sikhism'. One of these was written for Darayai Udasi and repeated to Prahlad Singh, and the other was written in reply to Bhai Nand Lal.

Among other things, these *Rahitnamas* talk of the Guruship of the *Granth* and the Panth, and Khalsa Raj.[87]

XI. APPENDICES FOR DEPTH

Cunningham's *History of the Sikhs* is remarkable for the number of its footnotes. These notes contain references to his sources, and it is possible to form an idea of what kind of reading and thought went into the making of his work. Some of the footnotes amplify or reinforce the points made in the text. Cunningham appears to be reluctant to criticize his predecessors in explicit terms but there are a number of footnotes which reveal his appreciation of or his disagreement with the views of the other historians. As in the text, so in the footnotes also he tries to give his own assessment of the actors and their actions. Thus, the footnotes form an integral part of his narrative.

Cunningham was familiar with all the works on Sikh history. He does not use them as authorities. He generally compares their statements and, wherever possible, also brings in his own additional evidence. This is how he uses the works of James Browne, John Malcolm, H.T. Prinsep, W.G. Osborne, W.L. M'Gregor, G.C. Smyth and H.H. Wilson. Two other works he uses are Henry Lawrence's *Adventures in the Punjab* and Steinbach's *Punjab*. It may be added that Cunningham was familiar with the major works on Indian history too. He refers to the *British India* of James Mill (edited by H.H. Wilson), Elphinstone's *History of India,* Grant-Duff's *Marathas,* and Tod's *Rajasthan*. Apart from these he refers to Orme's *History,* Francklin's *Life of Shah Alam* and his *Life of George Thomas,* Auber's *Rise and Progress of British Power in India,* Thornton's *History of India,* Smith's *Sketch of Regular Corps in the Service of Indian Princes,* Robertson's *Disquisition Concerning the Hindoos,* Bentley's *Astronomy of the Hindoos,* Ward's *Hindoos,* and H.M. Elliots's *Introduction* to Persian works on medieval India was published in 1849 itself.[88]

Apart from the Sikh works mentioned in the appendices, Cunningham used the source material available in print, like the travelogues of Bernier, Moorcroft, Forster, Masson, Burnes, Hugel, Barr, Sleeman's *Rambles and Recollections of an Indian Official,* and Sir Claude Wade's *Narrative of Personal Services.* The other sources referred to in Cunningham's *History* are Troyer's translation of the *Dabistan*, Ghulam Husain Khan's *Seirool Mutakkereen* (in Briggs' translation), the *Memoirs of Jahangheer*, the *Memoirs of Ameer Ali*, Shahamat Ali's *Sikhs and Afghans*, Shah Shuja's *Autobiography*, Mohan Lal's *Life of Dost Muhammad Khan*, Bahawalpur Family Annals (in manuscript), and Dr. Harlan's *India and Afghanistan*.

Cunningham tends to point out parallels in situations related to Indian or Sikh history and the history of Europe. This was made possible by his reading of works on European history. He refers to Edward Gibbon's *Decline and Fall of the Roman Empire*, Thirwall's *History of Greece*, Grote's *History of Greece*, Hallam's *Middle Ages*, Kemble's *Saxons in England*, Macaulay's *History of England*, Wade's *British History*, and Richard's *History of England*. Apart from modern historical works, Cunningham has used the classical works of Herodotus and Tacitus, and the epics of Homer, that is, the *Illiad* and the *Odyssey*. For cultural and religious history he refers to Hallam's *Literature of Europe*, and William Gray's *Sketch of English Prose Literature*, Ritter's *Ancient Philosophy* and Schleiermacher's *Introduction to Plato's Dialogues*, Waddington's *History of the Church*, Strausse's *Life of Jesus*, and Newman's *On the Development of Christian Doctrine*. These lists do not exhaust all the references. Cunningham was surely well read.

Cunningham refers to Elphinstone's *History of India* as 'most useful and judicious'. This remark is not without significance. Elphinstone's work, published in 1845, was sympathetic to both Hindu and Islamic civilizations in contrast with the harsh treatment of James Mill whose *History* was given a new lease of life, though toned down in editing, by H.H. Wilson.[89]

We may refer to a point of detail as an illustration of Cunningham's approach. Both Forster and Malcolm mention Talwandi of Rai Bhua as the birth place of Guru Nanak. Cunningham says that he was born 'in the neighbourhood of Lahore'. The reason given in the footnote is that 'one manuscript account' states that though his father lived in Talwandi, Guru Nanak was born in the house of his mother's parents in the village called Kana Kachh. That was why he was given the name 'Nanak'. Cunningham adds that it was quite common in the Punjab to give the name 'Nanak' or 'Nanaki' to a male or female child born in the home of the mother's parents (called *nanake*).[90]

Cunningham points out that Malcolm had given translations from the *Bachittar Natak* in his *Sketch of the Sikhs* but his own general narrative of the events was 'obviously contradictory and inaccurate'.[91] On the point of the distinct identity of the Sikhs, Cunningham states that Tacitus and Suetonius regarded the early Christians as a mere Jewish sect and failed to perceive the fundamental difference, 'and to appreciate the latent and real excellence, of that doctrine, which has added dignity and purity to modern civilization'. Among the scholars who had misunderstood the Sikhs were H.H. Wilson and John Malcolm.[92] Browne attached no significance to '*deg, tegh* and *fateh*', and therefore leaves it as 'meaningless'; he is more prudent than Sleeman who talks of 'the sword, the *pot* victory, and conquest being quickly found'.[93]

On *Gurmata,* Malcolm considers and Browne implies that Guru Gobind Singh directed 'the assemblage of Gooroomutta' but there was no authority for believing that he ordained 'any formal or particular institution, although, doubtless, the general scope of his injunctions, and the peculiar political circumstances of the times, gave additional force to the practice of holding diets or conclaves'.[94] Murray (in Prinsep's *Runjeet Singh*) was 'scarcely warranted' in making the Nishanias and the Shahids 'regular *Misls*'. In such matters of detail he merely expressed 'the local opinions of the neighbourhood of the Sutlej' where he gathered his information.[95] With reference to Malcolm's view that Guru Gobind Singh instituted the order of the Akalis, Cunningham says that there was nothing in the writings of Guru Gobind Singh to support this view.[96]

In a footnote in his *History,* Cunningham tells us that the entire account of Ranjit Singh was based primarily on the report which he himself had drawn up for the government. The political agents at Ludhiana, Captain Murray and Captain Wade, had each written a narrative of the life of Ranjit Singh. The one written by Murray was printed in 1834, with a few corrections and additions, and some notes, by Prinsep, secretary to the Indian government. Murray's account, and Wade's in a greater degree, was founded on personal recollections and oral reports 'rather than on contemporary English documents, which reflected the opinions of the times and existed in abundance after 1803'. Both Murray and Wade also used the accounts drawn up by intelligent Indians, like Bute Shah and Sohan Lal Suri.[97]

Cunningham's view of Ranjit Singh is different from that of H.H. Wilson who says that Ranjit Singh 'deposed Nanuk and Govind, and the supreme ruler of the universe, and held himself to be the impersonation of the Khalsa.' Cunningham points out that in writing or talking of his government Ranjit Singh always used the term 'Khalsa'. On his seal he wrote his name, with the prefix *akal sahai* (God the helper). This was a common practice of the Sikhs. Cunningham goes on to add:

> With respect to the abstract excellence or moderation, or the practical efficiency or suitableness of the Sikh government, opinions will always differ, as they will about all other governments. It is not simply an unmeaning truism to say, that the Sikh government suited the Sikhs well, for such a degree of fitness is one of the ends of all governments of ruling classes, and the adaptation has thus a degree of positive merit. In judging of individuals, moreover, the extent and the peculiarities of the civilization of their times should be remembered, and the present condition of the Punjab shows a combination of the characteristics of rising medieval Europe and of the decaying Byzantine empire,—semi-barbarous in either light, but possessed at once of a native youthful vigor, and of an extraneous knowledge of many of the arts which adorn life in the most advanced stages of society.

The fact that Amritsar city was a creation of the Khalsa refuted many charges of oppression and misgovernment. Also the lands under Sikh rule were cultivated with assiduity.[98]

With reference to his statement on the good qualities of the Sikh soldier, Cunningham describes the general constitution of a Sikh regiment in a footnote. He does not fail to mention that a Granthi, or reader of the scripture, was attached to each regiment. When he was not paid by the government, he was sure of being supported by the men. The *Granth* was usually deposited near the flag (*jhanda*) of the regiment which represented its headquarters.[99] With reference to the projection of general and comprehensive moral degradation of the Sikhs alleged by some European writers, Cunningham make the general observation that:

> The morals, or the manners, of a people, however, should not be deduced from a few examples of profligacy; but the Indians equally exaggerate with regard to Europeans, and, in pictorial or pantomimic pieces, they usually represent Englishmen drinking and swearing in the society and to use their weapons with or without a reason.

Cunningham concedes, however, that with the increase in the power of the nation 'luxuries and vicious pleasures' had followed wealth and indolence 'in numerous instances'.

With reference to the limitations of an individual and the far larger perspective of the British Parliament, Cunningham puts forth in a sense his own philosophy of imperial rule in a longish footnote. He appreciates men like Murray, Clerk, Ochterlony and Wade whose common purpose, despite their differences, was to enhance the general reputation of their countrymen. They gave adaptation and flexibility to 'the rigid unsympathising nature of a foreign and civilized supremacy'. Nevertheless, the best of subordinate authorities remained immersed in details and occupied with local affairs and they were liable to be biased by views which promised immediate and special advantage. Even the ablest among them resembled 'merely the practical man of the moment'. Their 'partial or one-sided' notions influenced the supreme authority intent upon some great undertaking. Cunningham goes on to add:

> The author has thus, even during his short service, seen many reasons to be thankful that there is a remote deliberative or corrective body, which can survey things through an atmosphere cleared of mists, and which can judge of measures with reference both to the universal principles of justice and statesmanship, and to their particular bearing on the English supremacy in India, which should be characterized by certainty and consistency of operation, and tempered by a spirit of forbearance and adaptation.[101]

General Allard had gone to France and returned to India by way of Calcutta in 1836. He had with him a document which accredited him to Ranjit Singh. It was assumed by the English that Allard would present this document to the Maharaja only if his life was in danger and then he could ask the British for help. When he presented the document to Ranjit Singh, the British authorities looked upon it as deceit 'or the vain effrontery of their guest'. Cunningham does not appreciate this attitude of the British authorities who had in a sense betrayed Ranjit Singh as their ally. Stating the French view on the authority of General Ventura, Cunningham goes on to add:

> Of the two views, that of the English is the less honorable, with reference to their duty towards Runjeet Singh, who might have justly resented any attempt

on the part of a servant to put himself beyond the power of his master, and any interference in that servant's behalf on the part of the British Government.

Sir Claude Wade thought that the real purpose of Louis Philippe was to open a regular intercourse with Ranjit Singh and to obtain a political influence in the Punjab. The Maharaja consulted the British political agent and ignored the overtures.[102]

Cunningham was not alone in looking upon Major Broadfoot as offensively aggressive. 'It was generally held by the English in India that Major Broadfoot's appointment greatly increased the probabilities of a war with the Sikhs'. There was an equally strong impression that if Clarke had remained the British agent, 'there would have been no war'. The letters of Broadfoot clearly showed that he was hostile to the Sikhs.[103] In support of his criticism of Lord Hardinge, Cunningham says that it was 'a common and just remark at the time' that if Lord Ellenborough had remained Governor-General, 'the army would have taken the field better equipped than it did'.[104] Cunningham underscores the treachery of Lal Singh and Tej Singh but he also makes the significant statement that had 'the English been better led and better equipped, the fame of the Sikhs would not have been so great as it is, and the British chronicler would have been spared the ungracious task of declaring unpleasing truths'.[105]

Finally, with reference to the Governor-General's idea of handing over Kashmir to Raja Gulab Singh, Cunningham says that if the English had indicated that they had desired to see Gulab Singh to remain minister and not bothered about Lal Singh, it was highly probable that 'a fair and vigorous government would have been formed, and also that the occupation of Lahore, and perhaps the second treaty of 1846, need never had taken place'.[106]

XII. IN THE FINAL ANALYSIS

If we turn to the three aspects of J.D. Cunningham's *History of the Sikhs* mentioned earlier, we can see that his sympathy with the Sikhs is quite palpable. There can be no doubt that he wrote with great empathy for Sikhism and the Sikhs. It is equally clear that he was a good historian: he was thoroughly familiar with the works published on the Sikhs, he tried to collect more evidence, including evidence coming from Sikh sources, and he interpreted all this evidence in the light of his understanding of European, Indian and Sikh history. His criticism of the British authorities in India was both explicit and implicit in his treatment of Anglo-Sikh relations. Significantly, he was addressing the British nation as against the East India Company. In all the three aspects he was different from his predecessors. His work proved to be a classic.

For half a century after the publication of his *History,* Joseph Davey Cunningham was totally ignored by the British authorities in India as a historian. He would be rediscovered in the twentieth century, but by the Indian historians.[107]

NOTES

1. Joseph Davey Cunningham, *A History of the Sikhs,* New Delhi: Rupa & Co., 2003 (third impression), Preface to the First Edition, pp. xvii-xviii.
2. Ibid., pp. xviii-xix.
3. Ibid., Preface to the Second Edition, pp. xv-xvi.
4. Ibid., p. xvi.
5. Gianeshwar Khurana, *British Historiography on the Sikh Power in Punjab,* New Delhi: Allied Publishers, 1985, pp. 122 & n.8, 123, 129, 130, 131, 132, 146.
6. Henry Lawrence Collection, British Library, London Eur. Mss. F. 85 (44).
7. Ibid.
8. *Calcutta Review,* vol. XI, no. XXII, January-June 1849, pp. 523-58. Gianeshwar Khurana states that Hardinge had persuaded G.W. Kaye to write this review: *British Historiography on the Sikh Power* in *Punjab,* p. 146.
9. *The Times,* 6 April 1849, p. 7.
10. *The Athenaeum,* 24 March 1847, p. 293.
11. Cunningham, *A History of the Sikhs,* pp. 1, 9, 10, 11, 13, 14, 15, 18.
12. Ibid., pp. 19-28.
13. Ibid., pp. 29-31.
14. Ibid., pp. 32-6.
15. Ibid., p. 36.
16. Ibid., pp. 37-41.
17. Ibid., pp. 42-5.
18. Ibid., pp. 46-8.
19. Ibid., pp. 48-50.
20. Ibid., pp. 50-2.
21. Ibid., pp. 53-7.

22. Ibid., pp. 58-68.
23. Ibid., pp. 68-80.
24. Ibid., pp. 81-3.
25. Ibid., pp. 83-7.
26. Ibid., pp. 87-8.
27. Ibid., pp. 89-93.
28. Ibid., pp. 94-9.
29. Ibid., pp. 99-101.
30. Ibid., pp. 101-3.
31. Ibid., pp. 103-10.
32. Ibid., pp. 111-18.
33. Ibid., pp. 119-20.
34. Ibid., pp. 121-30.
35. Ibid., pp. 131-3.
36. Ibid., p. 133.
37. Ibid., pp. 134-7.
38. Ibid., pp. 137-41.
39. Ibid., pp. 146-66.
40. Ibid., pp. 166-71.
41. Ibid., pp. 171-2.
42. Ibid., pp. 173-7.
43. Ibid., pp. 177-83.
44. Ibid., pp. 184-5.
45. Ibid., pp. 185-9.
46. Ibid., pp. 190-5.
47. Ibid., pp. 195-7.
48. Ibid., pp. 198-201.
49. Ibid., pp. 201-4.
50. Ibid., pp. 206-11.
51. Ibid., pp. 215-22.
52. Ibid., pp. 224-7.
53. Ibid., p. 227.
54. Ibid., pp. 229-37.
55. Ibid., pp. 237-41.
56. Ibid., pp. 241-4.
57. Ibid., pp. 245-6.
58. Ibid., pp. 252-60.
59. Ibid., pp. 261-3.
60. Ibid., pp. 264-70.
61. Ibid., pp. 271-3.
62. Ibid., pp. 274-9.
63. Ibid., p. 280.

64. Ibid., pp. 281-2.
65. Ibid., pp. 282-6.
66. Ibid., pp. 287-90.
67. Ibid., pp. 291-4.
68. Ibid., pp. 294.
69. Ibid., pp. 295-7.
70. Ibid., pp. 297-301.
71. Ibid., pp. 303-4.
72. Ibid., pp. 307-15.
73. Ibid., pp. 315-17.
74. Ibid., pp. 317-20.
75. Ibid., pp. 321-5.
76. Ibid., pp. 325-6.
77. Ibid., Appendix VIII.
78. Ibid., Appendix IX.
79. Ibid., Appendix X.
80. Ibid., Appendix XI.
81. Ibid., Appendix XII.
82. Ibid., Appendix XIII.
83. Ibid., Appendix XIV.
84. Ibid., Appendix XVII.
85. Ibid., Appendix XVIII.
86. Ibid., Appendix XIX.
87. Ibid., Appendix XX.
88. For James Mill and Mountstuart Elphinstone, see J.S. Grewal, *Muslim Rule in India: The Assessments of British Historians*, New Delhi: Oxford University Press, 1970, chapters V & IX.
89. Cunningham, *A History of the Sikhs*, p. 21n.
90. Ibid., p. 37n.
91. Ibid., p. 75n.
92. Ibid., p. 83n.
93. Ibid., p. 103n.
94. Ibid., p. 104n.
95. Ibid., p. 108n.
96. Ibid., p. 110n.
97. Ibid., pp. 131-2n.
98. Ibid., p. 172n.
99. Ibid., p. 177n.
100. Ibid., pp. 180-1n.
101. Ibid., pp. 144-5n.
102. Ibid., p. 219n.

103. Ibid., p. 290n.
104. Ibid., p. 297n.
105. Ibid., pp. 304-5n.
106. Ibid., p. 322n.
107. Gianeshwar Khurana, *British Historiography on the Sikh Power in Punjab*, p. 148 & nn. 122, 123. Completing a century of reprints, Rupa & Co. published a reprint of Cunningham's *History of the Sikhs* in 2002.

PART TWO

Under the Crown

CHAPTER SIX

Colonial Administrators and Army Officers on the Sikhs

The civil and military officers of the Punjab and the Indian army justified the annexation of the Punjab and admired its progress under the British rule. They were more interested in the contemporary Sikhs as their subjects than in the past achievement of the Sikhs. They had no serious interest in the Sikh religion but they could see its relevance in the changing contemporary situations. They relied largely on the works published earlier but interpreted their evidence selectively from their own perspectives. By far the most important writer of the late nineteenth century was Lepel Griffin who was interested primarily in the Sikh rulers and the former members of the Sikh ruling class. There were others in the early twentieth century who chose to write on the Sikhs as a martial people relevant for the Indian army. With the socio-religious awakening among the Sikhs, the British officers began to look at the political developments among the Sikhs as relevant for colonial politics and as possible collaborators. We propose to take up the concerns of these three sets of writers in separate sections.

I. THE SIKH RULERS AND THE SIKH CHIEFS

The nature of Lepel Griffin's interest is clearly reflected in the titles of his works: *The Punjab Chiefs* (published in 1865), *The Law of Inheritance to Chiefship as Observed by the Sikhs Previous to the Annexation of the Punjab* (published in 1869), and *The Rajas of the Punjab* (published in 1870). The interest of these works is centred in the Sikh rulers who had become subordinate to the British, and in the former *jagirdars* of the kingdom of Lahore who were still important in the Sikh social order. It was with them that the British administrators were chiefly concerned as rulers of the Punjab. Information on their present and past, therefore, was administratively useful. In fact, after the uprising of 1857-8, when the Punjabis provided crucial support to the British, 'the chiefs and families of note' came to be looked upon as the main prop of the colonial rule in the Punjab. The most historical of these works was *The Rajas of the Punjab*; it justified British policies and measures with regard to the princely states brought under British 'protection'.

Griffin became the obvious choice for writing on Ranjit Singh in the 'Rulers of India' series. Rather unexpectedly, he decided to treat the Sikh faith in his *Ranjit Singh* published in 1892. His reasoning is interesting. Ranjit Singh's career and character could not be properly understood without an understanding of the Sikh theocracy which, in turn, could not be appreciated without an understanding of the Sikh religious system. Therefore, 'a few words on the principles of the creed as expounded by Nanak' became necessary.[1]

Griffin observed that the Sikhs revered the *Adi Granth* 'as a direct revelation' to the same degree as Christians and Muslims regarded their respective scriptures. However, there was nothing novel or original in the compositions of Guru Nanak to entitle them to greater attention than the compositions of Kabir 'from whom it would seem that Nanak derived the greater part of his inspiration'. The dogmas of the *Adi Granth* did not differ appreciably from 'the esoteric teaching of Hinduism in its more ancient and purer form'. Guru Nanak desired to raise Hinduism from the degraded forms of superstition and polytheism. He was 'a reformer in the best and the truest sense of the word'. Sikhism could be placed very high among the philosophical religions of the civilized world because of its 'noble ideal' and its 'practical and social meaning'.[2] In his general view of Sikhism, Griffin relies upon his predecessors, except Cunningham.

For describing the Sikh faith in detail, Griffin summarizes Ernest Trumpp. The main point in the doctrine taught by Guru Nanak, according to Griffin, was the unity of the Supreme Being. Whatever the epithet used for the deity, Guru Nanak's God is incomprehensible, invisible, uncreated, eternal, and alone possessing any real existence. He is the root of all things, the primary cause from which all human beings and all nature have evolved. 'This doctrine is Pantheism, which in the *Granth* coexists with an exalted Theism'. On the whole, the teaching of the *Granth* is that the whole universe emanated from the divine essence. 'Nature apart from God is a shadow, a delusion, and a mirage'. Nevertheless, the more theistic view in the *Granth* represents God as altogether distinct from the creatures which emanate from Him. Polytheism is discountenanced in the *Granth* but Guru Nanak did not denounce 'the polytheistic theory' and accepted myriads of inferior deities. He also accepted the Hindu doctrine of transmigration, which in the *Granth*, is tantamount to 'denial of free will'. Paradoxically, escape from transmigration, promised by the Guru, attracted disciples to his creed.[3] With his better command of the English language, Griffin could summarize Trumpp rather neatly.

Exemption from the common lot of death-and-rebirth could be acquired by invoking the sacred Name. As in Calvinism so in Sikhism. There was a contradiction between the idea of predestination and the idea of free will. This logical contradiction was resolved in practice by not insisting on either the one or the other.

> Such fatalistic doctrine was not dwelt upon, for the obvious reason that the power of the Guru would diminish in proportion as it was understood that he could not relieve his followers from the burden of destiny, and it was generally taught that by religious exercises and by patient reception of the teaching of the Guru, the heart would be inclined to righteousness and a choice would thus be allowed which might counteract the fatalistic decree which was supreme over human will.

Reverence for the Guru and obedience to him is the 'most important doctrine of the Granth'.[4]

For Griffin, the teaching of Guru Nanak was highly ethical. Besides enjoining the practice of ablution, of giving alms and of abstinence from animal food, Guru Nanak denounced evil-speaking, unchastity, anger, covetousness, selfishness and want of faith. The position of the householder was honourable in the eyes of Guru Nanak and he 'strongly discouraged the idea that any special virtue was to be gained by the ascetic life'. True religion consisted not in the outward ceremonial but in the state of the heart; meditation was possible without retreating to the wilderness or the seclusion of a monastery. From this viewpoint, both the Udasis and the Akalis appeared to infringe the teaching of Guru Nanak. The *Adi Granth* is hostile to Brahmans. Though Guru Nanak did not directly enjoin the abolition of caste, he admitted disciples from all castes. The successors of Guru Nanak made little change of any religious or social importance till we come to Guru Gobind Singh 'whose teaching and book of conduct were a new starting-point for the Sikhs and did more than the authority of Nanak to form them into the military nation which they afterwards became'.[5]

Griffin pays a good deal of attention to the Sikh theocracy, devoting a whole chapter to its discussion, but virtually to refute J.D. Cunningham. 'Maharaja Ranjit Singh was so completely a product of the Sikh theocracy', says Griffin, 'and so embodied the spirit of the Khalsa, that no account of his character and career would be complete without a description of the religious system which had so powerful an effect upon the Jat cultivators of the Punjab in the eighteenth and the first half of the nineteenth century'. Griffin refers to the translation of the *Adi Granth* by Ernest Trumpp for a fuller understanding, telling the reader that the accounts of Sikhism given by Cunningham and Wilson were 'slight and defective'. For Griffin, as for Trumpp, the contents of the *Adi Granth* were 'involved, incoherent and shallow', with no relevance for understanding the Sikh theocracy. For determining the military and political constitution of the Sikhs the writings of Guru Gobind Singh were far more relevant. Guru Gobind Singh was more inclined to polytheistic ideas than to the refined pantheism of Guru Nanak; he abolished the custom of caste and promulgated a new faith with its own rules of conduct regarding dress, food and worship. He taught self-aggrandizement to his followers. A few of their customs were peculiar to the Jat Sikhs, relating to marriage and inheritance, that gave rise to the problem of succession and legitimacy. Sikh political activity and polity could be understood better in these terms. 'Ranjit Singh was merely the most successful among the robber chiefs, *primus inter pares*'.[6]

In a separate chapter on the state of Punjab at the time of Ranjit Singh's birth, Griffin outlines the development of the eighteenth century, largely in terms of *misls* or confederacies 'in which a number of robber chiefs agreed, after a somewhat democratic and equal fashion, to follow the flag and fight under the general orders of one powerful leader'. Of the six *misls* between the rivers Sutlej and Indus, the Sukarchakia was more important only than the Nakkai; it was less important than the Ahluwalia, Bhangi, Kanhiya and the Ramgarhia.

This supposed fact can be, and has been used to highlight Maharaja Ranjit Singh's achievement, but in the pages of Griffin it serves more to imply that he was an upstart.[7]

The confederacies fought against each other more often than against the common enemy. All Sikhs were theoretically equal, but in actual practice, 'the law of force, the keen sword and the strong hand were the foundations upon which the Sikh society, as indeed every other powerful society in the world, was founded'. The enthusiasm of the Sikhs for their faith gave them a certain dignity, and to their objects and expeditions almost a national interest. But their depredations were not always directed against others. 'No man could consider his land, his house, or his wife secure unless he was strong enough to defend them'.[8]

Griffin did not remain untouched by the high tide of imperialistic assumptions and attitudes. Talking of the administration of Maharaja Ranjit Singh, for example, he observes that his evidence 'will suffice to point the moral to those in India and in England who try to persuade the world that the British rule is harsh and oppressive'. He goes on to add: 'Anarchy, famine and rapine have been replaced by orderly and just administration, under which every man enjoys his own in peace, none making him afraid. Where, out of twelve shillings worth of produce, the Sikh government took six from the peasant as rent, the British government takes only two or one'.[9]

Griffin expresses himself strongly not only about the achievement of the British in India but also in his denigration of their predecessors:

If England were to withdraw her protecting hand, if she were to proclaim the *Pax Britannica* at an end and retire from India in a cowardly denial of her duties and her rights, is there any one of knowledge who doubts that in a very short time anarchy would return once more; that Sikhs, Marathas, and Afghans would again be fighting . . . that the children would again be tossed on the sword and spear-points of invaders, and the Punjab maidens again become the prey of the ravisher, while the light of flaming villages would nightly illumine the ancient walls of Delhi and Lahore?[10]

With these sentiments, it was a small matter for Griffin to justify British policies towards the successors of Maharaja Ranjit Singh. The downfall of the Sikh monarchy in his opinion was chiefly due to the fact that the authority of the Maharaja 'drew no part of its strength from the inherent respect of the people for an ancient house'. His dynasty could survive only if his successors had inherited his character and ability. The hands of the British were clean in the matter of Sikh wars and in the annexation of the Punjab, 'forced unwillingly upon them by the fierce and uncontrolled passions of the Sikh chiefs and people'. The question of supremacy over northern India 'must have occurred sooner or later'. It was fortunate both for England and the future of the Sikh people that the provocation and attack came from Lahore and not from Calcutta. In sum, the Lahore state eventually 'fell from inherent weakness and not from any designs on it by the British government'.[11]

It may safely be suggested that Griffin's primary concern was not to understand the Maharaja or his times but to present his case on the basis of plausible evidence. The political career of Ranjit Singh is narrated in three chapters, the last three, of Griffin's book. He felt confident that, having earlier worked on the 'Rajas of the Punjab' and the 'Chiefs of the Punjab', he did not have to look for any fresh evidence. In a chapter of 14 pages, an outline of the 'early conquests' of the Maharaja is given in relation to the Sikh chiefs. To his relations with the British up to the Treaty of Amritsar is given a chapter of 15 pages. Griffin was inclined to think that the Maharaja saved his cis-Sutlej territories by his 'great sagacity' and 'shrewdness' in making a show of war. It was only imperfectly known to the British at that time. In the last chapter, longer than the other two taken together, the 'later conquests' of Maharaja Ranjit Singh are outlined as his victories chiefly over his Muslim rivals and enemies. Griffin's comment on the whole of this political process is very telling: the kingdom of Ranjit Singh was founded on 'violence, treachery and blood'.[12]

In the opening sentence of his book, Griffin tells us that there is no more notable and picturesque figure among the chiefs who rose to power on the ruins of the Mughal empire than Maharaja Ranjit Singh. We may be sure that he did not mean it as a compliment. The Sikh monarchy was Napoleonic not only because of the brilliancy of its success but also because of the completeness of its overthrow. The bulk of Griffin's book is devoted nevertheless to aspects other than the politics of Maharaja Ranjit Singh. After the introductory first chapter, he takes up the position of the Sikhs under the British rule: their population, its composition and its numbers and distribution, underlining the importance of the Jats. The reason is not far to seek.

Of the many warlike races subject to the Queen Empress, the Sikhs indisputably take the first place as thoroughly reliable, useful soldiers. The backbone of the Sikh people were the Jats, 'by far the most important of all the Punjab races'. The British rulers of India would be wise to 'encourage and stimulate the military spirit of the Sikhs and employ them on active service on every opportunity, whether the campaign be in Europe, Asia, or Africa'.[13]

Griffin notices that even half a century after his death, Maharaja Ranjit Singh was 'a favourite subject' with the ivory painters of Amritsar and Delhi, by whom he was ordinarily represented in middle or old age. Baron Hugel's penportrait of the Maharaja was striking but unprepossessing. It described the Maharaja after he was worn down by his paralytic seizure in 1834. In his youth he was '*the beau ideal* of a soldier, strong, spare, active, courageous, and enduring'. Even when he was feeble and paralysed his dominance over his brilliant court of fierce and turbulent chiefs was complete. He was endowed with some of the most important characteristics of greatness. But of respectable virtues he had no part. He was selfish, false and avaricious; grossly superstitious, shamelessly and openly drunken and debauched.[14]

'Every age and people', says Griffin, 'have their own standard of virtue; and what is to-day held to be atrocious or disreputable may, one hundred years hence, be the fashion'. This, however, is not meant to mitigate the harshness of Griffin's judgement. 'Violence, fraud and rapacity were the very breath of the nostrils of every Sikh chief'. The Maharaja was very susceptible to feminine influence. Griffin does not miss the opportunity of dwelling on the notoriety of Maharani Jindan and the illegitimacy of Maharaja Dulip Singh in connection with the favourite women of the Maharaja. If Dulip Singh was not set aside in 1846, it was only because the British thought of the convenience of the *status quo*.[15] A whole chapter of Griffin's book is devoted to the character and personality of Maharaja Ranjit Singh to contrast the little good that was in him with the immensity of his foibles.

A chapter on the court of Maharaja Ranjit Singh is given on the assumption that a description of the courtiers would be more interesting to the reader than political activity and enable him to know what manner of a man the Maharaja was. His criterion for selecting his courtiers and servants was their competence and loyalty. They were allowed to squeeze the peasantry, provided they were not disloyal to the Maharaja. Not genuinely religious, he could afford to be liberal in employing Sayyids, Brahmans and Rajputs in preference to Jats. 'Against the cultured intelligence of these races what had the poor Jat cultivator, as stupid as his own buffaloes, to oppose?' They could do no more than keep the plough straight, or fight. That was why the Generals of the Maharaja were often Jats, while in council he gave preference to Brahmans, Rajputs, Khatris and Muhammadans like the Faqir Brothers; Jamadar Khushal Singh and his nephew Tej Singh; the Rajas Gulab Singh, Dhian Singh, Suchet Singh and Hira Singh; Raja Dina Nath; Misar Ralia Ram and his son Sahib Dayal; Hari Singh Nalwa; and Bhais Ram Singh, Gobind Ram and Gurmukh Singh.[16]

In a chapter on the army and administration of Maharaja Ranjit Singh, Griffin begins by saying that the military genius of the Maharaja was not so much shown in his Generalship as in the skill with which he raised a powerful, disciplined and well-equipped army, after realizing the superiority of the British military organization. The change was largely facilitated by the employment of European officers like General Ventura, General Allard, Colonel Court and General Avitabile, and a host of others. They were not entrusted with supreme command. The Punjabi generals too were very eminent, like Mohkam Chand, Diwan Chand, Fateh Singh Kalianwala, Nihal Singh Atariwala, Buddh Singh Sandhanwalia, his brother Atar Singh, and Hari Singh Nalwa. Griffin gives the figures of the army of Ranjit Singh, indicating numbers and expenditure for its various categories, and the pay of the soldiers.[17] He has little to say about the civil administration, which for him was a 'simple process of squeezing out of the unhappy peasant every rupee that he could be made to disgorge'. The only restraining factor was either the fear of revolt or the abandonment of cultivation. Custom duties were heavy, and the merchants were treated with utmost insolence and oppression. In support of his contention, Griffin simply quotes several extracts from the reports of the British settlement officers.[18]

The inclusion of Maharaja Ranjit Singh in the 'Rulers of India' series became at best a left-handed compliment. By yoking his interpretation to imperialistic purposes, Griffin made it worse than left-handed, not only for Maharaja Ranjit Singh but also for the whole Sikh movement and the Sikh people.

II. THE SIKHS AS A MARTIAL PEOPLE

Interest in the Sikh wars was reflected in G.B. Malleson's *Decisive Battles of India from 1746-1849 Inclusive,* published in two volumes by James Madden from London in 1888. In 1897, General Sir Charles Gough and Arthur D. Innes published from London their *Sikhs and the Sikh Wars: The Rise, Conquest and Annexation of the Punjab State.* Their account of the rise of the Sikhs and the establishment of a sovereign state under Ranjit Singh is rather brief and is based entirely on secondary sources. The account of the Sikh wars, however, is rather detailed and based on official records, official dispatches, and the diaries of Lord Hugh Gough, among other sources. Charles Gough was a nephew of Hugh Gough. This could be the source of inspiration for the former to write on the wars and also to defend his uncle who was the commander-in-chief during the Sikh wars. In any case, the authors take notice of the storm raised in England and of the angry voices raised in the British Parliament against the rashness of Gough in the battle of Pherushahr which resulted in a heavy loss of British lives. The Chairman of the Board of Directors, Sir Archibald Galloway, justified Gough's rashness with the following remark: 'Complaints are made that Sir Hugh Gough at Ferozeshah took the bull by the horns. But, gentlemen, in this case the bull was all horns'.

Furthermore, though Lord Hardinge had placed his services as a general officer under the commander-in-chief, at Pherushahr he overrode the chief's orders and waited for Sir John Littler's force. After the battle, 'the fate of India trembled in the balance'. If the Sikh army under Tej Singh had acted promptly, the British army could have been completely destroyed. But Tej Singh was ignorant of the actual state of affairs in the British camp. Thus, 'ignorance' exonerated Tej Singh from the charge of 'treachery'. Gough and Innes appreciate Lord Hardinge's decision to keep up the Sikh state in the same relation with the British as 'the Lahore State' under Ranjit Singh, and not to annex it or to bring it under the subsidiary system. They go on to add, nevertheless, that Jammu and Kashmir were sold to Gulab Singh, the Jalandhar Doab was annexed, the minor Maharaja was kept on the throne with a council of Sikh *sardars,* and a British Agent was appointed 'to exercise control over the council, and to act as the mouthpiece of the British Government'.

The Lahore state after the war can hardly be described as 'independent'. Nor was it strong. The strength of the Khalsa army was reduced to 20,000 infantry and 12,000 cavalry, without the artillery that had been used against the British.

The mutual trust so vital to the condominium was weakened by the removal of Maharani Jindan from the Punjab in 1847, the misunderstanding of the situation in Multan in 1848, and the over-reaching behaviour of the British agent at Hazara. The top executive in the British government came to favour annexation. It was Lord Dalhousie's strong and deliberate opinion that 'a wise and sound policy dictated that the British Government use all rightful opportunities of acquiring territory'. This in any case was his policy towards the Lahore state (which was actually a British protected state at the time). He announced rhetorically at a public banquet in Calcutta on 5 October 1848: 'Unwarranted by precedents, uninfluenced by example, the Sikh nation has called for war, and, on my words, sirs, they shall have it with a vengeance'. General Gough purposely waited for a general rising of the Sikhs and prepared a force competent enough 'to crush the whole Sikh nation in arms'. His strategy ensured decisive victory for the British. Annexation of the Lahore state was more than adequate compensation for the British losses in the second Sikh war. Thus, the authors of the *Sikhs and the Sikh Wars* not only defended and quietly glorified General Gough but they also justified all the measures adopted by the British government in relation to the Sikhs.[19]

General Sir J.H. Gordon published *The Sikhs* in 1904. He tells us that when the strength of the British empire was represented by soldiers from all parts of the world at the coronation of Edward VII, the soldierly bearing of the Sikhs won the admiration of all who beheld them. Therefore, a short sketch of their origins and their rise to power was necessary for understanding their transformation into loyal and hearty subjects of Queen Victoria. Without any pretension to research, General Gordon based his book on the published works of the writers like John Malcolm, W.L. M'Gregor, G.C. Smyth, J.D. Cunningham, Ernest Trumpp and Muhammad Latif. There are no specific references to any of the sources used and there is no bibliography. The book is a simple and straightforward narrative of what General Gordon understood of the Sikh faith and Sikh history.

As presented by General Gordon, Guru Nanak was essentially a reformer who wished to see Hinduism and Islam to be shorn of all accretions to regain theistic purity and to be reconciled to each other. Nonetheless he was the only Hindu reformer who established a national faith. To the religious base provided by Guru Nanak, political objective and organization were added by Guru Gobind Singh, imparting a distinct national character to the Sikhs. He thus laid the cornerstone of that national edifice which was raised by Ranjit Singh a hundred years later in the Punjab on the ruins of the Mughal empire to emancipate the land of his ancestors from thralldom and persecution. It is interesting to note that this basic thesis is the one presented by J.D. Cunningham.

The best qualities of the Sikhs as the subjects of Queen Victoria are seen by General Gordon as springing from their race and faith. He identifies 'Sikhs' with 'Jat Sikhs' more emphatically than any other writer before him. In fact, he regards even the Gurus as Jats. The racial characteristics of the Jats, who were descended from the Scythians, were totally different from those of the rest of the people in India; with their tenacious energy and militancy they had braved the storms of centuries and preserved continuity with the past. Wars and anarchy had failed to destroy their pristine traits. They fought stubbornly against the British and they fought gallantly for the British. As they had fought for their Guru and their Maharaja, so did they fight for Queen Victoria. Loyalty was in their blood.

A palpable and tendentious oversimplification of Sikh history is carried to its logical end by General Gordon in his assessment of the Sikhs as the subjects of the British empire. Guru Tegh Bahadur prophesies the replacement of Mughal rule by the British. Guru Gobind Singh is made to say in a devout prayer that loyalty to one's sovereign is a divine gift. The Raja of Nabha mentions three duties of a true Sikh: to live according to the precepts of the Gurus, to aid the state, and to pay personal homage to the suzerain. Baba Sir Khem Singh Bedi expresses his conviction that peace, justice and tolerance for which the Sikhs had fought in the past were realized by the British in India and, consequently, the Sikhs had placed themselves entirely at the service of the British. According to General Gordon's understanding of the situation, the policy of the British Indian government to enlist the Sikhs as soldiers and officers in increasing numbers was amply justified. Sikh history presented by him in *The Sikhs* appears to subserve a particular view of the Sikhs he wanted to project.[20]

Before the end of the nineteenth century, handbooks for the Indian army had begun to appear, like Captain R.W. Falcon's *Handbook on Sikhs for Regimental Officers*, published by the Pioneer Press from Allahabad in 1896. It takes into account Sikh religion, manners and customs of the Sikhs, and their history before the period of British rule. More popular was Captain A.H. Bingley's *A Class Handbook of the Indian Army*, first published by the Government of India from Simla in 1899 and then from Calcutta in 1918 as *Sikhs: A Handbook for Indian Army*.[21] It was reprinted by the Punjab government in 1970.

The first chapter of Bingley's book, 'history and origin', gives a brief history of the Jats and the Sikh movement. The political history of the Khalsa is briefly narrated up to the Sikh wars. On the termination of the first war, the British government of India decided to utilize for the native army the splendid fighting material which the conquest of the Punjab had placed at their disposal'. Such was the impression made by 'the stubborn valour displayed by the Sikhs'. Orders were issued in 1846 for the formation of two Sikh battalions at Ferozepore and Ludhiana. Besides these special corps, the commandants of regular regiments were directed to enlist 200 Sikhs for every battalion. The order was carried out, but only partially. In 1849, the policy was extended further: a corps of Guides and a brigade of all arms were formed for police and general purposes on the border. Composed largely of the former soldiers of the Khalsa', they served as the nucleus of the Punjab Frontier Force.[22]

The spirit of the Khalsa, which had been humbled by the defeats, was aroused 'at the thought of a combat between Sikhism and Islam'. This is how Bingley refers to the role of the Sikhs during 'the Sepoy Mutiny'. The Frontier Force earned distinction before Delhi, and the 14th and 15th Sikhs rendered splendid service in Oudh and the North-West Provinces. The reorganization of the Bengal Army which followed 'the Mutiny' led to a complete change in its composition. The Hindustanis were replaced by Sikhs, Dogras, Punjabis and Pathans. Bingley refers to 'the heroic band of Sikhs' who defended Saragarhi in the following words: 'True to the martial instinct of their faith, they died to a man at their posts, covering themselves with glory, and giving imperishable renown to the grand regiment to which it was their privilege to belong.'[23]

The classification and distribution of the Sikhs is the subject of the second chapter. Bingley talks of the limits of the Sikh recruiting ground, the differences between a Malwa and a Majha Sikh, and the races among the Sikhs who represent 'the great military brotherhood of the Khalsa'. Bingley writes about these Sikhs with an eye to the degree of their orthodoxy as the Khalsa, assuming its relevance for recruitment purposes. Included among them are Jats, Brahmans, Rajputs, Khatris, Aroras, Labanas, Mahtons, Sainis, Kambohs, Kalals or Ahluwalias, Tarkhans or Ramgarhias, Nais, Chhimbas, Jhiwars, Kahars or Chuhras, and Dakhani Sikhs.[24]

Bingley's third chapter relates to religion, customs, sects, and religious festivals. For religion, he talks of the change brought about by Guru Gobind Singh in the dispensation of Guru Nanak and his successors. He talks of 'modern' Sikhism in terms of its conformity to and diviation from the norms of the Khalsa of Guru Gobind Singh. He talks of the decay of Sikhism after the annexation and its revival after 1857. He refers to the encouragement received by Sikhism from the Indian army which keeps 'the advantages of the faith prominently before the eyes of the recruit-giving classes'. The influence of Hinduism over the Sikhs was not good in Bingley's eyes. He talks of popular religion and superstitions saying that these were common to both Sikhs and Hindus. The Sikh sects distinct from the Khalsa were Nanak-Panthis or Sahajdharis, Sultanis, Udasis, Niranjanis, Ram Raiyas, Nirmalas, Devi Sikhs, Gulabdasis, Nirankaris, and Namdharis or Kukas. The Akalis or Nihangs represented the Khalsa of the days of Guru Gobind Singh. Bingley gives the ceremonies related to birth, initiation, marriage and death. The required leave for birth ceremonies was three days and for marriage ceremonies ten. He gives Sikh and Hindu festivals, fairs, and places of pilgrimage in a tabulated form, mentioning the name and the time of occurrence and adding remarks. The relevance of the information in this chapter for the purposes of the British officers is quite obvious.[25]

The fourth chapter relates to characteristics of the Sikhs. In the case of the Jats, both racial characteristics and religious faith determined their traits as soldiers. The influence of the Sikhs faith was more important in their case. One of the highest qualities of Sikhism is its power to improve the social condition of its adherents, by removing the 'trammels of caste'. Even the despised chuhra or sweeper 'at once becomes valiant and valued soldier', and imbued with the spirit of his martial faith, loses all memory of his former degraded calling. However, Bingley gives far more space to the Jat Sikhs than to any other category of Sikhs for two main reasons: their larger numbers and their superior qualities as fighters.[26]

The last chapter in Bingley's *Handbook* is on recruitment in which he talks of the relative merit of the Majha and Malwa Sikhs as soldiers, and extends this evaluation to the Doaba Sikhs. However, the Sikhs of the submontane tracts were to be recruited very carefully, if at all. In Appendix A, Bingley gives a table of the Sikh districts and *tahsils* with their value as recruiting grounds. He goes into some detail of the process and method of recruitment. The presence of a British officer was regarded as a great advantage, though it was seldom possible to spare one. The cooperation of *zaildars* and *tahsildars* was necessary. Bingley gives a list of principal fairs held in each Sikh recruiting district in an appendix. It may be seen that whereas the last chapter and the appendices were directly related to recruitment, the other chapters were meant to facilitate good selection for recruitment.

In *The Sikhs of the Punjab*, published from London in 1921, R.E. Parry refers to Bingley's *Sikhs* as a 'handbook'. Parry's own book belongs to this category, with a large number of photographs and drawings. The first chapter relates to 'religion and history'. In five more chapters, Parry talks of the characteristics of the Jat Sikh, village life of the Sikhs, the economic geography of the Punjab, the control of environment, and agriculture and industries. Thus, only a very small part of his book relates to Sikh history and religion.[27]

In the Preface to his handbook Parry states its object: to give the general public some idea of 'one of our most loyal Indian sects', the Sikhs, who played 'no small share in upholding the traditions of the British Empire in no less than six theatres of war'. Parry believed that 'the Sikh character' was moulded at least partly by their environment, especially in the Ludhiana district where 'some of the finest types of Sikh manhood are met with'. That is why Parry has given a lot of attention to the environment in his account of the Sikhs. The characteristics of the Jat Sikh are summed up in three words: stubbornness, patience, and courage. 'These qualities are both hereditary and derived from environment and occupation'. Parry goes on to describe the various traits of the life of the Jat Sikhs, like their love of litigation, their dress, their tendency to hoard money, their fondness for travel, the condition of their women and children, their food, their gurdwaras and granthis, their ceremonies for betrothal, marriage and death, their sports and games, and their fairs and festivals. All this interesting information relates to the years of the First World War.[28]

Similarly, the information on 'Sikh village life' is very interesting. Apart from its physical appearance, Parry talks of the categories of people who provided various kinds of services for the landholders, the *dharamsala* which served both religious and social functions, the school, the local administration with its *lambardar*, *patwari*, and the *panchayat*. In the chapter on the physical geography of the Punjab and its climate, Parry offers a comparison of the Malwa, Majha and the Doaba Sikhs in terms of their physical and moral traits and their mutual attitudes. In the chapter on agriculture and industries, Parry talks of the laws of inheritance among the Malwa and Majha Sikhs, natural vegetation and crops, agricultural implements, minerals and manufactures, and domestic and wild animals. The Sikh was essentially a landowner and an agriculturist. Talking of population and density, Parry does not give any figures for the Sikhs. He also makes the general observation that the people of the Punjab were coming under Western influence.[29]

Parry refers to the growing need of recruitment for the Indian army during the War when new regiments were being quickly formed. 'The majority of people in England are not entirely ignorant of the procedure and methods adopted to obtain recruits for the high-caste regiments of the Indian Army.' Many parts of the Punjab were 'over-recruited' so that few were left to till the land. The 'white officers' aided by 'native officials' established central depots for recruitment on an unprecedented scale. Parry describes the procedures on the basis of his own experience in the Ludhiana district. He refers to the role played by the Sikhs in the then recent war with Afghanistan, and closes his book with the observation that the British army officers transformed the rough and rude material into superb soldiers. Clearly Parry seeks appreciation of the British public for the role of the British army officers like himself.[30]

Parry's book is interesting and in a way useful for the historians of the Punjab and the Sikhs during the early twentieth century but his account of the precolonial 'religion and history' of the Sikhs is of no use, not simply because it is very short and based entirely on secondary sources but chiefly because it contains a number of howlers which are Parry's own contribution. For him, the Sikhs are 'an order of militant Hindu dissenters' even though he refers to Macauliffe's work in the bibliography. Among the '5 Ks', *khanda* is mentioned instead of *kirpan*. Sikhism relapses into an ascetic tendency under Guru Angad. The *Granth Sahib* contains 'the writings of Nanak, with extracts from the works of Kabir and Ramanand'. Guru Arjan is imprisoned by 'the Emperor Sahangas'. Guru Hargobind was 'little more than a mercenary soldier'. Guru Tegh Bahadur was 'little more than a robber chief'. Guru Gobind Singh was sent by the Mughal emperor 'to put down the rebellious Mahrattas'. Incidentally, Parry reinforces the view that Sikhism had been kept alive in the Indian Army by fostering Guru Gobind Singh's tenets, especially in the Sikh regiments which had done much to preserve the traditions of the Khalsa. With his limited concern with the contemporary Sikhs and that too for a specific purpose, Parry had little interest in the Sikh past.

III. THE SIKHS AS COLLABORATORS

C.H. Payne was not exactly an admirer of the Sikhs as a community, though he was appreciative of their martial spirit which the British had wisely nurtured through their policy of recruitment. Payne's admiration was reserved for the British rulers of India whose policies he consistently justifies. He favours a collaboration between the British rulers and their Sikh subjects to the political advantage of the British, and the economic, social and cultural advancement of the Khalsa.

In *A Short History of the Sikhs,* which has the appearance of a text-book, Payne makes a brief statement on the political, social and religious situation of Baba Nanak, a short statement on his life, and refers for detail to Trumpp's *Adi Granth* or Macauliffe's *The Sikh Religion*. He presents Baba Nanak as essentially a reformer rather than the originator of a new faith. From a merely religious fraternity the Sikhs developed into a strong power due to the hostility of the Mughal emperors during the seventeenth century. Guru Gobind Singh instituted the armed Khalsa and abolished the caste system; the number of his followers began to increase. His democratic teaching and the military zeal of his followers brought him into conflict with the hill chiefs first and then with the Mughals. He was obliged to leave Anandpur. Before his death, he vested Guruship in the Khalsa and the *Granth Sahib*.[31]

Payne outlines the known events of the eighteenth century relating to the political struggle of the Khalsa and gives the familiar description of their government and political organization in terms of the *misl* system of the late eighteenth century. In the absence of a common danger the Sikh chiefs began to quarrel among themselves. The greatest of the Sikh leaders, Maharaja Ranjit Singh, welded the warring Khalsa into a nation. Payne refers to him as 'the national hero of the Sikhs', outlines his early rise to power, the expansion of his dominions, his administration and his court, and the last few years of his life. Mildly appreciative of Ranjit Singh, Payne refers to 'the shameless profligacy' of Maharani Chand Kaur and 'the vices and intrigues of her court'. The state was drifting from decline towards anarchy under the ministry of Hira Singh, ending in the murder of Jawahar Singh.[32]

The internal anarchy sapped the vitality of the state and the omnipotence of the army of the Khalsa led to its destruction. The attitude of the troops towards the British became increasingly hostile. This was due to their belief that the British were only waiting for a favourable opportunity to add the kingdom of Lahore to their dominions. For detail of the battles of the first Sikh war Payne refers to the work of Charles Gough and Arthur D. Inns, the work of R.S. Rait, and the biography of Hardinge. Payne tries to exonerate Tej Singh from the charge of treachery but in 'the honours of that great and glorious fight' at Sabraon he gives equal share to the Sikhs. He outlines the post-war developments till the treaty of Bhairowal which brought the kingdom of Lahore under British protection. This treaty led to a spirit of discontent practically in every section of the Sikh community. If there was no rebellion it was due to the Sikh belief that the term of British protectorate would expire at the end of Maharaja Dulip Singh's minority in 1854.[33]

For the second Sikh war, Payne adds Major Herbert Edwardes' *A Year on the Punjab Frontier* to his sources; he gives a detailed account of 'the last and gallant struggle of the Sikhs for national independence'. But this was their second blunder and it was greater than the first because it was irretrievable. Payne closes his account of the second Sikh war with the statement that the Sikhs gave no thought to the future.

They were conscious only that an alien hand was usurping their powers, restricting their liberties, and disbanding their armies, and in this they saw, not the future greatness of the Khalsa, but only their present humiliation. They had asked for the protectorate; but as soon as it became an accomplished fact, and they saw a British officer virtually in possession of the throne of Ranjit Singh, they repented of what they had done. The measures of the new administration galled them, not because they were strange or irksome, but because they were imposed by a foreign hand. The remedy seemed worse than the disease; and hence the Sikhs banded themselves together to oppose the only system which could possibly save their kingdom.[34]

The system to which Payne refers was the British protectorate under which the Punjab would have become peaceful and prosperous, as it became after the annexation. Payne's chapter on 'Annexation and After' starts with a statement that Hardinge and Dalhousie wanted the kingdom of Lahore to continue but the second Sikh war made such a course impossible. Payne shared Dalhousie's conviction of the 'expediency, the justice, and the necessity' of annexation. Soon after the annexation, the story of the Sikhs merged 'with the history of British India'. Many Sikhs were enrolled in the army and their prestige was revived. The Sikh civilians benefited from the material and cultural progress under the British rule. There were 30,000 Sikh troops now, and they constituted the 'flower of the Indian army'. With the establishment of Singh Sabhas, the Khalsa College at Amritsar, and the Chief Khalsa Diwan, the Khalsa had become more influential and stronger now than ever before.[35]

Major A.E. Barstow's *The Sikhs*, published in 1928, is introduced with the statement that, for many reasons, the Sikhs were of special interest 'to any body engaged in maintaining British rule in India'. His book can be seen as a revised and enlarged version of Bingley's *Sikhs*, but with a difference. The last chapter of the book is on 'recruitment', with a list of principal places where fairs were held. In another list given as an appendix are tabulated districts, states and *tahsils* with their relative value as Sikh recruiting grounds and the sub-divisions of Jat Sikhs in each. Some of the other chapters in the book have obvious relevance for this primary concern, like the one on the 'distribution of Sikhs' and 'ethnographic glossary of castes'. Very similar in purpose is the one on the 'Sikh sects and subdivisions of Jat Sikhs'. The chapter on 'customs' also has in focus the customs which were 'in practice amongst orthodox Sikhs' who were believed to be martial. Similar in interest is the chapter on 'characteristics and matters pertaining to village life'. No account of the Sikhs could be complete without reference to agriculture, says Major Barstow, because of its importance for 'the sepoys enlisted in the Indian Army'.[36]

One of the remaining four chapters of Barstow's book is introductory. The other three are on the 'origin of Sikhism and its history', 'salient features of the lives of the Gurus', and 'the Sikh religion'. Even for these chapters the purpose is the same: to put together all relevant information on 'the Sikh, his origin, history, customs, characteristics and modern developments which those, under whose charge or command he may be, it is so essential to maintain'. At the centre of Major Barstow's concern is evidently the Sikh soldier. His brief account of 'the origin of Sikhism and its history' ends with the Sikh wars. After the first war, orders were issued in 1846 for the formation of two Sikh Battalions at Ferozepore and Ludhiana because the Government of India was 'impressed by the stubborn valour displayed by the Sikhs'. To utilize this splendid fighting material for the army, the policy of giving military employment to the Sikhs was extended further in 1849 when 'the former soldiers of the Khalsa' came to form 'the nucleus of the Punjab Frontier Force'. In 1857-8, the Sikhs earned fame and distinction before Delhi, and rendered splendid service in Oudh and the North-Western Province. The Hindustanis were replaced largely by the Sikhs and the Punjabis in the Bengal army after 1858. Major Barstow goes on to add that it would be difficult to select 'a more striking example of military constancy and devotion' than that of the heroic band of Sikhs who defended Saragarhi. True to 'the martial instincts of their faith' they died to a man at their posts, 'covering themselves with glory, and giving imperishable renown to the grand regiment to which it was their privilege to belong'.[37]

Major Barstow refers to the famous prophecy of Guru Tegh Bahadur that a power rising in the west would sweep the Mughal Empire into dust, and goes on to add that the Sikhs never forget these prophetic words. This accounted largely for their loyalty to British rule. The sweepers who rescued the mutilated corpse of Guru Tegh Bahadur were admitted into the Khalsa, with the title of Mazhabi or faithful. Their descendants were recruited to the Pioneer regiments of the British Indian army. Guru Gobind Singh's decision to discard caste distinctions gained for him the support of the lower orders whom he inspired with military ardour 'with the hope of social freedom and national freedom'. Barstow saw the leaders of the Gurdwara Reform movement as following the example of Guru Gobind Singh 'in making use of religion as a stepping stone to political power'. Also, the tendency of modern Sikhism was 'to move away from Hinduism and popular religion. However, a number of petty superstitions were more or less in vogue amongst the Sikh population.'[38]

Major Barstow gives more attention than his predecessors to political developments among the contemporary Sikhs. He talks of the decay of Sikhism after the British conquest and the state of Sikhism in the late nineteenth and the early twentieth century under a number of sub-headings: influence of Hinduism on Sikhism, the pro-Hindu and the orthodox Sikh parties, present-day Sikhism and Hinduism, Sikhism in the Indian army, the Singh Sabhas and the Lahore and Amritsar Khalsa *diwans*, the Chief Khalsa Diwan, the Khalsa College, politico-religious movements of the twentieth century, the depressed classes movement among the Sikhs, effect of the Arya Samaj, the Ghadar movement, the disorders of 1919, Sikh non-cooperation, the Sikh League, the Gurdwara Reform movement, the Nabha affair, the Sikh Gurdwaras Act, and the Kirti movement which was closely associated with the Naujawan Bharat Sabha founded at Amritsar in 1926.[39]

There is hardly any doubt that this interest was closely related to his primary concern. Retired Sikh soldiers and non-commissioned officers had participated in the Gurdwara Reform movement, which made Sikh loyalty suspect in the eyes of the British. Barstow's analysis of the situation recognized the presence of both nationalist, or even revolutionary Sikhs, and loyal Sikhs in the Punjab. Therefore, he states that the modern developments among the Sikhs were difficult to understand and appraise aright. Nevertheless, his well considered view was that both 'overweening confidence' and 'undue suspicion' must be avoided. Not only statesmanship but also accurate knowledge of the history, characteristics, and general aspirations of the Sikhs was needed to guide, encourage or restrain them 'in their efforts to improve themselves'. The civil and military authorities could join hands for this common purpose.

Major Barstow was aware of the support which the Sikhs had provided for the British empire. In less than ten years from the second Sikh war, the British and the Punjabis 'saved India from the Mutineers'. Since then, more than ever, had India looked to the Punjab for a very large part of its fighting force. At the outbreak of the Great War the Punjab supplied half the Indian soldiers in the army. Of these, 33,000 were Sikhs. Their proportion gradually increased in the successive years of the war. From August 1914 to November 1918, no less than 88,924 Sikh combatants were enlisted. After the War, this fine record was somewhat overclouded. The common people were swayed by religious feelings and sentiments. It is often difficult to detect the division between religion and politics. A knowledge of one will assist to an understanding of the other: 'a comprehension of both should be within the radius of vision of every officer'.[40] Barstow's analysis of contemporary developments was meant to serve this purpose.

George Batley Scott in his *Religion and Short History of the Sikhs* gives less than 40 pages to 380 years of Sikh history from 1469 to 1849, and 50 pages to 80 years of colonial rule. In his Preface he refers to his memories of the second Sikh war when he was five years old, and of 1857-8 about eight years later, before he began to serve in the North-Western Frontier Survey party, having Sikh escorts and seeing Sikh regiments in camp and in action. He found Cunningham's *History of the Sikhs* useful for their early history, and for the years from 1913 to 1920 he looked upon Sir Michael O'Dwyer's *India As I Knew It* as the highest authority. In the Introduction to his book Scott refers to the Sikhs coming into contact with the British in 1839-42 as reluctant allies, as fierce and sturdy opponents of the British in 1845 and 1849, and then as brave and loyal soldiers under the Union Jack in many countries. More recently, however, a few of them were misled by 'designing politicians and anarchists' to become 'political malcontents and rioters'. Nevertheless, Scott believes that a close and strong bond of fellowship existed between the Sikh soldiers and their British officers.

It was natural therefore to ask how they differed from 'the hundred and one other races of India?'[41]

Scott goes into the background and context of the Sikh movement on the lines of J.D. Cunningham. He talks of Guru Nanak, called 'Nanak Chand', as the founder of a new group of followers on the basis of ideas which appealed principally to the peasantry; he spoke in Punjabi, and wrote in Gurmukhi. Within fifty years of his death he was proclaimed to be a divine emanation, a son of God, and numerous miracles were attributed to him. Scott cites the example of Panja Sahib.[42]

Guru Nanak was succeeded by nine Gurus, some nominated by their predecessors and some elected by the community. Several sons and disciples of the Gurus who were not appointed or elected ended in forming small communities of their own, like the Udasis, Minas, Ramdasis, Bedis, Sodhis, Bandapanthis and others, 'many at present in conflict with the Akhalis'. Furthermore, the peaceful sect was gradually transformed into 'a military power, largely owing to persecution'. That Scott had not read even his Cunningham carefully is evident from his statement that Guru Angad compiled the *Adi Granth*. Bhai Gurdas openly taught that Guru Nanak was 'a divinely commissioned successor of Mahomed and all the prophets', sent by God as a regenerator of mankind; and Guru Hargobind was said to have raided Lahore and abducted the daughter of its Muslim governor.[43]

The best account of Guru Gobind Singh (1675-1708), according to Scott, was given in the *Daswen Guru ka Granth* which was written by him. It was always placed with the *Adi Granth* in Sikh temples. Durga appeared in a vision and Guru Gobind Singh presented his sword to her; she told him that the Sikh religion would prevail throughout the world, but not in his lifetime. Guru Gobind Singh created the mystical body of the Khalsa to destroy the Turks. The Khalsa were distinguished from all others by the obligatory '5 Ks.' Victorious over minor chiefs, the Guru's cavalry was defeated again and again by the 'disciplined infantry' of the Mughals supported by artillery. Before his death, Guru Gobind Singh declared that the line of the ten ordained Gurus would end with him: 'Henceforth wherever five of the Khalsa meet, there will my spirit and that of all the Gurus, be with them.' Banda, a devoted follower of the Guru, led the remnant of the Khalsa to the Punjab, waited for the death of Aurangzeb, and then during the struggle for supremacy among the rival princes he burst with fire and sword over the province of Sirhind. His main objective was revenge. Otherwise, the Khalsa could have pushed on to Delhi and changed 'the whole course of Indian history'.[44]

At this point Scott talks of the Sikh sects in a separate chapter: the Akalis, the Sahajdharis, the Udasis, and the Minas. He brackets with them the Nikalsenis or the Sikhs who believed that General John Nicholson was 'a divine incarnation possessed by the spirit of Guru Nanak'. All the 'sectarian' Sikhs claimed to be and registered themselves as Sikhs but they were considered heretical, being as much Brahmanical Hindus as Sikhs. Scott goes on to state that the Sikhs barely exceeded 3 million in a total population of 25 to 30 million in the Punjab. They were found in all parts of India, and in Burma, South-East Asia, China, Canada and the United States of America. Scott is talking of the contemporary Sikhs here.[45]

The Mughal empire was tottering in the early eighteenth century due to internal revolts and external invasions. During the time of Ahmad Shah Durrani's invasions, Khalsa bands began to take possession of tracts close to their centres of activity. Jassa Singh, a distiller, organized the *Dal* of the Khalsa as 'a belligerent nation'. The Afghan governors were expelled and the Khalsa established their own confederacies called *misls*. The struggle for supremacy among them established the leadership of Patiala among the states between the Jamuna and the Sutlej and that of Ranjit Singh (called Bhanghi by Scott) on the other side of the Sutlej due to his wise diplomacy and able leadership. Organizing his forces on the Western models, he drove the Afghans back to their own mountains. His death in 1839 was followed by five years of strife and anarchy. Rani Jindan encouraged the Khalsa army to cross the Sutlej in order to get rid of them. They were defeated in two wars with the English.[46]

The Punjab under the East India Company and the Crown is presented by Scott in five chapters, covering five phases: 1849-59, 1859-1915, 1915-17, 1917-19, and 1920-30. The Sikhs figure in these chapters as a part of the general developments under the British rule. In the Board of Administration (1849-59), Henry Lawrence sympathized with the fallen *sardars* and great landholders, and John Lawrence preferred to make the peasantry loyal. Several regiments of infantry, cavalry and military police were recruited from the late Khalsa armies for the defence of the frontier. During the great mutiny, the Sikh princes supported the British, and more Sikhs were enlisted in the army. Both the princes and the people proved equally loyal to the British, justifying the policies of both Henry and John Lawrence.[47]

For half a century then, India enjoyed internal peace, security and prosperity, not experienced before for over two millennia. Sikh soldiers under British officers distinguished themselves in wars in China, Abyssinia, Afghanistan, Egypt and Burma. In general, the military spirit of the Jat Sikh peasantry gradually weakened. 'It would probably have died out entirely, and the whole community have reverted to Brahmanical Hinduism, but for the British officers and the Sikh states'. Scott refers to schools and colleges founded by the government and Christian missions. The members of the Sikh aristocracy soon saw the benefit of this new education for their sons. With the help of the enlightened rulers of the Sikh states and Sikh *sardars* and *babas*, a Khalsa College was founded at Amritsar. A great Sikh revival followed the publication of Macauliffe's translation of the *Granths*. After the retirement of Sir William Rattigan, who was elected President of the Committee for the Khalsa College (showing that the movement was at first pro-British), disputes arose in the Committee and the government took over the management, which was later denounced by the Sikhs 'as an interference with religion'.[48] Scott refers to the founding of the Indian Association (which came to be known as the National Congress) encouraged by Hume and Wedderburn. All 'English speaking mal-contents and eloquent gas-bags' entered the National Congress and 'paved the way for denunciation of all things British'. Sedition began to spread among the town mobs. Disaffection was expressed in vernacular and Anglo-vernacular press by educated Indians, especially members of the legal profession. After the partition of Bengal, assassination and violence began to be openly preached and this was followed by the actual murder of some English officials. Discontent and disturbances did not remain confined to Bengal. The more violent and abler demagogues saw that 'if a spirit of revolt could be started among the more virile natives of the north, especially Sikhs and other Punjabis, and a mutinous spirit among the Indian troops, much might be gained'. In this context Scott refers to the Arya Samaj which was meant to revive Hinduism on the basis of the Vedas, and to denounce Western civilization. It soon got infected with extremist political opinions, and its influence spread to the Punjab. Lajpat Rai and Ajit Singh, members of the Arya Samaj and noted demagogues, encouraged disaffection among the agitators against the Punjab government over increased assessments and protective regulations for the sale and mortgage of land. Rioting was accompanied by violent attacks on the police. The two leaders were promptly arrested and deported to Burma. Had they been kept out of India, much future bloodshed might have been avoided. Their releases resulted in their greater boldness and impunity.[49]

The Morley-Minto reforms satisfied the moderates for a time but not the extremists. Drastic measures had to be adopted to ensure peace. The Coronation Darbar at Delhi in 1911 demonstrated the loyalty of the princes to His Majesty (the King-Emperor), but rescinding of the partition of Bengal showed to the whole of India that even a Viceroy and Secretary of State could be coerced. 'The *Iqbal* was shaken if not lost'. The revolutionaries resorted to violence again. Meanwhile, a revolutionary society, called Ghadar, was formed at San Francisco where Indian malcontents had found a ready field for their teachings among Sikhs and other Punjabis who were more or less discontented with immigration laws and other government regulations. They could abuse all things British and spread 'accusations against the Punjab Government with no fear of contradiction or consequences'. Scott recounts the activities of the Ghadarites on the lines of Michael O'Dwyer's *India As I Knew It*, reinforcing his viewpoint as a die-hand imperialist.[50]

When Turkey joined the war, Muslim agents and Indian conspirators in Afghanistan and India began to spread reports that England was bent on destroying the Khilafat. This was the time for Hindus, Muslims and Sikhs to strike for liberty. But the Indian princes, especially the Sikh states and the Muslim rulers, were loyal to a man. The large Muslim population of the western Punjab was the most loyal of all the peoples of India. The bulk of the Sikh and Hindu Punjabis also were content under British rule. From the western Punjab 200,000 Muslims were recruited, and 30,000 Sikhs joined the army out of a total community of about 3,000,000. Practically the whole of the army was composed of agriculturists, and very few townsfolk joined up even in the Punjab cities.[51]

However, Montague, the Secretary of State for India, brought a resolution before the House of Commons in May 1917 to extend self-government in India. In November he visited India and presented to the Viceroy 'his wildcat scheme of Dyarchy and Representative Government'. According to this scheme, all the most important new appointments were to go to those who had openly or secretly opposed the government, and not to the men who had done good service to state. Montague and his colleagues, thus, threw away in a year the results of half a century of hard work. They conveyed the impression that the British government was determined to make over the country to Indians, and it approved of the doings of the revolutionaries. There was agitation against the Rowlatt Bills. Early in March 1919, when Montague's 'friend' Gandhi ordered a non-violent cessation of all work, there were violent disturbances. Instead of calling a few companies of British troops, the civil authorities opened a conference with the leaders of the rebellion. The outbreak had been skilfully organized in the Punjab. 'The populace were exhorted, in posters and speeches, to murder all Englishmen and dishonour all English-women, and to get rid of these devils'. The worst crimes and disorders occurred at Amritsar. In this holy city of the Sikhs, 'few, if any, Sikhs took part'. Brigadier General Dyer was placed in command and ordered to suppress the riots. Taking prompt action against a mob at Jallianwala Bagh he killed 300 men at the spot. All rioting in the Punjab ceased in four or five days. 'The Punjab was saved, and with it, India, and thousands of British and Indian lives'. The Sikhs were pleased with Dyer and the loyal section of the townfolk of Amritsar invited Dyer 'to join their community and initiated him with the sacred Pahal rites'.[52] We may add that this 'loyal section' was actually the Sikh manager of the Golden Temple who took all important decisions in accordance with the express wishes of the British authorities. In the present case, the suggestion could have come from Michael O'Dwyer.

Scott goes on to state that the bulk of the Sikh gentry and peasantry, and even townsfolk, on the whole had remained loyal to the British government up to the close of 1919. After the introduction of the Montague-Chelmsford reforms, however, a feeling was engendered among leading Sikhs that the only way to share the loaves and fishes of the office was to join in the opposition to all government measures.

To start a campaign against the government, they needed funds. The wealthy *mahants* of the various temples of the sectarians, and of the Golden Temple, could be removed from their positions of control and management for this purpose. The leaders of the Sikh revival around 1900 had expressed dissatisfaction with the management and functioning of the gurdwaras but the government, as usual, declined to interfere in religious disputes. In 1920, when the taunts and flatteries of the leading seditionists were proving to be effective, the Sikh leaders took possession of the Akal Takht, 'the most sacred portion of the Golden Temple'. The self-constituted Shiromani Gurdwara Prabandhak Committee (SGPC) decided to take forcible possession of all gurdwaras. Scott goes on to outline the main developments of the Gurdwara Reform or the Akali movement: forcible possession of the shrine of Tarn Taran, the gruesome tale of what happened at Nankana Sahib, the agitation for the keys of the Golden Temple, the *morcha* at Guru Ka Bagh, and the Jaito *morcha*. Scott reiterates O'Dwyer's view that the Raja of a Sikh state was 'forced' by the government to abdicate for 'misconduct', and that the SGPC had no right to interfere with the affairs of the Nabha state.[53]

The agitation of the Akalis was followed by five years of peace. Then, once again, the pernicious body called the National Congress held a conference at Amritsar 'in a style more suitable to a Viceroy's Durbar Camp'. A republic was proclaimed and 'a National Independence flag' replaced the Union Jack. 'But for the police, loyal Sikhs would have wiped out the camp'. Scott goes on to ask what good is a government that will not govern? That will not let its loyal officers do their duty, that will reward sedition and play cat-and-mouse with criminals? What is the use of a British steel frame if two-thirds of the steel supports are replaced by unreliable material and the other third not firmly fixed in their places? The Simon Report was awaited with wildest hopes by comparatively few 'enemies' and a far larger number of 'misguided patriots'. It was awaited with deepest misgivings by millions of Indian patriots. The activites of the National Congress made it clear that the Indian 'intelligentsia' of towns were absolutely unfitted for self-government or Dominion Status: The future welfare or ruin of the Indian Empire hung in the balance. Was loyalty or sedition to be rewarded? Were the leaders of the loyal peasantry or the revolutionaries to be placed in power? Was the British steelframe to be strengthened or scrapped? In sum, were the English or the Brahman lawyers to rule?[54]

Scott's sympathies, evidently, were with the English rulers of the empire and their loyal subjects. Despite minor deviations, the Sikhs fitted into the scheme of collaboration between the foreign rulers and the native subjects to perpetuate the British empire. Scott was more concerned about the empire than about the Sikhs.

IV. GENERAL CHARACTER

With the exception of Lepel Griffin, the administrators and army officers of the colonial period used published works for their books on the Sikhs. The use even of these secondary sources was not thorough. For most of them, Malcolm first and then Trumpp provided ready information and ideas. A few of them in the early twentieth century relied partly on Cunningham and Macauliffe. They were interested primarily in the contemporary problems of politics, government and administration, both civil and military. They tended to justify British rule in the Punjab as much as its annexation, praising all administrative measures and underlining peace and prosperity. In this situation, it was not possible for them to take any serious interest in Sikh politics of the past, and far less in Sikh achievement. Their interest in the early Sikh tradition was marginal. Their general attitude towards the Sikhs was anything but sympathetic. They had little appreciation for the Sikh tradition.

NOTES

1. Sir Lepel Griffin, *Ranjit Singh*, Delhi: S. Chand & Co., 1957 (rpt.), pp. 39, 51. This book was published in the Rulers of India series, Oxford: Clarendon Press, in 1905. Griffin's *Law of Inheritance* and his *Rajas of the Punjab* were published by the Punjab Printing Co., Lahore. His article on 'Sikhism' was published in the *Great Religions of the World*, New York, 1901. The only other administrator of the nineteenth century who took interest in Sikhism and Sikh history was Robert Needham Cust. His essays on various subjects, written between 1840 and 1903, were published by Trubner & Co., London, as *Linguistic and Oriental Essays*.
2. Griffin, *Ranjit Singh* (1957), pp. 51-2.

3. Ibid., pp. 52-5.
4. Ibid., pp. 55-6.
5. Ibid., pp. 56-8.
6. Ibid., pp. 39-69.
7. Ibid., pp. 70-83.
8. Ibid., pp. 83-4.
9. Ibid., pp. 144-51.
10. Ibid., p. 152.
11. Ibid., pp. 218-19.
12. Ibid., p. 219.
13. Ibid., pp. 9-18.
14. Ibid., pp. 88-91.
15. Ibid., pp. 94-5, 106-10.
16. Ibid., pp. 111-31.
17. Ibid., pp. 132-44.
18. Ibid., pp. 144-50. For Lepel Griffin, see also S.K. Bajaj, 'Lepel Henry Griffin', *Historians and Historiography of the Sikhs*, ed. Fauja Singh, New Delhi: Oriental Publishers, 1978, pp. 134-53.
19. *The Sikhs and Sikh Wars* was published by A.D. Innes & Co., London, 1897. J.S. Grewal, 'Sikhs and the Sikh Wars', *Encyclopaedia of Sikhism*, ed. Harbans Singh, Patiala: Punjabi University, 1998, vol. IV, pp. 183-5.
20. General John J.H. Gordon, *The Sikhs*, Punjab Languages Department, Patiala, 1970 (first published by Blackwood and Sons, London, 1904). Bingley's work was first published as *A Class Handbook for the Indian Army* (Simla: Government of India, 1899) and then as *Sikhs: A Handbook for Indian Army* (Calcutta, 1918). For Gordon, see also S.K. Bajaj, 'Gordon, Bingley and Payne', *Historians and Historiography of the Sikhs*, pp. 186-90.
22. A.H. Bingley, Captain, *Sikhs*, Punjab Languages Department, Patiala, 1970 (rpt.), pp. 1-36, 143-52. For Bingley, see also S.K. Bajaj, 'Gordon, Bingley and Payne', *Historians and Historiography of the Sikhs*, pp. 190-3.
24. Ibid., pp. 39-68.
25. lbid., pp. 69-120.
26. Ibid., pp. 121-42.
27. R.E. Parry, *The Sikhs of the Punjab*, Patiala: Punjab Languages Department, 1970 (rpt.), pp. 20-61.
28. Ibid., pp. 62-86.
29. Ibid., pp. 87-103.
30. Ibid., pp. 104-22.
31. C.H. Payne, *A Short History of the Sikhs*, Patiala: Language Department, Punjab, 1970 (rpt.), pp. 11-43. This work was first published by Thomas, Nelson & Sons, London, 1904.

32. Ibid., pp. 44-165.
33. Ibid., pp. 166-94.
34. Ibid., pp. 195-210.
35. Ibid., pp. 211-26.
36. A.E. Barstow, *The Sikhs: An Ethnology*, New Delhi: B.R. Publishing Corporation, 1985 (rpt.), pp. 1, 165. This book was first published as *Sikhs: Handbook for the Indian Army* in 1928.
37. Ibid., pp. 15-17.
38. Ibid., pp. 84-91.
39. Ibid., pp. 86-91.
40. Ibid., pp. 18-55.
41. George Batley Scott, *Religion and Short of the Sikhs 1469 to 1930*, New Delhi: Nirmal Publishers and Distributors, 1986 (rpt.), pp. 9-12. This book was first published by the Mitre Press, London, 1930.
42. Ibid., pp. 12-19.
43. Ibid., pp. 20-5.
44. Ibid., pp. 27-35.
45. Ibid., pp. 35-7.
46. Ibid., pp. 39-46.
47. Ibid., pp. 47-51.
48. Ibid., pp. 53-6.
49. Ibid., pp. 56-61.
50. Ibid., pp. 66-72.
51. Ibid., pp. 72-7.
52. Ibid., pp. 78-86.
53. Ibid., pp. 87-93.
54. Ibid., pp. 93-6.

CHAPTER SEVEN

Ernest Trumpp
The Adi Granth

I. A WESTERN VIEW OF TRUMPP

N. Gerald Barrier believed that Ernest Trumpp had devoted too much of his time and energy to the study of the Sikhs to deserve 'less than a critical new appraisal'. The Punjab officials were keen to know more about the Sikh faith to deal with the Sikhs. On their initiative, the Secretary of State for India approached Trumpp in 1869 to discuss the project of translating the *Adi Granth* and the *Dasam Granth*. He was teaching oriental languages at Tubingen, the university from which he had earlier received a degree in language and linguistics, and also passed some theological examinations. Under the aegis of the Christian missionary enterprise in Karachi, he had produced several studies on Sindhi and Pashto. If the India Office needed the services of a competent scholar, Trumpp needed the patronage of India Office to pursue his own interest further. He accepted the assignment and began to work on manuscripts in the India Office.[1]

Trumpp realized the difficulties involved in his task and felt the need to consult Sikh scholars. The India Office enabled him to visit the Punjab. He arrived in Lahore in 1870 but only to find that few scholars were able to assist him in translation. According to Barrier, many Sikh scholars themselves were in a confused state at this juncture. They lacked clarity on whether Sikhism was a separate religion or only a sect within Hinduism. There was no established 'theological tradition' among the Sikhs. Trumpp adopted 'an aloof attitude' and 'egotistically felt that he knew more about the real meaning of the *Adi Granth*, at least linguistically, than those revered for their ancient knowledge of the holy book'. Rather than cooperating with Sikh scholars, he decided to take help from 'Hindu *munshis*' and members of the Anjuman-i Punjab who 'helped locate and verify the authenticity of various manuscripts'. By April 1872 he had become frustrated as much with the intricacies of the material as by illness, and left for Europe. After protracted negotiations with the Secretary of State for India, he made arrangements to publish his *Adi Granth* in 1877. It contained a lengthy introduction on Sikhism and the Sikh Gurus together with the translation of approximately one-third of the *Granth* 'with extensive footnotes and commentary'.[2]

Barrier thought that Trumpp was not interested in 'the religious tenets of the Sikhs'; his main concern was with 'a linguistic study' of the Sikh documents made available to him. His 'religious intolerance' and Germanic orientation predisposed him to be unsympathetic towards 'things Indian', including Sikhism. He appears to have assumed from the outset that 'Sikhs were Hindus' though somewhat differentiated by certain symbols. He also believed that Sikhism is a waning religion, that will soon belong to history. In so far as he depended on Indians for assistance, Trumpp's work reflects the 'intellectual milieu' of the period. Despite the gratuitous remarks which dot his translation and introduction, he made important contribution to the study of Sikhism because his book constituted the first serious translation of the *Adi Granth*. It had a long-term influence and even today it is considered 'a useful source as one version of Sikh theology'. Barrier suggested that the tendency to look down upon Trumpp required rethinking.[3]

II. THE EARLY SIKH TRADITION

Ernest Trumpp's *Adi Granth* was the first important work on the Sikhs to appear after the annexation. He had worked in India as a linguist before but his knowledge of Sanskrit and north Indian languages proved to be inadequate for the task. With help from some native scholars in the Punjab, Trumpp prepared a grammar and a dictionary of his own. Having prepared his tools, he went through the entire *Granth* once, and returned to Europe. He worked distractedly for a few more years before he sent his work for publication.

Trumpp's *Adi Granth* was a monumental work. His translation covers more than 700 folio pages in print, though he did not translate the whole *Granth*. The reason he gives for his deliberate omissions is interesting: the Sikh *Granth* was 'incoherent and shallow in the extreme'. It was painful for Europeans to read even a single *Raga*. Therefore, it would have been 'a mere waste of paper to add also the minor *Ragas*, which only repeat, in endless variations, what has already been said in the great Ragas over and over again, without adding the least to our knowledge'.[4] This remark about variations adding little to our knowledge is rather obtuse.

Trumpp did not confine himself to translation. He added five 'introductory essays' of about 140 pages to the translation: one each on the life of Guru Nanak, the lives of the other Sikh Gurus, the religion of the Sikhs, the arrangement of the contents of the *Granth*, and its language and metres. Thus, the scope of Trumpp's work is much more than that of a translation. His *Adi Granth* presents in a way an interpretation of the early Sikh tradition. He looked upon his knowledge of the *Adi Granth* as a great advantage over all earlier writers, none of whom in his view had read the *Granth* personally, not even Professor H.H. Wilson.[5]

Trumpp was the first European scholar to study *Janamsakhis* for the life of Guru Nanak. During his stay at Lahore in 1870-2 he had come upon a lithographed edition of the *Janamsakhi* associated with Bhai Bala. He compared it with various other versions in manuscript. He felt convinced that the Sikh tradition concerning Guru Nanak 'could by no means be trusted'. He could detect very few historical facts in 'the rubbish of miraculous and often absurd stories'. The image of Guru Nanak which appeared to emerge from the *Janamsakhis* did not correspond to the image that emerged from his compositions. When Trumpp returned to Europe the authorities of the India Office brought to his notice a manuscript acquired originally by H.T. Colebrooke. The contents of this manuscript and its idiom suggested that it was very old. Trumpp thought that this was 'the fountain' from which all other *Janamsakhis* were largely drawn. He gives a summary of the events of Guru Nanak's life from this *Janamsakhi*, indicating at places how later versions embellished and enlarged the stories. A full translation in English is given. Extracts from other *Janamsakhi* are also given in translation for comparison. Trumpp got the impression that myths about the life of Guru Nanak had already progressed far when the original *Janamsakhi* was compiled. Later versions introduced the supernatural element on a much larger scale and tended to deify Guru Nanak. He was inclined to reject much even from the Colebrooke *Janamsakhi*.[6] This *Janamsakhi* came to be seen as a version of the *Puratan* tradition which became more important than the *Bala* tradition for most of the Sikh scholars.

Trumpp gives the lives of Guru Nanak's nine successors in thirty pages, making use of published works. His account of the Gurus from Guru Angad to Guru Tegh Bahadur is very brief. Even Guru Gobind Singh gets no more than eight pages. His comments on the Gurus reflect not merely his irreverent scepticism but also his desire to mark significant developments. Had Guru Nanak not appointed a successor before his death, his followers would have gradually dispersed and disappeared. Guru Amar Das built a *baoli* at Goindval with eighty-four steps. His verses are 'conspicuous for simplicity and clearness'. Guru Ram Das built the tank called *amritsar,* the temple called Harmandar, and the town called Ramdaspur, giving the Sikhs a fixed central place of worship. 'This was of the greatest importance for the firm establishment of Sikhism'. His verses formed 'the better compositions' of the *Granth* but there was no originality of thought in them. Guru Ram Das chose his son Arjan as his successor, and succession became hereditary, which added greatly to 'the wealth and the authority of the Gurus'. The Sikhs began to look upon them as 'their actual sovereigns'.[7]

For the history of the later Gurus, Trumpp felt specially handicapped by the paucity of sources and the character of the evidence available to him. Nevertheless, he highlighted the degree of transformation before Guru Gobind Singh appeared on the scene. Guru Hargobind was a man of warlike spirit and kept a strong band of armed followers. He entered the service of Jahangir and Shah Jahan before he fought battles against the Mughal administrators. He changed *faqirs* into soldiers, replacing the rosary with the sword. He attracted a large number of warlike Jats as his followers. He thus gave a different appearance to the Sikh community. His successor, Guru Har Rai, joined the rebellion of Prince Dara, giving Aurangzeb the chance to interfere in the affairs of the Sikhs. Guru Tegh Bahadur was taken prisoner on account of his predatory proceedings and executed 'as a rebel against the Government'.[8]

Guru Gobind Singh planned in the early years of his Guruship to avenge himself on the murderers of his father, to subvert the Muhammadan power, and to found a new empire. He invoked the Goddess at Naina Devi through a ceremony that involved human sacrifice. On his return to Anandpur he asked his followers to offer their heads for sacrifice. The five who offered themselves were given the baptism of the true religion (*sachche dharm ki pahul*) with water in which sugar was stirred with a two-edged dagger. They were given the name 'Khalsa', signifying that they were 'the Guru's own special property'. The epithet 'Singh' was added to their names. Whoever accepted this baptism was required to observe the Khalsa *rahit,* including the '5 Ks.' The caste system was abolished altogether and people from all castes were admitted to the order of the Khalsa on a footing of equality. The men of lower orders, among whom the Jats were predominant, felt attracted to the Khalsa, while the upper caste people decided to remain aloof. The latter, referred to as 'Sikhs', differed 'very little from the Hindus'. Guru Gobind Singh compiled a *Granth* in 1696. Its greater portion was 'made up by court poets'. It was meant to instill a new spirit in the Khalsa. Trumpp's account of Guru Gobind Singh's battles is brief, and rather confused. He then refers to the removal of the Masands who had become 'a regular plague to the Sikhs'. After this, Guru Gobind Singh went to the Deccan where he virtually invited attack from a Pathan and subsequently died deliberately by bending a strong bow. He did not succeed in his objective of overthrowing the Mughals, but he contributed substantially to their downfall by creating 'a distinct nation of fanatical soldiers'.[9] Trumpp's account of the Gurus makes little advance over those of his predecessors. And has all their shortcomings.

III. RELIGION OF THE SIKHS

Trumpp's 'sketch' of the religion of the Sikhs starts with a general observation on the Sikh doctrines. Guru Nanak was not 'an independent thinker', and he did not deliberately start a new religious sect. He followed the Hindu philosophy of his day in all essential points, and he was particularly indebted to Kabir whose writings in the language of the people were accessible to the unlearned masses. The obligation which Guru Nanak and his successors owed to Kabir is acknowledged by the inclusion of his compositions in the *Granth* compiled by Guru Arjan. Guru Nanak's successors did not deviate from his doctrines. These doctrines were never called into question after the compilation of the *Granth* which was held sacred 'as an immediate divine revelation'. The innovations introduced by Guru Gobind Singh did not touch the doctrines so much as the practical course of life. If anything, Guru Gobind Singh 'relapsed in many points' again into Hinduism, being a special votary of Durga.[10]

The chief point in Guru Nanak's doctrine, according to Trumpp, was the unity of the Supreme Being which had already been familiarized by the Hindu philosophical systems and the *bhaktas* like Kabir. Creation in Sikhism means 'the expansion of the same into a plurality of forms'. There is no teleological principle involved in this conception. There is a gross pantheism in the *Adi Granth* which identifies all things with the Absolute. However, there is also a fine pantheism which makes a distinction between the Absolute and finite beings; it 'borders frequently on Theism'. The supreme in its essence is light which, though diffused into all creatures, remains distinct. Trumpp sees a contradiction between gross pantheism and the conception of the Supreme as a 'self-conscious personality'. Though intellectual and moral qualities are attributed to this personality, Trumpp believed that logically there was no room for such qualities in the system of Guru Nanak.[11]

Emphasis on the unity of the Supreme Being did not mean that Guru Nanak forbade the worship of other gods: they became less important. Guru Nanak took over the whole Hindu pantheon and subordinated it to the Supreme. Only occasionally is idolatry ridiculed in the *Adi Granth*. It would also be wrong to assume that Guru Nanak attempted to unite the Hindu and Muslim ideas about God. He remained 'a thorough Hindu'. If Muslims became his followers, it was essentially because Sufism was nothing but pantheism derived from Hindu sources and only outwardly adapted to the forms of Islam. 'On these grounds tolerance between Hindus and Turks is often advocated in the *Granth* and intolerance on the part of the Turks rebuked.'[12]

The human soul is immortal as the light emanating from the Absolute. The aim of human life is to be reabsorbed in the fountain of light from which the human soul emanated. What keeps the human beings bound to the cycle of death-and-rebirth, and therefore to perpetual misery, is the influence of 'the three qualities' (*gunas*) and *maya*. Only the soul purified from all earthly desires can be reabsorbed in the eternal light. Man cannot attain to liberation unless he is freed from the error of duality. Trumpp brackets Guru Nanak with the *bhaktas* and looks upon their conception of emancipation as a clear proof of the pantheistic character of Sikhism. They all conceived of emancipation in terms of 'total dissolution of individual existence by the reabsorption of the soul in the fountain of light'. This aim is not different from the Buddhist Nirban (*nirvana*). It is the final proof of 'the pantheistic character of the tenets of the Sikh Gurus'.[13]

Guru Nanak announced that the name of Hari was the only means of final emancipation in the Kaliyuga. 'The name of Hari is the universal medicine for mankind; whoever mutters it, is saved in a moment.' The Sikh Gurus took good care to underline that the true Guru alone 'can bestow the right initiation and communicate the mantra of the name of Hari'. Renunciation, austerities, bathing at sacred places, and giving the alms were not denied to be meritorious acts; they were insufficient for gaining complete emancipation. Furthermore, emancipation is restricted to the elect who are chosen not according to their meritorious acts but according to pleasure of Hari. Strict predetermination was mitigated by the contradictory idea that men have the free will to come to the Guru. Neither Guru Nanak nor his successors give any proof of his being the true Guru. But the Guru is 'the only infallible guide' and the mediator between Hari and mankind. Indeed, he is 'the very fullness of Hari himself'. The actual teaching imparted by the Guru for final emancipation was 'contained in a few meagre sentences'. There were only three injunctions: muttering the name of Hari, singing his praises, and getting rid of the 'I'. The pantheistic 'I am that, I am identical with the Supreme' is the culmination of the Guru's teaching. The possibility of obtaining emancipation was there 'whilst being yet in the body'.[14]

Sikhism was not a 'moralizing Deism' for Trumpp. Nevertheless, he enumerates the moral duties enjoined upon the Sikhs: obedience to the Guru, service of the saints, remembering the name and giving alms and practising ablutions (*nam, dan, isnan*), abstaining from falsehood and slander, not coveting another's wife, and purifying the heart from the five vices (*kam, krodh, lobh, moh* and *hankar*). Charity to animals is frequently inculcated in the *Adi Granth* but only on pantheistic grounds. No sanctity is attached to the cow, but abstinence from animal food is inculcated. In due course, the Guru in Sikhism came to be identified with God. The abolition of Guruship by Guru Gobind Singh was good for a free and moral development of the Sikh community. The Sikhs did not become a narrow-minded sect of *faqirs* and developed instead into a political commonwealth because of the sound principle of Guru Nanak that there was no need to abandon secular occupation for emancipation.[15]

The goal of emancipation was not confined to the higher castes; it was made accessible to all men, even to the *chandals.* Guru Nanak received all men as his disciples without any regard to caste, recognizing the dignity of all human beings. However, he did not assail the institution of caste directly. It was left for Guru Gobind Singh to abolish caste altogether for his Khalsa. Though the teaching of the Brahmans and the authority of the Vedas and the Puranas were often reproved, the dignity of the Brahmans as family priests was left untouched by Guru Nanak and his eight successors. It was left for Guru Gobind Singh to prohibit the employment of Brahmans in any capacity.[16] Even if all the ideas expressed by Trumpp were based on his understanding of the *Granth,* it does not follow that they are sound or valid.

IV. TRUMPP'S TRANSLATION

Contrary to Barrier's impression, Trumpp's translation of the *Adi Granth* was seriously flawed. This may be illustrated with reference to his translation of the *Japuji* in detail. Trumpp's explanatory notes and comments constitute the most important part of his translation for an analysis of his treatment of the *Adi Granth.* In his translation there are more than eighty footnotes, which taken together, provide several clues to a proper understanding of his approach. About half of these footnotes refer to the sources of his information or explanation. Nearly four-fifths of these sources are Sikh. Besides a few references to the *Adi Granth* itself, Trumpp refers to 'Sikh' sources in a number of footnotes. However, the only Sikh author named is Mani Singh. There are more than half a dozen references to the Puranas.[17]

In his attitude towards the Sikh authorities, it may be noted that, occasionally, Trumpp passes on the received information to the reader without any comment. More often, however, he does not accept the Sikh interpretation. This does not necessarily lead to a correct interpretation. Even a categorical rejection of the Sikh tradition does not mean that Trumpp's own understanding was adequate or accurate. Sometimes it is not the context but 'grammar' that dictates the sense suggested by Trumpp. His inability to come out with satisfactory explanation makes him rather aggressive. The Sikh commentators are 'all totally unacquainted with the grammar of the old Hindui'. In another case he says: 'The Sikhs are in great trouble about the explanation of these words, and give all possible comments'. There is no hesitation on his part to deviate from the common explanations of the Sikhs which, in any case, are 'mostly ludicrous and pass in silence whatever offers particular difficulties'. Mani Singh held no special authority for Trumpp; he stands bracketed with the other representatives of the Sikh tradition.[18]

We can see that Trumpp accepts or rejects the Sikh tradition in the light of his own understanding of grammar and philology. He tended to prefer Sanskrit connotations of words. His indifferent command over the Punjabi language and its idiom proved to be a serious handicap. He failed quite often to make any distinction between the literal and the metaphorical use of words. The absence of any strong tradition of exegesis of the Sikh scriptures was another serious disadvantage. As a commissioned author, Trumpp was expected to produce an impressive work within a limited span of time. Dissatisfied with his achievement he tended to blame the text or its Sikh interpreters.

There was yet another factor which affected Trumpp's understanding of the *Adi Granth*: his familiarity with the Puranic tradition. The *Vishnu Purana* was available to him in H.H. Wilson's translation. Though Trumpp was aware that the terms used by Guru Nanak did not necessarily have the same connotation as in the *Vishnu Purana,* he tended to accept the Puranic signification of terms and concepts. Since he was writing for the Western readers he was anxious at times to explain simple terms. There are explanations which involve an element of interpretation. Then there are some longer explanations. In such footnotes Trumpp appears to make use of his knowledge of Sanskrit, or grammar, or simply the context. In a number of his footnotes Trumpp tries to get at the literal meaning and then to guess the sense. Occasionally, he can guess the import even when the literal meaning of a word alludes him. When Trumpp knows the literal meaning of words it does not follow that he can interpret the lines or passages correctly, or meaningfully. On the whole, the notes and comments of Trumpp leave the impression that he tended to lean on his understanding of Sanskrit grammar and the Puranic tradition. He was not familiar with the Punjabi idiom, and showed little appreciation for Persian vocabulary. Consequently, he could explain simple words and phrases for the benefit of the Western reader. But he failed to grasp complex or subtle ideas. Paradoxically, his strength became his weakness when he began to look for traditional ideas in Guru Nanak expecting no new concepts.[19]

The literal meaning of words does not necessarily lead to the sense of a line, and the literal meaning of lines does not necessarily lead to the import of a passage. A good translator tries to do justice to both the literal meanings of words and lines and the import of a whole passage. This could be done only with an understanding of the significance of Guru Nanak's basic concepts. In order to assess whether or not Trumpp succeeds in striking such a balance, we may turn to some passages in his translation of the *Japuji*. To avoid repetition, we may take up those passages to which Trumpp has provided no annotation. These obviously would be the passages which he thought were clear to him. The only help provided to the reader is through the addition of words in brackets which are meant to clarify the meaning. For our present purpose we can ignore the brackets.

One un-annotated passage is rendered as:

> By his order made the forms of all things, his order however cannot be told.
> By his order are made the living beings, by his order greatness is obtained.
> By his order some are pardoned, some are by his order always caused to wander about in transmigration.
> Everyone is under his order, exempt from his order is no one.
> O Nanak ! if one understand his order, he will not speak in self-conceit.[20]

Trumpp appears to be aiming at a literal translation. *Hukam* is rendered as 'order'; *akar* as 'forms of all things'; *kiha* as 'told'; *jia* as 'living beings'; *vadiai* as 'greatness'; *uttam* as 'the high' and *nich* as 'the low': *dukh* as 'pain' and *sukh* as 'pleasure'; *hukmai andar sabh ko* as 'everyone is under his order'; *bahir hukam na koi* as 'exempt from his order is no one'; *bujhai* as 'understand'; and *haumai* as 'self-conceit'. It is difficult to contest the literal meanings of words and phrases in this passage. However, the basic thrust of the idea expressed in this passage does not come out. What is sought to be underlined in this passage is not merely the greatness of God but the realization of his omnipotence by human beings so that they do not attribute things to themselves. The clue to this idea lies in the last line in which *bujhai* is better rendered as 'realized' and *haumai* as 'self-centredness'. This interpretation would harmonize with Guru Nanak's conception of *Hukam* and *haumai* in the *Adi Granth*.

Another passage in Trumpp's translation is:

> By having heard his name, truth, contentment and divine knowledge is obtained.
> By having heard, is obtained, the merit of the bathing of the sixty-eight Tirathas.
> By having heard and reading, reading the name they obtain honour at the threshold of God.
> By having heard, meditation comes naturally to them.
> O Nanak ! his worshippers are always happy.
> By having heard, pains and sins are annihilated.[21]

Here, *suniai* is rendered as 'by having heard his name'; *sat* as 'truth'; *santokh* as 'contentment': *gian* as 'divine knowledge'; *asnan* as 'the merit of bathing at *tirathas*'; *parh* as 'reading the name'; *man* as 'honour at the threshold of God; *sahaj* as 'naturally'; *dhian* as 'meditation'; *bhagat* as 'worshipper'; *vigas* as 'happy'; *dukh* as 'pain'; and *pap* as 'sin'. In this translation too the aim is to be literally accurate, but with much less success. The word *sat* in the context is better interpreted as 'charities'. The second line has no verb and, therefore, its meaning is left vague. The word *parh* is joined to 'heard' on the one hand and to 'the name' on the other, whereas in the original it is only repeated as *parh parh*. Consequently, Trumpp misses the literal meaning as well as the import of this line. The word *sahaj* is wrongly translated as 'naturally' and, therefore, the meaning of the line does not get across. This whole passage is intimately connected with Guru Nanak's conception of the Name. But Trumpp does not seem to be aware of its importance in the thought of Guru Nanak.

Yet another passage reads:

> If he mind it, he obtains the gate of salvation.
> If he mind it, he brings about the salvation of his families.

If he mind it, he is saved, and saves the disciplines of his Guru.
If he mind it, O Nanak! He does not wander about in begging. Such is the name of the Supreme Being.
If one mind it, he knows it in his heart.

The word *manne* is translated as 'if he mind it'; *mokh-duar* as 'the gate of salvation'; *parwar* as 'family' and *sadhar* as 'salvation'; *tarai* as 'is saved' and *tare* as 'saved'; *Gursikh* as 'disciples of his Guru'; *bhave* as 'wandering' and *bhikh* as 'begging'; *nam* as 'the name'; *niranjan* as the 'the Supreme Being'; *jane* is joined to *man* on the one hand and to man on the other. The sense of the last line changes. *Gursikh* is treated as one word; the alternative meaning 'the Guru saves his disciples' could not occur to Trumpp. The translation of the passage as a whole remains inadequate at best. The refrain of the passage given above occurs four times in the *Japuji*. Another of these four passages is un-annotated. It reads:

If one mind the name, understanding and wisdom is obtained in the heart.
If he mind it, the knowledge of the whole world.
If he mind it, he is not struck in the face.
If he mind it, he does not go with Yama.[22]

Here, *surt* is rendered as 'understanding' and *buddh* as 'wisdom'; *suddh* as 'knowledge'; *munh chota na khai* as 'is not struck in the face'; and *jam ke sath na jai* as 'does not go with Yama'. In the last two lines metaphors are rendered so literally that they do not make any sense. What does it mean to be 'struck in the face'? What is the implication of 'not going with Yama'? Trumpp has nothing to say as if the lines are self-explanatory. Both these lines can be interpreted in different ways. It may be suggested, however, that not to be struck on the face can mean not to receive punishment in the life hereafter. Not to go with Yama can mean release from the transmigratory cycle.

Another passage which is translated by Trumpp without any annotation is the following:

There is no end to his praises, in saying them there is no end.
There is no end of his works, in his giving there is no end.
There is no end in seeing his works, no end in hearing them.
No end is known, what counsel is in his mind.
No end is known, what his form is. No end nor limit is known.

> On account of not getting his end, how many lament!
> His bounds cannot be obtained.
> This end nobody knows. If much be said, much more is to be said.
> Great is the Lord, high his place. Higher than high is his name.
> If one be so high, he may know this high one.
> So great a one, as he himself is, he himself only knows.
> O Nanak! by his favourable look and by destiny the gift of knowing him is obtained.[23]

This probably is the simplest passage in the *Japuji*. Much of the translation given by Trumpp is literally accurate, but not all. The line 'on account of not getting his end, how many lament' is a little misleading, because the original line simply means 'how many there are who are yearning to understand his limits'. Similarly, the line 'so great a one, . . .' actually means that in order to know God's greatness one has to be as great (which is impossible). In the last line, which is really of crucial significance in this passage, the word *karmi* is misunderstood to mean destiny. This is the Persian *karm* which was confused by Trumpp with the Sanskrit *karma*. The word *karmi* here is meant to reinforce *nadari* to underline the crucial importance of God's grace.

The last un-annotated passage in the *Japuji* is:

> His seat are the worlds, his storehouses the worlds. Whatever is put down by him in them, is put down once and for ever.
> Having made all things the creator sees them. O Nanak! the work of the True one is true, that is real and lasting.
> Salutation to him, salutation! Who is first, spotless, without beginning, having the same dress through all ages.[24]

This is one of the several passages in the *Japuji* in which the terminology of the *jogis* is used in order to show that the right path is not Yoga but Guru Nanak's path. The first line is meant to convey the idea that what is provided by God in all the world is inexhaustible. The second line is meant to convey the idea that God looks after his creation, and just as only he truly exists so his creation alone is perfect. The refrain that follows is meant to underline that he alone, and not Shiva or Vishnu or Brahma, should be the object of devotion, he who existed before the beginning, who has no end, and who does not change his form. We can see that Trumpp's translation is neither literally accurate nor meaningful in the context in which this passage occurs.

At one place Trumpp fails to perceive that the ideas attributed to Guru Nanak were actually ideas current among his contemporaries. There are some other lines in his translation of the *Japuji* which can be interpreted in a similar way by the reader. For instance, Guru Nanak may appear to approve of the *pandit* reciting the Vedas in 'To thee sing Pandits and Rakhisars who read continually with the Vedas in their hands'. Similarly, *gurmukh vedang* is rendered as 'from the mouth of the Guru is the Veda'. In another line 'The Guru is *Isar*, the Guru is *Gorakh* (Vishnu), Brahma, the Guru is the Mother Parbati'. The reader may possibly get the impression that Guru Nanak believed in deities other than his God from the line 'By having heard his name, *Isar* (Shiva), Brahma and Indra have been made'. In the same way the reader may like to infer that Guru Nanak acknowledged the authority of the Brahmanical books from the line 'By having heard, the Shastras, the Smritis and the Vedas are obtained'. This may be reinforced by 'Recitations of innumerable books and of the Veda with the mouth'. Legitimacy for Yoga may be seen in 'Innumerable jogs of those, who remain secluded in their hearts'.[25] It must be pointed out that in order to put such interpretations on the lines cited above the reader will have to take them out of the context. It is quite clear that Trumpp does not try to distort the meaning deliberately. As elsewhere, in these lines too he tries to give a literal translation to the best of his understanding.

Indeed, Trumpp's objective of remaining literally accurate enables him to record Guru Nanak's attitude towards the traditional Indian beliefs and practices more or less faithfully. The Vedas are not the repository of all knowledge in the line 'Having sought the end, they have become tired, the Vedas say one word'. Similarly, 'the time is not found out by the Pandits, though it be written out of a Purana'. The reference here is to the time of the creation of the world. The Puranas are bracketed with the Qur'an: 'the time is not found out by the Kazis, though they write out a document from the Koran'. There is a more comprehensive statement in a passage that enumerates categories through which attempts are made to describe God's greatness and His attributes. Among these are the Vedas and the Puranas, the learned men and the Brahmans, Indra, the Gopis and Krishna, Shiva, the Siddhas, and the Buddhas. But 'nobody is able to tell his qualities'. The mention of deities and scriptures in multiples undermines the importance of each: 'There are many winds, waters, fires, many Kans (Krishnas) and Maheses (Shivas). Many Brahmas by whom creation is formed, . . . Many Indras . . . many disguises of the Devi. . . . Many Vedas, many worshippers, O Nanak! there is no end of the account.' Traditional practices too have little merit: 'Tirathas, austerity, mercy, gifts given: if one obtain their merit, it is the honour of a sesame-seed.' Furthermore, 'If the name of God be heard, minded and loved in the heart: he bathes inwardly as at a Tiratha.'[26] In these verses Trumpp tries to remain faithful to the text. The inadequacy or inaccuracy of his translation is not relevant for the present argument. In Trumpp's translation there is no deliberate attempt to minimize Guru Nanak's departure from the traditional beliefs and practices among his contemporaries. The problem lies in his lack of appreciation for the basic concepts of Guru Nanak.

V. AN ASSESSMENT OF TRUMPP'S WORK

Our analysis clarifies quite a few points in Trumpp's translation of the *Japuji*, which may in fact be relevant for his translation as a whole (though not for his entire work). He was familiar with the principle of internal comparison, but he did not use it on any considerable scale. He judged the Sikh tradition on its merit according to his lights but neither the acceptance nor the rejection of that tradition ensured accuracy. He made no deliberate attempt to distort the meaning of the text. However, he appears to have entertained the notion that Guru Nanak was a representative of the Hindu tradition as it was understood in missionary circles during the third quarter of the nineteenth century. This assumption, coupled with his familiarity with the Puranic tradition and his knowedge of Sanskrit, induced him to interpret Guru Nanak's concepts in traditional Hindu terms. Therefore, though he did not consciously minimize Guru Nanak's departure from Hindu beliefs, he failed to appreciate the importance of his basic concepts like the *name, shabad, hukam* and *nadar,* or the terms like *haumai* and *sahaj,* for his religious thought.

There are serious shortcomings in Trumpp's translation. He aims at a literal translation but fails to get at the meaning of words and phrases. His failure to recognize a metaphor when he came upon one was even more frequent. This could arise from his indifferent command over the language of the *Adi Granth.* Consequently, he did not succeed in grasping the essential import of a line or a passage at many places in his translation. He failed to elicit cooperation from Sikh scholars, either because he offended the Sikhs by his disrespect to the scriptures, or due to his assumption that he knew better than the Sikh scholars. Then there was the constraint of time and limited financial resources. All these difficulties, coupled with his theological assumptions and attitudes, made him aggressive in tone and expression. Writing for the Western reader, he did not realize that his work would be read by the Sikhs. His gratuitous remarks on the Sikh Gurus as well as the Sikh scriptures are denounced the most by his Sikh critics. What is much more important, however, is Trumpp's failure to give a correct or meaningful translation. Giani Badan Singh hit the nail on the head when he called it *ashuddh*.[27]

Ernest Trumpp brought the *Adi Granth* and the *Janamsakhis* to the centre of Sikh studies. He gave great importance to one of the earliest known *Janamsakhi*, the Colebrooke manuscript, and suggested that this was the original work to which myths and miracles were added later on a much larger scale. He was highly sceptical about the use of *Janamsakhi* materials for the historical life of Guru Nanak. For the lives of Guru Nanak's successors he used sources like the *Bachittar Natak* and the *Sakhi Book*, in addition to the *Dabistan-i Mazahib*, the *Siyar al-Mutakhirin* and Shardha Ram Philauri's *Sikhan de Raj di Vithia*. Trumpp's comments on certain developments in the Sikh Panth indicate that he saw a movement towards politicization. He looked upon the objectives of Guru Gobind Singh as clearly political. Guru Gobind Singh removed the Masands, abolished all distinctions of caste, and dispensed with all services performed by the Brahmans. Trumpp accepted the current view that Guru Gobind Singh invoked the Goddess for instituting the Khalsa.

In Trumpp's view, Guru Nanak was indebted to Hindu philosophy for all his important doctrines. For theistic ideas he was especially indebted to Kabir. Guru Nanak's insistence on the unity of God, thus, was not a new thing. He did not discard the gods of Hindu pantheon; he only made them subordinate to the Supreme Being. Guru Nanak was soft on idolatry. In his essentially pantheistic system, there was no teleological principle. Emancipation conceived as Buddhistic Nirban was a further proof of pantheism. There was no room for ethical life in this system. The attainment of Nirban did not affect one's attitude towards moral life. Guru Nanak, like the other reformers, adopted new means for attaining the old goal. It was little more than muttering the name of God and singing His praises. Traditional acts of piety were not discarded; they were looked upon as insufficient for emancipation. The Guru became indispensable; he demanded complete surrender; and prayers were offered to him. Abolition of Guruship largely explained the emergence of the Sikhs into 'a nation'. Sikhism strictly was neither theistic nor ethical. That was why it was wrong to see it as 'moralizing Deism'. Guru Nanak discarded neither the Hindu scriptures, nor the caste system, nor the Brahmanical priesthood. In short, Trumpp bracketed Guru Nanak not only with the medieval reformers but also with the Hindu thinkers in general. Trumpp's interpretation of Sikhism thus amounted to misrepresentation.

VI. A DIFFERENT VIEW OF SIKH RELIGION: PINCOTT

Frederic Pincott went to the other extreme and suggested that Sikhism could be regarded as 'the religion of a Muhammadan sect'. He contributed a special article to the *Dictionary of Islam* in 1885 in which he argued that Sikhism had not been studied so thoroughly as to warrant any assertion on its 'ultimate source', or 'sources'. Trumpp was the only author to have written on Sikhism with 'knowledge'. But his view that Sikhism had only 'an accidental relationship' with Islam did not find support in the early Sikh writings.

In Pincott's view, Trumpp was mistaken about the history of Sufism. Sufism was not a product of Indian environment. It represented essentially a Persian response to Islam. The great Persian poets were deeply influenced by Sufism and their poetry reflected its doctrines and attitudes. Pincott quotes Hafiz and Nizami to indicate the Zoroastrian origin of the refined spirituality of the Sufis. He calls it 'the Islamo-Magian creed'. The Persian conquerors of Hindustan carried with them the mysticism and spirituality of this 'Islamo-Magian' creed, and through it India received its flood of Islam. Therefore, when Pincott talks of Islamic source of Sikhism he has actually Sufism in view.

Pincott finds that the doctrines preached by the Sikh Gurus were distinctly Sufistic. Pincott quotes Jami and the *Adi Granth* to indicate almost complete correspondence of ideas on the unity of God. Some 'other technical terms of Sufism' were also reproduced in Sikhism. Pincott refers to the concepts of the 'light' and the 'beloved' in this connection. He goes on to add that the Sikh Gurus used a pen-name, 'Nanak', a practice that was common among the Persian poets in their *ghazals*. Guru Nanak refers to '*the Sofis*' as those who find the True One. The early Sikh Gurus assumed even the manners and dress of *faqirs*, and they carried small rosaries in their hands.

Pincott refers to the traditions of Guru Nanak preserved in the *Janamsakhi* for evidence on his 'alliance' with Islam. In his very early days he sought the society of *faqirs*. At Sultanpur, where he was serving a Muslim, he used to give all his salary to *faqirs*, keeping the bare minimum for himself. His experience of ecstatic exultation at Sultanpur is expressed in terms which are closely akin to those of the Sufis. His stress on the repetition of the name of God is akin to the Sufi practice of *zikr*. He is questioned by the *qazi* about his utterance: 'There is no Hindu, and there is no Musalman'. He tells the *qazi* how to become a true Muslim. He recites a few more verses, and both Hindus and Musalmans begin to say that God (Khuda) was speaking in Nanak. In another version, there was an outcry among Hindus and Musalmans that Nanak had become a 'Turk'. Pincott draws the inference that the early Sikhs believed that 'he went very close to Muhammadanism'.

Pincott attaches importance to Guru Nanak meeting several Shaikhs on his missionary journeys and responding to their greetings in the Muslim fashion. He is regarded as a *darvesh* even by Sultan Ibrahim Lodi. At Benares, the *pandit* greets Guru Nanak with 'Ram Ram' and calls him 'bhagat' but points out that he had 'none of the marks of a Hindu upon him'. Pincott draws the inference that Guru Nanak occupied 'an intermediate position between Muhammadanism and Hinduism'. Significantly, Pincott goes on to add that he converts both Muslims and Hindus to his way. Pincott wrongly assumes that Shaikh Farid was a contemporary of Guru Nanak, and that he accompanied him in his wanderings for twelve years. But the point he makes is that the compositions of the Sufi Shaikh were included in the *Adi Granth*. Guru Nanak and his immediate successors did not see any incongruity in their mixture of Hindu and Islamic ideas. This comes out clearly, again, in Guru Nanak's dialogue with Shaikh Ibrahim at Pakpattan. In his discussion with Mian Miththa, Guru Nanak lays emphasis on 'the Sufi doctrine of the Unity of God'.

Pincott looks upon Guru Nanak's visit to Mecca as 'an invention' but a very important one. His full confession of Islam in the episode showed how far the narrator thought it possible for Guru Nanak to go. In the incident of his meeting with Makhdum Bahauddin at Multan, 'we have an extraordinary admission from a Muhammadan that Nanak would succeed in breaking up the faith of Islam.' Finally, on the death of Guru Nanak both Hindus and Muslims owned him. The 'mixture' of Hinduism and Islam was in fact 'the establishment of a common basis of religious truth for both Muhammadan and Hindu; and thus he is shown to have accomplished with such dexterity that at his death no one could say whether he was more inclined to Hinduism or to Muhammadanism'.

Pincott emphasizes that Guru Nanak 'admitted to his fraternity men of all castes' and among his pupils were both Hindus and Musalmans. He used both Hindu and Muslim names of God. However, the chief point of his teaching was the Unity of God. No other being was associated with the Absolute Supreme. This exalted idea of God enabled Guru Nanak to treat with indifference the crowd of Hindu deities and caused them 'to subside into a condition similar to that of angels in modern Christianity'. They sink into utter insignificance.

Pincott maintains that pantheism and metempsychosis were common to the creed of a Hindu, a Buddhist, and a Sufi. As in Buddhism, the prime object of attainment in Sikhism was not paradise but 'the total cessation of individual existence'. Release from transmigration, or *nirvana*, was accomplished by perfect identity with the Supreme. Pincott talks of Buddhist influence on Sikhism in terms of freedom from caste, respect for animal life, importance attached to meditation, emphasis on charity, reverence for the Guru, respect for the lotus, Guru Nanak's missionary tours, and the curious union between the Guru and the Sangat. Gradually, the pantheistic idea of God changed into the notion of a self-conscious Supreme Being, the creator and governor of the universe. This could be due to the influence of Islam. Furthermore, Guru Nanak underlines that 'without the practice of virtue, there can be no worship'. At one place in his article, Pincott states that 'there is no Hindu, there is no Musalman' could mean that Guru Nanak's intention was to do away with the differences between the Hindu and Muslim creeds 'by instituting a third course which should supersede both of them'.[28]

Pincott's understanding of Sikhism became increasingly different from that of Trumpp two decades later. The earlier history of religion in India showed that Sikhism was not 'a violent reform due to the stupendous abilities of one man' but 'the natural outcome of previous ages of thought'. He outlines the history of religion in India from the earliest times to the time of Guru Nanak on the lines of J.D. Cunningham. The advent of Islam in India first cut-off the Punjab from the rest of India. With Islam, Sufism came to this region where the religion of the Vedas had originated and Buddhism had held an undisputed sway. The notions of the Sufis were 'practically the same as those of the Vedantists, or ancient Indian philosophers'. At that time, the religious mind of India had begun to be exceedingly active, with the work of Shaiva Shankaracharya, the Vaishnava Ramanuja, followed by the cults of Rama and Krishna. These waves of Hindu thought found their way into the Punjab. Gorakh Nath in the thirteenth century reconciled 'decaying Buddhism with reviving Hindusim'. Kabir flourished in the fifteenth century as 'a worshipper of Rama', but he rejected the worship of idols 'with all the energy of a Muhammdan'. He rejects the authority of the Islamic and Hindu scriptures and composed his own works in the language of the people. Above all, he addressed himself to both Hindus and Muslims. A new religious ferment prepared the way for Guru Nanak 'to build up a new and living faith'. He clearly perceived the errors of his predecessors and had the boldness to proclaim the truth. His principles can be reduced to a single formula: the Unity of God and the Brotherhood of man. These two ideas united all classes on a common basis and separated them from the rest of their countrymen. The practical application of freedom from prescribed trammels, equality before God, and the fraternity of mankind led to the formation of 'a new nationality'. Pincott was also aware that there was a desire among the contemporary Sikh leaders to revive the fading glories of Sikhism. The Khalsa were laying the foundation of an organized system of instruction, with the object of giving their fraternity a scholarly knowledge of their sacred books and enlarging their minds generally. He hoped that the Sikh faith would regain the simplicity and vitality with which it had been endowed by its noble-hearted founder.[29]

NOTES

1. N.G. Barrier, 'Trumpp and Macauliffe: Western Students of Sikh History and Religion', *Historians and Historiography of the Sikhs*, ed. Fauja Singh, Delhi, 1978, pp. 166-8, 185.
2. Ibid., pp. 168-70.
3. Ibid., 170-3, 184-5.
4. Ernest Trumpp, *The Adi Granth*, New Delhi: Munshiram Manoharlal, 1989 (rpt., first published in 1877), pp. v-vii.
5. Ibid., p. xcvii.
6. Ibid., pp. i- lxxvii, 55-60.
7. Ibid., pp. lxxvii-lxxx.
8. Ibid., pp. lxxx-lxxxix.
9. Ibid., pp. lxxxix-xcvi.
10. Ibid., p. xcvii.
11. Ibid., pp. xcvii-ci.
12. Ibid., pp. ci-cii.
13. Ibid., pp. cii-cvi.
14. Ibid., pp. cviii-cxi.
15. Ibid., pp. cix-cxi.
16. Ibid., pp. cxi-cxii.
17. Ibid., p. 9 n2.
18. Ibid., pp. 1nn.2, 5; 2n.4, 3n.4, 5n.2, 6n.2, 6nn.1, 5; 7n.3, 10n.8, 11n.2, 12nn.3, 5; 13nn.3, 8.
19. Ibid., 11 n3.
20. Ibid., p. 2.
21. Ibid., p. 4.
22. Ibid.
23. Ibid., p. 8.
24. Ibid., p. 11.
25. Ibid., pp. 3, 4, 6, 10.
26. Ibid., pp. 7, 8, 9, 12.
27. Giani Badan Singh, *Adi Sri Guru Granth Sahib Ji Steek*, Patiala: Punjab Languages Department, 1989 (rpt.), Introduction.
28. For this and the earlier paras in this section, see Thomas Patrick Hughes, *A Dictionary of Islam (Being a Cyclopaedia of the Doctrines, Rites, Ceremonies, and Customs, together with the Technical and Theological Terms, of the*

Muhammadans), Lahore: Premier Book House, 1984 (rpt., first published in 1885), pp. 583-94. Another work written by Pincott was *Sikhism in Relation to Mohammadanism*, London: W.H. Allen & Co., 1885. His article on 'The Arrangement of the Hymns of the *Adi Granth*, Holy Bible of the Sikhs', was published in the eighteenth volume of the *Journal of the Royal Asiatic Society*.

29. For this and the previous para, see Frederic Pincott, 'Sikhism' in '*Religious Systems of the World*, New York, 1901, pp. 70-83. Reprinted in *Sikh Religion: A Symposium*, Calcutta: Sushil Gupta (India) Private Ltd., 1958.

CHAPTER EIGHT

Max Arthur Macauliffe

The Sikh Religion

I. INTRODUCTORY

Max Arthur Macauliffe's *The Sikh Religion* was meant to replace Trumpp's *The Adi Granth.* His translation in Macauliffe's view was 'highly inaccurate and unidiomatic', and gave 'mortal offence' to the Sikhs because of the German missionary's *odium theologicum.* 'Whenever he saw an opportunity of defaming the Gurus, the sacred book, and the religion of the Sikhs, he eagerly availed himself of it'. Macauliffe wanted to give a simple and accurate translation, which should above all, be acceptable to the Sikhs. He submitted every line of his translation to 'the most searching criticism' of learned Sikhs. He was convinced that the language of the *Adi Granth* was exceptionally difficult to master for a single scholar. For this reason too he took help from Sikh scholars. Among them were eminent Sikh writers like Bhai Kahn Singh of Nabha and Giani Hazara Singh of Amritsar.

The Sikh Religion covers nearly 2,500 pages. About half of these are given to the lives of the ten Gurus and all the 'Bhagats' whose compositions are included in the *Adi Granth.* The space devoted to the compositions of the Gurus and the 'Bhagats' is more or less equal to the space given to their 'lives'. The first volume contains about eighty pages of 'preface' and 'introduction'. The rest of the volume is devoted to Guru Nanak. The third volume is devoted entirely to the life and compositions of Guru Arjan. The life and compositions of Guru Gobind Singh are given in the fifth volume. Among the Bhagats, the maximum space is given to the compositions of Kabir, followed at a great distance by Namdev and Farid. Macauliffe looks upon Shaikh Ibrahim, the Second Farid, as the author of these compositions.[1] Ravidas comes next, with more than twenty pages for his compositions. Most of the others get only five to one or even less than one page—Beni, Trilochan, Dhanna, Jaidev, Parmanand, Sadhna, Ramanand, Pipa, Sain, Bhikan, Surdas and Mira.[2]

Macauliffe used a much larger number and volume of source materials than any of his predecessors. It is quite remarkable that the bulk of his evidence consists of original sources. Much of this original evidence comes from Sikh sources: the *Adi Granth,* the *Dasam Granth,* the works of Bhai Gurdas, the *Janamsakhis,* the *Gurbilases* and the works of Bhai Santokh Singh. From amongst his Sikh contemporaries Macauliffe used the works of Giani Gian Singh and Bhai Kahn Singh of Nabha. He also used the well-known Persian works like the *Dabistan-i Mazahib,* the *Khulasat ut-Tawarikh* and the *Siyar al-Mutakhirin,* apart from the works translated by Elliot and Dowson in the *History of India As Told by Its Own Historians.* Macauliffe relied very little on his predecessors.[3]

Guru Arjan compiled the *Granth* which, in Macauliffe's view, supplanted the authority of the Vedas and the Puranas, and separated the Sikhs from the mass of the Hindus. He instructed his followers to accept the *Granth* alone as authentic and authoritative, and not any other composition even if it bore the pen-name 'Nanak'. The tradition regarding the space left vacant for the compositions of Guru Tegh Bahadur later was of course 'a prophecy *ex eventum*'. As a measure of great importance, Guru Arjan replaced voluntary offerings by a kind of tax to be regularly collected by his deputies called Masands. He engaged in trade in a grand style; he kept an establishment like a grandee, and he meddled with politics. In his time the Sikhs became accustomed to 'a kind of government of their own'. Guru Arjan's execution became a 'great turning-point in the development of the Sikh community'. It changed 'the whole character' of the movement initiated by Guru Nanak.[4]

Like Trumpp, Macauliffe wanted to avoid repetition in his translation but for a different reason. The Gurus used to address the people who clustered around them, and repetitions served to impress on them the instructions meant to be conveyed. In a printed work, however, repetition was not so necessary. Macauliffe's work does not contain translation of the entire *Adi Granth.* Equally important was his feeling that 'orthodox' Sikhs did not like the *Adi Granth* to be translated into another language 'in the order of the original' because of their fear that the respect which was due to the *Guru Granth* would not be accorded to the translated work. Therefore, he interspersed many of the sacred hymns in 'the lives of the Gurus'.[5]

II. SIKHISM AS THE MOST ORIGINAL DISPENSATION

Macauliffe's understanding of Sikhism was radically different from that of Trumpp. Whereas for Trumpp the inclusion of the compositions of the 'Bhagats' in the *Adi Granth* was one of the proofs that there was no difference between them and the Gurus, Macauliffe puts forward the view that Guru Arjan included their compositions in the *Adi Granth* to indicate 'the historical development of the Sikh reformation'.[6] In fact, 'the last great religion of the world' was not an extension of but a further improvement upon what had been done by others. The Gurus spoke to the people in their own language, and not in Sanskrit which was deemed to be 'the language of the gods' in Hinduism. Carefully preserved from the very beginning, the sacred hymns of the Gurus were the most authentic records in the world. The religion they embodied was totally unaffected by Semitic or Christian influence. Based on the unity of God, Sikhism rejected Hindu formularies and adopted an independent ethical system and rituals which were totally opposed to the theological beliefs of Guru Nanak's age and country. Macauliffe was convinced that the *Adi Granth* embodied all the elements of a new religion. Indeed, 'it would be difficult to point to a religion of greater originality or to a more comprehensive ethical system'.[7]

Macauliffe underlines that religion in India attained its 'monotheistic consummation' in the thought of Guru Nanak. The idea of one God was known since the *Rigveda*, but Guru Nanak gave 'expansion' to this idea. In response to Trumpp, Macauliffe states that the conception of God can be anthropomorphic, pantheistic or theistic. Logically, however, it is difficult to dissociate one from the other. In the writings of Guru Nanak, 'Pantheism' is distinctly implied in some passages, and in other passages 'matter is made distinct from the Creator' as an emanation from him. Macauliffe suggests that anthropomorphic theism which belongs strictly to 'religion' and pantheism which belongs strictly to 'philosophy' are inextricably blended by all sacred and profane writers. This was not a peculiarity of Guru Nanak, or of the Indian writers. Thus, Macauliffe tries to correct the view presented by Trumpp. In his discussion of Nirban (*nirvana*) too, Macauliffe appears to be improving upon Trumpp's view. Nirban and Sach Khand were practically the same, suggestive of the union of the human soul (*jivatma*) with the Supreme (*parmatma*), like light mingling with light or water with water. One could attain *Nirban* through meditation and conforming one's life to the teachings of the Guru. Only those who are sufficiently purified can be absorbed in the Absolute, or 'the all-dazzling fount of God's infinite perfection and love'.[8]

Unlike Trumpp, Macauliffe saw many 'moral and political' merits in the Sikh religion. It prohibited idolatry, hypocrisy, caste exclusiveness, concremation of widows, immurement of women, use of wine and other intoxicants, tobacco smoking, infanticide, slander, pilgrimages to the sacred rivers and tanks of the Hindus. It inculcated loyalty, gratitude for all favour received, philanthropy, justice, impartiality, truth, honesty, and 'all the moral and domestic virtues known to the holiest citizens of any country'.[9] Macauliffe differed with Trumpp on the bearing of the teachings of the Gurus on moral life as well as the nature and character of Sikhism, its relationship with Hinduism, the conception of God in Sikhism, and the Sikh idea of liberation. Far from looking at Sikhism as a form of Hinduism, Macauliffe wanted to see the comparatively young religion to escape the deadly embrace of Hinduism. He was opposed to the idea of the Sikhs being declared to be Hindus because this idea was in direct opposition to the teachings of the Gurus.[10]

III. VIEW OF SIKH SOURCES

Initially, Macauliffe had thought only of translating the *Adi Granth*. After the work on translation was over, he found it 'absolutely necessary' to give an account of the Sikh Gurus, and of the saints whose compositions were included in the *Adi Granth* for a correct interpretation of their writings. The current accounts of the Gurus were overladen with 'puerile, heterodox, or repulsive details' which were 'inconsistent with their sacred writings'. This was no less true of Bhai Santokh Singh's works than of the current *Janamsakhis*. However, Macauliffe's idea was to accommodate the 'orthodox' Sikh point of view, and even miracles find a place in his narratives. Just as in his interpretation of the Sikh faith his aim was to omit 'the debased superstitions and heterodox social customs of Sikhs who have been led astray from their faith by external influences', his aim in narrating the lives of the Gurus was to omit whatever was inconsistent with their true teachings.[11]

Macauliffe tried to work out a compromise between his own critical assessment and the Sikh attitude towards the sources for the life of Guru Nanak. The oldest authentic account was written by Bhai Gurdas not much more than sixty years after the demise of Guru Nanak. The detail given in his first *Var* could therefore be utilized rather unreservedly. Bhai Mani Singh expanded this *Var* in his *Gian Ratnavali.* After his death, however, the copyists 'interlarded several Hindu ideas in his works'. Tinctured with Hinduism from his early education and environment, Bhai Santokh Singh 'invented' several stories discreditable to the Gurus and their religion. 'His statements accordingly cannot often be accepted as even an approach to history'.[12]

The *Janamsakhis,* which professed to be biographies of Guru Nanak, were written at different times after his death and they give 'very different and contradictory details of his life'. All of them record 'miraculous acts and supernatural conversations'. They show the extent to which 'pious fiction' can fabricate details of the lives of religious teachers in all ages and countries. One of the most popular *Janamsakhis* was lithographed at Lahore as a large volume of 588 folio pages. Its editor claimed to have worked hard for collecting and collating materials for this compilation which, he claimed, could not have been produced by anyone else. It was apparently based on Bhai Santokh Singh's *Nanak Prakash.* Attributed to Bhai Bala, it was said to have been dictated to Paira by Guru Angad's order. But its language was not old, and no manuscript copy of the original was available. In fact, Bala was not even mentioned by Bhai Gurdas, or Bhai Mani Singh in his *Bhagat Ratnavali.* The *Janamsakhi* was claimed to have been written in 1535 or even in 1525. The implication is clear, that this *Janamsakhi* was not what it claimed to be.[13]

Macauliffe explains 'the falsification of old, or the compositions of new *Janamsakhis*' in terms of 'schisms' in the religion of Guru Nanak. The life of Guru Nanak written by an Udasi, Anand Ghan, presents Sri Chand as an incarnation of God and the only true successor of Guru

Nanak. Miharban wrote a *Janamsakhi* of Guru Nanak to glorify his own father, Prithi Chand, the eldest son of Guru Ram Das. Bhai Bala finds a place in this *Janamsakhi* for the first time. Bidhi Chand compiled a *Granth* and a *Janamsakhi* to exalt his father Handal and to degrade Guru Nanak by introducing fictitious narratives. Favoured by the Mughal administrators of the province, the Handalis apparently had sufficient influence to destroy nearly all older account of the life of Guru Nanak. The Mughal administrators on their own destroyed Sikh manuscripts in the process of persecuting the Sikhs.[14]

Of all the known *Janamsakhis,* Macauliffe placed the greatest reliance on the one written by Sewa Das in 1588. Its language was that of the Pothohar and its characters were unmistakably older than that of any other known work in Gurmukhi. It mentioned Mardana but not Bhai Bala. It was not free from 'mythological matter' but it was much more 'rational, consistent, and satisfactory' than any other narrative of Guru Nanak's life. It was 'the most trustworthy' record in existence. Macauliffe proposed to make 'this ancient Janamsakhi' the basis of his own account of the life of Guru Nanak. It could be supplemented by 'cullings' from the later accounts of Guru Nanak's life. Though conscious of the idea that the *Janamsakhis* provided settings for the compositions of Guru Nanak, Macauliffe himself makes ample use of his verses. He gives preference to early writings, and supplements his narrative by later materials. He does not entirely excise even the supranatural elements. But he keeps out elements which appeared to contradict Guru Nanak's teachings.[15]

For the life of Guru Gobind Singh, the main authorities mentioned by Macauliffe are the *Bachittar Natak,* Bhai Sukha Singh's *Gurbilas* and Bhai Santokh Singh's *Suraj Parkash.* He rejects the *Sau Sakhi* but finds Giani Gian Singh's *Panth Prakash* rather useful. He uses Bhai Nand Lal's *Zindagi Nama* and his *diwan* also for his account. He quotes at length from the *Zafarnama.* He refers to the letter of Guru Gobind Singh addressed to Tilok Singh and Ram Singh, and also to Khafi Khan's work, presumably on the basis of Elliot and Dowson's *History of India.* Several compositions of Guru Gobind Singh (other than the *Bachittar Natak* and the *Zafarnama*) are also used by Macauliffe. There is no doubt that he was the first European writer to use all this evidence for an account of Guru Gobind Singh.[16]

Macauliffe's attitude towards his sources is quite interesting. He was not uncritical but he tended to select evidence in support of what he regarded as the orthodox position. The *Krishan Avtar* was not a work of Guru Gobind Singh but of a bard named Shyam. Macauliffe refers to the report of a newswriter on the institution of the Khalsa, quoted by Ghulam Muhiyuddin, in which Guru Gobind Singh invites members of all the four castes to accept baptism of the sword and to discard the worship of Hindu deities in favour of the path shown by Guru Nanak and his successors.[17] Macauliffe's account of the invocation of the Goddess by Guru Gobind Singh is not based on Sukha Singh or Santokh Singh but on Giani Gian Singh's *Panth Prakash.* This account emphasizes that Guru Gobind Singh did not adore any gods or goddesses. He agreed to invoke the Goddess to expose the Brahmans. Guru Gobind Singh ordered all the materials to be thrown into the fire. A great flame shot up towards the heavens, and the people erroneously believed that the Goddess had appeared. Macauliffe finds enough of evidence in the *Akal Ustat, Bachittar Natak, Thirty-Three Savvayyas,* and the *Chandi Charitar* to prove that he was no worshipper of gods and goddesses. Macauliffe argues that *bhagauti* in the writings of Guru Gobind Singh meant the sword. Guru Gobind Singh selected Sanskrit literature for translation in order to inspire bravery and valour among his followers: 'he rendered in the vulgar dialect the tenth chapter of the *Bhagwat* with no other object than to inspire ardour for religious warfare'. Macauliffe accepts Bhai Ditt Singh's view that these translations could at the same time demonstrate that Hindu sacred writings were inferior to the compositions of the Gurus.[18] Enunciation of the *rahit* continued after the institution of the Khalsa. On one such occasion Guru Gobind Singh told his Sikhs not to associate with those who worshipped Sakhi Sarvar, Gugga, or any other *pir.* Guru Gobind Singh instructed Banda in the tenets of his religion and baptized him according to the new rite. Though he continued to be known as Banda he had been given the name Gurbakhsh Singh. Macauliffe relates the incident in which Guru Gobind Singh 'departed bodily for heaven'. Probably the contemporary Sikhs had no objection to this idea.[19]

Macauliffe's references to the *Adi Granth* appear to reflect the orthodox Sikh position. Guru Gobind Singh dictated the *Granth Sahib* to Bhai Mani Singh at Talwandi Sabo, adding for the first time the hymns and *shloks* of Guru Tegh Bahadur, and his own *shlok*. There were two other recensions of the *Granth Saḥib,* one written by Bhai Gurdas and the other associated with Bhai Banno. The former was still at Kartarpur in the Jalandhar district and the latter was at Mangat in the district of Gujrat. However, the recension prepared under the superintendence of Guru Gobind Singh, which was the most complete, was destroyed or taken away as booty by Ahmad Shah Durrani when he despoiled the Golden Temple.[20] Presumably, this was the recension that Guru Gobind Singh had opened just before his death, placed five *paisas* and a coconut before it, and solemnly bowed to it as his successor. He then circumambulated the sacred volume and said: 'O beloved Khalsa, let him who desired to behold me, behold the Guru Granth. Obey the Granth Sahib. It is the visible body of the Guru. And let him who desireth to meet me diligently search its hymns.' At the same time, Guru Gobind Singh told the Khalsa that 'the Guru shall be the Khalsa and the Khalsa the Guru'. The mental and bodily spirit of the Guru was thus infused into 'the Granth Sahib and the Khalsa'.[21]

Macauliffe was aware that the authenticity of the *Dasam Granth* was being debated by the contemporary Sikhs. In his view it was compiled by Bhai Mani Singh in 1734 from 'various materials'. Macauliffe's references to its contents indicate that he accepted the authenticity of the *Akal Ustat,* the *Jap,* the *Thirty-Three Savvayyas,* the *Bachittar Natak* and the *Zafarnama,* but he was not sure about the translations from Sanskrit works. Selections from the *Dasam Granth* for translation show that, apart from the works mentioned above, he looked upon the *Gian Prabodh,* remarks on the *Ram Avtar, Krishan Avtar* and *Parasnath Avtar,* all the *Hazare Shabad* and the *Benati Chaupai* as authentic. All the compositions are believed by Macauliffe 'to represent the Guru's own opinions and acts'. An early Sikh view was that the Persian tales (*Hikayat*) and the stories illustrating the deceit of women (*Triya Charitar*) should not have been included in the *Granth*.[22]

IV. MACAULIFFE'S TRANSLATION

If we compare Macauliffe's translation of the *Japuji* with that of Trumpp we get the impression that he was consciously trying to improve upon the latter. Macauliffe's translation and his annotations indicate that his understanding of the original was different from that of Trumpp. We may refer to those very passages which have been noticed in the case of Trumpp.

The stanza on *hukam* is translated as follows:

By His order bodies are produced; His order cannot be described.
By His order souls are infused into them; by His order greatness is obtained.
By His order men are high or low; by His order they obtain preordained pain or pleasure.
By His order some obtain their reward; by His order others must ever wander in transmigration.
All are subject to His order; none is exempt from it.
He who understandeth God's order, O Nanak, is never guilty of egoism.

In the footnotes Macauliffe explains that *akar* is supposed to refer to the non-sentient and *jiv* to the sentient world. Blending with God is the 'reward'. Macauliffe explains *haun main* as 'I exist by myself independently of God'; this is the sin of spiritual pride.[23]

In the passage related to *nam*, Macauliffe's rendering is the following:

By hearing the Name truth, contentment, and divine knowledge *are obtained.*
Hearing the Name is equal to bathing at the sixty-eight *places of pilgrimage.*
By hearing the Name and reading it man obtaineth honour.
By hearing the Name the mind is composed and fixed on God.
Nanak, the saints are ever happy.

In the footnotes, Macauliffe suggests alternative rendering: for line 3, 'On hearing the Name man obtaineth honour by the knowledge acquired'; for line 4, 'by hearing the Name man easily meditated upon God'.[24]

In the stanza on '*manne*', Macauliffe gives the following translation:

By obeying Him man's path is not obstructed;
By obeying Him man departeth with honour and distinction;
By obeying Him man proceedeth in ecstasy on his way;
By obeying Him man formeth an alliance with virtue
So pure is God's name
Whoever obeyeth God knoweth the pleasure of it in his own heart.

In the note on line 4, *bhave* and *bhikh* are explained as 'does not wander in transmigration'.[25]

Another stanza related to the same theme is translated by Macauliffe as follows:

By obeying Him wisdom and understanding enter the mind;
By obeying Him man knoweth all worlds;
By obeying Him man suffereth not punishment;
By obeying Him man shall not depart with Jam
So pure is God's name
Whoever obeyeth God knoweth the pleasure of it in his own heart.

The footnote, explains that Jam, also called Dharmraj, is the god of death. The meaning of the verse is that 'man shall not die again, but be absorbed in God'. Evidently, Macauliffe is far more perceptive than Trumpp.[26]

The stanza that relates to the inadequacy of praising God's greatness is given by Macauliffe as follows:

There is no limit to God's praises; to those who repeat them there is no limit.
There is no limit to His mercy, and to His gifts there is no limit.
There is no limit to what God seeth, no limit to what He heareth.
The limit of the secret of His heart cannot be known.
The limit of His cremation cannot be known; neither His near nor His far side can be discovered.
To know His limits how many vex their hearts.
His limits cannot be ascertained;
Nobody knoweth His limits.
The more we say, the more *there remains* to be said.
Great is the Lord, and exalted is His seat.
His exalted name is higher than the most exalted.
Were any one else ever so exalted,
Then he would know what exalted Being:
How great He is He knoweth Himself.
Nanak, God bestoweth gifts on *whom* He looketh with favour and mercy.

In the footnotes, the alternative rendering for the opening clause is given as 'There is no limit to the Praised One'. The 'far side' in line 5 is taken from the metaphor of the banks of a river. The literal meaning of *billah* in line 6 is 'cry in pain'.[27]

Finally, for the stanza addressed to the Jogis, Macauliffe gives the following translation:

His seat and His storehouses are in every world.
What was to be put into them was put in at one time.
The Creator beholdeth His creation.
Nanak, true is the work of the True One.
HAIL, HAIL TO HIM,
The primal, the pure, without beginning, the indestructible, the same in every age!

In the footnotes, the 'storehouses' meant to supply human necessities, and 'put in at one time' means 'before man is born, his portion is fully allotted to him.'[28]

The differences in the translation by Trumpp and Macauliffe in these passages may appear to be small but they are significant. In totality, the differences between them amount to two different interpretations of Sikh theology, doctrines, beliefs and ethics. In all fairness to the authors it may be added that neither in the case of Trumpp nor that of Macauliffe, the translator's understanding can be attributed entirely to their interactions with the men of learning in the Punjab.

V. MACAULIFFE'S INTERPRETATION REINFORCED IN THE WEST

Macauliffe's interpretation of Sikhism was reinforced by Dorothy Field in her *Religion of the Sikhs,* published in 1914. She was aware of the contemporary controversy about whether or not Sikhs were Hindus. A reading of the *Granth,* in Macauliffe's translation, strongly suggested that Sikhism was a world religion 'rather than a reformed sect of the Hindus'.[29] Acknowledging her great debt to Macauliffe, she could occasionally bring in ideas of some other scholars. The lofty monotheism of the Sikhs was the result of an attempt to reform and to simplify Islam and Hinduism. Though this attempt failed, it succeeded nonetheless in binding the Sikhs together and they became a nation by reason of their faith.[30] Guru Nanak assumed a critical attitude towards the three cardinal pillars of Hinduism: the priesthood, the caste system, and the Vedas. He was nevertheless a spiritual descendant of monotheistic reformers within Hinduism. At the same time, Islamic influences caused him to break away very much more from the older faith.[31] But, 'we must be careful not to attribute the Sikh doctrine of Divine Unity solely to the influence of Muhammadanism, for such doctrine had always been present within Hinduism.'[32] Dorothy Field hammers the point that Guru Nanak's religious system was autonomous: 'however much he may have borrowed in the matter of doctrine, his religion remains distinct and complete in itself, and is not in any way dependent on association with Hinduism.'[33] Dorothy Field's assessment of Sikhism remains close to Macauliffe's.

Like Macauliffe, Dorothy Field dwells on the supposed prophecies of Guru Tegh Bahadur and Guru Gobind Singh in favour of the English.[34] She favours the idea of preserving Sikh distinctiveness, and looks upon Sikhism as 'essentially a practical religion'. From this point of view, 'it would rank almost first in the world'. No other religion made a nation in so short a time as did Sikhism. It was little short of a miracle that this faith transformed the outcaste into 'a fine and loyal warrior'. This should interest the Englishmen 'who have so largely reaped the benefits of this grand faith.'[35]

In her discussion of the doctrines of Sikhism too Dorothy Field virtually repeats Macauliffe. Sikhism lays stress on the unity and omnipotence of God. His orders are absolutely binding and His ways are not to be questioned. The idea of incarnation is discarded in Sikhism, though the existence of Brahma, Vishnu and Shiva is admitted, together with a large number of demi-gods, in a manner that does not compromise monotheism in any way. God's transcendence is combined with a firm belief in the indwelling and all-pervading spirit. But god remains 'a being distinct from the world'. The theories of *karma*, transmigration, *maya* and *nirvana* were presented by Guru Nanak in a modified form. In the new way of liberation proclaimed by him, the first essential was 'a true Guru'. This true Guru was no other than Guru Nanak whose Guru was God Himself. He thus claimed direct revelation from God. The Name, uttered with meditation, was declared to be the best form of worship, making all the current rituals and rites irrelevant for emancipation. God's praises sung in the company of saints came next to meditation on the Name. Much stress was laid on all ethical virtues. Dorothy Field quotes a paragraph from Macauliffe to summarize Sikh ethics.[36]

VI. AN ASSESSMENT

Macauliffe includes in his narrative what may appear to be post-eventum prophecies without showing any scepticism. Guru Gobind Singh gave a written acknowledgement of debt to a Pathan, telling him that his Sikhs would pay this debt when they would come into power thirty years after his death. 'The debt was duly discharged by the Sikhs under happier and more prosperous circumstances'. Guru Tegh Bahadur had alluded before his martyrdom to the advent of the British. Guru Gobind Singh tells his Sikhs that the English would defeat the Sikhs in hard-fought battles when 'the Sikhs become entangled in the love of mammon', become self-seekers, unjust and corrupt, abandon the Guru's hymns to follow Shastras and the religion of the Brahmans, and when the Sikh rulers allow their states to be governed by 'evil influences'.[37] Such prophecies could be of advantage to the colonial state. Another prophecy of Guru Gobind Singh is to the effect that, after the arrival of the English, 'in every house there shall be wealth, in every house religion, in every house learning, and in every house happiness'. Macauliffe quotes a Sikh writer who underlines the loyalty of the Sikhs to their rulers even more than their unmatched bravery in the world. It may be added that Macauliffe has no hesitation in supporting the British policy of baptizing the Sikh recruits according to the rite prescribed by Guru Gobind Singh in spite of the professed civil policy of 'religious neutrality'. Punjabi could be recognized as an official or optional official language of the Punjab as 'a most powerful means of preserving the Sikh religion'.[38]

Macauliffe mentions several advantages of his study. The administrators could formulate correct policies on the basis of a better understanding of the Sikhs. Sikh studies could throw light on 'the state of society in the Middle Ages', and, thus, be useful also to the student of 'comparative theology'. Above all, a knowledge of the excellence of their religion throughout the world could serve practical as well as academic purposes, to the advantage of both the rulers and the ruled.[39]

Macauliffe's work found ready acceptance among Sikh scholars and Sikh organizations. A giani of the Golden Temple and two other eminent Bhais declared that his translation conformed to the religious tenets of the Sikhs. The editor of *The Khalsa* expected his work to introduce 'a new era' in Sikh history. The 'traitors' to the Panth would not be able to misrepresent the Sikh tradition in order to please their 'wealthier and more influential neighbours'. This oblique reference to the Sikh supporters of Hindu identity in the Hindu-Sikh controversy indicates that the editor was a supporter of an independent Sikh identity. The Singh Sabha of Amritsar felt gratified that Macauliffe's work would fulfil the great need of 'an accurate version' of the Sikh scripture, especially because Trumpp's translation was not only generally incorrect but also 'injurious to our religion'.[40] Macauliffe's anxiety to present an orthodox version of the Sikh tradition is understandable in this context. It is also understandable why many a Sikh scholar has been appreciative of his work.

Macauliffe widened the scope of the study of the early Sikh tradition on the basis of original sources, especially Sikh sources. That he was quite critical is evident from his rejection of certain sources, his analysis of the *Janamsakhis*, particularly his view that their composers looked for appropriate settings for the verses of Guru Nanak, and his analysis of the *Dasam Granth*. However, in his own narratives he not only used these verses but also included post-eventum prophecies and a few supernatural elements. It appears that he tried to find a middle ground between his own critical assessment and what he regarded as the 'orthodox' Sikh view.

Macauliffe's work can be seen as reflecting the views and attitudes of the Sikh scholars who were associated with the Singh Sabha movement. This can be seen in his opposition to Trumpp, his view of Sikhism as a totally independent world religion, his support for a distinct Sikh identity, his advocacy of Punjabi as the official language of the province, his rejection of the current belief that Guru Gobind Singh invoked the Goddess for instituting the Khalsa, his view that Guru Gobind Singh was opposed to the worship of gods and goddesses, demons, spirits, *pirs* and cemeteries, and his view that Guru Gobind Singh vested Guruship in the *Granth* and the Panth. Like the contemporary Sikh scholars of the Singh Sabha movement, he believed that there were three recensions of the *Adi Granth* which could be regarded as authentic. That appears to be the reason why he included Mira Bai among the 'Bhagats' of the *Adi*

Granth. It must be emphasized that Macauliffe was acceptable to the Sikhs primarily because his translation was closer to the original, and his interpretation of the Sikh tradition was faithful to the sources he used.

NOTES

1. Macauliffe's view of the authorship is not acceptable any more to a large number of scholars who have argued that Shaikh Farid, and not Shaikh Ibrahim, was the author.
2. Macauliffe himself says that Mira's hymn was included in the Banno recension but not in the *Granth* prepared by Guru Arjan: Macauliffe, *The Sikh Religion: Its Gurus, Sacred Writings and Authors*, Delhi: Low Price Publications, 1995 (rpt., first published in 1909), vol. VI, p. 342. Presumably, he accepted both the recensions as equally authentic.
3. Macauliffe refers only twice each to the works of Wilson and Trumpp, and only once each to the works of Malcolm and Cunningham: Ibid., vol. I, pp. xv and 82n.3; IV, p. 21n.1; V, p. 35n.; VI, pp. 104n.3 and 140n.1.
4. Ibid., vol. I, pp. vii, ix and xxix-xxx.
5. Ibid., pp. xvii-xviii.
6. Ibid., p. xxxii.
7. Ibid., pp. xl-xlix, lii-lv and p. I. Macauliffe quotes from the *Vars* of Bhai Gurdas to show that in his view the Sikh religion was 'distinct, and superior to other religions': Ibid., IV, pp. 241-74.
8. Ibid., vol. I, pp. lvii-lxix.
9. Ibid., p. xxiii.
10. Ibid., pp. xxiii and lvii.
11. Ibid., pp. ix, xiv-xvii.
12. Ibid., pp. lxxiii-lxxvii.
13. Ibid., pp. lxxvii-lxxviii.
14. Ibid., pp. lxxix-lxxxvi.
15. Ibid., pp. lxxxvi-lxxxvii.
16. Ibid., vol. V, pp. 1, 103-14, 201-6, 224n.1 and 254.
17. Ibid., pp. 22 and n. I, 93-4, 97 and 241.
18. Ibid., pp. 60-5 and 67-84.
19. Ibid., pp. 62, 122, 458-9, 238 and 245.
20. Ibid., p. 223.
21. Ibid., p. 224. Macauliffe tended to accept the *Pran Sangali* as authentic, though it was not included in the *Adi Granth*: Ibid., vol. I, p. 156; vol. III, pp. 53-5 and n. 1. The *Ragmala* was regarded as a part of the *Madhava Nal*

Sangit written in 1583 by a Muslim poet named Alam. But the list of *Ragas* and *Raginis* and their subdivisions given by Alam do not correspond with the *Ragas* of the *Granth Sahib*: Ibid., vol. III, pp. 64-5.

22. Ibid., vol. I, pp. li-lii; vol. V, p. 223 and n. 1, pp. 260-1 and n. 1.
23. Ibid., p. 196.
24. Ibid., pp. 200-1.
25. Ibid., p. 202.
26. Ibid., p. 201.
27. Ibid., p. 208.
28. Ibid., p. 214.
29. Dorothy Field, *The Religion of the Sikhs* (Wisdom of the East series), London: John Murray, 1914, Editorial Note. In her 'Acknowledgement' only the name of Macauliffe figures: Ibid., p. 11.
30. Ibid., p. 10.
31. Ibid., p. 9.
32. Ibid., p. 36.
33. Ibid., p. 42.
34. Ibid., pp. 28-31.
35. Ibid., pp. 34-5.
36. Ibid., pp. 44-60.
37. Macauliffe, *The Sikh Religion*, vol. V, pp. 107, 240, 245n.1.
38. Ibid., vol. I, pp. vii-viii, xxiv, xxv, 18, 20.
39. Ibid., pp. vii, x-xxiii.
40. Ibid., pp. x-xxiii.

CHAPTER NINE

J.C. Archer and C.H. Loehlin

American Missionaries on Sikhism and Sikh Scriptures

I. INTRODUCTORY

The missionary work in India created a certain degree of interest in the religions of India in North America. This interest extended to Sikhism and the Sikh scriptures far more conspicuously in the 1940s than earlier, even though the Sikhs were important in the eyes of the Christian missionaries since the establishment of the Ludhiana mission in the 1830s. The works of J.C. Archer and C.H. Loehlin stand distinguished from the earlier writings in terms of both scope and depth.

Before visiting the Punjab in the 1930s and the 1940s, John Clarke Archer had worked at Jubbalpur in 1907-12 as an educational missionary. Before his death in 1957 at the age of 75, he retired as Hobber Professor of Comparative Religion at the Divinity School of the Yale University. He was regarded as one of the best authorities on the religions of India. As a liberal Christian missionary Archer was opposed to the idea of establishing 'a distinctly American God' in India, and he was in favour of adapting the message of Christianity everywhere to 'the minds of men'. His interest in comparative religion was a reflection of his liberal outlook on non-Christian religions.

C.H. Loehlin, a younger contemporary of Archer, had stayed much longer in the Punjab, closely associated with the Baring Union Christian School and College at Batala. He believed in interfaith dialogue and he was interested primarily in the Sikh scriptures.

II. A COMPARATIVE STUDY OF THE SIKHS: J.C. ARCHER

Archer declares *The Sikhs in Relation to Hindus, Moslems, Christians and Ahmadiyyas*, published in 1946, to be 'a study in comparative religion' though a study in which 'prolonged attention' is given to the Sikhs and their religion. Archer was aware of the work done by Cunningham, Trumpp and Macauliffe; he was also familiar with the works published by Khazan Singh, Bhai Jodh Singh, Teja Singh, and Ganda Singh. But they had not undertaken a 'comparative appraisal'. The distinguishing feature of Archer's work was his comparative approach.[1]

Archer puts forth the familiar hypothesis that Sikhism originated in an effort toward 'reconciliation' of Hindu and Islamic order and ideas. He goes on to add, however, that 'somewhat at variance from initial purposes' Sikhism became 'an independent and conspicuous order of its own', comparable with Christianity, Hinduism and Islam. Paradoxically, therefore, the success of the Sikhs was the outcome of their failure to accomplish the original purpose of Sikhism. Archer observed that half of the Sikhs in the contemporary Punjab, could not readily be distinguished from their Hindu kinsfolk by 'outward signs'. But the other half bore distinctive marks, representing an enduring order which was 'at once non-Moslem and non-Hindu'. Archer's chief concern was with the rise of the Sikhs 'who are distinctive'.[2]

Archer makes a sharp distinction between 'the temporal and the spiritual' concerns of men, which somehow do not remain separate. Guru Nanak seemed to give no thought to politics, unless to reject it. But perhaps 'it was politics, primarily, which after a while gave Sikhism a much altered character in relation with the Mughals and the British'. That was why 'Sikhism as venture in the reconciliation of religions' issued ultimately in 'a distinct religious order and a separate political community'. Archer saw for this development some relevance of the Jats too. Ordinarily they were peaceably inclined and yet they were 'independent to a degree of impatience over too immediate government control'. The Jat Sikhs organized the Khalsa, and gave Sikhism 'most of its stolid and compelling substance'.[3]

For 'Sikh origins', Archer thinks of Kabir, whose teachings appeared to represent 'a reconciliation of the major doctrines of Islam and Hinduism'. About a dozen sects came to share his inheritance. Of them, the Sikhs were 'the most conspicuous, alert and virile'. Furthermore, the Sikh movement was at once related to and distinct from the movement initiated by Kabir.[8] Had there been no Guru Nanak, the memory of Kabir might have faded into the dim light of the common Hindu day. Kabir and Guru Nanak 'shared something of a common vernacular', but they were two 'distinct phenomena'.[4]

Guru Nanak is both factual and formless for Archer. 'This may be recognized at once as something common in the history of religions'. Guru Nanak was a 'historical person'; he was also a 'theological construction'. He was a real person and he was also 'a creature of religious fancy'. However, the two Nanaks are not always to be distinguished from each other. 'They are two in one, both in practice and in theory'. The formless Nanak is more important as a typical phenomenon in the total history of religion: 'It was the faith in him which made him a compelling figure'. Whereas records for the role of Nanak the formless are ample, records for the factual Nanak are meagre: 'no Sikh has yet examined the career of Nanak by the full means of modern, critical techniques'. What Mohan Singh had done for the life of Kabir, some Sikh 'must do the same one day for Nanak'.[5]

Imaginatively, Archer tries to make the best sense of the materials available to him. The round of Guru Nanak's early life was dictated largely by common custom. He received some formal education in the local elementary school, and learnt many things from observation, including both mosque and temple ceremonials. He seems to have displayed an unusual disposition toward religion. His piety was often more pronounced than his willingness for manual labour. He became acquainted in due course with portions of the Hindu Shastras and sacred writings, and with portions of the *Hadis* and the Qur'an, which were in circulation. He may have heard wandering Hindu and Muslim teachers discussing the unity of God. Breathing 'a lively atmosphere', he came under the influence of kindred expressions by different kinds of devotees. But it would be wrong to insist that 'he was merely acquiring the mind and the manner of imitation', or to say that when he expressed his teachings in any similar phraseology 'he was exhibiting dependence and not initiative'.[6]

Guru Nanak got married and took service, but he remained restless and unhappy. Possibly in his early thirties he took up an exclusively spiritual career. He may have been about fifty years of age when, in response to a special vision, he entered the final phase of his career; God offered him the cup of *amrit* as a token of favour and promise of his ultimate success. God commissioned him to 'repeat the Name', to inspire others also to repeat it, and teach all mankind the 'true religion'. The 'basic text' of Sikhism, the *mulmantar,* was uttered by Guru Nanak after this experience of illumination. He also proclaimed that 'there is no Hindu, nor is there a Musalman'. Archer takes it to mean that all men were 'only brethren' under God. If 'legend' was to be believed, Guru Nanak wandered widely throughout India and abroad. But we may assume that even his actual wanderings were 'extensive'. Informal groups of followers came into existence in 'loose, quasi-monastic bonds'.[7]

Archer attaches special significance to the travels of Guru Nanak. It was outside the Punjab that he had occasion to consider older atheisms of Buddhism and Jainism, to plead for 'a recognition of True Name' as the centre and object of devotion, and the sure ground of spiritual illumination. At Puri, he contended that Jagannath's *arati* was nothing in comparison with man's recognition of the divinity in all things. In his contest with the *yogis,* he revealed the 'miracle' of the True Name. He had no appreciation for yogic practices. Similarly, he agreed to one God of Islam but not in 'association' with Muhammad.[8] Guru Nanak had a message which 'revealed the hidden heart of things, and which could serve as a leaven for regeneration. He may be judged, therefore, not as one may judge Muhammad but as one may judge Christ. He left the creedal content of the movement largely undeveloped and its organization vague and incomplete. We have to judge 'this first Sikh in a fuller measure than himself, by other Sikhs and what came after him'. 'Was there something worldly after all in Nanak?'[9]

The psalms of Guru Nanak 'expound a socially and spiritually extensive and inclusive religion' in the name of One who makes no unfavourable distinctions among men, even though they themselves are born 'high and low by His will'. There is an optimistic note in Guru Nanak that was 'unusual in Hindu India'. 'It is Sat Nam that frees the devotee from the control of Karma and from the round of transmigration'. On the basis of his understanding of the *Japuji,* Archer comes to the conclusion that Guru Nanak proposed the superiority of the 'way of truth' over the 'way of knowledge' and the 'way of works'. He recommended the way of truth as superior even to the 'way of *bhakti*'.

Archer thinks that Guru Nanak was preaching the way of *bhakti* with the True Name as its inspiration. The *bhakti marga* was to Guru Nanak 'the true way if pursued in the true Name'. He proposed, 'even though not deliberately, a fourth way of salvation, more instrumental and effective than any one or all of the other three'.[10]

Guru Nanak introduced no formal legal code. Nor did he suggest any specific alterations in the immemorial legal usages of Indian tribes and clans. He took the state for granted. That is why Archer looks upon the appointment of a successor as of crucial importance. The successors of Guru Nanak gave Sikhism a form 'measurably in harmony with Nanak's legacy and his own intention'. The decades between the death of Guru Nanak and the martyrdom of Guru Arjan are seen by Archer as the 'period of adjustment'. Guru Nanak had made the public kitchen 'a distinctive feature of the Sikhs'. All the visitors and disciples ate 'as one family, regardless of race, wealth, sex, caste occupation or religion'. Guru Angad extended the operation of the public kitchen and enlarged his ministry. Guru Nanak had used essentially 'the language of the village folks' for his hymns. Guru Angad provided for these hymns their distinctive alphabet: 'through his effort arose Gurmukhi as a new language of religion'. [11]

Guru Amar Das's career in office gave further emphasis to the development of Sikhism as 'something more than a mere sect of Hinduism'. His verse became the channel of his message. He denounced the practice of *sati,* giving it a figurative spiritual meaning. Guru Amar Das composed his *Anand* to be commonly used at wedding festivals. In general terms too, the Sikh movement was marked by joy (*anand*) rather than sorrow (*udas*) to distinguish it from the 'mere negative asceticism' of Sri Chand.[12] Archer attributes to Guru Ram Das not only the founding of Ramdaspur but also the construction of the Harmandar amidst the 'pool of immortality'. Sikhism came to assume 'more definite proportions as an actually new community' during the time of Guru Arjan, 'the fashioner of a second sword'. His era was 'a time of utter transformation in the mission of the Sikhs'. Matters creedal, ritual, financial, political and social became public issues for the Sikhs in a special sense. Guru Arjan's noblest achievement was the assembling of the *Adi Granth* into a compact, coherent form, and its elevation as authoritative scripture. The Sikhs became a people of the book (*Granth*), like the Muslims with their Qur'an and Hindus with their Shastras. The governing principle was 'the Sikh communal consciousness'.[13] Guru Arjan had to deal with matters of importance other than ritual and scriptural matter. Voluntary offerings were no longer adequate to meet increased, legitimate expenses. 'A church and even a state were virtually in process of formation.' Every adult Sikh was asked to pay a tenth of his gross income to support the kitchens, the sanctuaries and the office of Guruship. Tithe-gatherers were appointed to work under supervisors (*masands*). 'Sikhs were getting acquainted with and practising self-government.' Then there was trade. Sikhs began to travel freely anywhere, uninhibited by any religious taboo. 'There were political considerations also, with their own social and religious implications.'[14]

The larger world of the Mughals took increasing notice of the Sikhs. Guru Arjan was fined, imprisoned, and tortured to death as 'the first martyr of the Sikhs'. However, it was not the martyrdom alone which made the Sikhs warlike. 'Sikhs were slowly getting organized and as an organism they came to be confronted by some circumstantial need of war.' The 'martial mood' was in the making in a situation of 'competition' between the Sikh church and the Mughal state. 'It was not long before rumor, whether couched in terms of the last "words of Arjun" or in others, began to pass through the Indian bazaars and along the pilgrim routes that a change of mood prevailed among the Sikhs.' In Archer's explanation of how a 'fellowship of reconciliation was assuming martial form', no single event and no single person is pinpointed. This transformation was the result of 'adjustment' that took place after 1539 in consonance with Guru Nanak's legacy and his intentions.[15]

The Sikh attitude under Guru Hargobind was not aggressive but the principle of mutual antagonism between Sikhs and Muslims by this time was well established. He asked for offerings of arms and horses as well as money. 'The nation in the making must defend itself, he thought, and be ready likewise for offensive, if necessary'. The 'communal consciousness' of the Sikhs made them feel distinct from Hindus as well. In Archer's view, the construction of Akal Takht (Throne of the Timeless), completed by Guru Hargobind, was begun by Guru Arjan. Archer was not interested in the battles of Guru Hargobind. But he does comment on the devotion of his Sikhs to him: several of his followers would have cast themselves into the very flames of his funeral pyre.[16] Archer takes notice of the *Vars* of Bhai Gurdas as evidence of a heightened sense of Sikh communal consciousness. Sikhism in the *Vars* is superior to all other faiths, and the Sikhs are different from all other communities, not just Hindus and Muslims. Archer saw nothing of great significance in the careers of Guru Har Rai and Guru Har Krishan but Sikhism under Guru Tegh Bahadur took on a 'martial character' so that he was more than a 'harmless' guide in spiritual concerns. The orthodoxy of Aurangzeb and the 'party' of Guru Tegh Bahadur were 'incompatible'.[17]

Guru Gobind Singh became a champion of the lowly peoples of north India and 'an irreconcilable foe' of Muslim rule. His measures resulted in 'further integration' of Sikhism and its 'ultimate expansion'. Archer has the institution of the Khalsa in mind in making this observation. In 1699 Guru Gobind Singh was 'a man of forty'; 'mature, seasoned and resourceful, with an enhanced sense of divine assistance in his discharge of sacred duty, and enjoying the confidence of a large following and the general public'. He summoned all Sikhs to Anandpur on the Baisakhi day, 'announcing that the goddess Durga has already bestowed her blessing upon his enterprise'. Guru Gobind Singh knew the value of appeal to her. He did not see anything in her worship that was 'necessarily incongruous with Sikhism'. Nor did it make Guru Gobind Singh 'a Hindu'. He was proceeding 'with some independence and sound judgment of his own'. Several unifying factors made the Khalsa Sikhs 'unique', and there was no violent departure from the earlier Sikh tradition. There was some telescoping in the code ascribed to Guru Gobind Singh. But one thing was certain: 'there was instituted an imposing order, adequately free, on the whole, of contaminations from Hinduism and Islam'. The concept of Guruship too was undergoing change. *Vaheguruji ka Khalsa, Vaheguruji ki Fateh* suggested to Archer that Guru Gobind Singh was thinking of putting an end to personal Guruship. The *Adi Granth* was a logical alternative to the personal Guru.[18] However, even after Banda Bahadur's death, the question of Guruship was still 'somewhat indeterminate'. This question was answering itself 'by a gradual but sure process'.[19]

In the early eighteenth century the Sikhs stood divided into a number of sects and parties: the Bandais, the Handalis, the Ram Raiyas, the

Minas, the Dhir Mallias, the Masandis, the Nanakpanthis, the Udasis, the Nirmalas, the Sewapanthis and the Akalis-Nihangs-Shahids (as a single category). Archer looked upon the last as the most important. Regarding themselves as the heirs of Guru Gobind Singh's tradition, the Akalis rallied many other Sikhs to build the Khalsa of Guru Gobind Singh's conception. Some active unity was forged against the Muslims by these members of the 'third religion'. From the middle of the eighteenth-century bands of Sikhs could be found all over the central Punjab. In 1764 a committee of the Akalis called a 'diet' in Amritsar to proclaim the independence of the Sikh state and religion. A theocracy (*gurmata*) was formed, consisting of a representative assembly sitting as a committee of the whole (*sarbat*) and taking counsel (*mata*) in the name of God the Guru. It provided unity of action, grounded in the theory of Sikh faith.[20]

Archer talks about the *misls* to emphasize the unity of action and sums up the position of the Sikh Panth before the end of the eighteenth century. To an outside observer, Sikhism was 'a loose collection of *misls* and *sardars,* of panths and mahants'. Politics among them was more apparent than religion. Observing the Sikhs closely, however, one could see that this loose confederacy was nonetheless, dominated by 'the ideal of the Khalsa', with religion as perhaps the chief of its ingredients. The men of action moved in a field 'so large and varied that no less than a threefold standard should be applied to its appraisal, namely, politics, religion and morality'.[21]

Maharaja Ranjit Singh gave Sikhism a state. His own religion was scarcely more than form. He made it political and diplomatic, 'an affair of man and not of God'. Yet he was punctilious in worship he was not only present regularly at public prayers but also listened daily to readings from the *Adi Granth.* Nevertheless, his Sikhism had something of a Hindu odour. He celebrated Hindu festivals, gave financial aid to Hindu holy places, and he countenanced *sati* among the Sikhs. On his own *samadh,* four wives and seven concubines are commemorated as *satis.* It may be argued that by maintaining gurdwaras and their custodians Ranjit Singh had met his obligation towards religion.[22]

For morality, however, Maharaja Ranjit Singh did not escape personal responsibility. He was promiscuous in sexual affairs. He was addicted to both liquor and *bhang* which were used frequently by the *sardars* and the rank and file of Sikhs. The Singhs were men of courage but they often simulated bravery with *bhang*. Sikhism had gained much, but at the cost of morals. Indeed, 'the Khalsa' had not been realized in terms commensurate with the larger plan of Guru Gobind Singh in which considerations of politics, morals and religion were held in delicate balance.[23]

Archer had visited the Punjab in the 1930s and 1940s. He had the privilege of seeing the original *Granth* prepared by Guru Arjan at Kartarpur in 1946. He contributed an article to *The Review of Religion* in 1949, carrying the title 'the Bible of the Sikhs'.[24] This article briefly described the Kartarpur manuscript and ended with the note that 'an altogether comprehensive and intensive study of the Bible of the Sikhs' may be undertaken. Archer was aware that several Sikh scholars were engaged in research 'in the history, composition, and authentic content of the Book' to seek answers to questions raised within the community. The scope of this research could be extended, he argued, to include linguistics and a comparative study of the various versions of the compositions of the *bhagats*. Reputable Sikh scholars could be encouraged to undertake historical and textual criticism of the Kartarpur manuscript.

Though Archer starts with the statement that he assumed the Kartarpur manuscript to be the original *Granth*, his description was meant to suggest that the 'problem of the book is, of course, acute'. The problem is summed up at the outset: 'it bears no date, nor the name of any scribe. Its history is not altogether clear, nor has the authenticity of all its contents been established'. The two other accepted versions of the *Adi Granth* did not improve matters. The Bhai Banno version contained a hymn of Mira Bai, besides being simply a copy of the Kartarpur recension. The *Granth* authenticated by Guru Gobind Singh contained his own verse and the *bani* of Guru Tegh Bahadur, in addition to what was there in the Kartarpur recension. But the copy authenticated by Guru Gobind Singh was lost. The printed *Granth* was 'for the most part, an uncritical reproduction of the Kartarpur original' together with the additions made by Guru Gobind Singh. With subdued scepticism, thus, Archer raised by implication the issue of the authenticity of the Kartarpur *Pothi*.

For Archer, Sikhism eventually emerged as a world religion. He isolates Kabir from Vaishnava *bhakti* and sees his relevance for Guru Nanak. Nevertheless, Guru Nanak is distinguished by his doctrine of the True Name. His movement was distinct from that of Kabir. Indeed, Archer talks of Guru Nanak's path as the fourth way which was more efficacious than all the other three: *karma, gian,* and *bhakti.* Archer raises the issue of the *Janamsakhis* to a different plane altogether by postulating a distinction between the factual and the formless Nanak. For Archer's purpose, there was no urgency for isolating the one from the other, but he did emphasize the need of a strictly historical biography of Guru Nanak. Archer does not see the Khalsa of Guru Gobind Singh as a sudden departure from the earlier Sikh movement. He attaches due importance to the *Japuji* as the nucleus of the Sikh scripture and to *langar* as the institution embedded in the idea of equality. The work of Guru Angad, Guru Amar Das, Guru Ram Das and Guru Arjan, in his view, made the Sikh Panth a state within the Mughal empire and brought it into competition with the Mughal state. This view makes Guru Hargobind an integral part of the élan of the Sikh movement.

III. THE SIKH SCRIPTURES: C.H. LOEHLIN

C.H. Loehlin published *The Sikhs and Their Book* in 1946. His doctoral thesis on the *Dasam Granth* was completed in 1957. An extended version of his first book was published in 1958 as *The Sikhs and Their Scriptures.* His doctoral thesis was published in 1971 as *The Granth of Guru Gobind Singh and the Khalsa Brotherhood.* Loehlin's interest in the Sikh scriptural literature is evident from his publications. In an article published in the *Proceedings Punjab History Conference* in 1966 he reinforced Archer's plea for historical and textual study of the *Kartarpur Pothi.*

In *The Sikhs and Their Scriptures,* Loehlin starts with the environment of tyranny in which Guru Nanak attempted a reconciliation of the two warring communities on the basis of a synthesis 'to form a new brotherhood'. The 'sect' of the Sikh Gurus had sprung from the teachings of Kabir. Like Kabir, Guru Nanak represented the *bhakti* tradition which was meant 'to synthesize Hinduism and Islam'. The synthesis produced by the Sikh Gurus resulted in an 'intermediate religion'. 'Sufism offered Bhakti Hinduism a congenial field of contact for this fusion'. According to Loehlin, Guru Nanak rejected the Vedas and other scriptures, priesthood of the Brahmans, caste, idolatry, pilgrimages, asceticism, *ahimsa* and animal sacrifice but he retained pantheism, *karma*, transmigration, *maya*, necessity of the Guru, repetition of the Name, *bhakti*, and salvation by grace. From Islam, Guru Nanak took the idea of One Absolute God, theocracy, repetition of God's name, fatalism, hatred of idolatry, a central shrine and daily prayers. The difference of Sikhism with Christianity related to ten Gurus instead of one Perfect Guru, baptism only of adults, no special recurring day of worship like Sunday, set prayers for everyday, and physical symbols. Nevertheless, Loehlin thinks that several ideas and practices could have possibly come from Christianity: salvation by grace, lay readers of scriptures, reality of sin and need of forgiveness, sacrifice in service, baptism and the communion meal, congregational hymn singing and worship by all men and women and children, and organization of local congregations. At the same time Loehlin thinks that congregational worship could have been taken from Buddhism.[25] Loehlin catalogued ideas and practices in terms of 'influences'. His work does not clarify any issue. Unlike Archer, he looks upon Sikhism as closely aligned with *bhakti*.

Loehlin's *Granth of Guru Gobind Singh and The Khalsa Brotherhood* was meant to correct the 'militaristic interpretation' of Guru Gobind Singh's mission.[26] A substantial portion of the book is devoted to the *Dasam Granth*. Loehlin discusses its status, purpose, character, form and language in two chapters. He underlines its importance by stating that the Sikhs have 'two books of scripture'. The *Adi Granth* was aimed at developing 'the mystical and contemplative side' of the Sikh character; the *Dasam Granth* was aimed at developing 'the martial side of the Sikhs'. These two books 'helped form the Sikh ideal man, the soldier-saint'. However, only 'a handful of extremists regard the *Dasam Granth* in its entirety as in any way equal to the *Adi Granth*'.[27]

The writings included in the *Dasam Granth* were composed by Guru Gobind Singh and his fifty-two bards and translators mainly in two phases: at Anandpur and Paonta before 1700, and at Damdama in 1705-6. While the others wrote in Braj, Guru Gobind Singh wrote in Punjabi and Persian as well. The *Granth* was compiled by Bhai Mani Singh in 1734. After his martyrdom in 1738, Sikh scholars assembled at Damdama expressed doubt about the spiritual value of much of its content. The issue was decided in favour of retaining the *Granth* as it was, but only because Mahtab Singh succeeded in killing Massa Ranghar and returning alive—a criterion which strictly speaking was extraneous to the terms of the debate and, therefore, arbitrary. The purpose of translating Hindu literature is stated explicitly by Guru Gobind Singh at the end of the *Krishan Avtar:* 'I have rendered in the vernacular the tenth chapter of the Bhagavat with no other purpose than to arouse desire for a holy war'. This militant purpose becomes clear from the various books of the *Granth.*[28]

Loehlin endorses the general agreement that the *Jap* was written by Guru Gobind Singh. The idea of incarnation is emphatically rejected in this composition. The *Akal Ustat,* a jumble of subjects, was a composition of Guru Gobind Singh, but not entirely. Loehlin does not like to believe that Guru Gobind Singh composed the section containing verses with 'amoral flavour'. But he is not surprised to see the Goddess riding the tiger in this 'praise of the Immortal'. Despite its invocations to the God of war, the composition ends with an attitude of universal tolerance. Loehlin is inclined to endorse the general agreement that the *Bachittar Natak* was composed by Guru Gobind Singh. He has reservations, however, about a section which 'seems far too Hindu in outlook and ideals', such as the exaltation of the Vedas and the sanctity of caste. This could not be 'the Guru's own work'. The twofold nature of Guru Gobind Singh's mission to create the warrior-saint is well exemplified in the *Bachittar Natak.*[29]

The epic of *Chandi* in Punjabi was another work of Guru Gobind Singh. The first verse of this *var* is always recited at the beginning of the Sikh prayer (*ardas*). Much of the *Gian Prabodh* seemed contrary to the authentic teachings of Guru Gobind Singh, but it was sought to be authenticated by the use of '*patshahi* 10' at its heading. Loehlin finds it hard to conceive that Guru Gobind Singh was the translator of the *Chaubis Avtar.* Its great mass must have been produced by the bards, some of whom must have been Hindus and 'probably all had imbibed the culture and mythology of Hinduism'. At the end of the *Ram Avtar,* Guru Gobind Singh makes it clear that he did not accept the opinions of the Puranas or of the Qu'ran, nor the doctrines of the Smritis, Shastras or the Vedas. The *Shabad Hazare* and *Thirty-Three Savvayye* were composed by Guru Gobind Singh. Another of his authentic compositions was the *Zafarnama.* Loehlin comes to the conclusion that the *Chaubis Avtar, Shastar Nam, Pakhyan Charitar,* and the *Hikayat* were probably the work of the bards. These may have been supervised by Guru Gobind Singh who sometimes added verses of his own. Thus, the Guru's authentic compositions cover only about 170 out of over 1,400 pages of the *Dasam Granth* compiled by Bhai Mani Singh.[30]

Loehlin compares the two *Granths,* reiterating that only the *Adi Granth* has the status of the Guru. In general, both the *Granths* accept the Hindu theology of the contemplative *bhakti* type. Both express boundless wonder at the Creator and His universe. However, Guru Nanak's God is the God of truth while Guru Gobind Singh invokes the immortal, deathless and unchanging God. Both the *Granths* reject Hindu practices such as pilgrimages, the sacred thread, caste, asceticism, and idolatry. And both seem at times to be tinged with Hindu pantheism, and with Muslim ideas of the absoluteness of God, and of fatalism. Both take for granted *karma* and transmigration. Both use the vernacular, and both are rhymed poetry. Their main difference is that of purpose. The *Adi Granth* 'aims at peace of mind, the *Dasam Granth* at readiness for war'. There is nothing in the *Japji* of Guru Nanak like the hundreds of negative attributes used to describe the immortal One in the *Jap,* nor like the dozens of Muslim names for God. There is nothing in the *Jap* like the emphasis of the *Japuji* on God's *hukam* or the mystical realms of Guru Nanak. 'Resting on a common theological foundation, the *Adi Granth* had taken form as a temple, the *Dasam Granth* as fortress.'[31]

Loehlin gives a whole chapter to *hukamnamas,* many of which were issued by Guru Gobind Singh. They have not merely a human interest but also historical importance. We may agree with Loehlin that these *hukamnamas* reveal religious, political, social, literary, and economic conditions 'in the intimate way letters do'. But Loehlin fails to relate this evidence in any appreciable way to either the life of Guru Gobind Singh or his creative writings. The chapter does not integrate with the rest of the book. Loehlin was probably tempted to talk of this fascinating evidence ready to hand in Ganda Singh's *Hukamname.*[32]

Loehlin points out some similarities between the writings of Guru Gobind Singh and the *Gita.* These similarities relate to the mission of Krishna on the one hand and that of Guru Gobind Singh on the other. Both hold out reward for death on the field of battle; both celebrate the destructive might of God; and both put emphasis on 'a mission of deliverance and mercy, and on a God who is supremely gracious'. Nevertheless, Guru Gobind Singh rejects the teaching of the *Gita* on caste duties, incarnation, action without desire, *nirvana*, and the value of Yoga and asceticism. Loehlin takes up Guru Gobind Singh's attitude towards Islam in order to correct the widespread opinion that he was an irreconcilable enemy of all Muslims. The Muslim terms used for God in the *Jap* appear to be relevant here. And so is the Guru's semitic outlook on the subject of incarnation. The dealings of Guru Gobind Singh even with the fanatical Aurangzeb 'show a singular lack of vindictiveness'. The Guru's relations with Bahadur Shah also indicate that he was not opposed to conciliation on fair terms. Loehlin concludes his discussion by referring to the *Akal Ustat* in which 'the temple and the mosque are the same, *puja* and *namaz* are the same'. Allah and Abhekh are the same; the Purana and the Qu'ran are the same; all are the creation of the One.[33]

Loehlin's Appendix on 'The Need for Textual and Historical Criticism' reproduces the short paper he had presented to the Punjab History Conference in 1965. It reinforces Archer's plea for historical and textual criticism. He had visited Kartarpur twice in 1946 and, like Archer, taken rough notes. Archer's note is quoted by Loehlin and he goes on to say that their observations were not superficial. Both of them were familiar with the 'textual criticism of the Christian scriptures', involving an effort to establish 'the original text with no original manuscripts of it extant'.

> If the problem of the *Adi Granth* is so acute, it should be evident from the preceding account, how much more so that of the Tenth Granth is. Who wrote it? How really was it compiled? What is its authentic text? What is the purpose of its various books?

There was a difference in the order and division of the contents in the various manuscripts of the *Dasam Granth* prepared by Bhai Mani Singh. The need of 'literary criticism' was evident from the fact that there was no general agreement as to what the Guru wrote himself, what he edited, what the bards wrote, and whether he approved of their writings or not. The Sikhs as well as Western scholars of Sikhism had noted lack of critical interest on the part of the Sikhs. 'Fortunately, many of their scholars and research experts are doing research on textual and historical problems.'[34] Truth was the main attribute of God for Guru Nanak: Guru Gobind Singh declared that he would not remain silent through fear of mortals. Loehlin saw no reason why the followers of Guru Nanak and Guru Gobind Singh should not pursue truth in a spirit of fearless independence.[35]

Like Archer, Loehlin emphasized the need of textual criticism in relation to both the *Adi Granth* and the *Dasam Granth*. Sikhism, for him, emerged as a world religion but in the beginning it stood equated with the *bhakti-marga* as a synthesis of *bhakti* Hinduism and Sufi Islam. Guru Gobind Singh gave Sikhism the final form by founding the Khalsa as a distinct order which provided the main cohesive force to the faith. Loehlin tends to subscribe to the view that Guru Gobind Singh propitiated the Goddess at Naina Devi. He argues that Guruship was vested by Guru Gobind Singh in the *Adi Granth*. He discusses the idea of equality in relation to the system of castes. The standard of equality set in the *Adi Granth* was high but the Sikhs still practised caste to some extent. They were not free from 'the caste system', but the war on caste was still going on.

IV. SOME GENERAL OBSERVATIONS

Both Archer and Loehlin were Christian missionaries interested in education. It may be interesting to compare their views on some important aspects of Sikhism and Sikh history. On the status of Sikhism they agree that Sikhism emerged as a world religion. However, they differ in their conception of the nature of the Sikh faith in the beginning. For Loehlin it was a synthesis of *bhakti* and Sufism, a form of *bhakti-marga*. For Archer, though influenced by Kabir, the Sikh faith was distinguished by the doctrine of the True Name as different from the *bhakti-marga* as well as the paths of *karma* and *gian*. Both Archer and Loehlin view the development of the Sikh Panth as evolutionary. For Archer, the martial activities of Guru Hargobind were a part of the élan of the Sikh movement. For Loehlin, Guru Gobind Singh completed the development of Sikhism. Both Archer and Loehlin subscribe to the view that Guru Gobind Singh went through the ritual of invoking the Goddess, and they agree that personal Guruship ended after Guru

Gobind Singh, and Guruship was vested in the *Granth Sahib*. Both Archer and Loehlin emphasized the importance of textual criticism in Sikh studies, suspecting the authenticity of the *Kartarpur Pothi* which was claimed to be the *Granth* originally compiled by Guru Arjan. It may be added that there are differences of emphasis and detail on these points between Archer and Loehlin.

Some other views are peculiar to Archer and Loehlin. Archer alone among the Western scholars postulated a difference between the factual and formless Nanak, the Nanak of history and the Nanak of faith. He suggested the need for a strictly historical biography. Archer was also the only Western scholar to suggest that the Khalsa *rahit* was not announced at one time; it developed during the course of the eighteenth century. Similarly, he suggested that the doctrines of *Guru Granth* and Guru-Panth came to be established gradually during the eighteenth century. Incidentally, these ideas would be pursued later on by W.H. McLeod. He also pursued a view expressed for the first time by Loehlin. Many historians had emphasized the ideal of equality in the Sikh social order. Loehlin too subscribes to the importance of the ideal. However, he points out that the Sikhs normally observed 'caste restrictions' for matrimony. Converts from the lower castes and the outcastes were not treated as 'social equals' and sometimes even 'equality of worship' was denied to them. Despite high standard of equality set in the *Granth Sahib*, the Sikhs did not come out of 'the caste system', though the war against caste was still on.

NOTES

1. J.C. Archer, *The Sikhs in Relation to Hindus, Moslems, Christians, and Ahmadiyyas: A Study in Comparative Religion*, Princeton: Princeton University Press, 1946, pp. v-vii.
2. Ibid., pp. v, 2.
3. Ibid., pp. 3, 5, 6.
4. Ibid., pp. 37-56.
5. Ibid., pp. 57-65.
6. Ibid., pp. 65-71.
7. Ibid., pp. 72-87.
8. Ibid., pp. 88-105.
9. Ibid., pp. 105-7.

10. Ibid., pp. 108-17.
11. Ibid., pp. 119-33.
12. Ibid., pp. 139-41.
13. Ibid., pp. 142-52.
14. Ibid., pp. 152-3.
15. Ibid., pp. 169-71.
16. Ibid., pp. 172-4.
17. Ibid., pp. 174-86.
18. Ibid., pp. 187-98.
19. Ibid., pp. 198-219.
20. Ibid., pp. 221-35.
21. Ibid., pp. 236-7.
22. Ibid., pp. 238-45.
23. Ibid., pp. 245-6.
24. John C. Archer, 'The Bible of the Sikhs', *The Review of Religion*, Columbia University, January 1949. For Archer, see also Jaswant Kumar Sharma 'In Comparative Context: Archer's Sikhs', *The Khalsa: Sikh and Non-Sikh Perspectives*, ed. J.S. Grewal, New Delhi: Manohar, 2004, pp. 170-86. J.C. Archer, 'The Bible of the Sikhs', *The Review of Religion*, 1949.
25. C.H. Loehlin, *The Sikhs and Their Scriptures*, Lucknow: Lucknow Publishing House, 1958, pp. 3 and 4.
26. Ibid., pp. 3, 4, 10, 35, 43-4, 54, 57-58, 59, 60, 61 and Table III.
27. C.H. Loehlin, *The Granth of Guru Gobind Singh and the Khalsa Brotherhood*, Lucknow: Lucknow Publishing House, 1971, Preface.
28. Ibid., pp. 9-10.
29. Ibid., pp. 18-20.
30. Ibid., pp. 20-32.
31. Ibid., pp. 9 and 57-9.
32. Ibid., pp. 61-7. Ganda Singh, *Hukamname*, Patiala: Punjabi University, 1967.
33. Loehlin, *The Granth of Guru Gobind Singh*, pp. 75-9.
34. Ibid., pp. 97-102.
35. Ibid., p. 103.

PART THREE

Punjabi Administrators and Professionals

CHAPTER TEN

Syad Muhammad Latif on the Sikhs

I. INTRODUCTORY

Muhammad Latif published his *History of the Panjab from the Remotest Antiquity to the Present Time* in 1891 as an Extra Judicial Assistant Commissioner in the Punjab. His book was presented to Queen Victoria and he was given the title of 'Khan Bahadur' in 1892. His *History* is divided into five parts. The first part relates to the early period, based on the works of European writers. The longest chapter in this part is on Alexander's invasion. All the ten chapters of the first part cover less than one-tenth of the book.[1] The second part, called 'the Mahommedan period', starts with the early Muslim invasions and ends with the death of Akbar Shah II in 1821. This part covers about one-fourth of the book in 25 chapters. The first chapter deals with the Arab invasions and Arab rule in Sind and Multan in two pages. In the rest of this part are given the reigns of a large number of rulers of the various dynasties. Separate chapters are given to the invasions of Timur and Nadir Shah. The longest chapters are on Akbar, Jahangir and Shah Jahan. Latif appreciates Akbar, who ignored the distinctions of race and creed. The memory of this 'ideal sovereign of India' was cherished equally by Hindus and Muslims.[2] Aurangzeb's bigotry and intolerance towards Hindus on the other hand revived religious animosities between the various classes of the population, which paved the way for a speedy dismemberment of the once powerful Mughal monarchy in India.[3] For this part of his *History of the Panjab*, Latif did not depend entirely upon the works of the British historians. He used some important sources in the original Persian or English translation. However, he did not form his general assessment of the past rulers on a criterion of his own. He was impressed much more by his own appreciation of British rule and the views presented by some of the British historians of medieval India.[4]

Latif formed a dim view of the rulers of India. What the much admired Shah Jahan did for his subjects was only 'a drop in ocean, compared with what British statesmen have done for the people of this country'. The rulers like Ashoka, Bikramajit, and Akbar presented brilliant examples of enlightenment and munificence, India prospered under them, and they were remembered as benefactors of their people and their country. But the later Mughal history revealed corruption, degradation, and treachery. The other epithets used by Latif in this connection are confusion and disorder, dissolution, vice, cruelty, extravagance, profligacy, plunder, murders, robberies, voluptuousness and debauchery. The money squeezed from poor peasants was wasted on feasts and peagants. The government was rapacious and tyrannical.[5]

The third part of Latif's book is related to the rise of the Sikhs; the fourth, to the life of Maharaja Ranjit Singh; and the fifth, to the period following the annexation, which includes an account of what the British did in and for the Punjab during the four decades of their rule. On the whole, Sikh history covers a little more than half of Latif's book. It constitutes a substantial volume by itself. That is why Latif was treated by many of the later historians as a historian of the Sikhs as well.

II. EARLY SIKH HISTORY

Latif refers to a wide range of sources for the history of the Sikhs. He acknowledges the use he made of the British historians of the Sikhs: Malcolm, Prinsep, M'Gregor, Smyth, Cunningham, and Griffin. Apart from Honingberger's *Thirty-five Years in the East,* he used the travelogues of Moorcroft, Burnes, Masson and Jacquemont, Thornton's *History of the Panjab,* and Trumpp's *Adi Granth.* In his view, Rai Kanhiya Lal's history of the Punjab in Urdu contained very little that was original. Sohan Lal Suri's *Umdat ut-Tawarikh,* in his view, was 'couched in a hyperbolic style and loaded with fiction'.[6] The other sources used for the history of the Sikhs were the *Memoirs* of Moulvi Mahomed Din of Batala, Diwan Amar Nath's *History of Lahore,* Mohan Lal's *Travels,* in addition to some of the works used for 'the Mahomedan period'.

However, Latif's account of the rise of the Sikhs was based mainly on the works of the European writers. Like them, he gives brief account of the contribution of each of the Gurus towards the development of the Sikh community, remaining close to his sources and repeating their mistakes. Guru Nanak's doctrines were those of pure deism, directed towards removing or reducing to a minimum those religious and social differences which had sprung up between Hindus and Muslims. He believed in the holy mission of Muhammad and in Hindu incarnations. There was a belief among the Sikhs that 'the spirit of Nanak was inherited by each successive Guru'.[7] Guru Angad strictly followed the path paved by Guru Nanak. He also recorded his own compositions which were incorporated in the *Granth*. Guru Amar Das established himself at Goindwal. The number of Sikhs increased during his time. His beautiful verses were included in the *Granth*. He separated the active and worldly Sikhs from the inert and torpid followers of Sri Chand, called Udasis. He disapproved of the practice of becoming *sati*. He built a *baoli* at Goindwal with the offerings received from Sikhs. Guru Ram Das received a grant of land from Akbar. He restored an old tank and called it *amritsar* or the 'pool of immortality'. Latif adds erroneously that in the midst of the tank, Guru Ram Das built a temple which he named Harmandar. On his request, Akbar remitted the revenue of one year for the peasants, which increased the Guru's popularity among the Jatts and the *zamindars*. The founding of the town of Amritsar by Guru Ram Das paved the way for the foundation of a commonwealth.[8]

Guru Arjan gave the Sikhs a religious code in the form of the *Granth* which was kept in the Harmandar. He organized a system of taxation and appointed delegates, or deputies, to collect contributions from the Sikhs and to present them to the Guru at the time of the annual assembly. The Sikhs were accustomed to a regular system of government. Guru Arjan also encouraged trade, especially in horses from Turkistan. He constructed two new tanks, one in Amritsar and the other at Tarn Taran. Guru Arjan refused to betroth his son Hargobind to the daughter of Chandu Shah, the *diwan* at Lahore, who made a malicious misrepresentation to Jahangir that the Guru had prayed for the rebel Prince Khusrau's success. Jahangir wanted to extort money. Guru Arjan died under torture.[9]

Latif gives more attention to Guru Hargobind who combined the qualities of a warrior, a saint, and a sportsman. He introduced animal food and took delight in hunting. He was the first Guru to organize a military system and prepare his followers for action on the field. He gave the same treatment to Chandu Shah as the latter had given to Guru Arjan. Like his British predecessors, Latif believed that Guru Hargobind entered the service of Jahangir; he appropriated the pay of the contingents for his own use and he was sent to the fort of Gwalior as a prisoner. After the death of Jahangir, Guru Hargobind entered the service of Shah Jahan. A horse brought by a Sikh from Turkistan for Guru Hargobind was appropriated by the emperor but the Guru managed to take it away from Lahore. Mukhlis Khan marched against the Guru with 7,000 troops but he was defeated near Amritsar. This was the first battle fought between 'the Mohamedans and the Sikhs'. Conscious of the strength of the Mughals, Guru Hargobind crossed the Sutlej into the jungles of Bhatinda. Kamar Khan and Lal Beg were sent against him but they were defeated. Guru Hargobind established himself at Kartarpur. Painda Khan was sent against him but he was killed. Towards the close of his life Guru Hargobind moved into the hills where he was succeeded by Guru Har Rai.[10]

Guru Har Rai supported Dara Shukoh against Aurangzeb. On ascending the throne Aurangzeb called Guru Har Rai to his court at Delhi. He sent a letter to the emperor with Ram Rai, his elder son, and Aurangzeb was satisfied but he kept Ram Rai as a hostage. Guru Har Rai made his young son, Har Krishan, his successor. Ram Rai raised the issue of succession and Guru Har Krishan was also called to Delhi. He got afflicted with smallpox and died in 1664, after telling the Sikhs that his successor would be found in the village Bakala near Goindwal.[11]

A Sikh merchant, Makhan Shah, supported Tegh Bahadur against Ram Rai and the Sodhis (of Kartarpur), and Tegh Bahadur was persuaded to accept Guruship. Following his British predecessors, Latif says that Guru Tegh Bahadur began to live in splendour and kept 1,000 horsemen in his employ. Ram Rai represented to Aurangzeb that Guru Tegh Bahadur's design was detrimental to the state. He was called to Delhi where the Raja of Jaipur interceded on his behalf and the Guru went towards Bengal with the Raja. He took up residence in Patna. Gobind Singh was born there. When the Raja returned to Delhi, Guru Tegh Bahadur came to Kahlur and founded Makhowal, close to Kiratpur. Here he became a regular freebooter and adopted a predatory career. Imperial troops were sent against him and he was brought to Delhi. Aurangzeb urged him to embrace Islam; his example was expected to induce hundred of Brahmans to accept Islam. After many religious disputations with Guru Tegh Bahadur, Aurangzeb asked him to show a miracle. He tied round his neck a paper with 'charms' written on it and said that no sword could harm him now. But his head rolled on the floor when the executioner gave a blow. The 'charm' on the paper was then read out. It said, 'he gave his head and not his secret'. Latif goes on to add that it was more likely that Guru Tegh Bahadur was executed as a rebel in 1675. The *Sakhis* published by the Sikh authors represented Guru Tegh Bahadur as a valorous Guru who made his disciples a martial people. He was called *Sachcha Padshah* or the true king. Thus, his aspirations in the latter part of his life were fully exhibited as kingly rather than priestly.[12]

Latif places the institution of the Khalsa soon after the sucession of Guru Gobind Singh. He retired to the mountains on both sides of the river Jamuna, and occupied himself with sports and archery, hunting tigers and wild boars. He longed to wreak vengeance and became an 'irreconcilable enemy of every Mahomedan'. He invoked the aid of the Goddess Durga. The Goddess asked for the heads of his four sons but five Sikhs volunteered themselves. They were given *pahul* and the Guru took *pahul* from them. He exclaimed that 'the Khalsa arose from the Guru and the Guru from the Khalsa. They were mutual protectors of each other.' Other Sikhs were then initiated, and rules for the conduct of life were written. The Khalsa were instructed to adopt the '5 Ks'. The Guru now embarked on his great enterprise. He remodelled 'the Hindu religion' and abolished the distinctions of caste. In less than a fortnight, 80,000 Sikhs flocked to Makhowal and Guru Gobind Singh addressed them explaining the beliefs and practices, and the duties of the Khalsa.[13]

According to Latif, Guru Gobind Singh organized his followers into troops and bands, and established forts along the skirts of the hills between the Sutlej and the Jamuna, besides military posts and strongholds. On the plains lower down the Sutlej, he got into difficulties with the Rajas of Nahan and Nalagarh, but had enough resources to defeat them. He allied himself with Bhim Chand, the Raja of Kahlur, who had refused to pay the annual tribute. His example was followed by others. Aurangzeb ordered the governors of Lahore and Sirhind to march against Guru Gobind Singh who was defeated and besieged. His mother and two younger sons made an escape to Sirhind where they were produced before Wazir Khan and, eventually, killed. Their grandmother died of grief. When the provisions of Guru Gobind Singh were exhausted, he evacuated the fort with 40 Sikhs and escaped to Chamkaur. His elder two sons died fighting in the battle at Chamkaur. Guru Gobind Singh left the place and, after various reverses, reached the wastes of Bhatinda. He was able to collect 12,000 men. Wazir Khan sent 7,000 troops against him. In the battle fought near Muktsar, the Sikhs were victorious. Then Guru Gobind Singh stayed at Damdama. Both these places had become places of pilgrimage for the Sikhs. Damdama became place of learning. Guru Gobind Singh went to Sirhind. The Sikhs were keen to destroy it, but Guru Gobind Singh told them not to. He lived in peace at Anandpur towards the end of Aurangzeb's reign. The emperor called him to his presence in the Deccan. Guru Gobind Singh composed a poem in Persian and sent it to the emperor who was pleased with its contents. He desired the Guru to repair to the emperor's presence and the Guru set out to meet Aurangzeb. On his way, however, he heard of the emperor's death in 1707.[14] The whole account is rather confused.

Latif goes on to state that Guru Gobind Singh reached the Deccan to find Bahadur Shah seated on the throne of his ancestor. He was received with distinction and made a commander of 5,000. During his stay in the Deccan, Guru Gobind Singh was provoked by the intemperate language used by a Pathan who was demanding payment for the horses he had supplied. His sons assaulted the Guru and wounded him. They were caught by the Sikhs but the Guru told them to release the culprits who had done well to avenge the death of their father who had been killed by the Guru. The wound had apparently healed when the Guru stretched a strong bow, and the wound got reopened. It was stitched again by the surgeons called from Delhi but the Guru remained restless. When he reached the town of Nander, he felt so exhausted that he asked his followers to stop there. Thousands of Brahmans were feasted. The Guru then ordered preparations to be made for cremation. The Sikhs were anxious to know who would guide them. Guru Gobind Singh said, 'I entrust my *Khalsa* to the bosom of the everlasting divine being. Whoever wishes to behold the Guru, let him offer *karah parsad* worth Rs. 1-4 or less, and bow before the *Granth* and open it, and he shall have an interview with the Guru. Whatever you ask shall be given to you.

The *Granth* shall support you under all your troubles and adversities in this world, and be a sure guide to you hereafter. The Guru shall dwell with the society of disciples, the Khalsa, and wherever there shall be five Sikhs gathered together, there shall the Guru be also present'. Guru Gobind Singh then mounted the funeral pyre and uttered a *savvayya* to the effect that he recognized only the One Supreme Lord. He expired during the performance of his devotions.[15] This account too is rather confused.

In Latif's assessment, Guru Gobind Singh was 'a lawgiver in the pulpit, a champion in the field, a king on his *masnad*, and a *faqir* in the society of the Khalsa.' He instituted a code that infused a spirit of valour in his followers and inflamed them with zeal for deeds of heroism. He laid the foundation of that vast fabric which the Sikh nation was enabled to build on 'the ruins of Mahomedan power' in the Punjab. Latif gives the principles from a book of guidance (*Rahitnama*) which forbade the Sikhs to follow the doctrines of the Vedas, Shastras, Puranas, and the Qur'an. The *Daswen Badshah ka Granth* raised the dormant energies of the Sikhs and urged upon them the necessity of leading an active and useful life.[16]

Latif gives some interesting information about Nander, called Abchal Nagar. Guru Gobind Singh's weapons were worshipped by the Sikhs. The *hukamnamas* issued by the *pujaris* at Abchal Nagar bore on it the seal of Guru Gobind Singh. It bore an inscription in three distinct units. At the top was '*ekankar sri satgur parsad*', in the middle, '*deg-o tegh-o fateh nusrat bedrang, yaft az Nanak Guru Gobind Singh*'; and at the bottom, '*Sri Akal Purkh ji sahai*'.[17] If correct, this information would be very significant.

III. SIKHS IN THE EIGHTEENTH CENTURY

After the history of the Sikh Gurus, Latif devotes a chapter each to Bairagi Banda, the political organization of the Sikhs into a theocratic confederate feudalism, and the twelve Sikh *misls* on the basis of his European and Persian sources. Guru Gobind Singh and Banda met for the first time in the Deccan and they became intimate friends. Banda was so impressed that he took *pahul* and became a disciple of the Guru. He was made the leader of the Sikhs. He issued orders to the Sikhs in the name of Guru Gobind Singh and they joined him in such large numbers that Banda could fight a battle with Wazir Khan who was defeated and killed. Sirhind was sacked and its people were put to the sword. Even the mosques were polluted and burnt down, and their custodians were subjected to the greatest indignities and tortures. Many other towns were devastated and their inhabitants plundered. Ten thousand men and women were mercilessly put to death in Samana. Latif gives more details about the sack of Batala and Kalanaur in the Bari Doab. He describes the campaign of Bahadur Shah against Banda who was obliged to escape from his fort during the night. Bahadur Shah went to Lahore and died there in 1712.[18]

In the anarchy and confusion that followed the death of Bahadur Shah, the Sikhs under Banda built a fort called Gurdaspur, and advanced towards Sirhind. Farrukh Siyar ascended the throne in 1713 and ordered Abd us-Samad Khan to take charge of the Punjab and punish the insurgents. Banda again fled to his hill fastnesses. Abd us-Samad went to Lahore. After a year's respite Banda reappeared and took possession of Kalanaur and Santokhgarh in the Gurdaspur area. He was joined by 35,000 warriors. Abd us-Samad Khan moved against them and they strengthened their position in the fort of Gurdaspur. The siege laid by the Mughal army was so thorough that the Sikhs were on the verge of starvation. Seeing no chance of escape, Banda opted for surrender. He and his supporters were brought to Lahore in chains. Put under the charge of Zakariya Khan, 740 of them were taken to Delhi. Banda was put in an iron cage. At Delhi they were treated with the greatest ignominy. One hundred of them were publicly beheaded in one day under the jeers and taunts of the mob. Each succeeding day saw the execution of a similar number until all of them paid the penalty of their crimes. Banda's execution was reserved for the last day. He was dragged from the cage like a wild beast and his son was placed in his lap and he was ordered to cut his throat. He complied. His own body was then torn to pieces with red hot irons. His name was never mentioned in any part of India without curses. His memory was held in the same detestation by the Sikhs as by the Muslims. He had introduced innovations in opposition to the policy of Guru Nanak and Guru Gobind Singh. Banda appeared to have been chosen by the Guru with a view to avenging the death of his father and two sons. And for this purpose 'he could not have singled out a better instrument than this ruthless bloodsucker'.[19]

Latif has nothing to say about the Sikh struggle for several decades; after the execution of Banda in 1716, he leaps to 1761, when Ahmad Shah Abdali returned to Kabul after the battle of Panipat. All the principal Sikh *sardars* appropriated lands to themselves. Hearing of their success, Ahmad Shah Abdali sent his general, Nuruddin Khan Bamzai, at the head of 7,000 horse to disperse the Sikh insurgents. He was repulsed with great loss. The Sikh *sardars* occupied more territories. They met at Amritsar and resolved to invest Jandiala; its chief was a supporter of Ahmad Shah. They ravaged Malerkotla, and invested Sirhind. Ahmad Shah Abdali came to Lahore and completed all his plans for surprising the Sikhs. He engaged them at Kot Rahira and gained a complete victory over them. Their killed and wounded were estimated at 12,000 to 30,000. It was a great disaster (*ghallughara*) for the Sikhs.

Latif goes out of his way to justify Ahmad Shah Abdali. Following the law of retaliation in Islam, Ahmad Shah avenged the outrages committed by the Sikhs on Muslim mosques and shrines by the demolition of the most sacred edifices in their most sacred city. Latif says that there can be no doubt that 'the Abdali acted in strict conformity with the law of his religion, and was actuated by a sense of duty, when he undertook the destruction of the sanctuaries of the Sikhs.' He vindicated Islam.[20]

Nevertheless, Lahore was captured by the Sikhs in 1764. The whole country from the Jhelum to the Jamuna was partitioned by the Sikhs among themselves.[21] Latif does not discuss in detail the late eighteenth-century Sikh polity, though he uses the term 'theocratic confederate feudalism' in the title of the chapter. Without any credible evidence, he underlines that Sikh rule was no good for the Muslims. 'When the Mahomedans were the predominating power in the Panjab, they treated the Sikhs with little consideration, and it was now their turn to suffer. They were employed by the ruling race in the most menial capacities, agriculture being about the most honourable profession in which they were allowed to engage, and, in this, only as tenants.' The Muslims were persecuted in every conceivable manner; their mosques were desecrated and turned into pigsties. The grandest of their shrines were utilized as magazines and arsenals. The Muslims dared not pray aloud and they were forbidden to use beef as an article of food. The majority of the well-to-do Muslims emigrated to the British territory where they were allowed to follow their religion unmolested.[22]

Latif was under the wrong impression that the use of intoxicants like opium, *bhang*, and spirituous liquors was allowed in the *Adi Granth*, that the only institution to administer civil and criminal justice was the *panchayat*, that the Sikhs compelled people to work without payment of any kind and that they believed in witchcraft and sorcery and the practice of *sati* was common among them.[23]

Following Prinsep, Latif gives the history of 12 *misls*, but in a different order: the Bhangi, the Ramgarhia, the Kanhiya, the Nakkai, the Ahluwalia, the Dallewalia, the Nishanwala, the Faizullapuria, the Karora Singhia, the Shahid and Nihang, the Phulkian, and the Sukarchakia. Latif mentions a new source of information, the Memoirs of Maulvi Mahomed Din of Batala, 'a contemporary historian'. The additional information is similar to what we find in the *Tarikh-i Hind* of Ahmad Shah of Batala. Some of the information given is new but Latif does not reflect on its significance. He tries merely to fit it into the received view of the *misaldari* system. Like some of his predecessors he looks upon the head of the supposed unit as *misaldar*. He makes the chiefs of Patiala as the head of the Phulkian *misl*, not knowing the fact that the chiefs of Nabha represented the senior line, and ignoring the fact that Phul was a chaudhari and his descendants functioned within the framework of the Mughal administration.[24]

The Sukarchakia *misl*, 'the last and by far the most important of the Sikh confederacies' to be taken up by Latif, serves as the link between the third and the fourth part of his book. Latif gives an elaborate genealogical table, showing the links of the Sukarchakias with the Sandhanwalias and the Majithias, and also with the Kanhiyas, Nakkais and Atariwalas. Buddha was the first ancestor of Ranjit Singh to take *pahul*, and to join the predatory excursions of the Sikhs. He built a large house at Sukarchak as his headquarters. He died in 1716, leaving two sons: Naudh Singh and Chanda Singh. Naudh Singh became a highway robber (*dharwi*). He joined the Faizullapuria *misl*. He died in 1752, leaving four sons: Charhat Singh, Dal Singh, Chet Singh and Mangi Singh. Charhat Singh separated himself from the Faizullapurias and began to plunder on his own. He married the daughter of Amir Singh who had also dissociated himself from the Faizullapurias. Charhat Singh formed a separate *misl* after 1756. He laid the foundation of the family before his death in 1774. His son, Mahan Singh, improved upon the legacy by extending his territory and increasing his resources and power. He possessed all the qualities of a *sardar*, and left behind him a high reputation for wisdom and bravery.[25]

IV. MAHARAJA RANJIT SINGH

For the life of Maharaja Ranjit Singh, Latif takes up the phase from his occupation of Lahore to his treaty with the British. He looks upon Sada Kaur as the ladder by which Ranjit Singh reached the summit of his power. She herself gained the Sardari of the Kanhiyas even though two younger brothers of her deceased husband were alive. Like his British predecessors, Latif dwells on scandals and talks of the grant received from Shah Zaman for the occupation of Lahore. He describes the political situation of the Punjab in 1799 in terms of the power centres at Lahore, Amritsar, Kapurthala, Wazirabad, Kangra, Chamba, Kasur, Pakpattan, Jhang, Multan, Mankera, Khushab, Attock, Peshawar, Bannu, Tank, Dera Ghazi Khan, and Kashmir. This is not a complete list but it does include the important centres. All these centres of power were either subjugated or subordinated to Ranjit Singh.[26]

Without any credible evidence, Latif states that Ranjit Singh formally assumed the title of Maharaja in 1801; an order was issued to establish a mint at Lahore; and a coin was struck with the inscription now familiar as '*deg, tegh, fateh*'. Not only in striking a coin but also in appointing *qazis* and *muftis* in Lahore, Ranjit Singh was following the example of 'the Mahomedan emperors'. But Ranjit Singh was simply following the Sikh chiefs of the late eighteenth century. For the events of this phase, Latif gives more details than Prinsep but follows him rather closely, mentioning his new sources. 'Ranjit Singh preferred to be called Khalsaji, signifying the whole body of the Sikhs; in all public documents this word signified *Maharaja* or *Sardar*'. His great successes had led that monarch to entertain notions that he was the lord of the whole Sikh nation.[27]

In the second chapter of this part, Latif takes up the events from the treaty of Amritsar to the conquest of Multan, Kashmir and Peshawar, that is, from 1809 to 1826. His narrative is more detailed than that of Prinsep, but follows more or less the same pattern. Latif refers to some new sources for his additional information, but does not contradict or disagree with his European predecessors. Prinsep's account of how Ranjit Singh treated Ram Singh, the *diwan* of Prince Kharak Singh and how he treated the Prince's mother is repeated in a somewhat different language. At the end of this phase, Ranjit Singh's dominions became more than twenty times larger than what he had inherited from Mahan Singh.[28]

The third chapter on Maharaja Ranjit Singh covers the phase from the rise of Syad Ahmad to the end of Ranjit Singh's reign, that is, from 1827 to 1839. Latif gives the early life of Syad Ahmad till he called upon the faithful to join him in a holy war against 'the infidel Sikhs'. He was careful to avoid complications with the British authorities and gave no cause of offence. In turn, he was not obstructed by the British when he started from Delhi with 500 followers in 1826. The Yusufzais in the Peshwar region acknowledged him as the leader of the faithful to wage a holy war against the Sikhs. Syad Ahmad's activities are mentioned by Latif till the death of the Syad. The meeting between Ranjit Singh and Bentinck is described in some detail. The rest of the events of this phase relate mostly to the trans-Indus, including the Peshawar campaign, the death of Hari Singh Nalwa at Jamrud, and the Tripartite Treaty. Latif does not omit to mention that Ranjit Singh married Gul Bahar, one of the *demi-monde* of Amritsar in 1833. Moran's sister, Mamola, adorned the bridegroom's neck with a necklace of pearls. When Rani Gul Begam died at Lahore in 1863, she was holding lands worth Rs. 12,380 a year. The marriage of Prince Nau Nihal Singh, celebrated in 1837, was marked by festivities, splendour and magnificence. Osborne's *Court and Camp of Ranjit Singh* was useful for the early negotiations between the British mission and the Maharaja. Latif reaffirms that Ranjit Singh wanted substantial concessions but the British did not agree to more than his claims to Shikarpur and Jalalabad. However, he goes on to add that Shah Shuja recognized Ranjit Singh's right over the Afghan territories he had conquered.[29]

Latif describes the death of Ranjit Singh before coming to an assessment of his character and achievement. This is no different from Prinsep's assessment. All that Latif has to say about Ranjit Singh's achievement is that 'he remoulded the political condition of the Sikhs, and consolidated numerous dismembered petty states into a kingdom'. Latif closes his account of Ranjit Singh by underlining that his relations with the paramount power of India remained cordial until his death. Latif's comment is a reflection of his almost exclusive concern with past politics.[30]

V. SIKH RULE REPLACED BY THE BRITISH

The period following the death of Ranjit Singh is treated by Latif in two informal parts. The last over 60 pages are devoted actually to the government and administration of the Punjab under the British. The earlier part of nearly 80 pages is divided into the regimes under Kharak Singh, Nau Nihal Singh, Chand Kaur, Sher Singh and Dulip Singh in the first chapter, the first Sikh War in the second, and the second Sikh War in the third and fourth chapters. The fourth chapter trails into the British period without any formal heading.

Kharak Singh, according to Latif, was a man of weak intellect. One of his first acts was to deprive Dhian Singh and Hira Singh of their privilege to enter the royal *zanana*. One Chet Singh was made the *wazir*. His opponents spread the rumour that Kharak Singh had agreed to acknowledge British supremacy. He was openly maligned and Nau Nihal Singh was re-called from Peshawar. Several persons close to Kharak Singh were murdered and he was induced to abdicate in favour of Nau Nihal Singh. Kharak Singh reigned for only three months. His reign was marked by 'the beginning of those numerous scenes of bloodshed and horror which have left an ineffable blot on the history of the Sikh regime in the Panjab'.[31]

Nau Nihal Singh was a promising youth of 18 when he was proclaimed ruler. He was thoroughly qualified for the position, but unrealistic ambition was his weak point. He detested the British and was reported to have collected an army for the invasion of British India. His 'mischievous designs' were frustrated by court intrigues. Kharak Singh died on 5 November 1840. Nau Nihal Singh heard the news of his death 'with open demonstrations of joy' when he was hunting near Lahore. He continued his amusement for two hours before returning for the funeral. As Nau Nihal Singh was returning from the funeral with Mian Udham Singh, son of Gulab Singh, the northern gate of the Huzuri Bagh fell as soon as they entered the arch way. Mian Udham Singh died at the spot and Nau Nihal Singh was found senseless. Dhian Singh took him into the fort and closed its gates. No one was allowed to go in, not even Nau Nihal Singh's mother Chand Kaur. The death of Nau Nihal Singh was kept secret for three days till the arrival of Sher Singh from Batala. Latif does not agee with those historians who think that the whole plan was premeditated. It appeared to him that it was a just retribution for Nau Nihal Singh's sins and wickedness: 'That this monstrous prince should have met with his death in this singular manner, cannot, I think, be attributed to any other cause but that of the Divine wrath.'[32] It was not enough for Latif to say that the cause of the calamity was natural.

With the support of Attar Singh Sandhanwalia, Chand Kaur began to exercise supreme power. Attar Singh was heading a council of four *sardars* as the prime minister. Dhian Singh, who was unhappy over this change, bided his time. In January 1841, Sher Singh came to Lahore again and he was welcomed by the Khalsa soldiery and declared to be the sovereign of the Punjab. He was joined by Suchet Singh and General Ventura. He entered the city and the gateways of the fort were bombarded. The siege lasted for five days. Dhian Singh arrived on the fifth day. Negotiations were started. On 18 Janurary 1841 Sher Singh was seated on the throne. During the days of the siege, the people of Lahore suffered all kinds of atrocities at the hands of the soldiery.[33]

The soldiery became intolerant and uncontrolable in the reign of Sher Singh. General Court escaped with his life but 'a brave young Englishman', Foulks, was murdered in cold blood. General Mahan (Mihan) Singh was slain in Kashmir and General Avitabile abandoned Peshawar and went to Jalalabad to save himself. The turbulence of the Khalsa army subsided only after the threat of British intervention. Sher Singh was addicted to pleasure and left the affairs of the state to Dhian Singh. The crafty Raja got rid of a potential rival in Jawala Singh who was imprisoned in the fort of Sheikhupura where he died under torture. In June 1842, Sher Singh got rid of Chand Kaur who had refused to marry him. His relations with Dhian Singh were no longer cordial. Sher Singh had put Lehna Singh Sandhanwalia in confinement while his brother Attar Singh and their nephew Ajit Singh had fled to the British territory. They were recalled and Lehna Singh was released. They conspired to murder Sher Singh. Eventually they murdered not only Sher Singh but also his son Partap Singh and Raja Dhian Singh. Raja Hira Singh secured the support of the army against the Sandhanwalias. Ajit Singh was beheaded, and Lehna Singh was killed afterwards. Attar Singh sought protection with Bhai Bir Singh, and crossed the Sutlej. In the whole process, the soldiery became all powerful. They could make or unmake a king.[34]

In September 1843, Dulip Singh was proclaimed Maharaja, with Hira Singh as his *wazir*. Pandit Jalla had great influence over Hira Singh. Dulip Singh's mother, Rani Jindan, favoured Suchet Singh. Hira Singh eliminated him with the help of the army, raising the pay of the soldiers by two and a half rupees a month. Attar Singh Sandhanwalia recrossed the Sutlej in May 1844 and joined Bhai Bir Singh. The disaffected princes, Kashmira Singh and Pashaura Singh also joined the standard of rebellion. Hira Singh sent a large force against them all. Bhai Bir Singh, Attar Singh, and Kashmira Singh died in defence. Pashaura Singh repaired to Lahore and made his submission. Hira Singh had now apparently reached the zenith of his power. But he was a tool in the hands of Pandit Jalla. The cunning Rani Jindan and her lover Lal Singh conspired against Hira Singh and Jalla and secured the support of the army which declared Jawahar Singh, Rani Jindan's brother, to be prime minister. Both Hira Singh and Jalla were cut down. Had the Khalsa army not acted under a mistaken notion of patriotism and blind zeal, much of the bloodshed and mischief might have been averted. 'But, as the affairs stood, the fate of the Panjab was sealed.'[35]

The new actors to appear on the scene were Rani Jindan's brother, Jawahar Singh, and her favourite Lal Singh. A golden necklace was given to every soldier in appreciation of their support. Gulab Singh agreed to pay Rs. 68,00,000 to the *darbar*, and the territory of Suchet Singh was taken back from him, along with the property of Hira Singh. Diwan Sawan Mal died in September 1844 and his son, Mul Raj, was appointed in his place. Mul Raj paid Rs. 1,80,000 as *nazrana*. Prince Pashaura Singh found some support among the soldiery and rose in rebellion. He was treacherously made prisoner and strangled in the fort of Attock. The Khalsa troops swore vengeance upon Jawahar Singh, and they killed him in the open. Rani Jindan assumed the charge of administration as Regent after the Dussehra of 1845. The power of the Khalsa army was now at its height. With the consent of the army, Rani Jindan made Lal Singh the wazir and Tej Singh the commander-in-chief of the army. The soldiers were cleverly incited against the British to prepare them to cross the Sutlej. The real purpose of Rani Jindan, Lal Singh and Tej Singh was to destroy the influence of the Khalsa army to make it possible for them to establish a Sikh government unrestrained by the army.[36]

The stage was set for the first Sikh war. On 8 December 1845, large detachments of Sikh troops appeared on the right side of the Sutlej, and the infux continued for two days more. On 13 December the British government declared that the Sikh army had recently marched from Lahore on the orders of the *darbar* to invade British territory; the Governor-General had to take measures to protect the British provinces, to vindicate the authority of the government, and to punish the violators of treaties and the disturbers of public peace. The possessions of Dulip Singh on the left bank of the Sutlej were annexed. It was asserted that the Sikhs aimed at causing a general rising against the British government and they had induced the chiefs of the protected Sikh states to join the Khalsa as soon as the Lahore army should cross the Sutlej. Latif gives a brief narrative of the battles and highlights Tej Singh's conscious decision not to go to the aid of Lal Singh until his force was defeated.[37]

On 31 December, the Governor-General declared that the Lahore government had commenced hostilities without any provocation, or a declaration of war. Their large army was repulsed and driven across the Sutlej; it had become necessary to take measures for punishing this unprovoked aggression, and for preventing similar acts of treachery in future by the government and army of the Punjab. On 9 March 1846, the treaty of peace was signed at Lahore. The whole of the plain and hill country between the Sutlej and the Beas was annexed; the hill territory between the Beas and the Indus, along with Kashmir and Hazara, was taken over by the British in lieu of Rs. 10,00,000 of indemnity; the strength of the Lahore army was reduced to 25 battalions of infantry, consisting of 20,000 men, and 12,000 cavalry. Two days later, it was agreed that a British force would be left at Lahore till the end of 1846. Through a separate treaty with Gulab Singh, the territory taken over in lieu of the indemnity was given to him for Rs. 1,000,000. 'Thus was the independence of the Sikhs as a nation broken, the monarchy formed by the genius of Ranjit Singh reduced to insignificance, and a contest brought to a close which in its origin and result had few parallels in history.' Rani Jindan was recognized as the Regent of the state and Raja Lal Singh as an executive minister. The advice and direction of Major Lawrence was available on all occasions. On 16 December 1846 a new treaty was executed and ratified on 26 December, by which the Sikh government agreed to pay Rs. 2,200,000 a year for the maintenance of 10,000 British troops in the Punjab till 4 September 1854 when the state was to be handed over to Dulip Singh as a sovereign ruler.[38]

Latif refers to the revolt of Mul Raj, and the delay in taking action against him in April 1848. Meanwhile, he was joined by Bhai Maharaj Singh, the successor of Bhai Bir Singh. Chattar Singh Atariwala, whose daughter was betrothed to Dulip Singh, was the governor of Hazara. Early in August 1848 his troops rose in revolt, killed Colonel Canora, who was employed in the Sikh army, and they marched in the direction of Attock. Raja Sher Singh, a son of Chattar Singh, decided to side with him. Rani Jindan too was active in her intrigues. The stage was set for the second Sikh war.[39]

The Multan rebellion was suppressed, but it served only as a prelude to 'a great national outbreak'. The whole of the Punjab was seething with disaffection. The avowed objective of the Khalsa army and the Sikh population was 'the restoration of Khalsa supremacy'. Latif had little sympathy for this aspiration. He describes the battles of Ram Nagar, Chillianwala and Gujrat, and comments: 'The British lion had effectually humbled the power of the Khalsa and the last deadly blow had been inflicted on the empire of Ranjit Singh.' The Sikhs surrendered unconditionally on 12 March 1849. Raja Sher Singh delivered up his sword, and his example was followed by the soldiery. As Lord Dalhousie put it, 'the victory gained was memorable, alike from the greatness of the occasion and from the brilliant and decisive issue of the encounter'. He went on to add that the completeness of the victory 'equalled the highest hopes entertained'.[40] Latif claimed to speak the truth on the basis of facts. But his facts justified everything that the British had done.

In the last chapter of the book, Latif reproduces the proclamation of 29 March 1849, announcing the annexation and the future policy of the British with regard to the Punjab. Latif goes on to talk of the administrative arrangements made by the new rulers and the measures adopted by them. The policy they initiated was crowned with success. The most important victories achieved by the British in the Punjab were the 'victories of peace and civilization' through the great work of pacification and amelioration. They did all they possibly could to mitigate the reverses of the feudal nobility of the defunct Sikh realm. Nor were the priestly and religious classes of the old regime neglected. Protection was afforded to the agricultural classes. Vast public works changed the face of the country. In the sepoy mutiny of 1857, the role of Punjab administrators earned the gratitude of others for rendering assistance in Hindustan. In the famine of 1860-1, the Punjab administrators provided commendable relief. The first exhibition of arts and manufactures was held at Lahore in 1864. Railway projects were started and so was female education. In 1865, a Chief Court was established at Lahore. The first Tenancy Act was introduced in 1866. An Oriental School and College at Lahore was a part of the movement for a university. The Kuka outbreak in 1872 was promptly handled with success. By an act of royal grace, Her Majesty Queen Victoria assumed the title of 'Empress of India'. The Punjab Chiefs' College, the Mayo School of Art, and Veternary School were established at Lahore. The Punjab Public Library was opened. At a meeting held to commemorate the Jubilee of Queen Victoria, it was resolved to establish a 'Technical Institute'. In 1889, Lord Lansdowne formally declared open the Lahore Mission College. Latif refers briefly to the reform movements among the Hindus, Muslims, and Sikhs of the Punjab during the late nineteenth century, and their educational programmes. All the three communities were united in their fidelity to the Crown. Loyalty to the rulers was a plant of indigenous and perennial growth in the Punjab. Latif ends his account in 1891, with the opening of the new Delhi-Ambala and Kalka Railway. The network of railways was developing fast. These were some of the blessings of the British rule in the Punjab.[41]

VI. ADMIRATION FOR BRITISH RULE

Latif had some appreciation for Ranjit Singh but none for his successors. He had no sympathy with the rulers of Lahore who came into conflict with the British. He changes his tone when he comes to the successors of Ranjit Singh. He begins to identify himself with the British. What he says about their successful policies and measures after the annexation was supposed to be the basis for his great appreciation for the British. And they presented a contrast to the former rulers.

In the opening sentence of his Preface, Latif says that no story in world history is so grand, so romantic and so pregnant with instruction as that of the British conquests in the East. In no part of the empire was British rule received with more genuine satisfaction than the country of the Five Rivers. Latif explicitly justifies the annexation of the Punjab. 'The aggressive policy adopted by the Sikhs towards the paramount Power of India, compelled the latter to take up arms against them.' The country was conquered, but generosity prevailed over policy, and the victors restored the territories they were entitled to hold by right of conquest to the recognized heir to the throne. 'The Sikh ministers and the Darbar, however, violated the treaty, and the Khalsa army waged a fierce war to destroy the benefactors of their race. The violatiors of the treaty were punished and the province was absorbed into the British empire.'[42]

The history of Punjab showed that the Punjabis had moved from an age of barbarism to an age of enlightenment; they shared with the rest of the Crown's subjects the benefits and blessings of a civilized government. Latif appeals to his countrymen to weigh carefully and calmly the facts narrated: 'Do not think that the Panjab of today is the Panjab of forty years back. Do not forget what the condition of your country was forty years ago, or to appreciate heartily the manifold blessings of the British rule and the influence of British civilization.' A humane nation from the far West, unrivalled among the nations of the world for its benevolence and sympathy with mankind, had been destined by the mysterious decree of Providence to rule over the vast empire. People were free to profess their religion openly. The days of calamity were over. The bands of fanatics, marauders and highway robbers were turned into peaceful cultivators and useful citizens. No longer were the weak the prey of the strong. Justice was impartially administered. 'It reaches equally the palace of the Nawab and the cottage of the peasant.' The various races and nationalities of India, putting aside their religious differences, had become moulded into a united people. The end and aim of British rule was 'the welfare of the people, not the personal aggrandizement of the rulers'.[43]

As the achievement of the British in the Punjab, Latif mentions the gigantic railway projects and the roads as the means of developing the trade and increasing the wealth, the grand schemes of irrigation which had converted thousands of acres of barren land into green smiling plains, the numerous charitable institutions like schools, colleges and hospitals, religious tolerance and freedom, the liberty of the press, prevention of epidemics and famines, Western learning, municipal institutions, and the protection of life and property. The Victorian age was unrivalled in history for the blessings of peace. Latif exhorts his young countrymen to respect the rulers, the benefactors of the country, and to identify themselves with their interest. They should not think of 'rivalry' with their rulers for that was sure to bring upon them the wrath of God and misfortune. Any idea of equality with the conquerors of the East was sure to lead to their own discomfiture and hurt. Latif's last advice to the young men of the Punjab was to fear God, love mankind, and honour the Empress. His dear countrymen should pray to God, with Latif: 'Long live our Gracious Queen, the Empress of India.'[44]

No British historian could have admired the British rule so enthusiastically as Latif and no British historian could have exhorted the Punjabis to be so deeply committed to loyalty as he did. He was opposed to any kind of political activity that could be seen as disloyalty by the British rulers. The Indian National Congress had been founded in 1885 and Sir Syed Ahmad had advised Muslims to stand aloof. Latif is giving the same advice to Punjabis, but not as a Punjabi patriot so much as a Punjabi Muslim. Throughout his work he appears to think in terms of religious communities. Even if he was genuinely concerned with all Punjabis, the foremost in his mind were the Punjabi Muslims. He wanted them to follow his own example of loyalty to the British to improve their lot. The British were seen as their saviours.

NOTES

1. Syad Muhammad Latif, *History of the Panjab from the Remotest Antiquity to the Present Times,* New Delhi: Eurasia Publishing House, 1964 (rpt., first published in 1891), pp. 1-74.
2. Ibid., pp. 148, 149.
3. Ibid., p. 179.
4. Ibid., Preface, p. vii.
5. Ibid., Preface, pp. xi, xii, xiv.
6. Ibid., Preface, pp. vi, vii.
7. Ibid., pp. 242-50.
8. Ibid., pp. 250-2.
9. Ibid., pp. 253-4.
10. Ibid., pp. 254-7.
11. Ibid., pp. 257-8.
12. Ibid., pp. 258-60.
13. Ibid., pp. 261-4.
14. Ibid., pp. 264-8.
15. Ibid., pp. 268-9.
16. Ibid., pp. 270-2.
17. Ibid., p. 270.
18. Ibid., pp. 274-9.
19. Ibid., pp. 279-81.
20. Ibid., pp. 281-4.
21. Ibid., pp. 284-7.
22. Ibid., pp. 290-1.
23. Ibid., pp. 292-5.
24. Ibid., pp. 296-334.
25. Ibid., pp. 334-45.
26. Ibid., pp. 346-51.
27. Ibid., pp. 372 n.
28. Ibid., pp. 381-436.
29. Ibid., pp. 436-92.
30. Ibid., pp. 492-6.
31. Ibid., pp. 497-8.
32. Ibid., pp. 498-501.
33. Ibid., pp. 501-7.
34. Ibid., pp. 507-20.
35. Ibid., pp. 520-32.
36. Ibid., pp. 532-9.
37. Ibid., pp. 539-44.

38. Ibid., pp. 544-56.
39. Ibid., pp. 556-67.
40. Ibid., pp. 567-71.
41. Ibid., pp. 571-635.
42. Ibid., Preface, pp. iii, iv.
43. Ibid., Preface, pp. ix, x, xii, xiii, xiv.
44. Ibid., Preface, pp. xv, xvi. For Muhammad Latif, see also S.K. Bajaj, 'Syad Muhammad Latif', *Historians and Historiography of the Sikhs*, ed. Fauja Singh, New Delhi: Oriental Publishers, 1978, pp. 199-219; Radha Sharma and Harish C. Sharma, 'Under the Shadow of Colonial Rule: The *Khalsa* for Latif', in *The Khalsa: Sikh and Non-Sikh Perspectives*, ed. J.S. Grewal, New Delhi: Manohar, 2004, pp. 137-67.

CHAPTER ELEVEN

The Early Sikh Responses

Sewaram Singh, Bhagat Lakshman Singh and Khazan Singh

By the beginning of the twentieth century educated Sikhs had begun to respond to Western interpretations of the Sikh tradition. They had good knowledge of the Sikh sources. They were not less critical in their attitude towards them, but they were sympathetic to the Sikh tradition. In fact, their faith served as a source of inspiration for their scholarship. Nevertheless, they did not address themselves to the Sikhs alone. They addressed themselves to all educated people.

I. SEWARAM SINGH ON GURU NANAK

The first major Sikh writer to appear on the scene was Sewaram Singh Thapar, a lawyer by profession. His *Critical Study of the Life and Teachings of Sri Guru Nanak Dev, the Founder of Sikhism* was published in 1904. As he says in the 'Preface', this work needed no apology. A number of Western writers had written on the Sikhs. However, writers like John Malcolm, W.L. M'Gregor and J.D. Cunningham had concentrated more on the political history of the Sikhs than on the earlier Sikh tradition. Their work did not clarify issues related to the early tradition. Indeed, there was a good deal of misunderstanding regarding 'the origin and development of the Khalsa Church'. Sewaram Singh was keen to clarify issues related to the early Sikh tradition, starting with Guru Nanak.[1]

Aware of the difficulties involved, Sewaram Singh says that the original sources for the life and work of Guru Nanak were 'chaotic and misleading'. The authenticity of the *Janamsakhis* had been seriously questioned. Their evidence could not be accepted in its entirety or on its face value. Many of them were full of 'mythological descriptions and fictitious tales'. None of the different versions of the *Bala Janamsakhi* appeared to be treated as 'perfectly correct'. This 'huddle muddle sort of material' obliged Sewaram Singh to be 'very cautious' in using evidence of the *Janamsakhis*.[2]

It is not without significance that Sewaram Singh's book was well received. Maharaja Hira Singh of Nabha sent a robe of honour (*khil'at*) for him. Tikka Ripudaman Singh of Nabha sent a copy of the work to the Deputy Commissioner of Amritsar to make it clear that idol-worship was no part of the Sikh tradition. The book was sold out in a few years. There was a great demand for literature on Sikhism in English in the late 1920s, and the Chief Khalsa Diwan wanted to reprint Sewaram Singh's book. However, more materials had become available to him. Besides, Bhai Vir Singh had written extensively in Punjabi. Aware of all these developments, Sewaram Singh, now a District and Sessions Judge, decided to take leave from his duties to revise his work. The revised version virtually became a new book. He published it in 1930 as *The Divine Master: Life and Teachings of Siri Guru Nanak Dev*.[3] It has been reprinted recently because the author appeared to have raised 'certain crucial issues' which have continued to engage the attention of scholars.[4]

Sewaram Singh's *Divine Master* is quite remarkable for its use of Sikh literature. He tried to use three *Janamsakhi* traditions: the *Bhai Bala*, the *Gian Ratnavali*, and the *Puratan*. In addition to these he used the works of Bhai Gurdas, the works of Bhai Santokh Singh and Giani Gian Singh, and the Baghdad inscription. For the teachings of Guru Nanak, understandably, he used his compositions. At the same time, he took the work of his European predecessors quite seriously, but not uncritically.

At a few places, Sewaram Singh takes his readers into confidence about the way he treated his evidence. For example, one *Janamsakhi* gave the middle of April as the date of Guru Nanak's birth but the November date was observed by the Sikhs everywhere as the date of his birth. Therefore, Sewaram Singh rejects the *Janamsakhi* evidence.[5] He rejects the view projected by the late *Janamsakhis* (and Bhai Santokh Singh) that Bhai Bala accompanied Guru Nanak on his travels. Bhai Santokh Singh himself looked upon the *Bala Janamsakhi* as full of interpolations introduced by the Handalis, including the story of Bala, but Sewaram Singh uses its evidence selectively. More crucial for rejecting Bala as a companion of Guru Nanak on his travels was the silence of the earliest known sources on the point: the *Vars* of Bhai Gurdas and the *Colebrooke Janamsakhi.*[6]

Sewaram Singh refers to the oldest *Janamsakhi* mentioning Sajjan's meeting with Guru Nanak in the southern Punjab before his first travel, while Bhai Santokh Singh specifically mentions Tulamba and places the incident after the four principal travels of Guru Nanak. Sewaram Singh does not decide on the time of the incident, in favour of one view or the other but he does point out that this evidence showed the kind of people Guru Nanak met and redeemed.[7] In spite of the statements of Bhai Santokh Singh on the point, Sewaram Singh rejects the idea that Guru Nanak met any Sultan named Karun, either in Turkey, Egypt, Sudan or Arabia, because no such Sultan finds mention in authentic histories of these countries. The *Nasihatnama,* said to have been addressed by Guru Nanak to Karun, is not included in the *Granth Sahib*; its language and sentiments do not inspire any confidence in its authenticity. Therefore, the *Nasihatnama* is also rejected.[8] Guru Nanak's visit to Mecca is accepted, but the work entitled *Makke di Gosht* is suspect because all the verses it contained were not included in the *Adi Granth.*[9] The visit to Baghdad is accepted on the basis of the Baghdad inscription.[10] Guru Nanak's meeting with Sultan Ibrahim Lodhi in Delhi is accepted on the basis of the *Colebrooke Janamsakhi.*[11] It must be pointed out that Sewaram Singh's references to the *Bala Janamsakhi,* though the most numerous, are less than a score in the whole work.

The chronology of Guru Nanak's travels presented a great difficulty to Sewaram Singh. The *Janamsakhis* give 'disconnected and mixed description'. The earliest authentic account, the first *Var* of Bhai Gurdas, is 'meagre and scrappy' and lacks chronological exactness. The chronology given in the *Colebrooke Janamsakhi* also cannot be accepted in its entirety. Its author had not paid that regard to the sequence of events 'which one would expect from a modern historian'. The later writers like Bhai Santokh Singh and Giani Gian Singh tried 'to formulate a connected account' but they seem to have drawn on conjecture; they have given no information about their sources, and no reasons for their formulation.[12] Sewaram Singh comes to the conclusion that only the incidents recorded in the earliest sources and supported by Guru Nanak's compositions in the *Granth Sahib* could be accepted as authentic. Allusions to contemporary events could be helpful in assigning dates to some of the incidents of his life. External evidence could also be used for fixing the dates of some events. There was some scope for surmise based on 'geographical position' of the places visited. Sewaram Singh held the view that the most important evidence for the incidents of Guru Nanak's life was provided by his own words. On the whole, one could be almost certain about incidents but not be so sure about their sequence.[13]

We find a large number of references to the *Adi Granth* in Sewaram Singh's work. Indeed, such references are far more numerous than all the other references put together. At several places he uses the evidence of Bhai Gurdas, and at a few places he refers to Bhai Banno's *Bir.* Occasionally, he is wrong in attributing verses to Guru Nanak, or Guru Gobind Singh. At a few places he refers to verses which are not included in the *Adi Granth.* By and large, however, he makes use of authentic compositions of Guru Nanak, giving his own translation in English.[14]

The outline of Guru Nanak's life that emerges from Sewaram Singh's treatment of his sources is clear and plausible. He appears to meet the challenge implicit in Trumpp's *Adi Granth* that a biography of Guru Nanak could not be written on the basis of the existing materials. However, the relative clarity and plausibility of this biography of Guru Nanak is gained by compromising a few known principles of historical research. First of all, the dates given by Sewaram Singh do not come from his sources in most cases and he does not advance any reasons for giving these dates. Secondly, he simply takes for granted that the compositions of Guru Nanak were his response to the situations in which he places them. This assimilates his biography actually to the *Janamsakhis,* with the only difference that he uses the compositions of the *Adi Granth.* Thirdly, he retains many supernatural elements in his account. He looks upon them as a proof of the 'divine' personality of Guru Nanak.[15]

Sewaram Singh gives a separate chapter to Guru Nanak's 'creed'. Three more chapters relate to his 'church', his 'method' and his 'personality'.

The chapter on his stay at Kartarpur in the 1530s is devoted largely to the institutions he founded. According to Sewaram Singh, Guru Nanak did not indulge in any philosophical discussions about the existence of God. 'He felt God within him and with him, and thus spoke of him with the authority of an eye-witness'. Therefore, he simply declares the existence of God and commands his disciples to accept it as the Reality. This answers Trumpp's question about a proof of Guru Nanak's divine mission. Guru Nanak was a prophet 'in the highest and truest sense of the word'. He wanted to rescue Hinduism from gross polytheism and Islam from aggressive Unitarianism, to free both of them from barren ceremonialism and mechanical conventionalism. At the same time, he wanted to preach 'a more exclusive monotheism, a nobler doctrine and a purer morality, based on solid foundations of Divine Grace'. His noble ideals had 'a practical and social meaning'.[16]

The first fundamental principle of the religion of Guru Nanak is the unity of God. As enunciated in the *mulmantar,* 'there is but one God, whose name is True, the Creator, the all-pervading, devoid of fear and enmity, Immortal, Unborn, Self-begotten'. Whatever the epithet used for him—Brahma, Hari, Ram, Govind or Allah—God is incomprehensible, invisible, uncreated, eternal, and alone possessing real existence. He alone is the true object of worship. The second fundamental principle of Guru Nanak's creed is the brotherhood of man, without distinctions of colour, race, caste or tribe. He knew that spiritual development, religious reform and social progress were not possible 'under a system of privileges, which vested the monopoly of spiritual evolution and religious sanctity in the higher castes, and debarred those of the lower castes from these advantages'. He denounced caste in unmistakable terms and established the equality of man before God. Emancipation, in theory, was open to all.[17]

Emancipation for Guru Nanak meant the attainment of everlasting happiness: it consisted of 'living with God and in God'; it could be attained 'even in this life'. Only they with whom God is pleased and on whom he bestows his favours are saved, but it is necessary to strive for liberation. Training one's consciousness (*surt*) for constant communion with God may lead to enfoldment of the soul. But this cannot be done without restraining the mind from indulgence in earthly cravings and low appetites. Devotion to God and meditation on his True Name with a heart full of faith were the means to deserving the grace of God. Guidance of the Guru was essential.[18]

Sewaram Singh underlines that man must bring 'all his actions into line with the will of the Supreme Lord of the Universe'. Without this, all austerities and good deeds are fruitless. The disciple whose mind is fixed on the ideal is called *Gurmukh*. The disciple of the Guru should seek the company of *Gurmukhs*. At the opposite end is *Manmukh*. Even his benevolent deeds are of no merit. The path suggested by Guru Nanak is not easy to pursue. For stepping on it, one had to place one's head on the palm of one's hand; one had to be prepared for 'the supreme sacrifice'.[19]

Individual and congregational prayer found a prominent place in the discipline evolved by Guru Nanak precisely because emancipation is ultimately a matter of divine grace. With the bestowal of grace all past sins are washed away. The world is not an illusion or a dream; its existence is real. 'It is in this real universe that individual soul has descended to work up its elevation and it is not by spurning it that the elevation can be attained'. The spirit should continuously remain in 'communion' with God and pray for mercy. Forgiveness of sins may then come of divine grace. In this lies 'the consolation of Sikhism'.[20]

Both for the life of Guru Nanak and his creed, Sewaram Singh wrote with reference to the work of the earlier writers. The view expressed by some European writers that Kabir was Guru Nanak's teacher was not acceptable to him because there was no evidence to support this view. Guru Nanak was likely to have met Kabir but by then he was fairly well advanced in his mission. About the position of the reformers who had gone before Guru Nanak, Sewaram Singh gives a long quotation from Cunningham's *History* which ends with the statement that it was reserved for Guru Nanak to perceive the true principles of reform and to lay the foundation of a nationality. Sewaram Singh does not accept the statement of the author of the *Siyar al-Mutakhirin* that Guru Nanak had passed his early life in the company of Sayyad Husain and learnt the moral maxims and doctrines of Islam to be subsequently expressed in his own language and formed into a book called the *Granth*. No Sayyad Husain is known to have been Guru Nanak's contemporary. The well-known mystic Shah Husain lived at Lahore in the time of Akbar, and his compositions are not consistent with the Sikh doctrines.[21]

On the unity of God, Sewaram Singh quotes Cunningham and refutes Trumpp's lengthy argument that Guru Nanak believed in the Hindu pantheon. He quotes Cunningham also to refute Wilson's view that the doctrines of Guru Nanak were based on the abstractions of Vedanta and Sufism. He refutes Trumpp's view that the institution of caste was not directly assailed by Guru Nanak. Trumpp's work in his view was marked by contradictions and inconsistencies; his conclusions and unwarranted opinions point to 'his scanty information and want of keen insight'. His study of the *Granth Sahib* was 'superficial' and he failed to comprehend the meaning of Guru Nanak's teachings. The 'absurdity' of Trumpp's remarks on Sikh ethics brings his grave errors into high relief. He was totally wrong in viewing Sikhism as devoid of ethical values. Trumpp had to be refuted because 'more than one European writer, and some of the Indian writers also, who have ever needed something to support a misrepresentation of the Sikh religion, have often drawn upon Dr. Trumpp's authority'.[22]

Sewaram Singh looked upon Guru Nanak as a unique person. That he was commissioned by God is clear from the character of his message and the influence he exerted on the lives of his followers. He himself says in his hymns that he was instructed by God. He set up a new dispensation and founded 'the true religion' in its pristine glory and purity. As regards other religious systems, 'he followed none and denounced none'. A perfectly spontaneous spiritual movement, Sikhism struggled for four hundred years 'for liberty of conscience'. To refresh itself it returns to the Master in the form of the Holy Book. The message of Guru Nanak 'came from the Divine'. That is why he is 'the Divine Master'. Among sons of men, 'none was born greater than Nanak'.[23]

According to Sewaram Singh, Guru Nanak established a number of centres (*manjis*) in different parts of the country, and even outside, before settling down at Kartarpur finally in the 1530s. There, he established a pattern of individual and congregational worship in which some of his compositions were used. A common kitchen was maintained for community meal on the basis of contribution made by the disciples themselves. Guru Nanak himself worked on a farm, and his wife and sons lived with him. Before his 'ascension', the spirit which had 'come unto him from above' was passed on to Guru Angad. The master remained at the head of his Church in the bodies of his successors for nine generations. After the tenth Master, the Word, as contained in the *Granth Sahib,* was installed in the supreme command of the Church.[24]

The congregation (*sangat*) was next to the Master in commanding respect in the Church. It was in the congregation that the *Gurmukh* imparted illumination to others. 'These Sangats were the noblest examples in history of assemblies of pious and spiritual enthusiasts, of truthful and mutually confiding seekers after Truth, and the humble and sincere servants of humanity.' The link between the *sangats* and the Guru was provided by his representatives who presided over the *sangats.* They were known as *bhais* or *babas.* In the Church of Guru Nanak, married life was no bar to spiritual progress. The householder who meditated on the name of the Lord was of equal merit with the hermit. No special virtue was attached to asceticism. The path was open to women. In the time of Guru Amar Das, women were allowed to preach as 'Mothers' (*mais*). A ceremony of initiation was instituted for all novices. Instruction in the principles of the faith and baptism (*charanghal*) constituted the basic features of initiation. It served as the prototype of the more elaborate baptism of the sword adopted by Guru Gobind Singh.[25]

Guru Nanak enunciated the basic principles for the guidance of his disciples. In matters of diet, for example, all food was pure as a gift from God. But eating for pleasure was 'impure' and the food which produced ailment in the body or evil thoughts in the mind was 'impure'. No ceremonials were set up, but when the need was felt by his successors the ceremonies introduced conformed to the principles of their Master. The composition which starts with *kita loriyey kamm,* for example, could be appropriately adopted for the Sikh rite of marriage. The *Kirtan Sohila* or 'the wedding song' could similarly be used on the occasion of death because of its metaphor for union. The sacred thread and the practice of sutak could be discarded on the basis of Guru Nanak's hymns. He was a man among men, a living example that could be followed: nowhere does he give the impression that 'his standard is beyond approach by mortal man'. Even today he speaks to men and women through his 'songs'.[26]

II. BHAGAT LAKSHMAN SINGH

The first Sikh biographer of Guru Gobind Singh was Bhagat Lakshman Singh. He had taught History and English Literature at Gordon Mission College at Rawalpindi, and edited *The Khalsa* in English before he thought of writing a book on the Guru who was acknowledged by millions in the Punjab as their 'saviour'. No European writer had given 'a comprehensive account of the life of Guru Gobind Singh', and the majority of the Indian writers had assumed that his principal role was of a political nature. Bhagat Lakshman Singh wanted to show that the great and lasting work of Guru Gobind Singh was 'to preach the fatherhood of God and the brotherhood of man'. The tenth Guru was a divine poet, a sage, and a reformer as much as a patriot.

Lakshman Singh's work was remarkable for its rational and humanistic approach to the life of Guru Gobind Singh. All miracles attributed to him were deliberately left out. Lakshman Singh believed that the working of the laws of nature can never be infringed. Guru Gobind Singh had openly discarded the theory of miracles, and characterized miraculous performances as 'trickeries'. Lakshman Singh was opposed to deifying heroes. Once deified, they ceased to be realizable ideals. They became objects of worship, creating an impassable barrier between them and their worshippers. Guru Gobind Singh clearly told his people to look upon him only as their spiritual father, a man among men. He took pride in acknowledging that his victories were due to his devoted disciples. The only object of adoration was the Timeless One.[27]

Guru Gobind Singh's achievement was made possible by the work of his predecessors. Guru Nanak had rejected 'ritualism', emphasized the importance of right living in complete dedication to God, and demonstrated that all human beings were equal in the eyes of God. With response from the lowly and the meek to this message of equality, a brotherhood was formed. A successor was needed to guide this brotherhood. Guru Angad, and his successor Guru Amar Das, faithfully followed Guru Nanak to consolidate 'the Church' established by him. Guru Ram Das added the ideals of benevolence and charity. Guru Arjan built the Harmandar, requesting Hazrat Mian Mir to lay its foundation, and compiled the Sikh scripture, which included the compositions of Hindu and Muslim saints. In the history of religion, this was the first example of equal honour being accorded to godly men of other creeds.

Guru Hargobind infused military spirit in his followers, took active part in politics, and fought and won battles. Guru Tegh Bahadur followed his example in displaying acts of bravery, culminating in the supreme sacrifice of his life. Guru Gobind Singh gave 'the finishing touch' to the dispensation of his predecessors by instituting the Khalsa.[28]

The Sikhs were different from the Hindus even before the institution of the Khalsa though mostly in doctrinal matters. Guru Gobind Singh sought to organize his followers into 'a real brotherhood' united by worldly interests as well as by common beliefs. He wanted to inspire his people with the feelings of love, manliness, and a sense of sacrifice. He evolved a 'new creed', the pure way or the *Khalsa Panth*.[29]

Lakshman Singh gives a 'rational' explanation of the origin of the idea that Guru Gobind Singh had invoked the Goddess for instituting the Khalsa. The Pandit who used to narrate stories of the *Mahabharata* to the Sikhs of Guru Gobind Singh dwelt generally on the blessings that all the great warriors had received from the Goddess. To show the absurdity of this notion the Guru gave his consent to the performance of *havan*. Despite elaborate preparations and profuse expenditure there was no result. The cunning priest fled during the night for fear of his life. All the ingredients of *havan* were thrown into the fire. The unusual illumination was attributed by the people to the appearance of the Goddess. But they were soon informed of what had actually happened.[30]

Guru Gobind Singh thought deeply about the predicament of his people. A voice from heaven told him that he had been commissioned to save humanity from sin and suffering as God's anointed son. With a naked sword in his hand he addressed a large assembly of his followers, telling them that this was the goddess that had appeared to him. He asked if any one was ready to sacrifice his life for the Guru and the community. The call had to be repeated before Daya Ram, a Khatri of Lahore, stood up. He was taken into the adjoining tent. Down came the sword and the sound of a thud. The Guru came out and demanded another head. Dharma, a Jat, came forward. He was taken into the tent and the thud was heard again. Three more Sikhs offered themselves for sacrifice: Himmat the water-carrier, Sahiba the barber, and Mohkam the washerman. A few minutes later all the five stood in new attire before their bewildered brethren. In their place, five goats had been slaughtered. On the following morning, which was the first day of Baisakh, 1699, all the five volunteers were administered *amrit* of the two-edged sword prepared by the Guru. Among other things, the epithet Singh was added to their names and they were duty bound to carry arms on their person. The Guru drank *amrit* from the same vessel and partook of the sacred food offered by them. These 'five beloved' (*panj piare*) formed the nucleus of the Khalsa. The hitherto neglected and down-trodden sections of the populace joined this order to contest power and position with the erstwhile privileged sections.[31]

Guru Gobind Singh taught belief in one God, rejected the theory of incarnation and worship of images, put no faith in austerities, and emphasized the efficacy of the Name of the Lord. Lakshman Singh quotes the well-known passage from Ghulam Muhiyuddin's *Tawarikh-i Punjab* to the effect that Brahmans, Kshatriyas, Vaishyas and Shudras were to be regarded as equals, that no place of Hindu or Muslim pilgrimage was to be visited, that Rama, Krishna, Brahma and the Goddess were not to be worshipped, and that all could learn from one another without any regard for caste. Many Brahmans and Kshatriyas refused to abandon the old religion of their ancestors and left the place. But 20,000 persons accepted baptism (*pahul*). Within a century, the low-caste Jats began to rule over Kshatriyas and Brahmans and to employ them 'as their gate-keepers and orderlies'.[32]

Personal Guruship ended with the death of Guru Gobind Singh. When he saw that his strength was failing and his dissolution was approaching, he collected his disciples and told them to regard the *Granth Sahib* as their Guru, and to submit all matters of moment to an assembly of five representative elders and to abide by their decision. Elsewhere Lakshman Singh states that the Guru left his *gaddi* to the whole community which consisted of men with brave souls united by noble ties, investing them with power 'to govern in matter spiritual and temporal'.[33] All were free to aspire to the highest rank in society. No one was deprived of the solace of religion because of his low origin. Hope was held out to all that God lifts all those who seek his aid.[34]

Lakshman Singh's interpretation of the mission of Guru Gobind Singh was interlinked with his view of the political and social problems in his own day. Guru Gobind Singh had lived for the people, worked for the people and died for the people. He was no friend of Brahmans and no enemy of Muslims. He inculcated 'a distinct creed, organized his followers into a distinct community with distinct symbols and distinct ways and beliefs'. However, diversity in matters of belief was no bar to an exchange of courtesies in matters social and political. A just Sikh social order and humanitarian relations of its members with others were issues of great importance.[35] The members of a religious denomination did not 'necessarily form one nationality'. Lakshman Singh visualized an 'Indian Nation' which would be neither Hindu nor Muslim, nor Christian, nor Sikh: it would include all the religious communities of India. True patriotism was based on the fatherhood of God and the brotherhood of man. Guru Gobind had laboured to ensure 'harmonious development of his country' as 'a patriot'. His patriotism was of a higher type, concerned with the downtrodden of the society and their upliftment. His example could serve as a source of inspiration for every Indian patriot of whatever race or creed.[36]

Lakshman Singh was not happy with the insistence that all Sikhs should take *pahul* and observe the Khalsa *rahit* on the argument that Guru Gobind Singh had made it obligatory for all Sikhs. This insistence was historically conditioned. The Sikh creed was 'Hinduized' after the establishment of Sikh rule. The high caste Hindus made advances for reconciliation with the new power and a compromise was effected by which the Sikhs abandoned their 'revolutionary programme' and the Hindus included the Gurus in the list of Vishnu's incarnations. The Nirmalas were mostly responsible for this. They had virtually gone over to Hinduism. In this situation the Sikh reformers began to insist more on the outward form than inward purity. In Lakshman Singh's view the Sikhs who took *amrit* and observed the five symbols (*kara, kachha, kirpan, kesh* and *kangha*) declared their determination to make sacrifices for the Panth. Guru Gobind Singh did not insist that all his followers must take *amrit:* the baptismal ceremony 'was not forced upon any one'. The insistence merely on the form with total disregard for the spirit could not serve the larger purposes of the Sikh community.[37]

Bhagat Lakshman Singh's monograph on the Sikh martyrs was complete in 1919 but it was published in 1928. In his 'Introduction' to this book he expounds his view of martyrdom in the Sikh tradition, a view that imparts a certain degree of unity to over a score of events that he treats in the book. He quotes passages from the *Rag Asa* which reflect Guru Nanak's anguish over the miseries suffered by both Hindus and Muslim due to Babur's sack of Saidpurs (Eminabad). Before this event, Guru Nanak had started his mission of 'peace and goodwill to all mankind'. Freedom from political and religious tyranny was his primary objective, and this called for moral and spiritual uplift. His basic principle was 'the Fatherhood of God and the Brotherhood of Man'. His gospel appealed to the common people. Guru Nanak's successors carried on the campaign 'against the old order of things', and created a distinctive 'church'.[38]

The alien rulers were not only tyrannical but also discriminatory in the treatment of their subjects. They chose to stand in opposition to the nascent Sikh 'church'. The struggle of the Sikhs against the Mughals was not 'religious'. Like Sikhism, Islam was seriously concerned with 'the depressed classes'. Indeed, there was much that was common between Sikhism and Islam. But the Mughal state treated the Sikhs harshly. For the Sikh Gurus the 'whole world was their home, and the wide universe their country'. But they were ready to defend themselves, and defend others, against injustice. Bhagat Lakshman had great admiration for Akbar, but he was an exception. The injustice and oppression of the Mughal rulers in general and their hostility towards the Sikhs in particular gave rise to Sikh martyrs. But they were not the passive products of their times: they changed the course of history. 'Men looked upon them in awe and wonder.'[39]

Bhagat Lakshman Singh saw a basic similarity between Sikh and Christian martyrs. 'Men have died all the world over, while exploiting land, wealth or women, but the credit of dying for the weak and the oppressed, and the upholding of Truth, belongs to the Christian and the Sikh martyrs alone'. Islam did a lot for rescuing people from a life of mental and moral degradation; it infused a wonderful love for one another in the believers. 'But it cannot be said that the men, who laid down their lives for it, were actuated altogether by pure motives'. They were attracted by the promise of sensual pleasures after martyrdom. 'The Christian and Sikh martyrs had no such temptation'. The hope of the Sikh martyr was to have an abode in 'Sach Khand', the region of Truth, to look at God and glorify him.[40] Thus, Bhagat Lakshman Singh postulates a close link between Sikh ideology and the Sikh tradition of martyrdom. He looks upon this tradition as quite distinct from the Islamic tradition of martyrdom.

Bhagat Lakshman Singh does not appear to be familiar with Ratan Singh Bhangu's *Panth Prakash*. He appreciates Giani Gian Singh for his long travels and arduous labour to write on the subject in Punjabi and Urdu. But his own purpose was to provide 'an abbreviated volume' in English, a language that was 'most widely understood throughout the world'. Obviously, he wanted the wider humanity to know something of 'the men who played so important a part in the world-drama, and who sacrificed their lives for the uplift of their downtrodden fellow-beings'.[41]

Among the Sikh martyrs are Guru Arjan, Guru Tegh Bahadur, Bhai Tara Singh, Bhai Mani Singh, Bhai Bota Singh, Sardar Mehtab Singh, Sardar Sukha Singh, Bhai Taru Singh, Sardar Subeg Singh and his son Shahbaz Singh, Baba Dip Singh, Baba Gurbakhsh Singh, Bhai Mati Das, Bhai Dayal Chand, Sahibzada Ajit Singh, Sahibzada Jujhar Singh, Bhai Sant Singh, Sahibzada Zorawar Singh, Sahibzada Fateh Singh, the forty immortals, Guru Gobind Singh himself, Haqiquat Rai, and Baba Ram Singh Bedi. Then there were thousand of other un-named martyrs who died for their faith due to persecution by the Mughal governors of Lahore and Ahmad Shah Abdali. The great *ghallughara* is specially underlined by Lakshman Singh as the event in which 30,000 Sikhs died in a single action.

We may notice only the asides and comments of Bhagat Lakshman Singh to see how his mind was working on the theme of martyrdom. Guru Arjan gave shelter and financial assistance to the rebel prince, Khusrau, in accordance with the Sikh conception of hospitality. He knew that he was giving mortal offence to Jahangir who, in any case, was looking for an excuse to take action against Guru Arjan because of his popularity and influence among the people. Hazrat Mian Mir showered imprecations on Jahangir and wished to pray for the overthrow of the Mughal rule. But Guru Arjan said that 'he would resignedly leave himself in the hands of God, who alone knew what was good'. He was right. 'Whatever dignity or nobility attaches to the name Sikh, is primarily due to this one of the most unostentatious, quietest and humblest of workers in the cause of Truth'.[42]

The Gurus were called *Sacha Padshah* because they were 'wholly devoted to the well-being of their fellowmen', and 'defended them from internal and external trouble'. This was the reason why the Brahmans of Kashmir approached Guru Tegh Bahadur for help against Aurangzeb's oppression. He must have felt deeply distressed to hear their tale of woe. The inhuman treatment accorded to Guru Tegh Bahadur was bound to provoke his people. Bhai Mati Das was sawn into two and Bhai Dayal Das was boiled to death. They faced the torture with unflinching courage to the admiration of both friends and foes.[43] Ajit Singh and Jujhar Singh died fighting; Zorawar Singh and Fateh Singh refused to accept Islam, which cost them their lives. Bhagat Lakshman gives the names of the forty immortals (*muktas*): 'Few names in history are remembered with greater fervour than theirs'. Guru Gobind Singh would have liked to die fighting in the thick of battle but his end was far nobler: 'He died while he was engaged in teaching and preaching his catholic creed, the basic principle of which was love for all mankind and wide tolerance, which gave all men the right to worship God as they chose.'[44]

Bhai Tara Singh, who had done many a brave deed to free his country from the yoke of the Yavanas, died gloriously and gave proof of 'the invincible spirit that the Khalsa then possessed'. On the spot where his remains were cremated stood a shrine, where 'the people of the surrounding villages, who still cherish his memory, assemble every year to do him honour'.[45] Bhai Mani Singh was asked to accept Islam but he never swerved from his loyalty to the Guru. His limbs were torn off. His remains were cremated at the spot called Shahidganj. 'The news of the cruel deed infuriated the Khalsa throughout the land'.[46] Bhai Bota Singh, with another comrade, courted martyrdom, fighting heroically with their foes. 'The way in which the two men had fought and met death elicited admiration, and the conviction grew upon the minds of the populace that the transfer of the Government to the hands of the Khalsa could not be long delayed.'[47]

The parents of Haqiqat Rai were pious Nanak Panthis. He was married to the daughter of Sardar Kishan Singh Uppal of Batala. 'Both these causes combined to instill deep spirituality into the mind of the young Haqiqat, and although he had not yet formally received baptism as a Khalsa, it was admitted, on all hands, that in religious zeal and devoutness, and in jealous regard for the honour of his creed and country, he was second to none of the professed baptized Sikhs of his time'. On being approached by Sardar Kishan Singh and his brothers, Mal Singh and Dal Singh, the Khalsa attacked Sialkot and killed the *mulla,* the *qazi* and the administrator responsible for Haqiqat Rai's death. The savage ruling classes soon came to know that 'some manliness was still left in the subject people, and that they could not exasperate them with impunity'.[48]

Bhai Taru Singh was arrested on the charge of harbouring dacoits. He plainly declared that he had given shelter to the Guru's followers and not done anything to be ashamed of; he deemed it a privilege that the Guru had placed him in a position that enabled him to serve the Sikhs. Zakariya Khan ordered that Bhai Taru Singh's head should be clean-shaved. A barber failed to cut his hair and a shoe-maker failed to remove his scalp. A carpenter used his adze to cut-off his head. His remains were cremated outside the Delhi Gate, at the place which later came to be known as Shahidganj. A *jagir* was set apart for its maintenance (in the time of Sikh rule). In the early twentieth century, both the offerings as well as the *jagir* were appropriated by a *mahant* who used them principally for his own private ends. The place was neglected. If revived as a place of pilgrimage it could be a source of perennial inspiration for the young generation of the Sikhs.[49]

A religious argument was the cause for which Subeg Singh and his son Shahbaz Singh were placed on the wheel and crushed. The news of this horrid deed spread like wildfire. The Khalsa came out of their haunts and wreaked vengeance on the tyrants and their supporters. The peacefully inclined people, irrespective of their faith, cursed the oppressor. 'Thus, quite unconsciously, the tyrannical rulers were losing their hold over the subject population. They were contributing to their own destruction and hastening the advent of the Khalsa rule.'[50] After the first *ghallughara,* the Khalsa increased tenfold in number, all burning with religious zeal and yearning for opportunities to wreak vengeance on the rulers and their supporters, whether Hindu or Muslim.[51]

The cause of Baba Deep Singh's martyrdom was the sacrilege of the Harmandar Sahib by the Afghans. Memorials were raised not only for Baba Deep Singh but also in honour of Dharam Singh, Kaur Singh, Mannu Singh, Sant Singh and Ram Singh, 'which stand to this day'.[52] Baba Gurbakhsh Singh and his companions too died fighting in defence of the Harmandar Sahib. They were cremated in the vicinity of the Akal Bunga and the place was named Shahidganj. A regular service was held there once a month.[53] The Khalsa who died fighting in the Great Holocaust made it impossible for Ahmad Shah Abdali 'to think of molesting the Khalsa again'.[54] The immense sacrifices made by the Khalsa led to their ultimate triumph.[55]

Bhagat Lakshman Singh underlines the cosmopolitan ideal of Guru Gobind Singh. He bought into being 'a separate fraternity, gave it a separate organization and made it a distinct self-contained, self-conscious entity'. But nowhere does he say that God is 'partial to the Khalsa alone' or that there need be 'any antagonism between the Khalsa and the Musalmans, or for that matter between any two peoples as a result of theological differences'.[56]

There is hardly any doubt that Bhagat Lakshman Singh looks upon martyrdom as an integral part of the Sikh tradition. The motivating force was supplied by religious ideology but the objective became increasingly political. The acts of the martyrs created a new awakening and a new courage among the common people and their sacrifices contributed towards the establishment of the Khalsa Raj.

III. KHAZAN SINGH ON SIKH HISTORY AND RELIGION

The first comprehensive work on the history and religion of the Sikhs was produced by Khazan Singh, an Extra Assistant Commissioner. He had a lot of appreciation for the 'splendid work' of Macauliffe, and he looked upon the work of Giani Gian Singh as extremely useful. However, most of the works published by European writers were 'extremely defective' and 'in many ways misleading'. A systematic account of the religion and history of the Sikhs, a truer and a fuller account, was needed. Towards this end, Khazan Singh published *The History and Philosophy of Sikh Religion* in two volumes in 1914.[57]

Khazan Singh was critical of the materials available to him. The Persian writers had their own biases and limitations. A *Janamsakhi* dictated by Bhai Bala and inscribed by Paira Mokha for Guru Angad did not have a large circulation because the Gurmukhi script was not known to many in those days. Before long, the disciples of Kabir corrupted and mutilated the *Janamsakhi* to show that Kabir was much higher in spiritual status than Guru Nanak. The Handalis introduced interpolations in the original *Janamsakhi* to exalt Handal. Eventually, the original *Janamsakhi* was destroyed and the corrupted one was made current. The *Colebrooke Janamsakhi,* compiled by a private individual independently of Bhai Bala, was not a continuous chronicle but a mass of isolated and detached *sakhis.* The extant *Janamsakhis* were either apocryphal, or corrupted, or incomplete. In spite of the excision of interpolated material by the editors, their texts contained much that should be discarded.[58]

The biographies of the sixth and the tenth Gurus, one written in the early decades of the eighteenth century and the other around its end, and Bhai Santokh Singh's *Nanak Parkash* and his *Suraj Parkash* appeared to have been written more or less 'under the influence of the priestly classes'. Bhai Santokh Singh was helped by many able *pandits* commissioned by the Sikh Chief of Kaithal; their conservative 'suggestions and insinuations' were incorporated in his works. Imperfection of knowledge among the Sikhs gave ample opportunity to the polytheistic *pandits* to mislead the Sikh authors who were not well educated. They were obliged to put 'wrong or misleading constructions' on the hymns of the Gurus. The compositions of Guru Gobind Singh, which have a peculiar style and rhyme, demanded a very deep and extensive knowledge.[59]

Khazan Singh suggests that the 'touchstone' for assaying any work on Sikhism was available in the *Adi Granth* and the *Vars* of Bhai Gurdas. The latter, which depicts the condition of Sikhism up to the time of Guru Hargobind, appears to be 'free from any foreign influence'. In the *Granth* associated with Guru Gobind Singh, his genuine compositions were 'few in number'. The rest of the book consisted chiefly of 'biographies' of the incarnations of Vishnu based on Sanskrit works. The Guru's personal remarks at the end of each translation indicate that he did not believe in these incarnations. Then there were abstracts from the *Ramayana* and the *Bhagavat.* About two-fifths of the book dealt with the viles of women. These three subjects occupied nearly two-thirds of 'the so-called Granth'. It was not 'a Holy Scripture in the true sense of the word'. It was a collection of scattered and unconnected fragments which fell into the hands of its unknown compiler.[60]

The *Granth* prepared by Guru Arjan contained the hymns of the first five Gurus and other votaries of God, irrespective of their caste or religion. Some space was left vacant at the end of each *Rag* to be filled up with the hymns of the Guru who should sacrifice his head for the sake of righteousness. This explanation of the inclusion of the compositions of Guru Tegh Bahadur in the *Granth*, which was characterized by Trumpp as a post-eventum prophecy, comes from the *Gurbilas Patshahi Chhevin*. This also explains for Khazan Singh why the hymns of Guru Gobind Singh were not included in the *Adi Granth*. Guru Arjan got books from Mohan, the son of Guru Amar Das, which contained hymns of the first three Gurus. Khazan Singh holds the view that not all the hymns of the Gurus were included in the *Granth* compiled by Guru Arjan, either because they were not procurable or because they were deliberately left out. The *Pran Sangali*, for instance, was procured from Ceylon (Sri Lanka) but it was not included in the *Granth* because Guru Arjan found it 'too difficult and complex for laymen to follow'.[61]

Khazan Singh believed that the process of selection was started by Guru Nanak himself, and there were various considerations for exclusion. Postulating thus, the existence of authentic but not canonized compositions, Khazan Singh suggests that a historian could utilize the genuine compositions not included in the *Adi Granth* 'for the purpose of illustration or explanation of facts'. For all writings, the ultimate criterion was whether or not an idea or a practice attributed to the Gurus was contrary to the teachings of the *Adi Granth*. Since the Gurus practised what they taught, their acts were never at variance with their teachings.

Bhai Banno's recension was 'brackish' (*khari*) because it contained hymns which did not have the prior approval of Guru Arjan. The Guru accepted his copy, signed it and sealed it, but he also remarked that it was *khari*. The volume prepared by the Guru was kept at Amritsar and Bhai Banno was allowed to take the other volume to his village Mangat in the district of Gujrat.[62]

Khazan Singh was interested far more in the early Sikh tradition than in the political history of the Sikhs. Within the early Sikh tradition he gives great prominence to Guru Nanak and Guru Gobind Singh. Virtually, therefore, he covers the ground covered by Sewaram Singh and Bhagat Lakshman Singh. His interpretation of the early Sikh tradition is not radically different from theirs.

As for the life of Guru Nanak, Khazan Singh pays special attention to the date of his birth. Karam Singh had argued at some length in favour of the Baisakh date. Khazan Singh points out that the various versions of the *Bala Janamsakhi* gave the date in the month of Kattak. These *Janamsakhis* were not free from interpolations, but they were not forgeries. Bhai Santokh Singh gives the Kattak date in his *Suraj Prakash.* After a careful study of Sikh sources Giani Gian Singh also comes to the same conclusion. The Kattak date was celebrated by the descendants of Guru Nanak at Dera Baba Nanak from the very beginning. The Baisakh date is given in the *Colebrooke Janamsakhi,* but this work was based on hearsay and not on 'any authority'. The strongest evidence in support of Baisakh appears to come from Bhai Gurdas who uses the word *vasoa* in his *Var:* this was interpreted as a reference to the celebration of Guru Nanak's birth on the first of Baisakh. In Khazan Singh's view this interpretation takes the word *vasoa* literally. But it was used by Bhai Gurdas metaphorically, to suggest that everyday was treated like the new year day (Baisakhi) for singing the praises of God. Khazan Singh comes to the conclusion that (there was no clear or credible evidence against the *puranmashi* of Kattak as the date of Guru Nanak's birth.[63]

For the teachings of Guru Nanak, Khazan Singh repeats the view expressed by Cunningham that the reformers like Shankaracharya, Gorakh, Ramanand and Kabir, had failed to promulgate the much desired 'reform' and it was left for Guru Nanak to remove oppression, to raise the morals of the people, and to direct them to righteousness. Guru Nanak and his successors insisted on the worship of the only True Lord, excluding all other objects of worship. The fatherhood of God and the brotherhood of man were the two cardinal principles of Guru Nanak. He never recognized any distinctions of caste or class, and he addressed himself to all classes of Hindus and Muslims. Khazan Singh elaborates three ideas in particular: the doctrine of the Divine Order, the theory of transmigration, and the law of *karma.* He emphasizes that Sikhism was meant to supersede all earlier religions. Designed for 'the whole world', the Sikh gospel was 'the essence of all revelation': Hindu, Muslim, Jewish, Christian, and others.[64]

There was no difference between Guru Nanak and his successors, or in their teachings. It is a mistake to think that 'Khalsa was an innovation of Guru Gobind Singh'. Guru Nanak's successors had prepared the way for the adoption of the Khalsa faith by Guru Gobind Singh 'on the lines chalked out by Guru Nanak'.[65] Indeed, everything was 'pre-arranged' by Guru Nanak, even the end of personal Guruship after the tenth Guru and the vesting of Guruship in the Khalsa theocracy and the holy scripture.[66]

The Khalsa Panth was meant to be distinct in all its 'domestic, social and political' functions but not necessarily sovereign.[67] The Gurus themselves had inculcated that there are 'always two sovereigns' in the world, and obedience to them was binding. The successors of both Baba Nanak and Babur, were created by God, the former as the spiritual and the latter as temporal kings. Khazan Singh goes on to add that the successor of Baba Nanak was now the *Granth Sahib* and that of Babur 'the British Government'. The Sikhs were 'enjoined' to be loyal to both.[68] This loyalty was not passive either. The Sikhs should help their sovereigns in 'carrying out the administration of the country'. Indeed, for a Sikh to be guilty of disloyalty was to fall from the faith of the Gurus.[69]

IV. SOME GENERAL OBSERVATIONS

All the three Sikh writers belonged to the Western-educated middle class. One was a lawyer who later became a judge; another was a teacher and a journalist; the third was a civil servant. They were aware of the context in which they were writing. They were dissatisfied with the existing work on the Sikh tradition. To improve upon it, they turned to original sources in addition to the works of Sikh and non-Sikh scholars. Reliance on Sikh sources became a remarkable feature of their work. Their attitude towards these sources was by no means uncritical, but they were far more sympathetic to the Sikh tradition than the bulk of non-Sikh scholars, whether Indian or European. In fact, they tended to look upon Sikhism and the Sikh Gurus as essentially unique. Thus, their interpretation of the Sikh tradition was closely linked to their faith in Guru Nanak and his successors.

According to Sewaram Singh, the existence of God for Guru Nanak was a matter of experience and not of proofs. His creed was monotheistic, egalitarian and ethical. Emancipation in Sikhism meant essentially living with God and in God. Devotion to God, meditation on the Name, and ethical living in accordance with the teachings of the Gurus embodied in the *Adi Granth* could lead to emancipation, but never without the grace of God. Guru Nanak emphasized the importance of congregational worship and prayers, and he established a number of centres for this purpose. The one at Kartarpur had a pattern of daily worship, and the whole community (*sangat*) ate in the common kitchen (*langar*) maintained by contributions made by individual Sikhs. Guru Nanak chose Angad as his successor to continue his work. The local communities of Sikhs (*sangats*) elsewhere were guided by *bhais* (brothers) and *mais* (mothers) appointed by the Guru. Novices were baptized through *charan-pahul*. The Sikhs being householders needed social institutions. These were evolved in due course on the basis of principles enunciated by Guru Nanak. Sewaram Singh appreciated Cunningham's view of Sikhism as a new and original dispensation, and he disagreed with Trumpp on several important issues, like Guru Nanak's conception of God and his attributes, the effect of Sikh beliefs on ethical living, the role of the Guru, and the concept of emancipation. On the whole, Sewaram Singh's exposition of the Sikh faith was more comprehensive than that of the earlier writers and it was based on a close study of Gurbani.

Bhagat Lakshman Singh looked upon the work of Guru Gobind Singh as the culmination of the work of Guru Nanak and his eight successors. Under them the differences between the Sikhs and the Hindus were spelt out as being of a religious nature. The egalitarian order of the Khalsa brought in differences which were social and political as well. Guru Gobind Singh agreed to invoke the goddess only to expose the Brahmans. He gave the awesome call for sacrifice much later, gave a new kind of *pahul* to the five beloved, and enunciated the *rahit* of the '5 Ks'. All those who accepted the baptism of the double-edged sword were told to believe in one God and not to worship Hindu gods and goddesses, not to worship idols, not to go to the sacred places of the Hindus, not to observe austerities of any kind, and not to observe any distinctions of caste. After the death of Guru Gobind Singh, they were to believe in the Guruship of the *Granth* and the Panth. On the whole, Bhagat Lakshman Singh's treatment of Guru Gobind Singh was more elaborate than that of the earlier writers and it was based on a rational interpretation of available evidence. Martyrdom was integral part of the Sikh tradition and it was intimately linked with Sikh ideology.

Khazan Singh believed that Guru Angad had prepared a *Janamsakhi* of Guru Nanak which was eventually lost because of the envy of the Kabir-Panthis and Handalis and the enmity of the Mughal administrators. Besides this official biography so to speak, *Janamsakhis* were compiled by private individuals—like the *Colebrooke Janamsakhi.* Just as *Janamsakhis* were corrupted by the rivals of the Gurus, much of the other Sikh literature was vitiated by the insidious influence of the conservative priestly class of Brahmans. Khazan Singh accepted post-eventum prophecies found in the early nineteenth-century Sikh literature. For him, not all the genuine compositions of the Gurus were included in the *Adi Granth.* These could be used by the historian as authentic evidence. Khazan Singh believed in the divinity of Guru Nanak and the originality of his creed. Guru Nanak was the seal of the prophets, and his revelation was the essence of all previous revelations. Sikhism was meant to transcend all earlier faiths. Without saying so, Khazan Singh tried to refute Trumpp in his exposition of the divine governance of the universe, the law of *karma,* and the doctrine of transmigration. He saw the work of the successors of Guru Nanak leading inevitably towards the institution of the Khalsa and the vesting of Guruship in the Panth and the *Granth.*

All the three writers appear to have cherished the Sikh tradition. Therefore, they were keen to correct what they regarded as 'misrepresentation' or 'misunderstanding'. They wanted to project their own understanding and interpretation of the Sikh tradition for Sikhs and non-Sikhs alike. All their concerns were not the same as the concerns of the European writers. Their concern for the uniqueness of the Sikh tradition was linked with their understanding of their own situation. The question of Sikh identity was important for all of them. Sewaram Singh, who looked upon the Udasis as a part of the Sikh tradition, was nonetheless clear that Sikhism was basically different from Hinduism. Bhagat Lakshman Singh believed that Sahajdharis were a part of the Sikh Panth, but his preference for the Singh identity was quite marked. Khazan Singh appears to equate the Sikh with the Singh.

For all the three writers, the Sikhs had an identity distinct from that of Hindus or Muslims. For Khazan Singh, there was no contradiction between a distinct identity of the Khalsa Panth and Sikh cooperation with and loyalty to the British government. In Lakshman Singh's view, Guru Gobind Singh's aim of social revolution was arrested by the political success of the Sikhs. His message was still relevant for social revolution, and it had a close bearing on the relations of the Sikhs amongst themselves and with non-Sikhs. The distinct and separate identity of the Sikhs did not mean that the Sikhs were a nation in the political sense. No religious community of India constituted a nation. The Indian Nation of the future would embrace all such communities. Concern for the Sikh present and future was not divorced from concern for the Sikh past for any of the three writers.

The attitude of the three writers towards Sikh sources was critical but not sceptical. They brought Sikh sources into high relief by a more or less critical use of these sources. Whatever their personal beliefs about Guru Nanak and Guru Gobind Singh, they tried to write their biographies in human and rational terms. It is not surprising that they produced biographies which can be treated as 'secondary works' by a present-day biographer of Guru Nanak or Guru Gobind Singh. They presented cogent arguments for treating Sikhism as a new faith with some important social implications. They tried to show that the institution of the Khalsa cannot be regarded as a rupture with the earlier Sikh tradition. They underlined the significance of the concept and the institution of Guruship in the Sikh tradition—its unity, continuity, and indivisibility leading to the doctrines of *Guru Granth* and Guru-Panth. They emphasized the importance of the norm of equality in relation to caste and gender. They insisted on looking at the pre-Khalsa as well as the Khalsa Panth as a distinct entity. However, they did not look upon Sikh identity as the basis of Sikh politics.

NOTES

1. Sewaram Singh, *The Divine Master: Life and Teachings of Guru Nanak*, ed. Prithipal Singh Kapur, Jalandhar: ABS Publications, 1988 (rpt.), pp. xi-xii.
2. Ibid., pp. xii-xiii.
3. Ibid., Preface to the Second Edition, pp. ix-x.
4. Ibid., Editor's Note, p. v.
5. Ibid., pp. 11-12 and 14-15.
6. Ibid., pp. 49-50. Sewaram Singh accepts the existence of Bala but rejects the view that he accompanied Guru Nanak on his travels.
7. Ibid., p. 62.
8. Ibid., pp. 101-2.

9. Ibid., pp. 102-3.
10. Ibid., pp. 104-8 and 110-11. A photographic reproduction of the Baghdad inscription is given. Sewaram Singh also states that the cloak (*chola*) received by Guru Nanak at Baghdad was still in the possession of his descendants at Dera Baba Nanak.
11. Ibid., pp. 117-19.
12. Ibid., pp. 53-4.
13. Ibid., p. 54.
14. Ibid., pp. 123, 145, 146, 185, 191 and 204.
15. Ibid., pp. 20, 36-38, 109, 117-19 and 155. Conversely, the 'divinity' of Guru Nanak induces Sewaram Singh to accept that he composed in his childhood verses like a learned and mature man; he could bodily ascend to the court of God; he could leave on a rock the impression of his palm; he could revive a dead elephant; a mill could grind without being handled by him; and his dead body could vanish after his death. The consistency of character and personality which Sewaram Singh discerns in the whole life of Guru Nanak also gets explained on the assumption of his 'divinity'.
16. Ibid., pp. 157-60.
17. Ibid., pp. 160-70.
18. Ibid., pp. 170-5.
19. Ibid., pp. 170-82.
20. Ibid., pp. 183-4.
21. Ibid., pp. 10-11, 23-4 and 25.
22. Ibid., pp. 164-6 and 176. According to Sewaram Singh, Trumpp misunderstood the idea of obedience to the Guru. Insistence on obedience was meant to teach humility: ibid., p. 171.
23. Ibid., pp. 207-16.
24. Ibid., pp. 147-55.
25. Ibid., pp. 147-55, 193-7.
26. Ibid., pp. 201-4, 208.
27. Lakshman Singh, *A Short Sketch of the Life and Work of Guru Gobind Singh*, Ludhiana: Lahore Book Shop, 1963 (rpt.), pp. 184-5, 193-4.
28. Ibid., pp. 190-2.
29. Ibid., pp. 28, 30, 48.
30. Ibid., pp. 30-1.
31. Ibid., pp. 32-7.
32. Ibid., pp. 39-55.
33. Ibid., pp. 136, 166.
34. Ibid., pp. 139-46.
35. Ibid., pp. 146-8.
36. Ibid., pp. 149-64.
37. Ibid., pp. 167-77, 181.

38. Bhagat Lakshman Singh, *The Sikh Martyrs*, ed. Prithipal Singh Kapur, Amritsar: Singh Brothers (in association with Delhi Sikh Gurdwara Management Committee), 2006, pp. 27-31.
39. Ibid., pp. 34-44.
40. Ibid., p. 44.
41. Ibid., p. 43.
42. Ibid., pp. 49, 50, 51.
43. Ibid., pp. 64-5, 67, 71, 80.
44. Ibid., p. 105.
45. Ibid., pp. 104-10.
46. Ibid., pp. 113-14.
47. Ibid., pp. 118-21.
48. Ibid., pp. 122-5.
49. Ibid., pp. 126-8.
50. Ibid., p. 135.
51. Ibid., pp. 153-5.
52. Ibid., pp. 156-7.
53. Ibid., p. 162.
54. Ibid., p. 102.
55. Ibid., p. 183.
56. Ibid., pp. 185-6.
57. Khazan Singh, *History of the Sikhs*, Patiala: Punjab Languages Department, 1970 (rpt.), pp. i-v.
58. Ibid., pp. 8-22.
59. Ibid., pp. 191-221.
60. Ibid., pp. 22-3 and 24-5.
61. Ibid., pp. 26-8.
62. Ibid., pp. 28-9.
63. Ibid., pp. 211-34.
64. Khazan Singh, *Philosophy of the Sikh Religion*, Patiala: Punjab Languages Department, 1970 (rpt.), pp. 31, 63-69, 103-91, 193, 204-6, 213, 218.
65. Ibid., pp. 224-7.
66. Ibid., p. 229.
67. Ibid., p. 323.
68. Ibid., p. 188.
69. Ibid., p. 178.

PART FOUR

Bengali Historians

CHAPTER TWELVE

Indubhusan Banerjee on the Early Sikh Tradition

The first volume of Indubhusan Banerjee's *Evolution of the Khalsa* was published in 1936, though its first draft was completed in 1920-1. The second volume appeared in 1947. Writing in the late 1970s, Professor A.C. Banerjee concluded his article on Indubhusan Banerjee as a historian with the remark that 'no student of Sikh history in the foreseeable future will fail to find in the *Evolution of the Khalsa* an indispensable guide and a source of inspiration.[1] My own impression was that Indubhusan Banerjee was 'on the way to be ousted from the respectable position he has occupied in the field of Sikh studies, partly due to the limitation of his conceptualization and partly due to the limitations of his source materials'.[2] More recently, Professor Indu Banga has argued that Indubhusan Banerjee subordinated his otherwise scholarly study of the Sikh movement to 'Hindu nationalism'.[3] We propose to concentrate on the text of the *Evolution of the Khalsa* for a proper appreciation of Banerjee's thought.

I. THE BASIC THESIS

Banerjee states that, originally, Sikhism belonged to 'the great family of popular religions' that made their appearance in the fifteenth and sixteenth centuries. Despite their differences in detail, Ramanand and Kabir, and Chaitanya and Guru Nanak, all agreed on the fundamentals: the message of love and truth, the message of peace, and the great panacea of the Name. However, Sikhism alone became a 'church-nation'. A simple monotheistic faith which had its origin in an unostentatious attempt at social emancipation and religious uplift became political in its aims and military in its methods. The whole character of the movement changed when 'a peaceful sect was gradually turned into a military order' and the devotee developed into 'the soldier saint'. Even though Sikhism had its origin in an extreme reaction against conventionalism of all kinds, it was not difficult to understand how it evolved conventions of its own. But the transformation of Sikhism into 'a military theocracy' presented a more complex problem and was much more difficult to understand.[4]

According to Banerjee, there were two distinct stages of development in this transformation. From the days of Guru Nanak to the year 1604, when the *Granth Sahib* was compiled, the movement ran on peaceful lines. During this phase, 'Sikhism gradually detached itself from Hinduism, developed ideals and institutions of its own, and the Sikh Panth came to acquire a more or less definite meaning'. There was no quarrel with Islam or the established state. The second phase started with the execution of Guru Arjan in 1606, followed by a sudden transition to militarism under his son and successor, Guru Hargobind. The more thorough militarism of Guru Gobind Singh was preceded by the execution of Guru Tegh Bahadur in 1675. The transformation of Sikhism could thus be explained 'primarily on the ground of Muslim persecution'.[5]

However, it was pertinent to ask what made it possible for Sikhism 'to react to the Muslim persecution in the manner it did'. The answer given by J.D. Cunningham was frequently quoted: Guru Nanak perceived the true principles of reform and laid the broad foundations for the work of Guru Gobind Singh. It was necessary for Banerjee to submit this view to 'a close examination'. In his view, Guru Nanak was concerned with 'fundamentals' rather than with 'a social programme'. He did not prohibit renunciation; the door to renunciation was barred by his successors. Sikhism became 'essentially a religion of householders' only under the successors of Guru Nanak. Banerjee conceded that Guru Nanak sought to strip religion of mythology and history to make Sikhism non-sectarian. But this could be said of Kabir as well, though most of the other sects reverted to mythology and tradition. In any case, Sikhism stood distinguished by the spiritualistic character of its worship and its moderation in regard to mythology. This comparative freedom from the shackles of tradition made it more mobile and more at liberty to adjust itself to the changing circumstances. Banerjee was keen to make the point absolutely clear. The future Sikh nation did grow on the foundation provided by Guru Nanak and he may be said to have planted the germs of a nation. But Cunningham's contention that the system of Nanak had 'some such original distinctiveness which alone could provide the basis of a nation and which was wholly absent in the other reform movements' was hardly tenable.[6]

Banerjee observes that the writers like Teja Singh and Kartar Singh saw in the *Babar-bani* verses a 'full-fledged Sikh nation of the future' contemplated by Guru Nanak. This showed how difficult it had become to study the history of the certain phases of Sikhism 'in their true historical setting and perspective' and how 'the later political and military successes of Sikhism' added largely to the difficulties of the historian. Banerjee goes on to add that since the days of Browne, most of the writings on the earlier phases of Sikhism had been coloured 'more or less by the reflected glory of its later days'.[7] This would apply to Cunningham as well.

For Banerjee, the nomination of a successor by Guru Nanak was 'a measure of far-reaching consequences'. The Guruship in Sikhism came to acquire a meaning quite its own, and the personality of the Guru supplied a nucleus around which the Sikh Panth could gradually arise. Sikhism developed a unique spirit of organization that produced practical results under Guru Nanak's successors. The compilation of the *Granth* completed the separation from mythology and tradition. Sikhism by the time of Guru Arjan had come to acquire a far-flung and yet a centralized organization through its *sangats* and *masands*. Together with the high intensity of the religious ideals of Sikhism, the strength of its organization 'gives us the measure of its reaction to Muslim persecution'. This reaction expressed itself in a sudden transition to militarism albeit of a purely defensive character.[8]

Guru Hargobind and his successors pursued a cautious policy in relation to the state, but never allowing the question of safety to get the better of duty and justice. Guru Tegh Bahadur found it impossible to stand by when he found that the proselytizing zeal of Aurangzeb was working havoc among 'the peaceful Hindu population'. His lofty religious ideals compelled him to throw all caution to the winds and openly to espouse the cause of the Brahmans of Kashmir. He was taken to Delhi and executed. The reaction was tremendous. The Sikhs realized that the limited militarism of the days of Guru Hargobind was no longer enough. A more vigorous policy had much greater chances of success. The outcome of this realization was the Khalsa, or the Sikh military theocracy.[9]

However, the explanation of 'transformation' did not end there. The question of 'race and religion' had received some attention in psychological and socio-anthropological studies, and it appeared to be well established that 'the innate characteristics' of a people were a very important factor in the modification of the religious system. Banerjee saw the relevance of this factor for Sikhism. Its democratic ideas had no attraction for the higher classes who valued their 'pride of birth' above everything else. Sikhism had to fall upon the low caste Jats for swelling its ranks. The character of the Jats 'imperceptibly modified the system, as it was bound to do'. Banerjee saw a close correspondence between the major traits of the Jat character and some of the developments associated with the Khalsa. The transformation of Sikhism was thus an example of 'the assimilation of the form of the religious system to the innate tendencies of the people'.[8] On the whole, thus, for Banerjee the transformation of Sikhism could be explained in terms of 'Muslim persecution', the ideological and institutional developments under the successors of Guru Nanak, and the innate traits of the Jats. The implication is clear: nothing in the ideology of Guru Nanak could lead to this transformation.

II. THE LIFE OF GURU NANAK

Banerjee's *Evolution of the Khalsa* is an elaborate exposition of the thesis put forth in the foregoing paragraphs. In the first volume of this work are discussed the age of Guru Nanak, the life of Guru Nanak, the message of Guru Nanak, the foundation of the Sikh Panth under his first four successors, and the ideals and institutions of the Sikhs. There is an appendix on Guru Nanak and the caste system, and another on Hindu divinities in the *Japuji*. In the second volume are discussed Guru Hargobind and his three successors before coming to the 'early adventures' of Guru Gobind Singh, 'the reformation' introduced by him, and the last phase of his life. There is an appendix on the chronology of

Guru Hargobind, another on the chronology of Guru Gobind Singh, and the third on the *Bachitar Natak.*

Banerjee shows interest in the social, religious and political milieu of Guru Nanak, making ample use of his compositions. He comes to the conclusion that 'at the time of Guru Nanak's advent, religion there was none'. The spirit of both Hinduism and Islam was hidden under formalities and extraneous observances. There was tyranny all around: tyranny of forms, tyranny of names and tyranny of might. The unity of Godhead was lost in the worship of numerous *avtars* and divinities, and *pirs* and *dargahs.* Pilgrimages and empty ritualistic practices had taken the place of real devotion of the heart. Blind faith and superstition had driven truth away. Hindus and Muslims quarrelled, the Brahman and the *mulla* wrangled, social and political inequalities reigned rampant and there was strife, eternal strife, everywhere. All aspects of life presented the same spectacle.[11]

Banerjee refers to the difficulties involved in reconstructing Guru Nanak's life: 'the materials that we possess are scanty when reliable, and unreliable when abundant'. Therefore, any 'critical account' on the basis of available materials was 'almost beyond possibility'. The earliest known record was the *Janamsakhi* of Sewa Das written in 1588, about half a century after Guru Nanak's death. The *Var* of Bhai Gurdas came next, written around 1600. These two, the most reliable records, were not free from supranatural touches. The *Janamsakhi* of Sewa Das contained settings invented for the verses or sayings of Guru Nanak. 'If we leave out these details, as we certainly must, and those that savour of the mythical and supernatural, only a bare skeleton would remain which can hardly be regarded as even the necessary minimum'. The later *Janamsakhis* were practically useless. In the *Nanak Prakash,* written in 1823, imagination assumes 'almost complete control'.[12]

The testimony of the *Dabistan* could be of special value as he was a contemporary of the fifth, sixth and seventh Gurus, but his account of Guru Nanak was on the whole disappointing. His information came from the Sikhs of his own days and confirmed the evidence of Bhai Gurdas that 'deification had already made startling progress'. According to the belief of the Sikhs, as stated in the *Dabistan,* 'Baba Nanak was a god, and the world his creation'. The evidence of the *Dabistan* did not amount to much for the life of Guru Nanak. An interesting study of the *biographies* of Guru Nanak could be conducted, but 'a satisfactory biography on critical lines' could not be written. The only two dates known more or less definitely were those of his birth and death. For the interval of about seventy years in between there was the dim reflected light of only one or two independent references. The hymns of Guru Nanak were of no help on dates. Banerjee makes it very clear that he could try to provide only a broad framework.[13]

For Banerjee, the earliest phase of Guru Nanak's life started with his birth at Talwandi in 1469 and ended with his resignation from the office he had held under Daulat Khan Lodhi at Sultanpur. Whereas the *Janamsakhis* seemed to suggest that Guru Nanak was practically an uneducated man, his own compositions showed that he had become a fairly good Persian scholar. The details of investment with the sacred thread come from the *Asa di Var.* Speaking historically, the first significant utterance of Guru Nanak was: 'There is no Hindu and there is no Musalman'. With this he began his career as a religious teacher and reformer. An interview with the Almighty Lord could establish a divine sanction for his mission. Guru Nanak made a great stir in Sultanpur on this occasion.[14]

For the second phase of Guru Nanak's life, the phase of his travels, Banerjee did not feel sure about the general sequence or the main trend of events. Only two dates were known: Guru Nanak's visit to Baghdad in 1520-1 and his presence at Saidpur in 1524. The 'travels in the east' appeared to have ended some time about 1507. If the miraculous elements and the settings for the verses were taken out, these travels amounted to a series of names of places visited by Guru Nanak: Kurukshetra, Hardwar, Panipat, Delhi, Benares, Nanakmata, and some place in Kamrup. Whereas the *Janamsakhis* placed a detailed tour of the Punjab immediately after the 'travels in the east', Banerjee was inclined to place it later.[15]

For his second *udasi* (journey) Guru Nanak proceeded towards the south and reached the Dravidian country. The *Janamsakhi* narrative was so grossly overloaded with fabulous myths that it was difficult to blame Trumpp for discrediting its authenticity. Except for the Guru's meeting with a Jain priest and some aspects of his relations with Raja 'Shivnath' of Ceylon, the whole account appeared to be a long excursion into the realm of the supranatural. However, Banerjee was inclined to accept the main story of Guru Nanak's journey to south India and Ceylon on the basis of the discovery of a new manuscript.[16]

The third journey of Guru Nanak was towards the north. He went direct to Kashmir where he humbled Pandit Brahm Das. Then he ascended Sumeru where he is said to have come across an assembly of *siddhas*. Banerjee agrees with Trumpp that the Guru's visit to Sumeru and his discussion with the *siddhas* belong to 'the realm of fiction'. However, Guru Nanak's journey to the west and his visit to Mecca and Baghdad was definitely established by the discovery of the inscription at Baghdad. After 1520, Guru Nanak began an intensive propaganda, travelling through the province almost district by district. He arrived at Saidpur in 1524 on the eve of its capture by Babur. A personal meeting with Babur was not impossible but it was not very probable. From Saidpur, Guru Nanak went to Sialkot and then to Mithankot in the district of Dera Ghazi Khan. From there he came to Lahore where the millionaire Duni Chand turned into a great admirer of the Guru and founded a village which came to be known as Kartarpur.[17]

With this, Banerjee comes to the third and the last phase of Guru Nanak's life. At Kartarpur, Guru Nanak busied himself with the work of consolidation, living with his family as a householder to demonstrate how 'to abide pure amidst the impurities of the world'. A Sikh society was in the making and its divine services were more or less clearly formulated. 'Guru Nanak had not remained satisfied by merely pointing out to his followers that singing the *Name* with true devotion was the very best of religious practices but attempted to give them something more definite'. Guru Nanak visited Achal where he told Jogi Bhangar Nath that he had no miracle other than the True Name. 'Here at last we get a glimpse of the real Nanak, the man fighting the mighty forces of ignorance and superstition with simple devotion, sincerity and truth'. His visit to Multan for a discourse with Pir Bahavadin (Bahauddin) was of no importance.[18]

Banerjee says explicitly that we can divide the life of Guru Nanak into three well-defined periods: the period of inward struggle and enlightenment, the period of travels and propagation, and the period of consolidation. When Guru Nanak saw that his end was approaching, he appointed Angad to be his successor to continue his mission after his death. The tradition that the Hindus wanted to cremate him and the Muslims wanted to bury him testified to the wide tolerance that characterized the teachings of Guru Nanak.[19]

III. THE TEACHINGS OF GURU NANAK

Guru Nanak's career as a teacher, according to Banerjee, began with the utterance. There was no Hindu and there was no Musalman. It was interpreted as the gospel of the universal brotherhood of mankind: everybody was primarily a human being, and a Hindu or a Musalman only afterwards. However, it should be interpreted as a criticism, that there was no true Hindu and no true Musalman. Guru Nanak had first to make it clear what religion was not before he could make it clear what it was. Without the essential condition of surrender to God, all formal observances were of no avail. Without effacing himself, a Musalman could not be a true Musalman. The *jogis* were told plainly that a few external marks of holiness could not make them what they pretended to be. Guru Nanak tried to transcend all transitory forms to make men aware of the ultimate reality.[20]

Guru Nanak attacked blind adherence to sacred texts and mechanical pursuit of rites and rituals. The way to true religion may to be found by abiding pure amidst the impurities of the world. Impurity consisted in chronic pride, the refusal to recognize the supremacy of God's will, and the wanton pursuit of worldly desires. The antidote to this chronic disease was to be found in the Word, the Guru's instruction, and the support of the Name. Guru Nanak preached the glory and greatness of God whose creation was also real in a limited sense. The two essential requisites for a pure and virtuous life were the love of the Name and obedience to God. The Guru's instruction was needed for being imbued with a true love of the Name and a spirit of surrender. The spiritual regeneration of man depended initially on divine pleasure. The idea of Divine grace is repeatedly stressed by Guru Nanak like the doctrines of the unity of the Supreme Self and the indispensability of the Guru. Thus, the main elements of Guru Nanak's message were three: the Supreme Lord, the Guru, and the Name. Salvation lay in the Word of God and it could be known only under the instruction of the Guru.[21]

Banerjee was aware of 'the trend of modern Sikh opinion' and the view of Macauliffe on the independent status of Guru Nanak's message. He concedes that Sikhism gradually developed on certain distinctive lines and eventually stood clearly differentiated from the older creeds. But the important point was 'to understand its start'. Several important facts had to be explained and accounted for before one could accept 'the views of modern writers like Macauliffe and Bhai Kahn Singh'. One of these was the question of caste. In order to understand the issue Banerjee brings in the question of the sacred thread. On the second issue, he takes the view that Guru Nanak did not seek to abolish the custom but 'vigorously denounced the untenable claims advanced on the strength of the thread alone'. In his anxiety to show that the successors of Guru Nanak had not given up the sacred thread, Banerjee quotes Bhai Gurdas Bhalla (in Malcolm's translation) to the effect that the family of Guru Gobind Singh wore the holy cord as Kshatriyas. There were other examples of individual Sikhs wearing the sacred thread. The conclusion was 'irresistible that no abolition of the custom had at all been attempted'. On this analogy, Banerjee argues that Guru Nanak made a distinction between caste and caste pride. He warned his listeners that 'exclusive reliance on caste was absolute foolishness'.[22]

Banerjee states that much was made of the statement of Bhai Gurdas that Guru Nanak reduced the four castes into one. This statement could not be interpreted literally. There were no known instances of intercaste marriage among the Sikhs. On the contrary, marriages between Sikhs and non-Sikhs took place on caste considerations. There was no solid ground to contend that Guru Nanak had attempted the abolition of 'the caste system'. The Name was thrown open to all persons, irrespective of birth. This was a much needed reformation of the times and not an attempt at destruction of 'the old order'. Banerjee brings in the question of pilgrimages and ritualistic observances to clarify Guru Nanak's attitude towards caste. In his view Guru Nanak was laying stress on the limited utility of the practices of pilgrimage, penance, alms-giving, and the like, and the superiority of true inward devotion. Without the latter, the former were of no avail. The seemingly 'destructive' tone of Guru Nanak could mislead the unwary. Banerjee cites the examples of Guru Amar Das and Guru Tegh Bahadur for pilgrimage to Kurukshetra and Prayag. He goes on to suggest that 'the question in hand' was a complicated one. Any conclusion 'based solely on the utterances and compositions of Guru Nanak may very well be misleading'.[23]

Banerjee argues that even in relation to deities and scriptures Guru Nanak's attitude cannot be regarded as 'destructive' without any qualification. The *Granth Sahib* contains hymns of several saints of various orders. Guru Arjan had the catholicity enough to appreciate that what really mattered was 'sincerity of purpose, earnest devotion and the spirit of surrender'. The worship of *avtars* and divinities was not 'entirely valueless' if it was performed in the right spirit of devotion and surrender. Guru Nanak placed the divinities in their proper position in relation to the One Supreme Lord. With regard to the sacred texts too 'the position was not dissimilar'. It was necessary to make a distinction between an attack on scriptures and scripturalism. Guru Nanak merely pointed out the uselessness of relying on scriptures without the saving grace of devotion and piety. That the sacred books played little or no part in the subsequent development of Sikhism was easy to explain. In order to be understood by the common people Guru Nanak had to use their language and it remained in use for that very reason.[24]

The whole issue of the status of Guru Nanak's message was so important to Banerjee that his two appendices were also related to it. In the appendix on 'Guru Nanak and the caste-system' Banerjee states that the two essentials of the caste were the prohibition against intermarriage and eating in common. There was hardly any evidence to show that intermarriage was practised or even encouraged among the Sikhs. The *langars* of the Gurus knew no caste distinctions. But this could not prove anything. Sacred food was distributed from a public sanctuary even among the most orthodox of Hindus without following the caste rules. As for the meat diet among the Sikhs, Guru Hargobind permitted it as a concession to the traditional habits of the Jats who had been entering Sikhism in ever increasing numbers. Many Muslims had come under the influence of Sikhism but it was doubtful that they became Sikhs in the true sense, and it was certain that they formed a class apart within the community.[25]

In his appendix on 'Hindu divinities in the *Japji*' Banerjee reiterates that Sikhism enjoined the worship of the One True Lord alone. However, Guru Nanak's attitude towards the divinities like Brahma,

Vishnu and Shiva was not one of total denunciation. He merely pointed out their limited and secondary character. However, they had no chance of survival in view of the insistent emphasis on the unity of Godhead. Banerjee goes on to add that the position in Hindu philosophy was similar. Furthermore, if the various features of Sikhism were taken separately, there were not many which 'we do not come across in the past history of Hinduism'. Guru Nanak selected 'certain aspects and put an almost exclusive emphasis on them, with the result that the whole, as it emerged, appeared, more or less, new'. For Banerjee, Sikhism in its metaphysical aspects 'preached the Vedanta of the Vaisnavite brand'.[26]

Banerjee came to the general conclusion that there was no satisfactory evidence that Guru Nanak denounced almost everything that he had found in existence and that it was his object to build an entirely novel structure on the ruins of the old. On the contrary, his primary concern was to provide a new viewpoint and an attitude which would enable his contemporaries to understand the relative value of things in religious matters and to distinguish the fundamental from the secondary. Sikhism had its start in a protest, but a protest against conventionalism and not against Hinduism. There was no satisfactory evidence to show that he intended to overturn the social order. Guru Nanak had the vision to perceive that any unnecessary attack on time-honoured institutions and practices 'would only intensify the prevailing bitterness and strife and thus defeat his own object of extending the spirit of equality and fellowship'. Guru Nanak was 'out not to kill but to heal, not to destroy but to conserve'.[25] In other words, he was a Hindu reformer, more radical than the Vaishnavas but nonetheless a Hindu.

IV. SIKH PANTH AND ITS IDEALS AND INSTITUTIONS

For the foundation of the Sikh Panth, Banerjee takes up the work of the first four successors of Guru Nanak and the ideals and institutions of Sikhism. The nomination of Angad as the Guru placed the Sikh movement under the guidance and control of a definite and indisputable leadership to clothe Guru Nanak's message with some distinctive emblems which might give it an individuality of its own. Paradoxically, new forms were forged to preserve the spirit. Guru Angad worked unswervingly in the path chalked out by Guru Nanak. His pontificate was more or less uneventful but not unimportant. He 'modified and adopted' a script for recording the hymns of Guru Nanak. This script, called Gurmukhi, proved to be a weapon of unforeseen possibilities in a variety of other ways. The characteristically Sikh institution of the free kitchen (*langar*) was maintained by Guru Angad with the offerings of the Sikhs. Apart from being the instrument of advertisement and popularity, this institution served as a bond of union among the Sikhs and helped to mitigate caste prejudices to some extent. With the Guru as the sole and supreme religious leader, the Guru's hymns and the *langar*, the Sikhs could now claim a certain degree of individuality of their own.[28]

Guru Amar Das declared that the domestic Sikhs were wholly separate from the reclusive Udasis. Sikhism became essentially a religion of householders. Henceforth, while new religious ties were added one after another, there was a gradual drifting away from the orthodox Hindu society. Attempts were made through innovations to bring into existence 'a new brotherhood, social as well as religious, self-sufficient and independent'. All the visitors were asked to eat from the *langar* before they were allowed to see the Guru. The hymns of the first three Gurus were recorded. Since Sikhism made a considerable headway during his time, Guru Amar Das introduced the *manji* system, dividing the entire following into 22 units with local centres, each placed in charge of a pious and devout Sikh. Goindwal became a central place of pilgrimage, with a *baoli* constructed by Guru Amar Das. The Emperor Akbar made a grant of several villages to the Guru's daughter, Bibi Bhani. Pilgrims tax was remitted on the Guru's party visiting Kurukshetra. The Sikhs were asked to come to Goindwal at the time of Baisakhi, Diwali and Maghi. An attempt was made to reform the traditional ceremonies of marriage and death. The *Sadd* of Sunder Das left no doubt that Guru Amar Das wanted to dispense with the elaborate Hindu ceremonies on his own death. The practice of *sati* was prohibited. Drinking of alcohol was forbidden. On the whole, the pontificate of Guru Amar Das became a turning point in the history of Sikhism. The difference between a Hindu and a Sikh became more pronounced.[29]

Guru Amar Das chose his son-in-law, Ram Das, to be the Guru. He laid the foundations of the tank at Amritsar and the city of Ramdaspur. The work was completed by his son and successor, Guru Arjan. The elder brother of Guru Arjan, called Prithia, remained his bitter enemy and conspired against him whenever he could. Guru Arjan constructed the Harmandar in the midst of Guru Ram Das's 'tank of nectar'. A central place of worship was thus fixed. It became the most important place of Sikh pilgrimage. Guru Arjan introduced the *masand* system in which his authorized representatives began to collect fixed contributions from the Sikhs. New towns were founded at Tarn Taran and Kartarpur. At Lahore, a *baoli* was constructed in the Dabbi Bazar. Akbar's visit and his partial remission of the revenues at the Guru's request must be regarded as the high watermark in Guru Arjan's career. However, his crowning achievement was the compilation of the *Granth Sahib*. Included in it were selections from the compositions of various saints, both Hindu and Muslim, whose teachings agreed with those of the Gurus in their fundamentals. The *Granth Sahib* was placed in the Harmandar in 1604, ending the first phase of Sikhism. The progress in this phase was entirely peaceful, and it was conducive to the development of Sikh ideals and institutions.[30]

The most important institution evolved by Guru Nanak and his successors was the Guruship itself. The criterion for nomination to succession was devotion and obedience even when the distinction was made hereditary by Guru Ram Das. Banerjee equates the ideal of implicit obedience to the Guru with complete self-sacrifice for the Guru. As Bhai Gurdas put it, 'to be a Sikh was to be dead'. The crucial importance of the Guru in Sikhism was a corollary of the position assigned to him in Sikh thought. 'Without the *Word* none could be saved and it is the Guru who communicates the *Word*.' The concept of the Guru as the mediator between man and God never lost ground. The Guru was without a rival, and the Gurus were one and the same. From the very beginning the impersonal character of Guruship was recognized. Indeed, Guruship was impersonal, indivisible and continuous.

There were some other features of Guruship. The *Shabad* came to mean the essentials of Sikhism as propounded by Guru Nanak and his successors. The *Shabad* and the *Nam* merged in a sense in the *bani* or the hymns of the Gurus. In the next place, the *Shabad* was identified with the Guru, foreshadowing the possibility of the abolition of personal Guruship by Guru Gobind Singh. Furthermore, Guruship was regarded as of divine origin. For Guru Ram Das, 'the Guru is God and God is the Guru'. For Guru Arjan, the Guru is the creator, he is the Supreme God. This identification was made possible by a conception of the ultimate essence of the Guru as distinct from his person. In order to make this clear Guru Gobind Singh warned his followers that all who would call him the Supreme Being shall fall into the pit of hell; he was merely a servant of God, sent to this world to see the wonders of creation.[31]

The conception of the Guru in Sikhism had yet another dimension in relation to the ideal of Sikh brotherhood. Everyone of the Guru's followers was something of a saint; Guru Ram Das says that he is 'a slave to the slaves of those disciples of the Guru who perform his work'. Bhai Gurdas says that 'where there are five Sikhs there is God'. Logically, service to the Guru was expanded into service to the Sikhs in general. Guru Hargobind tells his disciples: 'Deem the Sikh who comes to you with the Guru's name on his lips as your Guru'. Bhai Gurdas asserts that 'the Guru is the Sikh and the Sikh *is* the Guru'. There was no difference between them. In this perspective, the abolition of the personal Guruship by Guru Gobind Singh and his dictum that 'the Khalsa is the Guru' no longer appear to be either accidental or cataclysmic.[32]

The ideal for the Sikh way of life was 'renunciation in the midst of worldly occupation' or, as Bhai Gurdas puts it, *maya vich udas*. On a practical level, the essentials of Sikhism were represented by the formula of *nam, dan, isnan*. *Nam* stands for devotion to God and His worship; *dan* represents the idea of service; *isnan* stands for purity. These ideas became associated with certain practices. A detailed and a somewhat formal scheme of daily observances was evolved, including both personal and congregational forms of worship. The idea of purity in the abstract was never lost but *isnan* came more particularly to mean ablutions in holy tanks. Similarly, *dan* was given the tangible form of offerings to the Guru and the maintenance of the *langar*. The responsibility for the *langar* rested on the entire Sikh community. It was in Sikhism alone that a sense of corporate unity gradually evolved. The *langar* was actually a component part of one single institution which went by the name of *sangat*. A whole network of *sangats* brought into existence the *masand* system which enabled the Guru to undertake enormous projects. The Sikhs began to regard their Guru as a temporal and spiritual ruler.[33]

Banerjee comes to the conclusion that the ideological, institutional and material resources of the Sikhs acquired a certain degree of visibility. The *masand* system was gradually familiarizing the Sikhs with a kind of self-government of their own, and the Guru at the centre with his unchallenged authority, his magnificent *darbar*, and his control over the entire organization of the *sangats*, was 'a symbol of unity and of something mystical, beyond all ordinary considerations'. A community with such a leadership, with such high ideals of discipline and self-sacrifice and institution which gave practical meaning to those ideals 'could not, but react on the government of the day'. A situation was arising in which a conflict between the forces of the state and those of Sikhism was becoming more or less inevitable. 'The state could not but regard the Sikh organization as one of immense possibilities, which might at any time become a rallying point of disaffection, and for the Sikhs too, there could be no getting back, no reversion to a line of policy less liable to be misunderstood.'[34]

V. CONFLICT WITH THE STATE AND INTERNAL CLEAVAGE

According to Banerjee, conflict with the state was inherent in the position of the Sikh community as a separate polity within the Mughal empire. The crisis was precipitated by the rebellion of Prince Khusrau in which Guru Arjan became implicated. This became the ostensible cause of action against the Guru but there could be little doubt that Guru Arjan was 'primarily a victim of religious bigotry'. Banerjee strongly disagreed with Jadunath Sarkar who had looked upon Guru Arjan as merely a political offender and revenue defaulter.[35]

Guru Hargobind acquired a body of troops and told the *masands* that he would be pleased to receive offerings of arms and horses. He turned his attention to the hunt and other warlike occupations. He permitted and encouraged animal diet. His disciples began to imitate in his robust practices. He was soon called to Delhi and then imprisoned in the fort of Gwalior. After about two years he was released in 1611. He lived in peace with the government, holding a minor position in the administration. Henceforth he was anxious to have an army by his side and the old force was revived. Apparently the Sikhs of the old school did not like his innovation. Banerjee thinks that Bhai Gurdas refers to the people's allegations in one of his *Vars.* There can be little doubt that Sikhism was undergoing a transformation in the hands of Guru Hargobind. His new policy attracted numbers of warlike Jats. At the same time the system of *sangats* and *masands* was supplemented by several Udasi hearths (*dhuans*) for spreading the message of Sikhism and broadening its organization.[36]

The friendly cooperation with the government lasted till the end of Jahangir's reign. Early in the reign of Shah Jahan, an expedition was sent against Guru Hargobind and a battle was fought in and around Amritsar (Ramdaspur). A few other battles were fought before the battle of Kartarpur. After this, Guru Hargobind moved first to Phagwara and then to Kiratpur where he lived in peace. His eldest son, Gurditta, died and the latter's eldest son, Dhir Mal, became insubordinate to his grandfather. Guru Hargobind chose his younger grandson, Har Rai, to be his successor before he died in 1645. Banerjee thinks that Guru Hargobind played a clever and well-conceived part in exceptionally difficult circumstances. His connection with the government served as a cloak and he succeeded in seeing his plans mature without any interference from the authorities. His victories were not useless. The Sikhs were inspired with self-confidence. 'They had hitherto been kept under heels by the Mussalmans, but they learnt, for the first time, that under proper guidance and control they could meet the Mussalmans on an equal footing or even gain the better'. Guru Hargobind demonstrated the possibility that the Sikhs could openly assume an attitude of defiance against the government. He prepared the way for 'the thorough reformation' later brought about by Guru Gobind Singh.[37]

Banerjee maintains that the nature of the Guru's following had been changing as a result of the propaganda work, particularly of Guru Arjan. He was said to have converted the entire Jat peasantry of the Majha tract. A new situation was arising which called for new methods. By the time of Guru Hargobind the Jats formed by far the most preponderant element in the Sikh community. Their character and temperament, and their traditions and tendencies, were relevant for reaction to the situation. Banerjee goes into the question of their origin, their distribution in the Punjab, the importance of their tribal kinship and freedom, the strength of their tribal cohesion and exclusiveness, and their marauding instinct. The Jats were habitual plunderers. A predatory trait in their character made them impatient of control and prone to aggrandisement. At the same time they were fighters *par excellence.* The essential traits of the Jats did not change on entering the Sikh fold. In order to accommodate them in the Sikh Panth certain readjustments were bound to occur. The policy of 'non-resistance' to aggression would hardly have suited the tradition and temper of the Jats.[38]

The march of consolidation and progress which had been the chief characteristic of Sikhism under the successors of Guru Nanak received a set-back after the death of Guru Hargobind. A period of disintegration started. By the time Guru Gobind Singh ascended the *gaddi*, centrifugal tendencies were very much in evidence. This state of affairs was the result of the continued absence of the Guru from Amritsar, the rise of dissentient sects and rivals to the Guru, the deterioration of the *masand* system, the intervention of the state, and some other factors. Guru Har Rai did some work for the propagation of Sikhism before he joined Dara Shukoh who was preparing for a battle with Aurangzeb. The supporters of Dara melted away and Guru Har Rai too returned to Kiratpur. Nevertheless, he was summoned by Aurangzeb to Delhi. Guru Har Rai sent his eldest son Ram Rai who did not hesitate to distort a word in a verse of Guru Nanak in order to please the emperor. He earned the displeasure of his father who nominated the younger son, Har Krishan, as his successor.[39]

Barely six years old, Guru Har Krishan was summoned to Delhi where he had an attack of smallpox and expired in 1664. The dispute about succession gave Aurangzeb the opportunity to intervene in the matter, and divided the *masands* who availed themselves fully of the opportunities that the situation presented to them. Both the claimants to Guruship were minors.[40]

Before his death, Guru Har Krishan uttered 'Baba Bakale' to indicate that his successor would be found in the village Bakala. Twenty-two kinsmen of the Guru claimed Guruship. Tegh Bahadur, the youngest son of Guru Hargobind, was discovered to be the true Guru. He succeeded to a position of great difficulty. Ram Rai and Dhir Mal were hostile towards him. He bought a piece of land from the Raja of Kahlur and established himself in the village of Makhowal. For several years then he travelled in 'the east'. After his return to Makhowal he busied himself in propagating the faith. Before long, however, he was caught in the situation created by Aurangzeb's religious policy. The emperor ordered the temples of the Sikhs to be destroyed and the *masands* expelled from the cities. The governor of Kashmir was forcibly converting Hindus to Islam. The Brahmans of Kashmir approached Guru Tegh Bahadur with their tale of woe and it was agreed that they should tell the emperor to convert the Guru first. Guru Tegh Bahadur was summoned to Delhi and asked to accept Islam. On his refusal to accept Islam, he was asked to show a miracle. On his refusal to show a miracle he was beheaded in Delhi in 1675. As recorded in the *Bachittar Natak* he protected the frontal mark and sacrificial thread of the Hindus and suffered martyrdom for the sake of religion. It was a self-sought martyrdom, a willing sacrifice for religion to assist the Hindus against the religious persecution of Aurangzeb. Banerjee refutes the views of all previous writers who attributed overt political activity to Guru Tegh Bahadur. In his view, the Guru fell a victim to religious bigotry. His execution strengthened the resistance against Aurangzeb's religious policy. It prepared the way for the final stage in the evolution of Sikhism.[41]

At the time of Guru Tegh Bahadur's martyrdom, there were dissensions within the Sikh Panth and dangers from without. The Udasis were friendly but the Minas, the Dhir Mallias and the Ram Raiyas were hostile. Aurangzeb had raised a whirlwind throughout the empire. There remained no method of self-defence other than with the aid of arms. Moreover, Sikhism had acquired certain adjuncts in the course of its development which it could neither completely assimilate nor entirely discard. 'A purely religious movement had gradually acquired certain accretions which were distinctly of a socio-political character'. Both the character of the Sikhs themselves as well as external dangers demanded further development. 'The future of Sikhism, therefore, depended on how these contradictory forces were synthesized under the banner of a common ideal and how uniformity was secured within the system itself in order to better assure the cohesion of the secular movement that was to be based on it'.[42]

VI. INSTITUTION OF THE KHALSA

Guru Gobind Singh revived the policy of his grandfather. Armed resistance became predominant under him. However, the early measures for self-defence were considered inadequate and he retired farther into the hills and took up residence at Paonta in the territories of the Raja of Nahan. A few years later he fought the battle of Bhangani and defeated Raja Fateh Shah of Srinagar (Garhwal). The battle is described in the *Bachittar Natak* but the causes of conflict are not clear. Banerjee suggests that the Guru had seriously alarmed the hill chiefs. He represented a faith which inculcated liberal ideas and most of his followers were Jats whom the Rajputs looked down upon. The hill chiefs presented a united front against Guru Gobind Singh due to political privilege, social exclusiveness and tribal pride. This explains why the Guru never succeeded in maintaining a lasting alliance with them and why Sikhism never made any headway in the hills.[43]

The immediate cause of the battle could be the traditional boundary disputes between the rulers of Nahan and Garhwal. In any case, Guru Gobind Singh was victorious. He returned to Kahlur and founded Anandpur. Those who had kept away from the battle of Bhangani were driven out. He was apparently living on friendly terms with Raja Bhim Chand of Kahlur. He joined Bhim Chand's side in the battle of Nadaun which was fought between the Mughal *faujdars* and their local supporters on the one hand and Bhim Chand and his allies on the other. Bhim Chand had probably refused to pay tribute, which was regarded as an act of revolt by the state. By direct participation in the battle, Guru Gobind Singh compromised himself in the eyes of the government. While a regular and a systematic campaign was carried on against the hill chiefs, expeditions were sent against the Guru at Anandpur. Eventually Prince Muazzam was sent to the Punjab. He took up his position at Lahore and sent Mirza Beg Mughal to reduce the hill tracts. Four other relentless officers were sent to punish the rebels. The rebellion was completely crushed. Guru Gobind Singh remained untouched, but he passed through very anxious times.[44]

Banerjee refers to the institution of the Khalsa as 'the reformation', the central climacteric that divided Guru Gobind Singh's career into the pre-Khalsa and post-Khalsa phases. During the pre-Khalsa phase his object seemed to have been to enter into the fraternity of the hill chiefs and establish himself as one of their equals. He identified himself with their cause but his differences with them were fundamental. When they returned to the old allegiance to the Mughal empire, he found himself completely isolated. Therefore, he began to set his own house in order and to bring about 'a transformation in the ideology of his followers'. To meet the situation with their unaided strength he brought the Khalsa into existence.[45]

The mission of Guru Gobind Singh is explained in the *Bachittar Natak*. The essence of its mythology was to claim a direct divine sanction for his mission. The essentials of Sikhism are reiterated but Guru Gobind Singh strikes an entirely new note when he says that he was sent into the world to 'seize and destroy the evil and the sinful'; he had assumed birth for the purpose of spreading the faith and saving the saints by 'extirpating all tyrants'. Banerjee hears an echo of the *Gita* in this note but there is a difference: Guru Gobind Singh merely claims that he is the chosen instrument of God for the redemption of the world. He points out that he is the slave of the Supreme Being, come to behold the wonders of the world, and not the Supreme Being. His familiarity with Hindu literature relating to incarnations and other divinities 'must have fired his imagination'. For his new mission the old weapons of service, humility and prayer were wholly out of place. He makes his position clear at the outset that his reliance is on God and the Holy swords. Banerjee argues at some length that Guru Gobind Singh did not invoke Durga in connection with the institution of the Khalsa, though possibly he had worshipped the goddess at an earlier stage.[46]

In order to put an end to the process of disintegration that had started after Guru Hargobind and to revitalize the Sikhs by giving them a new ideology, Guru Gobind Singh tackled the question of the *masands* first of all. Far from being the foremost auxiliaries of the Guru, they had become the greatest counterpoise to his authority. He depicts their degeneration into a disruptive force, needing a desperate remedy. The *masands* were denounced and excommunicated from within Sikhism. Closely connected with this was the question of the Minas, the Dhir Mallias and the Ram Raiyas. Their activities weakened Sikhism in a variety of ways. Rejected by the majority of the Sikhs they sought the support of government officials and created a good deal of misunderstanding between the imperial authorities and the Sikh Gurus. Guru Gobind Singh denounced the dissidents, and the Sikhs were prohibited from having any social intercourse with them.[47]

It was necessary at the same time to provide for 'a new integration'. On the first of Baisakh in 1699, Guru Gobind Singh addressed a large gathering at Keshgarh and called for volunteers to lay down their life for him. Each of the first five volunteers was taken into a tent by turn where a goat was slaughtered, adding to the consternation of the gathering at every call. With these 'Five Beloved', Guru Gobind Singh proceeded 'to lay anew the foundation of Sikhism'. They were baptized afresh by the new rite of the double-edge dagger, given the appellation of Singh, and asked to repeat *Vahguru ji ka Khalsa, Vahguru ji ki Fateh*. The old ideal of humility and surrender was changed into a new one of self-assertion and self-reliance. More remarkably, the Guru stood up in an attitude of supplication and prayed to the 'Five Beloved' to initiate him in the same manner. They were told that 'the Khalsa is the Guru and the Guru is the Khalsa'. There was no difference between them. When the Guru thus merged himself in the Khalsa, 'the whole sect was invested with the dignity of Gurudom'. Banerjee quotes the words used by Guru Gobind Singh as reported by 'the newswriter of the period' (actually quoted by Macauliffe). This address of the Guru underlined that all distinctions of caste and creed were obliterated. The Khalsa were enjoined to wear the '5 Ks.' As recorded in a composition of Guru Gobind Singh, all beliefs, rituals or ceremonies that implied the recognition of anything but the One True Lord were categorically rejected. The objective was to create 'a compact brotherhood in faith' which was also 'a brotherhood in arms'. The Name was still the chief object of adoration but blessed in this world was his life who repeated God's Name with his tongue and meditated war in his heart. The Khalsa were taught to regard the sword as God and God as the sword. Thus, soldierly qualities were given the foremost place in the Khalsa created by the Guru.[48]

In the writings of Guru Gobind Singh there is nothing about dominion or sovereignty. His war was with tyranny and oppression. The quarrel with 'the Muhammadans' and the achievement of political dominion by the Sikhs followed as more or less inevitable corollaries of this basic concept. Militarism was now adopted as an article of creed.

The leadership of the community was left to the community itself. Thus was brought into existence 'a military commonwealth with the fullest democratic freedom'. Not in its enunciation but in its consequences 'the Khalsa is the Guru and the Guru is the Khalsa' proved to be revolutionary. The Khalsa of Guru Gobind Singh's conception was meant to be 'a fully democratic compact community, armed to the teeth, struggling to maintain what it conceived to be the right path and fighting incessantly and without compunction tyranny and injustice in all their forms'.[49]

The ideology was new but the structure was built on the old and many of the ideas associated with the Khalsa had developed long back in Sikhism. The importance given to 'the five', for example, had been emphatically stated by Bhai Gurdas: 'Where there are five Sikhs, there is God'. Even the military ideals had been associated with Sikhism since the days of Guru Hargobind. But ideas had existed side by side without any apparent coherence. They were now synthesized in 'a new concordance' and made to flow in 'one single channel'. The Khalsa of Guru Gobind Singh were required to abnegate the caste principles. Most of the Khatris left the fold, thereby leaving the leadership of the movement to the Jats. At the same time, the outcaste like the Chuhras were inducted into the Khalsa as Ranghretas.[50]

Banerjee underlines that the essentials of Guru Nanak's teaching still formed the core of Sikhism. Indeed, Guru Gobind Singh admonishes his followers to consider their houses altogether as the forest and remain anchorites at heart. Nevertheless, it would be idle to deny that 'in the Khalsa we breathe a new spirit'. It was marked by the 'clear assumption of a more positive role in human affairs'. The Jats largely contributed to the process of change that had already commenced. Guru Gobind Singh recognized this change and 'synthesized it with all that was best in the old tradition, thus assuring a new lease of life to the movement'. The Khalsa was a compound of the Sikh and the Jat; the religious fervour of the Sikh was united with the warlike temper of the Jat. After this new synthesis, 'Sikhism became more uncompromizing and consequently more sectarian in character'. The free and untrammelled growth of the Sikhs was thereby arrested but it was 'in the logic of events and could not be otherwise'.[51]

VII. FINAL CONFLICT WITH THE MUGHAL STATE

The institution of the Khalsa spread consternation among the hill chiefs. The chief of Kahlur in particular saw the integrity of his dominion seriously threatened. He formed a combination against the Guru and laid siege to Anandpur. Unable to overpower the Khalsa, the hill chiefs took an oath on the cow that they would remain friendly if the Guru left Anandpur for a while and came back later on. Guru Gobind Singh moved to Nirmoh and his troops plundered the villages of Kahlur. The chief of Kahlur decided to enlist the assistance of the Mughal government. The governor of Lahore and the *faujdar* of Sirhind were ordered by Aurangzeb to march against Guru Gobind Singh. The combined forces of the Mughal commandants and the Raja of Kahlur attacked Nirmoh but failed to take it. Guru Gobind Singh decided to leave the place and cross the river Sutlej. Another battle was fought on the bank of the river in which the allied forces were defeated. The Guru went to Basali across the Sutlej. The chief of Kahlur attacked him there but only to be defeated. After the battle of Basali Guru Gobind Singh plundered Kalmot, and the chief of Kahlur was unnerved. He agreed to Guru Gobind Singh's return to Anandpur where he built the fort of Anandgarh.[52]

The Khalsa brought the villages around Anandpur under their own control, and began to levy contributions by force. The chief of Kahlur sent an ultimatum that Guru Gobind Singh should leave Anandpur. It went unheeded, and the combined forces of the hill chiefs attacked Anandpur but proved unequal to the task. They again applied to the Mughal authorities, and troops from Lahore and Sirhind were sent to their assistance. The allied forces failed to take Anandpur and laid siege to it. All ingress and egress were completely stopped. As the situation of the besieged became desperate, the allies offered safe evacuation on oath. Despite Guru Gobind Singh's reluctance, the Sikhs favoured evacuation and took the responsibility for its consequences.[53]

Soon after the evacuation of Anandpur, Guru Gobind Singh and his followers were attacked by the allies. He reached Chamkaur with a small number of the Khalsa and his two elder sons. Nearly all of them died fighting in the battle of Chamkaur, but Guru Gobind Singh left the place unhurt and was helped by Nabi Khan and Ghani Khan to travel safely from Machhiwara towards Raikot. At Jatpura he heard of the execution of his two younger sons aged only 9 and 7. From Dina he wrote a letter to Aurangzeb. At Khidrana he defeated the Mughal troops. The brunt of the attack fell on those Sikhs who had deserted Guru Gobind Singh at Anandpur but had come to join him again. Due to their sacrifice, Khidrana came to be known as Muktsar. Guru Gobind Singh travelled to Talwandi Sabo and stayed there for some time. The place came to be known as Damdama or the breathing place. Many Sikhs were baptized here and brought more thoroughly into the Khalsa, like Tiloka and Rama who were the ancestors of the Nabha and the Patiala Houses. A new recension of the *Granth Sahib* was brought out at Damdama.[54]

There were conflicting views about the last two years of Guru Gobind Singh's life, mainly because the sources were either inadequate or untrustworthy. Three points appeared to emerge from the Sikh and Muhammadan accounts taken together: that the Guru had sent a communication to the emperor, that some sort of an understanding had been arrived at, and that as a result the Guru started for the south. In Sainapat's *Gursobha,* the Guru's complaint was primarily against the officials who had wantonly broken their pledges; the emperor should accept the responsibility for their actions. An appeal is made to the emperor's sense of justice and to his religious integrity. However, the tone and substance of the *Zafarnama* are entirely different. Nevertheless, the Guru had begun to move about freely a few months before the emperor's death. After Aurangzeb's death, he met Bahadur Shah. In a letter written to the Sikhs of Dhaul in October 1707, Guru Gobind Singh says that the old negotiations were progressing well and he expected to return to the Punjab rather soon. Within a month, however, Bahadur Shah had to leave for Rajputana and the Guru had to accompany him. The latter avoided the issue under one pretext or another. When Guru Gobind Singh saw that his efforts had failed, and his end was near, he commissioned Banda Bahadur to accomplish by force what he had failed to achieve by an appeal to justice.[55]

Banerjee suggests that Guru Gobind Singh wanted appropriate action taken against Wazir Khan. In any case, though Guru Gobind

Singh remained close to the camp of Bahadur Shah, moving with him for more than ten months, 'we find no reference anywhere that the Guru participated in any of the actions in which the emperor engaged and it seems more probably that he had been travelling as a mere companion than that, as some writers say, he had been given a command'. At Nander, after his separation from the emperor, he was assassinated by a Pathan. Banerjee argues that there is nothing unbelievable in the story that Wazir Khan was the real instigator of the murderous attack that led to the Guru's death on 18 October 1708.[56]

Banerjee goes on to argue that 'the transformation of Sikhism' presented a rather striking example of 'the assimilation of the form of the religious system to the innate tendencies of the people'. The Jat love of freedom and their martial spirit received the fullest recognition in the new dispensation together with all that constituted the glory of Sikhism—the worship of the One True Lord, the Word and the Name, the spirit of brotherhood and self-sacrifice. The Sikh gave Guru Gobind Singh the ideal, the Jat the material, and combining the two he forged a dynamic force. 'Speakingly dialectically, we may say that the Sikh was the thesis, the Jat the antithesis, and the synthesis came in the Khalsa.'[57]

Banerjee criticized Jadunath Sarkar for belittling the achievement of the Sikhs. In his view, Sarkar had misconceived the entire issue of the Sikh war of independence, completely ignoring the ideological factors. Banerjee quotes N.K. Sinha on the point: 'a nation was up in arms against its enemies and it is the collective efforts of the masses rather than individual achievements that ultimately made the revolution a success'. Sarkar's relative appreciation for Ranjit Singh is not acceptable to Banerjee: 'Ranjit Singh was in reality an aberration because a military monarchy was far off from anything that the Guru had contemplated'. The Guru's ideals would have led to 'something like a federated republic'.[58]

In Banerjee's estimate Guru Gobind Singh 'must be counted among the greatest of Indians of all ages'. He was first and foremost a great religious leader. He was a litterateur. He was also a great soldier and a great general. He was a builder *par excellence*. The Khalsa carved its way to renown and glory and played a noble part in the arena of Indian history.[59]

VIII. THE BASIC LIMITATION

Compared to the earlier writers, Indubhusan Banerjee's *Evolution of the Khalsa* was more scholarly and more comprehensive in its treatment of the early Sikh movement. It was divided into two volumes, each dealing with a distinct period of Sikh history: the period of peaceful development up to 1604, and the period of increasing militarization from 1606 to 1708. This periodization is closer to the contours of the past than the stereotype of the dramatic contrast between the 'pacifist' Guru Nanak and the 'militant' Guru Gobind Singh. The major developments of the two periods are carefully outlined.

However, there is a more significant, though informal, division: between Guru Nanak and his early successors. Whatever the label appropriate for the latter, Guru Nanak was clearly a Hindu reformer. His thought in its metaphysical aspects was 'Vedanta of the Vaishnavite brand' and it provided the core of Sikhism in the time of his successors as well. For Banerjee, Guru Nanak was an advanced Vaishnava.

By making Guru Nanak a Hindu reformer, Banerjee could appropriate the Sikh past in the cause of 'nationalism'. The *Evolution of the Khalsa* ends formally at 1708, but Banerjee reveals his view of the later Sikh history on this point. The greatest contribution to the cause of India was the wresting of the Punjab and the adjoining land up to the frontier from the clutches of the Afghans: 'no service could have been greater'. Banerjee talks of 'Muslim persecution' and the 'religious bigotry' of Jahangir and Aurangzeb. The rulers of medieval India are virtually seen as 'tyrants', and equated with 'Muslims'. Referring to the followers of the Gurus, he states that they were 'kept under heel by the Mussalmans'. It may not be wrong to suggest that Banerjee's nationalism is Hindu nationalism.[60]

The scholarly device used by Banerjee for appropriating the Sikh past accounts for both the merit and the limitation of his *Evolution of the Khalsa*. His account of Guru Nanak in terms of his 'age', 'life' and 'message' is, on the whole, more detailed than what we find in any earlier non-Sikh work. However, the age of Guru Nanak depicted by Banerjee is 'darker' than what may be warranted by credible evidence. The 'tyranny' of the age of Guru Nanak appears to be linked with some unquestioned assumptions about 'Muslim rule'. For the life of Guru

Nanak, Banerjee's attitude is both critical and positive, but he leaves out the core of the message of the *Janamsakhis:* the uniqueness of Guru Nanak's mission. The significance of Guru Nanak's comments on the known scriptures, deities and incarnations, the sacred thread, and the caste is sought to be minimized. In his discussion of these issues Banerjee becomes rather eristic. He quotes Bhai Gurdas who had died in the 1630s on the time of Guru Gobind Singh who was born several decades later.

The assumption, or the argument, that Guru Nanak was a Vaishnava reformer, obliged Banerjee to explain the later developments meticulously in terms of the importance of the nomination of a successor and the whole concept of Guruship, the institution of the *sangat*, the *Granth* as a scripture, social rites and ceremonies, and organization. The ideological, institutional and material resources of the Gurus made the Sikh Panth a visible entity, which the state could not fail to notice. A conflict was inherent in the situation. Relevant for the strong Sikh reaction to the martyrdom of Guru Arjan and Guru Tegh Bahadur was the changing composition of the Sikh Panth in favour of the Jats. The evidence available to Banerjee on the Jats actually did not amount to much but he assumed the Jats to be an unchanging monolith with fixed characteristics. His explanation of 'militarization' is logical but lacks adequate empirical base. The assumptions which inspired his research induced him to force on his evidence an interpretation that it was not strong enough to support.

NOTES

1. A.C. Banerjee, 'Indubhusan Banerjee', *Historians and Historiography of the Sikhs*, ed. Fauja Singh, New Delhi: Oriental Publishers, 1978, pp. 239-57.
2. J.S. Grewal, 'Indubhusan Banerjee's Evolution of the Khalsa', ibid., pp. 258-63.
3. Indu Banga, 'In the Service of Hindu Nationalism: Banerjee's Evolution', *The Khalsa: Sikh and Non-Sikh Perspectives*, ed. J.S. Grewal, New Delhi: Manohar, 2004, pp. 187-200.
4. Indubhusan Banerjee, *Evolution of the Khalsa*, vol. I (*The Foundation of the Sikh Panth*), Calcutta: A. Mukherjee & Co., 1963, 2nd edn., Preface to the First Edition, pp. 1-3.
5. Ibid., pp. 3-4.
6. Ibid., pp. 4-9.

7. Ibid., pp. 9-10.
8. Ibid., pp. 10-11.
9. Ibid., pp. 12-14.
10. Ibid., pp. 14-21.
11. Ibid., pp. 22-51.
12. Ibid., pp. 52-7.
13. Ibid., pp. 61-4.
14. Ibid., pp. 64-74.
15. Ibid., pp. 74-82.
16. Ibid., pp. 82-3.
17. Ibid., pp. 84-8.
18. Ibid., pp. 88-91.
19. Ibid., pp. 91-3.
20. Ibid., pp. 94-101.
21. Ibid., pp. 101-12.
22. Ibid., pp. 113-21.
23. Ibid., pp. 122-32.
24. Ibid., pp. 132-41.
25. Ibid., pp. 267-76.
26. Ibid., pp. 277-80.
27. Ibid., pp. 141-5.
28. Ibid., pp. 146-59.
29. Ibid., pp. 162-83.
30. Ibid., pp. 183-215.
31. Ibid., pp. 216-41.
32. Ibid., pp. 241-9.
33. Ibid., pp. 250-63.
34. Ibid., pp. 265-6.
35. Indubhusan Banerjee, *Evolution of the Khalsa,* vol. II (*The Reformation*), Calcutta: A. Mukherjee & Co., 1962, 2nd edn., pp. 1-7.
36. Ibid., pp. 7-19.
37. Ibid., pp. 19-34.
38. Ibid., pp. 34-45.
39. Ibid., pp. 47-52.
40. Ibid., pp. 52-4.
41. Ibid., pp. 54-63.
42. Ibid., pp. 64-7.
43. Ibid., pp. 67-73.
44. Ibid., pp. 73-91.
45. Ibid., p. 92.
46. Ibid., pp. 92-108.
47. Ibid., pp. 108-13.

48. Ibid., pp. 113-17.
49. Ibid., pp. 118-19.
50. Ibid., pp. 119-21.
51. Ibid., pp. 123-5.
52. Ibid., pp. 126-30.
53. Ibid., pp. 130-4.
54. Ibid., pp. 134-9.
55. Ibid., pp. 139-45.
56. Ibid., pp. 145-52.
57. Ibid., pp. 152-3.
58. Ibid., pp. 153-5.
59. Ibid., pp. 156-61.
60. In this respect, Banerjee is closer to G.C. Narang than to N.K. Sinha.

CHAPTER THIRTEEN

N.K. Sinha on the Eighteenth Century and Ranjit Singh

I. THE SIKH STRUGGLE FOR INDEPENDENCE

In his *Rise of the Sikh Power* N.K. Sinha traces the history of the Sikh struggle for independence and Sikh rule in the eighteenth century before the advent of Ranjit Singh. First published in 1936, it was meant to illumine 'an obscure corner of Indian history' which had been outlined in Cunningham's 'brilliant work'. Sinha's book was dedicated to Joseph Davey Cunningham, the conscientious and faithful historian whose *History of the Sikhs* 'still remains a source of inspiration'.[1] Only a year earlier had appeared Ganda Singh's *Banda Singh Bahadur* based on a wide range of sources, especially Persian and Sikh. Sinha's book begins with 1716, after the execution of Banda Bahadur.[2]

Sinha narrates the Sikh struggle for independence in three phases: Mughal disintegration and the Afghan menace from 1716 to 1752, the Punjab as the cockpit of anarchy and confusion from 1752 to 1761, and the rise of the Sikhs into political power from 1761 to 1767. However, the political story does not end there. Sinha dwells on the feeble opposition of the Afghans to the *de facto* sovereignty of the Sikhs after 1767. A separate chapter is given to the cis-Sutlej Sikhs who were fighting against their neighbours on the Delhi side. The relations between British imperialism and Sikh Confederate Feudelism are discussed in yet another chapter. The last chapter deals with the polity, economy and military organization of the Sikhs under the *misls*. Thus, the scope of Sinha's *Rise of the Sikh Power* is quite comprehensive. It is based on Persian, Gurmukhi, English and Marathi sources. Its second edition came out in 1946, and the third in 1960.

What is of interest to us now are the asides and reflections of N.K. Sinha. The history of India in the eighteenth century for him was mainly a record of anarchy and confusion, selfishness, cowardice and treachery, unpatriotic betrayals and horrible reigns of terror. The depth of this gloom was 'relieved by the story of the rise of Sikh political power, as a result of the collective endeavour of a united people'. The Sikh struggle, like the Maratha struggle for independence, was remarkable for the 'successful leadership of comparatively obscure men'. In both cases, 'a nation was up in arms against its enemies'. The collective efforts of the masses ultimately made 'the revolution a success'. Unfortunately, the germs of its failure were present in the success of this collective struggle. The 'theocratic confederate feudalism' of the eighteenth century degenerated into 'a military monarchy' which was destined to fail.[3]

The fortunes of 'the Sikh nation' were at their lowest ebb in 1716. Abd us-Samad Khan, the Mughal governor of the Punjab, followed a relentless policy of persecution for ten years as the 'sword of the state'. He was succeeded by his son Zakariya Khan, an active soldier and an excellent administrator who followed a dual policy of firmness and kindness. One of the most important events of his time was the martyrdom of Bhai Mani Singh in 1738. This supplied the much needed fillip to the Sikh struggle for independence. A year later, Nadir Shah's invasion of India proved to be very important for the rise of Sikh power. Difficult under all circumstances, it became even more difficult now to suppress the Sikhs. Within a few years of Zakariya Khan's death then, Ahmad Shah Abdali took up the work begun by Nadir Shah. His inroads from 1748 to 1767 exercised a very decisive influence in the history of the rise of the Sikh power. Even if it was possible for the Mughal governor Muin ul-Mulk to crush the Sikhs in 1750-2, it was no longer possible after 1752 when Ahmad Shah Abdali became more earnest about his Indian expeditions and secured from the Mughal emperor the cession of the Punjab, Multan and Sirhind. Henceforth, the Sikhs were concerned not so much with the Mughals as with the Afghans.[4]

Muin ul-Mulk died in November 1753, leaving the Punjab in a state of lawlessness. The Sikhs plundered and looted everywhere. In 1757, Ahmad Shah Abdali's son Taimur Shah occupied Amritsar and desecrated the holy shrine. However, the commandants he left behind were overpowered by the Sikhs. Adina Beg Khan invited the Marathas. The possibility of a combination between the Marathas and the Sikhs was created but there was no far-sighted leader among them. After ousting the Afghans from the Punjab, the Marathas entrusted its administration to Adina Beg Khan. At the time of his death in September 1758, Adina Beg was hard pressed by the Sikhs. Their territorial ambition seemed to find full scope now. Ahmad Shah Abdali invaded the Punjab and the Maratha commandants retreated before him. He was in a hurry to measure his sword with the Marathas. They were eventually defeated in the battle of Panipat in 1761. Ahmad Shah Abdali then turned to the Sikhs but only to find that a defeat inflicted on them was like 'a sword slash through a pond'.[5]

The 'most glorious chapter of Sikh history and one of the most glorious chapters of Indian history' began after the battle of Panipat. We come upon 'a duel in which the all-powerful Afghan conqueror was worn out by an obscure people who successfully wrested from his closed fist that part of India which the house of Timur had failed to preserve'.[6] The Afghan governor of Lahore was in no better position than 'the commander of an outlying post'. To make him effective, Ahmad Shah Abdali decided to inflict a death blow on the Sikhs. He succeeded in killing thousands of Sikhs in a single action in February 1762, remembered as the great massacre (*ghallughara*). Nevertheless, the governors he left behind were defeated, and the Sikhs occupied the entire Sarkar of Sirhind in 1764. Before the end of the year Ahmad Shah Abdali came personally to establish his control but only to find that the Sikhs were now in a position to fight him in regular battle formation. He was obliged to retreat without a fight. In April 1765, Lahore was occupied by three Sikh leaders. A coin was struck as a public declaration of Sikh sovereignty. The great Durrani emperor failed to stop them.[7]

The success of the Sikhs was due in the first place to their method of warfare, a golden mean between precipitate action and total inaction. Qazi Nur Muhammad's *Jangnama* testifies to their tried tactics. Ahmad Shah Abdali could not spare a sufficient number of soldiers in the Punjab to prevent the Sikhs from recovering their possessions and power. His lieutenants in the Punjab were unequal to the task assigned to them. 'An individual, however gifted, however great, is always at a disadvantage in fighting with a nation in arms, fired by a consciousness of its own destiny'. The Khalsa Dal became a great instrument for the assertion of the supremacy of the Khalsa. Their religious fervour was matched by their high ethics in war. For its successful termination the credit went to 'the entire nation, not to any individual'. However, an exception could be made in favour of Jassa Singh Ahluwalia, a leader who was willingly followed by others.[8]

Sinha underlines the fact that the coins of the Sikh Commonwealth were struck for the first time in 1765, and not in 1758 or 1761. A different inscription was used for a coin struck in 1778. A coin of 1784 bore the word *ahad* but its significance was not clear. In any case, between 1767 and 1773, the Sikhs extended their power from Saharanpur to Attock, and from Multan to Kangra and Jammu. They formed themselves into twelve *misls* or confederacies. Taimur Shah recovered Multan in 1780 but he realized the weakness of his position in relation to the Punjab. His successor, Shah Zaman, made several attempts to reconquer the Punjab before his reign came to an inglorious end in 1799: he was blinded by his half brother, Shah Mahmud. The designs of Shah Zaman proved to be 'empty schemes of ambition'.[9]

Between the Sutlej and the Jamuna, four *misls* were established: the Phulkian with all its branches, Karora Singhia, Shahid and Nihang, and Nishanwala. Two aspects of their history are of interest to the students of Indian history: they were both on the offensive and the defensive. They made Najib-ud-Daula feel that he was beaten. The ebb and flow of the tide of their invasion eastward was felt from 1773 to 1783. Towards the close of the century, however, they were on the defensive against the Irish adventurer George Thomas. He was eliminated from politics by the French Generals of the Marathas who themselves were to be replaced very soon by the British.[10]

Warren Hastings recorded in 1784 that the Sikh power extending from 'the most western branch of Attock to the walls of Delhi' was a new object worth serious contemplation. He visualized a change in their polity with the rise of a single individual to supremacy. In that case, the Sikhs would present a threat to British imperialism. Bussy saw in the Sikhs a potential enemy of the British and a friend of the French. Some of the Sikh chiefs, however, were hobnobbing with Colonel Cumming against the Marathas. But in 1787 the British were thinking of reducing the Sikhs with the support of Mahadji Sindhia. The invasions of Shah Zaman made the British rather sympathetic to the Sikh chiefs as allies. Shah Zaman disappeared from the political arena. The adventures of George Thomas showed the way to the British to the region between the Jamuna and the Sutlej.[11]

II. SIKH POLITY

For Sikh polity of the late eighteenth century, Sinha underlines the relevance of 'the transformation of Sikhism' associated with Guru Gobind Singh. The Sikh brotherhood had become supreme like the Guru. The final step in the transformation was the declaration that 'the Khalsa is the Guru and the Guru is the Khalsa'. Devotion to God had already become merged with devotion to the Guru, and now love of God, obedience and service to the Guru and love for one another—all would consist in the service of the Khalsa or the Commonwealth. In this transformed system there was an element of theocracy along with a strong sense of brotherhood. The Sikhs were now a religious-minded warlike fraternity, with an intense consciousness.[12]

The central government of the Sikhs during the late eighteenth century consisted of a tumultuous 'diet', the *Sarbat Khalsa*. It met at Amritsar twice a year and chose a leader by majority of votes as the first among equals during his temporary elevation. The confederacy was called *Khalsaji* and the grand army was called *Dal Khalsaji*. The resolutions passed by the Sarbat Khalsa in the presence of the holy *Granth* were *gurmatas*. From the Sikh point of view, the grand 'diet' of the confederation deliberated and took decisions under the inspiration of the invisible being. During the interval between the general meetings of the Sarbat Khalsa, local gathering were held to resolve on important matters. For all practical purposes, in both the situations, only a few *sardars* really decided matters. Therefore, the constitution was democratic in its spirit and aristocratic in its actual working. In spite of its theocratic character, the central government of the Sikhs was very weak.[13]

Though a component part of the confederation, every *misl* was for all intents and purposes independent. Through a process of voluntary association with a leader chosen for collective action, including territorial occupation, emerged twelve very powerful feudal chiefs of *misls* as confederacies of equals. The feudalism of the Sikhs was different from the feudalism of medieval Europe and of contemporary Rajputana. With its distinctive characteristics, the *misl* reminded Sinha of the *Ayudhajibia Sanghas* of 'the Hindu period', mentioned by Panini and confirmed by Kautilya, in the Vahika country comprising the Sind valley and the Punjab. Thus, the military confederacies of the Sikhs had their prototype 'even in the early Hindu period'.[14]

The economic condition of the Punjab under the Sikh rule could be appreciated with reference to the desolation and misery caused by the Persian and Afghan invasions from 1739 to 1767. The greatest task of the Sikh chieftains was to induce the people to settle down to peaceful avocations. The Sikh chiefs acquitted themselves well. The Bhangi Sardars Gujjar Singh and Sahib Singh were ideal chiefs in this respect. 'They seem to have followed an enlightened liberal policy, sparing no effort to induce the people harassed by twenty years of constant spoliation to settle down to peaceful occupations.' Not only agriculture but also trade and commerce were revived. Following Prinsep, Sinha refers to four kinds of land tenures. His description of the Sikh army was based on the evidence of the contemporary Europeans.[15]

According to Sinha, the dissolution of the *misl* organization was inevitable. The presence of an external foe alone could keep such a loose confederation in working order. After 1767, there was no such danger, and this became a signal for 'disorders within'. Concord became conspicuous by its absence. The central government practically ceased to function. The sense of brotherhood ceased to be operative 'in a political sense'. A struggle for supremacy began in the 1770s and the chiefs degenerated into 'self-seeking free booting barons'. In the struggle for ascendancy the Sukerchakia *misl* prevailed over others, except in the Sutlej-Jamuna Divide where 'the separatist tendency' triumphed with the help of a foreign power. Theocratic confederate feudalism was already a decayed institution in 1768 and it went on decaying from day-to-day. The rise of a man like Ranjit Singh was only a matter of time.

Nevertheless, Sikh theocratic confederate feudalism had great triumphs and grand achievements to its credit. Ranjit Singh gave half a century more of glorious political life to the Sikhs. But the *Dal Khalsa* had been largely responsible for stemming the tide of Durrani invasions.

The part played by the Sikhs in removing the Durrani menace 'must not be minimized'. The prospects of the Durranis in north-western India were definitely shattered by the Sikhs who settled down 'like a wall of concrete, a dam against the encroachments of the northern flood'. What was almost equally important, the establishment of Sikh power in the Punjab 'put an end to the peaceful immigration of adventurers from Persia and Turkistan'. For Sinha, the rise of the Sikh power was a nationalist enterprise, both Indian and Hindu.

III. RISE OF RANJIT SINGH

N.K. Sinha's *Ranjit Singh* was published in 1933. It was revised 'thoroughly and re-written' in 1945. Sinha says that he was 'almost ashamed' of his first publication. There was much that was new in the second edition. However, the main conclusions remained 'more or less the same'. In the third edition in 1951, only 'piecemeal additions' were made and there was 'nothing remarkably new in this edition'.[16] It was reprinted in 1960 and then in 1968. Thus, five editions of *Ranjit Singh* appeared in 35 years. Like his own *Rise of the Sikh Power* and Banerjee's *Evolution of the Khalsa*, Sinha's *Ranjit Singh* was received as a scholarly work.

Sinha reiterates that Guru Gobind Singh was 'the father of Sikh militarism'. The Khalsa or the commonwealth became the most potent force in Sikh life. The visibly increasing weakness of the Mughal monarchy encouraged the Sikh warriors to organize themselves into small bands. The invasions of Nadir Shah and Ahmad Shah Abdali enabled the Sikhs to increase their strength. After 1767, they were left alone to establish Sikh independence in the form of 12 *misls* or confederacies. Sinha subscribes to Cunningham's conception of their polity as 'theocractic confederate feudalism'. After the foreign danger was over, there began to appear dissensions, discords and mutual plunderings among the leaders. 'Then came the man of destiny Ranjit Singh to establish a military monarchy on the ruins of feudalism.'[17]

In his early life Ranjit Singh had no lofty religious and moral ideas to imbibe. He was brought up more or less as a spoilt child. His early life presented a contrast to the early life of Shivaji. Ranjit Singh was betrothed to Mahtab Kaur in 1785. After his father Mahan Singh's death in 1790, he was helped by Sada Kaur as well as his mother and Diwan

Lakhpat Rai. But he was 'headstrong and ungovernable by nature'. As he told C.M. Wade, he used 20,000 rounds of shot left behind by Mahan Singh. Before long, Ranjit Singh married a Nakkai princess Raj Kaur. Sinha refutes 'scandals and rumours' attached to Ranjit Singh in relation to his mother and Diwan Lakhpat Rai.[18]

Ranjit Singh began his career of petty warfare in the seventeenth year of his life. During the invasion of Shah Zaman in 1797 he played no part, but in 1798 he rushed upon the Lahore fort and shot down some Afghans. He told Wade in 1827 that he used to attack the Shah's army every night to distress him. Sinha argues that Ranjit Singh did not secure Lahore on the strength of a grant from Shah Zaman. The seemingly submissive attitude of Ranjit Singh, like the conciliatory attitude of Shah Zaman, was a 'mere diplomatic camouflage to hide the real objectives'. Each wanted to make use of the other. Since the British entertained the possibility of cordiality between Shah Zaman and Ranjit Singh, they sent Yusuf Ali in 1800 to counteract 'the insidious proposals of the Durrani prince'. By the time he reached Lahore, Shah Zaman was no longer on the throne.[19]

The first important achievement of Ranjit Singh was the occupation of Lahore. It was a very easy conquest, and a valuable prize. It brought Nizamuddin of Kasur, Gulab Singh Bhangi of Amritsar, Sahib Singh of Gujrat, and Jassa Singh Ramgarhia together in a temporary alliance against Ranjit Singh. The two sides remained encamped near Bhasin for two months. Gulab Singh's death due to excessive drinking proved to be a signal for the dispersal of the allies. They could not unite again. Ranjit Singh remained in undisputed possession of Lahore. For four or five years then, Ranjit Singh's campaigns were directed against Jammu, Dal Singh of Akalgarh, Sahib Singh of Gujrat, Nizamuddin of Kasur, Sansar Chand of Kangra, Jassa Singh of Chiniot, the Nawab of Multan, Ahmad Khan of Jhang, and Mai Sukhan, the widow of Gulab Singh Bhangi, at Amritsar. Sinha himself sums up the result. Ranjit Singh now was in possession of Lahore and Amritsar, in alliance with Fateh Singh Ahluwalia and Sada Kaur, realizing tribute from Jammu Kasur, feeling his way in the hilly country and in the Jhang-Sahiwal-Khushab-Rawalpindi region, and in the direction of Multan.[20]

In 1805, Ranjit Singh got rid of 'two troublesome visitors': the Marathas under Jaswant Rao Holkar and the British army under Lord Lake. Ranjit Singh offered support to neither but helped them to come to an understanding. Before the end December, Holkar had committed himself to leave the Punjab. Lake left early in 1806. After his departure, Jaswant Rao let loose his troops upon the country. Ranjit Singh paid him the compliment of being a 'determined rascal'. The phrase actually used by Ranjit Singh was closer to 'bloody bastard' (*pakka haramzada*).[21]

Lord Lake showed no interest in the affairs of the chiefs between the Jamuna and the Sutlej. From this Ranjit Singh drew the inference that the British had no suzerain claims over the region. He was allowed to march south of the Sutlej without any reaction. If he did not establish his firm grip over this region it was only because he could not foresee that British interest in it would revive. In any case, in 1806 and 1807 he demonstrated his supremacy in the region in terms of overlordship and actual occupation of a considerable territory. Metcalfe recorded: 'The cis-Sutlej Rajas and chiefs in the Maharaja's camp were as submissive as if they had been used to his authority.' He was not in a position to admit that British policy had changed before the end of 1808. The arguments put forth by Metcalfe in December 1808 did not appear to accord with the facts in connection with Ranjit Singh's activity in the Sutlej-Jamuna Divide till March 1808.[22]

Sinha refers to the changes in the diplomatic situation in Europe, the Near East and Middle East to account for the change in British attitude towards the Sikh chiefs and Ranjit Singh. The Governor-General now claimed that the cis-Sutlej chiefs 'according to the established custom, are and will remain under the protection of the British Government'. Ranjit Singh was not prepared for this 'sudden change'. Nothing but the show of force by the British induced him to relinquish his suzerainty over the Sutlej-Jamuna Divide. But he insisted on a treaty and Metcalfe also argued in favour of a formal treaty. It was on their initiative that the British government signed the Treaty of Amritsar in April 1809. 'Ranjit Singh suffered a diplomatic defeat and had to put his pride in his pocket and eat the humble pie.'[23]

IV. TERRITORIAL EXPANSION AND RELATIONS WITH FOREIGN POWERS

Sinha takes up Ranjit Singh's conquests and consolidation from 1810 to 1824. Most of these conquests were made at the cost of the Afghans. Sinha outlines Ranjit Singh's relations with Afghanistan prior to 1810 to explain the later events. The Durrani monarchy gradually sank into anarchy and decay in the time of Shah Zaman (1793-1800), Shah Mahmud (1800-3), and Shah Shuja (1803-9). Defeated by Wazir Fateh Khan Barakzai, who brought Shah Mahmud back to the throne, Shah Shuja fell into the hands of the Afghan governor of Attock who sent him to Kashmir where he was kept as a close prisoner. Ranjit Singh supported Wazir Fateh Khan in his expedition to Kashmir with the idea of getting hold of Shah Shuja because his wife had promised Koh-i Nur in return. Diwan Mohkam Chand brought him to Lahore. Fateh Khan was now keen to occupy Attock but Mohkam Chand defeated the Afghans, and Attock was taken over by Ranjit Singh. The year 1813 was thus favourable for him.[24]

In 1814, Ranjit Singh's expedition to Kashmir against its new governor, Muhammad Azim Khan, ended in a failure. His sway in the hills was also shaken. The hill chiefs were completely subdued in 1815 and 1816. Multan was conquered in 1818 and Kashmir in 1820. In 1820 Ranjit Singh conquered Dera Ghazi Khan. He crossed the Indus to reconquer Peshawar from the Barakzais. The occupation of Jahangira fort and the battle of Naushehra, fought in March 1823, were the most important events of the campaign. Mankera was conquered before the end of 1823. Like Yar Muhammad Khan, who was given Peshawar as a feudatory, the chiefs of Bannu and Tank were obliged to pay tribute in 1824.[25]

During these years, Ranjit Singh annexed a number of principalities in the former Mughal province of Lahore too. Among those who lost their territories were Jodh Singh of Wazirabad, Buddh Singh Faizullapuria, Sahib Singh of Gujrat, the Nakkais, Nidhan Singh Kanhiya, Jaimal Singh Kanhiya, the Ramgarhias, and Sada Kaur. Thus, all the *misls* on the right of the Sutlej were gradually absorbed, with only one exception: Fateh Singh Ahluwalia of Kapurthala. He had exchanged turban with Ranjit singh and they had together entered into a 'treaty of friendship and amity' with the British. From this complete equality he gradually sank into the position of a subordinate. He crossed the Sutlej in 1826 to seek protection with the British. But they did not intervene and Ranjit Singh persuaded him to return. More than half of his territory was restored to him. Sinha observes at the end that the Sikh 'military monarchy' was created and consolidated between 1797 and 1823. Ranjit Singh was cautious and conciliatory, depending more on diplomacy than force. Most of the chiefs whom he dispossessed were given sufficient *jagirs* to maintain themselves in comfort and even high ranks in state service if they were willing to serve him.[26]

Talking of Ranjit Singh's relations with the British government, Sinha refers to the Treaty of Amritsar (1809) which deprived Ranjit Singh of his cherished ideal to be the sole ruler of the Sikhs. He remained suspicious of the British up to 1812. However, Anglo-Sikh relations continued to be satisfactory till 1823. There were some disputed territories in the Sutlej-Jamuna Divide. Sinha takes up the disputes relating to Wadni and Ferozepore to illustrate British attitude towards Ranjit Singh at this stage. The former place was in the control of Sada Kaur who had got it herself in 1807 and later received a *sanad* from Ranjit Singh on the condition of paying Rs. 15,000 a year. The Governor-General decided after reading the arguments of his Agents that the place should be regarded as liable to escheat to the British after Sada Kaur's death. Later, however, Ranjit Singh's claims were admitted. Ranjit Singh's claim to Ferozepore was disallowed even though it had been regarded as his possession. Ferozepore was occupied by the British in 1835 because of its strategic importance, and a cantonment was established there in 1838.[27]

Sinha emphasizes that Ranjit Singh was convinced of his utter inability to contend with the British arms. He refused to help the Gurkhas in 1815; he did not respond to the appeal of the ex-Peshwa Baji Rao II in 1820; and he refused to respond to the appeals from Bharatpur in 1825-6. After 1831, when Ranjit Singh turned his attention to Sind he was forestalled by the British. In spite of the exhortations of his *sardars*, Ranjit Singh yielded once again. His ready acquiescence on the Sind question 'enables us to realize how impotent was Ranjit Singh in his relations with the British'. He was an unwilling partner in the Tripartite Treaty of 1838. His own trans-Indus possessions were secured but the treaty also gave protection to the ruler of Kabul against any possible designs of Ranjit Singh. On the whole, Ranjit Singh profited by British friendship in 1809-24. After that, he had to yield on all vital matters.[28]

After a brief outline of Ranjit Singh's relations with the British, Sinha gives his comment. Ranjit Singh could see clearly enough that his kingdom would be absorbed in the British empire before long. He did not gain anything by continuing to yield to the British. Towards the end of his reign, however, there was a change in his tone and temper. The sense of deference to the British government was gone. Ranjit Singh's impatience was also clearly discernible. 'The English were too strong even for a nation of warriors like the Sikhs.' But war with the British would have come sooner or later. Ranjit Singh should have declared war over the issue of Sind even if he had no chance of success against the British. He 'chose instead the policy of yielding, yielding and yielding'.[29]

For Ranjit Singh's relations with Afghanistan, Sinha refers to the political situation at Kabul in which Dost Muhammad Khan Barakzai became the ruler. Shah Shuja, who had taken refuge with the British at Ludhiana, was keen to get back the throne of Kabul. In 1831 he sought Ranjit Singh's support, but the terms proposed by Ranjit Singh would have made Shah Shuja a vassal of the Maharaja: (a) that the Shah should prohibit cow slaughter in Afghanistan, (b) that he should deliver the gates of Somnath (supposed to have been carried away by Mahmud of Ghazni), and (c) that the heir-apparent of the Shah should attend the Maharaja with an auxiliary force. Shah Shuja rejected these proposals. But in 1833 he signed a treaty with Ranjit Singh by which he recognized his sway over the Kabul territories conquered by Ranjit Singh in return for his neutrality, and some financial assistance. Peshawar was annexed by the Maharaja in this context.[30]

A new phase of Sikh-Afghan relations started in 1834 after Dost Muhammad Khan's victory over the army of Shah Shuja. Dost Muhammad was keen on the recovery of Peshawar. He made colossal preparations to measure his strength with the Sikhs. He assumed the title of Amir al-Muminin to give his campaign the character of a *jihad*. He collected a force of 40,000 men, with a strong artillery. 'It was a great crisis in Sikh history.' But Ranjit Singh's diplomacy and his disciplined army enabled him to gain 'a bloodless victory'. The battle of Jamrud is briefly described by Sinha: 800 Sikhs and 500 Afghans were killed in this battle. Though much was made of this battle, the action at Jamrud in itself was of no importance. The death of Hari Singh Nalwa, 'that flower of Sikh chivalry', cast a gloom over the Punjab. The Afghans were exultant, but they never succeeded in capturing Jamrud, Shabkadar or Peshawar. Dost Muhammad was not in a position to do any real harm to Ranjit Singh.[31]

Sinha states that a study of Ranjit Singh's western frontier policy had some significance for those interested in the problem of India's defence. Ranjit Singh spoke sometimes of invading Afghanistan but he did not really want to conquer Afghanistan, except perhaps for a short time after the death of Hari Singh: 'the mere warrior within him never got the better of the statesman'. Sinha refers to the *jihad* of Sayyad Ahmad and his battles. After the annexation of the frontier territories Ranjit Singh pursued the policy of sending military columns into the territory of an aggressively refractory chief to inflict the damage they could and then to pull out. 'The mountaineers were kept down by a movable column constantly in the field.' A memorable part was played by Hari Singh Nalwa in the Hazara region where he built a number of forts for the subjugation of its unruly chiefs. While Hari Singh followed an aggressive policy as the governor of Peshawar, Ranjit Singh gave *jagirs* to the Barakzais to reduce their annoyance to the minimum. The whole frontier region was dotted with forts, and Ranjit Singh kept boats on the Indus in readiness to form a bridge. At the same time, he allowed a large degree of local autonomy, his main purpose being the collection of revenues in addition to the concerns of defence.[32]

In Sinha's assessment, Ranjit Singh was to a large extent successful in the solution of his western frontier problem. The tribes were not brought under direct control. His aim was to make the high road to Peshawar safe even for private individuals. The moderation of Sikh rule in the Derajat was acknowledged by C.M. Wade when he wrote that the paucity of troops maintained by the Sikhs in the newly-acquired country was 'the clearest evidence of their role in tranquillising and subduing the insurrectionary spirit of the chiefs of the Derajat'.[33]

Sinha goes into Ranjit Singh's relations with Bahawalpur, Sind, Nepal and other Indian states. In the early 1820s, Sadiq Muhammad Khan of Bahawalpur was obliged to pay a heavy *nazrana* after the battle of Tibbi and to transfer his allegiance from the Afghans to Ranjit Singh. Most probably for military reasons, the Sikh territory conquered beyond the Indus was given to the Khan of Bahawalpur on payment of Rs. 3,00,000 a year in addition to tribute. In 1831, this territory was brought under direct control. The Amirs of Sind began to send their envoys regularly to the court of Ranjit Singh after his conquest of Multan. Ranjit Singh was keen to occupy the strategic and commercial town of Shikarpur about 100 miles from his territory. At Ropar In 1831 he tried to elicit from the Chief Secretary, British views on Sind. But there was no response, even though Bentinck had already sent Pottinger to the Amirs to negotiate a commercial treaty with them. Ranjit Singh did not oppose the British on the issue of the commercial treaty though it implied partial British protection for the Amirs. But he did not abandon the idea of conquering Shikarpur. In 1835, he began preparations for an attack on Sind. The Mazaris had provided the immediate cause by attacking Mithankot for plunder. Prince Nau Nihal Singh was sent against them and to tell the Amirs that it they did not shift their allegiance from the Afghans to Ranjit Singh, Shikarpur would be occupied. In deference to the wishes of the British government, however, Ranjit Singh did not press the Amirs any harder and recalled his army on the way to Shikarpur. The idea of advancing in the direction of Sind was finally defeated by the Tripartite Treaty of 1838.[34]

Ladakh was not an unprofitable country to conquer because of its trade in shawl wool, which had been opened to the British by Moorcroft in 1820. In the 1830s the British were more keen to check Ranjit Singh's advance into the plains of Sind than into the hills. In 1834, Gulab Singh conquered Ladakh with Ranjit Singh's tacit approval. General Zorawar Singh fixed a tribute of Rs. 30,000 from Ladakh. Through Ladakh, Ranjit Singh wanted to be in the neighbourhood of the Nepal ruler. He did not encourage Gulab Singh and Zorawar Singh against Iskardu or Tibet. He had a sound sense of limits. A mission from Nepal came to Amritsar in 1834, followed by a regular mission in 1837. Ranjit Singh wrote to the ruler of Nepal, acknowledging his presents, expressing his pleasure over his 'friendship', and desiring its continuation. His changed attitude towards Nepal may be regarded as a real change of policy. Wade rightly suspected that the motive of the Nepalese mission was more substantional than a mere exchange of compliments.[35]

V. GOVERNMENT AND ADMINISTRATION

Sinha states that the *Catalogue of Khalsa Darbar Records* gives a good idea of Ranjit Singh's system of government and its actual working, and there were other sources as well. In theory, and to some extent in practice, Ranjit Singh was not the supreme embodiment of all economic and political authority. The living principle of the commonwealth was one great limitation. Some check was also exercised by the Akalis and the martial nobility of the Punjab, and even by the common people possessing arms. Ranjit Singh professedly regarded himself as nothing more than 'a mere drum of the commonwealth for the assertion of the political supremacy of the Khalsa'. He always acted in the name of the Khalsa. He did not assume the title of King; the source of his orders was 'Sarkar Khalsa'. He dared not defy the religious susceptibilities of his people and abolish the order of the Akalis.[36]

As the supreme ruler of the Punjab, Ranjit Singh wanted to have the big *sardars* under his complete control. His standing army overawed the nobility. The new nobles created by him became a powerful check on the old Sikh chiefs. Due to the fatuity of his later years, the Jammu brothers firmly established themselves in the hills. However, 'patriotism', defined as the instinct of self-preservation being raised to a moral duty, characterized the Sikh people who could not altogether sink into the languid indifference of private life. They could not be easily ignored.[37]

Ranjit Singh established an elaborate civil secretariat, a Toshakhana and the office of the *deodidar*. The Punjab was divided into seven great districts: Kashmir, Multan, Peshawar, Wazirabad, Pind Dadan Khan with the salt mines, and Kangra with a portion of the Majha, and the Jalandhar Doab. The governors of these districts were allowed to do whatever they liked. The affairs of the country were in the hands of (a) men of wealth, position and influence who were sent to the distant provinces as farmers of revenue; they managed the whole business of their territories with reference to the court; (b) the military chiefs who held feudal demesnes on the condition of sending contingents in the field; and (c) the Kardars whose power varied according to their influence at the court, and who lived by the perquisites of their own office. In the cities, *kotwals* were appointed and the *mohalladari* system was revived. The village communities were left undisturbed in the enjoyment of their ancestral rights.[38]

In financial matters there was a great scope for embezzlement. Ranjit Singh sometimes called upon his servants to pay him fees or aids and, if they refused, to plunder them. When he confiscated the properties of his dead officials, in most cases it 'merely balanced his accounts'. The rate of assessment generally ranged from two-fifth to one-third, but it could be 50 per cent or even a little more of the gross produce. The methods of assessment were *batai, kankut* or cash. The revenue collected from land amounted to about Rs. 1,34,00,000. There was a network of excise duties, town duties, customs duties and transit duties. Commerce flourished. There were eight salt mines. The income from this source amounted to over Rs. 24,00,000. On the whole, 'the government gave back with one hand what it took with the other'.[39]

Sinha had the impression that there was no special officer for the dispensation of civil justice or the execution of criminial law. The chiefs generally judged both civil and criminal cases and thus no regular courts of law were required. There was no written law. Private arbitration was common. The *qazis* and *qanungos* exercised their traditional functions privately and indirectly; the former performed marriages, registered testaments, and attested deeds, and the latter expounded local customs. The Maharaja made extensive tours and heard appeals. He also heard appeals in court, but justice was 'not so much a national as local concern'. It was left to the feudatories. Fines were levied in almost all cases. Capital punishment was rare, except in the disturbed areas like Hazara and Peshawar. There were many 'defects' in Ranjit Singh's judicial and police system. But Punjab under Ranjit Singh was safer even than the British territories in India.[40]

Ranjit Singh kept himself informed of the affairs of his dominions by news-writers who reported independently of the governors, *kardars* and *jagirdars*. They served as a great check upon the local agents. Ranjit Singh was also one of the best informed men about the affairs of the countries in which he was interested. His curiosity was in striking contrast to 'the general apathy of the nation'. In all important international transanctions, Faqir Azizuddin played a prominent part. Sinha is particularly interested in Ranjit Singh's attitude towards his Muslim subjects. He appointed a *qazi*, a *mufti* and a Muslim *kotwal* in Lahore. He had a number of trusted Muslim officers. State patronage was extended to Muslim shrines and to individuals known for their learning or piety. Ranjit Singh tried to ensure that his Muslim subjects enjoyed as much religious freedom as did the Hindus or the Sikhs. 'The great Sikh ruler was superior to communal prejudices.'[41]

According to Sinha, there were many defects in the administrative system of Ranjit Singh. Forms and institutions were evolving but they were yet in their infancy. The kingdom was not united by laws, nor was it adorned by arts. The treasury was filled in many cases with the help of the standing army. But Ranjit Singh knew where to let men and things alone. He was not obsessed with the idea of centralization, except in the financial sphere. Sinha refers to the testimony of a contemporary traveller and a later British administrator who have recorded their appreciation for the government of Ranjit Singh. The system was rough but firm. Its yoke was onerous but not galling. Its justice was rude but people had access to redress. The landowners were jealous of their rights. Property in land survived all changes and the village communities preserved their constitution.[42]

Sinha closes his discussion of the government of Ranjit Singh with a note on the administration of Kashmir. It was divided into 22 *parganas* under 20 collectors, with 10 *thanas* and 400 villages. Different kinds of coinage was in use in Kashmir: the old rupee, the rupee associated with Hari Singh, and the Nanakshahi rupee. The total revenue amounted to Rs. 36,00,000 a year. The military establishment in Kashmir consisted of 4,000 men of whom 1,000 were horsemen. The Afghan force earlier had 16,000 to 20,000 men. Moorcroft was not 'a friendly critic' of Ranjit Singh. He talks of 'rackrent' in Kashmir. Some of the governors of Kashmir were rapacious. Because of the difficulties of access, no adequate relief could be sent to the people of Kashmir in times of famine.[43]

VI. THE ARMY AND THE *DARBAR*

Sinha talks of the army of Ranjit Singh and his *darbar*. Ranjit Singh created 'a regular disciplined professional Sikh army' in place of part-time levies of predatory horsemen. The strength of the regular army in 1811 was 4061; it consisted of infantry and artillery. In 1838, the number had risen to 38,242, including regular cavalry. The total expenditure on this army amounted to Rs. 3,74,101 per month.[44]

The system of monthly cash payment was introduced by Ranjit Singh for the regular army, following the example of the East India Company. However, the troops were kept in arrears for five or six months. Sinha gives the average salaries from the commandant (Kumedan) to the soldier in a footnote. There was no regular pension but in 30 per cent of cases a member of the family of the retiring soldier was employed in his place. A kind of allowance was sometimes given to the members of the family of the dead or wounded. The Maharaja was liberal to those who had been wounded in his service.[45]

Besides the regular army, there was the *be-qawaid fauj* or irregula cavalry, the salaried *Ghurcharhas*. Their number in 1838 was 10,795. They were divided into *deras* which were subdivided into *misls*, each varying from 15 to 70 horsemen. They provided themselves with horses and if a trooper lost his horse he drew the pay of a foot soldier. Then there were contingents of the *jagirdars*, generally employed on rather unimportant punitive expeditions. European visitors to the Punjab differed in their assessment of the army system. In Sinha's view, irregularity of payment was one of the greatest defects of Ranjit Singh's military organization. In actual practice, the monthly system was something midway between the old bi-annual system and the British system of payment.[46]

Sinha pays special attention to European officers in Ranjit Singh's army. Ranjit Singh followed the tradition of the Peshwa Balaji Baji Rao and the Maratha chiefs who had employed Europeans in their armies. Before Ventura and Allard were employed in 1822, there were two white officers in the Punjab army. It is not true to say that Ventura and Allard introduced the new system for the first time. The Khalsa Darbar records show that as early as 1807 there were three battalions trained in the European fashion. Ventura, Allard and Court gave a moderate degree of precision and completeness to 'a system already introduced'. It was only gradually that the Sikh *sardars* turned friendly towards the European officers. Apart from Europeans of various nationalities, there were some American and Russian officers in the army. They were all encouraged to develop permanent interest in the Punjab. Ranjit Singh was aware that Ventura, Allard and Court had fulfilled their mission, no more foreigners were needed, and even these three were given additional duties. After Ranjit Singh's death the foreigners found themselves in an atmosphere of suspicion and treachery. They had begun to take interest in politics. The Sikhs formed the bulk of the regular army and they possessed a strong *esprit-de-corps*. The way in which they fought in the two Sikh wars showed that 'Ranjit Singh's mistake was the postponement of an inevitable war, not the introduction of trained battalions'.[47]

Sinha does not agree with those who regarded the courtiers of Maharaja Ranjit Singh as 'adventurers'. Most of them were able men whose loyalty to the Maharaja was beyond question. Sinha outlines the careers of Mohkam Chand, Diwan Chand, Hari Singh Nalwa, Khushal Singh, the Jamwal brothers, and Azizuddin to make his point. Some of the other important persons were Bhawani Das, Ganga Ram, and Dina Nath. All policy matters were decided by the Maharaja. No 'favourite' dared to undertake anything on his own. No rivalry or enmity between individuals was allowed to prejudice the Maharaja in favour of one or the other. He rose above 'communal narrowness'. His administration was the nearest approach to 'the ideal of popular monarchy that was possible in those days and in those circumstances'. The *Umdat ut-Tawarikh*, according to Sinha, gives a vivid picture of the Maharaja in the midst of his courtiers. The informal decorum of the court went on increasing with the passage of time. Sinha concedes that Ranjit Singh departed from his usual attitude of vigilance in the case of the Jamwal brothers. Gulab Singh and Dhian Singh were not so committed to the state as were the other courtiers of their time. The successors of Ranjit Singh paid very dearly 'for the engrossing and prejudicial influence which he had allowed the Dogra brothers to attain'.[48]

VII. RANJIT SINGH AS A RULER

Sinha looks upon Ranjit Singh as a crude, dynamic, and vigorous despot who was the subject of many anecdotes which did not build-up into a legend. He had many demonstrable and conspicuous defects. He showed a puerile curiosity combined with remarkable intelligence and rare sagacity. Habitually reserved in matters of business, he used to joke with dancing girls in the open court, which ill-behoved a monarch. Accustomed to act singly and independently practically in every important matter, he used to make a show of consulting his courtiers whenever it suited his interests. He knew the name, position and history of 10,000 to 12,000 villages in his kingdom. His conversation was a 'nightmare' even to a man like Jacquement. The book of military *parwanas* covering the period from 14 November 1833 to 18 December 1834 reveals how indefatigable he was in his work, how thorough his grasp of detail was, how keen his solicitude for his men was. Few rulers exercised more rigid control over the conduct of their troops than Maharaja Ranjit Singh.[49]

In the emergence of Ranjit Singh as a powerful monarch, Sinha saw the logic of history. 'The exclusively military turn given to the Sikh character resulted after the Sikh wars of liberation and the establishment of a theocratic confederate feudalism in the founding of a military monarchy, when a strong man arose who could compel the entire system to gyrate round himself and Sikh valour flared up brightly.' The Jats formed the backbone of the Sikh community. They were principally soldiers and became even more so as a result of the reforms of Guru Gobind Singh. Therefore, power, as understood by Ranjit Singh, the last great constructive genius among the Sikhs, was not moral but military. Nevertheless he secured the support of Sikhs, Hindus and Muslims; he defended the North-West Frontier against a powerful Afghanistan; he trained an army that could fight the British; and to a certain extent he furnished 'Indian nationalism' with what it greatly needed, 'a tradition of strength.' Therefore, Maharaja Ranjit Singh 'must always stand in the forefront of great men of Indian History.'[50]

Among Ranjit Singh's principal achievements, for Sinha, was his very successful defence of his kingdom against the Afghans. At one time Afghanistan was a part of India. But India lost it once for all. The North-West Frontier, the Punjab, and Kashmir would also have been lost, but for Ranjit Singh.[51]

Maharaja Ranjit Singh presented a supreme example of 'an intellect without conscience'. He did not breathe any noble sentiments into the hearts of his people which could have held them together after his death. 'Shivaji like Ranjit Singh had incapable succesors. But the history of Maharashtra presents a striking contrast to that of the Punjab after the death of Ranijt Singh.' The imperfections of Ranjit Singh as the builder of a state were apparent. He centralized everything pertaining to his government in himself. His disappearance caused a void into which the entire structure of government collapsed. He left the *jagirdars* weak, and the army too powerful for his weak successors to control. The army considered itself as the visible embodiment of the Khalsa or the commonwealth. But the soldiers were very unfit guardians of a legal or even civil constitution. The able Generals of Ranjit Singh died in his lifetime and they were replaced by crafty and designing men who were either weaklings or worse traitors. Disputed successions encouraged intrigue, and the Punjab became a scene of the wildest disorder.[52]

One great external cause of Ranjit Singh's weakness is found by Sinha in his relations with the British government. In almost all cases, the Maharaja was the horse and the British government was the rider. A collison between the military monarchy and British imperialism was inevitable and imminent. Ranjit Singh hesitated and hesitated, forgetting that in politics, as in war, time is not on the side of the defensive. 'In his relations with the British government, Ranjit Singh is seen at his worst. He never grandly dared. He was all hesitancy and indecision.' At the same time, Sinha emphasizes that Ranjit Singh's failure was inherent in the very logic of events. The opponents of British imperialism were doomed to go down. Sinha's regret seems to be that Ranjit Singh did not go down fighting against the British.[53]

VIII. FINAL ASSESSMENT

Sinha defends Ranjit Singh against some of the statements made by European writers. He refutes scandals and rumours attached to Ranjit Singh's mother and Diwan Lakhpat Rai. The chiefs whom Ranjit dispossessed were treated humanely by him: They were either given *jagirs* or taken into service. His western frontier policy was not a failure. He was not a despotic ruler: neither in theory nor in practice was he the supreme embodiment of authority. The Punjab under Ranjit Singh was a safer place than British India. He was far above communal prejudices. Sinha does not accept Moorcroft's judgement that Sikh rule in Kashmir was oppressive. Ranjit Singh's courtiers were not really adventurers'. His principal achievement was that he saved the Punjab, Kashmir and the North-West Frontier for India. For Sinha, Maharaja Ranjit Singh was in the forefront of great men of Indian history.

Nevertheless, Sinha is critical of Ranjit Singh on several scores. He had no lofty religious or moral ideas. There were many defects in his administration. He himself had many demonstrable and conspicuous defects. For example, he used to joke with dancing girls in the open court. He presented a supreme example of an intellect without conscience. He did not breathe any noble sentiments into the hearts of his people. That was why after his death the Punjab presented a contrast with Maharashtra after the death of Shivaji. As the builder of a state Ranjit Singh showed imperfections.

Sinha is most critical of Ranjit Singh for his attitude towards the British. In 1809, Ranjit Singh had to put his pride in his pocket and eat the humble pie when the British gave a jolt to his cherished ideal to become the sole ruler of the Sikhs. Sinha expected Ranjit Singh to help the Gurkhas in 1815, Baji Rao in 1820, and Bharatpur in 1825-6. But he was convinced of his utter inability to contend with the British arms. In 1835 the British took over Ferozepore which was in his possession. The question of Sind showed that Ranjit Singh felt improtent in his relations to the British. Even when he knew that the British would take over his kingdom he did not oppose their aggressive policy. Sinha wished him not to have followed a policy of yielding but to have declared war over the issue of Sind even if he had no chance of success against the British. In other words, he should have become a martyr to the ideal of freedom at the cost of his country and his people. Sinha speaks as a votary of Indian nationalism. Both his appreciation and his criticism of Ranjit Singh sprang from the same source.

NOTES

1. Narendra Krishna Sinha, *Rise of the Sikh Power,* Calcutta: A. Mukherjee & Co., 1973 (rpt.), 1st edn., 1936, pp. 1-2.
2. Ibid., pp. 3-17.
3. Ibid., pp. 18-31.
4. Ibid., p. 32.
5. Ibid., pp. 33-48.
6. Ibid., pp. 48-53.
7. Ibid., pp. 54-75.
8. Ibid., pp. 76-98.
9. Ibid., pp. 99-106.
10. Ibid., pp. 107-8.
11. Ibid., pp. 108-10.
12. Ibid., pp. 110-12.
13. Ibid., pp. 112-16.

14. Ibid., pp. 116-17.
15. Ibid., pp. 118-19.
16. Narendra Krishna Sinha, *Ranjit Singh*, Calcutta: A. Mukherjee & Co., 1968 (rpt.), Preface.
17. Ibid., pp. 1-4.
18. Ibid., pp. 7-9.
19. Ibid., pp. 9-13.
20. Ibid., pp. 13-17.
21. Ibid., p. 18.
22. Ibid., pp. 21-3.
23. Ibid., pp. 24-33.
24. Ibid., pp. 41, 43-53.
25. Ibid., pp. 53-63.
26. Ibid., pp. 63-9.
27. Ibid., pp. 71-7.
28. Ibid., pp. 77-88.
29. Ibid., pp. 88-91.
30. Ibid., pp. 92-5.
31. Ibid., pp. 95-102.
32. Ibid., pp. 104-12.
33. Ibid., pp. 112-14.
34. Ibid., pp. 116-23
35. Ibid., pp. 123-32.
36. Ibid., pp. 136-8.
37. Ibid., pp. 138-9.
38. Ibid., pp. 139-41.
39. Ibid., pp. 141-7.
40. Ibid., pp. 147-8.
41. Ibid., pp. 148-50.
42. Ibid., pp. 150-2.
43. Ibid., pp. 152-3.
44. Ibid., p. 157.
45. Ibid., pp. 157-8.
46. Ibid., pp. 158-60.
47. Ibid., pp. 160-72.
48. Ibid., pp. 174-85.
49. Ibid., pp. 187-9.
50. Ibid., pp. 189-90.
51. Ibid., p. 190.
52. Ibid., pp. 190-1.
53. Ibid., pp. 191-2.

PART FIVE

Punjabi Historians

CHAPTER FOURTEEN

Gokul Chand Narang

Transformation of Sikhism

I. INTRODUCTION

Born in 1878, Gokul Chand Narang matriculated from the Mission School, Gujranwala in 1896. After getting his Master's degree in 1901-2, he taught at D.A.V. College, Lahore, where he came in close contact with Mahatma Hans Raj and other Arya Samajists; he wrote a small book entitled *Message of the Vedas*. He went to Oxford for research but got the degree of Ph.D. from the University of Berne in Switzerland. He published his doctoral thesis in 1912 as *The Transformation of Sikhism*.

Narang's book covered the period from Guru Nanak to 1799. His intention was to write a second volume on Maharaja Ranjit Singh and his successors. However, he published only a revised version of the book in 1945 which was reprinted in 1946. It contained a chapter on Maharaja Ranjit Singh, and another on his successors. In the third additional chapter he talked of the Namdharis. The fourth chapter related to the history of the Sikhs from 1849 to 1946. There was also a chapter on the future of the Sikhs. The book was revised and enlarged again in 1956. The fifth edition, brought out in 1960, included a discussion of the demand for the creation of a Punjabi-speaking state. Gokul Chand Narang died in 1969. A new edition of his book was published in 1972 under a new title, *Glorious History of Sikhism: From Spiritualism to Militarism*. All the chapters related to the period after 1849 were excluded from this edition. Only the first edition of the book was based on research. The later additions are helpful for providing insights into the outlook and attitudes of Gokul Chand Narang.

II. THE SIKH MOVEMENT: A HINDU REVIVAL

Gokul Chand Narang's *Transformation of Sikhism* was meant to be neither 'a chronicle of the Sikhs' nor 'a dissertation on Sikhism'; it was intended to be a brief narrative of 'the various stages' through which the Sikhs passed to become 'the sovereign power' in the Punjab. Narang claimed to be 'impartial' in presenting the results of his 'long and careful study' of the early history of the Sikhs.[1]

The starting point of this study is Guru Nanak's mission of 'spiritual emancipation'. Narang subscribes to the view that all religious movements were in reality political movements. Finding the Hindus in a most deplorable condition Guru Nanak thought of 'a religious revival' as the only remedy. Hinduism had never been able to shake off the accretions it had received from Buddhism and Jainism: the worship of idols, and the doctrine of incarnation. The Hindu reformers who preceded Guru Nanak were more or less sectarian, ritualistic, narrow-minded and bigoted. Guru Nanak's system stood distinguished from other reform movements by its non-sectarian character and its reconciliation with secular life. It leavened 'the whole Hindu thought' in the Punjab. Guru Nanak proved to be 'the first Hindu hero' to command allegiance of all parties. He showed to the Hindus that 'the highest worldly ambition was not incompatible with the purest and godliest life'.[2]

Though the object of Guru Nanak was simply to leaven the social and religious thought of the Hindus, and not to found a sect, it was necessary that his work should continue after his death. Had he died without a successor there would have been 'no Sikhism today or at best simply another Kabirism'. His successor, Guru Angad, followed Guru Nanak's policy of not cutting himself off from the Hindu community. However, it was necessary that a community should serve as an 'advance guard' of the Hindus. Guru Angad gave 'individuality' to Guru Nanak's followers through the introduction of Gurmukhi characters, compilation of Guru Nanak's memoirs, and starting a free kitchen (*langar*). The Sikhs now began gradually to drift away from 'the orthodox Hindu society' to form a sort of new brotherhood by themselves: 'in the simplicity of their faith, their ardour and earnestness they rather resembled their Aryan ancestors'. However, like the Udasis, they were still prone to believe that the world was all a delusion and a mirage. Guru Amar Das appealed to the people to follow the example of Guru Nanak by living 'in the world' without being 'of the world'. He also took the first step towards organization by instituting 22 *manjis* to take care of the whole country inhabited by the Sikhs.[3]

The power and influence of the Guru increased in the time of Guru Ram Das. Guru Nanak had built a *dharamsala* and started a dining hall; Guru Amar Das had founded Goindwal and constructed a *baoli* as the first important place of pilgrimage of the Sikhs. Guru Ram Das founded the city of Amritsar in the midst of 'the sturdy Hindu peasantry' which was later to prove to be the bulwark of his warlike successors. Amritsar also proved to be a source of vast revenues due to its commercial importance. Akbar's friendly relations with the Gurus increased their prestige and made their mission more popular. They also obtained popular concessions from Akbar in the form of remission from pilgrims tax and land revenue. Guru Ram Das made the office of Guruship hereditary so that the Guru henceforth was looked upon by his followers 'not only in the light of a spiritual guide but also as a worldly lord and a ruling sovereign'. [4]

The organizational steps taken by Guru Arjan resulted in the foundation of Sikh theocracy: compilation of the *Adi Granth*, construction of the Harmandar as the chief place of Sikh pilgrimage; transfer of his headquarters to Amritsar to make it the centre of Sikh activity; propagation of Sikhism among the Jats of Majha by founding Tarn Taran; introduction of an important measure of political organization by placing the revenue system on a sound basis; the encouragement of trade in horses from Turkistan which broke down the prejudice against crossing the borders, and enriched the Sikh traders and introduced the practice of horse riding among the Sikhs. The Church developed into a sort of State. The Guru's *darbar* became a place of splendour and magnificence, and the palatial buildings, tents and horses, and the treasure gave it the look of a princely court. With the Guru as *Sachcha Padshah* at their head, the Sikhs became accustomed to 'a form of self-government within the empire'.[5]

Before taking up the beginning of armed resistance under Guru Hargobind, Narang talks of the persecution to which the Sikhs were systematically subjected by 'the Muslim government' of the day. He mentions not only the martyrdom of Guru Arjan due to the bigotry of Jahangir but also of the 'deportation' of Guru Hargobind to Gwalior, the martyrdom of Guru Tegh Bahadur, the slaughter of the innocent children of Guru Gobind Singh, the execution of Banda Bahadur and his companions, the general persecution of the Sikhs ordered by Farrukh Siyar, the martyrdom of Bhai Mani Singh and Bhai Taru Singh, the execution of a large number of other Sikhs at a place which came to be known as Shahidganj, and the young martyr Hakikat Rai.[6] Among the causes of Guru Hargobind's military preparations was the feeling of revenge for his father's death, and its objective was 'the destruction of Islam and of the Muslim government'. Guru Hargobind fought three battles as the first Guru to have entered upon a military career. After him, the Sikhs were in little danger of relapsing into the limited merit of monks and mendicants.[7]

Narang did not have much to say about the three successors of Guru Hargobind. His grandson, Guru Har Rai, was endowed with a peace-loving nature and reflective mind. The only time he had recourse to arms was when he was called upon to defend Dara Shukoh 'who was all but a Hindu'. The Bhai families of Kaithal and Bagarian, and the Phulkian rulers, traced their origin to Guru Har Rai. His elder son, Ram Rai, was a favourite at the court of Aurangzeb. He complained to the emperor when his younger brother, Har Krishan, was installed on the *gaddi*. Guru Har Krishan was called to Delhi. He was confirmed in the succession but he died soon afterwards. He had sent the insignia of Guruship to his grandfather's younger brother, Tegh Bahadur, a man of great humility. Nevertheless, Guru Tegh Bahadur's *darbar* always possessed royal splendour and magnificence, and he was always addressed as *Sachcha Padshah*. On a representation made by Ram Rai, Aurangzeb called him to Delhi. The Raja of Jaipur interceded on his behalf and took Guru Tegh Bahadur with him to Assam. On his return to the Punjab Guru Tegh Bahadur founded Makhowal but he was again summoned to Delhi. On refusing to accept Islam, he was put to death by the emperor's order. Guru Tegh Bahadur was generally looked upon as 'a champion of the Hindus'. This execution was universally regarded by the Hindus as a sacrifice for their faith. It stirred up 'once more the dying embers of Hindu hatred of the Muslim rule'.[8]

The bigotry of Aurangzeb and the Deccan wars afforded a great advantage to Guru Gobind Singh. He built fortresses and called together great *pandits* from Patna and Benares and great Persian scholars from the Punjab. He went through the whole range of epic literature. He was deeply impressed by the Puranic idea of 'a saviour appearing from time to time to uphold righteousness and destroy unrighteousness, to uproot evil and establish good, to destroy the oppressor and rescue the weak and the innocent'. The stories of Rama, Krishna and Durga filled his heart with hope and confidence. While strongly believing in his heaven ordained mission, he humbly declared that he was 'but a servant of the supreme being, and anybody calling him God will be thrown into the cauldron of hell'. After an education, training and reflection of twenty years, Guru Gobind Singh realized the miserable condition of 'his race' and thought of the amelioration of 'his nation'. His object now was 'to infuse a new life into the dead bones of Hindus', to make once more 'a living nation of them and enable them to regain their lost independence'.[9]

At this time there was 'no such thing as a Hindu nation or any Hindu striking force in the Punjab'. Guru Gobind Singh had first 'to forge the sword with which he was to fight'. All that was calculated to foster 'a national sentiment' was incorporated in the new creed. Its first element was unity. Since caste was a great barrier to unity, he struck at the very root of the evil by declaring that 'caste was an after-growth in the Hindu social system' and no body could call himself a true Sikh if he did not give up the prejudice of caste. Guru Gobind Singh tried not only to make one caste out of four but also to remove all unevenness of religious privileges to establish 'a theocratic democracy'. The other means employed to bring about unity were common worship, common place of pilgrimage, common baptism for all classes, and common external appearance. He inspired his Sikhs with the belief that they were now under the direct control and protection of God, that God was always present in the general body of the Khalsa, and that wherever even five Sikhs were assembled the Guru would be with them. They were impressed with the idea that they were born to conquer. Guru Gobind Singh did not believe in any deity except the true and deathless one. But he ordered a great sacrifice to be performed with the ostensible object of making the goddess appear. The ceremony lasted for a year but the goddess did not appear. The presiding priest decamped and the Guru flung all the remaining material into the fire. The blaze was taken as a sign of propitiation and the sword brandished by the Guru was seen as a gift of the goddess. He appealed to the people to worship the sword.[10]

Guru Gobind Singh's immediate object was to achieve a commanding influence among the hill Rajas and to establish a principality in the hills to serve as a base of operations against the Mughal empire. Seeing the Rajas apathetic, he made up his mind to coerce them. They made a grand alliance but only to be defeated in the battle of Bhangani. The Rajas hastened to make an offensive and defensive alliance with him and refused to pay tribute to the Mughal authorities. The Mughal forces sent against them were defeated. Aurangzeb sent Prince Muazzam to realize tribute from the Rajas. They realized that it was dangerous to provoke Aurangzeb's wrath and returned to their former allegiance. In fact, they formed a coalition against Guru Gobind Singh and sought help from the emperor. Eventually, a long siege was laid to Anandpur. The Guru evacuated the place and made his way to Chamkaur where his two eldest sons died fighting. He defeated the Mughal troops at Khidrana (Muktsar). At Damdama he compiled the *Dasam Granth*. Aurangzeb summoned him once more but the emperor died while the Guru was on his way to the Deccan. Guru Gobind Singh accompanied Bahadur Shah to the Deccan but the allegation that he had accepted service with the emperor seemed to be groundless. He died at Nander after instructing his followers to look upon the *Granth* as their Guru incarnate and assuring them that he would himself be there wherever five Sikhs were assembled.[11]

Guru Gobind Singh did not live to see his high aims accomplished but his labours were not lost. He broke the charm of sanctity attached to the lord of Delhi and destroyed the awe and terror inspired by 'the Muslim tyranny'. He had seen what was still vital 'in the Hindu race' and relumed it with Promethean fire. He was the first Indian leader to teach democratical principles. The Khalsa were taught to regard themselves as the chosen of the Lord, destined to crush tyranny and oppression, and look upon themselves as the future rulers of the land.[12]

Commissioned by Guru Gobind Singh to carry on his work as a temporal leader, Banda Bahadur came to the Punjab and thousands of Jats flocked to him. He defeated Wazir Khan, the Mughal *faujdar* of Sirhind, and plundered the city. He appointed Sikh governors in the territories he conquered. He was 'now looked upon as the champion of Hinduism'. If Guru Gobind Singh breathed a new life into the Sikhs, Banda taught them how to fight and conquer. Banda's great success gave Sikhism 'a prestige and a power which had never been associated with it'. Banda failed, firstly because the Mughal state was still very strong and secondly because of his own conduct. He did not fully realize that Guru Gobind Singh had given Sikhism a distinct individuality. He tried to tamper with it and modify it in such a manner as to make it appear 'less sectarian and more nationalistic in its character'. The protection of the cow as an outstanding feature of Banda's mission had rallied the Hindus to his banner. In his opinion there was something 'exotic' in Sikhism which detracted from its value as a lever for uplifting the Hindus. 'Accordingly he tried to give it a more decidedly Hinduistic tone by altering some of its distinctive institutions'. Furthermore, Banda did not fully understand the democratic character of Sikhism. He failed to carry the entire body of the Khalsa with him. Banda's promising career was cut short by his sacerdotal ambition and incomprehension of the true nature of Sikhism as much as by Farrukh Siyar's persecutory measures and the machinations of the Mughal administrators.[13]

There are three appendices in Narang's book: one on the Sikh scriptures, another on whether or not Sikhism was a syncretic creed, and the third on the distinctive features of Sikhism. Turning to these appendices we find that the main body of the *Adi Granth,* in his view, was composed in Hindi, and the tone of the whole compilation was Hindu in all its details. The constitution of the *Granth* appeared to resemble that of the *Rigveda*. The *Dasam Granth* did not command much respect among cultured Sikhs who looked upon most of its contents as spurious. Its poetic and literary merit, however, was very great and some of its parts deserved the highest place in the ranks of Hindi poetry of the narrative and epic kind. The book served as an index to the part played by Hindu theology, mythology, philosophy, history and literature in the life and activities of Guru Gobind Singh. Like the *Adi Granth,* the *Dasam Granth* was written in Gurmukhi but in other respects there was a radical difference between them. Just as Guru Gobind Singh set a sort of new dispensation in religion, so he struck a new line in poetry, so much so that he did not use 'Nanak' in his compositions.[14]

Narang thought it necessary to explode the widely prevailing myth that Sikhism was 'a mixture of Hinduism and Muhammadanism'. Islam had much to do with the advent of Sikhism but nothing to do with Sikh thought. Sikhism was 'the embodiment of Hindu reaction against Islam'. The method adopted by Guru Nanak and his followers, was 'to discard the vulnerable points, give up the rusty swords and battered armour of rotten beliefs and corrupted practices, and fight in the open field with flashing swords and thrice tempered steel of the theistic doctrines of vigorous, manly, moral and philosophical Hinduism'. Narang invokes the authority of Trumpp in support of his view. Islam had very little to do with the reformed system of Nanak. Though precipitated by Islam, Sikhism owed nothing to Islam. It was 'a phase of Hindu revival' and had retained 'all essential features of real Hinduism'.[15]

What distinguished Guru Nanak's doctrine from the 'vulgar Hinduism' of his times was the unity of the Supreme Being. The Hindus had borrowed the doctrine of divine incarnation from the Jains and no Hindu leader had the courage to question its correctness. Rama and Krishna had received the homage of everyone as Divine Beings. Guru Nanak boldly questioned their divinity and brought them down to the level of mortals; he declared that the Almighty who created and controlled the whole universe could not add anything to his greatness by assuming human shape to destroy the wretches like Ravana and Kansa. The next important point of difference between Sikhism and 'common Hinduism' was the absence of idol-worship among the Sikhs. But a strange kind of worship which Guru Nanak could not foresee was the worship of the *Granth*. A characteristic of Sikhism as founded by Guru Nanak was 'the utter disregard for form'. However, this beauty of Sikhism as a religious system was lost when Guru Gobind Singh 'felt himself forced by circumstances' to turn Sikhism into a political weapon. The fourth and the last special feature of Sikhism was the doctrine of *Nam*. Though borrowed from Vaishnavism, it was given the foremost position. These four points distinguished Sikhism from the 'other Hindu sects'. In the social polity of the Sikhs and the Hindus, there was not much difference. But the Sikhs were not strict in the observance of caste restrictions in eating and drinking and in matrimonial affairs. Except in theory, Sikhism was not a proselytising religion. The festivals of the Sikhs were the same as those observed by the Hindus. 'The chief peculiarity of the Sikh, however, lies in his soldierly habits and qualifications'.[16]

The foregoing paragraphs reveal three major features of Narang's treatment of the Sikh movement. In the first place, it was a Hindu movement. Guru Nanak was a 'Hindu hero' whose mission was to leaven 'the whole Hindu thought'. The Sikhs formed a new brotherhood but only as an 'advance guard' of the Hindus. Guru Tegh Bahadur was 'a champion of the Hindus'. His martyrdom was for their sake. Guru Gobind Singh's purpose was 'to infuse a new life into the dead bones of Hindus' to make them 'a living nation'. His objective was to enable the Hindus 'to regain their lost independence'. Banda Bahadur taught the Hindus how to conquer and rule. He tried to make Sikhism 'less sectarian and more nationalistic' in its character. Here, the word 'sectarian' is used for the Sikh Panth and 'nationalistic' for the Hindu nation. Narang leaves no doubt that the Sikhs represented a Hindu sectarian dispensation.

However, Narang had greater appreciation for the Sikhs than for the other Hindu sects of medieval India. He looked upon the Sikhs as prototypes of the Arya Samajists. For Narang, Sikhism was not influenced by Islam in any way; it was a 'Hindu revival', with all the essential features of 'real Hinduism'. The idea of incarnation had entered Hinduism from the Jains and the practice of idol-worship had come from the Buddhists. Guru Nanak had the unique courage to discard both of these. The early Sikh movement had shown utter disregard for form. The *Adi Granth* was comparable in some ways with the *Rigveda*. The this-worldly orientation of Sikhism, including politics, distinguished the Sikhs from the followers of other Hindu sects. The early Sikhs reminded Narang of 'their Aryan ancestors'. Though influenced by Hindu theology, mythology, history, and literature, Guru Gobind Singh did not have to invoke the goddess. His reliance was on the sword in his fight for independence.

Independence, obviously, meant the subversion of Mughal authority and Mughal rule. However, Narang prefers to talk of 'the Muslim government'. Guru Hargobind's objective was the 'destruction of Islam' as well as the destruction of 'the Muslim government'. Narang talks of 'Muslim tyranny'. Guru Har Rai came to Dara Shukoh's help because Dara was 'all but a Hindu'. Guru Tegh Bahadur's martyrdom stirred up 'the dying embers of Hindu hatred of the Muslim rule'.

III. SIKH POLITICAL ACHIEVEMENT

The 'process of transformation' did not end with the institution of the Khalsa or the death of Banda Bahadur. Narang talks of a long, life-and-death struggle of the Khalsa, and its ups and downs, till the establishment of the supremacy of the Khalsa in the Punjab. The process was completed in 1768 'when the Sikhs occupied Lahore'. Narang's comment on the result of the long struggle is not without significance:

> Thus in 1768 the Khalsa Commonwealth extended from the Jamuna to the Indus. The seed sown by Nanak had now, thanks to the talents of his successors, the great military genius of Govind and the unconquerable spirit of Banda, blossomed into a rich crop. The nation started with the rosary and ended by snatching the scepter from the oppressing hands of its tyrannical masters. The political organization of the Sikhs was now complete and the sovereignty of the Land of Five Waters had now completely passed to the children of the Khalsa.[17]

Narang goes on to give a brief account of the *misls* which ruled simultaneously in various parts of the Punjab to fill up the gap between the occupation of Lahore and 'Ranjit Singh's accession' to serve as a link between this volume and the intended 'second volume on Sikh history'.[18]

Narang looked upon Ranjit Singh as a common hero of Sikhs and Hindus. With no new fact at his disposal, he makes a general statement on Ranjit Singh which is far different from his image drawn by any of Narang's predecessors:

> Not only the Sikhs but the whole Hindu nation felt that in him the sun of Hindu glory had once more risen on the political horizon of India. They showered upon him their heartiest blessings. They looked upon him as their

> liberator and their protector, one who after centuries of barbarious attacks from the North, hurled back the invaders and raiders to their mountain lairs. They bestowed their unstinted love and affection on him and reversed him as a God-sent guardian of their hearths and upholder of their national honour.

The author approvingly quotes one of his aunts as having remarked that 'the Maharaja was an Avtarji, gifted with miraculous powers'. Even around 1900, the hearts of the Hindus turned to Ranjit Singh 'as a national hero'.[19]

The successors of Ranjit Singh were small men, 'sadly lacking in political sense'. The Sikh soldiers were illiterate peasants with no sense of patriotism. There leaders were selfish or cowardly, devoid of national spirit. 'Like rats deserting a sinking ship they slank away to save their own skins.'[20] The decade after Ranjit Singh's death is treated by Narang as 'after him the deluge'.

Significantly, Narang talks about the Namdharis, but only in a few pages. The original movement was 'purely religious' but with its increasing influence over a large number of people the protagonists of the movement began to preach the revival of Khalsa Raj and the ouster of the British. Narang appears to approve of 'Guru Partap Singh' who kept the Namdharis aloof from political agitation in connection with the linguistic controversy and the demand for a Punjabi-speaking state, and under whose guidance the Namdharis remained loyal to the government and cooperated with the authorities.[21]

For the history of the Sikhs from 1849 to 1946, Narang dwells on the theme of loyalty. The British were hostile to the Sikhs till 1857 when, on an appeal from the rulers, the Sikhs came to their rescue and performed great service in a difficult situation. They became famous for loyalty and, therefore, special favourites of the British government. In 1913, however, the issue of the Gurdwara Rakab Ganj gave a serious jolt to Sikh attitude. The relations of the Sikhs deteriorated further over the issue of Gurdwara Reform. The Akalis triumphed but the relations between the Sikhs and the British became strained. The British trust in Sikh loyalty was shaken. The strength of the Sikhs in the Indian army was reduced. With the Second World War, however, the relations between the Sikhs and the British improved and the government began to show favours to them.[22]

Narang responds to Jogendra Singh's remark in his Foreword to the second edition of Narang's book about the author's 'divided loyalties' by asserting: 'No such question can arise so far as the rule as a writer of history is concerned. As historian his first loyalty is to truth. He cannot play the part of an apostle either to one community or the other, nor suggest or institute any measure to promote or hinder any particular movement'. Narang still looked upon himself as a 'missionary of Hindu-Sikh unity'. Narang reiterates that the Hindus of the Punjab could 'never forget their obligation to Guru Nanak and his successors' who conveyed 'the ancient teachings to Hindu masses'. It may be noted that Narang acknowledges an old debt: in the present the Sikhs were no longer the vanguard of the Hindus.

In 1956, Narang talks of the Sikh struggle for 'Khalistan', the Regional Formula, the Akali agitation for a Punjabi-speaking state and the counter-agitation of the Hindus. He identifies himself completely with the Hindus who were opposed to the Akali demand for territorial reorganization of the state on linguistic basis. He looked upon this demand as anti-Hindu. He had no hesitation in asserting that the Sikhs had 'no political future as an independent community'. With no Sikh princely states, separate electorates or reservation of seats, they were a small minority completely dependent on the central government. The only sound option for them was to remain 'on the right side of the central government'. The Akalis had done well to give up politics after their acceptance of the Regional Formula, and to confine their activities to educational, cultural, religious and economic matters.[23]

However, the constitutional provisions of the Regional Formula were never implemented and the Akalis reiterated their demand for a linguistic state. In 1960, Narang had no sympathy for this demand and underlined that there was no possibility of its being accepted by the government. Both the Chief Minister of the Punjab and the Prime Minister of India were strongly opposed to the demand. A deputation of the Arya Samajists and Sanatanists of the Punjab, headed by Virendra, editor of the *Daily Pratap*, had met Jawaharlal Nehru who made the categorical statement that 'under no circumstances the demand for a Punjabi Suba would be acceptable to the country'.[24] Narang remained pessimistic about the future of the Sikhs.

IV. RECENT ASSESSMENTS OF NARANG'S *TRANSFORMATION*

The first edition of Gokul Chand Narang's *Transformation of Sikhism* appeared to Fauja Singh to be 'the best from the angle of historical discipline'. The later additions can be seen as 'a journalistic exercise' or as 'a piece of political writing rather than a writing of history'. Even the work published in 1912, which is the best is 'an interpretation rather than a detailed analytical work'. Furthermore, the interpretation does not flow from the historical data. It appears to spring essentially from 'certain pre-conceived ideas and tendencies'. By far the most relevant tendency was the upsurge of 'religious nationalism'. In Narang's work it appears as 'Hindu nationalism'.[25]

In a recent article, K.L. Tuteja has taken note of Gokul Chand Narang's *Transformation of Sikhism*.[26] The purpose of his article is two-fold: (a) to examine how Narang's ideological framework was deeply infused with Hindu consciousness, and shaped his approach to Sikh history and (b) to show that a section of Hindu intelligentsia made a selective use of historical consciousness to consolidate Hindu identity, and projected Muslims as 'the other'.[27]

According to Tuteja, Narang represented a liberal-bourgeios position with a strong Hindu orientation given by the Hindu resurgence under colonial rule. The Brahmo Samaj was the first organization to aim at reconstructing Hindu religious identity in support of the aspirations and goals of the newly-educated middle classes. The Arya Samaj aimed at purging Hinduism of all those elements which appeared to be retrogressive and irrational. A section of the Arya Samajists ultimately became the carriers of Hindu consciousness in the early twentieth century. Narang belonged to this section of Hindu society in the Punjab. He believed in the glorious past of the Hindus as a monolithic entity and looked upon Islam as barbaric and destructive. Tuteja goes on to add that Narang consciously adopted a Hinduized communal framework, with Muslims as the opponents, for his study of the Sikhs. The relations between the Arya Samajists and the Sikh reformers who claimed independent identity for themselves, were not exactly amicable but he looked upon the Sikhs as Hindu because the founder of Sikhism was a born Hindu.[28] We know, however, that Narang regarded the whole Sikh movement as Hindu.

In his analysis of Narang's work, Tuteja refers to his contention that Guru Nanak was concerned with revitalizing the contemporary Hindu society which had degenerated largely due to the onslaught of Islam. He tried to 'emancipate the Hindu mind from the fetters of mythology'. Guru Nanak owed his success to a 'non-sectarian' approach and rejection of the path of renunciation. He did not want to cut himself off from the Hindu community. However, his successors developed institutions and attitudes which led the Sikhs to view themselves as a different religious community by the time of Guru Arjan. By the early eighteenth century the Sikhs appeared to have constituted a community with a distinct set of beliefs and practices. They remained nonetheless an offshoot of the 'Hindu race'. Narang looked upon the 'Tat Khalsa' of the early twentieth century as 'separatist' but he was more concerned with Muslims as the 'other'.[29] Tuteja appears to minimize the importance of Narang's assumption that the Sikhs were Hindu.

According to Tuteja, Narang constructed his whole account of the origin and growth of Sikhism by juxtaposing Islam in its political form as the opponent. The emergence of Sikhism in the Punjab was closely related to the threat posed by Islam as a 'religion of the sword'. The Hindus were left with the option to accept Islam or face death. Islam led to the birth of Sikhism, but Sikhism did not have any element of Islam. Narang projects the Sikh Gurus essentially as fighting the cause of the Hindus. Guru Tegh Bahadur was an obstacle in the way of Aurangzeb's coercive policy as an acknowledged head of Punjab Hindus. Guru Gobind Singh was a 'defender of Hindus', like Shivaji.[30] However, this projection is not meant simply to show that the Muslims represented the 'other'.

Tuteja points out that Narang's treatment of Sikh history had serious flaws. In his presentation of Islam he totally ignores the role of the Sufis and their influence on the people of India. Islam was not insignificant in terms of its imprint on the thought of Guru Nanak either. Narang equates Islam with the Mughal empire. It is difficult to accept his contention that the Sikh Gurus were motivated by the desire to oppose Islam and to safeguard Hindus from 'the tyranny of Muslim rule'. In order to show that Narang's interpretation of the Sikh movement was seriously flawed, Tuteja largely uses the works of Harjot Oberoi, W.H. McLeod, J.S. Grewal and Richard M. Eaton.[31] The flaws in Narang's work are the outcome of his assumptions and approach.

Tuteja comes to the conclusion that Narang's work, on the whole, represents a curious example of Hinduized consciousness that was fast gaining strength in north India at the turn of the twentieth century. The Sikh past is presented by Narang with a Hinduized perspective positing Hindu-Muslim divide as a central aspect of Indian society, past and present. His work differs not only from the Singh Sabha view of the Sikh past but also from the writings which offered 'a nationalist perspective on the Sikh past'.[32]

For 'nationalist' writings, Tuteja refers to Himadri Banerjee's *The Other Sikhs: A View from Eastern India* which relates to the work of historians but more to the work of poets, playwrights, litterateurs and others concerning Sikh history and religion. For both historical and non-historical literary works, Banerjee uses the term 'Sikh studies'. For a comparison with Gokul Chand Narang, we can think only of historical literature. Banerjee himself postulates a difference between the works of history in regional languages and English in terms of methodology and the use of sources. Thus, Narang remains comparable only to the historians of the Sikhs writing in English, like Indubhushan Banerjee, N.K. Sinha, Niharranjan Ray and A.C. Banerjee. All of them are academic or professional historians. Only N.K. Sinha is isolated by Banerjee as a 'nationalist' historian.[33] But an apt comparison of Narang can be with Indubhushan Banerjee who has been shown to be a 'Hindu nationalist' in a well-argued article by Indu Banga.[34] Indeed, whereas Indubhushan Banerjee makes Guru Nanak an advanced Vaishnava, Narang makes Guru Nanak's reform a prototype of the reform advocated by the Arya Samaj. Both Banerjee and Narang tried to appropriate the Sikh past for the purposes of 'Hindu nationalism'.

NOTES

1. Gokul Chand Narang, *Transformation of Sikhism,* New Delhi: Kalayani Publishers, 1989 (rpt. of 5th edn.), Preface to the First Edition, pp. 12-13.
2. Ibid., pp. 17-26.
3. Ibid., pp. 27-33.

4. Ibid., pp. 34-9.
5. Ibid., pp. 40-5.
6. Ibid., pp. 46-59.
7. Ibid., pp. 60-5.
8. Ibid., pp. 66-72.
9. Ibid., pp. 73-8.
10. Ibid., pp. 79-87.
11. Ibid., pp. 88-98.
12. Ibid., p. 98.
13. Ibid., pp. 99-114.
14. Ibid., pp. 243-8.
15. Ibid., pp. 249-55.
16. Ibid., pp. 257-62.
17. Ibid., p. 44.
18. Ibid., preface to the first edition.
19. Ibid., p. 177.
20. Ibid., p. 187.
21. Ibid., pp. 188-9.
22. Ibid., pp. 191-7.
23. Ibid., p. 242.
24. Ibid., p. 235.
25. Fauja Singh, 'Gokul Chand Narang', *Historians and Historiography of the Sikhs*, pp. 283, 285, 287-8.
26. K.L. Tuteja, 'Interpreting Sikh History: A Study of Gokul Chand Narang's *The Transformation of Sikhism*', in *Historical Diversities: Society, Politics and Culture,* ed. K.L. Tuteja and Sunita Pathania, New Delhi: Manohar, 2008, pp. 401-2. Narang's thesis was submitted to the Oxford University but not approved for the award of the Ph.D. degree. Narang succeeded in securing the degree from one of the universities in Switzerland.
27. Tuteja, 'Interpreting Sikh History', pp. 403-4.
28. Ibid., pp. 403-8.
29. Ibid., pp. 408-14.
30. Ibid., pp. 414-18.
31. Ibid., pp. 418-23.
32. Ibid., pp. 423-5.
33. Himadri Banerjee, *The Other Sikhs: A View from Eastern India,* New Delhi: Manohar, 2003, particularly pp. 21, 227, 231, 235-7.
34. Indu Banga, 'In the Service of Hindu Nationalism: Banerjee's Evolution', *The Khalsa: Sikh and non-Sikh Perspectives,* ed. J.S. Grewal, New Delhi: Manohar, 2004, pp. 187-200.

CHAPTER FIFTEEN

Hari Ram Gupta on the Eighteenth-Century Sikhs

Hari Ram Gupta published his doctoral thesis in 1939 as *History of the Sikhs,* covering the period from 1739 to 1768 and the area between the Indus and the Jamuna. It was followed by two more volumes in 1944: one on the Sikh chiefs of the cis-Sutlej area and the other on the Sikh chiefs of the trans-Sutlej area, from 1769 to 1799. All the three volumes were published in 1952 as *A History of the Sikhs* in three volumes in a more or less revised form. All the three volumes reveal his concern for contemporary evidence in Persian, English, Gurmukhi, and Marathi sources, and his interest in factual detail. We may take up these three volumes one by one in order to form a fair idea of Gupta's treatment of Sikh history during the eighteenth century.

I. RISE OF SIKH *MISLS* TO POLITICAL POWER: 1739-1768

Hari Ram Gupta's *History of the Sikhs* was dedicated to 'the brave and noble Sikh heroes of the mid-eighteenth century through whose valour, resourcefulness and cheerful endurance a grave peril threatening the country was averted'. Gupta, thus, appreciates the political success of the Sikhs against the Afghans under Ahmad Shah Abdali in the context of Indian history. Jadunath Sarkar appreciated Gupta's doctoral work as 'a model to other workers on Indian history'. One period of the history of the Punjab, and that of the Delhi empire too, had been 'set up on a granite foundation'. Gupta had 'left no source untapped' and he had 'taken nothing without a critical examination'. The strong features of Gupta's work were his 'erudition' and the reliability of his narrative'.[1] There is no reason to disagree with Jadunath Sarkar, but in the light of later research by a number of scholars it is possible to see some limitations of Gupta's work.

In his preface to the first volume, Gupta says that the period of Sikh history from 1716 to 1799 had not received the attention it deserved. It was during this period that the genius and ambition of the Sikhs enabled them to carve out 'independent principalities on the ashes of the Mughal Empire'. They played the most important part in the politics of northern India from 1739 to 1799 and rendered 'the most invaluable services to the cause of our country by putting a dead stop to all foreign invasions from the north-west'. The importance of this period induced Gupta to take it up for study. However, for the years 1716-38 the material available was very scanty. In fact, there was no contemporary evidence on record. Also, the year 1739 was marked by the invasion of India by Nadir Shah (the first invasion after more than two centuries) which induced the Hindu peasantry of the Punjab to join the ranks of the Khalsa, the only people who could offer stout opposition to their oppressors. Their struggle became 'a fight for the ideal of independence and sovereignty'. By 1768, they had established themselves as 'a political and territorial power'.[2]

The period from 1739 to 1768 is covered in 17 chapters. The last two relate to 'the life and manners' of the Sikhs and 'the condition' of the country. The remaining 15 chapters relate to political history. The first two decades of this period are seen in six phases: 1739-45, 1745-8, 1748-53, 1753-7, 1757-8, and 1758-9. Each of these phases marked the progress of the Khalsa towards political power. What helped them in this process were the foreign invasions with all their political and economic implications, and 'the intrinsic worth of the Sikhs': their firm and high hopes, and their power of resistance and tenacity of purpose.[3]

During the five months of 1739 when Nadir Shah was in India, the Sikhs constructed a small mud fort at Dallewal and laid under contribution the neighbouring countryside in the upper Bari Doab. They organized a number of light cavalry bands and plundered Nadir Shah's flanks on his return from Delhi in May. Nadir Shah warned the governor of Lahore, Zakariya Khan, against 'these rebels' who were most likely to raise their head. Zakariya Khan razed their fort to the ground, and killed many of them. The entire official machinery was set in motion, and the *chaudharis* and *muqaddams* were obliged to cooperate in an all-out effort to suppress the Sikhs. Due to persecution, the Sikhs left the Punjab plains to seek shelter elsewhere. Zakariya Khan died on 1 July 1745. His sons, Yahiya Khan and Shahnawaz Khan, were both keen to succeed to his position. The Sikhs got the respite to strengthen themselves. They formed *deras* in open defiance of the ruling authority. Gupta quotes Anand Ram Mukhlis who was present in the Punjab on 13 August 1746 to the effect that disorder was raging throughout the province of Lahore due to the activity of 'lawless men, plunderers and adventurers'. The Sikhs had divided themselves into 25 groups of about 100 persons each in October 1745 when they visited Amritsar at the time of Diwali. This organization into regular bands was 'a significant starting point in the military career of the Sikhs'.[4]

Enlarged and developed further, this organization formed the basis of 'the first regularly organized national army of the community, popularly known as Dal Khalsa'.[5] In March 1746, the Sikhs killed Jaspat Rai, the *faujdar* of Eminabad, and his brother, Diwan Lakhpat Rai, retaliated by killing thousands of Sikhs in a single campaign in April-June. The massacre is known as *ghallughara*. About five months later, Shahnawaz Khan, who was in charge of the province of Multan, advanced upon Lahore to oust his brother, Yahiya Khan. In March 1747, he made Yahiya Khan captive. Meanwhile, 'the Sikh bands sallied out of Amritsar and fell upon the Bari and Rachna Doabs'. At the time of Baisakhi in 1747 they assembled at Amritsar and built a fort called 'Ram Rauni' (God's shelter). Without any hope of approval of his usurpation from Delhi, Shahnawaz Khan invited Ahmad Shah Abdali, who had succeeded Nadir Shah in Kandhar and Kubul after his murder on 9 June 1747, with the title of Durrani. However, Shahnawaz did not submit to Ahmad Shah Abdali when he approached Lahore. Unable to oppose Ahmad Shah, he fled to Delhi. Ahmad Shah marched towards Delhi but he was defeated by the Mughal army in the battle of Manupur, near Sirhind. The Sikhs plundered the rear of Ahmad Shah Abdali on his return to Kabul in March 1748. They met at Amritsar on 30 March, and formed the Dal Khalsa, uniting the whole body of the fighting Sikhs as a national army. As many as 65 units were combined to form eleven larger units, and Jassa Singh Ahluwalia was chosen as the commander of the Dal Khalsa to offer a bold front to the enemy, or to undertake a predatory enterprise. A kind of federal union was established, with the leader of the Dal Khalsa as 'the head of the Church and State'. This proved to be a step of the greatest significance in the history of the Sikhs.[6]

The Mughal emperor appointed Muin-ul-Mulk as the governor of Lahore. Reaching Lahore in April 1748, he started sending punitive expeditions against the Sikhs. The siege of Ram Rauni in October 1748 was raised in February 1749 due to Diwan Kaura Mal's intercession and one-fourth of the revenues of *pargana* Patti was assigned to the Khalsa as the condition of peace. They remained peaceful for the rest of the year. During the second invasion of Ahmad Shah Abdali in December 1749-February 1750, they plundered the suburbs of Lahore. Muin-ul-Mulk renewed persecutory measures against the Sikhs in March 1750. Faced with the revolt of Shahnawaz Khan, he sought support from the Sikhs and after his defeat and death he gave a *jagir* worth Rs. 1 lakh to the Sikhs in appreciation of their services. However, he remained wary of them and renewed his policy of repression in 1751. They were driven out of the Punjab. During the third invasion of Ahmad Shah in December 1751-March 1752, Muin-ul-Mulk was obliged to submit to him. By the terms suggested by Ahmad Shah and accepted eventually by the Mughal emperor, the Punjab and Multan were lost to the Mughal empire. During these months the Sikhs spread their depredations over a wider area, acquired a lot of rich booty and gained large numbers of fresh recruits. Appointed as the governor of Lahore by Ahmad Shah Abdali, Muin-ul-Mulk persecuted the Sikhs with a greater vigour and persistence till his death on 3 November 1753, but the Sikhs gained strength due to the increasing discontent among the peasantry. They were far from being suppressed despite the harshest measures against them.[7]

From the death of Muin-ul-Mulk in November 1753 to the invasion of Ahmad Shah Abdali in April 1757, the Sikhs remained unhampered due to factional tussle for power at Lahore between the widow of Muin-ul-Mulk, called Mughlani Begam, and others, resulting in rebellions and weakening of administration. The Sikhs were active in the Bari, Rachna and Jalandhar Doabs, and in the cis-Sutlej area under the leadership of Jassa Singh Ahluwalia, Charhat Singh, and Jai Singh. They established the 'Rakhi' system which led them to 'the final stage of their becoming a political power'. By paying one-fifth of their income twice a year, the villagers could come under the protection of the Dal Khalsa against all others. During the fourth invasion of Ahmad Shah Abdali in November 1756-April 1757, the Sikhs attacked his army several times between Delhi and the river Chenab. In retaliation, Ahmad Shah pulled down the sacred buildings of the Sikhs at Amritsar, and filled the tank with dirt and refuse. Before returning to Kabul, he appointed his son Timur Shah as the governor of Lahore, with his commander-in-chief Jahan Khan to assist the prince.[8]

Jahan Khan tried to suppress the Sikhs. They were forced to seek shelter in the hills and in the desert of Malwa. About 5,000 Sikhs under the leadership of Deep Singh reached Amritsar to celebrate the Diwali of 1757. Jahan Khan marched against Amritsar and he was attacked by the Sikhs. He would have been defeated if Haji Atai Khan had not arrived in time to his support. Their joint forces defeated the Sikhs and they retreated to Amritsar. The Afghans attacked the city. Deep Singh and five *jathedars* lost their lives, with a large number of other Sikhs, in defence of the holy place. Jahan Khan destroyed and polluted all the places of worship and filled up the tank at Amritsar. Another victim of Jahan Khan's wrath was Sodhi Badbhag Singh of Kartarpur. The Sikh temple at Kartarpur was destroyed and polluted, and all women were converted to Islam. Gupta quotes Miskin to the effect that the peace and orderly rule established recently in the country now disappeared and 'the Sikhs rose in rebellion on all sides'. In concert with Adina Beg Khan, they defeated the Afghans in December 1757. Adina Beg Khan invited the Marathas and they welcomed the opportunity to extend their influence to the Punjab. In April 1758, the Afghans were expelled from the Punjab jointly by the Marathas and the Sikhs. Raghunath Rao decided to place the Punjab under Adina Beg Khan for Rs. 75,00,000 a year. Gupta does not subscribe to the idea that the Sikhs occupied Lahore in 1758 or that a coin was struck in the name of Jassa Singh 'Kalal'.[9]

From June 1758 to October 1759, the Sikhs began to acquire territories. Adina Beg Khan died on 15 September 1758, without curbing the Sikhs. Dattaji Sindhia came up to the Sutlej in April 1759 and sent Sabaji to Lahore where the Sikhs were 'predominant and commanded a vast force'. Sabaji defeated Jahan Khan with the help of the Sikhs. In October 1759, Jahan Khan crossed the Indus with a much large force, and the Marathas retreated before him. However, the Sikhs 'did not fail in their national duty, which the Marathas had so disgracefully shirked'. They fought a battle with Ahmad Shah Abdali in which 2,000 Afghan troops were slain and Jahan Khan was wounded. Gupta places the establishment of a feudal system under the *misls* in 1758-9. A new 'self-formed aristocracy' came into existence. The possessions of the Sikhs at this time covered the major portion of the Jalandhar Doab and the northern parts of the Bari Doab.[10]

At this point, Gupta takes up the 'peaceful progress of Malwa Sikhs' under Ala Singh from 1739 to 1761. The Sikhs of the Malwa pursued 'a different line of action', always adopting a diplomatic tone and never defying the government of the day openly. They had received grants of land, founded villages, and become wealthy. In the early eighteenth century, they began to increase their power and territory. Their acknowledged head was the Phulkian house. Besides Ala Singh, Gupta refers to the families of Bhadaur, Nabha, Jind, Malaud, Badrukhan, Jiundan, Dayalpura, Laudgharia, Rampur, and Kot Duna. The house of Faridkot was more distantly connected. Ala Singh had succeeded Rama in 1714 in 'the lordship of a few villages'. In 1723, the number of villages under him was 30. He supported the imperial army against Ahmad Shah Abdali and won approbation of the Crown Prince. During the next ten years he extended his territory. In 1758 he helped the Mughal emperor with food and fodder. Before the end of the year, however, he conquered Sunam which was in the imperial domain. In 1759 he came into conflict with the governor of Sirhind. In March 1761, he became a formal tributary of Ahmad Shah Abdali as a vassal chief with autonomous control over 726 towns and villages. The Dal Khalsa was annoyed with Ala Singh for his submission to Ahmad Shah but Jassa Singh Ahluwalia pacified the other leaders by imposing a fine on Ala Singh.[11]

From October 1759 to January 1761, Ahmad Shah Abdali was occupied with the Marathas. Their activity in the Punjab had enraged him and he had resolved to settle the score with the Marathas once for all. Finally, on 14 January 1761 the Marathas were defeated at Panipat and most of them were massacred. They would come to Delhi ten years later but only to find that the Sikhs were too securely established to be ousted. The Sikhs had to contend with only the Durranis now. They had built forts in Ahmad Shah Abdali's absence from the Punjab, attacked Lahore in November 1760, and got a tribute of Rs. 30,000. They harassed the retreating Durranis in April-May 1761. They spread havoc over the Punjab in June-July, ousting the Afghan administrators of the Jalandhar Doab and plundering Malerkotla. Ahmad Shah Abdali's General, Nuruddin, was defeated in August, and Khawaja Abed, the Afghan governor of Lahore, in September 1761. In November, the Sikhs captured Lahore and coined money in the name of 'Jassa Kalal'. Gupta discusses the issue of the coin at some length to refute the arguments of N.K. Sinha.[12]

Gupta devotes a whole chapter to the 'Ghallughara and after'. In January 1762, the Sikhs had besieged Jandiala which was held by the supporters of Ahmad Shah Abdali. He arrived at Jandiala and pursued the Sikhs who were encamping now at Kup near Malerkotla, numbering about 50,000, including non-combatants. Jassa Singh Ahluwalia and Charhat Singh organized the defence. A running fight went on the whole day on 5 February 1762, and about 12,000 Sikhs lost their lives. Ala Singh was taken prisoner and paid Rs. 5,00,000 as ransom. Ahmad Shah destroyed the sacred buildings of the Sikhs at Amritsar. He stayed in the Punjab for the rest of the year, and re-conquered Kashmir. However, the Sikhs were not demoralized. They attacked Zain Khan, the Afghan governor of Sirhind, in May 1762, and he paid Rs. 50,000. In August, the Sikhs visited Amritsar, and ravaged the neighbourhood of Lahore. Their tactics frustrated Ahmad Shah Abdali. He fought an indecisive battle with the Sikhs near Amritsar in October and retreated to Lahore. He led an expedition against them in November across the Sutlej, which produced no result. In December 1762 he decided to return to Kabul, leaving Kabuli Mal as his governor at Lahore. The Sikhs frightened Kabuli Mal and replanted their military post at Lahore.[13]

Within a year, then, the Sikhs conquered the Sirhind territory. They attended to the work of reconstruction at Amritsar. In May 1763, they sacked Kasur and collected rich booty. In June, they ran over the Jalandhar Doab. In November, they defeated Jahan Khan who had been sent against them. In December, they attacked Malerkotla and killed

Bhikhan Khan, the chief support of Ahmad Shah Abdali in 1762. The Sikhs plundered Morinda early in January 1764, and massacred the Ranghars whose ancestors had captured the younger sons of Guru Gobind Singh. Finally, on 14 January 1764, they attacked Sirhind, killed Zain Khan, and occupied all the territories of Sirhind. Gupta does not fail to mention that they erected a platform at the spot where the younger sons of Guru Gobind Singh had been bricked up alive. A *granthi* was appointed for the gurdwara built there. It was named Fatehgarh.[14]

Gupta mentions the territories of over 32 Sikh chiefs in the cis-Sutlej region in 1764. Rai Kalha at Raikot, and the Afghans at Kunjpura, Malerkotla, Mamdot, and Kotla Nihang were the only non-Sikh chiefs in the plains of the cis-Sutlej.[15] Gupta talks of the Sikh 'ravages' in the Punjab and the Gangetic Doab in February 1764 to January 1765. As a result they extended their domains, subjugated pockets adjacent to their possessions, defeated some Afghan functionaries, and collected booty through plunder. They formed an alliance with the Jats of Bharatpur against Najib-ud-Daulah. Thus, they were fighting on all sides to increase their power and resources.[16]

The year 1765 was remarkable for the fact that the Sikhs issued coins from Lahore as a mark of their sovereignty. Ahmad Shah Abdali had tried hard in 1764-5 to crush the Sikhs but without any success. After his departure from the Punjab, they met at Amritsar at the time of Baisakhi and decided to occupy their old territories and to acquire new ones. Gujar Singh Bhangi, Lahna Singh, and Sobha Singh divided the city of Lahore and its neighbourhood among themselves. Charhat Singh arrived late and asked for a share in the spoils; he got the Zamzama gun. A coin was struck on 16 May in the name of the Gurus. Gupta thinks that this coin was called 'Gobindshahi'. The term 'Nanakshahi' came into use later in May-July 1765. The Sikhs extended their territories in all the four Doabs between the Beas and the Indus.[16]

For nine months then the Sikhs tried to extend their influence towards the Gangetic Doab and Delhi. In October 1765, they marched against Najib-ud-Daulah and fought an indecisive battle near Shamli, 12 miles east of Karnal. They marched towards Delhi. The Jat Raja of Bharatpur, Jawahir Singh, submitted to them, paid Rs. 7,00,000 and hired 25,000 of their horse to fight the Marathas. The Sikh leaders and Jawahir Singh plundered Rewari and sacked Kot Putli, a possession of Raja Madho Singh of Jaipur. The combined forces of Sikhs and Jats defeated the Marathas near Dholpur in March 1766, and Jawahir Singh occupied Dholpur. In April, the Sikhs plundered the country of Najib-ud-Daulah east of the Jamuna. Hard pressed by him, they crossed the Jamuna and plundered his districts on this side.[17] It appears that Gupta had collected this information and given it to the readers without bothering much about its contextual significance.

Gupta presents the events of the period from June 1766 to December 1768 as 'triumphant emergence of the Sikhs'. He refers to two expeditions in 1766: one, led by the Nakkai chief Hira Singh against Pakpattan and the other, led by the Bhangi chiefs against Multan. Hira Singh was killed in a battle, but Jhanda Singh and Ganda Singh Bhangi captured Pakpattan. Then they marched upon Multan but failed to capture it. Towards the end of the year, Ahmad Shah Abdali crossed the Indus and reached Lahore on 22 December. After a week he left for Sirhind. The Sikhs plundered his baggage. In a battle near Amritsar, Jahan Khan was defeated by the Sikhs. Ahmad Shah pursued the Sikhs in all directions, but they avoided open engagement. Raja Amar Singh of Patiala received the title of Raja-i Rajgan from Ahmad Shah Abdali at Sirhind. Ahmad Shah went to Lahore on his way back to Kabul. The Sikhs again spread all over the country and occupied their old possessions. In 1767, the Sikhs were trying to extend their possessions to the Sind Sagar and the Gangetic Doabs. They defeated Najib-ud-Daulah in March and December 1768. The major portion of the Punjab, from the right bank of the Jamuna to the left bank of the Indus, and from the neighbourhood of Multan and Sind to the foot of the Shiwaliks, came under their direct control. They triumphed over three external enemies of theirs: the Mughal governors at Lahore, Ahmad Shah Abdali, and his greatest lieutenant Najib-ud-Daulah in Delhi. They owed their triumph to 'the tenacity of purpose and resourcefulness of mind'. They placed themselves at the head of 'the nation', and showed themselves as protectors of 'the rights of the people'. The tide of foreign aggression which had run its course for 800 years was turned back. To them the people of northern Indian in general, and of the Punjab in particular, 'owe a deep debt of gratitude'. Amritsar played a crucial role in the achievement of the Sikhs. To them, Amritsar was 'a symbol of their mother country as well as their religion'.[18]

The last chapter in *History of the Sikhs* is divided into two sections (which appear as separate chapters in the table of contents): 'Life and Manners of the Sikhs' and 'The Condition of the Country'. The first relates to the Sikhs alone and the second, to all the people of the Punjab. In both, Gupta tries to put the information available in his sources under heads which appeared to be relevant for the themes. In the first section, the number of such heads is 15 and in the second 12. It is possible to co-relate a number of them to a few major themes, but Gupta does not try to do that. In the first section, the heads mentioned are physique, disposition, character, recruitment, drill and discipline, modes of payment, equipment, method of warfare, raids, horses, food, dress, amusements, women, and fairs. Ten of these heads relate to the army, three relate to individual traits, and one each to gender and a religious activity.

The heads for 'the condition of the people' given by Gupta are: anarchy and confusion, character of the people, the village, the villages measures of defence, village functionaries, the *panchayat*, education, modes of irrigation, poverty of the people, fairs, trade, and the Sikh rule. Four of these heads may be seen as related to village communities, three to the people, two each to politics and economy, and one to intellectual culture. If we were to think of the broad rubrics to which all the 27 heads get related, we could think of polity, economy, society and culture. Thus, the scope of the chapter is in a sense quite wide, but the information even on each broad rubric does not amount to very much. We may notice what Gupta has to say about the Sikhs.

Under 'the Sikh rule', Gupta points out that in 1768 the administration was being set up. The end of foreign invasion was 'a blessing' for the people. The Sikhs now established 'a kind of feudal government' under twelve big chiefs who had under them a number of minor *sardars*. Villages were assigned to them. Each chief was independent. The Akalis were in charge of the Harmandar and managed ecclesiastical affairs, without interfering with the authority of the chiefs. The chief enjoyed 'absolute' power in theory but his rule was mild. The assessment of land was very lenient. Whether a landowner or a tenant, the actual occupant of the land paid the revenue. The social structure of the village was left unchanged. The situation with regard to trade also did not change. Heavy duties had to be paid by traders passing through the territories of various chiefs. For education, there were Gurmukhi schools.[20]

Gupta gives the largest space to the army. For recruitment, no consideration was paid to the original caste or creed of the person. Enlistment was voluntary and the chief tried to keep the soldiers in good humour. There was no training in drill but the Sikhs were not wanting in war tactics. Their religious zeal, single-minded devotion to the Panth, an intense feeling of self-respect, and passion for revenge were great assets. They were allowed to retain a portion of the booty acquired. Land revenue was assigned to them in lieu of salary. Gupta describes their weapons, methods of warfare, their love for horses, their food, their dress, and their amusements. His Sikhs are largely the politically and militarily active Khalsa. They enjoyed good physique, and they were unusually independent in their attitudes. They were brave and honourable, cheerful and open, sociable and upright; they adapted themselves to all circumstances, and they possessed enough vigour of body and mind to meet all calamities with courage and perseverance. They subordinated their personal interest to the good of the Panth. They served their country of their own free will. A 'hero' in times of misfortune, the Sikh was a 'brother' in halcyon days. Gupta quotes Qazi Nur Muhammad at some length on the martial and moral traits of the Singhs.

The Sikh women were generally fine-looking, tall, and graceful. The girls were married at an early age. On festive occasions there was a good deal of ostentation. The Sikh women played no small part in the struggle for independence. The principal fairs of the Sikhs were the Diwali and the Baisakhi at Amritsar. Two large fairs were held at Tarn Taran too. Religious fairs were held at Goindwal, Khadur, Dera Baba Nanak, and other Sikh shrines.[21]

II. POLITICS OF THE CIS-SUTLEJ SIKH CHIEFS: 1769-1799

The first two chapters of the second volume relate to the political state of India and the position of the Sikhs in 1769. The next two chapters narrate Sikh activities against Jats, Mughals and Rohillas and the relations of the Sikhs with Zabita Khan Rohilla, covering the years from 1769 to 1779. In three chapters then Gupta takes up the campaigns of Abdul Ahad and Shafi against the Sikhs in 1779-81. Sikh activities in the Doab and Delhi from 1781 to 1783 are taken up in two chapters. These activities alarmed the British, a theme taken up in the tenth chapter. The Sikh-Maratha relations from 1785 to 1794 are discussed in three chapters. The last three chapters relate to Sikh devastation of the Doab in 1794-6, their clash with George Thomas and Perron in 1997-9, and the submission of the cis-Sutlej Sikh chiefs to Shah Zaman in 1997-9. The narrative does not remain well connected all the time because of lack of information. Gupta does not say so, but a certain pattern of political developments appears to emerge from the account he gives in several phases.

India in 1769 was in a state of disintegration and decay. The central government was paralysed and its provinces had become independent. There was the Durrani kingdom in the north with its capital at Kabul. The Sikhs were supreme in the Punjab. The Mughal emperor Shah Alam II was in Allahabad and Delhi, the imperial capital, was under the control of Najib-ud-Daulah as the plenipotentiary of Ahmad Shah Abdali. The Maratha chiefs still owed nominal allegiance to the Peshwa, with the exception of the Bhonsle of Nagpur who had declared his independence. After the death of Peshwa Madho Rao in 1772, the other Maratha chiefs became virtually independent: the Sindhia at Gwalior, the Gaekwar at Baroda, and the Holkar at Indore. The Jats had carved out a small kingdom in the close neighbourhood of Delhi with their capital at Bharatpur, but there was no strong man at the head of the State. Most of the Rajput chiefs were under Maratha domination. The most important among them were the chiefs of Jaipur, Marwar and Udaipur. The Rohillas too had several independent chieftains. The most important were three: Najib-ud-Daulah in Delhi, Hafiz Rahmat Khan with his headquarters at Etawah, and Ahmad Khan Bangash with his headquarters at Farrukhabad. Their power was on the decline. Nawab Shuja-ud-Daulah of Awadh was an ally of the English who had established their garrisons at Chunar and Allahabad; they were virtually the rulers of Bengal, Bihar and Orissa. The Nizam of Haidarabad was almost their permanent ally due to his fear of the Marathas and Haidar Ali of Mysore. The Nawab of Carnatic was a nominal ruler, having delivered up the revenues of his territories to the English at Madras. Gupta provides a general picture of the political powers in India and regrets that 'nobody thought of the country as a whole'. The Sikh chiefs of the cis-Sutlej fit into this general picture.[22]

There was 'no central government' in the Punjab. There was disunity among the Sikh chiefs and they fought among themselves. 'The national character of the Sikhs had greatly degenerated at this time'. They had become 'a gang of robbers' with the sword' as the only law. The lust for power led to corruption; conflicts of temper, ambition and avarice led to discord and dissension. Gupta refers to the military resources of the Sikh chiefs of the cis-Sutlej in terms of 6 *misls*: Bhangi, Dallewalia, Nishanwala, Karorasinghia, Shahid and Phulkian. He refers also to the resources of individual chiefs, with Sahib Singh at the top (4,500 horse and 1,500 foot) and Saundha Singh of Khanna at the bottom (225 horse and 75 foot). Gupta refers to the tenures of *pattidari, misldari, jagirdari* and *tabadari*. For the distribution of territories, he mentions 35 chiefs, indicating in most cases their affiliation to a *misl*, and their revenues in some cases. Some of the Sikh chiefs of the trans-Sutlej had their territories in the cis-Sutlej, like Jassa Singh Ahluwalia, Tara Singh Ghaiba, Khushal Singh Singhpuria, and Tara Singh Kakar. Then there were the non-Sikh chiefs: Rai Ilias of Raikot and the Afghan Nawab of Malerkotla, both in alliance with the Raja of Patiala, the Afghans of Kunjpura and Kotla Nihang, and the chief of Mamdot. Gupta's description, though quite detailed, is not complete but it leaves no doubt that the number of the centres of power in the cis-Sutlej was pretty large, and there was a great difference between the most powerful and the weakest chief. Most or many of the chiefs felt free to follow the dictates of their own interest or inclination. Gupta's use of the general term 'the Sikhs' for individual Sikh chiefs, or a few Sikh chiefs in combination, becomes a source of confusion. But this is a flaw that was from his sources.[23]

Gupta appreciated the Sikhs who, 'inspired by a sense of patriotism', had set themselves free from the political bondage after 'nearly eight hundred years of subjection and slavery to foreign rule'. After 1769, however, they were impelled by some other motives. They had to defend themselves against others to remain in power, to fight against them to enhance their political prestige, and to plunder the rich Doab and the Delhi province to increase their material resources. They had also to settle their disputes with the other Sikh chiefs. Gupta narrates Baghel Singh Karorsinghia's fight with Raja Amar Singh of Patiala in 1769. Najib-ud-Daulah died in October 1770 to be succeeded by his Zabita Khan in the upper Gengetic Doab. The Sikhs plundered the district of Panipat. In 1772, they defeated Mughal Ali Khan, the son of Asaf Jah Nizam-ul-Mulk of Haidarabad, who was appointed as the governor of Sirhind, even before he could reach Sirhind. In December 1773, the Sikhs invaded the Gangetic Doab and plundered the people. Karam Singh Shahid overran the territory of Zabita Khan. In January 1774, the Sikhs devastated Shahdara. The emperor sent *khil'ats* to the chiefs and offered revenues for the service of 10,000 men. This did not materialize. Abdul Ahd was appointed as the *faujdar* of Sirhind but he was defeated before he reached Karnal. The Sikhs were again hovering around Shahjahanabad. Mulla Rahimdad Khan Rohilla, who was appointed to Panipat, laid siege to Jind, the capital of Gajpat Singh. Amar Singh of Patiala, Hamir Singh of Nabha, and the *bhais* of Kaithal supported Gajpat Singh and the *mulla* was killed in a battle. The allied chiefs conquered Gohana, Hissar, Hansi and Rohtak. But they had to surrender these territories to Najaf Quli who was supported by the *wazir* of the Mughal empire. Gajpat Singh retained only seven villages. Thus, for five or six years the Sikh chiefs tried to increase their resources and power at the cost of the Rohillas and the Mughal territory but without much addition to their possessions.[24]

For about four years the Sikhs remained concerned with Zabita Khan who incited them to turn their attention to the crown lands. The Sikhs gathered near Karnal and divided their forces under Rai Singh Bhangi, Bhagat Singh Karorasinghia and Tara Singh Ghaiba. They crossed the Jamuna into the territory of Zabita Khan and subdued several places. At Ghausgarh Zabita Khan paid Rs. 50,000 to them and accompanied them to Delhi. In July 1775 they destroyed Paharganj and Jai Singhpura before recrossing the Jamuna. In March 1776, Zabita Khan and the Sikhs killed Abul Qasim Khan, Abdul Ahad Khan's brother, who was appointed as the *faujdar* of Saharanpur. In June 1776, the Sikh allies of Zabita Khan extended their activity up to Aligarh. In October and November, they created disturbance near Delhi. In 1777 the Sikhs were fighting against the Mughal forces as allies of Zabita Khan. Najaf Khan was initially unable to take effective action against them due to the jealousy of Abdul Ahad Khan, but eventually he obliged them to cross the Jamuna into Karnal. In a desperate situation, Zabita Khan declared himself to have become a Sikh as Dharam Singh. With Sikh support, he penetrated the Doab as far as Khurja. They were defeated by Najaf Quli and recrossed the Jamuna. In December 1778, the Sikhs went up to the banks of the Ganges, crossed the river, and plundered several villages in the area of Najibabad. Then they recrossed the Ganges and continued their activity in the Doab. In 1779, Zabita Khan established a friendly alliance with Najaf Khan, and offered his daughter in marriage to him, without consulting the Sikhs. They came to look upon him as a renegade.[25]

Abdul Ahad, a Kashmiri Muslim, tried to arouse the emperor's religious sentiment against Najaf Khan who was an Irani and a Shia'. To strengthen his own position he also sought help from the Sikhs. At this time, Raja Amar Singh of Patiala petitioned the emperor to help him against his Sikh opponents. Abdul Ahad marched from Delhi in June with 50,000 horse and foot and 200 guns, and Mirza Farkhund Bakht as the nominal commander. Several Sikh chiefs joined him at Karnal. Gajpat Singh promised to pay Rs. 2,00,000. After the rainy season, Abdul Ahad marched towards Patiala. Desu Singh paid Rs. 3,00,000 and his son, Lal Singh, was taken as a hostage. Abdul Ahad insisted on Raja Amar Singh's personal presence. But Amar Singh appealed to the chiefs like Jassa Singh Ahluwalia, Khushal Singh, and Tara Singh Ghaiba. Abdul Ahad could not make any effect on Patiala. With the news of the Sikh army having encamped at Malerkotla, Abdul Ahad began to retreat. Had he not been helped by his Sikh allies, he would not have returned alive.[26]

Abdul Ahad's failure encouraged the Sikhs to invade the Doab. Najaf Khan appointed his grand-nephew, Mirza Shafi, in January 1780 to campaign against the Sikhs in the upper Doab. Several Sikh chiefs conveyed their goodwill to Najaf Khan. The Sikh chiefs began to fight among themselves. Desu Singh died in September 1780 and his son, Lal Singh, was released for Rs. 50,000. Mirza Shafi maintained his ground at Kunjpura early in February 1781. The Sikhs entered the Doab.

Shafi reached Saharanpur and fought well, and some of the Sikh recrossed to Jamuna. Thus, the masters of Delhi were able to contain the Sikhs in 1780-1.[27]

Shafi felt encouraged to cross into the cis-Sutlej before the end of February 1781. He was joined by Ghulam Qadir, son of Zabita Khan. Skirmishes went on between the Sikhs and the Mughals. Shafi marched towards Buriya. Raja Amar Singh of Patiala offered help to Shafi against the Sikhs. But he was attacked by Jassa Singh Ahluwalia and Tara Singh Ghaiba, and he had to recall his contingents. The Mughal troops occupied Mustafabad and Sadhaura, but disaffection spread in Shafi's army. He was short of money too. Nevertheless he kept on fighting against the Sikhs and in April 1781 he inflicted heavy losses on them. Shahabad was seized by his troops. Before the end of the month, Shafi was obliged to retreat from Sadhaura. The Mughal *amil* of Shahabad was defeated by the Sikhs in May, and the Sikhs laid siege to Buriya. Shafi continued to reside in Kunjpura till June 1782, but he could not take any effective measure against the Sikhs.[28]

While Shafi was trying to deal with the Sikhs in the cis-Sutlej, the Sikhs increased their activity in the Doab in February-June 1781. They plundered Lakhnauti and Gangoh and attacked Sardhana, the estate of Begum Samru. Najaf Khan and Zabita Khan failed to check the Sikhs. The Sikh invasion of the Doab was the chief cause of Shafi's failure. Zabita Khan and Gajpat Singh interviewed the Sikh chiefs and persuaded them to come to an agreement with the government in Delhi. The terms offered were that they would formally be confirmed in the possession of their estates in the region north of Panipat and they would have the right to one-eighth of a rupee in the revenues as *rakhi* in the region from Panipat to the walls of Delhi and the upper Doab; their obligation would be to serve in the Delhi army for pay when called upon to do so, and they would not raid the imperial territory. 'Thus the Mughal Emperor of India formally accepted the sovereignty of the Sikhs over the country situated to the west of the Jamuna, and admitted their right of blackmail in the upper Gangetic Doab. In this way their sway became de jure as well as de facto'. This was a very remarkable success for the Sikhs. But for their disunity and dissention, they would have superseded the Marathas in supremacy over northern India. Gupta does not say so, but this agreement provides a clue to the aspiration of the Sikhs.[29]

The agreement did not last long. There was mutual mistrust. After the rainy season of 1782 the Sikhs marched into the Doab and approached Anupshahr on the Ganges. The Raja of Garhwal paid tribute to them. In March 1783, after plundering Aligarh and Bulandshahr, the Sikhs advanced upon Delhi and attacked its suburbs. They retired after receiving Rs. 3,00,000, and Baghel Singh remained behind with 4,000 Sikhs to build gurdwaras at places associated with Mata Sundari and Mata Sahib Devi, Guru Har Krishan, and Guru Tegh Bahadur. In May and June, the Sikhs moved into the Doab with 15,000 horse and 20,000 foot. There was no power to oppose them effectively. In 1782-3, thus, the Sikhs appeared to be dominant in the Doab. They also entered into negotiation with Mahadji Sindhia and the English.[30]

The dominant presence of the Sikhs in the Doab created uneasiness in the mind of James Browne who had been deputed by Warren Hastings to Delhi. He wrote about the threatening attitude of the Sikhs in the neighbourhood of Delhi in February 1784. He wanted the Sikhs to side with the British and proposed a plan of joint conquest and three-eighths of the conquered territory as the share of the Sikhs. But Warren Hastings favoured an alliance with the emperor to contain the Sikhs, looking upon the imperial territory as a buffer between the Sikhs and the Nawab of Awadh. In June 1784, the Sikhs collected *rakhi* from the Doab. In December 1784, Warren Hastings told the Council that Sikh domination extended from the Indus to the walls of Delhi, and they presented a serious danger. He proposed a plan to bring the Mughal emperor under British protection. But he failed for various reasons.[31]

Shah Alam II was aware of Mahadji Sindhia's capacity to be his support. In a public *darbar* on 1 December 1784, he appointed the Peshwa as his deputy and commander-in-chief with the stipulation that only Mahadji Sindhia would perform the functions of these high offices as the Peshwa's agent. Three days later he made the announcement that Mahadji was the *Vakil-i Mutlaq* of the empire. The greatest difficulty of Mahadji was that the Sikhs roamed unchecked in the Doab and plundered Chandausi early in 1785. The *vakil* of Ghulam Qadir who had succeeded Zabita Khan offered to pay the usual *rakhi* but asking them to withdraw from his territory. They decided not to invade Rohilkhand across the Ganga. Mahadji Sindhia sent his agents to the Sikhs, and also made arrangements to check them. On 30 March 1784, a treaty of unity and friendship was concluded between Raja Ambaji and the Chiefs of the *Khalsaji* (Baghel Singh, Karam Singh, Dulcha Singh, Bhag Singh, Mohar Singh and others) to the effect that the latter would forego their *rakhi*, serve Mahadji Sindhia, and receive one-third of any territory occupied other than the royal territories. The British were opposed to the alliance but not willing to enter into a direct agreement with the Sikhs. In May 1785, Sindhia concluded a treaty with the Sikhs. It was agreed that the Sikhs would receive allowances and a *jagir* of Rs. 10,00,000 and the territories of the Nawab of Awadh and the English were not to be molested. Gupta remarks that the treaty was bound to fail because the Sikhs respected only superior physical force, and not any policy of persuasion and conciliation. It seems, however, that not all the Sikh chiefs were willing to be contained in their political aspirations.[32]

Mahadji appointed officers to various places with the instructions to keep an eye on the Sikhs. In June 1785, the Sikhs entered to Doab to collect *rakhi*. In August, Gurdip Singh of Ladwa plundered the Meerut district. The Sikhs ravaged the Doab in January 1786. Towards the end of the year they were spread over the Doab held by Sindhia. The point of contention between the Sikhs and the Marathas was the *rakhi*. In February 1787 the Sikhs plundered Ghulam Qadir's territory because he had refused to pay *rakhi*. Mahadji sent Ambaji towards Panipat with a considerable force. He wanted to secure favourable terms through negotiations with the Sikh chiefs. Ghulam Qadir joined Ambaji at Karnal, and Ambaji marched towards Patiala to collect tribute from the cis-Sutlej chiefs. But he was recalled by Mahadji. He was back in Delhi before the end of June. The Sikhs attacked Shahdara and plundered the country between Delhi and Agra. Ghulam Qadir entered Delhi in September with the help of the Sikhs. Mahadji's power was declining and he was not capable of taking effective steps against the Sikhs. They ransacked the Doab and ravaged the territory of Ghulam Qadir in the summer of 1788. They decided to attack Delhi after the rains. In August, Ghulam Qadir entered Delhi, blinded the emperor, and sat on the throne. Mahadji Sindhia ousted him from Delhi and pursued him closely. He was captured before the end of 1788 and put to death early in March 1788.[33]

The Sikh chiefs acknowledged Sindhia's supremacy and some of them accepted the role of peaceful feudatories in the Doab. In 1790, however, they began to disturb Sindhia's territory. Mahadji was much perturbed. The Sikhs renewed their depredations in the Doab in Janaury 1791. At Anupshahr, they captured Lt. Colonel Robert Stuart who was guarding the forts on the Ganges on behalf of the Nawab of Awadh. Despite the Governor-General's efforts to get him honourably released, Bhanga Singh insisted on getting Rs. 60,000 as ransom, and it was paid through Begum Samru in October 1791. The Sikhs raided the Doab again in January 1792. We hear of their expulsion from the Doab and the Delhi province before the end of 1793. Mahadji Sindhia died in February 1794, without success in his avowed object of establishing peace in northern India with the active cooperation of the Sikhs. He had no chance of success with the Sikhs who were totally ignorant of the value of treaties and engagements. 'But his failure is the failure of heroes who fight against their times'. Gupta's sympathies are clearly with Mahadji Sindhia.[34]

In 1794 the Sikhs tried to seize the Saharanpur district but Baghel Singh fell ill. Jassa Singh Ramgarhia offered help to Ghulam Muhammad Khan, the Rohilla Chief of Rampur. He hired 10,000 Sikh troops, but he eventually surrendered to the English. The Sikhs wished to visit Nanakmata near Bareilly but the Ganga was flooded in June and they did not cross the river. In September and October 1795, Nana Rao marched into the cis-Sutlej to realize tribute from the Sikh chiefs, but he got tired of useless fighting which brought him no gain, and returned to Delhi through Ambala. The Sikhs invaded the Doab, and the Maratha commandants had to fight against them. In April 1796, some Udasis of Hardwar were killed by the Gosains. On the following day, the Sikhs present in Hardwar attacked all mendicants, whether Gosain, Bairagi or Nanga. About 500 of them were put to the sword. The massacre stopped only when two companies of British troops under Captain Murray appeared on the scene to intervene. Three Sikh chiefs were involved in this affair: Raja Sahib Singh of Patiala, Rai Singh of Buriya, and Sher Singh. Hardwar was an important source of income for both the Sikhs and the Marathas. This incident, like the general course of

Sikh history, showed that feelings of cupidity and vindictiveness made a Sikh oblivious of 'distinction between proper and improper, fair and unfair, religious and irreligious, human and inhuman, strong and weak, man and woman.'[35]

In 1797-9, the Irish adventurer George Thomas established a small principality of 800 villages worth Rs. 2,86,000 a year with his headquarters at Hansi. Gupta describes his earlier career and his experience of fighting against the Sikhs on behalf of others. While the French General Perron was trying to collect tribute from the cis-Sutlej Sikh chiefs on behalf of Daulat Rao Sindhia, Thomas led campaigns against Bhag Singh of Jind. Some of the other Sikh chiefs came to the support of Bhag Singh and Thomas had to retire from Jind in February 1799 after a blockade of three months. Eventually, he negotiated for peace and *status quo ante* was established. However, Thomas continued his aggressive career for a couple of years more before he was defeated and expelled from the Punjab by Perron.[36]

In Janaury 1797, Raja Sahib Singh of Patiala told Shah Zaman in a letter through the agent sent to the Raja, that he was Shah Zaman's 'nurtured slave'. This was with reference to the suzerainty of Ahmad Shah Abdali and his son over Ala Singh and Amar Singh. Shah Zaman acknowledged his letter and appreciated his loyalty. In 1797-8, Sahib Singh did not join Shah Zaman at Lahore but he maintained communication with him, assuring him of his loyal support. Early in December 1798 he wrote to Shah Zaman that he would wait on him after he crossed the Sutlej. But Shah Zaman never crossed the Sutlej. The attitude of Sahib Singh towards him was the same as his attitude towards the Mughal emperor and the Marathas: to acknowledge their supremacy but to act according to his own perceived interests.[37]

III. POLITICS OF THE TRANS-SUTLEJ SIKH CHIEFS: 1769-1799

The third volume of Hari Ram Gupta's *History of the Sikhs* continues the story of the trans-Sutlej Sikhs from 1769 to 1799. The Afghan danger greatly disappeared with the death of Ahmad Shah Durrani in 1772. The Sikhs began to extend and strengthen their political control and, in this process, to quarrel among themselves. However, they displayed the noble trait of their character in resisting the invader from the north-west. The last 'Muslim invasion' of India took place in 1799 and this was also the year of the foundation of Sikh monarchy in the person of Ranjit Singh.

The first chapter of this volume depicts the territorial possessions of the Sikh rulers in 1769. The second relates to the expansion of their territories in the plains and the third, to their conquest of Kangra and Jammu hills. The fourth chapter goes into the detail of their internecine warfare. Three chapters then relate to the conflict with Shah Zaman from 1793 to 1799. After chapter 8, which describes the beginning of the monarchy of Ranjit Singh in 1799, there are two chapters on the nature and character of Sikh administration and the social and economic life of the people. Thus, though largely political, the volume does not ignore the government of the Sikhs and its effect on the life of the people. Like the first volume, it is based on a wide range of sources in English, Persian, Marathi, and Gurmukhi, both in print and in manuscripts.

Gupta talks of the territorial possessions of the Sikhs in 1769 in terms of *misls* for each of the five Doabs.[38] The Bhangi *misl* held possessions in four Doabs: Bari, Rachna, Chaj and Sind Sagar. Among their chiefs were Jhanda Singh and Ganda Singh, with a number of the less important ones, like Nidhan Singh Hattu, Bhag Singh Hallowalia, Dhanna Singh Kalalwalia, Karam Singh Chhina, Nahar Singh Chamyari, Sahib Singh and Jodh Singh. Sahib Singh was actually a son of Gujjar Singh who held territories in three Doabs, with Milkha Singh Thehpuria as his captain in Rawalpindi. The amount of the revenue collected by any Bhangi chief is not mentioned. The Kanhiya *misl* held territories in three Doabs: Jalandhar, Bari and Rachna. The chiefs named are Jai Singh, Jaimal Singh, Amar Singh Bagga, Tara Singh, Desa Singh, Mirza Singh, Natha Singh and Sudh Singh Dodia.

The Dallewalia *misl* had territories only in the Jalandhar Doab, with Tara Singh Gheba as the most important chief having nearly Rs. 8,00,000 a year as revenue. Two other chiefs were Hari Singh and Massa Singh. The Nakkai *misl* had territories in two Doabs: Bari and Rachna. Its chiefs named are Ran Singh and Kamar Singh, with an annual income of more than Rs. 10,00,000 from their possessions in the Bari Doab. Thus, four *misls* had more than one chief, but the relationship which the chiefs of a *misl* had with one another is not clear.

The Sukerchakia *misl* had territories in three Doabs: Rachna, Chaj and Sind Sagar. Its only chief was Charhat Singh. The Ahluwalia *misl* had territories in two Doabs: Jalandhar and Bari. Its only chief was Jassa Singh whose territory in the Jalandhar Doab yielded about Rs. 10,00,000 a year. The Ramgarhia *misl* held territories in two Doabs: Jalandhar and Bari. Its only chief was Jassa Singh. His possessions in the Jalandhar Doab yielded about Rs. 10,00,000 a year. The Singhpuria Khushal Singh held territory worth Rs. 3,00,000 in the Jalandhar Doab. Karora Singh, whose *misl* is called Kararosinghia, held territory in the Jalandhar Doab, with Mian Muhammad Khan as his tributary at Talwar. Thus, five *misls* had only one chief each. Three of them belonged to the first generation of chiefs. All the five *misls* were known after the founder.

For the expansion of Sikh territories in the plains, Gupta looks at five sub-regions of the Punjab: the central, the southern, the south-western, the western, and the north-western. Among the non-Sikh rulers of the Punjab plains were largely Afghans, Baloches, and Muslim Rajputs and Jats. In the central Punjab, Jassa Singh Ahluwlia took a part of Rai Ibrahim of Kapurthala (who lost all his territory later). Jointly with Jhanda Singh Bhangi, Jassa Singh Ahluwalia attacked the Afghan stronghold of Kasur and obliged the Afghan chiefs to pay Rs. 4,00,000. The Pathans of Saurian and the Rajputs of Chamyari, like the Randhawa *zamindars* submitted to them. Gujjar Singh Bhangi obliged Ahmad Khan Chaththa of Ramnagar to submit to him. In the southern Punjab, Kamar Singh Nakkai expelled the Hans from Kot Kamalia and gave a share in the revenues to the Kharals who had invited him for help against the Hans. Buddh Singh Bhangi defeated the Wattus who held territories on both sides of the Sutlej. In the south-west Punjab, Jhanda Singh and Ganda Singh Bhangi led expeditions against its Afghan governors and conquered much of their territory in 1772. Taimur Shah, the son and successor of Ahmad Shah Abdali at Kabul, besieged Multan early in 1780, captured it, and appointed Muzaffar Khan as his governor. In the western Punjab, the Baloch chiefs of the Jhang area and the Nawab of Mankera were made tributary by Jhanda Singh Bhangi. In the north-western Punjab, Gujjar Singh Bhangi and Charhat Singh Sukarchakia conquered the territories of the Gakhars, Janjuas, Goleras and others up to Attock. Thus, the Sikh chiefs were engaged in conquering and subduing the non-Sikh rulers all over the Punjab plains.[39]

At the same time, some of the Sikh chiefs extended their power and influence in the Punjab hills. All the states between the Indus and the Jhelum were ruled by Muslim chiefs. Between the Jhelum and the Ravi, there were 22 states. Eight of these, between the Jhelum and the Chenab had Muslim chiefs. Fourteen of these were ruled by Hindu Rajputs, all between the Chenab and the Ravi. Nine of these were offshoots of Jammu which was the oldest. Between the Ravi and the Sutlej there was only one Muslim principality, that of Shahpur. Thirteen states were ruled by Hindu Rajputs, with Kangra as the most important, having four offshoots. Almost all the hill states had acknowledged the suzerainty of Ahmad Shah Abdali. After his death, several of the hill states tended to assert their independence against the Afghan authority.[40]

Gupta says that the prosperity of the hill chiefs attracted the attention of the Sikhs. The trade routes passing through the hills provided the prospect of plundering the merchants. The Sikhs were familiar with the hills. Gupta does not say so, but they were also aware of the tributary status of the hill chiefs. Therefore, they could think of getting tribute from them. In 1770, the Kangra hills became tributary to Jassa Singh Ramgarhia whose territories were adjacent to the hills. His brother, Mali Singh, was stationed at Talwara with 4,000 horse for the collection of tribute which amounted to Rs. 2,00,000. In 1775, Jassa Singh Ramgarhia was displaced by Jai Singh Kanhiya who claimed tribute from most of the Kangra states. The fort of Kangra was famous for its strength and it had been held by a Mughal *faujdar* since the time of Jahangir. Raja Sansar Chand of Kangra invited Jai Singh Kanhiya and Baghel Singh Karorasinghia to help him against Saif Ali Khan, the Mughal *faujdar*. Sansar Chand took it from Jai Singh later in exchange of territories he had conquered in the plains. Gupta refers to the evidence of George Forster for the Sikh influence in the Kangra hills before the fort of Kangra came into Sansar Chand's possession in 1786. Brij Raj Dev had succeeded his father, Ranjit Dev, at Jammu in 1781. The state came under complete subjection of the Sikhs for an annual tribute of Rs. 30,000. It was sacked twice by Mahan Singh Sukarchakia. Brij Raj Dev was killed in a battle in 1787, and the power of the Sikhs was fully established in the region. Shah Zaman's assertion of suzerainty over the hill chiefs in 1797 did not affect the general position of Sikhs in relation to the hills.[41]

All this time the Sikh chiefs were fighting among themselves too, taking opposite sides in disputes among non-Sikh chiefs and also in direct conflict with one another. According to Gupta, the principle of equality could serve their selfish purposes of self-assertion and aggrandizement. Factional spirit increased with the passage of time. The last three decades of the eighteenth century were marked by petty warfare and petty feuds among the Sikh chiefs, which produced important changes in 'the Sikh State'. Gupta gives several important examples of warfare. In 1774, there was fighting over Jammu when Charhat Singh Sukarchakia and Jai Singh Kanhiya supported Brij Raj Dev against his father Ranjit Dev who was supported by Jhanda Singh Bhangi. Charhat Singh was killed by the bursting of his own gun, and Jai Singh bribed a Ranghreta Singh to kill Jhanda Singh. The murder of Jhanda Singh rankled in the mind of his brother Ganda Singh and he declared war upon Jai Singh in 1775. During this conflict Ganda Singh died due to illness. Before the end of the year, Jassa Singh Ahluwalia and Jassa Singh Ramgarhia fought over Zahura on the Beas and the latter was wounded in the battle. In 1776, Jassa Singh Ahluwalia was captured by Mali Singh but released by Jassa Singh Ramgarhia. Before the year ended, Jassa Singh Ramgarhia was expelled from his territories by the Ahluwalia chief with the support of Jai Singh and Haqiqat Singh Kanhiya. In 1782, Haqiqat Singh realized Rs. 30,000 as tribute from Brij Raj Dev in return for supporting him in recovering some territory of Jammu occupied by the Bhangis. Before the end of the year, the Kanhiyas and the Bhangis made up their differences and the territory restored to Jammu was again seized by them. Brij Raj Dev invited Mahan Singh for help. In the fighting that followed, Jassa Singh Ahluwalia supported the Bhangis and the Kanhiyas. After several days of fighting, the Ahluwalia chief prevailed upon both the parties. The fortress of Dinpur remained in the possession of Brij Raj Dev but the neighbouring territory was handed over to Haqiqat Singh. Soon afterwards, however, Mahan Singh plundered Jammu. Jai Singh Kanhiya insisted on getting a share for the Kanhiyas and he fought a battle with Mahan Singh near Majitha but only to be worsted. Mahan Singh invited Jassa Singh Ramgarhia to return to the Punjab and fight for his territory with his support. In a battle fought near Achal, Jai Singh's son Gurbakhsh Singh was killed. In 1787, Jai Singh attacked Batala which had been occupied by Jassa Singh Ramgarhia but he had to raise the siege after three weeks. In 1791, Mahan Singh laid siege to Sodhra which was held by Sahib Singh Bhangi. But he fell ill and he was taken back to Gujranwala where he died. Thus, we find that even the most eminent Sikh chiefs fought among themselves from 1774 to 1791. Mahan Singh Sukarchakia appears to have increased his power during these years. This was the legacy he left to his son and successor Ranjit Singh.[42]

The invasions of Shah Zaman are discussed by Gupta in three phases: 1793-5, 1796-7, and 1798-9. He discusses the position of the Sikh chiefs on the eve of Shah Zaman's invasions. There was complete disunity among them. Ranjit Singh's dominions in three Doabs yielded Rs. 30,000,000 a year, and the Raja of Jammu was his tributary. He possessed 15 forts, and in an emergency he could raise 11,000 horse and 6,000 foot. Sahib Singh Bhangi was an independent chief in Gujrat with a territory worth Rs. 13,00,000 a year. He owned 12 forts, and he could raise 8,000 cavalry and 4,000 infantry. There were other chiefs with smaller resources. Karam Singh Dulu, the Bhangi chief of Jhang, could raise 6,000 horse and 3,000 foot, with an annual revenue of approximately Rs. 14,00,000. Karam Singh Dodia, with a territory worth Rs. 8,00,000 could raise 2,000 horse and 1,000 foot. Sahib Singh of Sialkot possessed territory worth Rs. 9,00,000 a year, and he could raise 3,000 cavalry and 1,000 infantry. Three chiefs in Lahore (Lehna Singh, Sahib Singh and Mohar Singh) could raise 7,000 cavalry and 4,000 foot, with revenues approximating Rs. 15,00,000 a year. Gulab Singh Bhangi at Amritsar, with revenues about Rs. 10,00,000 a year, could raise 4,000 cavalry and 2,000 infantry. The most notable chiefs of the Jalandhar Doab were Jassa Singh Ramgarhia and Tara Singh Gheba. They could raise 5,250 horse and 1,750 foot. The other chiefs were Baghel Singh of Nurmahal, Tara Singh Kakar, Khushal Singh of Garhshankar, and Mahan Singh of Jalandhar. They could raise 5,025 cavalry and 1,675 infantry. The estimates of the total military strength of the Sikh chiefs ranged from 50,000 to 73,000. But this force could not be used against Shah Zaman because of the disunity among the Sikh chiefs due to their individual interests and political outlook.[43]

Shah Zaman had ascended the throne of Afghanistan in May 1793 with the ambition of establishing an empire in India. He sent several emissaries to the courts of influential Indian rulers, notably the Mughal emperor and Nawab of Awadh. Before the end of 1793, he left Kabul but he did not go beyond Peshawar. He sent several agents to India. Shah Alam II was in regular correspondence with him, pressing Shah Zaman to invade India and relieve him of the Maratha Control. Shah Zaman moved to Peshawar again before the end of 1795.

Ranjit Singh, the first Sikh chief on his way to Lahore, looked at foreign invasion 'from national point of view'. It was 'disgraceful to all Indians and to the Sikhs in particular' who controlled the north-western frontier. He was determined to oppose Shah Zaman but he was not in a position to fight a pitched battle with the Afghan forces. His garrison at Rohtas evacuated the fort, and it was occupied by the Afghans. The Sikh gave a short battle to the Afghans at Pind Dadan Khan and then crossed the Jhelum. Shah Zaman's brother, Mahmud, raised a revolt at Herat and Shah Zaman decided to return to Kabul early in 1796.[44]

In July 1796 Shah Zaman's emissaries waited upon Shah Alam II, and they delivered his letter to Daulat Rao Sindhia in which it was declared that his conquests would be confined to the territories of the Sikhs. Shah Zaman negotiated with the Sikh chiefs too. Ranjit Singh's response was to the effect that he would meet the Durrani in the field of battle. Shah Zaman collected an army of 80,000 horse and foot, 63 pieces of cannon, and 700 pieces of camel artillery. The Marathas were the strongest power in India but they too were disunited like the Sikhs. The Muslim chiefs were in sympathy with Shah Zaman. The Sikh chiefs of Malwa, headed by Raja Sahib Singh of Patiala, were not prepared to go against Shah Zaman. He left Kabul in October 1796, stayed at Peshwar for a month, reached the Indus opposite Attock, and sent an advance guard of 12,000 across the river. Milkha Singh defended Rohtas. Shah Zaman crossed the Indus, and Ranjit Singh took up his position at Miani where he was joined by Milkha Singh.

When the Durrani advance guard crossed the Jhelum, the Sikh chiefs crossed the Chenab and began to collect troops on its southern bank. Shah Alam II offered to pay Rs. 50,000 to Shah Zaman for every march and Rs. 25,000 for a halt. Shah Zaman tried to pacify the Sikh chiefs, particularly Lehna Singh, the old chief of Lahore, whom he promised all concessions and favours. He entered Lahore on 1 January 1797, and he was greeted by the people. He learnt that Sikhs were assembled at Amritsar. On 11 January a desperate battle was fought near Amritsar, with great losses on both sides, and the Durranis were pursued by the Sikhs to the gates of Lahore. The Sikh chiefs eventually decided to cut-off supplies to the Afghan camp. After much thought, Shah Zaman decided to retreat, collecting Rs. 22,00,000 from Lahore. The Durrani Governor, Ahmad Khan Shahanchi Bashi, was defeated in April 1797; his head was cut-off and sent to Ranjit Singh at Ramnagar.[45]

An intelligence officer sent by the English to Kabul wrote in June 1797 that the Muslim chiefs of the Punjab had sent their *vakils* to Shah Zaman for inviting him to expel the Sikhs from power. Wazir Ali Khan of Awadh sent his emissaries to Kabul to persuade Shah Zaman to expel the English from Awadh. Shah Zaman sent his agents to India to assess the situation. Seeing his letter of 1798 addressed to Sir John Shore, Marquis of Wellesley expressed his 'entire disapprobation' of Shah Zaman's projects. The Marathas were watchful on account of Shah Zaman's hostile attitude towards them. Shah Zaman reached Rohtas by the middle of November. The Sikh chiefs gathered at Amritsar and resolved to oppose him. He was moving towards Lahore by slow marches. In a battle near Amritsar, the Afghans were forced to retreat to Lahore. Ranjit Singh, Gulab Singh, Chet Singh, and Sahib Singh marched from Amritsar towards Lahore. They could not make a concerted attack and decided to cut-off supplies coming to the Afghan camp. A few of the Sikh chiefs received *khil'ats* from Shah Zaman. They were instructed to encourage other chiefs to do so. However, Shah Zaman failed to induce the Sikh chiefs to accept his suzerainty. Sahib Singh Bedi said on their behalf that they had taken the country by the sword and they would keep it with the sword. The Sikhs grew so bold as to attack the suburbs of Lahore in broad daylight. The Afghan soldiers were becoming increasingly restless when they were not allowed to plunder. In the first week of January 1799, Shah Zaman held several conferences and finally decided to go back. He reached Peshawar before the end of the month. This proved to be his last invasion. He was dethroned and blinded. Gupta makes the following observation on 'the last Muslim invasion of India':

> Thus ended the stream of immigration of needy adventurers from Turkistan, Iran, Afghanistan and Baluchistan which had supplied to various Muslim kingdoms in this country nearly all their distinguished statesmen, eminent politicians, illustrious administrators and celebrated generals, the Indian Musalmans producing almost no celebrity during this long period.[46]

According to the British records, Ranjit Singh indicated to an agent from Shah Zaman that if appointed to the charge of the fort of Lahore, he would pay Rs. 1,00,000 as *nazrana*. On Shah Zaman's return to Afghanistan, Ranjit Singh recovered Rohtas, and captured the forts of Hasan Abdal and Attock. For establishing his sway over the Punjab, he thought of seizing Lahore. His idea was to weld the Sikh *misls* into 'one commonwealth with himself as the head'. He tried to please Shah Zaman by extricating eight of his twelve guns which had fallen into the river Jhelum. Meanwhile, Nizamuddin Khan of Kasur tried to seize Lahore with the help of its Muslim leaders. He failed because the plan had leaked out. Ranjit Singh sent his own agents to the Muslim leaders of Lahore and a plan was formed. Ranjit Singh marched to Batala before attacking the Lohari Gate of Lahore, while Mai Sada Kaur attacked the Delhi Gate. The Lohari Gate was opened for Ranjit Singh and he dashed into the city. Mohar Singh escaped from the *haveli* of Lakhpat Rai, his place of residence in Lahore, but he was captured and allowed to retire safely to his lands with all his moveable property. The Delhi Gate also fell and Chet Singh shut himself in the fort. But he was unable to cope with the situation, and opened negotiations; he was allowed to retire to Waniki as his *jagir*. Before the end of 1799, Ranjit Singh received a rich *khil'at* from Shah Zaman in acknowledgement of his service for conveying the guns to Kabul. The British records state that Ranjit Singh interpreted it as his appointment by Shah Zaman as the chief of Lahore 'to acquire greater authority and to legalize his usurpation of Lahore'. Gupta suggests that Ranjit Singh's occupation of Lahore formed a landmark in the history of the Sikhs. 'It marks the beginning of the independent Sikh chiefs on the one hand, and the establishment of Sikh monarchy on the other'. However, if 'monarchy' is taken to mean the concentration of political power in the hands of one individual, the occupation of Lahore made no difference to the position of Ranjit Singh who was a born prince and had succeeded to his father's position as a matter of course. Probably, what Gupta wishes to underline by the use of the term 'monarchy' is the large extent of the dominions of Ranjit Singh. The vast extent of his possessions and the vast number of his subjects brought about a revolution in his human and material resources and made him a powerful ruler. Historians refer to his dominions also as a 'kingdom' though he never declared himself to be a 'king'.[47]

Gupta says in a footnote that the last two chapters of his book 'apply to all the Sikhs of the Punjab between the Indus and the Jumna'.[48] One of these two chapters is on the 'nature and character of Sikh administration'. The Sikh chiefs showed much concern for the prosperity of the peasant and the trader, and the contemporary evidence cited by Gupta indicates that they succeeded reasonably well in making people happy and contented. Capital crimes were rarely perpetrated, and justice was mild and equitable. The Sikh chiefs had shown good governance in their own possessions despite internecine warfare. They were tolerant in matters of faith. They did not interfere with an individual's property in land. The *batai* system, which was popular among the cultivators, was the most prevalent system. Fixed rates in cash were applied only to a few crops. There were additional cesses but the total burden was not heavy. The *panchayats*, the chiefs, eminent *jagirdars*, and '*adalatis* appointed by the chiefs administered justice. By way of state charity, the Sikh chiefs maintained *langars* or free kitchens for all people. Transit duties were a hindrance to trade but the chiefs tried to regulate trade caravans led by the descendants of Guru Nanak for safety. Trade routes through Patiala connected the Punjab with the Gangetic Doab and Rajasthan. Sikh and Ahmad Shahi coins were current, the latter in Patiala, Jind and Kaithal but not in Nabha. The Sikh coins bore two inscriptions in Persian; both of these are given by Gupta.[49]

The last chapter relates to 'social and economic life of the people'. Gupta talks of the rural population which was numerically predominant. Their general condition was prosperous. There was no 'Hindu, Muslim and Sikh problem' in the sense in which it existed in the 1940s. 'All the three communities as a rule lived peacefully, and in social and religious matters they often followed the practices of others'. Gupta talks of the daily life of the villagers, their food, life of the women, polygamy, infanticide, *sati*, dancing girls, language of the people, fairs, and manufacture of arms. Thus, Gupta tries to put together the information in his sources on various aspects of social and economic life. The scope of the description is pretty large but the information on each aspect of life is rather small. No attempt is made to relate these aspects with one another.[50]

IV. SOME GENERAL OBSERVATIONS

All the three volumes of Hari Ram Gupta's *History of the Sikhs* are remarkable for their factual details based on a large volume and variety of sources. He may be seen as interpreting eighteenth-century Sikh history largely through his facts, especially in the first and the third volumes. The period chosen for these two volumes from 1739 to 1799 is marked by important events: the invasion of India by Nadir Shah and the occupation of Lahore by Ranjit Singh. However, the first volume does not end with 1765 when the Sikhs struck a coin as the formal declaration of their sovereignty. This may be partly due to the fact that, according to Gupta, a coin was struck earlier also. He was also concerned with the situation on the ground. The Sikhs were securer in power in 1768 than in 1765.

In any case, Gupta does not conceal his admiration for the Sikhs who established sovereign rule in the Punjab. Their struggle for independence was a kind of national service. They regarded the recovery and defence of the frontier region of 'our country' as a 'national duty'. They turned the tide of 'foreign' aggression after 800 years. Gupta refers to the last invasion of Nadir Shah as 'the last Muslim invasion'. The equation of Muslims with foreigner' carries implications for 'Indian' nationalism. Foreign invasions did help the Sikhs to come into power because their enemies were weakened and discontent among the peasantry of the Punjab induced them to join the Khalsa. However, it was the 'intrinsic worth' of the Khalsa which enabled them to overpower their opponents. Gupta talks of the 'genius and ambition' of the Khalsa, and their 'tenacity of purpose and resourcefulness'. He also refers to their institutions as a helpful factor. The *rakhi* system made them popular with the peasantry. Amritsar played a crucial role in the Sikh struggle for independence: they looked upon it as the 'symbol of their mother-country'.

The trans-Sutlej Sikhs in 1769-99 fought among themselves and there was no unity among them, but they were still patriotic However, this was not true of the cis-Sutlej Sikhs. In fact, in the whole of India in the late eighteenth century there was no patriotic prince except Mahadji Sindhia. The Sikh chiefs of the cis-Sutlej subordinated collective interest to their individual interests and they degenerated into selfish plunderers due to their lust for power. Gupta brings out the complexity of politics in the relations of the Sikhs among themselves, and their relations with the Jats, the Marathas, the Rohillas, the Mughals, and the English. The frequent use of the term 'the Sikhs' instead of individuals concerned becomes a source of confusion and one fails to see any pattern. However, Gupta's own evidence does not leave any doubt about the independent stance of the Sikh chiefs and their ambition to extend their power and influence.

Hari Ram Gupta makes a distinction not only between the Sikh chiefs on the two sides of the Sutlej but also between the chiefs who belonged to the trans-Sutlej and those who belonged to the cis-Sutlej. He talks of 'a different line of action' adopted by the latter. They never openly defied the Mughals, the Afghans or the Marathas. Gupta does not say so but his evidence shows that the Phulkian chiefs were different in their origins also. With the exception of Nabha they made use of the Mughal administrative framework to increase their resources and power and had no hesitation in accepting political subordination as vassals. They made Ahmad Shahi coin current in their dominions. Like other historians, Gupta talks of the Phulkian *misl*, though there is no evidence for treating the Phulkian chiefs as a single unit. Gupta fails to see that all the important Sikh chiefs were acting independently of others. They were acting as 'monarchs' and Ranjit Singh was a born 'monarch'.

What we have said about the choice of the period covered by Gupta in the first and the third volume of his *History* does not apply to the cis-Sutlej. Neither 1739 nor 1768 nor 1799 are important dates in the history of the cis-Sutlej Sikhs. Also, all the factual information given in the second volume does not contribute to our understanding of the political processes. Occasionally, a whole chapter does not enhance our understanding of political developments. In all the three volumes, Gupta is meticulous about persons, places and events but his understanding of 'contemporary evidence' is rather broad. Anything that came from the eighteenth century, and even the early decades of the nineteenth century, is treated as contemporary. Thus, the evidence of the European writers is used for the 1740s and the 1750s. On the whole, Gupta makes a clear and substantial advance over Sinha in terms of factual detail and authenticity and in terms of political development phase by phase. However, the scope of his *History* too is almost exclusively political. It does not contribute anything serious even to polity. Some of economic, social and cultural aspects are barely mentioned.

NOTES

1. Hari Ram Gupta, *History of the Sikhs*, vol. I (*The Confederacies*), Simla: Minerva Book Shop, 1952, 2nd edn., Foreword by Jadunath Sarkar, pp. v-vi.
2. Ibid., Preface, pp. vii-ix.
3. Ibid., p. 1.
4. Ibid., pp. 2-23.
5. Ibid., p. 24.
6. Ibid., pp. 25-57.
7. Ibid., pp. 58-84.
8. Ibid., pp. 85-105.
9. Ibid., pp. 106-24.
10. Ibid., pp. 125-36.
11. Ibid., pp. 137-43.
12. Ibid., pp. 144-68.
13. Ibid., pp. 169-90.
14. Ibid., pp. 190-203.
15. Ibid., pp. 203-13.
16. Ibid., pp. 225-38.
17. Ibid., pp. 238-48.
18. Ibid., pp. 249-58.
19. Ibid., pp. 259-83.
20. Ibid., pp. 320, 325-8.
21. Ibid., pp. 284-305.

22. Gupta, *History of the Sikhs,* vol. II (*The Cis-Sutlej Sikhs 1769-1799*), pp. 1-15.
23. Ibid., pp. 16-35.
24. Ibid., pp. 36-56.
25. Ibid., pp. 57-77.
26. Ibid., pp. 78-92.
27. Ibid., pp. 93-105.
28. Ibid., pp. 106-24.
29. Ibid., pp. 125-35.
30. Ibid., pp. 136-56.
31. Ibid., pp. 157-68.
32. Ibid., pp. 169-89.
33. Ibid., pp. 190-219.
34. Ibid., pp. 220-48.
35. Ibid., pp. 249-68.
36. Ibid., pp. 269-85.
37. Ibid., pp. 286-91.
38. Gupta, *History of the Sikhs,* vol. III (*Trans-Sutlej Sikhs 1769-1799*), Lahore: Minerva Book Shop, 1944, pp. 1-6.
39. Ibid., pp. 7-19.
40. Ibid., pp. 20-1.
41. Ibid., pp. 21-32.
42. Ibid., pp. 33-45.
43. Ibid., pp. 46-52.
44. Ibid., pp. 52-9.
45. Ibid., pp. 60-86.
46. Ibid., pp. 87-120.
47. Ibid., pp. 121-9.
48. Ibid., p. 130.
49. Ibid., pp. 130-51.
50. Ibid., pp. 152-70.

CHAPTER SIXTEEN

Gulshan Lal Chopra

The Panjab as a Sovereign State (1799-1839)

In 1928, G.L. Chopra published his Ph.D. thesis approved by the University of London. In his Foreword to the work, H.L.O. Garrette refers to it as 'an exhaustive study of the reign of Maharaja Ranjit Singh, his court, his army and his policy' and points out that it was based on original and unpublished sources at the India Office and British Museum.[1] Chopra himself has provided a bibliography, divided into four sections: Persian manuscripts, unpublished English documents, published works of contemporary writers and travellers, and secondary works. Among the 21 manuscripts listed are the works of Sohan Lal Suri, Mufti Aliuddin, Bute Shah, Khushwaqt Rai, Ganesh Das, Bakht Mal and Buddh Singh Arora. The English documents are Bengal Political Consultations 1800-45, Bengal Secret and Political Consultations 1800-34, India Secret Proceedings 1834-9, and Lord Auckland's Private Letters 1836-42. Among the 41 contemporary writers and travellers are Burnes, Barr, Browne, Cunningham, Forster, Hugel, Jacquemont, Lawrence, Malcolm, Moorcroft, Masson, M'Gregor, Mohan Lal, Osborne, Prinsep, Shahamat Ali, Smyth, and Vigne. Among the 24 secondary works are those by Sir Lepel Griffin, Sir John Gordon, Muhammad Latif, G.C. Narang, C.H. Payne, and Sita Ram Kohli.[2]

The scope of Chopra's work is indicated by his chapterization: unification of the Punjab, Ranjit Singh's relations with the Afghans and the British, his army, his civil administration, his court and camp, and an assessment of Maharaja Ranjit Singh. There are three maps: the Punjab in 1799, 1809, and 1823-39. There are six appendices: pay-scales of Ranjit Singh's officers and men, the artillery at different periods, list of European and American officers, estimate of the revenues, the etiquette and ceremonial at the court, and a brief account of the Sikhs and extracts from archival materials. To these may be added footnotes and an index to complete the list of contents of *The Panjab As a Sovereign State*. The tone as well as the format of the work is scholarly and its scope, as indicated in the title itself, is confined to the state.

I. A BROAD OUTLINE OF RANJIT SINGH'S POLITICAL CAREER

For the events leading to the unification of the Punjab under Ranjit Singh, Chopra has used both English and Persian sources: Forster, Malcolm, Prinsep, Cunningham, Latif, Hugel, some archival material, and the works of Sohan Lal Suri and Mufti Aliuddin. Covering the period from 1716 to 1839 in 22 pages, Chopra gives only a broad outline. He talks of the emergence of the *misls* and the *misldari* system, Ranjit Singh's conquests in the central Punjab, occupation of the province of Multan, conquest of the Kashmir Valley, and conquests in the trans-Indus region. The use of both English and Persian sources enables him to correct some wrong impressions. For example, Chopra does not find any evidence in Persian sources for the impression that Sada Kaur was an ambitious woman who thought of schemes against Ranjit Singh's health and prevented him from receiving the benefits of education. Nor was Ranjit Singh involved in the murder of Diwan Lakhpat Rai.[3]

Chopra makes the general observation that the principal writers appeared to think that the expansion of Ranjit Singh's authority was not the outcome of a systematic design or policy but of indiscriminate and haphazard encroachment. 'This in reality was not the case'. Chopra suggests three well-marked phases. From 1799 to 1809, Ranjit Singh established himself in the Central Punjab; between 1809 and 1822, he incorporated into his kingdom most of those lands which 'he had first harried by fire and sword'; the borders were extended to its geographical limits in other directions by the conquest of Multan and Kashmir. The third phase opened in 1824 and ended with Ranjit Singh's death. The suppression of Syad Ahmad and the annexation of Peshawar and advance up to Jamrud were the only events of military significance during this phase. Within forty years Ranjit Singh broke the opposition of a hundred chieftains, and removed every vestige of alien influence from within the borders of the Punjab. Rising from a petty *sardar* to the rulership of an extensive kingdom, he brought the scattered people of the Punjab under a uniform and consistent system of government. He thus evolved 'a young and vigorous nation'. Chopra appears to be talking of 'Punjabi nationalism'.[4]

Chopra pays special attention to Ranjit Singh's relations with the Afghans and the English because a study of this theme reveals the factors influencing the growth of the Sikh kingdom up to 1839, enables us to grasp some of the fundamental issues which led to the downfall of the kingdom, and elucidates several points concerning Ranjit Singh's character and policy.[5]

Chopra observes that there was a tendency among the writers on Ranjit Singh 'to attribute the rapid expansion of his kingdom entirely to his own political genius'. However, the political situation at Kabul in the early nineteenth century which precluded the possibility of Afghan intervention in the affairs of the Punjab, gave a favourable opportunity to Ranjit Singh, to carry out his designs. Political power in Afghanistan was ultimately acquired by the Barakzai brothers at the cost of the Saḍozai descendants of Ahmad Shah Abdali. The Barakzais controlled the titular rulers of Kabul first and then established their own power. In this process, the Sadozai governor of Multan became independent and Kashmir became independent under a Barakzai. A similar situation developed in Attock, Peshawar and the Derajat. Each one of the rulers of these territories had to fend for himself against Ranjit Singh whose power was increasing all this time. Before Dost Muhammad established a tolerably strong and stable government at Kabul, Ranjit Singh occupied Peshawar and retained it despite Dost Muhammad's attempts to recover it. Hari Singh Nalwa played a crucial role in this context and even lost his life.[6]

For Ranjit Singh's relations with the English, Chopra outlines the late eighteenth-century background before coming to the first decade of the nineteenth century when some important changes took place in the attitude of the East India Company towards the Sikh chiefs. When Holkar was pursued by Lord Lake into the Punjab in 1805, Ranjit Singh refused after some hesitation to join Holkar against the British. In fact, Ranjit Singh and Fateh Singh Ahluwalia signed an agreement in 1806, pledging 'friendship between the Honourable East India and Sardars Ranjit Singh and Fateh Singh'. Soon after the arrival of Lord Minto as the new Governor-General, the situation in Europe changed radically after the Treaty of Tilsit between Napolean and Russia, and it affected British policy in India. In February 1808 Lord Minto wrote that this change called for a change of policy towards the Punjab. Aware of the policy of non-intervention, he suggested that it appeared to have become necessary to intervene in the affairs of the cis-Sutlej chiefs who were subjugated by Ranjit Singh. In fact, he attributes Ranjit Singh's penetration into the Sutlej-Jamuna Divide as a result of the policy of non-intervention. Thus, his views were formed before Metcalfe's mission. Minto did not wish to press the issue of the cis-Sutlej states, telling Colonel Ochterloney merely to be prepared for advance. However, the situation in Europe appeared to have changed so that there was no possibility of a French invasion of India. There was no need of an alliance with Ranjit Singh at the cost of the cis-Sutlej lands. He was told to regard the Sutlej as the eastern boundary of his dominions. Ranjit Singh, eventually, signed a treaty in 1809. His dream of uniting the Sikh people under his umbrella remained unrealized but the treaty enabled him to expand his dominions on his side of the Sutlej. In the long run, it proved to be unfavourable for expansion beyond certain limits and also for the stability of the state.[7]

After 1809, a crisis arose in 1822 about Wadni in the cis-Sutlej area. The place had been given by Ranjit Singh to Sada Kaur in 1808. The British Agents at Ludhiana and Ambala treated Sada Kaur as an independent ruler and wanted her territory on the left side of the river. When a quarrel arose between Sada Kaur and Ranjit Singh, she was imprisoned and Ranjit Singh's troops occupied Wadni. But the British Agent ordered their ejection. Ranjit Singh made a representation to the Governor-General and he accepted his claim to the place. About a decade later, while Ranijt Singh wanted to expand his dominions towards Sind, he was asked to endorse the British commercial relations with Sind. It was with great hesitation and reluctance that Ranjit Singh yielded to the suggestion made by Captain Wade on behalf of the Governor-General.[8]

Finally, when the British mission to Kabul for an alliance against Russia failed, they thought of replacing Dost Muhammad by Shah Shuja as Ranjit Singh had thought of it earlier but Shah Shuja had not agreed to relinquish his claim to Peshawar. In 1838, Ranjit Singh was approached to be a party to the British enterprise. He was indifferent to the supposed danger from Russia and, therefore, not enthusiastic about a scheme which appeared to result in British influence over the ruler of Afghanistan. When he was told that the British would go ahead with the scheme without his support, he agreed to sign a tripartite treaty after some minor modifications suggested by him. Many of the *sardars* and Generals were not in favour of this treaty. Against the view of several other writers, Chopra does not subscribe to the view that Ranjit Singh's policy of reconciliation was the result of a genuine feeling of trust or goodwill. It was during this phase that glancing at an English map of India he exclaimed: 'All will be red'. During the last three years, he showed a marked disposition to follow an independent line of policy, and he was supported by several ministers, notably Dhian Singh.[9]

II. THE ARMY OF RANJIT SINGH

Chopra looks upon Ranjit Singh as primarily a conqueror and military organizer. Both temperament and necessity induced him to raise a strong and well-trained army not only for the establishment of a large state but also to protect its integrity. The army of the *misls* consisted principally of cavalry. The infantry formed an inferior branch, and the *sardars* knew little of artillery. After Holkar's visit to the Punjab, Ranjit Singh raised some battalions, and became more serious about a trained army after the skirmish between the Akalis and Metcalfe's escort in Amritsar in 1809. Ranjit Singh's regular army came to have three wings: infantry, cavalry and artillery. In the beginning, the bulk of this army consisted of Afghans, Gurkhas, and *Purbia Hindostanis*. However, by 1818 both Sikh and other Punjabis, had come to dominate the army. In 1822, Ranjit Singh employed European officers who organized and trained an efficient army.[10]

The strength of the infantry battalions went on increasing from the range of 400 to 600 each in 1819 to the range of 700 and 900 in 1829. The uniform of the infantrymen was scarlet, with blue cotton trousers and turbans and black leather belts. They were usually armed with sword, musket and bayonent. A company consisted of 100 men and a section, of 25 men. The chief officer of the battalion was the commandant who was assisted by an adjutant and a major. Each company was under a *subedar* who was assisted by two *jamadars*. Each section was headed by a *havaldar* assisted by a *naik*. In the non-combatant establishment were a *munshi*, a *mutasaddi* and a *granthi*. Then there were menial workers like the *khalasi, sakka, ghariali, beldar, jhanda-bardar, mistri, kama,* and *tahliya*.[11]

The *Fauj-i Khas* formed the model brigade of the Sikh army. It was raised by Ventura and Allard in 1822. It consisted of four battalions of infantry, two regiments of cavalry, and 24 guns under General Ilahi Bakhsh. The eagle and the tricolour flag, with a verse of Guru Gobind Singh embroidered upon it, was the emblem of the *Fauj-i Khas*. It was also called the French Brigade, French Legion or Fransisi Campu. The four Sikh battalions wore turbans of different colours. Captain Wade highly appreciated the infantry section when he saw it on parade.[12]

The regular cavalry trained by General Allard and other European officers was less important. It consisted of a few regiments of dragoons and lancers. Until 1822, there were only 4 trained regiments of cavalry as against 14 battalions of infantry and 8 *deras* of artillery. The total number of trained horsemen was about 1,000 as against 10,000 foot. By 1829, the number of trained horsemen had increased to 4,000 or 5,000, and remained much the same in the rest of Ranjit Singh's reign. The pay of the cavalry regiments was higher than that of the infantry. In due course, Sikhs had begun to join the cavalry. Chopra quotes a description given by Lieutenant Barr. Osborne commented in 1838 that cavalry was not comparable with the infantry, neither in appearance nor in reality.[13]

In the beginning, two guns were usually attached to each infantry battalion and there was no distinct detachment of artillery. In 1810, a separate corps was raised and placed under the *Darogha-i Topkhana*. Two years later it formed the principal unit of artillery called *Topkhana-i Khas*. It was commanded by Mian Ghaus Khan, and was divided into four sections: *Aspi* (driven by horses), *Gavi* (driven by bullocks), a separate horse battery, and guns distributed over infantry battalions. In 1814, a fresh battery was raised under Ilahi-Bakhsh, and the old separate battery was assigned to the regular army. In 1826, the number ofbatteries attached to the regular army was 7, and the number of guns and swivels was 200. General Court was employed in 1827 and Colonel Gardner in 1832. The entire *Topkhana* was reorganized and divided into three sections: *Topkhana-i Jinsi* (heavy and mixed batteries), *Topkhana-i Aspi* (horse and light field-batteries), and *Zamburkhanas* (swivel batteries). In 1835, when the army was organized into brigades, the artillery branch was further modified. One horse battery was assigned to each brigade. A few *Jinsi* siege trains remained a distinct corps, first under Sultan Mahmud and then under Lehna Singh Majithia. Chopra quotes Barr's description of the uniform of artillerymen. In less than a decade the training and organization of the artillery was accomplished on European lines. Osborne carried a good impression of its perfection.[14]

The Irregular Army, called *Fauj-i Be-qawaid,* followed no prescribed rules. It was principally composed of *Ghurcharhas* (horsemen). In the early part of his reign, Ranjit Singh had constituted a regiment of *Ghurcharha Sawars,* and to this he added *Ghurcharha-i Khas.* Both were paid cash salaries, but they remained free from the discipline to which the regular cavalrymen were subjected. The general body of irregular horse was divided into two sections: *Ghurcharha-i Khas* and *Misldars.* The former supplied their own horses and equipment, and they were paid first in *jagirs* and then in cash. The *Misldars* consisted of the petty chiefs, who had been dispossessed of their territories by Ranjit Singh, at the head of their bands of horsemen. At the end of the reign, they completed the greater portion of the irregular cavalry. The men of a *misl* generally belonged to a single tribe, clan or community. Their strength ranged from 25 to 75 men. Several *misls,* combined together to form a *dera.* The Jat Sikh element was in a large majority among the *Ghurcharhas,* followed by Hindu Rajputs of lower Kashmir and Muslims of the districts lying along the Jhelum River. Socially respected, they formed the conservative element in the state, ever eager to uphold its political independence and territorial integrity. They enjoyed the fullest confidence of Ranjit Singh. Europeans like Hugel, Wade and Osborne had appreciation for the *Ghurcharhas* for their picturesque appearance. A part of the irregular horsemen, but a distinct part, were the Akalis; their personal courage and recklessness proved to be advantageous in hazardous enterprises.[15]

Chopra takes up recruitment and pay, arms and accoutrements, mobilization, animal transport, the growing strength of the army of Ranjit Singh, and its general estimate. Due to Ranjit Singh's personal attitude towards the fighting services, the prestige attached to soldiering, and the presence of martial sections in the Punjabi population, there was no problem of recruitment. Starting with payment through *jagirs,* the practice of cash payment became general before the end of Ranjit Singh's reign. The army remained in arrears for four to six months, partly due to inefficiency and partly due to deliberate policy to check insubordination and desertion. The irregulars were paid by the *diwan,* and the regulars by the *bakhshi,* from a separate treasury called *Peti Khazana-i Fauj.* The soldiers in garrisons were paid by the *thanadars* of the forts. The pay scales were not uniform. However, a few general statements could be made. The pay of the artillery and cavalry was higher than that of the infantry. The payment made to *Ghurcharhas* was even higher than what was paid to the regular cavalry. Occasional *jagirs* and rewards were given in lieu of pension. No provision was made for the widows and children of these who had died in service.[16]

The *Ghurcharhas* were armed with swords, spears and matchlocks, like regular cavalrymen. The principal arm of the infantry was the musket. Swords, spears, matchlocks, pistols, helmets, coats of mail, shields, breast-plates and gauntlets were manufactured in the Punjab. The artillery consisted of heavy cannons, light guns, and swivels. Most of the guns were six-pounders, but the pieces of artillery were on the average greater in weight than those of the English. All these came to be manufactured in the Punjab. The soldiers could be ordered to march at any hour of the day or night at a short notice. They could traverse long distances in rapid marches. The troops on the move had their own regimental bazaars to supply articles of private use. The drum, the fife and the bugle were used by the infantry, and bands were introduced in certain units. The artillery horses and mules were good, and fort-artillery was drawn partly by horses and partly by bullocks. The army wagons were drawn by bullocks only. Camels were used to transport ammunition packed in boxes, and sometimes small pieces of artillery, and fuel and forage.[17]

Chopra refers to the estimates of the numbers by Burnes, Masson, Lord Auckland, Wade and Griffin among the Europeans and to figures given in the *Tazkirat al-Umara,* the *Catalogue of the Khalsa Darbar Records,* and by Shahamat Ali. These estimates and figures show slight variations. Nevertheless, they provide sufficient data for drawing approximately correct conclusions. The disciplined army of the Punjab at the time of Ranjit Singh's death ranged from 35,000 to 40,000 men. To these may be added an equal number of irregulars of all classes, taking the total to about 75,000 men. Sir Henry Fane, the Commander-in-Chief of the army of the East India Company, described what he saw of the *Ghurcharhas*, the regular cavalry, and the infantry in 1837, as well-clothed, armed and accoutred, completely organized, and brigaded and placed under proper officers; 'their movements were as good as those of our own troops could be'. Lord Auckland too observed that Ranjit Singh's army was 'in no respect inferior to our own army'.[18]

Thus, in a single generation, Ranjit Singh raised an army of less than 8,000 untrained troops to a magnificent force of 75,000 men, at least half of whom were regularly trained, disciplined and equipped. The regular infantry attracted the pick of the youth and represented the flower of the Punjab. The artillery also became a regular part of the army. Ranjit Singh created such an efficient engine of war that he could have fought on equal terms with the East India Company. The conduct of the army of the Punjab in the two Sikh wars far excelled anything of the kind witnessed before on the Indian soil. This would remain an ample vindication of the reforms undertaken by Ranjit Singh, 'the war-lord of the Punjab'.[19]

III. RANJIT SINGH'S CIVIL ADMINISTRATION

G.L. Chopra's account of the army of the Punjab is more elaborate and systematic than that of any of his predecessors. It is based on Persian manuscripts as well as sources in English. However, he refers to the *Catalogue of the Khalsa Darbar Records* only twice. In his account of the civil administration of Ranjit Singh he makes no reference to the *Catalogue*. It is based on the work of the earlier historians, European travellers, archival records and Persian works. On the basis of this evidence he suggests that Ranjit Singh was compelled to devote more attention to his civil and revenue administration after 1823 than what he had done earlier.[20] It was a financial necessity. Chopra discusses the financial and departmental organization of the kingdom of Ranjit Singh, land revenue system, territorial divisions and local administration, judicial arrangements, and governance.

According to Chopra, Ranjit Singh had no state treasury for nearly a decade of his rule; his accounts were kept by Rama Nand, a banker of

Amritsar. In 1808, he appointed Bhawani Das as his *diwan*, or finance minister, who divided the work into several departments, like *Daftar-i Abwab al-Mal* or *Daftar-i Maliyat, Daftar-i Abwab al-Tahwil* also called *Daftar-i Tahwilat, Daftar-i Taujihat, Daftar-i Mawajib,* and *Daftar-i Roznamcha-ikhrajat.* The first of these five departments dealt with revenue receipts and it was sub-divided into two sections: one called *Jama' Kharch-i Ta'aluqat,* dealing with land revenue, and the other called *Jama' Kharch-i Sairat,* dealing with all other sources of income, like tribute and presents, escheats and forfeitures, excise, registration fees and customs, and transit duties. Chopra gives a brief outline of these sources of income.[21]

Chopra gives more importance to the land revenue system which brought in by far the greater part of the income of the state. In the beginning of Ranjit Singh's career, the system of *batai* was 're-introduced on the old Mughal plan'. It was a simple division of the crop, and the share of the state was collected in kind. This system continued till 1823. The second phase began in 1824 when *kankut* replaced *batai.* In the new system the share of the state was reckoned out of a standing crop and collected in cash. This was a distinct improvement. However, *kankut* was also defective because the income of the state was estimated only a short time before the end of the harvest. After 1834, Ranjit Singh encouraged farming out revenues to the highest bidder. Such arrangement was sometimes made directly with the village to eliminate the profits of the farmers as middlemen.[22]

Chopra refers to the statements on the share of the government in the produce from land by Lawrence and Douie, and in the Punjab Administration Report of 1849-50. He comes to the conclusion that the share of the gross produce which belonged to the state varied from place to place according to the productivity of the soil, the nature of the crop, the means of irrigation, and other facilities for cultivation. At some places the share of the state could be half of the gross produce; elsewhere it varied from two-fifths to one-third; it was seldom lower than one-third in central Punjab. In Multan, it was rarely one-half and it could be as low as one-third to one-sixth of the gross produce. The total amount of *abwab* (taxes other than the land revenue) ranged from 5 to 15 per cent of the revenue. The chief officer for collecting revenue in the *ta'aluqa* was the *kardar* who was assisted by *muqaddams, patwaris* and *kanungos*. Some of these officials had the right to a commission, amounting to 5 per cent of the revenue. There was a special treasury under the *kardar*. The revenue was collected twice a year, a month after harvesting. It was either sent to Lahore or disposed of in accordance with the orders of Ranjit Singh.[23]

The second department was concerned with the records of accounts of income and expenditure sent by officials. The third department was concerned with the accounts of the royal household, *khil'ats* and entertainment of guests. In the fourth department, the accounts of the pay of the army, the civil staff, the official establishment, and the menials were kept. The fifth office was set-up to register accounts of daily expenditure under various heads. These *daftars* passed through several changes. Towards the end of Ranjit Singh's reign there were 12 principal *daftars*, each controlled by one of the prominent courtiers, working more or less directly under the personal direction of the ruler.[24]

The Punjab was divided into four provinces for local administration: Lahore, Multan, Kashmir and Peshawar. The territories of the tributary chiefs were not included directly in these four provinces. Each province (*suba*) was divided into *parganas* and each *pargana* into *ta'aluqas*, containing 50 to 100 villages each. This system was close to the Mughal system of territorial divisions. The administration of the province was entrusted to a governor (*nazim*), with a number of *kardars* under him. Usually there was a *kardar* in every *ta'aluqa*, and he was more important in the local administration than the governor whose functions were largely of an appellate character and of a general nature. The *kardar* performed a number of functions as a revenue collector and supervisor of land settlement, a treasurer and accountant, a judge and magistrate, an excise and customs officer, and a general supervisor of the people on behalf of the state. The European writers and Indian chroniclers refer to cases in which due efficiency and honesty were combined, and there was a striking degree of prosperity among the people. There are instances of maladministration too. The difference lies in the general estimate of the *kardars*: the European writers condemned them as a class and the Indian chroniclers only the individuals. The judgement of the former was conditioned partly by their European background. The effects of the local administration on the people varied with the personality of the official. There was also a difference between the administration of the provinces of Lahore and Multan and the other two which were rather distant from the capital. The attitude of the people in Peshawar and Kashmir towards their rulers was also different from the attitude of the people of Lahore and Multan.[25]

Chopra points out that there was very little information on the administration of justice. The European writers did not fully comprehend the working of an institution which was not based on codified law but on customary rules. There was no uniformity. The procedure was simple and no distinction was made between civil and criminal cases. Village disputes were settled by the *panchayat,* a court of five. It was more of an arbitration court than a judicial tribunal. Its decisions could be revised by the *kardar*. In the towns, justice was administrated by the *kardars.* In the cities, important cases were decided by the governor. Separate officials (*'adalatis*) were appointed sometimes for exclusive judicial work. Sohan Lal refers to the *Adalat-i Ala,* but its constitution was not clear. It was probably an appellate court, analogous to the High Court of the British times. Judicial authority was delegated to prominent ministers of the ruler. Finally, the Sikh ruler himself held his *darbar* and heard petitions and appeals against the lower courts or officials.[26]

Ranjit Singh's judicial system was 'crude and simple' only in appearance. In actual practice it suited the political temperament of the people. Abuse of authority by local officials was restrained by several considerations. Their arbitrary action could displease the ruler, which was not in their interest. Ranjit Singh himself took personal interest in the representations and complaints of the people in the countryside. The practice of appointing touring *adalatis* to hear complaints had a restraining influence on the local officials. Instances of capital punishment given by *kardars* are known but generally a fine was imposed on murderers. Mutilation was not common. On the whole, the rigour of punishment depended upon the nature of the crime, the disposition of the magistrate, and the likelihood of his action being reported to the ruler. The locality in which the crime was committed also had an important bearing on the punishment awarded.[27]

Chopra subscribes to the view that Ranjit Singh destroyed the *misls* and allowed the *gurmata* to decay; he transformed the whole constitution of the Sikhs from an irregular theocratic commonwealth of a loose federal type into a military monarchy based on personal rule. He established 'a pure and unmitigated despotism'. Under his despotism, the Punjab was governed in a manner that generally suited the existing state of society. There was little interference in village life, except matters related to land revenue. The humblest subject could aspire to a position of wealth. Ranjit Singh never arrogated any high sounding titles; his aggressive designs were presented as enhancing the glory of the Khalsa, the whole Sikh Church. He appeared to be an embodiment of the high purpose of the *gurmata*. His rule presented a counterblast to Muslim bigotry. From the viewpoint of his subjects his despotism was benevolent. He was not a foreign ruler and there was no drain of wealth. Compared with the conditions before the establishment of his large state, his rule was a distinct improvement in terms of law and order, peace and prosperity. However, Ranjit Singh had inherited no elaborate system or settled principle of government, and he evolved no constitution for his state. There was no constitutional check on the absolute power of the ruler. In the case of Ranjit Singh it worked well, but under his successors it led to a state of anarchy and confusion.[28]

IV. THE COURT OF RANJIT SINGH

For the 'court and camp of Ranjit Singh', Gulshan Lal Chopra divides the leading personalities into six groups: Dogra Rajputs, Sikhs, Hindus, Brahmans, Muslims, and Europeans. The Dogras were represented by the brothers Dhian Singh, Gulab Singh and Suchet Singh, and Hira Singh, the son of Dhian Singh. The three brothers entered Ranjit Singh's service in 1811 as mere troopers. Within three years, they became *ghurcharhas*. Before long, Gulab Singh was given a *jagir* and Dhian Singh succeeded Khushal Singh as the *deoridar* (keeper of the palace). In 1818, all the three were created Rajas with a considerable territory. Dhian Singh was ultimately made Raja-i Kalan Bahadur, a title signifying the first minister of the state. Chopra goes on to outline the careers of Raja Dhian Singh, Raja Gulab Singh, Raja Suchet Singh and Raja Hira Singh.[29]

The Sikh courtiers represented the landed aristocracy. Some of them descended from the chiefs of the old *misls*, while others had newly risen to eminence. They mostly served in the army and seldom employed in civil administration. They were often attached to diplomatic missions. Chopra gives 'a short sketch' of some prominent members of this class. From amongst the Majithias he selects Lehna Singh. The Sandhanwalias were Ranjit Singh's collaterals. The first to join Ranjit Singh's service was Buddh Singh, followed by his two brothers, Atar Singh and Lehna Singh. Their total *jagirs* amounted to nearly Rs. 1 million a year. After Ranjit Singh's death, they represented the chief opposition against the Dogras, with no better motives. Two other Sikh *sardars* noticed by Chopra are Shyam Singh Atariwala and Hari Singh Nalwa.[30]

Among the Hindu members of the court to be noticed by Chopra are Diwan Mohkam Chand, Diwan Bhawani Das, and Diwan Karam Chand. Among the Brahmans are Jamadar Khushal Singh, Tej Singh, Diwan Ganga Ram, Diwan Dina Nath, Misar Diwan Chand, and Misars Beli Ram and Rup Lal. To be noticed among the Muslims are Fakirs Azizuddin, Nuruddin and Imamuddin. The most important Europeans were Ventura, Allard, Court, and Avatibile. As Chopra points out, all the courtiers are noticed not simply because of their own importance but also due to their representative position. He is deliberately selective and not comprehensive.[31]

The courtiers of Ranjit Singh did not form a homogeneous body: they represented various creeds, diverse races, and different traditions. They who controlled the administrative machinery of the state were essentially adventurers. The indigenous element was confined to the army almost exclusively. A court constituted on such a basis could hardly secure any identity of interests or unity of purpose. Most of the members of the aristocracy were not imbued with a genuine regard for the safety of the state or its people. In other words, they were not activated by 'patriotism'. The lines of demarcation between the aristocracy were a source of strength for Ranjit Singh who could use their personal loyalty to his advantage, but after his death they did not feel the same kind of loyalty for his successors.[32]

Chopra finds the study of Ranjit Singh especially instructive because, in spite of its benevolent character under him, his despotism was soon followed by decline and fall. Chopra observes that Sohan Lal, Moorcroft, Burnes, Hugel, Jacquemont, M'Gregor, Osborne and others had noticed almost every phase of Ranjit Singh's career. However, there is some repetition in their accounts and divergence of their views, particularly between the European writers and the Indian chroniclers. Their differences enable the historian to draw his own independent conclusions. Chopra has tried to follow a critical and comparative approach for a correct estimate of Ranjit Singh as a man and a ruler.[33]

Chopra provides an outline of Ranjit Singh's boyhood, his personal appearance and conversation, his dress, private habits and inclinations, his religious views, his generosity, acquisition of the Koh-i Nur, his qualities as a soldier, and his statesmanship. Chopra does not omit the information which does not present Ranjit Singh in a good light, particularly his personal morals. However, Chopra suggests that this side of his life should be seen in relation to his social environment. Moreover, he was not a habitual drunkard and did not exhaust his energies by sensual pleasures. Referring to the sharp difference between the Indian and European writers on the issue of Ranjit Singh's religious views, Chopra states that he inherited the religious beliefs of his forefathers, and he was enlightened enough to comprehend, or even to criticize, the Sikh creed. He readily accepted its more obvious features with 'implicit faith and superstitious reverence'. In fact, he appeared to the contemporary Sikhs as a staunch defender of their faith. He refrained from interfering with the religious rights of his subjects, nor did he approve of such interference by the ruling class.[34]

Ranjit Singh created the Punjab as a sovereign state, involving all its communities in the venture, in place of a mere geographical region divided into a large number of petty states. Yet he has been held responsible for the ultimate decline of the Sikh power. Chopra addresses himself to this question in the concluding chapter of his book. There is a substantial element of truth in the charge that Ranjit Singh allowed the Dogras to acquire vast territorial power and influence. However, this was only one among several causes of the ruin of the Sikh kingdom. The most important was the despotic and personal rule of the Maharaja. His death created a sort of vacuum at the centre, which led to pursuit of individual gains and advantages rather than collective benefit. The presence of the East India Company, a power with moral and material standards and political ideas different from those of the

Sikhs, on the frontiers of the Punjab was another cause. Thus, 'we find that such subtle and fundamental causes were working against the independence of the Punjab, as the ruler of the Sikhs could not possibly provide against, even if he had displayed a better political genius.' The word 'he' in this quotation is for Ranjit Singh. In other words, for G.L. Chopra, to hold Maharaja Ranjit Singh responsible for the decline and fall of the Sikh kingdom is to take a superficial view.[35]

Like the concluding section of Chopra's book, most of the appendices are related to the main body of the book. The first appendix is related to the chapter on the army. The second appendix is actually a table giving the strength of the artillery in terms of men, guns and swivels in 1819-20, 1828-9, and 1838-9, showing the increase, respectively, from 834 men in 1920 to 4,535 in 1839, from 22 guns in 1820 to 188 in 1839, and from 190 swivels in 1820 to 280 swivels in 1839. The third appendix gives the names of 54 'Europeans' employed by Ranjit Singh. Their largest bulk was in the army. The fourth appendix gives a table of the sources of state income, amounting to Rs. 1,48,81,500. The amount of revenue alienated by way of *jagirs* was Rs. 1,09,28,000, bringing the total to Rs. 2,58,09,500. In the fifth appendix are given the time, place and manner of holding *darbars*, dresses of the courtiers, and the official language of the court.[36]

The sixth appendix contains a brief account of the Sikh coins. In the body of the book there is very little about coins. This account was based on a personal examination of the collections preserved in the British Museum and the museum at Lahore. There was no coin of 'Jassa Kalal' in these collections. Chopra thinks, however, that this coin was struck, in 1758. The coin struck at Lahore in 1765 was actually examined by Chopra. It was struck from Amritsar in 1778. No coins of 1790-6 were found. Ranjit Singh did not strike any coin in 1799 when he occupied Lahore. Coins of 1803 and 1807 were there, and then every year coins were struck at Lahore and Amritsar. The coins of 1804, 1805 and 1809 are seen by Chopra as 'Moran Shahi', after Moran, because these coins appear to bear symbols of the peacock's tail and thumb-mirror (*arsi*). These coins appeared to have continued to be struck till 1827. A coin in the British Museum contained the figures of Guru Nanak and Mardana. Coins were also struck at Multan and Kashmir (Srinagar). A coin struck at Peshawar in 1837 is attributed by Chopra to Hari Singh Nalwa. Gold coins (*mohars*) were struck in 1804. Copper coins were struck at various places.[37]

The seventh appendix contains letters and extracts from the Bengal Political Consultations. The letter of C.M. Wade to Sir C.T. Metcalfe, dated 11 January 1827, contains the reports sent by Doctor Murray, who had been sent to attend on Maharaja Ranjit Singh, written in December 1826, and then his reports written on 1 June 1827, 22 May, 25 May, 31 May, and 19 June 1831. Another letter was addressed to Sir C.T. Metcalfe on 1 August 1827. It is a detailed report on the British mission to the Maharaja in May 1827. Both the reports and letters of Doctor Murray and C.M. Wade provide information on Ranjit Singh, his courtiers, his army, his political concerns, and his personality. This information has a direct bearing on what Chopra states at different places in the body of his work. Thus, all the appendices except perhaps the one on coins appear to support and illumine the text.[38]

V. GENERAL REMARKS

Gulshan Lal Chopra's approach and treatment of the subject is scholarly or what may be called academic. As the title indicates, it is meant to be confined to politics and polity; he talks of political events, diplomacy, government and administration. There is hardly anything about society, economy or culture. In all this, he is akin to his British predecessors. He does not enter into any controversy with them but his disagreement on certain important issues is very clear.

Significantly, Chopra does not accept the scandals associated with Ranjit Singh and his family. He emphasizes that there was a method or systematic policy in his conquests. Ranjit Singh's success was partly due to the political situation of the north-west, especially the position of the rulers of Kabul, which was helpful to him. His relations with the British did not remain the same throughout his reign. His policy of reconciliation was not the result of trust or goodwill. Chopra is appreciative of the magnificent force raised by Ranjit Singh in a short time. He could have fought the British on equal terms. Even after his death, the British met the toughest resistance from the Sikhs in their entire political career in India. Chopra points out that the European writers did not comprehend the working of the administration of justice under Ranjit Singh because it was not based on codified laws but custom. The system appeared to be crude and simple but it suited the political environment of the people. There was a large degree of local autonomy in social matters, and there was no religious discrimination. Opportunities were open to the humblest subject. Chopra does not hesitate to state that Ranjit Singh was not a 'foreign' ruler and, therefore, there was no drain of wealth. Evidently, Chopra has little appreciation for colonial rule.

Chopra does not feel happy about the members of the aristocracy lacking patriotism. In the context of the state of Ranjit Singh, it could mean regional patriotism more than anything else. Chopra does not give preference to any European view of the functionaries of the state under Ranjit Singh. He does not accept their view of Ranjit Singh's religion. He emphasizes that the Maharaja was a good Sikh according to the notions of his time and he defended the Sikh faith. But he did not interfere with the religious rights of his subjects. He did not allow others to interfere with the religious affairs of other people. He involved all the communities of the Punjab in creating a sovereign state. It was a mistake on his part to allow the Dogras to acquire vast territorial power and influence. It is possible to discern an undercurrent of 'Punjabi nationalism' in *The Panjab as a Sovereign State.*

NOTES

1. Gulshan Lal Chopra, *The Panjab As a Sovereign State (1799-1839),* Hoshiarpur: Vishvesharanand Vedic Research Institute, 1960, 2nd edn., Foreword.
2. Ibid., Preface and Bibliography.
3. Ibid., pp. 7-8, nn. 1, 3.
4. Ibid., pp. 21-2.
5. Ibid., p. 23.
6. Ibid., pp. 24-9.
7. Ibid., pp. 29-41.
8. Ibid., pp. 42-5.
9. Ibid., pp. 45-9.
10. Ibid., pp. 50-4.
11. Ibid., pp. 55-6.

12. Ibid., pp. 56-7.
13. Ibid., pp. 57-9.
14. Ibid., pp. 60-3.
15. Ibid., pp. 63-7.
16. Ibid., pp. 67-9.
17. Ibid., pp. 69-71.
18. Ibid., pp. 71-4.
19. Ibid., pp. 74-5.
20. Ibid., p. 76.
21. Ibid., pp. 76-8.
22. Ibid., pp. 78-80.
23. Ibid., pp. 80-2.
24. Ibid., pp. 82-4.
25. Ibid., pp. 84-8.
26. Ibid., pp. 88-90.
27. Ibid., pp. 90-1.
28. Ibid., pp. 91-4.
29. Ibid., pp. 95-100.
30. Ibid., pp. 100-2.
31. Ibid., pp. 104-7.
32. Ibid., p. 118.
33. Ibid., pp. 119-20.
34. Ibid., pp. 121-8.
35. Ibid., pp. 139-41.
36. Ibid., pp. 142-51.
37. Ibid., pp. 152-5.
38. Ibid., pp. 156-225.

CHAPTER SEVENTEEN

Sita Ram Kohli on Ranjit Singh and his Successors

I. INTRODUCTORY

Sita Ram Kohli's *Maharaja Ranjit Singh,* written in Punjabi, was published in 1953. His *Sunset of the Sikh Empire* was published posthumously in 1967. However, both these books were essentially the product of the work done by Kohli much earlier. Born in 1889, he had matriculated from Government High School, Bhera (his birth place) and passed the Master's examination in Hisotry from Government College, Lahore, in 1910 or 1911. He was given Alexandra Research Scholarship to pursue historical studies, and then taken into service as a Lecturer in History at Government College, Lahore. In 1915, he was assigned the task of preparing a catalogue of the Khalsa Darbar Records in the Punjab Archives at Lahore. The first volume of his *Catalogue of the Khalsa Darbar Records* was published in 1919.

In 1918, Kohli had already written a paper for the Indian Historical Records Commission on the records of the 'Sikh Government', and presented a paper to the Punjab Historical Society on land revenue under the Sikhs which was published in the *Journal* of the Society. In 1922, Kohli began to contribute articles to the *Journal of Indian History* on the army of the Sikhs. The second volume of his *Catalogue* was published in 1927. In 1928 he edited the text of Diwan Amar Nath's *Zafarnama-i Ranjit Singh.* In 1932 he published the *Trial of Mul Raj* which was based largely on archival sources. In 1933 appeared his book on Maharaja Ranjit Singh in Urdu, written for the Hindustani Academy, Allahabad. At that time, Kohli was familiar with the *Fatehnama Guru Khalsa Ji Ka* (which he edited in 1952). In 1936, he published a thoroughly annotated *Var* of Shah Muhammad. In 1940, he wrote a paper on 'A Book of Military Parwanas' which was a compilation of about 450 orders of Maharaja Ranjit Singh issued to Sardar Tej Singh as commander of the *Kampu-i Mu'alla* (the army of the Maharaja) during the Peshawar campaign of 1833-4.[1] Thus, we can see that Kohli had worked on sources and written on the period of Ranjit Singh and his successors for nearly four decades before the two books, which we propose to analyse, were published.

II. APPROACH TO MAHARAJA RANJIT SINGH

Sita Ram Kohli's *Maharaja Ranjit Singh* has 20 chapters, two portraits of the Maharaja, a photograph of the medal called 'The Star of the Punjab' (*Kaukab-i Punjab*), two maps (of the Punjab in 1800 and the Punjab in 1839, clearly showing the vast expansion of his dominions), and six appendices. One appendix contains a list of books to which reference is made in the footnotes.

This list includes the *History of the Punjab* by Muhammad Latif and 10 others books used by him. However, Kohli makes much greater use of Sohan Lal's *Umdat ut-Tawarikh* than Latif. Instead of M'Gregor, Kohli's preference is for Cunningham. Some of the new Persian sources used by Kohli are the *Khalsa Darbar Records*, Ahmad Shah of Batala's *Tarikh-i Hind* (in manuscript), a manuscript relating to the affairs of Multan, the *Kitab-i Naql-i Parwanajat* (a collection of more than 450 orders of the Maharaja mentioned earlier), and Bute Shah's *Tarikh-i Panjab*. The other manuscripts he uses are the *Fatehnama Guru Khalsa Ji ka* by Ganesh Das, the *Khalsanama* of Raizada Ratan Chand, and the *Shir-o Shakar* of Pandit Daya Ram Kashmiri. A number of new printed works have also been used by Kohli. Important among them are Bawa Prem Singh's *Maharaja Ranjit Singh* in Punjabi, Shahamat Ali's *The Sikhs and the Afghans* in English, the correspondence of Sir Charles Metcalfe, Lepel Griffiin's *Maharaja Ranjit Singh*, the *Sikh Wars* by Sir C. Gough, and Kohli's own six articles on the army of Ranjit Singh published in the *Journal of Indian History* in 1922 and 1923, apart from the *Gazetters* of Multan and Peshawar. Sita Ram Kohli has not treated any work as an authority, and he differs with his predecessors on several points. His approach has been empirical and critical and his attitude empathetic.

The background chapters, four in all, have some relevance for what follows but Kohli does not try to establish or state explicit links. This relevance appears to increase as we move through these chapters towards the beginning of Ranjit Singh's reign. Kohli accepts the classification of *misls* into twelve and uses the *misldar* in the sense of Prinsep's *sardar*. Ranjit Singh, therefore, is seen as starting his career as a *misldar*. He agrees with George Forster that the possibility of one *sardar* emerging as the supreme power in the Punjab was inherent in the *misldari* system itself. The fourth chapter deals with the ancestors of Ranjit Singh and shows that Charhat Singh and Mahan Singh left a substantial legacy for Ranjit Singh in terms of territory, resources, and troops.

In the next ten chapters, Kohli follows the pattern set by Prinsep of mentioning events in their chronological order. However, he is more meticulous and gives greater details. He treats the reign of Ranjit Singh in several phases: 1793-9, 1800-2, 1803-6, 1806-8, 1809-11, 1812-14, 1815-18, 1818-22, and 1822-33. The remaining years of his reign are not formally treated as a phase presumably because the dominions of Ranjit Singh had reached their utmost limits by 1833. Kohli's interest in details is reflected in the number of sub-headings he gives in these ten chapters: no less than 250. Over 200 of them relate to political events and diplomacy.

The remaining 'events' relate to births, betrothals, marriages and deaths of individuals connected with Ranjit Singh or his state, directly or indirectly; arrival of new courtiers and army officers; the Koh-i Nur diamond; European visitors to the court; conferment of titles and territories; natural or man-made disasters and a few other 'events'. The births of Princes Kharak Singh, Sher Singh, Tara Singh, Kashmira Singh are mentioned in different phases. The only betrothal to be mentioned as a sub-heading is that of Prince Kharak Singh. Apart from Ranjit Singh's own marriages in 1796 and 1798 and the marriage of Prince Kharak Singh in 1812, the marriage of General Ventura figures in the sub-headings. The death of Diwan Mohkam Chand in 1814, of Rama Nand Sarraf in 1823, and of Misar Diwan Chand in 1825 are given. The arrival of new courtiers, army officers and European visitors is mentioned in the case of Jamadar Khushal Singh, Teja Singh, Ram Singh, Diwan Ganga Ram, Dina Nath, Pandit Bir Dhar, Ventura, Allard,

William Moorcroft, and an English doctor. The persons to receive titles and territories are Mian Kishora Singh, Dhian Singh and Hira Singh. Evidently, the sub-headings do not cover all the persons of any particular category. The earthquake of 1826 in Kashmir, the outbreak of cholera in Lahore, and the famine in Kashmir are the three calamities mentioned by Kohli. The scuffle between the Akalis and the soldiers of Metcalfe in Amritsar is mentioned as a significant happening.

Men and events figuring in the sub-headings are regarded as important by Kohli for the nature of their connection with Ranjit Singh or their bearing on the state. Faced with a critical financial position he discovers a hidden treasure. He changes the name of the Shalimar Garden to Shala Bagh and repairs it. He goes to Katas for bathing. He rebukes Prince Kharak Singh for the mismanagement of his *jagirs* and sends his *diwan*, Bhayya Ram Singh, to prison, to be released later. Kohli does not dwell on scandals. Though not emphatically in each case, he is critical of the scandals attached to the ladies of Ranjit Singh's family and to the legitimacy of his sons.

In connection with diplomatic matters, Kohli refers to the exchange of presents and missions between Ranjit Singh and the British, and his meeting with the Governor-General at Ropar in 1833. The only other matter mentioned in connection with diplomacy is that Ranjit Singh received agents of the ruler of Nepal when the Gurkhas were fighting against the British, but he refused to give any support. By far the largest number of events mentioned by Kohli are essentially political. He talks of campaigns, conquests, and occupation of territories in the plains and the hills, making no distinction between Sikh, Hindu and Muslim chiefs. After subjugation, they were given the option of serving Ranjit Singh as *jagirdars* or receiving *jagirs* for subsistence. Quite often, their troops were incorporated in the army of Ranjit Singh. The most important of his campaigns were organized for the conquest of Multan and Kashmir and the occupation of Peshawar. After the Treaty of Amritsar in 1809, he could expand his territories only on his side of the river Sutlej. All the *misldars* (Sikh chiefs) lost their territories to him, except Fateh Singh Ahluwalia who was made a subordinate chief. When he fled into the British territory in 1826 and was persuaded to return in 1827, he felt reconciled to his position as a subordinate chief.

Many of the Muslim chiefs in the plains were obliged to pay tribute in acknowledgement of the superior political status of Ranjit Singh before their dominions were annexed to the Lahore state. Many of the chiefs in the hills lost their territories but a considerable number accepted Ranjit Singh's suzerainty, paid tribute and served him with their armies. Ranjit Singh created new vassal chiefs like Gulab Singh, Dhian Singh and Hira Singh, among others. Kohli is quite clear that in the 1830s the British were trying to put a stop to any further expansion of the Lahore state.

III. RELATIONS WITH OTHER POWERS

Some of the political events of the reign of Ranjit Singh are mentioned in connection with his relations with the rulers of Kabul in the chapter on his relations with his neighbours.[2] The other 'neighbours' to figure in this chapter are the British, the ruler of Nepal, the Nizam of Hyderabad, the rulers of Balochistan and Herat, the Nawab of Bahawalpur, and the Amirs of Sind. In the case of Nepal, the Maharaja was probably thinking of having better relations but till this time matters were confined to the induction of the Gurkhas who wished to join the army of Lahore. The Nizam of Hyderabad sent his *vakil* to the court of Ranjit Singh with costly presents, including the canopy which was later presented by the Maharaja to the Darbar Sahib. The Agents of Herat came to the court of Ranjit Singh with presents. The Agents of the Nawab of Balochistan brought presents and sought help to recover some forts taken over by the Nawab of Bahawalpur who had come under the protection of the British for his territory on the east of the Sutlej when he had felt threatened by Ranjit Singh. After the conquest of Dera Ghazi Khan in 1820, Ranjit Singh had given it to the Nawab of Bahawalpur for a stipulated amount of *ijara* in addition to the tribute he paid as a vassal chief in his territory on the west of the Sutlej. The Maharaja brought Dera Ghazi Khan under his direct control in 1831, the Nawab was paying Rs. 5,00,000 as *ijara*. He remained a tributary chief after 1831.

Kohli's interest in the Amirs of Sind and the rulers of Afghanistan gets linked up with his account of the Maharaja's relations with the British. He refers to the Treaty of Amritsar (1809) which confined Ranjit Singh's political activity to the west of the Sutlej. His sovereign status was also recognized, which enabled him to establish a large state in the north-west of India in fifteen years. With the increasing power of Ranjit Singh, the British became increasingly concerned with containing his power. In 1835, they took possession of Ferozepore and three years later made it a cantonment. This place had earlier been recognized as falling within Ranjit Singh's sphere of influence, like Wadni, Anandpur and Chamkaur. The British Resident ignored Sayyad Ahmad's activities which were known to be anti-Sikh. In 1827, the presents sent by the King-Emperor for the Maharaja were deliberately brought through the river Indus to explore the possibility of its navigation and to have a commercial agreement with the Amirs. For such a commercial treaty, it was necessary to have Ranjit Singh's consent. Already, before meeting Ranjit Singh at Ropar in 1831, Bentinck had ordered Colonel Pottinger to negotiate with the Amirs. The terms of the treaties with the Amirs of Haidarabad, Khairpur and Mirpur were worked out in 1832 without Ranjit Singh's knowledge. In December 1832, Captain Wade was instructed to go to Lahore to induce the Maharaja to enter into a commercial treaty with the British, recognizing their treaties with the Amirs. The Maharaja agreed to sign the treaty but rather reluctantly. The British knew that he was conscious of their superiority in arms and used the garb of 'friendship' to persuade him. In this situation, the only alternative for Ranjit Singh was to increase his military power.

Ranjit Singh had assumed direct control of Dera Ghazi Khan with the idea of expanding his dominions in the direction of Sind. A few forts were taken by Ventura to clear the way to Shikarpur. Ranjit Singh tried to befriend the Talpuria Baloches who had ruled in Sind before the ruling Kalhura Amirs. The Talpurias were given financial support and residential accommodation at Rajanpur, near Multan. In 1835-6, the Mazari Pathans raided the Multan territory and the Maharaja got the chance to move against them. Diwan Sawan Mal occupied Mithan Kot before Hari Singh Nalwa arrived there with the army. He had instructions from the Maharaja to tell the Amirs to send tribute to Lahore instead of to Kabul. If they refused, Shikarpur was to be occupied. The Governor-General advised Colonel Pottinger that the Amirs were likely to come under British protection in view of the threat from Ranjit Singh. Captain Wade was asked to persuade the Maharaja not to send his troops to Shikarpur because the British had promised protection to the Amirs. The Maharaja recalled Hari Singh but did not relinquish his control over the fort of Rojhan.

In 1834, Ranjit Singh took possession of Peshawar to keep it under direct administration. Prince Nau Nihal Singh was made its governor, with Hari Singh Nalwa as his *mushir*. Two new forts were built: one at Shabqadar, and the other at Jamrud, close to the Khaibar Pass. Dost Muhammad, the Barakzai ruler at Kabul was never reconciled to the occupation of Peshawar. He approached the British with the proposition that he would enter into treaty against Russia if Peshawar got restored to him. Disappointed in this mission, he sent an army against Jamrud. Hari Singh succeeded in repelling the Afghans but he was killed by a stray shot. Peshawar in a way became all the more important for Ranjit Singh. In 1838, the British were doubtful about Dost Muhammad in relation to Russia. They thought of placing Shah Shuja on the throne of Kabul. Ranjit Singh agreed to help if Shah Shuja as the ruler of Kabul would recognize the right of Ranjit Singh to hold all the territories in his possession on the west of the Indus. At the same time he refused to accept the proposition that the British army accompanying Shah Shuja for his restoration might pass through the Punjab. Thus, Ranjit Singh ensured his *de jure* right to hold Peshawar.

IV. ARMY AND CIVIL ADMINISTRATION

For the revenue and civil administration of Maharaja Ranjit Singh, Kohli states that approximately 1,40,000 sq. miles of his dominions were divided in official records into the provinces of Lahore, Multan, Kashmir and Peshawar. The total income of the state in 1838-9 was about Rs. 2,88,89,000, coming from land revenue (Rs. 1,75,57,741), *nazrana* (Rs. 6,03,657), miscellaneous taxes (Rs. 15,31,634), and alienated *jagirs* (Rs. 91,96,000). A further split-up is given for the first three items and the detail of the expenditure of the civil establishment is similarly provided under 13 items, with the total coming to Rs. 33,70,300. This information is based on the Khalsa Darbar Records. Kohli talks of the central and provincial administration, the central secretariat (*Daftar-i Mu'alla*) with its six wings and the personnel handling these departments from time to time, methods of assessment and collection of the revenue from land, measures adopted for the protection and aid of the peasantry, criminal courts, and the religious policy of the Maharaja. Thus, the account given by Kohli is quite comprehensive.[3]

The chapter on the army of Maharaja Ranjit Singh is based on five articles which had been published in the *Indian Historical Journal*.[4] He talks of the infantry, the artillery, the new cavalry, the old *Ghurcharha* army, the *Jagirdari* troops, arms and weapons, garrisons in the forts, recruitment, payments, and the views of European on the troops trained on the European model. The total number of the army in 1838-9 is given at 59,437 men, with break-up into trained infantry, cavalry and artillery (35,242), *deras* under the *sardars*, *Ghurcharha-i Khas*, and *Jagirdari Deras* (14,194), and garrison troops (10,000). The expenditure on each wing of the army amounted to Rs. 95,80,006. The salary of the French and English officers was Rs. 2,00,000. The average expenditure on a battalion under Hari Singh Nalwa, consisting of 632 men, was Rs. 82,130. The emoluments of officers and other personal of the army are given: Rs. 100 for the *kumedan*, Rs. 60 for the *ajetan*, Rs. 21 for the *subedar*, Rs. 15 for the major, the *jamadar*, the *munshi* and the *granthi*, Rs. 12 for the *nishanchi*, Rs. 11 for the *havaldar*, Rs. 9 for the *naik*, Rs. 8 for the *havaldar* quater Gard and the *tamburchi*, Rs. 7 for the *khalasi*, the *sair sipahi* and the *mistri* (*lohar* or mason), Rs. 6 for the *beldar*, Rs. 5 for the *sarban*, and Rs. 4 for the *mashki*, the *jhanda-bardar*, the *ghariali*, the *langari* and the *harkara*. Kohli talks of transportation, rations and commisariat. The orders of Ranjit Singh forbade the troopers to do harm to the peasants in any way. Much of this detail came only from the Khalsa Darbar Records.

Maharaja Ranjit Singh wore no crown and used no throne, the traditional symbols of royalty. None prostrated before him. However, his state processions were marked by splendour and he conferred titles and gave robes of honour (*khi'lat*) to distinguished servants of the state. Kohli gives some details of these. The title of Raja was given to only a few persons. Raja Dhian Singh was given the title of 'Raja-i Rajgan Raja-i Kalan'. He was made *wazir* in 1838. The 'Kaukab-i Iqbal-i Panjab' was introduced in 1837, with Ranjit Singh's portrait at the centre. Kohli talks of the courtiers who were selected without regard to their creed, caste, class or country. However, most of the important functionaries belonged to a small number of families. Later on their mutual rivalries came to the fore. The language of administration was Persian to which some Punjabi terms were added. In the daily conduct of affairs Punjabi was frequently used.[5]

Maharaja Ranjit Singh was fond of hunting and exercise. His daily routine is described by Kohli. Ranjit Singh found peace in Gurbani and he had great veneration for the *Guru Granth Sahib* which figured regularly in his routine. His breakfast was generally rather simple. He worked hard. He was not literate but he promoted education and learning. He had the qualities of a good general and a good administrator. Kohli does not omit to mention that the Maharaja used to take opium, drink spirituous liquors, and enjoy watching dance. His relations with Moran and Gul Begum were the result of his interest in drinking and dance parties. Nevertheless only a few individuals in the history of the world had risen from a small position into great prominence, and Ranjit Singh was one of them. He never took life, and he was generally popular with all kinds of people.[6] Kohli's assessment of Maharaja Ranjit Singh is very different from that of the European historians except Cunningham.

Ranjit Singh gave peace and prosperity to a large part of the country, basing his administration on sound principles. His greatest service to the country was the unification of the Punjab. He was quick to see the superiority of the 'modern' European armies and to mould his army on their model. That was why the army of Lahore could give such a tough fight to the British as to make the Anglo-Sikh wars the most remarkable in their career of conquest in India. Had he lived longer he would probably have modernized some of the other departments too. He was a statesman as well as a good administrator. There was complete peace in his dominions at the time of his death but there was also a potential for political factions at his court. Towards the end of his life his court was full of 'the new courtiers' who were more concerned with their personal interests than those of the state. The successors of the Maharaja did not have his qualities and there was no administrative machinery to function without guidance from the top. The presence of the British in the neighbourhood was a source of weakness. They were keen to take over the Punjab at the earliest opportunity.[7] Kohli is distinguished from the other historians of Maharaja Ranjit Singh by a meticulous regard for facts and a great admiration for the Maharaja.

V. FROM THE DEATH OF RANJIT SINGH TO THE ASSASSINATION OF SHER SINGH

Sita Ram Kohli gives the story of the successors of Maharaja Ranjit Singh in his *Sunset of the Sikh Empire,* edited by Khushwant Singh and published in 1967 after Kohli's death. Khushwant Singh says that no historian of the Punjab, dead or living, set the same standard for his research, or achieved it in the same measure as Sita Ram Kohli. His *Sunset of the Sikh Empire* presents a detailed narrative with a meaningful interpretation. However, Kohli's manuscript was incomplete. The last three chapters were terribly mutilated and Khushwant Singh tried to do his best, deleting repetitions and filling in omissions. He provided the account of the battles of the second Anglo-Sikh War from his own *Fall of the Kingdom of the Punjab.*[8]

Kohli's primary purpose is to explain 'how the kingdom of the Punjab lost its sovereignty.' He tries to do this with the help of factual information and his comment on events and persons. The first chapter, 'The Builders', provides the background based on his *Maharaja Ranjit Singh* and presented in a simple and lucid manner. The chapter ends with a statement on the factions among the Jat Sikhs and the 'foreign' elements in the ruling class. As Kohli puts it, adventurers from European countries, Dogra Rajputs from the Jammu hills, Gaur Brahmans for Uttar Pradesh, and Kashmiri Pandits had come to occupy very high positions in the Darbar. The Jat Sikhs, represented by the Attariwalas, the Sandhanwalias, and the Majithias, were resentful of 'the foreigners who had gained predominance in their land'. When the Maharaja died on 27 June 1839, these factions came to a head-on clash.[9]

The second chapter deals with the events after the death of Ranjit Singh to the death of Prince Nau Nihal Singh early in November 1840, following the death of Maharaja Kharak Singh who had lost *de facto* power early in October 1839, that is, within four months of Ranjit Singh's death. However, the events of these four months were not without significance. Prince Sher Singh, who aspired to the throne, sent a confidential message to the British Agent at Ludhiana, 'urging his superior merits' and promising a cession of territory on the left of the Sutlej. But he was not encouraged by the British. For the ceremony of his investiture, Prince Kharak Singh did not wait for the arrival of

Prince Nau Nihal Singh even for a day or two. It was surmised that Kharak Singh apprehended some mischief from the Prince. Maharaja Kharak Singh doted on the young Chet Singh who had offended Dhian Singh and other dignitaries by his pretensions and arrogance. Dhian Singh plotted Chet Singh's elimination; the senior Maharani, Chand Kaur, agreed to a change of government in favour of her son, Prince Nau Nihal Singh. Chet Singh was murdered and the Maharaja was placed under virtual imprisonment. The murder of Chet Singh proved to be the first of a series of violent acts which led ultimately to the dissolution of the kingdom.[10]

Kohli remarks that Prince Nau Nihal Singh was not actuated by 'any sordid motive but the good of the state'. With his *de facto* power, he tried to set the affairs of the state in order. He took action against Baba Bikram Singh Bedi who had murdered his nephew. He tried to pacify the north-western districts. The governors of Multan and Kashmir were ordered to clear their arrears. The Dogra General Zorawar Singh succeeded in making Iskardu a tributary of Lahore in May 1840, which created complications with the British. Despite Macnaughten's 'anti-Sikh activities', Nau Nihal Singh handled relations with the British rather tactfully. In the internal administration of the state, Dhian Singh was so conscious of his independent power that he began to bargain for terms instead of giving cooperation to the Prince. The courtiers inimical to Dhian Singh tried to widen the gulf but the Prince tried to get on with the *wazir*. Suddenly then, on the day of Kharak Singh's cremation, Prince Nau Nihal Singh met a fatal accident and died early in November 1840, crushed by the fall of a gate of the Huzuri Bagh. There were speculations about the cause of the fall, but Kohli treats it as an accident, 'a bolt from the blue' that cut short the career of a promising ruler.[11]

In the tussle for succession, Rani Chand Kaur succeeded against Prince Sher Singh. The work in civil administration was marred by a factional spirit. Dhian Singh went on leave, and the administrative machinery went out of gear. Prince Sher Singh came to Lahore from his residence in Batala to make a bid for power. He had the support of Dhian Singh and the bulk of the army in cantonments. When Sher Singh entered the city, Gulab Singh prepared his men for defence of the fort. It was bombarded by Sher Singh. Dhian Singh arrived for mediation.

Chand Kaur's misrule came to an end. In the whole process of the wooing of the army they gave its men an exaggerated notion of their importance as kingmakers. Furthermore, both Sher Singh and Chand Kaur had offered slices of territory to the British. This proved to be the 'heel of Achilles' which the British would use to their advantage.[12]

Sher Singh was formally installed as Maharaja on 20 Janurary 1841 amidst hopes of peace which were soon belied. The army demanded the promised rewards, but there was little money in the treasury. When their demands were ignored the soldiers made it a practice to leave their posts, assemble in bazaars, and plunder shops and homes. In the words of Sohan Lal Suri, the city was turned into a veritable hell for eight to ten weeks. Insubordination spread to other places. The governor of Kashmir was hacked to pieces; Commandant Faulkes was murdered in Mandi and Major Ford was murdered in Hazara. General Avitabile was obliged to leave Peshawar and take shelter in Jalalabad. Kohli comments that the root cause of the trouble was the devotion of Sikhs to the ideals of the Panth. They were resentful of the willingness of their rulers 'to dismember the state in order to ingratiate themselves with the British.' They formed *panchayats* to save the state. They assumed that they represented the Sarbat Khalsa, which gave them the right to intervene in the affairs of the state.[13]

Feeling insecure, Maharaja Sher Singh first got rid of Prince Nau Nihal Singh's widow who was pregnant, and then of Maharani Chand Kaur. He formally assumed the title of Maharaja and ordered the minting of coins bearing his name. These were significant innovations. Dhian Singh caused a misunderstanding between Maharaja Sher Singh and his old *diwan*, Jawala Singh. The latter was arrested and tortured to death. In October 1841, the British insisted that General Zorawar Singh's campaign against Tibet was against the agreement of 1840 by which the jurisdiction of the Lahore Darbar had been confined to Ladakh. After Shah Shuja's death in April 1842, the British troops were allowed to pass through the Punjab for recapturing Kabul. Like Maharaja Sher Singh, the British Agent at Ludhiana wanted the ouster of Dhian Singh for his own reasons. He interceded with the Maharaja on behalf of the Sandhanwalias and Ajit Singh was allowed to return to Lahore. Lehna Singh and Kehar Singh Sandhanwalia were released from the prison. Ajit Singh began to show his old friendly attitude towards

Sher Singh and succeeded in shooting the Maharaja while apparently presenting a gun to him. Lehna Singh murdered Prince Partap Singh. Dhian Singh too was assassinated. It was suspected that the British were behind these murders. Sher Singh's reign of two years and eight months was marked by events that accelerated the dissolution of the kingdom.[14]

The British became more serious now about the conquest of the Punjab. William Osborne had suggested annexation of the Punjab upon Maharaja Ranjit Singh's death. In February 1841, the Governor-General's Agent at Ludhiana suggested 'armed intervention' in the affairs of the Punjab. Ten to eleven thousand men were actually kept in readiness to move into the Punjab, but the scheme was eventually abandoned for various reasons. Henry Lawrence's wife wrote in a private letter in May 1841 that there were rumours of war, referring to the long suspended question of occupying the Punjab. Before sailing for India, Lord Ellenborough consulted the Duke of Wellington in October 1841 about the manner in which 'a campaign against the Punjab could be successfully conducted'. Ellenborough tried to draw Avitabile, Ventura and Allard into the circle of his informers. Ventura kept him posted about events in Lahore and even helped to shape them in accordance with the wishes of the British. Ellenborough wrote to the Duke that if the Sikhs accepted Jalalabad they would be obliged to keep their principal forces in that area and he could assemble an army in twelve days at any time to invade the Punjab. 'The state of Panjab will be under my foot.' At this time the Sikhs were actually helping the British and Ellenborough was arranging to have a personal meeting with Maharaja Sher Singh to decide upon a policy towards Afghanistan.[15]

VI. HIRA SINGH'S MINISTRY

After the assassination of Maharaja Sher Singh, Prince Partap Singh and Raja Dhian Singh, the issue to be settled was whether the Sandhan-walias or the Dogras were to wield power at the Sikh court. This issue was settled in favour of Hira Singh who had won the support of the army, first approaching the troops under Court, Avitabile and Ventura. Hira Singh presented himself to the Khalsa as a champion of sovereign rule and the Sandhanwalias as traitors who wanted to hand over the Punjab to the British. Lehna Singh and Ajit Singh were killed. Prince

Dulip Singh was proclaimed Maharaja at the age of five. The claims of two other princes, Pashaura Singh and Kashmira Singh, were ignored because it did not suit Hira Singh's purpose. He wanted to be a virtual ruler of the state. He appointed Pandit Jalla as his *mashir-i khas*. The salary of the soldiers and junior officers of the army was raised by Rs. 2 or 3 a month, and Hira Singh retained charge of the army for himself.[16]

The first trouble for Hira Singh came from Jawahar Singh who had been made guardian of the Maharaja. He intrigued with Raja Suchet Singh to oust Hira Singh from prime ministership. Suchet Singh was prepared to make a bid for the office, but he was dissuaded by Raja Gulab Singh. Jawahar Singh was sent to the *haveli* of the late Maharaja Kharak Singh for imprisonment, and it was planned to eject Princes Kashmira Singh and Pashaura Singh from their *jagirs* on the suspicion that they were in league with the Sandhanwalias. Hira Singh's action against the princes roused the Khalsa against the Dogras. On behalf of the Sarbat Khalsa, the army *panchayats* conveyed to Hira Singh the order (*hukam*) not to ill-treat the princes in future. If he hesitated or refused to obey the order he himself was to be seized. Despite this evident contempt for the authority of the government, Hira Singh readily promised compliance. The army solicited Raja Suchet Singh to come to Lahore, but before his arrival Hira Singh won over the army. Suchet Singh decided to fight and he died fighting, along with his forty devoted comrades.[17]

Tension between Hira Singh and Gulab Singh came into the open when Hira Singh threatened him that, if he did not relinquish control over the estates of Dhian Singh and Suchet Singh in the hills, he would seize Gulab Singh's property in the plains. Gulab Singh retaliated by threatening to seize Hira Singh's brothers. Eventually, however, a semblance of amity was restored. Gulab Singh sent his son Sohan Singh to reside at Lahore. In the early months of 1844, Hira Singh's ministry was threatened by activities at the *dera* of Bhai Bir Singh who was popular among the Sikhs, and his place became a refuge for disaffected persons. In May 1844, Hira Singh sent Khalsa troops against the *dera*. When he got the news that Attar Singh Sandhanwalia had crossed the Sutlej on the advice of the British and joined Bhai Bir Singh. Among the others to join him were Jawahar Singh Nalwa, Ratan Singh Gharjakhia,

Diwan Basakha Singh and the Princes, Pashaura Singh and Kashmira Singh. In the action that followed Attar Singh Sandhanwalia and Bhai Bir Singh were killed. Pashaura Singh had deserted their side earlier and reached Lahore.[18]

In view of the anti-British feeling in the army, Hira Singh dismissed all Europeans in the service of the Darbar. The army in Lahore looked upon the troops sent against Bhai Bir Singh as 'murderers of a guru'. Hira Singh tried to appease them by gifts of gold medals and ornaments. Meanwhile, Gulab Singh fomented disaffection in the border districts of the north-west. These districts had to be 're-conquered' in November 1844. By this time the total strength of trained wings of the army had risen to 51,452 from 35,242 in 1839-40, and their salaries rose to over Rs. 87 lakh from over 42 lakh. No attempts were made to increase the revenues of the state. The rude and overbearing conduct of Pandit Jalla was a source of alienation of the nobility. In December 1844, the army demanded the surrender of Pandit Jalla, but this was refused. Hira Singh tried to escape the wrath of the army but he was overtaken and killed, along with Pandit Jalla, Mian Sohan Singh and Mian Labh Singh. Major Broadfoot, Agent to the Governor-General, wrote to Lord Ellenborough in England in January 1845 that 'both Sardars and army suddenly uniting, overthrew the Pandit and the Raja and revived anarchy'.[19]

During Hira Singh's ministry the relations between the Lahore Darbar and the British government deteriorated further. Like his father Dhian Singh, he was anti-British. The issue of the treasure stored by Suchet Singh at Ferozepore before his death became a constant source of irritation. It was claimed by both the Darbar and by Suchet Singh's heirs. After a good deal of correspondence, the Darbar came to the conclusion that the British had no intention of parting with the treasure. Another issue was related to the village Mauran in the Nabha state. Maharaja Ranjit Singh had persuaded Raja Jaswant Singh to give this village to his General Dhanna Singh Malwai in return for one in the dominions of Ranjit Singh given to the Raja's sister. After Dhanna Singh's death in May 1843, Raja Davinder Singh of Nabha made a representation to the Agent to the Governor-General who agreed that the village could be resumed. Nabha troops occupied the village and seized the personal property of Hukam Singh, son of Dhanna Singh.

On receiving a representation from Hukam Singh the British took over the village on the plea that Raja Jaswant Singh had no right to give it to Maharaja Ranjit Singh without the formal consent of the paramount power. Another offence related to Attar Singh Sandhanwalia. The British Agent at Ludhiana had allowed him to traverse freely over a 100 miles of British territory to join Bhai Bir Singh unchecked. The most serious source of tension, however, was the movement of British troops and the building of additional barracks in the cantonments at Ferozepore, Ambala, Kasauli, Sabathu, Simla and Meerut. Hira Singh moved 4,000 horse and foot and 16 pieces of cannon to Kasur. When the British Agent remonstrated with Hira Singh he replied that he would consider recalling the Lahore troops from Kasur after the additional British troops at Ferozepore had left Sind.[20]

VII. THE ARMY *PANCHAYATS*, RANI JIND KAUR, AND THE FIRST SIKH WAR

With the death of Hira Singh on 21 December 1844 ended the Dogra hegemony at the court of Lahore. All military dispositions were now made under the sole authority of the army *panchas*. Soldiers prowled in the streets maltreating citizens. Sikh chiefs, relatively secure in their feudal domains behaved as 'irresponsible petty sovereigns'. The districts of Hazara, Chhachh and Kalabagh were in a state of ferment. The governor of Kashmir threatened to become autonomous like Gulab Singh whose accounts were in arrears. The Khalsa army marched against Gulab Singh and after long negotiations he agreed to pay Rs. 4,00,000 as an earnest of the full discharge of his obligations to the state. He was brought to Lahore. Rani Jind Kaur offered prime ministership to him but he politiely declined. He paid Rs. 2,700,000 by way of arrears but got the lease of his revenue-farms extended for two years. Early in July 1845, he obtained leave to return to Jammu.[21]

Rani Jind Kaur installed her brother, Jawahar Singh, as the *wazir*. He did not mend his old evil ways; rather, he misused his new position. The Rani sent General Mehtab Singh to seize the estate of Prince Pashaura Singh who declared himself to be the ruler and entered into correspondence with Dost Muhammad of Kabul. Jawahar Singh sent Sardar Chattar Singh Attariwala and Fateh Khan Tiwana against him.

On 31 August Pashaura Singh was seized, thrown into a dungeon, and strangled to death. The army *panchayats* resolved on 19 September that Jawahar Singh must die as a traitor. He was put to death in the presence of Maharaja Dulip Singh and Rani Jind Kaur. The army committee began to use their seal of authority with the words *Panth Khalsa Jeo* and, above this, the invocation *Akal Sahai*. A remarkable development that followed the assumption of real authority by the Khalsa was an enforcement of a very rigid discipline among the soldiers.[22]

Early in 1845, both Rani Jind Kaur and Gulab Singh had made overtures to the British for her and his own reasons. The Rani was prepared to accept British suzerainty. The ruling party was willing 'to undertake the filthy job of prompting the Khalsa troops to commit a number of acts, direct or indirect, which might provide an ostensible cause for British interference'. Gulab Singh proposed to muster inhabitants of the hills against the Sikhs, to break relations with Lahore and transfer allegiance to the British; and to raise 40,000 or 50,000 men to destroy the Sikh army. The British then could occupy Lahore without firing a shot. In return, he asked for the enjoyment of his present possessions worth Rs. 1,200,000 a year, during his life and then by his heirs in perpetuity. The Rani and a chosen coterie of chiefs set about invidious propaganda to influence Khalsa soldiers against the British. Then a great army council was held in November and Diwan Dina Nath confirmed some of reports which were current. At the end he offered the Rani's proposal to make Lal Singh the *wazir* and Tej Singh the commander-in-chief. This was accepted by the Khalsa army.[23]

According to the plan of the Rani's junta, the army was to be divided into seven divisions, each with a strength of about 8,000 men. One of these was to remain at Lahore, one was to go to Peshawar, one towards Sind, and four divisions were to cross the river Sutlej and march towards Ropar, Ludhiana, Harike and Ferozepore. Each division was, severally, to engage the enemy and not to make a concerted effort. The soldiers and *sardars* were invited to assemble at the *samadh* of Maharaja Ranjit Singh where Lal Singh and Tej Singh were formally installed in their new posts. Everyone present was required to pledge in the presence of *Guru Granth Sahib* his fidelity to the government of Maharaja Dulip Singh and his officers in the field. The authority of the *panchayats* was suspended. Sir Henry Hardinge was not yet prepared for action.

He authorized Major Broadfoot to inform the Lahore Darbar that if Maharaja Dulip Singh was deposed by force the Governor-General would not recognize the successor. Major Broadfoot remained in touch with Gulab Singh and other possible defectors.[24]

Major Broadfoot was aggressive in his dealings with the Lahore Darbar. One of his first actions as Agent to the Governor-General had been to claim for his government the protection of all the cis-Sutlej estates. On the basis of the claim he actually intervened in a domestic quarrel of the Sodhis of Anandpur. In March 1845, a judge of the Lahore state, Lal Singh Adalati, who had crossed the Sutlej to go into the territory of the Darbar, was ordered by Broadfoot to return. Broadfoot sequestered two villages of the Darbar on the plea that they were harbouring criminals from British territory. All this activity of the Agent was tacitly approved if not encouraged by the Governor-General. The strength of the British troops on the Punjab frontier was increased from 17,612 men and 66 guns to 40, 612 men and 94 pieces of cannon. In September 1845, 60 large boats were delivered at Ferozepore to form a flotilla or a bridge.[25]

Sikh troops began to move towards the Sutlej on 24 November. The Governor-General issued a proclamation on 13 December declaring war on the Darbar. The cis-Sutlej territories of the Darbar were annexed. A day earlier, Lal Singh's confidential messenger, Shamsuddin of Kasur, had told the Assistant Political Agent at Ferozepore that both Lal Singh and the Rani were friends of the British and desired nothing more than that 'the Sikh army be destroyed'. Lal Singh promised to keep back his army for two days after they had been required to join the regular force. On 16 December, he reaffirmed that no harm would come to the small British garrison at Ferozepore. He marched from Pherushahr with only half the force, reached Mudki, opened the attack, and disappeared from the field. Nevertheless, 'the Sikhs fought as if they had everything at stake'. British losses in men and officers were 215 killed and 657 wounded; among the dead were Sir Robert Sale, Sir Joseph McGaskill and two aides of the Governor-General. The battle of Mudki dispelled the British notion that the Sikhs were no great force to be reckoned with. They were able to retire to Pherushahar without any hindrance from the British.[26]

Relying on the assurances given by Lal Singh and Tej Singh, Sir John Littler left his strategic post poorly defended despite the fact that 20,000 trained Sikhs were hovering at a distance of only 6 miles. He joined the main British force, raising its number to 17,000 men and 69 guns. The Khalsa soldiers at Pherushahr had thrown up earthworks without any guidance from their senior officers or expert technicians; this information was conveyed to the enemy by Lal Singh's emissary, Shamsuddin. At one stage in the battle some of the British officers advocated retreat to Ferozepore. The letters of the Governor-General show that he was aware of the delicacy of his position. Lal Singh had spent the day of the battle hidden in a ditch, and he stole away to Amritsar at night. On the second day, the Khalsa were soon in full retreat. Meanwhile Tej Singh was pretending to guard Ferozepore even though Sir John Littler had left it in broad day light on 21 December. When he arrived on the scene the Khalsa army was already in flight. He made a feint attack and withdrew at the very moment when the British had exhausted their last round of ammunition. British losses amounted to 2,200, killed and wounded, and they had only a few siege guns with them. The Sikhs were able to recross the river into their own country.[27]

The theatre of war shifted towards Ludhiana. Ranjodh Singh Majithia had crossed the Sutlej on 17 December with 10,000 men and 60 pieces of artillery, but there was no action. He came face to face with Sir Harry Smith near Baddowal and a brief skirmish ended in victory for the Sikhs. This was not followed up by Ranjodh Singh. He was joined by a brigade of four battalions, raising the strength of his men to 15,000. Harry Smith was joined by Brigadier Wheeler. In a hotly contested battle at Aliwal in January 1846 the Sikh infantry engaged the British cavalry in hand-to-hand fight. The Sikhs were forced to recross the Sutlej, after losing more than 50 guns. However, after the battle it was found that 'the ground was more thickly strewn with the bodies of the victorious horsemen than of the beaten infantry'.[28]

The decisive battle of the campaign was fought at Sabraon on 10 February 1846. Lal Singh and Tej Singh having been discredited, Rani Jind Kaur brought in Gulab Singh who was known to have negotiated with the enemy. He had offered his allegiance to the British in return for a guarantee of his possessions. The British appreciated his wisdom in not taking up arms against them, and assured him that 'his interests would be taken into consideration'. The battle of Sabraon was fought under circumstances of 'shameless treason' on the understanding that the Sikh army would be attacked by the British and, when beaten, it would be abandoned by its own government, and the road to Lahore would lay open to the victors. Gulab Singh persuaded the Khalsa to fight. They crossed the river into the Lahore territory near Sabraon, with 20,000 to 25,000 men and 70 guns. Lal Singh was re-imposed on the army. Shamsuddin gave information to Henry Lawrence about the dispositions of the Sikh army. On 11 February 1846, the British opened assault with heavy cannonading which lasted for three hours, but the Sikhs did not yield. Hand-to-hand fight started. A large number of British soldiers were killed. Sham Singh Attariwala fought to death. Eventually, the Sikhs were driven to the river, and they found that the bridge of boats had been blown up by Tej Singh who had fled across the river after the first assault. They tried to swim across and the British horse-artillery fired at them to kill 5,000 men. Not a single Sikh soldier in arms remained on the British side of the river by the afternoon.[29]

The British signed separate treaties with the Lahore Darbar and Gulab Singh. The Treaty of Lahore was signed on 9 March. It was a blend of 'confiscatory, retributive and repressive clauses'. The army of Lahore was to be reduced to a third of its strength. The territory on the east of the Beas was to be taken over by the British. On 11 March, a supplementary treaty was added as if at the instance of the Darbar; it provided for an adequate British force in Lahore for the protection of the Maharaja and for the services of an experienced political officer to help in reconstructing the government. As Hardinge told his Agent at Lahore in October 1846, the Punjab was never intended to be an independent state by the treaty of March 1846. A clause in the treaty made the Maharaja subordinate to the paramount power of the British in his foreign relations. As Hardinge put it, 'the native prince is in fetters and under our protection, and must do our bidding'. The Lahore Darbar was prepared to pay indemnity in cash but the British insisted on having territory, asserting that the Darbar had offered it. Gulab Singh's role, which was in accordance with the intended policy of the British, was rewarded. Their arrangement with Gulab Singh was in keeping with the long term project envisaged by Lord Ellenborough and implemented by

Lord Hardinge. He was given Jammu and Kashmir, and the stipulated indemnity was never fully realized.[30]

VIII. DELIBERATE SUBVERSION OF A PROTECTED STATE

The 'experienced officer' to give 'advice and guidance' to the Darbar was Henry Lawrence who was posted at Lahore with a British force. There was no Sikh army in the capital. Lal Singh was confirmed as *wazir* and Tej Singh as commander-in-chief. But the real power was in the hands of Henry Lawrence. Rulia Dutt was executed for agitating over the injury inflicted on cows by a British sentry. Prompt action was taken against the *thanadar* of the Kangra fort who had shown defiance. Shaikh Imamuddin, the governor of Kashmir, refused to hand over Kashmir to Gulab Singh. But when a large force was sent against him under Brigadier Wheeler, he tendered his resignation on 31 October. It was discovered that Imamuddin had acted on Lal Singh's suggestion, Lal Singh was dismissed after an enquiry and a council of four was formed in his place, consisting of Tej Singh, Sher Singh, Dina Nath, and Nuruddin. In December 1846, Hardinge encamped at Bhyrowal, a few marches from Lahore. On 14 December he wrote to Henry Lawrence that he may order Sir John Littler to move all British troops as close to the citadel as convenient, if the *sardars* were disposed 'to assent to our view', and to pledge their support to Hardinge's scheme of leaving a British force in the Punjab at the cost of the Lahore Darbar (instead of withdrawing the British troops before the end of 1846 in accordance with the treaty of March 1846) on a request from the *sardars*. In other words, the *sardars* were to be persuaded, or coerced if necessary, to accept Hardinge's scheme.[31]

By a treaty signed at Bhyrowal in the presence of Maharaja Dulip Singh on 24 December 1846, the Regency Council was to be doubled by the addition of Attar Singh Kalianwala, Shamsher Singh Sandhanwalia, Ranjodh Singh Majithia, and Bhai Nidhan Singh. No change was to be made without the consent of the British Resident who was to be assisted by an efficient staff and also 'shall have the full authority to direct and control the duties of every department'; the allowance of the Maharani was fixed at Rs. 1,50,000 a year; the arrangement was to continue till

4 September 1854 when Maharaja Dulip Singh was to attain the age of 16. The British Resident 'virtually became the successor of Ranjit Singh on the throne of Lahore'.[32] The 'Kingdom of Lahore' had finally lost its 'sovereignty'. The British would annex a state that had constitutionally come under their 'protection'.

Six months later, Rani Jind Kaur's allowance was reduced to Rs. 48,000 and she was sent to the fort of Sheikhupura. She had tutored Maharaja Dulip Singh not to place the saffron mark on the foreheads of certain *sardars* who were to be honoured by the State. She had no part now in the administration of the country, and she was not given much opportunity to see her son. However, Henry Lawrence was not at ease with her presence in the Punjab. Without being told, she was secretly sent to Ferozepore. Early in 1847, the army was retrenched; Lawrence claimed to have saved Rs. 60,00,000 a year from retrenchment in the army and other institutions. He appointed a number of British officers to 'help and advise' the governors and collectors of the state: Edwardes in Bannu, James Abbot in Hazara, Herbert in Attock, and George Lawrence in Peshawar. Younger officers were selected to 'settle the country, assess lightly, make the people happy and instill confidence into them as to the good intentions of the British'. They were also to collect information regarding the resources in the district under their charge. Kohli comments that each of these men began 'to exercise his authority in a manner which took for granted that the Punjab had passed into the hands of the British, and he at his headquarters was the representative of his government'.[33]

The last three chapters of the *Sunset of the Sikh Empire* were more substantially edited by Khushwant Singh. However, the basic narrative was provided by Kohli, except for the last chapter which deals largely with the battles of the second Sikh war. Kohli narrates the rising at Multan and its first siege, with an occasional comment of his own. The revolt of Mul Raj as the governor of Multan was not premeditated. Sir Frederick Currie, the acting Resident at Lahore, delayed action. Lord Dalhousie wanted to watch the developments 'to see the flame of rebellion spread' so that the Punjab could be seen as 'conquered'. These long-term designs, fully accepted by the Commander-in-Chief and the Resident, were not a secret. The conduct of events serves to reveal clearly the deviousness of the policy at work. Having decided to postpone major operations till the cold weather of 1848-9, Currie had to devise measures only for the intervening period.[34]

Meanwhile, Sardar Chattar Singh Attariwala, the governor of Hazara, was obliged to defy the British authority due to the aggressive and overbearing attitude of Major James Abbot who was supported by the higher authorities. His son, Raja Sher Singh, was distrusted by Major Edwardes. He made up his mind to leave his side on the night of 12-13 September 1848 and to join hands with Mul Raj. Major Edwardes' cunning made Mul Raj and Sher Singh part company for ever. Sher Singh left Multan on 9 October, moving first towards Lahore and then to join his father. Early in November, Lord Gough crossed the Sutlej with his army for the invasion of the Punjab treating Maharaja Dulip Singh as an enemy though he was still under British protection. The battles of Ram Nagar, Chillianwala and Gujrat are described by Khushwant Singh, resulting in the formal annexation of the Lahore state to the British empire towards the end of March 1849.[35]

IX. ASSESSMENT OF KOHLI'S WORK

According to Professor Fauja Singh, Sita Ram Kohli's approach was marked by 'intellectual honesty'. He presents historical facts logically, and his interpretation emerged largely from his facts. These qualities make his style lucid and readable. He avoided controversies but did not hesitate to express his view when it differed from that of others. We may add that Kohli's understanding of Ranjit Singh and his successors is appreciably different from that of his predecessors, especially Griffin and Muhammad Latif. In terms of empathy with the subject, only J.D. Cunningham is a comparable predecessor.

Professor Fauja Singh thinks that Kohli 'did not penetrate far below the surface' to see the diverse forces that shaped the society and accounted for the success of Ranjit Singh and the downfall of his successors. Furthermore, he failed to comprehend the mechanism of British foreign policy which was a major factor in the disintegration and final extinction of the independent kingdom of the Punjab. We may, however, point out that Kohli's exposition of the decline and fall of the kingdom of the Punjab in a short time is more adequate than that of any of his predecessors, and he does not ignore the change in the foreign policy of the British. It may be added that hardly any historian has related the political history of the early nineteenth-century Punjab to 'social forces'.

Finally, Professor Fauja Singh looks upon Kohli as 'essentially a pioneer'.[36] He is a pioneer in bringing new sources to light. His *Catalogue of* the *Khalsa Darbar Records* alone would justify the statement. His well-annotated editions of the *Zafarnama-i Ranjit Singh,* the *Var* of Shah Muhammad, and the *Fatehnama Guru Khalsa Ji Ka* reinforce the justification. Kohli is also a pioneer in giving special attention to the army of Ranjit Singh, and his revenue administration. The first trail has been followed by Fauja Singh himself in his *Military System of the Sikhs* and the second trail has been followed even more amply by Indu Banga in her *Agrarian System of the Sikhs* which goes far beyond the mere issues of revenue administration.

NOTES

1. Sita Ram Kohli prepared these *parwanas* for publication with an English translation before his death in 1962. He left this material with his former student, S.N. Rao, who looked around for a historian to finalize it for publication. Fifteen years later it was substantially revised and published as the *Civil and Military Affairs of Maharaja Ranjit Singh: A Study of 450 Orders in Persian,* ed. J.S. Grewal and Indu Banga, Amritsar: Guru Nanak Dev University, 1987.
2. Sita Ram Kohli, *Maharaja Ranjit Singh,* Delhi: Atma Ram and Sons, 1953, pp. 184-203.
3. Ibid., pp. 204-23.
4. Ibid., pp. 224-43.
5. Ibid., pp. 244-55.
6. Ibid., pp. 256-69.
7. Ibid., pp. 270-5.
8. Sita Ram Kohli, *Sunset of the Sikh Empire,* ed. Khushwant Singh, New Delhi: Orient Longman, 1967, 'About this Book'.
9. Ibid., pp. 1-9.
10. Ibid., pp. 10-17.
11. Ibid., pp. 17-29.
12. Ibid., pp. 30-8.
13. Ibid., pp. 39-42.
14. Ibid., pp. 42-66.

15. Ibid., pp. 57-9.
16. Ibid., pp. 67-70.
17. Ibid., pp. 71-5.
18. Ibid., pp. 76-9.
19. Ibid., pp. 79-80, 85-9.
20. Ibid., pp. 80-3.
21. Ibid., p. 94.
22. Ibid., pp. 94-7.
23. Ibid., pp. 97-100.
24. Ibid., p. 100.
25. Ibid., pp. 101-5.
26. Ibid., pp. 105-8.
27. Ibid., pp. 108-11.
28. Ibid., pp. 111-12.
29. Ibid., pp. 112-16.
30. Ibid., pp. 117-20.
31. Ibid., pp. 121-31.
32. Ibid., pp. 131-2.
33. Ibid., pp. 132-7.
34. Ibid., pp. 137-49.
35. Ibid., pp. 149-84.
36. Fauja Singh, 'Sita Ram Kohli', *Historians and Historiography of the Punjab*, New Delhi: Oriental Publishers, 1978, pp. 336-7.

CHAPTER EIGHTEEN

Teja Singh and Ganda Singh

A Short History of the Sikhs

I. SIKH SCHOLARSHIP GAINS MOMENTUM

Like Sita Ram Kohli, Teja Singh and Ganda Singh have published their major work on Sikh history after Independence but on the basis of interests pursued in the colonial period. The work of Sewaram Singh, Bhagat Lakshman Singh and Khazan Singh was followed by a number of important publications by several Sikh scholars who continued to write after 1947. Their work represents a kind of transition from the colonial to contemporary Sikh studies. *A Short History of the Sikhs* by Teja Singh and Ganda Singh is the most important publication on Sikh history of this transitional phase.

The *Encyclopaedia of Sikh Literature* (*Gurshabd Ratnakar Mahan Kosh*) by Bhai Kahn Singh Nabha, published in 1930, contained more than 60,000 entries explaining all the words of the *Adi Granth* and the *Dasam Granth,* besides a dozen other works of Sikh literature. Essentially a product of the Singh Sabha movement, the *Encyclopaedia* came to be seen as the most authentic representation of Sikhism and Sikh history. Bhai Jodh Singh, who was intimately connected with the Akali movement, published his *Religion and Religious Life as Conceived by Guru Nanak* in 1925. Seven years later came out his well-known *Gurmat Nirnai.* A very different kind of work appeared in 1947, *Prachin Biran Bare Bhullan di Sodhan.* It was written in response to G.B. Singh's *Sri Guru Granth Sahib dian Prachin Biran,* published in 1944 as a textual study. Bhai Jodh Singh published *Some Studies in Sikhism* in 1953 and *The Japji* in 1956. But more interesting in retrospect is his *Sri Kartarpuri Bir de Darshan,* published in 1968. It was written in response to the controversial issue of the *Ragmala* in *Guru Granth Sahib* and published partly in response to scholarly demand for a textual study of the *Kartarpuri Bir*. Bhai Jodh Singh was deeply interested in *Gurbani* and its interpretation, a subject on which he was regarded as a great authority from the 1930s. Printed posthumously for the third time in 1993, his *Bani Bhagat Kabir Ji Steek* bears ample evidence of his scholarship in this area of Sikh studies.

Interest in biographical, philosophical and scriptural studies in the last quarter of colonial rule in the Punjab was reflected in works like Sir Jogendra Singh's *Thus Spake Guru Nanak*, Kartar Singh's *Life of Guru Nanak Dev*, Giani Sher Singh's *Philosophy of Sikhism*, Bishan Singh's *Sri Guru Granth Sahib Steek*, Narain Singh's *Dasam Guru Granth Sahib Steek*, and the anonymous *Sri Dasam Granth Sahib Ji*. In this context we can appreciate the publications of Sahib Singh. He published his *Gurbani Viakaran* for the first time in 1939. This work, he thought, was essential for a proper understanding of *Gurbani*. He wrote a number of articles on the *Adi Granth*. The manuscript of his *Adi Bir Bare* was completed in 1950, though it was actually published in 1970. It contains a new hypothesis about the compilation of the *Adi Granth*. In Professor Sahib Singh's view, Guru Nanak recorded his own *bani* and left it for Guru Angad. His example was followed by all his successors so that Guru Arjan had the *bani* of all his predecessors with him for compiling the *Granth* in 1604. Professor Sahib Singh is known to the scholarly world primarily for his later work which is really monumental: *Sri Guru Granth Sahib Darpan*. It was published in ten volumes in 1962-4, reflecting his understanding of the grammar of *Gurbani*.

Professor Teja Singh had assisted Bhai Kahn Singh in finalizing the *Encyclopaedia* of Sikh Literature. Its warmly appreciative Foreword was in fact written by Teja Singh. The *Gurdwara Reform Movement*, published in 1922, reflected some of the ideas Teja Singh had expressed earlier in *Guru Nanak and His Mission*. He brought out *Asa di Var* in English translation in 1924, followed by an English translation of the *Japuji*. He published an English translation of the *Sukhmani* in 1937. At the same time, he published his *Sikh Religion* and the better known *Sikhism: Its Ideals and Institutions*. Teja Singh's *Growth of Responsibility in Sikhism* came out in 1942, and his *Essays in Sikhism* in 1944. In all these publications, he had two concerns: to interpret Sikhism as an original system and to propagate this interpretation among Sikhs and non-Sikhs alike. The most scholarly work of Teja Singh was the *Shabadarth Sri Guru Granth Sahib Ji* which is indispensable for any serious study of the Sikh scripture and the Sikh faith.

The first historian to represent the Singh Sabha's concern for Sikh history was Karam Singh who came to be known as 'the historian'. Sikh history became a passion of his life (1884-1930). A few months before the final examination for graduation at Khalsa College, Amritsar, he left the college to collect information on the last phase of Sikh rule because the men who had participated in the events were dying one by one. He collected the daily diaries (*roznamchas*) too of this phase. He wrote a large number of articles in Punjabi on Sikh history and the importance of writing Sikh history on the basis of contemporary sources in Punjabi, Persian and English which were known to be extant. He analysed Qazi Nur Muhammad's *Jangnama* in detail, and discussed the date of Guru Nanak's birth in his *Kattak kih Visakh*. He published two monographs, one on Banda Bahadur and the other on Raja Ala Singh of Patiala. Rational interpretation of empirical evidence was the hallmark of Karam Singh's work as a historian. His ambition was to write a comprehensive history of the Sikhs during the eighteenth century but he died prematurely in 1930. His mantle fell upon Ganda Singh.

Ganda Singh looked upon Karam Singh 'the historian' as his predecessor. He had great appreciation for Karam Singh's interest in empirical evidence and his open minded research. In 1935, Ganda Singh published three works: *The Life of Banda Singh Bahadur,* with an exhaustive bibliography; the *Mirat ut-Tawarikh-i Sikhan,* a bibliographical work; and the *History of the Gurdwara Shahidganj, Lahore,* which related to a contemporary issue. In 1938, he published three more works: the Persian text of Qazi Nur Muhammad's *Jangnama,* an English translation of the *Dabistan-i Mazahib's* section on the Nanak-Panthis; and the *Contemporary Sources of Sikh History (1469-1707)*. In 1939, Ganda Singh contributed three articles to *Maharaja Ranjit Singh: First Death Centenary Memorial Volume* which he co-edited with Teja Singh. Before 1947, he published six more books, all in Punjabi: *Maharaja Kaura Mal Bahadur, Sardar Sham Singh Attariwala, Kukian di Vithia, Sikh Itihas Bare, Punjab dian Varan,* and *Sikh Itihas Wal.* Ganda Singh's interest in biography, original source materials, and issues or themes of contemporary interest stayed with him throughout his academic life.[1]

II. SCIENTIFIC APPROACH

In the Preface to *A Short History of the Sikhs*, Teja Singh and Ganda Singh claim that their work was the first attempt to write a history of the Sikhs from 'a secular stand-point'. In their view, the foundations of the character of the Sikhs were laid by their Gurus 'who were their temporal and spiritual guides'; the political institutions of the Sikhs grew out of their religious origins and 'national needs'; and suffering intensified their character and moulded their 'national aim', the deliverance of their country from 'the grip of the foreigner'. The Sikh cause was the country's cause. A patient struggle of over a century ultimately gave them the sovereignty of the Punjab. 'The whole movement was gradual and at no stage was there any sudden or uncalled for departure from the original aim.' There was no dichotomy between what was called the 'peaceful and saintly' character of the Sikhs and the 'worldly' or 'military' character of the Khalsa. The Sikhs were not merely 'good fighters' but also 'good farmers, carpenters, artisans, engineers, doctors, merchants, poets and painters'. Rather than mystical fervour or religious obscurantism, the distinctive trait of the Sikhs was common sense and hard thinking. In other words, Sikh history made a better sense in terms of the Sikh character (their ideas, attitudes, ethics and values), enabling them to respond to the changing situations in a constructive way for the attainment of their aims and objectives, without invoking supranatural or external influences for explanation.

Teja Singh and Ganda Singh emphasize that they had used contemporary sources and quoted the later authorities only in support of the earlier ones. The Sikh scripture, known as the *Guru Granth Sahib*, is used as a source and 'drawn upon more widely than ever before'. Indeed, 'the implications of its text are brought out more intimately than could be expected from those whose knowledge of Sikh scriptures is only second-hand'. In other words, Teja Singh and Ganda Singh have used the evidence of the *Guru Granth* in a way that no earlier historian could have done. The main source material for the period of 'Sikh-Muslim clash' was in Persian, and produced in many cases in a partisan spirit. The echoes of their disparaging and strong terms could be heard in the works of some Hindu writers too. The source material in Persian was indispensable but it had to be used with a sense of discrimination. The English translations of Persian works were often unsatisfactory and sometimes misleading. Therefore, it was necessary to consult the original works for necessary amendment. Coming to the Sikh works, Teja Singh and Ganda Singh state that they have preferred the earlier works over the later. Consequently, Kesar Singh Chhibber and Ratan Singh Bhangu are more important for them than Bhai Santokh Singh and Giani Gian Singh.

Finally, Teja Singh and Ganda Singh state that they have tried to be just and impartial and left the result to be judged by just and impartial readers. 'In dealing with the whole story of the Sikhs and their life-and-death struggle against social and political tyranny, we have put down nothing in over-praise or malice'.

A remarkable feature of *A Short History of the Sikhs* is its bibliography. Most of the major works in Gurmukhi are listed, many of them in manuscript form. Besides nearly all the relevant works in Persian are mentioned, including many manuscripts. Nearly all the relevant works in English are also listed, including what may be regarded as contemporary. Only the Urdu works listed are later writings. Thus, Teja Singh and Ganda Singh reveal greater familiarity than did their predecessors with the evidence on Sikh history from the sixteenth to the eighteenth century in Gurmukhi, Persian and English. This distinguishes them clearly from the other historians, whether Western or Indian, Sikh or non-Sikh.

III. RELIGIOUS FOUNDATIONS OF THE SIKH PANTH: THE TEN GURUS

A Short History of the Sikhs is divided into three parts. The first part covers the period from 1469 to 1708 as the 'religious foundations' under the ten Gurus, from Guru Nanak to Guru Gobind Singh. The second part covers the years 1708-16 as the 'political foundations' laid by the 'Sikhs under Banda'. The third part covers the period from 1716 to 1765, seen as 'persecution leading to power'. Almost equal space is given to both the first and the third parts, though the period covered in the first part is much longer. The second part is the shortest, and it covers less than eight years.

According to Teja Singh and Ganda Singh, Sikh history reveals 'the gradual making and development of a nation'. The Sikh Gurus had much in common with other contemporary reformers, but with a difference. They had in mind 'the duties of a nation as much as the duties of an individual'. It is explicitly stated that the Sikh Gurus were different from the Vaishnavas. Studied from the perspective, Sikh history revealed no apparent contradictions, no break, and no digression. Like an organism, Sikh life was experiencing change and developing new organs and functions when challenged to exercise new energies. The principle of life remained the same, though it underwent a constant 'transfiguration'.[2] The response of each Guru to the challenge of his situation, therefore, was important to note. Teja Singh and Ganda Singh take up all the ten Gurus, one by one.

Teja Singh and Ganda Singh accept 15 April 1469 as the date of Guru Nanak's birth, accepting Karam Singh's conclusion. They underline the importance of Guru Nanak's early education which made him 'a scholarly writer'. Many of the *sakhis* which became current were 'only settings provided for the word-pictures drawn by him in his verses'. The *sakhi* of Guru Nanak's spiritual experience at Sultanpur is taken by Teja Singh and Ganda Singh as his communion with 'the spirit pervading the whole universe'. Guru Nanak 'felt' that he stood before the throne of the Almighty, and received from him the message of his mission. Guru Nanak's enunciation, 'there is no Hindu, no Musalman', proclaimed his mission 'to reconcile the two warring communities of India into one brotherhood'. This was 'a turning point' in his life. He travelled far and wide in India and abroad. Against Trumpp's scepticism about Guru Nanak's visit to the South and Ceylon, Teja Singh and Ganda Singh refer to the evidence of the *Hakikat Rah Makam*. For Guru Nanak's visit to Baghdad, they cite the evidence of the Baghdad inscription. One of his own hymns makes him an eye-witness to the sack of Saidpur by Babur.[3] For most of the incidents of Guru Nanak's life, Teja Singh and Ganda Singh use the evidence of the *Janamsakhis*, interpreting each *sakhi* in rational terms.

Guru Nanak was not only 'a man of devotion and peace' but also a leader who thought of 'the worldly needs of the people'. He felt concerned with their 'social and political disabilities'. He declared that woman, having an equal responsibility for her actions before God, was not inferior to man. To give a practical shape to the idea of equality, Guru Nanak 'instituted the custom of inter-dining in a common mess attached to every place of worship'. He roused 'the national sentiment of the people' by adopting their spoken language for religious purposes. 'That the Guru was not a mere reformer but the founder of a new religion is clear from the fact that he travelled abroad to non-Hindu countries, established Sangats or Sikh organizations in different centres under the charge of Manji-holders, and took special care to test and appoint a successor who should continue his work after him.' Guru Nanak actually installed Guru Angad in his own place and 'saluted him' as the Guru before he died on 22 September 1539.[4]

Guru Angad explained the mission of Guru Nanak through 'regular meetings', wrote on the same themes, maintained the common kitchen, and 'gave definiteness and distinction to the general ideals laid down by Guru Nanak'. He got the *bani* of his master recorded in a special script called Gurmukhi. Thus, a nucleus of the Sikh scripture began to be formed, leading to the consciousness that the Sikhs were 'distinct from the mass of Hindus'. Like his predecessor, Guru Angad chose his successor before he died on 29 March 1552.[5]

Guru Amar Das told his Sikhs 'to reject the path of renunciation' and to think of the life of the householder as 'the only' approved way of practising religion. When Goindwal became a big religious centre, Guru Amar Das constructed a *baoli* with 84 steps 'for the use of visitors'. The *langar* became a great institution. Guru Amar Das asked all visitors to sit in a line and eat together. 'No distinction of caste or creed, high or low, was made'. Guru Amar Das prohibited the practice of committing *sati*. He divided his spiritual domain into twenty-two provinces (*manjis*) and appointed his representatives for each of these. His own compositions and selections from the compositions of some *bhagats* were added to the compositions of his predecessors and put together by his grandson Sahansar Ram. These volumes were later used by Guru Arjan for the compilation of the *Granth*. Ceremonies of marriage and death came to be performed with the help of *Gurbani*. Guru Amar Das wanted only the praises of God to be sung on his death. He consecrated his son-in-law, Ram Das, as his successor before he died on 1 September 1574.[6]

Guru Ram Das laid the foundation of the city of Amritsar, then called Chak Guru, Chak Ramdas or Ramdaspur. He invited traders and craftsmen to reside in the town. 'Possession of wealth was no longer to be considered as Maya, but as a very salutary and helpful thing in the conduct of human affairs'. Guru Ram Das died at Goindwal on 1 September 1581 to be succeeded by his youngest son, Guru Arjan, who completed the work of building the tank and the city with the manual and material help of the Sikhs. Every Sikh was expected to set aside one-tenth (*dasvandh*) of his income for the Guru's fund as a voluntary contribution. This could be remitted through an accredited *masand*. Guru Arjan laid the foundation of the central shrine, now called the Golden Temple, in the midst of the tank of *amritsar.* He founded Tarn Taran and Sri Hargobindpur not far from Amritsar, and he founded Kartarpur in the Jalandhar Doab. He constructed a *baoli* at Lahore.[7]

According to Teja Singh and Ganda Singh, 'the greatest work' of Guru Arjan was compilation of the *Granth*. Some work in this direction had already been done by Guru Angad and Guru Amar Das. Guru Arjan went to Goindwal personally to borrow the volumes from Baba Mohan and to bring them reverentially to Amritsar. He had to consult some other sources too to complete the work. Guru Arjan's own contribution to the *Granth* was the largest. He also included selections from the writings of fifteen Hindu and Muslim saints, most of whom belonged to the so-called depressed or untouchable classes. The basis of selection was not doctrinal but 'the lyrical and living values of the pieces'. The idea was inherent in the 'cosmopolitan nature of Sikhism'. Guru Arjan was not the first Guru to think of making a collection of the verses of the *bhagats*. He enlarged the scope of inclusion and gave 'a scriptural position' to their writings. The compositions of men like Kanha, Chajju, Shah Husain and Pilu were rejected either because of their Vedantic leanings or because of their hatred for the world, or for women. Guru Arjan wanted 'only healthy optimism and joy in worldly duties and responsibilities and not mere tearful asceticism or otherworldliness'. The huge material assembled was reduced to writing by Bhai Gurdas at the dictation of Guru Arjan. The *Granth* was completed and installed in the Harmandar at Amritsar in 1604. Teja Singh and Ganda Singh refer to the arrangement of the contents of the *Granth* with some interesting comments. The *Granth* was brought to its final form by Guru Gobind Singh at Damdama Sahib (Talwandi Sabo) in 1705. A new recension was prepared, not by dictating it from memory, nor by adding the *bani* of Guru Tegh Bahadur for the first time, but by re-editing an existing recension.[8]

Jahangir had formed a prejudice against the Sikh movement. As he states in his *Tuzk*, he had thought of putting an end to 'this false traffic' or to bring Guru Arjan into the fold of Islam. He got a chance during the rebellion of Prince Khusrau. After the prince was captured and punished, Jahangir was told that Guru Arjan had put a saffron mark on Khusrau's forehead as the mark of his blessings in favour of the rebel. No enquiry was made, nor any trial held. Jahangir asserts that he knew the Guru's 'heresies'. He ordered 'that his house and children be made over to Murtaza Khan, that his property be confiscated, and that he should be put to death with tortures'. The allegation seems to have been concocted by the Guru's enemies, and Jahangir got the pretext he needed. Guru Arjan was handed over to Chandu Shah who had a private grudge against him. Subjected to all sorts of tortures in the burning heat of Lahore, the blistered body of Guru Arjan was thrown into the cold water of the Ravi to be carried away. This occurred on 30 May 1606.[9]

The martyrdom of Guru Arjan convinced the Sikhs that they must arm themselves and fight if they wanted to survive. Guru Hargobind wore two swords on the occasion of his accession, one to represent spiritual and the other temporal interests. He asked the *masands* and the Sikhs to bring arms and horses as offerings. A fortress, called Lohgarh, was constructed in Amritsar. A meeting place for the Sikhs was also built. It was called Akal Takht, or the Throne of the Almighty. In the courtyard in its front, physical feats were performed, visitors were received, and complaints were heard and redressed. Jahangir summoned the Guru and sent him to the fort of Gwalior as a state prisoner. Later, however, the emperor seems to have been convinced that he had been misled. Guru Hargobind was released and he resumed his mission. He built the town of Kiratpur in the hills. Jahangir's death in 1627 brought the phase of peace to an end. Shah Jahan, prohibited the conversion of Muslims and ordered the demolition of temples. The *baoli* at Lahore was filled up and a mosque was erected on the site of the free kitchen attached to it. In this situation even a slight cause could result in a clash of arms. This cause was provided in 1628 by an altercation over a hawk between the Sikhs and some men of the royal hunting party. The Mughal noble

Mukhlis Khan was killed. Guru Hargobind left Amritsar for Kartarpur where he was attacked by the Mughal *faujdar* of Jalandhar. The *faujdar* was killed in the battle. Two other commandants, Painde Khan and Kale Khan, were killed in yet another battle fought near Kartarpur in 1632. 'A new heroism was rising in the land', its object, then dimly seen, was to create the will to resist 'the foreign aggressors'. This accorded well with the intentions of Guru Nanak. Active measures for the service of mankind were not inconsistent with their religious ideals. The assumption of *miri-piri* by Guru Hargobind was a logical development, and not a deviation.[10]

The time of Guru Har Rai (1644-61) was rather uneventful. Towards its end, however, his partiality for Dara Shukoh attracted Aurangzeb's attention. Summoned to Delhi the Guru sent Ram Rai who compromised his integrity to please the emperor. Guru Har Rai appointed his younger son, Har Krishan as the Guru. He too was called to Delhi for arbitration. There he died in 1664 after indicating that his grand uncle, Tegh Bahadur, would be his successor. Guru Tegh Bahadur met opposition from Dhir Mal at Kartarpur, Harji at Ramdaspur, and Suraj Mal at Kiratpur, and founded a new town called Anandpur. Teja Singh and Ganda Singh pay serious attention to Guru Tegh Bahadur's long tour up to Assam in the late 1660s. Meanwhile Aurangzeb adopted a hostile policy towards Hindus and Sikhs. Guru Tegh Bahadur returned to the Punjab and preached the message of 'frighten not and fear not' among the peasantry of the Malwa region. On a misrepresentation of his position by the newswriters, he was arrested at Agra, taken to Delhi, and tried. He refused to perform a miracle or to accept Islam. He was beheaded in the Chandni Chowk area of Delhi. The event recorded by his son and successor in the *Bachittar Natak* shows that he laid down his head for his principles, he suffered martyrdom for the sake of religion, and protected the frontal mark and the sacrificial thread of the Hindus.[11]

Born at Patna in 1606, Gobind Das was only nine years old at the time of this event. He retired into the state of Nahan and founded a fort at Paonta on land offered by the ruler of Nahan. There, he went through the whole range of epic literature in Sanskrit and learnt to compose in Hindi and Punjabi. He practised the manly exercises of riding, hunting, swimming, archery, and sword-play. His increasing influence excited the jealousy and fear of the hill chiefs. Headed by Bhim Chand of Kahlur they came to attack him. He met them in Bhangani and won the battle. He returned to Anandpur and built four forts. Called upon to support the cause of Bhim Chand against the Mughal *faujdars,* he agreed to take part in the struggle 'which he considered national'. The Mughal *faujdars* were defeated in a battle at Nadaun. Guru Gobind Singh's success caused some anxiety to the emperor. In 1693 he had warned Guru Gobind Singh not to assemble his Sikhs. Now he sent Prince Muazzam to the Punjab to deal with the disorders. Bhai Nand Lal interceded on behalf of the Guru and he was left alone. The refractory rulers were severely punished. This was the situation in which Guru Gobind Singh thought of instituting the Khalsa.[12]

Going through Puranic literature, Guru Gobind Singh was deeply impressed by the idea that God had been sending a saviour from time to time to uphold righteousness and to destroy evil. He came to feel that he himself was the man required by the times. As he states in the *Bachittar Natak,* he believed that God had commissioned him 'to advance righteousness, to emancipate the good, and to destroy all evil-doers root and branch'. The keynote of literature preserved in the *Dasam Granth* is optimism; the heroic deeds of gods and goddesses are glorified 'to inspire ardour for religious warfare'. On 30 March 1699, he gave the dramatic call for sacrifice and baptized the first five volunteers with sweetened water stirred with a dagger. He spoke of his mission to the assembly. For the speech of Guru Gobind Singh, Teja Singh and Ganda Singh quote Ghulam Muhiyuddin *alias* Bute Shah. The Guru begged the Five Beloved to baptize him in the same way as he had baptized them. 'After this there remained no difference between him and his baptized Sikhs'. They were 'quite competent to take his place after him'. About 80, 000 men were baptized in a few days. Guru Gobind Singh ordered that all those who called themselves Sikhs should get themselves confirmed by receiving the new baptism, and follow the *rahit* he enunciated. Guru Gobind Singh expressed great admiration for the Khalsa. To serve them pleased his heart, and no other service was so dear to his soul. 'All the substance in my house, nay, my soul and body are at their disposal.' The Guru poured his life into the Khalsa and invested them with his own personality.[13]

Teja Singh and Ganda Singh give a factual narrative of events from the death of Guru Hargobind to the institution of the Khalsa by Guru

Gobind Singh. They highlight the effect of the *Zafarnama* on the mind of Aurangzeb, resulting in an invitation for a personal meeting. This is followed by Guru Gobind Singh's meeting with Bahadur Shah at Agra in 1707, his intention to return to Anandpur, disillusionment with Bahadur Shah after a year's stay near his camp, the conversion of Banda Bahadur, and an attack on Guru Gobind Singh by a hired assassin. The wound had not yet fully healed when the Guru tried to bend a stiff bow. The wound burst open. On 7 October 1708, a couple of hours after midnight, he roused his Sikhs from sleep to bid them farewell. There was to be no personal Guru after him. 'The whole Sikh community, in the organized form called the *panth,* was to guide itself by the teaching of the Gurus as incorporated in the Holy Granth, and also by the collective sense of the community.'[14]

IV. POLITICAL FOUNDATIONS: BANDA SINGH BAHADUR

After the death of Guru Gobind Singh, the political leadership of the Sikhs came into the hands of Banda Singh who had been baptized by Guru Gobind Singh as 'a regular Sikh' and sent to the Punjab to continue the struggle with the Mughal rulers. He was instructed to look upon himself as a servant of the Khalsa who represented the Guru. He had with him five Singhs to advise him in all matters. Among them were Baj Singh, Binod Singh and Kahan Singh. As the commander of the Khalsa, Banda Singh dispatched the *hukamnamas* of Guru Gobind Singh to the leading Sikhs of the Punjab, calling them to join him to punish Wazir Khan, the Mughal *faujdar* of Sirhind. The Sikhs flocked to him. Marching towards Sirhind, he plundered and destroyed a number of places, like Samana, Kapuri and Sadhaura. Apart from the Khalsa volunteers, Banda Singh had the support of men sent by the sympathizers. Some others joined him for plunder or private revenge. The Sikhs from the Majha and the Doaba had to fight against the Malerkotla Afghans near Ropar before they could join Banda Singh near Banur. The number of his followers was probably larger than the troops of Wazir Khan but the latter were better trained and much better equipped with artillery and cavalry. The battle of Chhappar Chiri, fought on 12 May 1710, went in favour of the Khalsa. Wazir Khan was killed and Sirhind was captured and ransacked. Sucha Nanad, the *peshkar* of Wazir Khan, who had instigated the murder of the sons of Guru Gobind Singh, was put to death.[15]

The conquest was followed by setting up of a new administrative machinery. Baj Singh was appointed governor of Sirhind, with Ali Singh of Salaudi as his deputy. Fateh Singh was given charge of Samana. Baj Singh's brother Ram Singh was given the charge of Thanesar, jointly with Binod Singh. The whole tract from Ludhiana to Karnal, worth about Rs. 36,00,000 a year, was brought under control. Banda fixed upon Mukhlispur, a hilly place near Sadhaura, as his headquarters. Its old fort was repaired and renamed Lohgarh. 'He assumed royal authority, and struck coins in the name of the Guru.' He also introduced an official seal, with an inscription that expressed his deep sense of devotion to his master. Banda abolished the *zamindari* system. The tillers of the soil became masters and the curse of the *zamindari* system was lifted from the Punjab which was now considered as 'the heaven of peasant proprietors'.[16]

The fall of Sirhind was a signal for a general rising of the Sikhs all over the country. Teja Singh and Ganda Singh take up first the movement led by Banda Singh. He crossed the Jamuna and occupied the city of Saharanpur and half of the Sarkar. Nanauta was razed to the ground and Jalalabad was besieged. In the meantime, the Sikhs of the Jalandhar Doab began to oust the petty officials; they occupied the fort of Rahon on 12 October 1710. Shams Khan, the *faujdar* of the Doab, declared *jihad* against them. In the Bari Doab, the Khalsa turned out the Mughal officials from Batala and Kalanaur and established their own *thanas* in the upper Bari Doab. The Mughal governor of Lahore, Aslam Khan, declared *jihad* against the Sikhs. The *ghazis* were defeated by the Khalsa. The Sikhs were now masters of the Punjab east of Lahore.[17]

Bahadur Shah, the Mughal emperor, left Ajmer on 27 June, collected a huge army, and marched towards the Punjab. The Sikhs left Thanesar and Sirhind, and took their stand at the fort of Lohgarh. It was invested by over 60,000 horse and foot. On 10 December 1710, Banda made a determined sally and disappeared with all his men into the hills of Nahan. On the day following, the Mughal commander, Mun'im Khan took the fort but he was disappointed to find that 'the hawk had flown'. The emperor was extremely displeased. Raja Bhup Prakash of Nahan was made a prisoner and sent in a cage to Delhi. Banda Singh made the northern hills his home and occasionally descended on the plains, as in the upper Bari Doab in June 1711. Bahadur Shah died at Lahore on 18 February 1712. The time of internecine struggles offered a favourable opportunity to Banda Singh to re-establish his power. He took Sadhaura and Lohgarh. Farrukh Siyar appointed Abdus Samad Khan as the governor of Lahore with the express objective of dealing with Banda Singh. The Sikhs were obliged to evacuate Sadhaura and Lohgarh in October 1713. Banda took refuge in the Jammu hills.[18]

Banda Singh appeared in the plains in 1715. After an indecisive battle with Abdus Samad Khan, he took a defensive position at Gurdas Nangal, near Gurdaspur. Abdus Samad Khan drew the siege closer and the Khalsa began to suffer extremes of hunger. Binod Singh favoured the idea of cutting through the besiegers but Banda was opposed to it. Eventually, Binod Singh rode out of the enclosure and fought his way through the Mughal troops. Banda and his companions were obliged to surrender on 7 December 1715. They were first taken in a procession to Lahore and then to Delhi, providing a spectacle for the people in both the cities. However, most of the Sikh prisoners appeared to be happy and cheerful, merrily singing their sacred hymns when they were carried on camels in Delhi. Their execution began in March 1716 and ended in June with the execution of Banda close to the *dargah* of Khwaja Qutbuddin Bakhtiyar Kaki near the Qutub Minar. Teja Singh and Ganda Singh refer to a Sikh youth whose mother wished to save him on the plea that he had been forced to join the Khalsa but who declared that his mother was a liar, and died willingly at the hands of the executioner.[19]

The revolution led by Banda Singh had been started much earlier by the Sikh Gurus against the Mughal power, but it was he who effectively organized it as a political force to pull down the Mughal edifice and 'to give a foretaste of independence to the people of the land'. This was the primary reason for the harsh judgement against him by the Persian writers who were generally aligned with the Mughal state. He was no 'monster' as he is made out to be. And even his enemies bear witness to his coolness of courage and dauntless bravery against all odds. He followed the *rahit* of the Khalsa. The differences between the Khalsa and the followers of Banda arose after his death. He introduced *fateh darshan* only as 'a war cry' and not as the Sikh salutation. That was why he dropped it when it was pointed out to him that it might replace *Vaheguru ka Khalsa, Vaheguruji ki Fateh.* The introduction of vegetarian diet could not have created a split. 'The aim of Banda was nothing short of liberation of the country from the Mughal rule, which was still foreign in most of its essentials.' He was the first man among the Sikhs to think of 'founding a political *raj*'. He set an example for the Khalsa to follow in darker days of persecution. 'The idea of a national state, long dead, once again became a living aspiration, and although suppressed for the time being by relentless persecution, it went on working underground like a smouldering fire, and came out forty years later with a fuller effulgence.'[20]

V. SECTARIAN DIVISIONS AND THE EMERGENCE OF THE KHALSA: 1716-1748

The period from 1716 to 1765 is divided by Teja Singh and Ganda Singh into four phases. The first, from 1716 to 1721, was marked by 'divisions among Sikhs'. The Mughal authorities adopted every possible measure not only to destroy the power of the Sikhs but also to extirpate the community as a whole. The adoption of Khalsa symbols amounted to courting death. Therefore, those who believed in Sikhism began to go about without long hair. 'They were called *Khulasas* or irregulars —now known as *Sahajdharis* or slow adopters'. They believed in the same principles as 'the regular Sikhs' whom they helped with money and provisions in times of need and whom they joined as soon as they found themselves ready to make sacrifice. The 'genuine Sikhs' took shelter in hills and forests, gradually coming out of their hiding places.[21]

With the return of the Sikhs to the plains, their visits to the gurdwaras increased, particularly to the Darbar Sahib at Amritsar where they assembled in large numbers at the time of Baisakhi and the Diwali. This created a new problem: who was to guide the services and to control income and expenditure? Teja Singh and Ganda Singh turn here to various categories of the Sikhs, the Khalsa and the others. Among the latter were the *Gulab Raiyas,* the *Gangu Shahyas,* and the *Handalias.* Then there was Ajit Singh in Delhi, and the older orders of the Minas, the Dhir Millias, and the Ram Raiyas, besides the Udasis. None of them was active against the state. The baptized Nirmalas were also safe because their missionary activities were confined to the Malwa region, though they were one with the Khalsa in matters of belief. The main clash of the Khalsa was with the followers of Banda who looked upon him as Guru Gobind Singh's successor. They demanded equal share in the management of gurdwaras. Both the Khalsa and the 'Bandeis' tried to assert their claims over the Darbar Sahib by a show of force in 1720. Kahan Singh, son of Baba Binod Singh, tried to postpone the settlement of their differences. Meanwhile, Mata Sundari sent Bhai Mani Singh to Amritsar, along with Kirpal Singh, the maternal uncle of Guru Gobind Singh, to restore peace among the Sikhs. Bhai Mani Singh became the *granthi* of the Darbar Sahib and began to organize service in the temple and to manage its affairs in 1721. But this did not put an end to the differences between the Khalsa and the 'Bandeis'. At the time of Baisakhi in 1721 they came to a clash in which the Khalsa had the upper hand. 'From that day the Bandeis assumed a quieter role and practically disappeared from the pages of history.'[22]

The second phase started after the elimination of the 'Bandeis'. The Khalsa began to consolidate their strength at Amritsar. They were able to withstand a contingent sent against them from Lahore by its Mughal governor. A police post was now established at Amritsar to keep the Sikhs in check. They were sometimes harassed and dispersed. Their sufferings added to their strength. The imperial court thought of placing the province of Lahore in the hands of a strong man. Abdus Samad Khan was transferred to Multan in 1726 and his more energetic son, Zakariya Khan, took his place as the governor of Lahore.[23]

Zakariya Khan adopted strong measures to root out the Sikhs once for all. They were captured, tortured, and beheaded at the horse market known as *Nakhas*. It came to be known as Shahidganj or 'treasure-trove of martyrdom'. The severity on the Sikhs created sympathy for them among the people and they joined the Khalsa in large numbers. They had no hearths, no homes, no property but they lived in the hope that one day the Khalsa shall rule (*Raj Karega Khalsa*), as prophesied by Guru Gobind Singh. Tara Singh of Van, who had won laurels in the campaign of Banda, died fighting as a martyr, along with 22 other Singhs. In retaliation, the Khalsa captured government treasuries and plundered caravans. Zakariya Khan tried now to placate the Sikhs.[24]

In 1733, Zakariya Khan's proposal to the Mughal court that a grant be made to the Sikhs and a title conferred on their leader was accepted. Subeg Singh, a government contractor, was sent to the Khalsa assembled at the Akal Takht, Amritsar. He accepted the penance (*tankhah*) imposed by the Khalsa and he was allowed to make an offer on behalf of the Mughal governor: the title of 'Nawab' for their leader and the *parganas* of Jhabal, Kanganwal and Dipalpur, worth Rs. 1,00,000 a year, as *jagir*. Diwan Darbara Singh, a prominent leader, declined the title on the plea that the Guru had promised a kingdom and he would accept nothing shorter. Kapur Singh of Faizullahpur, who was waving a large fan over the assembly at that time, was selected for the honour. He accepted the robe after it had been sanctified by the touch of the feet of five Singhs. 'Nawab' Kapur Singh organized the Khalsa into two main divisions: the Buddha Dal or the Army of Elders, and the Taruna Dal or the Army of the Young. After Diwan Darbara Singh's death in 1734, it became difficult to control the young Khalsa at one place. Five centres were established for them, each under one or two leaders. They resumed their old activity in the countryside, and Zakariya Khan rescinded the *jagir* in 1735.[25]

Once again the Khalsa came into clash with the Mughal authorities. The Buddha Dal was driven out of the Bari Doab by Diwan Lakhpat Rai. When the Dal came to Amritsar at the time of Diwali it was defeated but soon afterwards the combined Dals inflicted a heavy defeat on the enemy. Two *faujdars* and the nephew of Lakhpat Rai were killed in a battle near Hujra Shah Muqim. The Darbar Sahib at Amritsar was now taken over by the Mughal officials and military men were posted to prevent the Sikhs from assembling there. In 1738, Bhai Mani Singh approached the Lahore governor for permission to hold the Diwali festival. He was allowed to do so on the condition that he would pay Rs. 5,000 after the fair which was to last for ten days. Zakariya Khan sent Lakhpat Rai with a force to be stationed at Ram Tirath and to disperse the Sikhs on the days of the fair. Bhai Mani Singh failed to pay Rs. 5,000 to the treasury. He was given the option of Islam or death; he chose to die as a martyr. A few of Bhai Mani Singh's companions were also executed. Renewed persecution drove the Sikhs into hills and forests.[26]

Nadir Shah sacked Delhi in the early months of 1739 and took the route along the Shiwaliks on his return. At Akhnur the Sikhs descended from the hills, fell upon his rear, and relieved him of much of his booty. He called a halt at Lahore and questioned Zakariya Khan about the whereabouts of the people who had dared to interfere with his march. Zakariya Khan told him that they were a group of devotees who visited their Guru's tank twice a year for bathing, and their homes were their saddles. Nadir Shah warned him that they would take possession of his country. Zakariya Khan became rigorous in his persecutory measures. Even the *chaudharis* and *muqaddams* were mobilized to crush the Sikhs. A *chaudhari* called Massa Ranghar took charge of the Darbar Sahib and began to use it for dance (*nauch*) by professional female singers. Mehtab Singh of Mirankot and Sukha Singh of Mari Kambo disguised themselves as peasants to reach the Darbar Sahib and, there, they cut-off Massa Ranghar's head in August 1740.[27]

Before Zakariya Khan's death on 1 July 1745, Bota Singh Sandhu of Padhana died fighting against a Mughal contingent to make his presence felt. Bhai Taru Singh of Poola used to help the Khalsa in their exile. In June 1745 he was arrested and taken to Lahore. He was asked to accept Islam and to cut-off his hair. On his refusal to do so, Zakariya Khan ordered the removal his scalp. He died on 1 July 1745, Zakariya Khan on the same day. Zakariya Khan's son and successor Yahiya Khan was as relentless as his father. Shahbaz Singh and his father Subeg Singh died as martyrs due to his policy of persecution.[28]

Even more disastrous was the *ghallughara* of 1746. Diwan Lakhpat Rai's brother, Jaspat Rai, was the *faujdar* of Eminabad. A band of Sikhs wanted to purchase provisions from the town, but Jaspat Rai fell upon them. During the fight a Ranghreta Sikh, named Nibhau Singh, got on to his elephant and cut-off his head. Lakhpat Rai vowed vengeance upon the Sikhs. With a large number of troops he marched against the Sikhs who were about 15,000 in number and had taken shelter in the reedy marshes of Kahnuwan. They were pushed out towards the Ravi which they crossed and headed towards Parol and Kathua. Hard pressed by Lakhpat Rai they tried to recross the Ravi but found it difficult due to its flooded state. The Khalsa in desperation attacked the Mughal troops. Their leader, Sukha Singh, was wounded in the leg in an effort to get at Lakhpat Rai. The Khalsa crossed the Ravi, the Beas, and the Sutlej to move out of the province of Lahore. In this campaign at least 7,000 Sikhs lost their lives, besides 3,000 were taken as prisoners to Lahore.

Yahiya Khan was ousted from Lahore by his brother Shah Nawaz Khan who invited Ahmad Shah Durrani to invade India. However, when the Durrani marched towards Lahore in January 1748, Shah Nawaz Khan went to Delhi. Ahmad Shah was defeated in the battle of Manupur in March 1746 and Mir Mannu became the governor of Lahore and Multan.[29]

VI. CONFLICT WITH AHMAD SHAH ABDALI

The third phase, from 1748 to 1758, started with the Sikhs taking advantage of the confusion reigning in Lahore and Delhi and emerging from their hide-outs. The Durrani was pursued by Charhat Singh's band up to the Indus and relieved of a number of horses and other property. Jassa Singh Ahluwalia killed Salabat Khan, the officer-in-charge of Amritsar, in a battle and took possession of the town. 'This proved to be a landmark in the history of the Sikhs, not because it was an occasion of great victory but becaue it ushered in a new era in which the Sikhs knit their scattered bands into a more homogeneous organization, and provided it with a local habitation in the form of a fort.' On the Baisakhi day of 1748, Jassa Singh Ahluwalia was chosen the supreme commander of the Dal Khalsa which was re-organized and declared to be a state. Near Ramsar, was built a small enclosure of a mud wall, called Ram Rauni after the name of Guru Ram Das. The leaders of the Khalsa began to assert their rule over different parts in the Bari, Jalandhar and Rachna Doabs.[30]

Mir Mannu took notice of this development, and he laid siege to Ram Rauni on the Diwali of 1748. The reign went on for three months, till December, and about 200 Sikhs were killed. Jassa Singh (Ramgarhia), who was with the besiegers joined the Khalsa with a hundred followers. The invasion of Ahmad Shah Durrani obliged Mir Mannu to leave Amritsar. He did not receive any help from the Mughal court and agreed to meet the Durrani's demand that the trans-Indus territories be regarded as a part of the Afghan empire, and the revenues of four *parganas* of the province of Lahore be paid to him. This was the arrangement made by Nadir Shah with the Mughal emperor in 1739. Against Mir Mannu's wishes, Shah Nawaz Khan was made the governor of Multan by the Mughal court, and Mir Mannu took help from the

Khalsa under Jassa Singh Ahluwalia for defeating Shah Nawaz who was killed in the battle. The Sikhs got some respite. Many of the oppressed peasantry and downtrodden menials felt encouraged to join the Khalsa under one leader or another.[31]

During Ahmad Shah Durrani's invasion of 1751-2, a large number of Sikhs under the leadership of Sangat Singh and Sukha Singh supported Mir Mannu, and Sukha Singh got killed in a battle. Diwan Kaura Mal too was killed and Mir Mannu was defeated. However, he was reinstated as the governor of Lahore and Multan on behalf of Ahmad Shah Durrani. The cession of these two provinces to Ahmad Shah was ratified by the Mughal emperor in April 1752. Feeling secure in his position, Mir Mannu adopted harsh measures to remove the causes of disturbance within the country. The Sikhs too returned to their old ways and began to bid for independence. Mir Mannu resorted to vigorous measures against them. Even Sikh women were seized and tortured. However, Mir Mannu died early in November 1753. For over three years then, the Afghan administrators did not feel strong enough to suppress the Sikhs.[32]

In January 1757 Ahmad Shah Durrani came and entered the Red Fort. The *sarkar* of Sirhind was ceded to him by the Mughal emperor. Before returning to Kabul, he appointed his son, Prince Taimur, as the Viceroy of Sirhind, Lahore, Kashmir, Multan and Thatta. The Sikhs had organized a protective system, called *rakhi,* under which they protected Hindu and Muslim *zamindars* against all others for a levy of one-fifth of the annual rent. The system was acceptable to most of the people in the distracted areas, which passed under the control of the Sikhs. It became the basis of the administration called 'the *misaldari* system'. A number of Sikh leaders had already carved out principalities for themselves in the Chaj, Rachna, Bari and Jalandhar Doabs. At the end of March 1757, the Sikhs harassed the Afghan army under Taimur and Jahan Khan. The Afghans retaliated by destroying Kartarpur in the absence of Sodhi Vadbhag Singh. A *jihad* against the Sikhs was proclaimed, and the Sikhs felt the urge to defend Amritsar under the leadership of Baba Dip Singh. The Afghans defeated the Sikhs and Jahan Khan returned to Lahore. Soon afterwards, however, the Sikhs joined forces with Adina Beg Khan and plundered Jalandhar. Adina Beg paid Rs. 1,25,000 as *rakhi.*[33]

Adina Beg Khan invited the Marathas to oust the Afghans from the Punjab at his expense. Raghunath Rao accepted the offer and the Maratha army reached Sirhind on 9 March 1758 to find that the Sikhs had already entered the city. On 19 April, the Sikhs and Marathas entered Lahore. Some of the leading Sikhs who took part in this campaign with 10,000 to 15,000 horse were Charhat Singh, Tara Singh Gheba, Jassa Singh Ahluwalia, Jassa Singh Ramgarhia, and the Bhangi leaders Hari Singh, Lehna Singh, Gujjar Singh and Jhanda Singh.[34]

VII. THE KHALSA EMERGE AS A SOVEREIGN POWER

The last phase, in which the 'Sikhs become sovereign power', started with the realization by Raghunath that the Marathas could not hold the country in the face of the rising power of the Sikhs. He decided to leave the government in the hands of Adina Beg for an annual tribute of Rs. 75,00,000. On 10 May 1758 the main army of the Marathas moved out of Lahore. Adina Beg died in September 1758. The detachments left behind were driven out by the Afghans in 1759. The Maratha garrisons fell like nine pins before the advancing army of the Afghans under Jahan Khan. In a battle with the Sikhs, however, 2,000 Afghans were killed and Jahan Khan was wounded. Ahmad Shah Durrani moved on towards Delhi. The historic battle of Panipat, fought on 14 January 1761, sealed the fate of the Maratha empire in the north. In March 1761, Ala Singh of Patiala submitted to the Durrani and agreed to pay Rs. 5,00,000 as the annual tribute. He was condemned by the Dal Khalsa for this submission to the Durrani. 'The Khalsa wanted nothing less than sovereignty.' On the Diwali of 1760, the Sarbat Khalsa had gathered at Amritsar and resolved by a *gurmata* to take possession of Lahore. The governor, Muhammad Khan paid Rs. 30,000 for *karha prasad* and the Sikhs retired. On the Durrani's march back to Kabul the Sikh pursued the Afghan army up to the Indus and rescued 2,000 Hindu women.

In May 1761, the Sikhs spread themselves over most of the Punjab and into the Shiwalik hills. They killed the Afghan *faujdar* of four *mahals* and defeated the Afghan General Nuruddin Bamzai. The Afghan governor of Lahore, Khwaja Ubaid Khan, marched against Charhat

Singh but he was defeated by the Sikhs and he returned to Lahore, leaving a considerable number of guns, horses, camels and stores in their hands. Led by Jassa Singh Ahluwalia, the Sikhs entered Lahore and proclaimed him king with the title of *Sultan ul-Qaum*. He coined money in the name of the Guru with the inscription that had appeared on the official seal of Banda Singh. The fort was still in the hands of Ubaid Khan. The Khalsa moved into the Jalandhar Doab, and ousted the Afghan *faujdars,* Sa'adat Khan and Sadiq Khan Afridi. The entire Punjab from the Indus to the Sutlej passed into the hands of the Sikhs.[35]

On the Diwali of 1761 in October the Sarbat Khalsa gathered at Amritsar and resolved to reduce the strongholds of all the allies and supporters of Ahmad Shah Durrani. The nearest at hand was Aqil Das of Jandiala, the Guru of the Niranjanias, who was an avowed enemy of the Sikhs. He wrote to Ahmad Shah Durrani for help. Already on his way to India, the Durrani hurried to Jandiala to discover that the Sikhs had raised the siege and gone away towards Sirhind. The Afghan chief of Malerkotla, Bhikhan Khan, informed the Durrani that the Sikhs were gathering in villages close to Malerkotla. He left Lahore on 3 February 1762 and reached the village Kupp, near Malerkotla on the 5th, where about 30,000 Sikhs were encamped with their families and all their belongings. The Sikh leaders tried to protect the non-combatants, moving and fighting. At least 10,000 Sikhs, mostly women and children, were killed in this *ghallughara*. On 10 April 1762 the Durrani blew up the Harmandar with gun powder.[36]

On the Diwali of 1762, when the Sikhs gathered at Amritsar, the Durrani marched against them from Lahore. He reached Amritsar on 16 October. The Sikhs attacked him on the day following, and compelled him to withdraw his forces and escape to Lahore under cover of darkness. On Ahmad Shah's return to Kabul the Sikhs reoccupied their territories. He deputed Jahan Khan to march against them. But he was forced to return to Kabul in November 1763. Early in 1764, under the leadership of Jassa Singh Ahluwalia, the Sikhs occupied Sirhind after killing Zain Khan in a battle. The whole of the *sarkar* was partitioned among the conquerors. The Afghan governor of Lahore was now threatened by the Sikhs. Ahmad Shah came for the seventh time in 1764. The Sikhs were gathered at Amritsar. He resolved to slay them and level the Chak to the earth, as he had done before. He found only about thirty Sikhs, led by Gurbakhsh Singh Shahid, ready to defend the sacred place. They died as martyrs and a Shahidganj was built over the spot of their cremation behind the Akal Takht.[37]

Ahmad Shah Durrani tried to work out a relationship with the Sikh leaders as he had done with Ala Singh of Patiala. But the Sikhs were not inclined to accept rulership from the hands of a foreigner. When he recrossed the Sutlej, his advance guard was set upon by the Sikhs. He ordered the army to be ready in battle formation. The Sikhs too organized themselves for a pitched battle, with Jassa Singh Ahluwalia and Jassa Singh Ramgarhia in the centre, Charhat Singh on the right, along with Jhanda Singh and Lehna Singh Bhangi, and Jai Singh Kanhiya, on the left, along with Hari Singh. They followed their usual tactics. Skirmishes went on for seven days. The Durrani was now anxious to return to Kabul. After his departure in March 1765, the Sikhs met at Amritsar on the Baisakhi day and resolved to occupy Lahore. Three Sikh leaders occupied the city and partitioned it among themselves. The whole country, liberated from foreign rule, passed into the hands of the Sikhs. They looked upon this success as a mark of the Guru's special favour. They struck a coin with the inscription which had appeared on the seal of Banda Singh and the coin of Jassa Singh:

Deg o tegh o fateh o nusrat be-dirang
Yaft az Nanak Guru Gobind Singh.[38]

VIII. SOME GENERAL OBSERVATIONS

Teja Singh and Ganda Singh underline that Sikhism was founded as a new faith from the very beginning. The Sikh social order developed on the basis of Sikh ideology and institutions. This view is based on their study of the compositions of Guru Nanak and his first four successors. The visible success of the movement and the nature of its influence was at the root of the Sikh confrontation with the state. The response of Guru Hargobind and his successors, especially Guru Gobind Singh, was meant to meet the challenge. The establishment of Sikh rule was prophesied by Guru Gobind Singh himself.

To these religious foundations, Banda Singh Bahadur added the political foundations by conquering territory, evolving his own administration, and declaring the sovereignty of the Khalsa by striking a coin.

He demonstrated the possibility of establishing Khalsa Raj. For the first time in the history of historical writing Ganda Singh had provided comprehensive information on Banda Bahadur and the whole account of Banda in *A Short History of the Sikhs* was based on Ganda Singh's work.

For the political history of the Sikhs during the eighteenth century from 1716 to 1765, Teja Singh and Ganda Singh postulate four phases. In the first phase the Khalsa re-emerge as the most conspicuous component of the Sikhs in control of Ramdaspur as the locus of their religious and political institutions. In the second phase they survive repressive persecution by the Mughal authorities, and re-emerge as a political entity. In the third phase they begin to occupy territories, especially after the death of Mir Mannu, and join hands with the Marathas to oust the Afghans from the Punjab. In the fourth phase, the Khalsa occupy territories on a larger scale and come out successful in their contest with Ahmad Shah Abdali. Once again they strike a coin as the declaration of their sovereign rule. Teja Singh and Ganda Singh try to make sense of this eventful period, marked by rapid changes, with the help of both Sikh and Persian sources. They stand distinguished from the other historians of the Sikhs for the use of these sources. However, they do not make a distinction between strictly 'contemporary' and 'near-contemporary' evidence.

A Short History of the Sikhs has served as a good introduction to Sikh history for six decades, and it is still read. However, during the recent decades, the scope of Sikh history has expanded. Furthermore, our understanding even of political history has improved. The authors look upon Guru Gobind Singh as the creator of a nation and yet they are reluctant to ascribe any political purposes directly to him. The activity of the Khalsa under the leadership of Banda was actually an extension of their activity in the time of Guru Gobind Singh who conceived the idea of sovereign rule. On a matter of detail, Teja Singh and Ganda Singh accept that Guru Gobind Singh agreed to perform *hom* for the Goddess even though to disillusion the people, but there is no credible evidence for the *hom* itself. They do not cite any evidence in support of their statement that Banda Singh abolished the *zamindari* system. In fact, they equate the *zamindars* with large proprietors of land without any support in contemporary evidence. Similarly, they do not cite any evidence for the *rakhi* system and its difference from the occupation of territories. More factual information has come to light on the period from 1716 to 1765. The authors accept the concept of *misldari*. The fact that the system is not described anywhere suggests that, like their predecessors, they use the term *misldari* for the period of Sikh rule during the late eighteenth century which is not covered in their *History*.[39]

NOTES

1. Hira Singh Dard, *Karam Singh Historian di Itihasik Khoj* (Punjabi), Amritsar: Sikh Itihas Research Board, SGPC, 1974, 2nd edn.
2. Teja Singh and Ganda Singh, *A Short History of the Sikhs*, vol. I (*1469-1765*), Patiala: Punjabi University, 1999, 3rd edn., pp. 1 & n. 1, 2.
3. Ibid., pp. 13-17.
4. Ibid., pp. 17-19.
5. Ibid., pp. 19-24.
6. Ibid., pp. 24-8.
7. Ibid., pp. 29-33.
8. Ibid., pp. 33-5.
9. Ibid., pp. 35-46.
10. Ibid., pp. 44-56.
11. Ibid., pp. 56-63.
12. Ibid., pp. 46-70.
13. Ibid., pp. 71-7.
14. Ibid., pp. 78-83.
15. Ibid., pp. 83-6.
16. Ibid., pp. 86-90.
17. Ibid., pp. 90-4.
18. Ibid., pp. 94-100.
19. Ibid., pp. 100-4.
20. Ibid., pp. 105-6.
21. Ibid., pp. 106-12.
22. Ibid., pp. 112-13.
23. Ibid., pp. 113-16.
24. Ibid., pp. 116-18.
25. Ibid., pp. 118-20.
26. Ibid., pp. 120-2.
27. Ibid., pp. 122-5.
28. Ibid., pp. 125-30.

29. Ibid., pp. 130-2.
30. Ibid., pp. 132-7.
31. Ibid., pp. 137-45.
32. Ibid., pp. 145-52.
33. Ibid., pp. 152-4.
34. Ibid., pp. 154-9.
35. Ibid., pp. 160-1.
36. Ibid., pp. 161-4.
37. Ibid., pp. 165-73.
38. Ibid., pp. 175-7.
39. See also, Anurupita Kaur and J.S. Grewal, 'A Modern Sikh View: Teja Singh and Ganda Singh', *The Khalsa: Sikh and Non-Sikh Perspectives*, ed. J.S. Grewal, New Delhi: Manohar, 2004, pp. 205-16.

PART SIX

Contemporary Historical Writing

CHAPTER NINETEEN

Widening Range

In the past six decades a wide range of historical literature on Sikhs has been produced in English and Punjabi. A few bibliographies and a considerable number of texts and translations have been published. Apart from archival documents, a couple of books on Sikh coins have also appeared. Books on popular Sikh themes have continued to appear and an increasing number of professional historians have produced monographs and anthologies. More specifically a number of areas or themes have been studied: religious and secular figures of Sikh history, Sikh thought and ethics, the Sikh movement under the Gurus, Sikh politics and polity of the eighteenth and the early nineteenth century, the Sikh scripture and various forms of Sikh literature, Sikh institutions, Sikh social order with reference to caste and gender, the Sikh tradition of martyrdom, Sikh identity, and historical writing on the Sikhs. A number of general histories of the Sikhs have also appeared in recent decades. Furthermore, the recent decades have witnessed a protracted debate on most of the basic issues related to Sikh studies.

It is not easy to introduce this wide range of literature satisfactorily in a short space. We would deal with the basic issues debated in the recent controversies in the next chapter. Here we will take up the works which are not directly connected with the controversies. Even so, we have to be selective. The criterion for selection can be the academic importance of a work or the degree to which a work is representative of a period, an area, a form, or a theme. This will enable us to cover all the well marked periods of Sikh history, and for each period take up works on major themes or areas. For the early Sikh tradition, we take up a few studies of Guru Nanak and Guru Gobind Singh, and the period of the Sikh Gurus as a whole. For the eighteenth and early nineteenth centuries we take up works on Sikh polity, agrarian economy and society. For the colonial period, there are several important themes: socio-religious re-awakening among the Sikhs, social transformation, the Akali movement for the control of gurdwaras, and Akali politics before 1947. For the contemporary period, the dominant themes are related to politics: the movement for Punjabi-speaking state, and militancy leading to the movement for Khalistan, generally discussed in terms of Sikh ethnicity or Sikh ethno-nationalism. All the themes taken up in this section would in a way be complemented by the basic issues to be taken up in the next chapter.

Of the studies of Guru Nanak, J.S. Grewal's *Guru Nanak in History* (1969), is important for its approach, methodology, and its main conclusions. The study is divided into two parts. The first part deals with the politics and polity, social order, and religious systems of the time of Guru Nanak based entirely on sources other than the Guru's own compositions. The second part deals with Guru Nanak's response to this environment embodied in his own compositions. This approach reveals a rare kind of social awareness. For the first time we also realize that his appreciation of the Sufis and the Vaishnavas was relative and not really unqualified. His criticism of their beliefs and practices is rather serious: it arises from his own values and principles. Guru Nanak did not identify himself with any of the established religious systems or any of the new movements. He claims emphatically and explicitly to have enunciated a new system. This approach takes the study of Guru Nanak out of the grooves of 'influences' and 'parallels', and makes a case for the importance of 'creative response'. Indeed, Guru Nanak can be revisited through this approach for further insights into his life and mission.[1]

Guru Gobind Singh: A Biographical Study (1967) by J.S. Grewal and S.S. Bal was meant to be a study of Guru Gobind Singh on the basis of contemporary and near contemporary evidence entirely in rational and human terms. The framework of the Mughal empire, the polity of the Punjab hills, and the background of the Sikh heritage of Guru Gobind Singh are kept in view for his early life and battles. For the institution of the Khalsa the relevance of the ideas expressed in several of the compositions in the *Dasam Granth* are taken into account. That the institution of the Khalsa precipitated the conflict with the Mughal state is emphasized, but no political aspirations for the Khalsa are postulated in this work. They appear to be fighting merely a defensive war. The last few years of Guru Gobind Singh, after the evacuation of Anandpur, are seen in terms of a truce, a view supported by the *Zafarnama* of Guru Gobind Singh, his *hukamnamas*, and the orders of Aurangzeb. The book emphasizes that Guru Gobind Singh's presence near the camp of Bahadur Shah need not be explained in terms of his having taken service with the emperor. Guru Gobind Singh vested Guruship in the collective body of the Khalsa and the Sikh scripture before his death at Nander in 1708. The failure of Bahadur Shah to restore *status quo ante* resulted in Banda Bahadur's armed campaign against the Mughal authorities and the establishment of sovereign Sikh rule in the Sarkar of Sirhind for a few years. His failure did not dampen the spirit of the Khalsa to seek political power on their own. The approach adopted in this study can lead to a better understanding of Guru Gobind Singh and the Khalsa with the new evidence that has come to light since 1967.[2]

For a work on the early Sikh movement as a whole we may turn to Niharranjan Ray's *The Sikh Gurus and the Sikh Society: A Study in Social Analysis* (1970). It is a frankly interpretative work from a broad humanistic standpoint and with a strictly academic approach in which the author uses 'the concepts and methods and tools and techniques of modern intellectual disciplines used in the humanities and the social sciences in an interdisciplinary manner'. Sikhism or Sikh society was not Ray's field of special study and he was not 'a man of religion'. His focus is on the socio-religious and socio-economic aspects of the teachings and activities of the Gurus, and he pays special attention to Guru Nanak, Guru Arjan and Guru Gobind Singh. According to him, they represented three great turning points in the history and culture of the Sikhs, their religion and their society 'which happens to be an integral part of the large Indian society, and yet a definitely distinct, definitely identifiable community of people with an integrity of their own'.

Ray approaches the early Sikh movement in terms of the political, social, and religious milieu of the ten Gurus, and the production system of their times, the message of Guru Nanak and of his successors in relation to the other religious movements, and the mission of Guru Gobind Singh. Throughout the study Ray tries to bring out the distinctive features of Sikhism and the Sikh social order. The Sikh

Gurus steered clear of austerities, self-mortification and of general negativism of the ascetical orders on the one hand, and of the orders of the emotionally oriented and surcharged Vaishnavas of the Bhakti movement on the other. The process of transformation was slow but nevertheless detectable, and by the time of Guru Gobind Singh the cumulative effect was all but clear. At the back of the transformation from a purely religious group to a highly organized body with a militant spirit was 'the economic strength' of the entire Sikh community consisting largely of agriculturists and other productive sections, and traders. The material resources of the Sikhs and their allegiance to Guru Gobind Singh as their spiritual and temporal leader made the Sikh community a small 'state' within the bigger state of the Mughal emperors.

Sikhism was just not 'Kabirism', according to Ray, nor was it just a continuation of the north Indian Sant tradition. Passing through the crucible of Guru Nanak's actual, imaginative and intellectual experience his inheritance became 'an entirely new thing altogether' and it called for a new label. Moreover, he had a clear social purpose in view and he adopted the ways and means to work it out effectively. Guru Nanak and his successors were able to maintain a balance between the temporal and the spiritual. 'The cohesion and solidarity of the community has not been a little due to the attention Guru Nanak, his successors, and the community they reared up, paid to the spatio-temporal aspects of human life and society.' Guru Nanak, Guru Arjan, and Guru Gobind Singh reveal a rare kind of social consciousness in their social criticism and protest. 'It is difficult to believe that there was no conscious and deliberate attempt to build up the Sikh community as a distinct and different one from that of the Hindus.' This distinctiveness was heightened by Guru Gobind Singh through the corporate community of the Khalsa who were different from both Hindus and Muslims even in their external appearance. An analysis of Guru Gobind Singh's writings shows very clearly that he elaborated, in a somewhat different socio-political situation, what Guru Nanak had stood for. An ideology of action integrated with piety was basic to both. This helped to create 'a new image of a new faith and a new society'. No document is so pregnant with social significance as the one in which Guru Gobind

Singh sings 'the praise and glory of his people in full-throated voice, his love and concern for the common man'.[3]

On Sikh polity we may take up Bhagat Singh's *Sikh Polity in the Eighteenth and Nineteenth Centuries* (1978), the most voluminous work on the subject. For the 'genesis' of Sikh polity he goes back to Guru Nanak's response to contemporary politics, society and religion. His ideals and his comment on the contemporary situation are relevant for polity. Similarly, the 'Khalsa commonwealth' is traced to the socio-economic and institutional framework evolved by Guru Nanak and strengthened and elaborated by his successors. Bhagat Singh looks upon Banda Bahadur as introducing political institutions but not evolving 'a concrete form of government'. Liquidation of the *zamindari* system is ascribed to Banda Bahadur but without any credible evidence. Sikh political organization began in the 1730s and 1740s, resulting in the foundation of the Dal Khalsa at Amritsar in 1748. The '*rakhi* system' established by the Dal Khalsa was virtually a parallel government of the Sikhs in the 1750s. For giving protection to the peasants of an extensive area, the Dal Khalsa was divided into units called *misls*. In 1765, the Sikhs assumed sovereignty, and there was the inevitable need of establishing some sort of a regular government. Bhagat Singh talks of the '*misldari* system' in this context.

According to Bhagat Singh, the head of a unit of the army first and then of a territory was called *misldar*, and the leaders subordinate to him were called *sardars*. In the last quarter of the eighteenth century the difference between the *misldar* and the *sardar* was obliterated; there was no *misldar* but so many *sardars* of major or minor consequence. The *sardar* ruled in the name of the Guru and the Khalsa, and thought of justice as their primary duty, making no distinction between a Sikh and a non-Sikh, and giving primacy to the welfare of the people. Thus, their political ideology was remarkably different from that of the Mughal rulers. The meetings of the Sarbat Khalsa became rare after 1765 and there was no need of *gurmata* after the rise of Ranjit Singh as a sovereign ruler. Bhagat Singh makes no distinction between the organization of the *misl* before and after territorial occupation. He talks of the transition from *misldari* to monarchy, the latter represented by the state of Ranjit Singh. He goes on to discuss the Sikh concept of the state as a welfare state. He dwells on the non-sectarian character of the state of Ranjit Singh as an enlightened and benevolent monarchy. He talks of the Darbar of Ranjit Singh and the structure of his administration. There is much narration and description, and there are references to the views of other writers, both European and Indian. Also, there is much information which strictly is not relevant for discussion of the polity. Moreover the issues do not get clarified for want of clear conceptualization and rigorous analysis.[4]

Indu Banga's *Agrarian System of the Sikhs: Late Eighteenth and Early Nineteenth Century* (1978) also includes a discussion of Sikh polity in terms of the rulers and the vassals. The 'institutions' of *rakhi*, *gurmata*, Dal Khalsa and *misl* are briefly described and it is argued that all these institutions played a vital role in the third quarter of the eighteenth century. During the last quarter, a large number of *sardars* exercised the powers and prerogatives of an independent ruler. In the inscriptions of the Sikh coins sovereignty was derived from the Gurus. By the same token, each *sardar* could rule independently of others. 'For all practical purposes, the individual chief became a sovereign ruler not in spite of the coin but because of it.' The term 'Sarkar Khalsaji' referred to the government of the individual Khalsa and it was used for several of the late eighteenth-century Sikh chiefs. The rule of the individual allowed him to have recourse to suzerain-vassal relationship, a practice started by the late eighteenth-century Sikh chiefs. The suzerain-vassal polity was strengthened by Ranjit Singh not only by recognizing existing rulers as his vassals but also by creating new vassal chiefs like the Jamwal brothers. The whole system is discussed in detail.

The *Agrarian System of the Sikhs* has a chapter on 'the land and the people' under the Sikh rule. The other chapters relate to the units and functionaries of the Sikh revenue administration, the methods of assessment and collection of land revenue, the *jagirdars*, the *dharmarth* grantees, and land tenures. It is suggested that there was a large degree of structural continuity and similarity with the Mughal times but there were some important differences also. Though the Sikh rulers did not make a conscious distinction between Sikhs and non-Sikhs and both Hindus and Muslims were employed in the civil administration and the army, a large share of *jagirs* and *dharmarth* grants went to Sikh individuals and institutions. No other scholar has improved upon this study. The *Agrarian System* can be revisited in the light of additional information.[5]

For socio-religious re-awakening, historians of the Sikhs talk about three movements: the Nirankari, the Namdhari, and the Singh Sabha. The first two originated in the time of Ranjit Singh, and the third during the colonial period. It is easy to see the imprint of the historical situations in which these movements originated and developed. Both the Nirankaris and the Namdharis have written on their past in their own way. But a few historians have taken interest in the Nirankaris and, even more so, in the Namdharis. However, the greatest attention has been given to the Singh Sabha movement which is regarded as by far the most important.

For the Nirankaris we may take notice of *The Nirankari Sikhs* (1979) by John C.B. Webster. He argues that the labels 'movement', 'sect', and 'community' are not appropriate for the Nirankaris. Because of their 'shared rites and ceremonies', it is somewhat legitimate to use the term 'cult' with reference to them. Webster sought to apply 'modern critical methods' to the study of Nirankari history. He has paid more attention to the 'cult' than to the Nirankari *gurus*, and concentrated on developments which appeared to him to be historically important. He points out that contemporary evidence on the early phase of the Nirankaris comes from missionary and official sources. The first Nirankari source is a *hukamnama* signed by Sahib Rattaji, the second successor of the founder of the cult, Baba Dayal, but it was certainly issued before 1873. Then there are a few more documents till 1909. All these source materials, reproduced in appendices, cover less than 40 pages in print. Webster bases his account of the Nirankaris up to 1909 on these sources.

Webster talks of Baba Dayal and the origin of the Nirankaris, developments under Baba Darbara Singh (*c.* 1855-70) and Sahib Rattaji (1870-1909). He gives special attention to the support of the Nirankari *gurus* for the Anand Marriage Bill of 1908 which was passed in 1909. Webster comes to the conclusion that the early Nirankaris were both urban and rural, and they included both *keshdharis* and *sahajdharis*, probably Khatris, Aroras, Bhatias and Suniars. Leadership was vested in the *guru* and the succession remained in the family of Baba Dayal. What set the Nirankaris apart from others were their distinctive ceremonies rather than beliefs. This was an important development within Sikhism. However, the influence of the Nirankaris remained confined to thousands, and did not extend to tens of thousands during their later history. The whole account of the Nirankaris by Webster is brief and elementary but it still serves as the best starting point for further research on the Nirankaris.[6]

Fauja Singh Bajwa in his *Kuka Movement* (1965) underlines the political importance of the Namdhari movement as 'an important phase in Punjab's role in India's struggle for freedom'. It was 'a religious, social and political movement, all rolled into one'. Baba Ram Singh's ideas of religious and social reform could be traced to Baba Balak Singh. The source of his political outlook was the 'Khalsa nationalism' of Bhai Maharaj Singh, for whom Baba Ram Singh had great respect. However, the ultimate source of inspiration for him were the Gurus, especially Guru Gobind Singh. Four things were important for Baba Ram Singh: the Name, social equality, the Khalsa *rahit*, and 'Sikh nationality'. The new order of the 'Sant Khalsa' was enjoined to observe a strict code of discipline. The followers of Baba Ram Singh began to regard him as a reincarnation of Guru Gobind Singh, and they were anxious to bring back the Khalsa Raj. Spiritual and moral uplift in their view, was a pre-condition for regaining political power and freedom.

Fauja Singh points out that the new features of the 'Sant Khalsa' were the result of changed circumstances. They had to pursue their objective secretly. They evolved their own arrangements for communication. An independent judicial system was developed to deal with internal disputes. After 1872 the principle of boycott was extended to service under the government. Similarly, the educational institutions of the government were avoided, particularly because the Kukas (as the Namdharis came to be called popularly) were opposed to the system introduced by the foreign rulers. The hatred for the British (referred to as *mlechh*) induced them to wish for the end of their rule. They could think of Khalsa Raj as the only substitute. There was no conception of 'Indian nationalism' in the third quarter of the nineteenth century. The Kuka movement was 'a people's affair'. Its membership in the nineteenth century was predominantly rural and Jat. This was a source of concern for the British. Certain sections within the Indian society were opposed to the Kukas. This included Sikh princes, aristocrats, village headmen, custodians of historic gurdwaras, and government officials. The British bureaucracy had no doubt about the essentially political character of the Kuka movement. The vigilance of the government and their decisive action in 1872 crippled the movement. After this the Kukas could never recover their old vigour. Significantly, however, they aligned with the Congress in the Gandhian era. Fauja Singh emphasizes that the Singh Sabha movement 'simply carried forward the work begun by the Kuka movement, giving in the process a new interpretation to the Sikh doctrine in the light of Western influences'. Fauja Singh's *Kuka Movement* is based largely on the original source materials preserved in the National Archives of India and the Punjab State Archives. In his detailed treatment of the movement, the author takes into account the works written in Punjabi and Urdu as well.[7]

A few Sikh historians had begun to take interest in the Singh Sabha movement when N. Gerald Barrier published *The Sikhs and Their Literature* (1970) as a guide to tracts, books and periodicals from 1849 to 1919, underlining the importance of this source material for fresh research and interpretation. In his 'Introduction' to this volume he briefly refers to the first two phases of Sikh history 1469-1708 and 1708-1849, and moves on to 'a period of Sikh resurgence' as 'one phase of the Sikh revival' from 1849 to 1919. He talks of an intellectual crisis and revitalization, and the emergence of new Sikh institutions during this period. He refers to the opposition of the Namdhari sect to idol-worship and its advocacy of marriage reform. This tradition was continued and elaborated by the Namdharis or Kukas who, under the leadership of Ram Singh, moved toward more militant reforms. However, but 'a new chapter in the evolution of Sikhism' was inscribed by the Singh Sabhas. Unlike the earlier sectarians, the leaders of the Singh Sabhas remained within the fold of Sikhism.

Barrier refers to the Amritsar Singh Sabha and the Lahore Singh Sabha, their leadership and their membership, and their enterprise in journalism. The leaders of the Singh Sabhas established their own presses to print their newspapers, periodicals and other materials. An increasing number of Singh Sabhas raised the problem of co-ordination. Khalsa Diwans had been established at Amritsar and Lahore before the Chief Khalsa Diwan (CKD) was founded in 1902 as the most representative Sikh institution. The CKD founded other institutions like the Khalsa Tract Society, Khalsa Orphanage, and the Sikh Educational Conference. The radical leaders of the Singh Sabhas, called Tat Khalsa, entered into controversies with others, like the Arya Samaj, the Christian missionaries and Muslims. The Tat Khalsa also came into confrontation with the custodians of the Golden Temple. There was resistance to the CKD from organizations like the Bhasaur Singh Sabha. Its leader, Babu Teja Singh, was much more radical than the most eminent leader of the CKD, Sunder Singh Majithia. In fact, Barrier suggests that the Singh Sabha period produced a range of institutional and ideological positions without resolving key issues.

Barrier goes on to talk about 'the Sikhs and communal politics' to examine their relations with Hindus, especially with regard to the issues of conversion and language. Sikh-Muslim conflicts are also referred to. Finally, Barrier talks of 'the Sikhs and the British Raj', and the way in which the colonial institutions influenced the Sikhs and other religious communities of the Punjab. On the whole, loyalty typified the style and tone of Sikh politics. The Ghadarite Sikhs were not supported by the Sikhs in general. However, the Tat Khalsa were becoming restive in the matter of Khalsa College, the Anand Marriage Bill, and the restoration of the Rakabganj Gurdwara wall. Within seventy years the Sikhs were sufficiently revitalized to confront others, including the British. Thus, Barrier gives a simple but comprehensive account of the Singh Sabha to make a clear case for further research.[8]

With his sustained interest in the half century from 1870 to 1920, Barrier continued to reiterate, re-inforce, elaborate and refine his ideas about the Singh Sabha through successive articles, with growing focus on Sikh identity and Sikh diaspora. On the issue of Sikh identity he refers to Harjot Singh Oberoi's work as a specialist in support of his own view that in the middle of the nineteenth-century Hindus and Sikhs were quite similar in terms of social networks, ritual, and religious understanding. The British views of communal patterns in the Punjab led them to balance the interests of the religious communities. On occasions they used divide-and-rule tactics to deal with specific situations but not as a long range policy. The British policy towards the Sikhs was marked by both trust and suspicion, though they tried to avoid their being seen as either favoured or distrusted. Barrier's interest in the Singh Sabhas has not resulted in a sustained study of any of its aspects.[9]

Ethne K. Marenco's *The Transformation of Sikh Society* (1976) is 'an enquiry into the social stratification of the Sikhs' with special reference to 'the coexistence of caste and class'. At the beginning of the colonial period there was a caste system among the Sikhs, broadly similar to the Hindu caste system but weaker in some ways. Marenco discusses the structure of Sikh caste hierarchy and corporate caste change in the first half of the nineteenth century. The political supremacy of the Sikhs under Ranjit Singh raised the Jat Sikhs to 'the highest level of the newly designated hierarchy'. The economic, technological, educational, and other changes brought about by the British rule resulted in corporate caste change and 'the emergence of social classes' among the Sikhs. The Jat Sikhs came to be regarded as the most important agriculturist caste. The Tarkhan Sikhs advanced economically and socially (as Ramgarhias), like the Kalal Sikhs as Ahluwalias. The Mazhabi Sikhs too raised their corporate status. Individuals from several castes joined the professions and services, even industry, to become part of a new class or classes. The Khatri and Arora Sikhs were important, among other things, for becoming a part of the professional class. Thus, social classes emerged with members from heterogeneous castes. Marenco compares the caste system among the Sikhs with the Hindu caste system, and social classes among the Sikhs with the class system in Western societies. Whereas castes were marked by homogeneity, classes were marked by heterogeneity. Both were hierarchical. In the colonial Punjab, they existed side by side. The limitations of Marenco's work appear to come from the nature of the evidence used. Contrary to the view of the contemporary British writers and many later scholars, there was no normative or theoretical recognition of hierarchy among the Sikhs as a community. The notions and claims of superior status by various segments of the community, a part of their pre-Sikh socio-cultural baggage, were not based on any common authority or even consensus of the community.[10]

The movement that overshadowed the CKD and the Singh Sabha was the Gurdwara Reform movement of 1920-5. Mohinder Singh deliberately refers to his study of this movement as *The Akali Movement* in order to project its political aspect. It was not a mere 'movement of Gurdwara reform', nor was it an 'organization working towards treasonable ends'. It was a peaceful struggle against the *mahants* and other vested interests in the Sikh shrines on the one hand, and against the repressive administration in the Punjab on the other. It changed the course of history in the Punjab and strengthened the forces of nationalism in the country. Mohinder Singh refers to the various strands in its background, founding of the Shiromani Gurdwara Prabandhak Committee (SGPC) and the Shiromani Akali Dal, different phases or *morchas* of the movement, and its implications for the loyalty of the Sikhs in British India and the Punjab states. He also goes into its links with the Congress leadership and its programme of non-cooperation.

Mohinder Singh discusses the organization and the base and leadership of the Akali movement with reference to the SGPC and the Shiromani Akali Dal. While the bulk of the Akali volunteers came from the Sikh peasantry, leadership was provided by the educated middle-class nationalists, consisting of barristers, college and school teachers, military pensioners, and middle-level landlords. The differences among the moderate and extremist Akali leaders, and the tactics of the Punjab Governor, Malcolm Hailey, resulted in a split over the acceptance of the conditional release of the Akali leaders in prison, which widened the breach in the Akali camp. Despite efforts, real unity was never again achieved. Power-politics became a poor legacy of this great movement. The Akali leadership became enmeshed in mutual wrangles, never to regain the power and prestige that it had enjoyed during the heyday of the Akali movement. Mohinder Singh takes up the Babbar Akali movement which, though not a part of the Akali movement, increased the bargaining power of the Akali leadership and demoralized the loyalists.

Mohinder Singh comes to the conclusion that of all the movements in the Punjab, the Akali movement was, perhaps, the biggest and the strongest, as also the most popular with a broad base and active mass participation. The losses faced by the Sikhs in life, property, careers, and suffering were also enormous. The Sikh Gurdwaras Act made SGPC a statutory body of its own kind in the world, with control over 200 important gurdwaras with an income of over Rs. 25 lakh in 1925. The Indian National Congress extended help to the Akali movement and the Congress leadership in turn continued to exercise a good deal of influence over the Akali leaders for taking the Congress programme to the Sikh masses. The ideology of non-cooperation took deep roots among the Akalis. Their movement became a part of the national movement. It shattered the myth of Sikh loyalty to the British. The pro-British feudal leadership of the Sikhs was replaced by educated middle-class nationalists. The SGPC and the SAD acquired a unique position of power in the religious and political life of the Sikhs. Mohinder Singh's study of the Akali movement is thorough and comprehensive. Subsequent research has added to our understanding of the various facets of the movement but Mohinder Singh's book remains the best introduction to the subject.[11]

K.L. Tuteja in his *Sikh Politics (1920-40)* covers part of the same ground as does Mohinder Singh, but he looks at the politics of the Sikhs and not of the Akalis alone. In view of the impending Muslim domination in the Punjab the Sikhs had to struggle for survival. In the backdrop of the Simon Commission Report, Communal Award and the Act of 1935, Sikh leadership was divided into three major groups: the CKD as the Khalsa National Party, the Shiromani Akali Dal, and the Congressite Sikhs. Tuteja emphasizes the complexity of Sikh politics in the 1930s arising out of electoral alliances, Sikandar-Jinnah Pact, outbreak of the world war, and the Lahore Resolution of the Muslim League. Not only were the Sikhs surrounded by external forces, there were also important differences within the Sikh community itself. The loyalist CKD derived its strength from landed interests, attracting a sizeable section of the middle class. The Akali leadership mainly came from the middle class but had the support of the peasantry. The Central Sikh League was markedly aligned with the Congress. The Akalis appeared to be sailing in two boats but their double loyalties did not seem inconsistent to a large body of the Sikhs because devotion to sectional interests did not mean alienation from the nation. But the Akalis tried to woo the government as well. The Sikhs were always at pains to emphasize their separate identity. For Tuteja, this study of Sikh politics in 1920-40 is a story of competition and struggle for gaining political power and influence. It furnishes 'a curious example of the use of religion as a cementing force, and that too for extra-religious purposes'. Tuteja looks at Sikh politics from the nationalist angle.[12]

Baldev Raj Nayar's *Minority Politics in the Punjab* (1966) was meant to be a study of the problem of what has been referred to as 'nation-building'. Since the demand for the formation of a new linguistic state had overshadowed the politics of the Punjab, Nayar's study of 'the basis and dynamics' of the demand constituted in effect the first full-scale study of the politics of the Punjab since Independence. Nayar thinks that the Congress leadership was committed to the ideals of national unity, parliamentary democracy, and the secular state. The Akali demand for a Punjabi-speaking state was seen as 'merely a camouflage for the eventual creation of a Sikh theocratic state'. There was also the fear of 'future secessionist claims' in a border state in view of the past Akali demands for a sovereign Sikh state. The reform movements in Sikhism had laid emphasis on a separate political entity of the Sikhs. The nationalist leadership refused to concede the demand, and the Akali leadership pursued it with great vigour, claiming to represent the Sikh Panth. They used three major strategies: constitutional, infiltrational, and agitational. But they encountered stubborn opposition even from within the state, and from within the Sikh community. Writing in 1965, Nayar does not see any possibility of a linguistic state being created. He is also of the view that, though the Congress should redress genuine grievances of the various groups in the society, it should remain 'firm and determined when attempts are made to undermine the basic political framework'. Apart from its obvious hostility to the Akali demand, Nayar's view remains an 'outsider's view' of the Akali demand for a Punjabi-speaking state.[13]

An 'insider's view' and 'a chronicle of events' leading to the formation of the Punjabi-speaking state are presented by Ajit Singh Sarhadi in his *Punjabi Suba* (1970), written after the formation of the new state in 1966. It was entirely incorrect, he says, to think of the demand as struggle for a Sikh State. Tracing its background Sarhadi suggests that 'The story of the struggle' goes back to Sikh resurgence in the colonial period. He further states that Master Tara Singh's idea of a Sikh state was contingent upon the creation of Pakistan, and his disillusionment with the hopes held out by the Congress leadership might have 'motivated Master Tara Singh to demand Punjabi Suba in the postpartition India'. Early in 1949, the arrest of Master Tara Singh and of the rest of the Akali leadership 'initiated some re-thinking of the policies and programmes by the Sikh leadership, as to their position in the future set-up of the country'. At a Sikh convention in April the demand for 'the creation of a linguistic State for Punjabis' was adopted. On Master Tara Singh's direction Hukam Singh clarified that the demand was neither communal nor undemocratic. The conception of 'Punjabi Suba' was not that of 'a Sikh State'. This allegation was brought forth by the Arya Samaj Press. Partap Singh Kairon announced his opposition to a linguistic state in the Punjab and the Congress openly started opposing it. Thus, two forces were opposing the creation of the Punjabi Suba in 1950. In his 'chronologically compiled' story of events Sarhadi brings out the internal divisions among the Akalis and the growing opposition to their demand from the Punjabi Hindus led by the Arya Samaj and supported by the Congress party. He refers to the dubious role of Indira Gandhi as the prime minister, which resulted in the creation of a Punjabi-speaking state with serious problems built into its formation: the exclusion of Chandigarh and other areas, and the central control over water and power resources.[14]

Harnik Deol's *Religion and Nationalism in India: The Case of the Punjab* (2000) traces the historical roots of Sikh communal consciousness in three phases: 1469-1708, 1708-1849, 1849-1947. During the first phase, the Sikhs came to have separatist symbols, a doctrinal discourse, and distinct and separate practices. In the second, the political triumph of the Sikh movement imbued Sikh identity with the symbolic memory of Sikh rule. In the phase of colonial rule, the social and religious reform movements among the Sikhs resulted in the establishment of an institutional framework that provided the base for Sikh separatism. Disagreeing with Richard G. Fox and Harjot Oberoi, she argues that the interplay between the general growth in literacy, communications and expansion of imperial bureaucracy on the one hand, and the socio-religious reform movements, on the other, gave birth to religio-linguistic nationalism at the end of the nineteenth century in the Punjab.

Deol goes on to state that the Punjabi *suba* movement consolidated the process of religion-based linguistic differentiation. The enormous impact of the policies and activities of the central government on the

Sikh communal perception radicalized the moderate demands of the well-to-do peasants. This radicalization was reinforced by the tendency of the Sikh peasantry to turn to religious notions for legitimizing their economic, political and social grievances. The growing Sikh unrest in the Punjab was due to the intransigency of the central government in conceding the seemingly legitimate demands of the Akali Dal. After June 1984, the exploited Sikh peasantry constituted the vanguard of the struggle for Sikh national independence. The lack of tacit support for their guerrilla resistance by a broad cross-section of the rural and the urban Sikh population and the Sikh professional class led to the virtual disintegration of the movement. Another factor that contributed to the failure of the movement was the lack of proper organizational structure to coordinate the activities of the guerrilla cadres.

Deol emphasizes the importance of two factors for explaining the timing of the Sikh ethno-nationalist struggle. The transition to commercial agriculture induced widespread dislocation and alienation, resulting in a section of the Sikh peasantry becoming politically mobilized. Second, the spread of literacy in the late twentieth century coincided with a revolution in communications through the vernacular press and oral communication through devices like audio cassettes. She makes the general statement that dramatic shifts in the prevailing material conditions of existence generate mass discontent in society and unleash political forces. 'However, in many late-industrializing societies there is a tendency to turn to religious notions emanating from religious faith in legitimizing economic, political and social grievances. This is because these societies have not experienced a revolutionary break with the past and religion continues to be the dominant worldview.' Deol suggests that there is a need to revise Western theories of nationalism in the light of the proliferation of 'religious nationalisms'. In the context of the cultural and historical specificities of non-European state formation, and the persistence of beliefs and symbols as integrative in South Asia, it is necessary to reconsider the very nature of nationalism.[15]

Jugdep S. Chima's *The Sikh Separatist Insurgency in India: Political Leadership and Ethnonationalist Movements* largely deals with Sikh politics of 1978-97 as the phase of Sikh separatist insurgency. He concentrates on the emergence of the Sikh ethno-nationalist movement from 1978 to 1984 (the beginning of Sikh extremism in 1978-81, the emergence of ethno-nationalist violence in 1981-3, and ethnic insurgency and Operation Bluestar in 1983-4). He moves on to the sustenance of the Sikh ethno-nationalist movement from 1984 to 1992 (talking of failed political compromises and re-marginalization of the militants for armed struggle for Khalistan in 1986-8, the divided state and electoral victory of the extremists in 1988-90, and the escalating factionalism and internecine violence within the separatist movement in 1990-2). Then, from 1992 to 1997 he talks of the demise of the Sikh ethno-nationalist movement in two short phases: crushing of the violent Sikh movement by the state in 1992-3, and return to normalcy in the Punjab during 1993-7. Altogether, more than two-thirds of the text narrates factual events of two decades in nine short phases, making the narrative itself a substantial contribution to systematic study of a contemporary movement.

Chima puts forth a hypothesis too. Intellectually unsatisfied with the existing theories in the field, especially in relation to the sustenance of ethno-nationalist movements, he has constructed a theory of 'how patterns of political leadership' affect the trajectory of ethno-nationalist movements. He argues that 'violent subnationalist movements arise when competing ethnic and state elites cannot resolve their political differences'. Regarding the sustenance of ethno-nationalism, he argues that in the absence of a negotiated settlement, violent subnationalist movements persist when ethnic militants remain 'united' and retain a viable political front, while state elites become internally divided and factionalized traditional ethnic elites engage in competitive 'ethnic-outflanking'. For the demise of ethno-nationalism, Chima suggests that violent subnationalist movements decline when ethnic militants 'factionalize' and lose a viable political front, and the unified state elites pursue coordinated politics prompting traditional ethnic elites to unite, moderate, and re-enter the 'normal' political process. The important conclusion drawn by Chima is that ethno-nationalist movements are largely the products of the interaction between self-interested political elites. This proposition holds a key to understanding the trajectory of violent ethno-nationalist movements, and it makes self-interested political elites accountable for the consequences of their actions. This could obviate the 'potential re-emergence of violent Sikh separatism in united India'.[16]

Emergence of general histories of the Sikhs in the contemporary period reflects the growing interest in Sikh studies. A number of amateur and professional historians have written general histories of the Sikhs, starting with Harbans Singh's *The Heritage of the Sikhs* published in the early 1960s, revised and enlarged in 1983, and then in 1994.[17] Khushwant Singh's *A History of the Sikhs* in two volumes, also published first in the 1960s, has been reprinted, revised and enlarged several times as, perhaps, the most popular general history of the Sikhs.[18] It was followed by Gopal Singh's *A History of the Sikh People* in 1979.[19] Two general histories written after the high tide of the movement for Khalistan are Sangat Singh's *The Sikhs in History* (1995)[20] and Patwant Singh's *The Sikhs* (1999).[21] They are all Sikh historians keen to interpret the Sikh tradition for the world in the light of their understanding of their history and the degree of their commitment to the Sikh faith. They write well, or with passion. They make use of both original evidence and secondary works but with little pretension to serious scholarly credentials.

Two professional historians have also written general histories: Hari Ram Gupta and J.S. Grewal. The first volume of Gupta's *History of the Sikhs* (1973) covers the period of the ten Gurus (1469-1708). Three more volumes published till 1982 are actually reprints or re-organized versions of his earlier published works on the eighteenth century. The fifth volume of his *History of the Sikhs* (1991) relates to *Maharaja Ranjit Singh*. All the five volumes are based on research but not integrated as a general history.[22]

J.S. Grewal's *The Sikhs of the Punjab* (1990), a volume of 'The New Cambridge History of India', takes into account the major works of research on the period of the Gurus, the period from the death of Guru Gobind Singh in 1708 to the annexation of the Punjab in 1849, the colonial period from 1849 to 1947, and the contemporary period from the partition of the Punjab to the Operation Bluestar of 1984, with an epilogue on the later developments. Written alike for the general reader and the researcher, and based on research, it is both concise in treatment and comprehensive in scope.[23]

In the foregoing paragraphs we have taken notice of works selected from a large number of books which figure in the Bibliography. Their discussion provides the major contours of Sikh history for five centuries. Debate on a number of issues by scholars across the globe in recent decades, taken up in the next chapter, adds depth to the study of the subject.

NOTES

1. J.S. Grewal, *Guru Nanak in History*, Chandigarh: Panjab University, 1969 (2nd. rpt. in 1998).
2. J.S. Grewal and S.S. Bal, *Guru Gobind Singh: A Biographical Study*, Chandigarh: Panjab University, 1967.
3. Niharranjan Ray, *The Sikh Gurus and Sikh Society: A Study in Social Analysis*, Patiala: Punjabi University, 1970.
4. Bhagat Singh, *Sikh Polity in the Eighteenth and Nineteenth Centuries*, New Delhi: Oriental Publishers & Distributors, 1978.
5. Indu Banga, *Agrarian System of the Sikhs: Late Eighteenth and Early Nineteenth Century*, New Delhi: Manohar, 1978.
6. John C.B. Webster, *The Nirankari Sikhs*, New Delhi: Macmillan, 1981.
7. Fauja Singh, *Kuka Movement: An Important Phase in Punjab's Role in India's Struggle for Freedom*, Delhi: Motilal Banarsidass, 1965.
8. N. Gerald Barrier, *The Sikhs and Their Literature*, New Delhi: Manohar, 1970.
9. Ibid.
10. Ethne K. Marenco, *The Transformation of Sikh Society*, New Delhi: Heritage Publishers, 1976.
11. Mohinder Singh, *The Akali Movement*, New Delhi: Macmillan, 1978.
12. K.L. Tuteja, *Sikh Politics (1920-1940)*, Kurukshetra: Vishal Publications, 1984.
13. Baldev Raj Nayar, *Minority Politics in the Punjab*, Princeton: Princeton University Press, 1966.
14. Ajit Singh Sarhadi, *Punjabi Suba: The Story of the Struggle*, Delhi: U.C. Kapur & Sons, 1970.
15. Harnik Deol, *Religion and Nationalism in India: The Case of Punjab*, London: Routledge, 2000.
16. Jugdep S. Chima, *The Sikh Separatist Insurgency in India: Political Leadership and Ethnonational Movements*, New Delhi: Sage, 2010.
17. Harbans Singh, *The Heritage of the Sikhs*, New Delhi: Manohar, 1994 (2nd edn., first published in 1983).
18. Khushwant Singh, *A History of the Sikhs*, 2 vols., New Delhi: Oxford University Press, 1999 (rev. paperback edn., first published in 1963 & 1966).

19. Gopal Singh, *A History of the Sikh People, 1649-1988*, New Delhi: Allied Publishers, 1993 (rpt., first published in 1979).
20. Sangat Singh, *The Sikhs in History*, New Delhi: Uncommon Books, 1996.
21. Patwant Singh, *The Sikhs*, New Delhi: HarperCollins Publishers India, 1999.
22. Hari Ram Gupta, *History of the Sikhs*, 5 vols., New Delhi: Munshiram Manoharlal, 1973-91.
23. J.S. Grewal, *The Sikhs of the Punjab* (The New Cambridge History of India, II. 3), Cambridge: Cambridge University Press, 1998 (2nd. edn., first published in 1990).

CHAPTER TWENTY

Recent Controversies

The emergence of recent controversies could be traced to the publication of W.H. McLeod's *Guru Nanak and the Sikh Religion* in 1968.[1] He was criticized rather harshly by some Sikh scholars on account of his treatment of the *Janamsakhis* for the life of Guru Nanak. On the publication of *The Evolution of the Sikh Community* (1975)[2] he was seriously criticized by a professional historian, Fauja Singh, and rather severely by Daljeet Singh, an administrator turned scholar.[3]

By that time, South Asian area study programmes had been launched in North America, and a few graduate students became 'Punjab Specialists'. Among the 'Punjab Specialists' was N. Gerald Barrier, to whose *The Sikhs and Their Literature* (1970) we have referred earlier. The first conference on Sikh studies in the United States was held at Berkeley in 1976. The papers presented at the conference were published as *Sikh Studies: Comparative Perspectives on a Changing Tradition* (1979). The increasing presence of Sikhs in the United States had become relevant for Sikh studies. The major concern of the conference was how to develop Sikh studies in North America.[4]

John C.B. Webster took note of the criticism of McLeod's work on the Sikhs by warning the Western scholars interested in Sikh studies that they should be prepared for the charge that they were foreign scholars who did not understand the Sikhs or Sikhism, and need methods which did not apply to Indian religious traditions.[5] In Canada, the first conference on Sikh studies was held at Toronto in February 1987. The presence of a large 'diaspora' of Canadian Sikhs in the province of Ontario, especially in Toronto, and their keenness to encourage the study of Sikh history and religion provided the general context for this conference. Serving as a kind of 'catalyst' for the conference was the presence of W.H. McLeod at the University of Toronto as a

Commonwealth Fellow. The papers presented at the conference were published as *Sikh History and Religion in the Twentieth Century* (1988).[6]

In the Punjab, meanwhile, the growing conviction that McLeod's formulations were seriously flawed was reflected clearly in the *Perspectives on the Sikh Tradition* (1986). The purpose of this publication was to present a thorough refutation of McLeod's propositions: one, that Guru Nanak can be placed within the *sant* tradition; two, that his successors did not preach one set of doctrines, at one stage even giving up his teachings in favour of militancy; three, that the Panth took to arms not because of any decision of Guru Hargobind but because of the Jat influx; four, that the traditional account of the founding of the Khalsa cannot be accepted; five, that the Sikh code of discipline and Sikh symbols evolved during the eighteenth century, and not promulgated by Guru Gobind Singh on the Baisakhi of 1699; six, that the Gurus denounced caste system but they were not sincere or serious in removing caste differences; seven, that the succession of *Granth Sahib* as the Guru after Guru Gobind Singh was a subsequent adoption and not due to his injunction; eight, that the authenticity of the current version of *Guru Granth Sahib* is open to question. The contributors to this volume included Noel Q. King, Daljeet Singh, Hari Ram Gupta, Ganda Singh, Harbans Singh, and Jagjit Singh. The editor, 'Justice' Gurdev Singh, dwelt on the motives of McLeod as a Christian missionary. Many of McLeod's critics would later invoke his missionary motive to explain his lack of empathy with the Sikh tradition and lack of its understanding.[7]

Two years later, a conference of Sikh studies was organized by the Sikh community of North America at the California State University, Long Beach. Apart from contributors to the *Perspectives on the Sikh Tradition,* some scholars from the Panjab, Punjabi and Guru Nanak Dev universities made their presentation at this conference. In the volume of conference proceedings published as *Advanced Studies in Sikhism,* it was stated that the recent Western writings in the area of Sikh studies had generally been 'quite peripheral in their scope and inadequate in their approach'. Daljeet Singh criticized W.H. McLeod and Harjot Oberoi. Among the other critics of McLeod were S.S. Kohli, Madanjit Kaur, and Gobind Singh Mansukhani.[8]

Towards the end of 1990, seven 'international' conferences were held in England and North America at London, Toronto, Vancouver, Berkeley, Chicago, Washington and New York, sponsored by a number of Sikh organizations. Nearly half of the participants who presented papers were those who had contributed to the *Perspectives on the Sikh Tradition* and the *Advanced Studies in Sikhism*. They contributed a score of papers while an equal number was contributed by new scholars. At least three of the new scholars were associated with universities and formal study of the Sikh tradition. Others were independent scholars with or without any connection with academic institutions. Apart from the old themes, some new themes were taken up for discussion. Some old and new works were also criticized, especially the publications of McLeod and Oberoi, but on the whole, a number of expositions were marked by positive projection. The papers were published in two volumes in 1992 as *Fundamental Issues in Sikh Studies* and *Recent Researches in Sikhism.*[9]

The issue of textual criticism in relation to the Sikh scripture and the issue of Sikh identity were debated more furiously in the early 1990s than ever before. Piar Singh's *Gatha Sri Adi Granth* appeared in 1992 as a scholarly search for the genuine contents of the *Granth* prepared by Guru Arjan. The Kartarpur manuscript in his view was not the *Granth* prepared by Guru Arjan.[10] Within a month, the sale of the book was suspended by Guru Nanak Dev University as its publisher. Two weeks later, the SGPC imposed ban on research on the *Guru Granth.* Piar Singh was summoned to appear at the Akal Takht and ordered to do penance for forty days. In his *Gatha Sri Adi Granth and the Controversy* (1996), Piar Singh stoutly maintains that the *Kartarpuri Bir* was 'a fake copy and not the original *Adi Granth* prepared by Bhai Gurdas'.[11] Another scholar summoned to the Akal Takht was Pashaura Singh whose doctoral thesis, 'The Text and Meaning of the Adi Granth', was supervised by W.H. McLeod and submitted to the University of Toronto in 1991.[12] A book published as *Planned Attack on Aad Sri Guru Granth Sahib: Academics or Blasphemy* (1994) was meant to denounce Pashaura Singh and his research as reinforcing McLeod's efforts to cast doubt on the authenticity of the *Kartarpuri Bir* and, therefore, on the *Guru Granth.*[13]

Both Pashaura Singh and Piar Singh were criticized by Trilochan Singh in his *Ernest Trumpp and W.H. McLeod As Scholars of Sikh History, Religion and Culture* (1994).[14] Balwant Singh Dhillon in his *Early Sikh Scriptural Tradition: Myth and Reality* (1999) has argued not only against Pashaura Singh but also against Gurinder Singh Mann who has published two books related to the making of the Sikh scripture. Textual criticism and textual studies on the whole have come a long way.[15]

Concern for Sikh identity explains the response to Harjot Oberoi's *The Construction of Religious Boundaries: Culture, Identity and Diversity in the Sikh Tradition* (1994).[16] The *Invasion of Religious Boundaries* (1995), 'a critique of Harjot Oberoi's work', contains 32 articles and reviews and 8 appendices, questioning, among other things, the legitimacy and justification of appointing Harjot Oberoi to the Chair of Punjabi and Sikh Studies at the University of British Columbia. Titles of many of the reviews indicate the drift of their argument: 'journey into obscurity'; 'academics or imagination'; 'a stranger to Sikhism'; 'an attempt at destruction'; 'scholar or saboteur'; 'an unpardonable excess'; 'mischievous propaganda is not research'. Oberoi's work appeared to undermine a distinct Sikh identity. His exposition of 'Sanatan Sikhism' was extremely misleading. Contemporary evidence refuted his assumption and argument that there was no dominant Sikh identity before the advent of the Singh Sabhas.[17]

The critics of McLeod, Oberoi, Pashaura Singh and others feel convinced that they have successfully exposed misrepresentations of Sikh history and Sikhism, and produced considerable literature as an alternative reading. A large number of Sikh scholars appear to agree with them. But this is not the view of those who have been criticized or those who appreciate their work. A conference held at Columbia University in 1989 resulted in the publication of *Studying the Sikhs: Issues for North America* (1993). The editors, John Stratton Hawley and Gurinder Singh Mann, noticed the 'marked tensions between academics and believers' that had affected the field of Sikh studies in recent years and created a concern that surfaced in 'almost every chapter of the book'.[18]

Mark Juergensmeyer observed that the subject matter of religious studies had changed dramatically in the 1960s and 1970s to make the field less pious and 'religious' in its orientation and more objective and 'intellectually respectable'. The rallying cry of this new trend was 'methodology'. The tendency of the scholars of religious studies to align their field with the Enlightenment ethos of a secular university had serious implications for Sikh studies. In Sikh scholarship in the Punjab the main thrust was to show the distinctiveness of the faith rather than its connections and similarities to other traditions, and to demonstrate solidarity with the community in projecting an integral, unified, and autonomous culture. This set the stage for an unhappy confrontation between two views of scholarship. Juergensmeyer cites McLeod's *Guru Nanak and the Sikh Religion* as one of the most controversial works. Juergensmeyer's explanation becomes an unqualified defence of McLeod's position. Indeed, he supports McLeod's view of the Sikh tradition as derived from the *sants* and brackets Guru Nanak himself with the *sants*.[19]

N. Gerald Barrier postulates two approaches to Sikh historiography, the one more familiar in the Punjab and the other more at home in Western universities. The former, with certain shared preconceptions and commitments, tended to reinforce a respect for the Gurus, a sense of historical continuity, a clear differentiation between Sikhism and Hinduism from the time of the first Guru, and a hagiographic treatment of Sikh historical figures. The scholars trained in the Western universities questioned traditional sources and applied rigorous textual analysis in treating documents that related to other historical and religious traditions. They tended to regard Sikhism as an evolving religious and cultural tradition, one that mirrors and in turn affects the environment in which it was evolved. McLeod's critical research had aroused a strong reaction among the Sikhs. The issues raised by this debate had to be carefully considered (in the light of Barrier's observations). Harjot Singh Oberoi's work was criticized by Sikh historians who claimed a single line of authoritative practice from Guru Gobind Singh up to the present. The way in which Barrier presents the debate indicates that he does not attach much importance to the criticism of McLeod or of Oberoi.[20]

J.T. O'Connell observes that there was a network of vocal Sikhs who were evidently troubled by 'the thrust of rigorous critical scholarship' with a bearing upon the religious history of the Sikhs. Some of the writers failed to distinguish between criticizing views and imputing motives or otherwise attacking the personal integrity of those with whom they disagreed or whom they just did not fathom. There has always been some degree of tension between those committed to scholarly inquiry and those committed to preserving and fostering a religious way of life. Clearly, for O'Connell too, the criticism by Sikh scholars was of no consequence.[21]

In his *Autobiography*, McLeod says that he regards himself as a historian of religion who follows the established methods of historical research. Trained in the Western methods of historical research, he adheres to Western notions of historiography. His primary objective has been to communicate 'an understanding of the Sikh people and their religion to educated *Western* readers'. Western understanding underlines all that he has written 'and no apology is offered for it'. This candid statement is interesting in view of the charge of Eurocentrism that his critics have levelled against McLeod. He postulates a simple dichotomy between the 'Western historian' and the 'traditionalist historian'. The attitude of the former is firmly rooted in the Enlightenment, which dictates that all conclusions should be rational and based on sound sources. 'This is light years away from the attitude that takes its stand firmly on revelation and accepts as true that which is divinely revealed.' The two world-views stand in complete opposition to each other. However, what is relevant for debate is the bearing of a world-view on historical writing, and not the world-view itself. The comments of his critics do not make much sense to McLeod. He tells the readers: 'My works stand as I have written them, and readers will need to decide whether they are acceptable or whether the comments of my critics make better sense.'[22]

The controversy is comprehensive enough to cover what are called the 'fundamental issues in Sikh Studies'. A large volume of Sikh studies produced in the past four decades relates to this controversy, directly or indirectly. One side presents it in terms of Enlightenment *versus* religious faith, or 'critical historians' *versus* 'traditional historians'; the other side presents it in terms of deliberate misrepresentation of the Sikh tradition, lack of empathy and linguistic competence, and use of inappropriate methodology. There is little mutual appreciation. Consequently, what we hear largely are two sets of assertions. However, one hopes that an understanding of their contentions may result in a kind of dialogue for the researcher.

W.H. McLeod was not the first historian to treat the *Janamsakhis* critically. But he was the first to adopt a peculiar approach to the life of Guru Nanak. Out of the known sources for his life, he looks upon the *Janamsakhis* as by far the most important. But the *Janamsakhis* are concerned more with the religious ideas and ethics of Guru Nanak than with his secular life. Divorced from these concerns there is only a broad chronology of his life. McLeod conducted an elaborate analysis of each *sakhi* to establish facts with regard to the events of Guru Nanak's secular life. He found the *Janamsakhis* wanting and abandoned the project. Thus, starting with the idea of reconstructing the life of Guru Nanak he ends up with the conclusion that *Janamsakhis* give us only a broad outline. He appears to imply that no historical biography of Guru Nanak can be written.

McLeod has been criticized primarily for rejecting a large number of *sakhis*. But even if all the *sakhis* were to be accepted in terms of incidents and events of Guru Nanak's life, the total information would not yield a historical biography of Guru Nanak, particularly if his thought and concerns are excluded. Guru Nanak's life is important precisely because he was a religious figure. If his biographer is not interested in his ideology he or she cannot go far with a biography. Another point made against McLeod is that he has ignored the real import of the *sakhis* in his search for facts. McLeod himself argues that the *Janamsakhis* present the 'myth' of Guru Nanak. But he does not appreciate that the 'myth' of Guru Nanak is in fact an interpretation of his life and mission and, therefore, the core of a *Janamsakhi*.[23]

McLeod lost interest in the life of Guru Nanak but not in the *Janamsakhis*. His later works, especially the *Early Sikh Tradition*, deal with several aspects of the *Janamsakhis*. This work has been simply ignored by his critics. He wonders why the *Early Sikh Tradition* sank like a stone. At least a part of the answer lies in the fact that he has ignored the heart of the matter, the 'myth' of Guru Nanak. Furthermore, he is aware of the existence of sectarian groups within the Sikh Panth and their *Janamsakhi* traditions, but he does not relate the two. Consequently, he remains unaware that there are 'myths', and not 'the myth' of Guru

Nanak, created or projected by different sections of Sikhs. A study of this 'stuff of Sikh history' can be fascinating and rewarding and it can also become alive. McLeod has not done this. Possibly, that is the reason why his scholarship on the *Janamsakhis* appears to run in 'neutral gear'.[24]

More important than the issue of Guru Nanak's 'life' is the 'faith' of Guru Nanak, the starting point of the Sikh movement, and of Sikh Studies. On this issue, Daljeet Singh's understanding is radically different from that of McLeod. Whereas the message of Guru Nanak for McLeod is liberation through *nam simran* as the supreme purpose of human life, for Daljeet Singh liberation-in-life results in altruistic social action. Consequently, whereas the institutionalization of the Sikh movement for McLeod was due to later historical developments, for Daljeet Singh it was built into Guru Nanak's conception of the purpose of life. Whereas Guru Nanak's originality for McLeod lies in giving coherence to the *sant* 'synthesis', for Daljeet Singh Guru Nanak's dispensation was something new in which spiritual and temporal concerns were two sides of the same coin of faith. It must be emphasized that the use of common concepts by Guru Nanak and the *sants* does not mean that they occupy the same position. Indeed, no institutionalization can be attributed to any *sant* before we come upon the Sikh movement. For the *sants,* liberation-in-life was a personal project; for Guru Nanak it was a social project for the redemption of others. The foundation of the Sikh faith and Sikh Panth can thus be attributed to Guru Nanak. The later Sikh history was intimately linked with this foundation.[25]

McLeod tends to assume that there was no institutionalization in the time of Guru Nanak and Guru Angad. 'Innovations' started under pressure from the changing circumstances in the time of Guru Amar Das, with the *langar,* pilgrimage centre, compilation of *pothis,* and appointment of intermediaries. McLeod does point out that the place of pilgrimage was Goindwal (and not Hardwar or Kashi) yet he refers to 'Hindu' influence as if only Hindus used to have places of pilgrimage. The pull of the environment is of crucial importance for McLeod. His Jat theory of militarization and his 'hypothesis of the Devi cult' appear to spring from this assumption rather than the empirical evidence at his command.[26]

McLeod's impression that Sainapat's *Sri Gur Sobha* and the *Rahitnamas* were composed several decades after the time of Guru Gobind

Singh reinforces his general assumption about environment determining his treatment of the Khalsa *rahit* and doctrines. By now, however, it is clear that this impression is wrong and all the arguments put forth by McLeod about the evolving character of the Khalsa *rahit*, the doctrines of Guru Panth and Guru Granth, and even the ideal of *raj karega khasla*, have no validity. The most important features of the *rahit* were in place during the time of Guru Gobind Singh or soon afterwards, including the five symbols which later constituted the '5 Ks'. On the whole, McLeod's hypotheses about the evolution and transformation of the Sikh Panth are the weakest in his treatment of Sikh history. His flawed hypotheses are linked to his partial understanding of Guru Nanak.[27]

In his exposition of the early Sikh identity, McLeod assumes that the Sikhs were distinct from Muslims but their distinct identity in relation to Hindus was not 'uniform'. For Oberoi, it was not 'fixed'. For Daljeet Singh, the early Sikh identity was clearly distinct from that of Hindus and Muslims just as the Sikh faith was distinct from 'Hinduism' and Islam. None of the three scholars have, however, gone into the issue of 'Hindu' identity in the precolonial times; they assume it to be known. They are agreed upon the objective differences of the Sikhs from the others around and they talk of the Sikh subjective awareness or consciousness of distinct identity. In the compositions of the Gurus, Bhai Gurdas and the *Janamsakhis* the Sikh faith and the Sikh Panth are essentially distinct from all the religious and social entities around. This self-image is supported by the evidence of the *Dabistan-i Mazahib*. Significantly, though there is an awareness of separation, neither Hindus nor Muslims are seen as the 'other' in the sense of an opponent or an enemy.[28]

McLeod, Oberoi and Daljeet Singh subscribe to the distinct identity of the Khalsa of Guru Gobind Singh based on a unique form of initiation, outward appearance, doctrines and rites, martial ideals and egalitarian ethos of the Khalsa. The Khalsa identity became the dominant Sikh identity during the course of the eighteenth century. For McLeod and Daljeet Singh, this was the dominant identity of the Sikhs during the time of Sikh rule as well. For Oberoi, however, it was replaced by 'Sanatan Sikhism' in the late eighteenth and the early nineteenth century. Even McLeod appears to have adopted this view in his later years. It is clear from the contemporary evidence, however, that

'Singh' identity was the dominant identity among the Sikhs throughout the period of Sikh rule. Oberoi is not clear about the Sahajdharis and even McLeod is unaware of the presence of the non-Singh Khalsa in the early eighteenth century. The relationship of the Singhs with the non-Singhs, therefore, is misconceived. The situation calls for a better conceptualization of the dominant Singh identity with its operative limitations.[29]

Both McLeod and Jagjit Singh agree in theory about the egalitarian ideal of the Gurus. Jagjit Singh emphasizes it more than McLeod. Both agree on the relevance and importance of commensality and connubium in a discussion of equality and caste. They agree that the old patterns of matrimony in terms of endogamous *jatis* and exogamous *gotras* continued among the Sikhs. McLeod emphasizes the intractability of the custom for connubium, but Jagjit Singh refers to the absence of any felt need for change, particularly when there was no 'caste system' among the Sikhs on the basis of hierarchy. McLeod talks in terms of high and low castes among the Sikhs, but no hierarchy was upheld in principle. Hierarchy was not the accepted norm in the Sikh Panth. On commensality, McLeod underlines the sharing of food by all in the sacred space. Jagjit Singh makes the practice more universal during the eighteenth century. Thus, there is a certain measure of agreement between McLeod and Jagjit Singh but there are important differences as well. On the whole, for the pre-colonial Sikh Panth, the evidence used by McLeod and Jagjit Singh is rather limited. It appears that a distinction can be made between the pre-Khalsa Sikhs and the Khalsa Singhs for a study of equality and caste. But the whole issue calls for a thorough analysis of the entire range of Sikh literature and other contemporary evidence. It also calls for a new paradigm.[30]

This is equally true of the issue of equality and gender. While Kapur Singh emphasizes the importance of the principle of equality, McLeod underlines the importance of empirical continuities. Doris Jakobsh tries to suggest two phases in the pre-Khalsa period: one, from Guru Nanak to Guru Amar Das, when women gained some ground in terms of gender relations; and two, from Guru Ram Das to the institution of the Khalsa by Guru Gobind Singh when the ground gained was lost to the rising ethos of masculinity. The institution of the Khalsa with its martial ideals turned it hyper-masculinity. Though interesting, this hypothesis is flawed due to the use of limited evidence partially interpreted and the importance given to a theoretical assumption. Jakobsh appears to support a preconceived notion. The evidence available for analysis suggests a far more complex situation in which there is a constant tension between the ideal of equality and the inegalitarian institution of the family which is taken for granted. If anything, the issue of gender relations in the Sikh social order calls for a thorough research.[31]

The Singh Sabha movement is seen by McLeod as a reformation of the Khalsa tradition, by Oberoi as a rupture with the 'Sanatan tradition', and by G.S. Dhillon as a revival of the early Sikh tradition. They all agree that the Khalsa tradition was re-vitalized and Singh identity was successfully espoused. The environment created by the colonial rule was certainly relevant for the success of the Singh Sabha movement but so was the earlier Sikh tradition from which the leaders of the movement derived all their important doctrines and most of their concerns. Their interpretation of the earlier Sikh literature has not yet been seriously studied, nor the literature which they produced. Instead of a selective use, a thorough study of this literature can lead to a better understanding. What was new to the situation was not Sikh identity but the conscious argument that a distinct identity turned the Sikhs into a political entity. No attention had yet been paid to the changing conception and consciousness of Hindu identity in the nineteenth century.[32]

The view that the Singh Sabha movement produced a radical re-interpretation of the earlier Sikh tradition amounting almost to a kind of 'invention' is reflected in the treatment of the conception and tradition of martyrdom by Oberoi, McLeod, and Louis Fenech. They do not see any relevance of Sikh ideology for the tradition of martyrdom. Several other scholars on the other hand look upon Sikh ideology as the basis of martyrdom. Both sides look for a direct statement on martyrdom in the Sikh scripture, some finding it there and others not finding it anywhere before the nineteenth century. In a historical approach to martyrdom, it is relevant to see the implications of Sikh ideology. The theory of 'heroic tradition' does not explain the martyrdom of Guru Arjan and Guru Tegh Bahadur before the institution of the Khalsa, and of Bhai Mani Singh and Bhai Taru Singh afterwards. The evidence of Sikh literature of the precolonial period does not support the view that the Singh Sabha Movement 'created' the tradition of martyrdom or re-defined it radically for their own religious or political purposes.[33]

Textual criticism entered an important phase with doubts about the authenticity of the *Kartarpur Pothi* expressed by McLeod, which meant doubts about the authenticity of the *Guru Granth Sahib*. Understandably, much of the literature on this subject relates to the issue of *Kartarpur Pothi*. By now the issue seems to have been settled in favour of its authenticity on the basis of detailed analysis not only of the *Kartarpur Pothi* itself but also of a large number of manuscripts produced before and after. As Gurinder Singh Mann's works shows, the *Guru Harsahai Pothi*, the *Goindwal Pothis* and the *MS 1245* are still controversial but their evidence has provided a historical view of the process that led to the compilation of the *Kartarpur Pothi*. Scriptural manuscripts of the late seventeenth century show clearly that the *Damdami Bir*, based on the *Kartarpur Pothi*, had come into existence in the time of Guru Tegh Bahadur and Guru Gobind Singh before the end of the seventeenth century. Guruship was vested in the *Damdami Bir*. Thus, the historical lines of development from the *Kartarpur Pothi* to the *Damdami Bir*, and from the *Damdami Bir* to the *Guru Granth Sahib*, are clear. Pashaura Singh's 'draft theory' and 'power hypotheses', and his view that Maharaja Ranjit Singh made the *Damdami Bir* the authorized version, are more conjectural than empirical, and rather misleading.[34] The view made current by McLeod and Oberoi that the *Dasam Granth* had come to be regarded as the Guru before the advent of colonial rule in the Punjab has no empirical basis. The influence of the *Dasam Granth* among the Sikhs during the eighteenth and nineteenth centuries is an area yet to be seriously explored. For this, it would also be necessary to go into the history of the *Dasam Granth* and its authorship much more thoroughly than has been done so far.[35]

We have thus seen the bearing of these controversies on our perspective on the life of Guru Nanak, his ideology and his status, the evolution of the Sikh movement in terms of the relative roles assigned to ideology and environment, the Khalsa *rahit* and the doctrines of Guru Granth and Guru Panth, the issues of caste and gender in the Sikh social order, Sikh identity, and making of the Sikh scripture, apart from the character of the *Janamsakhi* and *Rahitnama* literature. For a serious student of Sikh history and a researcher in Sikh studies, an awareness of the issues involved in the controversies can certainly be helpful.

Finally, a good deal of importance is given to methodology both by the academia and the intelligentsia involved in the controversies.[36] No one has denied the importance of empirical evidence, or the need of verification of generalizations. Therefore, the distinction between the 'critical historians' and 'traditional historians' is a difference of degree but not of kind. What is relevant for our purpose is not the world-views in themselves but their bearing on one's approach and method. It is quite evident that methodology by itself does not ensure veracity or validity. The historical method is not Western simply because it was initially developed in the West: it is not culturally rooted. The assumptions and purposes of the contestants, generally, have not been clearly separated from their method. A historian would be poorer to the extent he or she ignores ideas or 'mentalities'. A dialectical relationship between ideas and environment can ensure a better historical understanding.[37]

NOTES

1. W.H. McLeod, *Guru Nanak and the Sikh Religion*, Oxford: The Clarendon Press, 1968.
2. W.H. McLeod, *The Evolution of the Sikh Community*, New Delhi: Oxford University Press, 1975.
3. For criticism of McLeod's *Evolution* by Fauja Singh see, *The Panjab Past and Present*, vol. XI, part 1, pp. 178-85, and by Daljeet Singh, see *Journal of Sikh Studies*, vol. IV, no. 1 (February 1977), pp. 166-9.
4. Mark Juergensmeyer and Norman Gerald Barrier (eds.), *Sikh Studies: Comparative Perspectives on a Changing Tradition*, Berkeley: Graduate Theological Union, 1979.
5. John C.B. Webster, 'Sikh Studies in the Punjab', *Sikh Studies: Comparative Perspectives on a Changing Tradition*, ed. Mark Juergenesmeyer and N. Gerald Barrier, pp. 25-32.
6. Joseph T. O'Connell et al. (eds.), *Sikh History and Religion in the Twentieth Century*, Toronto: University of Toronto, 1988.
7. Gurdev Singh (ed.), *Perspectives on the Sikh Tradition*, Patiala: Siddharth Publications, 1986.
8. Jasbir Singh Mann and Harbans Singh Saraon (eds.), *Advanced Studies in Sikhism*, Irvine: Sikh Community of North America, 1989.

9. Kharak Singh, Gobind Singh Mansukhani and Jasbir Singh Mann (eds.), *Fundamental Issues of Sikh Studies,* Chandigarh: Institute of Sikh Studies, 1992.
10. Piar Singh, *Gatha Sri Adi Granth,* Amritsar: Guru Nanak Dev University, 1992.
11. Piar Singh, *Gatha Sri Adi Granth and the Controversy,* Michigan: Anant Education and Rural Development Foundation, 1996.
12. Pashaura Singh, 'The Text and Meaning of the Adi Granth', Ph.D thesis, University of Toronto, 1991.
13. Giani Bachittar Singh (ed.), *Planned Attack on Aad Sri Guru Granth Sahib: Academics or Blasphemy,* Chandigarh: International Centre of Sikh Studies, 1994.
14. Trilochan Singh, *Ernest Trumpp and W.H. McLeod as Scholars of Sikh History, Religion and Culture,* Chandigarh: International Centre of Sikh Studies, 1994.
15. Balwant Singh Dhillon, *Early Sikh Scriptural Tradition: Myth and Reality,* Amritsar: Singh Brothers, 1999.
16. Harjot S. Oberoi, *The Construction of Religious Boundaries: Culture, Identity and Diversity in the Sikh Tradition,* New Delhi: Oxford University Press, 1994.
17. Jasbir Singh Mann, Surinder Singh Sodhi and Gurbakhsh Singh Shergill (eds.), *Invasion of Religious Boundaries,* Vancouver: Canadian Sikh Study and Teaching Society, 1995.
18. John Stratton Hawley and Gurinder Singh Mann (eds.), *Studying the Sikhs: Issues for North America,* Albany: State University of New York Press, 1993.
19. Mark Juergensmeyer, 'Sikhism and Religious Studies', *Studying the Sikhs: Issues for North America,* ed. John Stratton Hawley and Gurinder Singh Mann, pp. 9-23.
20. N. Gerald Barrier, 'Sikh Studies and the Study of History', *Studying the Sikhs: Issues for North America,* ed. John Stratton Hawley and Gurinder Singh Mann, pp. 25-45.
21. Joseph T. O'Connell, 'Sikh Studies in North America: A Field Guide', *Studying the Sikhs: Issues for North America,* ed. John Stratton Hawley and Gurinder Singh Mann, pp. 113-27.
22. W.H. McLeod, *Discovering the Sikhs: Autobiography of a Historian,* Delhi: Permanent Black, 2004.
23. For McLeod's statement on the *Janamsakhis,* see 'The Janamsakhis', *The Evolution of the Sikh Community,* pp. 20-36. He has upheld his position in *The Sikhs: History, Religion and Society,* New York: Columbia University Press, 1989, pp. 19-20; *Discovering the Sikhs: Autobiography of a Historian,* pp. 150-1.

    McLeod's view is unacceptable to a number of scholars. For example, Kirpal Singh refers to scepticism about the value of *Janamsakhis* for the life of Guru Nanak and asserts that his own studies lead him to conclude that the

Janamsakhis 'shall ever remain the most important source of information on Guru Nanak if we study them carefully and intensively'. See his *Janamsakhi Tradition: An Analytical Study*, Amritsar: Singh Brothers, 2004, pp. 7-10. For a much more focused critique, see Gurinder Singh Mann, 'Guru Nanak's Life and Legacy: An Appraisal', *Journal of Punjab Studies*, vol. 17, nos. 1 & 2 (Spring-Fall 2010), pp. 3-44.

24. W.H. McLeod, *Early Sikh Tradition: A Study of the Janamsakhis*, Oxford: The Clarendon Press, 1984. For a critique of this work, see J.S. Grewal, 'The *Janamsakhi* Traditions', *Lectures on History, Society and Culture of the Punjab*, Patiala: Punjabi University, 2007, pp. 141-66. See also, J.S. Grewal, 'The *B40 Janamsakhi*', ibid., pp. 167-217.
25. McLeod, *Guru Nanak and the Sikh Religion*, pp. 163-32; *The Evolution of the Sikh Community*, p. 5; *The Sikhs: History, Religion and Society*, pp. 18-19, 22-31. For critiques of McLeod's view, see Gurdev Singh (ed.), *Perspectives on the Sikh Tradition*, pp. 15-21; Daljeet Singh, 'Origin of Sikh Faith', *Perspectives on the Sikh Tradition*, ed. Gurdev Singh, pp. 55-8; Daljeet Singh, *The Sikh Ideology*, Amritsar: Singh Brothers, 1990, pp. 112-13; J.S. Grewal, 'The Bani of Guru Nanak', *Lectures on History, Society and Culture of the Punjab*, pp. 101-29; J.S. Grewal, 'Guru Nanak and His Panth', *The Sikhs: Ideology, Institutions and Identity*, New Delhi: Oxford University Press, 2009, pp. 3-21.
26. McLeod, 'The Evolution of Sikh Community', *The Evolution of the Sikh Community*, pp. 1-19. For a different interpretation, see Jagjit Singh, 'The Militarization of Sikh Movement', *Perspectives on the Sikh Tradition*, ed. Gurdev Singh, pp. 325-80; Jagjit Singh, 'Sikh Militancy and Jats', *Advanced Studies in Sikhism*, ed. Jasbir Singh and Harbans Singh Saraon, pp. 214-33.
27. McLeod, 'Cohesive Ideals and Institutions in the History of the Sikh Panth', *The Evolution of the Sikh Community*, pp. 37-58. For a different view, see Ganda Singh, 'Guru Gobind Singh Designates Guru Granth Sahib To Be Guru', *Perspectives on the Sikh Tradition*, ed. Gurdev Singh, pp. 183-210; Harbans Singh, 'The Guru Granth Sahib', ibid., pp. 211-24. It may be added that McLeod's treatment of the Sikh *rahit* in his *Sikhs of the Khalsa: A History of the Khalsa Rahit*, New Delhi: Oxford University Press, 2003, has been ignored by his critics and so has been his translation of the *Prem Sumarag as The Testimony of a Sanatan Sikh* (New Delhi: Oxford University Press, 2006).
28. McLeod, *Who is a Sikh? The Problem of Sikh Identity*, Oxford: The Clarendon Press, 1989, pp. 7-22. Oberoi, *The Construction of Religious Boundaries*, pp. 50-8. Daljeet Singh, 'The Sikh Identity', *Essentials of Sikhism*, Amritsar: Singh Brothers, 1994, For a discussion of the views of these three scholars, see J.S. Grewal, *Historical Perspectives on Sikh Identity*, Patiala: Punjabi University, 1997, pp. 1-14.
29. McLeod, *Who is a Sikh?*, pp. 23-61. Oberoi, *The Construction of Religious Boundaries*, pp. 92-138. For a discussion of the views of McLeod, Oberoi

and Daljeet Singh see J.S. Grewal, *Historical Perspectives on Sikh Identity*, pp. 15-32.

30. McLeod, 'Caste in the Sikh Panth', *The Evolution of the Sikh Community*, pp. 83-104. Jagjit Singh, 'Caste System and the Sikhs', *Perspectives on the Sikh Tradition*, ed. Gurdev Singh, pp. 231-320. J.S. Grewal, 'Caste and the Sikh Social Order', *The Sikhs: Ideology Institutions and Identity*, pp. 189-205.
31. Kapur Singh, *Parasharprashna: An Enquiry into the Genesis and Unique Character of the Order of the Khalsa with an Exposition of the Sikh Tenets*, ed. Piar Singh and Madanjit Kaur, Amritsar: Guru Nanak Dev University, 1989. W.H. McLeod, 'Gender and the Sikh Panth', *Essays in Sikh History, Tradition and Society*, New Delhi: Oxford University Press, 2007, pp. 191-6. Nikky-Guninder Kaur Singh, *The Feminine Principle in the Sikh Vision of the Transcendent*, Cambridge: Cambridge University Press, 1993. Doris R. Jakobsh, *Relocating Gender in Sikh History: Transformation, Meaning and Identity*, New Delhi: Oxford University Press, 2003. J.S. Grewal, *Guru Nanak and Patriarchy*, Simla: Indian Institute of Advanced Study, 1993. J.S. Grewal, 'Sikhism and Gender', *The Sikhs: Ideology, Institutions and Identity*, pp. 206-25.
32. McLeod, *Who is a Sikh*?, pp. 62-121. Oberoi, *The Construction of Religious Boundaries*, pp. 102-4, 105-8, 126-30, 139, 203, 207-57, 260-303, 305-51, 351-76, 382-92, 397-401, 422-4. G.S. Dhillon, 'Singh Sabha Movement: A Revival', *Advanced Studies in Sikhism*, ed. Jasbir Singh and Harbans Singh Saroan, pp. 234-42; 'Sikh Identity: A Continuing Feature', *Recent Researches in Sikhism*, ed. Jasbir Singh Mann and Kharak Singh, Patiala: Punjabi University, 1992, pp. 226-46. For a discussion of the views of McLeod, Oberoi and Dhillon, see J.S. Grewal, *Historical Perspectives on Sikh Identity*, pp. 33-96.
33. Oberoi, *The Construction of Religious Boundaries*, pp. 328-30. W.H. McLeod, *Sikhism*, Harmondsworth, Penguin Books, 1997, pp. 128-31. Louis E. Fenech, *Martyrdom in the Sikh Tradition: Playing the 'Game of Love'*, New Delhi: Oxford University Press, 2000. Kharak Singh, 'Martyrdom in Sikhism', *Abstracts of Sikh Studies*, Chandigarh: Institute of Sikh Studies, January 1994. J.P.S. Uberoi, *Religion, Civil Society and the State*, New Delhi: Oxford University Press, pp. 61, 88-9, 93-4, 96-7, 114-23, 135, 151. J.S. Grewal, 'Martyrdom in Sikh History and Literature', *The Sikhs: Ideology, Institutions and Identity*, pp. 42-75.
34. W.H. McLeod, 'The Sikh Scriptures', *The Evolution of the Sikh Community*, pp. 59-82. Daljeet Singh, *Essays on the Authenticity of Kartarpur Bir and the Integrated Logic and Unity of Sikhism*, Patiala: Punjabi University, 1987. Daljeet Singh, 'Authenticity of Kartarpuri Bir', *Advanced Studies in Sikhism*, ed. Jasbir Singh Mann and Harbans Singh Saraon, pp. 138-60. Gurinder Singh Mann, *The Goindval Pothis: The Earliest Extant Source of the Sikh Canon*, Cambridge (Massachusetts): Harvard University Press, 1996; Gurinder Singh Mann, *The Making of Sikh Scripture*, New York: Oxford University Press, 2000.

Pashaura Singh, *The Guru Granth Sahib: Canon, Meaning and Authority*, New Delhi: Oxford University Press, 2000. J.S. Grewal, *A Study of Guru Granth Sahib: Doctrine, Social Content, History, Structure and Status*, Amritsar: Singh Brothers, 2009.

35. W.H. McLeod, 'The Sikh Scriptures', *The Evolution of the Sikh Community*, pp. 79-81. C.H. Loehlin, *The Granth of Guru Gobind Singh and the Khalsa Brotherhood*, Lucknow: Lucknow Publishing House, 1971. Gurtej Singh, 'Two Views on Dasam Granth', *Fundamental Issues in Sikh Studies*, ed. Kharak Singh, Gobind Singh Mansukhani and Jasbir Singh Mann, pp. 179-83; Gurtej Singh, 'The Mystique of the Dasam Granth', *Sikh Studies Quarterly*, Chandigarh: Institute of Sikh Studies, July 1994, pp. 81-4. Daljeet Singh, 'Dasam Granth: Its History', *Abstracts of Sikh Studies*, July 1994, pp. 81-93; Jagjit Singh, 'The Historical Identity of Dasam Granth', ibid., pp. 95-9. Gurinder Singh Mann, 'Sources for the Study of Guru Gobind Singh's Life and Times', *Journal of Punjab Studies*, vol. XV, nos. 1 & 2 (Spring-Fall 2008), pp. 229-84.
36. Noel Q. King, 'Orientalism, Critical Scholarship and the Sikh Religion', *Perspectives on the Sikh Tradition*, ed. Gurdev Singh, pp. 41-52; 'CAPAX IMPERII? Scripture, Tradition and "European Style" Oriental Method', *Advanced Studies in Sikhism*, ed. Jasbir Singh Mann and Harbans Singh Saraon, pp. 1-13. Daljeet Singh, 'Issues of Sikh Studies', *Advanced Studies in Sikhism*, ed. Jasbir Singh Mann and Harbans Singh Saraon, pp. 16-28. Mansukhani, Gobind Singh, 'The Origin and Development of Sikh Studies', *Fundamental Issues in Sikh Studies*, pp. 127-35; Gobind Singh Mansukhani, 'An Integrated Methodology for Appraisal of Sources in Sikh Studies', *Recent Researches in Sikhism*, pp. 109-20.
37. For a general discussion of the controversies, see J.S. Grewal, *Historical Perspectives on Sikh Identity*, Patiala: Punjabi University, 1997; *Contesting Interpretations of the Sikh Tradition*, New Delhi: Manohar, 1998; *Recent Debates in Sikh Studies*, New Delhi: Manohar, 2011. For an analysis of most of the major works of Sikh literature, see J.S. Grewal, *History, Literature and Identity: Four Centuries of Sikh Tradition*, New Delhi: Oxford University Press, 2011.

Glossary

'adalati: associated with justice; legal, judicial, just; an officer specially appointed under Sikh rule for administering and supervising justice.

Adi Granth: the Sikh scripture known as the *Adi Sri Guru Granth Sahib Ji*, the epithet '*Adi*' indicating that it was in existence earlier than the *Dasam Granth* generally associated with Guru Gobind Singh even though compiled after his death.

ahimsa: non-injury to living beings; the principle of non-violence, rejected by the Sikh Gurus.

Akal Takht: 'eternal throne'; a large and high platform built by Guru Hargobind close to the Harmandar Sahib for conducting temporal affairs of the Sikh people; with a structure raised over the spot, the Akal Takht was adopted in the eighteenth century as the seat of the collective authority of the Khalsa.

Akali: pertaining to God as the Immortal Being (Akal); a staunch follower of Guru Gobind Singh, dedicated totally to the Guru and God.

'amil: a performer, an operator; a functionary of the Mughal government, especially for collecting revenues from a *pargana*.

amrit: nectar; the water used for initiation into the Khalsa order, also called baptism of the double-edged sword (*khande di pahul*).

arati: praise of a deity; the Vaishnava ritual praise of the divinity performed with lighted lamps in a tray containing flowers and incense presented in circular motion in front of an idol.

bairagi: a renunciate, generally a Vaishnavite mendicant who remains celibate.

baoli: a step well for easy access to water; the step well constructed by Guru Amar Das at Goindwal which later became a place of pilgrimage.

bhaddan: tonsure; ritual shaving of the hair of the head, especially on the death of the father.

bhagauti: a sword; the sword as the symbol of the power of the omnipotent God.

bhang: cannabis, hemp, hashish; its leaves and pistils, ground with almonds and sugar and mixed with water, used as an intoxicant.

chaudhari: a local agent commissioned for the collection of revenues from a number of villages; the office tended to become hereditary during the Mughal times.

daftar: a part, section or volume of a book; more generally, an office.

Dal Khalsa (or *Khalsaji*)*:* the joint forces of the leaders of the Khalsa under a single commander selected for a campaign.

Damdami Bir: the recension of the *Granth Sahib* prepared by Guru Gobind Singh at Damdama (Talwandi Sabo) in 1706 or the Damdama at Anandpur, in the 1680s; this recension is believed to have been lost but its early copies are extant.

darbar: a court; the court of a king; the court of the Guru; also used for the Harmandar Sahib at Amritsar, and the gurdwara at Tarn Taran.

dargah: a great house; a court; the burial place of a *pir*; the divine court.

darogha: headman of an office, an overseer or superintendent.

Dasam Granth: the Book of the Tenth Guru compiled during the eighteenth century with a large number of religious and secular writings; attributed to Guru Gobind Singh and the poets at his court, it was venerated by the Sikhs but never treated as the scriptural Guru and, therefore, never bracketed with the *Adi Granth.*

dasvandh: one-tenth; the share of annual income of a Sikh expected to be spent for the welfare of others in the name of the Guru.

deg, tegh, fateh: these three words, literally meaning 'a cauldron for cooking food', 'the sword', and 'victory', were inscribed on the seal of Guru Gobind Singh in a couplet in Persian, and came to stand for the spirit of charity, physical might in righteous causes, and conviction of victory through God's grace.

deodidar: keeper of the royal gate; the minister-in-charge of a royal palace.

dharamsal (*dharamsala*): a metaphor used by Guru Nanak for earth as the place for earning merit; came to be used for the place of Sikh congregational worship and community meal; from the eighteenth century onwards this term was replaced by *gurdwara*.

dharmarth: by way of charity; land-revenue alienated in favour of a religious institution or an individual known for religious merit; called *madad-i ma'ash* during the Mughal times.

dhuan: smoke, fire; an Udasi establishment.

faqir: one who pursued religious merit through austerities and a life of resignation; a mendicant or a beggar.

faujdar: keeper of troops; the officer for keeping law and order and helping the civil authorities in the collection of revenues from refractory *zamindars*.

five Ks: the five articles enjoined upon the Khalsa as a part of their *rahit*, each starting with the letter k (*kakka* in Gurmukhi): *kesh, kangha, kirpan, kara* and *kachh* (uncut hair, comb, sword, iron bangle, and short breeches); all these articles are mentioned in the early *Rahitnamas*, individually or in groups, but the formulation of '5ks' appeared later, from the late eighteenth century onwards.

gaddi: a throne; the seat of a religious guide; the office of Guruship in the Sikh tradition.

granthi: a reader of the *Granth Sahib*, generally employed in a gurdwara for performing various religious duties.

ghallughara: literally, a stream of blood; a great massacre or carnage; used for two such events in Sikh history, one in 1746 and the other in 1762.

ghazi: a Muslim warrior, especially the one fighting against infidels and prepared to die fighting.

ghurcharha: rider of a horse, a cavalryman; the individual trooper in the cavalry of Ranjit Singh, whether regular or irregular.

gurmata: a resolution passed by a Sikh congregation in the presence of *Guru Granth Sahib*, and therefore having the morally binding force even for those Sikhs who were not physically present.

haumai: 'I am'; the psychic state of self-centredness in oblivion of God's omnipotence.

havan: a fire sacrifice, involving animal slaughter at one time but later only the burning of incense or organic materials.

haveli: a large mansion, generally of an affluent member of the society in towns and villages.

Hindostani: used in the Punjab for a person belonging the Ganges plains.

hukam: an order; a royal order; the divine order.

hukamnama: a written order; used for the letters of the Sikh Gurus addressed to their followers, and by other religious authorities among the Sikhs.

jagir: a piece of cultivated land with its revenue alienated by the state in lieu of salary for service.

jagirdar: the holder of a *jagir*; a servant of the state authorized to collect revenues from a piece of land, a village, or several villages, directly or indirectly through his agents.

jagirdari: the system of paying the servants of the state by alienating land-revenue in their favour.

Janamsakhi: 'Life's testimony', a form of literature on Guru Nanak generally regarded as biographical; its nature, character and importance have been discussed by a number of scholars.

kam-krodh-lobh-moh-hankar: desire-anger-greed-attachment-pride as the five adversaries of human beings.

kankut: a method of determining the state's share in the produce from land on the basis of estimated yield from a standing crop.

kanungo (*qanungo*): one who states the law or custom in relation to matters agrarian; a functionary of the government above the village accountant (*patwari*), in the land revenue administration.

karah parsad: the sacred food distributed in the Sikh *dharmsal* or gurdwara, ideally prepared with equal quantities of flour, ghee, and sugar.

kardar: a functionary of the state, especially the person in-charge of the administration of a *pargana*, or a number of *parganas*, with wide powers to maintain law and order, to collect land revenue, and to perform judicial functions.

karm (*nadar*): kindness and mercy; divine grace; several other terms are used to underline this basic attribute of God in Sikh thought.

karma: a deed, an action; linked with the idea of transmigration as the law of *karma,* it accounts for the distinctions of birth.

karma-gian-bhagti: the three well-recognized paths to the goal of emancipation (*mukti* or *moksha*), that is, the path of prescribed social practices and ritual worship, the path of knowledge, and the path of devotion.

Kartarpur Pothi: the *Granth* compiled by Guru Arjan in 1604, now in the possession of the Sodhi descendants of Dhir Mal at Kartarpur in the Jalandhar district.

katha: a narrative; a narrative related to an event in the life of Guru Nanak; exposition of a verse or verses from the sacred scripture of the Sikhs.

Khalsa: an epithet used for a Sikh, or a Sikh congregation, directly linked with the Guru and not through the mediacy of a *masand*; it came to be used for the Sikh who took *pahul* of the double-edged sword and adopted a specified way of life.

Khalsaji: refers to an individual member of the Khalsa order as well as the collectivity of the Khalsa.

khanda: a double-edged sword; it figures metaphorically in early Sikh literature, and it was used literally by Guru Gobind Singh for the new form of baptism he introduced; it is seen as the symbol of *miri* and *piri* (temporal and spiritual authority) rolled into one.

khil'at: a robe of honour, actually consisting of a number of pieces, conferred by a ruler.

khulasa: in contrast with the *khalsa,* used for a Sikh who did not take *pahul* of the double-edged sword and, therefore, did not observe the Khalsa *rahit.*

kirpan: a sword; it has acquired a great sanctity for the Sikhs as one of the 5ks.

kirtan: singing of God's praises, especially through the hymns embodied in the *Guru Granth Sahib.*

kotwal: keeper of a walled place; the official in charge of a city for maintaining peace, and observance of moral and social norms.

kurimar: killer of an infant daughter, liable to be excommunicated by the Khalsa.

lambardar (*numberdar*): the village headman in the colonial Punjab, earlier called *muqaddam.*

langar: a kitchen, a community kitchen; a community meal; generally, a feature of the Sikh sacred space for congregational worship.

mahal: a unit for revenue administration; also used for the *pargana.*

manji: literally a cot, but used as a symbol of authority to preach the Sikh faith on behalf of the Guru; later, this intermediary came to be called Ramdas and more popularly, *masand.*

masand: the term used for the Guru's representatives in the time of Guru Arjan, appointed for collecting *dasvand* and other voluntary offerings from the local Sikh *sangats* to be brought to the Guru at the time of Baisakhi and Diwali.

mashir-i khas: a special or a close advisor of the ruler, meant actually for consultation.

mata: a decision, a resolution by a group of people.

maya: the material world with all its fascinating attractions which stand in the way of exclusive devotion to God; it is not an illusion in Sikhism but nonetheless an obstacle in the way of liberation.

mir: a leader, a ruler; an individual holding temporal power.

miri-piri: the idea that the temporal and spiritual authority is combined in the office of the Guru among the Sikhs; consequently, the Sikhs are duty bound to be concerned with both spiritual and temporal life.

misl: groups of men and their leaders combined under a leader for political activity.

misldar: the leader of a *misl,* who could join other *misldars* for a concerted action under a single leader or *sardar.*

misldari: generally refers to the system of polity established by the Sikh leaders in the late eighteenth century; though much discussed, the concept is still not very clear.

morcha: a trench; used metaphorically for a non-violent agitation over a specific issue or a number of issues.

mufti: the official who formally propounded the Islamic law for the consideration of the *qazi* to pronounce judgement.

mukta: one who attains liberation (*mukti*).

mulla: a person learned in Islamic law, but generally the person in-charge of a mosque who performed various religious and social functions for the local Muslims; a symbol of Muslim orthodoxy.

mulmantar: the opening statement in the *Granth Sahib* embodying the Sikh conception of God, an affirmation serving the purpose of invocation.

munshi: a writer, a clerk, a secretary.

muqaddam: a leader, chief, commander; a title of respect; the village headman who collected revenues on behalf of the government.

Nakhas: a place where cattle, horses, camels, and slaves were sold; the marketplace in Lahore where Sikhs were executed by the order of the governors of the province in the late 1740s and the early 1750s.

nam: the name; refers to the simultaneously transcendent and immanent states of God; a concept of a crucial importance in Sikh thought.

namaz: a prayer; one of the five daily prayers in Islam; an additional prayer.

nazim: an organizer, an administrator; generally the Mughal provincial governor, also called *subedar*.

nazrana: offering of a gift to a superior; also tribute.

Nirmala: a Singh of Guru Gobind Singh who devoted himself to learning and not to arms; generally, the Nirmalas gave a Vedantic interpretation of Gurbani.

pahul: the baptismal water for the rite of initiation into the Khalsa order, stirred with the double-edged sword.

panchayat: a body of five or more persons to represent a whole group, section, caste or community.

panj piare: the five beloved Sikhs of the Guru who offered their lives on a call from Guru Gobind Singh; any five Sikhs who represent the whole congregation.

Panth: a path; the path shown by Guru Nanak and his successors; the body of the followers of that path.

pargana: a unit of administration, especially revenue administration, with a large number of villages.

pattidar: the holder of a share; a shareholder in a joint conquest by a Sikh leader during the eighteenth century; a land-tenure.

pattidari: the system in which the rights of a shareholder in conquest were recognized.

patwari: a village accountant; there could be one *patwari* for several villages.

pir: a spiritual guide; the Sufi Shaikh who guided others on the path towards union with God.

pirzada: the son of a *pir*; the descendants of a well-known *pir*.

puja: worship; ritual worship of an idol performed by a Brahman; any form of ritual worship.

Purbia: of the east; used in the Punjab for individuals coming from the Gangetic plains.

qazi: the officer who gave judgement in accordance with the provisions of the Islamic law expounded by the *mufti*.

qiladar: garrison commander of a fort.

rahit: a way of life essentially in terms of religious beliefs and practices.

Rahitnama: a written document containing the injunctions for what should be or should not be done, outlining a whole way of life.

rakhi: protection; protection offered by the Sikh leaders in the eighteenth century to the cultivators of land on the condition that they would pay one-fifth of the produce.

raj-jog: power and renunciation pursued together; the ideal of detachment in the midst of social commitments.

Sahajdhari: now used for non-baptized Sikhs of all shades, but originally for the Khalsa (Sikhs directly linked with the Guru) who had not yet taken *pahul*; the term did not apply to Udasis or to any group declared to have been excommunicated by the Guru.

samadh: the structure raised on a spot of cremation, generally in honour of an important individual in religious or secular terms.

sangat: association; a Sikh congregation; the entire body of the Sikhs.

Sarbar Khalsa: the entire body of the Khalsa; refers generally to the meetings of the Khalsa at Amritsar for taking collective decisions.

sardar: a leader; the head of a group of people; the chief Sikh leader accepted by other leaders voluntarily to lead a particular campaign.

sardari (*sirdari*): the share of the chief leader in the lands conquered jointly with others.

Sarkar Khalsaji: the government of the Khalsa; also an individual representing the Khalsa Panth, or ruling on behalf of the Khalsa.

sarkarda: a leader.

sati: the widow who burns herself on the funeral pyre of her deceased husband, traditionally treated with great veneration.

shabad: the word; the divine word; a hymn of the *Guru Granth Sahib.*

Shahidganj: the site where a number of Sikh martyrs were cremated; generally a *gurdwara* was built on such sites.

suba: a province.

subedar: a provincial governor.

Sufi: a Muslim mystic.

sutak: the notion of impurity and pollution associated with the untouchables and with women in the time of menstruation and child birth.

ta'aluqa: a tract of land belonging to a particular chief; a unit area for administration in Sikh times.

tabadari: a tenure mentioned by Prinsep first and then by others on his authority, but its distinction from *jagirdari* is not clear.

tahsil: a unit of administration within a British district.

tahsildar: the officer-in-charge of a *tahsil* for the collection of revenue, with some executive and judicial powers.

Udasi: a renunciate and a celibate vaguely associated with the Sikh movement but representing an essentially different tradition.

Vaheguruji ka Khalsa, Vaheguruji ki fateh: 'The Khalsa belongs to God, and His is the ultimate triumph' used as a form of salutation by the Khalsa.

wazarat: office of the *wazir* as the foremost minister.

zaildar: the head of a number of village headmen under the British as a weak counterpart of the *chaudhari* of the pre-colonial times.

zamindar: the holder of land, a proprietor; used more often for the intermediary who collected revenues from a number of villages on behalf of the government.

Select Bibliography

Aggarwal, Partap C., *The Green Revolution and Rural Labour*, New Delhi, 1973.

Ahluwalia, M.L., *Sant Nihal Singh alias Bhai Maharaj Singh: A Saint Revolutionary of the 19th Century Punjab*, Patiala: Punjabi University, 1972.

———, *Gurdwara Reform Movement 1919-1925: An Era in Congress-Akali Collaboration*, New Delhi: Ashoka International Publishers, 1985.

Ahluwalia, M.M., *Kukas: The Freedom Fighters of the Punjab*, Bombay, 1965.

Archer, J.C., *The Sikhs in Relation to Hindus, Moslems, Christians, and Ahmadiyyas: A Study in Comparative Religion*, Princeton: Princeton University Press, 1946.

———, 'The Bible of the Sikhs', *The Review of Religion*, January 1949.

Archer, W.G., *Paintings of the Sikhs*, London: HMSO, 1966.

Arshi, P.S., *The Golden Temple: History, Art and Architecture*, New Delhi: Harman Publishing House, 1989.

Ashta, D.P., *The Poetry of the Dasam Granth*, New Delhi: Arun Prakashan, 1959.

Avtar Singh, *Ethics of the Sikhs*, Patiala: Punjabi University, 1996 (3rd edn.).

Badan Singh, Giani, *Adi Sri Guru Granth Sahib Ji Steek* (Punjabi), Patiala: Punjab Language Department, 1989 (rpt.).

Bal, Sukhmani, *Politics of the Central Sikh League*, Delhi: Books N' Books, 1990.

Bal, S.S., *British Policy Towards the Punjab 1944-49*, Calcutta, 1971.

Banerjee, A.C., *Guru Nanak and His Times*, Patiala: Punjabi University, 1971.

———, *Guru Nanak to Guru Gobind Singh*, Allahabad, 1978.

Banerjee, Himadri, *The Other Sikhs: A View from Eastern India*, New Delhi: Manohar, 2003.

Banerjee, Indubhusan, *Evolution of the Khalsa*, vol. I (*The Foundation of the Sikh Panth*), Calcutta: A. Mukherjee & Co., 1963 (2nd edn., first published in 1936).

———, *Evolution of the Khalsa*, vol. II (*The Reformation*), Calcutta: A. Mukherjee & Co., 1962 (2nd edn., first published in 1947).

Banga, Indu, *Agrarian System of the Sikhs: Late Eighteenth and Early Nineteenth Century,* New Delhi: Manohar, 1978.

———, 'Crisis of Sikh Politics, 1940-47', in *Sikh History and Religion in the Twentieth Century,* ed. Joseph T. O'Connell et al., Toronto: Centre for South Asian Studies, University of Toronto, 1988, pp. 233-55.

———, 'Social Structure, Religious Ideology and Political Articulation: The Sikhs of the Punjab', Presidential Address: Modern Section, *Indian History Congress,* 49th Session, Dharwad 1988.

———, 'Recent Studies on the Martyrdom of Guru Arjun: A Critique', in *Guru Arjun's Contribution, Martyrdom and Legacy,* ed. Prithipal Singh Kapur and Mohinder Singh, Amritsar: Singh Brothers, 2009, pp. 162-79.

———,'Raj-Khalsa: Ideology and Praxis', *Journal of Punjab Studies,* Special Issue on Guru Gobind Singh, vol. 15, nos. 1-2, 2008.

Banga, Indu and J.S. Grewal, 'The Study of Regional History', in *Different Types of History,* ed. Bharati Ray (History of Science, Philosophy and Culture in Indian Civilization, vol. XIV, pt. 4), New Delhi: Pearson/Centre for Study in Civilizations, 2009, pp. 199-228.

Barrier, N. Gerald, *The Sikhs and Their Literature,* New Delhi: Manohar, 1970.

———, 'The Role of Ideology and Institution Building in Modern Sikhism', in *Sikh Studies: Comparative Perspectives on a Changing Tradition,* ed. Mark Juergensmeyer and N. Gerald Barrier, Berkeley: Graduate Theological Union, 1979, pp. 41-51.

———, 'Sikh Politics in British Punjab Prior to the Gurdwara Reform Movement', in *Sikh History and Religion in the 20th Century,* ed. J.T. O'Connell et al., Toronto: University of Toronto, 1988, pp. 174-90.

———, 'Sikh Emigrants and their Homeland: The Transmission of Information Resources and Values in the Early Twentieth Century', in *The Sikh Diaspora: Migration and Experience Beyond Punjab,* ed. N. Gerald Barrier and Van Dusenbery, Columbia Mo: Smith and Asia Books/ Delhi: Chanakaya Publications, 1989, pp. 49-89.

Barstow, A.E., *The Sikhs: An Ethnology*: New Delhi: B.R. Publishing Corporation, 1985 (rpt., first published in 1928).

Bhagat Singh, *Sikh Polity in the Eighteenth and Nineteenth Centuries,* New Delhi: Oriental Publishers & Distributors, 1978.

Bingley, A.H., *Sikhs,* Patiala: Punjab Language Department, 1970 (rpt., first published in 1899 as *A Class Handbook of the Indian Army*).

Brass, Paul R., *Language, Religion and Politics in North India,* Delhi: Vikas, 1975 (published in London in 1974).

———, 'Ethnic Groups and Ethnic Identity Formation', in *Ethnicity and Nationalism,* ed. Paul R. Brass, New Delhi: Sage, 1991.

Browne, James, 'History of the Origin and Progress of the Sicks', in *Early European Accounts of the Sikhs*, ed. Ganda Singh, Calcutta: Firma K.L. Mukhopadhyaya, 1962.

Chima, Jugdep S., *The Sikh Separatist Insurgency in India: Political Leadership and Ethnonationalist Movements*, New Delhi: Sage, 2010.

Chopra, Barkat Rai, *Kingdom of the Punjab*, Hoshiarpur: Vishvesharanand Vedic Research Institute, 1969.

Chopra, Gulshan Lal, *The Panjab As a Sovereign State (1799-1839)*, Hoshiarpur: VVRI, 1960 (2nd edn., first published in 1928).

Cole, W. Owen, *Sikhism and its Indian Context, 1464-1708*, Indian edn., Delhi: D.K. Agencies, 1984.

Cunningham, Joseph Davey, *History of the Sikhs*, New Delhi: Rupa & Co., 2003 (3rd impression by Rupa; first published in 1849).

Daljeet Singh, *Sikhism: A Comparative Study of its Theology and Mysticism*, New Delhi: Sterling, 1979.

———, *The Sikh Ideology*, New Delhi: Guru Nanak Foundation, 1984.

———, *Essays on the Authenticity of Kartarpuri Bir and the Integrated Logic and Unity of Sikhism*, Patiala: Punjabi University, 1987.

———, *The Sikh Ideology*, Amritsar: Singh Brothers, 1990.

———, *Essentials of Sikhism*, Amritsar: Singh Brothers, 1994.

Dard, Hira Singh, *Karam Singh Historian di Itihasik Khoj* (Punjabi), Amritsar: Sikh Itihas Research Board, SGPC, 1974 (2nd edn.).

Darshan Singh, *Western Perspectives on the Sikh Religion*, New Delhi: Sehgal Publishing Service, 1991.

Deol, Harnik, *Religion and Nationalism in India: The Case of Punjab*, London: Routledge, 2000.

Dhillon, Balwant Singh, *Early Sikh Scriptural Tradition: Myth and Reality*, Amritsar: Singh Brothers, 1999.

Dhillon, Gurdarshan Singh, *Insights into Sikh Religion and History*, Chandigarh: Singh and Singh Publishers, 1991.

———, *India Commits Suicide*, Chandigarh: Singh and Singh Publishers, 1993 (2nd edn.).

Fauja Singh, *Military System of the Sikhs*, Delhi: Motilal Banarsidass, 1964.

———, *Kuka Movement: An Important Phase in Punjab's Role in India's Struggle for Freedom*, Delhi: Motilal Banarsidass, 1965.

———, *Some Aspects of State and Society under Ranjit Singh*, New Delhi: Master Publishers, 1982.

———, *After Ranjit Singh*, New Delhi: Master Publishers, 1982.

Fauja Singh and Gurbachan Singh Talib, *Guru Tegh Bahadur: Martyr and Teacher*, Patiala: Punjabi University, 1975.

Fenech, Louis E., *Martyrdom in the Sikh Tradition: Playing the 'Game of Love'*, New Delhi: Oxford University Press, 2000.

———, *The Darbar of the Sikh Gurus*, New Delhi: Oxford University Press, 2008.

Field, Dorothy, *The Religion of the Sikhs* (Wisdom of the East Series), London: John Murray, 1914.

Forster, George, *A Journey from Bengal to England, through the Northern Part of India, Kashmire, Afghanistan, and Persia, and into Russia by the Caspian Sea*, 2 vols., Patiala: Punjab Language Department, 1970 (rpt., first published in 1798).

Fox, Richard G., *Lions of the Punjab: Culture in the Making*, Berkeley: University of California Press, 1985.

Ganda Singh, *Life of Banda Singh Bahadur*, Patiala: Punjabi University, 1990 (first published in 1935).

———, (ed.), *Early European Accounts of the Sikhs*, Calcutta: Firma K.L. Mukhopadhayaya, 1962.

———, *A Bibliography of the Panjab*, Patiala: Punjabi University, 1988 (rpt., first published in 1966).

———, *Sardar Jassa Singh Ahluwalia*, Patiala: Punjabi University, 1990 (Punjabi version published in 1969).

Gobinder Singh, *Religion and Politics in the Punjab*, New Delhi: Deep & Deep Publications, 1986.

Gopal Singh, *A History of the Sikh People, 1469-1988*, New Delhi: Allied Publishers 1993 (2nd edn., first published in 1979).

Gordon, General John J.H., *The Sikhs*, Patiala: Punjab Language Department, 1970 (rpt., first published in 1904).

Goswamy, B.N., *Painters at the Sikh Court: A Study Based on Twenty Documents*, New Delhi: Aryan International, 1999 (expanded Indian edn.).

———, *Piety and Splendour: Sikh Heritage in Art*, New Delhi: National Museum, 2000.

Goswamy, B.N. and Caron Smith, *I See No Stranger: Early Sikh Art and Devotion*, New York/India: Rubin Museum of Art, in association with Mapin Publishing, 2006.

Grewal, J.S., *Guru Nanak in History*, Chandigarh: Panjab University, 1998 (2nd reprint, first published in 1969).

———, *Muslim Rule in India: The Assessment of British Historians*, New Delhi: Oxford University Press, 1970.

———, *The Sikhs of the Punjab* (The New Cambridge History of India, II. 3), Cambridge: Cambridge University Press, 1998 (2nd edn., first published in 1990).

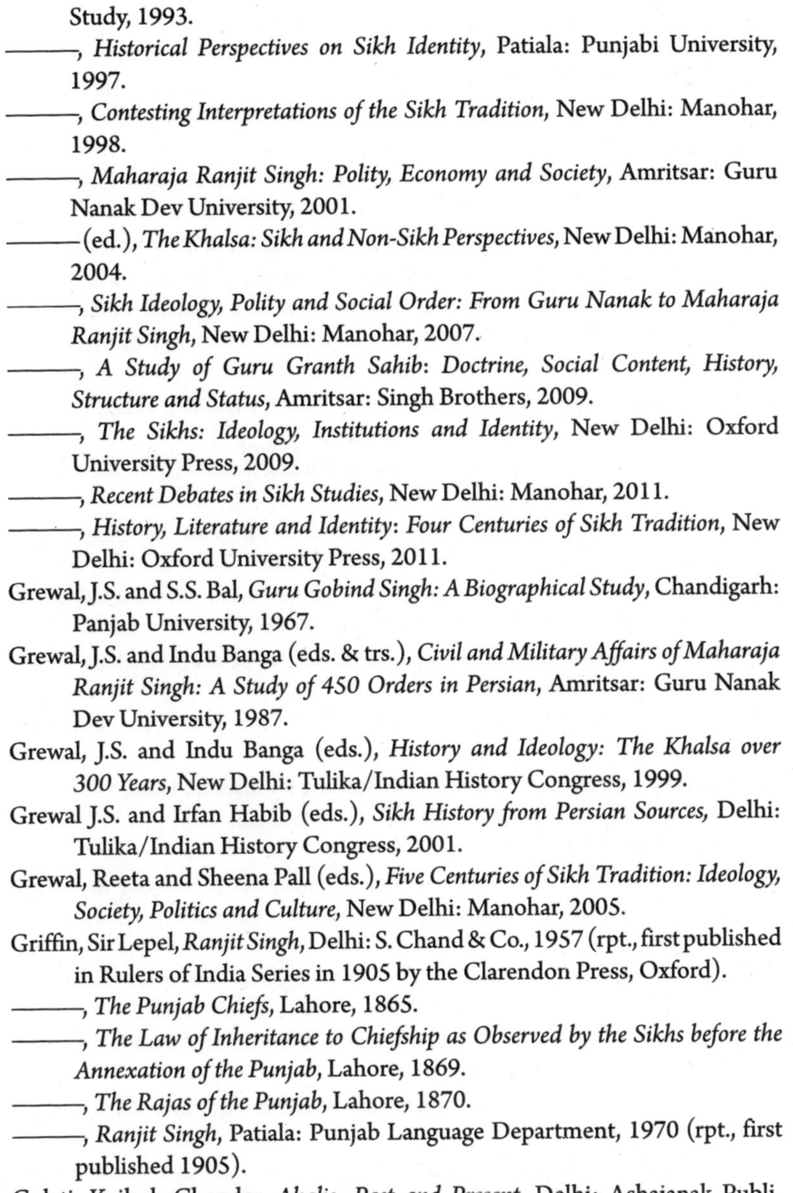

———, *Guru Nanak and Patriarchy*, Simla: Indian Institute of Advanced Study, 1993.

———, *Historical Perspectives on Sikh Identity*, Patiala: Punjabi University, 1997.

———, *Contesting Interpretations of the Sikh Tradition*, New Delhi: Manohar, 1998.

———, *Maharaja Ranjit Singh: Polity, Economy and Society*, Amritsar: Guru Nanak Dev University, 2001.

——— (ed.), *The Khalsa: Sikh and Non-Sikh Perspectives*, New Delhi: Manohar, 2004.

———, *Sikh Ideology, Polity and Social Order: From Guru Nanak to Maharaja Ranjit Singh*, New Delhi: Manohar, 2007.

———, *A Study of Guru Granth Sahib: Doctrine, Social Content, History, Structure and Status*, Amritsar: Singh Brothers, 2009.

———, *The Sikhs: Ideology, Institutions and Identity*, New Delhi: Oxford University Press, 2009.

———, *Recent Debates in Sikh Studies*, New Delhi: Manohar, 2011.

———, *History, Literature and Identity: Four Centuries of Sikh Tradition*, New Delhi: Oxford University Press, 2011.

Grewal, J.S. and S.S. Bal, *Guru Gobind Singh: A Biographical Study*, Chandigarh: Panjab University, 1967.

Grewal, J.S. and Indu Banga (eds. & trs.), *Civil and Military Affairs of Maharaja Ranjit Singh: A Study of 450 Orders in Persian*, Amritsar: Guru Nanak Dev University, 1987.

Grewal, J.S. and Indu Banga (eds.), *History and Ideology: The Khalsa over 300 Years*, New Delhi: Tulika/Indian History Congress, 1999.

Grewal J.S. and Irfan Habib (eds.), *Sikh History from Persian Sources*, Delhi: Tulika/Indian History Congress, 2001.

Grewal, Reeta and Sheena Pall (eds.), *Five Centuries of Sikh Tradition: Ideology, Society, Politics and Culture*, New Delhi: Manohar, 2005.

Griffin, Sir Lepel, *Ranjit Singh*, Delhi: S. Chand & Co., 1957 (rpt., first published in Rulers of India Series in 1905 by the Clarendon Press, Oxford).

———, *The Punjab Chiefs*, Lahore, 1865.

———, *The Law of Inheritance to Chiefship as Observed by the Sikhs before the Annexation of the Punjab*, Lahore, 1869.

———, *The Rajas of the Punjab*, Lahore, 1870.

———, *Ranjit Singh*, Patiala: Punjab Language Department, 1970 (rpt., first published 1905).

Gulati, Kailash Chander, *Akalis: Past and Present*, Delhi: Ashajanak Publications, 1974.

Gupta, Dipankar, *The Context of Ethnicity: Sikh Identity in a Comparative Perspective*, New Delhi: Oxford University Press, 1996.

Gupta, Hari Ram, *A History of the Sikhs*, vol. I, Simla: Minerva Book Shop, 1952 (2nd edn., first published in 1939); vol. II on *The Cis-Sutlej Sikhs*; and vol. III on the *Trans-Sutlej Sikhs*, published by the Minerva Book Shop, Lahore in 1944.

———, *History of the Sikhs*, 5 vols., New Delhi: Munshiram Manoharlal, 1973-91.

Gurdev Singh (ed.), *Perspectives on the Sikh Tradition*, Patiala: Siddharth Publications (for Academy of Sikh Religion and Culture), 1986.

Gurharpal Singh, 'Sikh Ethnicity and Panjab', in *Ethnic Conflict in India: A Case Study of Punjab*, ed. Gurharpal Singh, London: Macmillian Press Ltd., 2000.

Gurharpal Singh and Darshan Singh Tatla, *Sikhs in Britain: The Making of Community*, London: Zed Books, 2006.

Gurtej Singh, *Tandav of the Centaur: Sikhs and Indian Secularism*, Chandigarh: Institute of Sikh Studies, 1996.

———, 'Rise of the Sikh Power as seen through the eyes of Ratan Singh Bhangu', in *History and Ideology: The Khalsa over 300 Years*, ed. J.S. Grewal and Indu Banga, New Delhi: Tulika/Indian History Congress, 1999 (rep., first published in 1967), pp. 48-54.

Harbans Singh, *Guru Gobind Singh*, Chandigarh: The Guru Gobind Singh Foundation, 1966.

———, *Guru Nanak and Origins of the Sikh Faith*, Bombay: Asia Publishing House, 1969.

———, *Guru Tegh Bahadur*, New Delhi: Sterling Publishers, 1982.

———, *The Heritage of the Sikhs*, New Delhi: Manohar, 1994 (2nd edn., first published in 1983).

Hawley, John Stratton and Gurinder Singh Mann (eds.), *Studying the Sikhs: Issues for North America*, Albany: State University of New York Press, 1993.

Helweg, Arthur W., *Sikhs in England: The Development of a Migrant Community*, New Delhi: Oxford University Press, 1986 (2nd edn.).

Herrli, Hans, *The Coins of the Sikhs*, New Delhi: Munshiram Manoharlal, 2004 (2nd edn., first published in 1993).

Hues, Thomas Patrick, 'Sikhism', *Dictionary of Islam*, Calcutta: Rupa & Co., 1988 (rev. edn.), pp. 583-94.

Jaggi, Rattan Singh and Gursharan Kaur Jaggi (eds.), *Sri Dasam Granth Sahib*, New Delhi: Gobind Sadan, 1999, 5 vols.

Jagjit Singh, *The Sikh Revolution: A Perspective*, New Delhi: Kendri Singh Sabha, 1981.

———, *Perspectives on Sikh Studies*, New Delhi: Guru Nanak Foundation, 1985.

Jakobsh, Doris R., *Relocating Gender in Sikh History: Transformation, Meaning and Identity*, New Delhi: Oxford University Press, 2003.

——— (ed.), *Sikhism and Women: History, Text, and Experience*, New Delhi: Oxford University Press, 2010.

Jodh Singh, *Varan Bhai Gurdas: Text, Transliteration and Translation*, 2 vols., Patiala: Vision and Venture, 1998.

Jodh Singh, Bhai, *Sri Kartarpuri Bir de Darshan* (Punjabi), Patiala: Punjabi University, 1968.

Joginder Singh, *The Sikh Resurgence*, New Delhi: National Book Organization, 1997.

Joshi, Chand, *Bhindranwala: Myth and Reality*, New Delhi: Vikas 1984.

Juergensmeyer, Mark and Norman Gerald Barrier (eds.), *Sikh Studies: Comparative Perspectives on a Changing Tradition*, Berkeley: Graduate Theological Union, 1979.

Kapur, Prithipal Singh, *Jassa Singh Ramgarhia* (Punjabi), Amritsar: Singh Brothers, 1998 (5th edn., first published in 1957).

Kapur, Prithipal Singh and Mohinder Singh (eds.), *Guru Arjan Dev: Life, Martyrdom and Legacy*, New Delhi: Delhi Sikh Gurdwara Management Committee, 2006.

Kapur, Rajiv A., *Sikh Separatism: The Politics of Faith*, Delhi: Vikas, 1987 (published in London in 1986).

Kapur Singh, *Parasharprashna: An Enquiry into the Genesis and Unique Character of the Order of the Khalsa with an Exposition of the Sikh Tenets*, ed. Piar Singh and Madanjit Kaur, Amritsar: Guru Nanak Dev University, 1989.

———, *Sikhism: An Oecumenical Religion*, ed. Gurtej Singh, Chandigarh: Institute of Sikh Studies, 1993.

Kavita Singh (ed.), *New Insights into Sikh Art*, Mumbai: Marg Publications, vol. 54, no. 4, June 2003.

Khalsa, Gurudharam Singh, *Guru Ram Das in Sikh Tradition*, New Delhi: Harman Publishing House, 1997.

Kharak Singh, Gobind Singh Mansukhani and Jasbir Singh (eds.), *Fundamental Issues of Sikh Studies*, Chandigarh: Institute of Sikh Studies, 1992.

Khazan Singh, *History of the Sikhs*, Patiala: Punjab Language Department, 1970 (rpt., first published in 1914).

———, *Philosophy of the Sikh Religion,* Patiala: Punjab Language Department, 1970 (rpt., first published in 1914).

Khurana, Gianeshwar, *British Historiography on the Sikh Power in Punjab,* New Delhi: Allied Publishers, 1985.

Khushwant Singh, *Ranjit Singh, Maharaja of the Punjab,* London: George Allen & Unwin, 1962.

———, *A History of the Sikhs,* 2 vols., New Delhi: Oxford University Press, 1999 (rev. paperback edn., first published by Princeton University Press in 1963 & 1966).

Kirpal Singh, *Baba Ala Singh: Founder of Patiala Kingdom,* Amritsar: Guru Nanak Dev University, 2005 (2nd edn., first published in 1954).

———, *Janamsakhi Tradition: An Analytical Study,* Amritsar: Singh Brothers, 2004.

Kohli, Sita Ram, *Maharaja Ranjit Singh* (Punjabi), Delhi: Atma Ram and Sons, 1953.

———, *Sunset of the Sikh Empire,* ed. Khushwant Singh, New Delhi: Orient Longmans, 1967.

Kohli, Surinder Singh, *A Critical Study of the Adi Granth,* New Delhi: Motilal Banarasidas, 1961.

———, *Philosophy of Guru Nanak,* Chandigarh: Panjab University, 1969.

La Brack, Bruce, *The Sikhs of Northern California: 1904-1986,* New York: American Migration Series, 1988.

Lafont, Jean-Marie, *Maharaja Ranjit Singh: Lord of the Five Rivers,* New Delhi: Oxford University Press, 2002.

———, *Fauj-i-Khas: Maharaja Ranjit Singh and His French Officers,* Amritsar: Guru Nanak Dev University, 2002.

Lakshman Singh, Bhagat, *A Short Sketch of the Life and Work of Guru Gobind Singh,* Ludhiana: Lahore Book Shop, 1963 (rpt., first published in 1909).

———, *The Sikh Martyrs,* ed. Prithipal Singh Kapur, Amritsar: Singh Brothers (in association with Delhi Sikh Gurdwara Management Committee), 2006 (first published in 1928).

Latif, Syad Muhammad, *History of the Panjab from the Remotest Antiquity to the Present Times,* New Delhi: Eurasia Publishing House, 1964 (rpt., first published in 1891).

Loehlin, C.H., *The Sikhs and Their Scriptures,* Lucknow: Lucknow Publishing House, 1958 (first published in 1946).

———, *The Granth of Guru Gobind Singh and the Khalsa Brotherhood,* Lucknow: Lucknow Publishing House, 1971.

Macauliffe, Max Arthur, *The Sikh Religion: Its Gurus, Sacred Witings and Authors*, 3 vols., New Delhi: Low Price Publications, 1971 (rpt., first published in 6 vols. by the Clarendon Press, Oxford in 1909).

Madra, Amandeep Singh and Paramjit Singh (eds.), *'Sicques, Tigers or Thieves': Eyewitness Accounts of the Sikhs (1606-1809)*, New York: Palgrave Macmillian, 2004.

Malcolm, Lt. Col. (John), *Sketch of the Sikhs*, New Delhi: Asian Educational Services, 1986 (rpt., first published in London in 1812).

Malhotra, Karamjit K., 'The Earliest Manual on the Sikh Way of Life', in *Five Centuries of Sikh Tradition: Ideology, Society, Politics and Culture*, ed. Reeta Grewal and Sheena Pall, New Delhi: Manohar, 2005, pp. 55-81.

———, 'History, Literature and Ideology: A Historiographical Perspective on the Rahitnamas', *Journal of Regional History*, vols. XIII-XIV, 2007-8, pp. 75-96.

———, 'Sikh Rites and Rituals', *Journal of Punjab Studies*, University of California, Santa Barbara, vol. 16, no. 2 (Fall 2009), pp. 179-97.

———, 'Social and Cultural Life of the Sikhs during the Eighteenth Century', Ph.D. thesis, Panjab University, Chandigarh, 2009.

Manmohan Singh, *Sri Guru Granth Sahib* (English & Punjabi Translation), 8 vols., Amritsar: SGPC, 2000-8 (6th edn., first published in 1962-9).

Mann, Gurinder Singh, *The Goindval Pothis: The Earliest Extant Source of the Sikh Canon*, Cambridge (Massachusetts): Harvard University Press, 1996.

———, *The Making of Sikh Scripture*, New York: Oxford University Press, 2000.

———, 'Sources for the Study of Guru Gobind Singh's Life and Times', *Journal of Punjab Studies*, vol. XV, nos. 1 & 2 (Spring-Fall 2008), pp. 229-84.

Mann, Jasbir Singh and Harbans Singh Saraon (eds.), *Advanced Studies in Sikhism*, Irvine: Sikh Community of North America, 1989.

Mann, Jasbir Singh and Kharak Singh (eds.), *Recent Researches in Sikhism*, Patiala: Punjabi University, 1992.

Mann, Jasbir Singh, Surinder Singh Sodhi and Gurbakhsh Singh Shergill (eds.), *Invasion of Religious Boundaries*, Vancouver: Canadian Sikh Study and Teaching Society, 1995.

Mansukhani, Gobind Singh, *Guru Ramdas*, New Delhi, 1979.

Marenco, Ethne K., *The Transformation of Sikh Society*, New Delhi: Heritage Publishers, 1976.

McLeod, W.H., *Guru Nanak and the Sikh Religion*, Oxford: The Clarendon Press, 1968.

———, *The Evolution of the Sikh Community*, New Delhi: Oxford University Press, 1975.

———, *Early Sikh Tradition: A Study of the Janamsakhis*, Oxford: The Clarendon Press, 1980.

———, *Textual Sources for the Study of Sikhism*, Manchester: Manchester University Press, 1984.

——— (ed. & tr), *The Chaupa Singh Rahit-Nama*, Dunedin: University of Otago, 1987.

———, *The Sikhs: History, Religion and Society*, New York: Columbia University Press, 1989.

———, *Who is a Sikh? The Problem of Sikh Identity*, Oxford: The Clarendon Press, 1989.

———, *Popular Sikh Art*, New Delhi: Oxford University Press, 1991.

———, *Sikhism*, Harmondsworth: Penguin Books, 1997.

———, *Exploring Sikhism: Aspects of Sikh Identity, Culture and Thought*, New Delhi: Oxford University Press, 2000.

———, *Sikhs of the Khalsa: A History of the Khalsa Rahit*, New Delhi: Oxford University Press, 2003.

———, *Prem Sumarag: The Testimony of a Sanatan Sikh*, New Delhi: Oxford University Press, 2006.

———, *Discovering the Sikhs: Autobiography of a Historian*, Delhi: Permanent Black, 2004.

———, *Essays in Sikh History, Tradition and Society*, New Delhi: Oxford University Press, 2007.

M'Gregor, W.L. *The History of the Sikhs*, 2 vols., Patiala: Punjab Language Department, 1970 (rpt., first published 1846).

Mohinder Singh, *The Akali Movement*, New Delhi: Macmillan, 1978.

———, *The Akali Struggle: A Retrospect*, New Delhi: Atlantic Publishers, 1988.

Nahar Singh, Bhai and Kirpal Singh (eds.), *Rebels Against the British Rule*, New Delhi: Atlantic Publishers, 1995.

Narang, A.S., *Storm Over the Sutlej: The Akali Politics*, New Delhi: Gitanjali Publishing House, 1983.

Narang, Gokul Chand, *Transformation of Sikhism*, New Delhi: Kalyani Publishers, 1989 (rpt. of 5th edn, first published in 1912 by the Tribune Press, Lahore, with the extended title 'How the Sikhs became a Political Power').

Nayar, Baldev Raj, *Minority Politics in the Punjab*, Princeton: Princeton University Press, 1966.

Nikki-Guninder Kaur Singh, *The Feminine Principle in the Sikh Vision of the Transcendent*, Cambridge: Cambridge University Press, 1993.

Nripinder Singh, *The Sikh Moral Tradition*, New Delhi: Manohar, 1990.

Oberoi, Harjot S., *The Construction of Religious Boundaries: Culture, Identity and Diversity in the Sikh Tradition*, New Delhi: Oxford University Press, 1994.

O'Connell, Joseph T., Milton Israel, Willard G. Oxtoby, W.H. McLeod and J.S. Grewal (eds.), *Sikh History and Religion in the Twentieth Century*, Toronto: Centre for South Asian Studies, University of Toronto, 1988.

Parry, R.E., *The Sikhs of the Punjab*, Patiala: Punjab Language Department, 1970 (rpt., first published in 1921).

Pashaura Singh, *The Guru Granth Sahib: Canon, Meaning and Authority*, New Delhi: Oxford University Press, 2000.

———, *Life and Work of Guru Arjan*, New Delhi: Oxford University Press, 2006.

Pashaura Singh and N. Gerald Barrier (eds.), *Sikh Identity: Continuity and Change*, New Delhi: Manohar, 2001 (paperback, first published in 1999).

Patwant Singh, *The Sikhs*, New Delhi: HarperCollins Publishers India, 1999 (Murray, London: John 1999).

Payne, C.H., *A Short History of the Sikhs*, Patiala: Language Department, Punjab, 1970 (rpt.).

Pettigrew, Joyce, *Robber Noblemen: A Study of the Political System of the Sikh Jats*, Boston: Routledge and Kegan Paul, 1975.

Piar Singh, *Gatha Sri Adi Granth*, Amritsar: Guru Nanak Dev University, 1992.

———, *Gatha Sri Adi Granth and the Controversy*, Michigan: Anant Education and Rural Development Foundation, 1996.

Prinsep, Henry T., *Origin of the Sikh Power in the Punjab and Political Life of Maharaja Ranjit Singh with an Account of the Religion, Laws and Customs of the Sikhs*, Patiala: Punjab Language Department, 1970 (rpt., first published in 1834).

Purewal, Shinder, *Sikh Ethnonationalism and the Political Economy of the Punjab*, New Delhi: Oxford University Press, 2000.

Randhawa, M.S., *Green Revolution*, Ludhiana, 1974.

Randhir Singh, Bhai (ed.), *Prem Sumarag Granth* (Punjabi), Jalandhar: New Book Company, 1965 (2nd edn.).

Ray, Niharranjan, *The Sikh Gurus and Sikh Society: A Study in Social Analysis*, Patiala: Punjabi University, 1970.

Sachdeva, Veena, *Polity and Economy of the Punjab During the Late Eighteenth Century*, New Delhi: Manohar, 1993.

Sahib Singh, *Sri Guru Granth Sahib Darpan*, 10 vols., Jalandhar: Raj Publishers, n.d. (rpt. of 3rd edn. published in 1972).

Sangat Singh, *The Sikhs in History*, New Delhi: Uncommon Books, 1996 (from New York in 1995).

Sarhadi, Ajit Singh, *Punjabi Suba: The Story of the Struggle*, Delhi: U.C. Kapur & Sons, 1970.

Scott, George Batley, *Religion and Short History of the Sikhs, 1469 to 1930*, Patiala: Punjab Language Department, 1970 (rpt., first published in 1930).

Sewaram Singh, *The Divine Master: Life and Teachings of Guru Nanak*, ed. Prithipal Singh Kapur, Jalandhar: ABS Publications, 1988 (rpt., first published in 1904).

Shackle, Christopher, *An Introduction to the Sacred Language of the Sikhs*, New Delhi: Heritage Publishers, 1999 (rpt., first published in London in 1982).

Shackle, Christopher, Gurharpal Singh and Arvindpal Singh Mandair (eds.), *Sikh Religion, Culture and Ethnicity*, Richmond: Curzon Press, 2001.

Sinha, Narendra Krishna, *Ranjit Singh*, Calcutta: A Mukherjee & Co., 1968 (rpt., first published in 1933).

———, *Rise of the Sikh Power*, Calcutta: A. Mukherjee & Co., 1960 (3rd edn).

Smyth, G. Carmichael, *A History of the Reigning Family of Lahore*, Patiala: Punjab Language Department, 1970 (rpt., first published 1847).

Stronge, Susan (ed.), *The Arts of the Sikh Kingdoms*, London: Victoria and Albert Museum, 1999.

Surinder Singh, *Sikh Coinage: Symbol of Sikh Sovereignty*, New Delhi: Manohar, 2004.

Talbot, Ian and Shinder Thandi (eds.), *People on the Move: Punjabi Colonial and Post-Colonial Migration*, Karachi: Oxford University Press, 2004.

Talib, Gurbachan Singh, *Guru Nanak: His Personality and Vision*, Delhi: Guru Das Kapur & Sons, 1969.

———, *Sri Guru Granth Sahib in English Translation*, 4 vols., Patiala: Punjabi University, 1997-2001 (3rd edn.).

Tatla, Darshan S., *Theses on Punjab* (A Bibliography of Dissertations Submitted to Universities Outside India and Pakistan), Coventry: Association of Punjab Studies (UK), 1996.

Tatla, Darshan Singh and Eleanor M. Nesbitt, *Sikhs in Britain: An Annotated Bibliography*, Warwick: Centre for Research in Ethnic Relations, University of Warwick, 1987.

Teja Singh and Ganda Singh, *A Short History of the Sikhs*, vol. I (1469-1765), Patiala: Punjabi University, 1999 (3rd edn., first published in 1950).

The Sikh Religion: A Symposium, Calcutta: Susil Gupta Private Ltd., 1958.

Trilochan Singh, *Guru Tegh Bahadur: Prophet and Martyr,* Delhi: Gurdwara Prabandhak Committee, 1967.

———, *Ernest Trumpp and W.H. McLeod as Scholars of Sikh History, Religion and Culture,* Chandigarh: International Centre of Sikh Studies, 1994.

Trumpp, Ernest, *The Adi Granth,* New Delhi: Munshiram Manoharlal, 1989 (rpt., first published in 1877).

Tully, Mark and Satish Jacob, *Amritsar: Mrs Gandhi's Last Battle,* New Delhi: Rupa & Co., 1985.

Tuteja, K.L., *Sikh Politics (1920-1940),* Kurukshetra: Vishal Publications, 1984.

———, 'Interpreting Sikh History: A Study of Gokul Chand Narang's *The Transformation of Sikhism*', in *Historical Diversities: Society, Politics and Culture,* ed. K.L. Tuteja and Sunita Pathania, New Delhi: Manohar, 2008.

Uberoi, J.P.S., *Religion, Civil Society and the State,* New Delhi: Oxford University Press, 1996.

Webster, John C.B., *The Nirankari Sikhs,* New Delhi: Macmillan, 1981.

Wilson, H.H., *The Vishnu Purana: A System of Hindu Mythology and Tradition,* Calcutta: Punthi Pustak, 1961 (3rd edn., first published in 1840).

Index of Names

Index of Places

Subject Index